Digital Identity and Access Management:

Technologies and Frameworks

Raj Sharman
State University of New York at Buffalo, USA

Sanjukta Das Smith
State University of New York at Buffalo, USA

Manish Gupta
State University of New York at Buffalo, USA

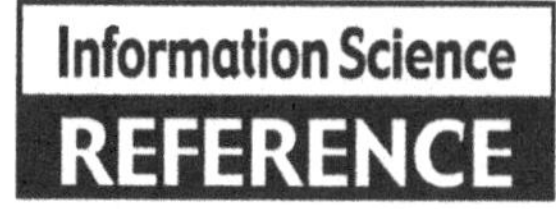

Managing Director:	Lindsay Johnston
Senior Editorial Director:	Heather Probst
Book Production Manager:	Sean Woznicki
Development Manager:	Joel Gamon
Development Editor:	Joel Gamon
Acquisitions Editor:	Erika Gallagher
Typesetters:	Mackenzie Snader
Print Coordinator:	Jamie Snavely
Cover Design:	Nick Newcomer, Greg Snader

Published in the United States of America by
Information Science Reference (an imprint of IGI Global)
701 E. Chocolate Avenue
Hershey PA 17033
Tel: 717-533-8845
Fax: 717-533-8661
E-mail: cust@igi-global.com
Web site: http://www.igi-global.com

Library of Congress Cataloging-in-Publication Data

Digital identity and access management: technologies and frameworks / Raj Sharman, Sanjukta Das Smith and Manish Gupta, editors.

p. cm.

Includes bibliographical references and index.

Summary: "This book explores important and emerging advancements in digital identity and access management systems, providing innovative answers to an assortment of problems as system managers are faced with major organizational, economic and market changes"--Provided by publisher.

ISBN 978-1-61350-498-7 (hbk.) -- ISBN 978-1-61350-499-4 (ebook) -- ISBN 978-1-61350-500-7 (print & perpetual access) 1. Computer networks--Security measures. 2. Computer networks--Access control. 3. Computer security. 4. Online identities. 5. Online identity theft--Prevention. I. Sharman, Raj. II. Smith, Sanjukta Das, 1978- III. Gupta, Manish, 1978-

TK5105.59.D54 2012

005.8--dc23

2011036891

British Cataloguing in Publication Data

A Cataloguing in Publication record for this book is available from the British Library.

List of Reviewers

C. Warren Axelrod, *Delta Risk LLC, U.S.A*
Ivonne Thomas, *Hasso-Plattner-Institute, Germany*
Christoph Meinel, *Hasso-Plattner-Institute, Germany*
Athanasios Karantjias, *University of Piraeus, Piraeus, Greece*
Nineta Polemi, *University of Piraeus, Piraeus, Greece*
Rajanish Dass, *Indian Institute of Management, Ahmedabad, India*
Sujoy Pal, *Indian Institute of Management, Ahmedabad, India*
Daisuke Mashima, *Georgia Institute of Technology, USA*
David Bauer, *Georgia Institute of Technology, USA*
Mustaque Ahamad, *Georgia Institute of Technology, USA*
Douglas M. Blough, *Georgia Institute of Technology, USA*
Ryan Kendrick, *State University of New York, USA*
Gábor Gulyás, *Budapest University of Technology and Economics, Hungary*
Róbert Schulcz, *Budapest University of Technology and Economics, Hungary*
Sándor Imre, *Budapest University of Technology and Economics, Hungary*
Takao Kojima, *Institute of Information Security, Japan*
Yukio Itakura, *Institute of Information Security, Japan*
Peter White, *Charles Sturt University, Australia*
Alessandro Armando, *University of Genova, Italy*
Roberto Carbone, *Fondazione Bruno Kessler, Italy*
Luca Compagna, *SAP Research Sophia-Antipolis, France*
Giancarlo Pellegrino, *Eurécom, Sophia-Antipolis, France*
Valer Bocan, *Alcatel-Lucent, Romania*
Mihai Fagadar-Cosma, *Alcatel-Lucent, Romania*
Waleed Alrodhan, *Imam Muhammed Ibn Saud University, Saudi Arabia*
Hany F. EL Yamany, *Suez Canal University, Egypt*
David S. Allison, *The University of Western Ontario, Canada*
Miriam A. M. Capretz, *The University of Western Ontario, Canada*
Jacques Wainer, *University of Campinas, Brazil*
Fabio Negrello, *University of Campinas, Brazil*
Igor Ribeiro de Assis, *University of Campinas, Brazil*
Pradeep Kumar KB, *SRM University Chennai, India*

H.R Rao, *State University of New York, USA*
Andreas Pashalidis, *Katholieke Universiteit Leuven, Belgium*
Chris J. Mitchell, *Royal Holloway, University of London, UK*
Peter Haag, *Utrecht University, The Netherlands*
Marco Spruit, *Utrecht University, The Netherlands*

Table of Contents

Detailed Table of Contents

Managing digital identities and computer and network access rights is difficult at the best of times. But today's rapidly changing organizational structures and technology dependencies make for even greater challenges. In this chapter the authors review the various stages in the identity and access management (IAM) lifecycle from the particular perspective of organizations undergoing substantial change from mergers and acquisitions, business expansions and contractions, as well as internal structural and technological changes. The chapter also looks at the impact on IAM of incidents originating from outside organizations, such as natural disasters (earthquakes, hurricanes, volcanic eruptions, etc.) and manmade catastrophes (terrorist bombings, major oil spills, etc.). The authors address the question of how one might prepare for and respond to such events by managing and controlling identification and authorization in fast-moving, difficult-to-control situations.

This chapter will focus on this contradiction and its reasons. One of the main reasons is the problem of establishing trust relationships between independent parties - a problem, which is inherent to open environments with multiple trust domains. In open environments participants often do not know each other, but nevertheless require an existing trust relationship to perform critical transactions. Governments, commercial organizations, and academia alike have addressed this issue by providing better assurance guidelines for identity management. The outcome is a number of identity assurance frameworks that identify and cluster certain security criteria into levels of trust or levels of assurance (LoA). These approaches are described, compared, and assessed with regard to their role towards a reliable identity management across the Internet. Limitations are identified and trust levels for attributes are proposed as potential fields for further research.

Identity and Access Management (IAM) systems are considered as one of the core elements of any sound security electronic framework for electronic business processes. Their ability to quickly and reliably verify who is trying to access what service, and what they are authorized to do, is both a business enabler and a core requirement for meeting regulatory demands. However, IAM systems are difficult to implement since they touch virtually every end-user, numerous business processes as well as every IT application and infrastructure component of an enterprise, and therefore most of the times IAM implementations fall short of expectations. This chapter proposes an effective way of approaching, designing, and implementing a constructive, user-centric, standards-based, centralized and federated IAM system, with which a trust relationship among the involved entities is established in a secure and interoperable way, enabling end-users to easily gain electronic and/or mobile (e/m) access to advanced business services, and Service Providers (SPs) to effectively enhance their infrastructures by easily adopt it in their systems. In addition, a collective knowledge of IAM systems' implementation best practices is presented.

National identity projects in various countries around the globe, which manage unique identification of citizens, have captured attention of late. Although the perceived benefits in terms of public administration are numerous, the challenges and bottlenecks for a successful rollout are also many. The objective of this chapter is to identify the drivers and inhibitors for adopting a common identity management system across various organizations for public administration and to suggest a model for determining the feasibility and sustainability of such a system. The authors reveal the various factors affecting successful implementation of the system and the probable impact of these factors. The model suggested would allow public organizations and policy makers to determine the critical factors for the implementation of an identity management system on a large scale.

The pervasive use of digital identities in today's cyberspace has led to an increasing interest in the area of identity management. Recently proposed user-centric identity management systems have accomplished higher-level of user control over online identity credentials. However, while the lack of a central authority that governs the entire system requires users to be responsible for their own digital identity credentials, the existing user-centric identity management systems still have problems in terms of security, privacy, and system availability. In this chapter, the authors present an identity management architecture that solves these problems. The scheme relies on user-controlled identity agents. Identity agents realize fine-grained control over online identity disclosure by using a minimal-disclosure identity credential scheme and also improve users' awareness over their credential usage via an identity-usage monitoring system that includes a real-time risk scoring mechanism. A proof-of-concept implementation is shown and evaluated in terms of security, user-centricity, and performance.

Identity management (IdM) systems are information systems that help to manage an individual's credentials. This occurs through the establishment, description, maintenance, and eventual destruction of an identity. There are numerous IdM systems in place today that follow a general framework, yet provide users of the system with different solutions. This chapter will present architecture and applications that will help in establishing and analyzing the framework that IdM system follow. It will define the role of IdM systems in today's electronic age, while examining challenges that arise during implementation, management, and integration of the systems. The latter part of the chapter examines eighteen commercial off-the-shelf IdM software solutions. The authors provide brief discussion on each of the solutions to highlight differences and advantages. The discussions and presentations in the chapter can aid system managers and security professionals in understanding current landscape of Identity Management Solutions and Technologies and analyses provided can significantly facilitate their decision making and risk management.

As various information technologies are penetrating everyday life, private and business matters inevitably mingle. Separating private and business past records, public information, actions or identities may, however, be crucial for an employee in certain situations. In this chapter, the authors review the interrelated areas of employee privacy, and analyze in detail two areas of special importance from the viewpoint of the separation: web and social network privacy. In relation to these areas, the chapter discusses threats and solutions in parallel, and besides surveying the relevant literature, it also presents current Privacy Enhancing Technologies applicable in each area. Additionally, the authors briefly review other means of workplace surveillance, providing some insight into the world of smartphones, where they expect the rise of new privacy-protecting technologies as these devices are getting capable of taking over the functions of personal computers.

Herein the authors propose the concept of "Identity and Access Management Architectures," comprising a policy-oriented management system that enables the utilization of user identity-related data. This policy-oriented management system encourages users to take the initiative in providing their own identity-related data and encourages awareness of the usage of such data by entities. This architecture is designed to allow users to initiate "user policies" for identity-related data protection (user intention providing user data), just as entities have policies describing their intention to consume the data. We have developed a "Privacy Policy Matching Engine" as a component of the Identity and Access Management Architectures. This engine enables the matching of a user's intention to provide his/her identity-related data with an entity's own privacy policy. Also, it automatically analyzes the policies with a focus on the types and handling method for identity-related data.

The chapter argues that an enterprise should develop its own Identity Management Architecture (IdMA) before attempting any Identity Management implementation. It begins with a discussion of the development of the Reference IdMA. It also discusses the issues of how to incorporate existing enterprise workflows and processes and other specific needs of an enterprise into an IdMA. It proposes the incorporation of existing information security controls into the IdMA by the use of chokepoints to monitor identified security hotspots. The issues surrounding the privacy of personal data as well as the protection of corporate data and assets are discussed and it is shown how these issues may be addressed and included in the Reference IdMA. Finally, there is a discussion of how to include federation with other enterprises as part of the enterprise's IdMA.

Single-Sign-On (SSO) protocols enable companies to establish a federated environment in which clients sign in the system once and yet are able to access to services offered by different companies. The OASIS Security Assertion Markup Language (SAML) 2.0 Web Browser SSO Profile is the emerging standard in this context. In previous work a severe security flaw in the SAML-based SSO for Google Apps was discovered. By leveraging this experience, this chapter will show that model checking techniques for security protocols can support the development and analysis of SSO solutions helping the designer not only to detect serious security flaws early in the development life-cycle but also to provide assurance on the security of the solutions identified.

Cryptographic authentication systems are currently the de facto standard for securing clients access to network services. Although they offer enhanced security for the parties involved in the communication process, they still have a vulnerable point represented by their susceptibility to denial of service (DoS) attacks. The present chapter addresses two important aspects related to the security of authentication systems and their resistance against strong DoS attacks, represented by attack detection and attack prevention. In this respect, the authors present a detailed analysis of the methods used to evaluate the attack state of an authentication system as well as of the countermeasures that can be deployed to prevent or repel a DoS attack.

In this chapter, the author provides an overview of five of the most widely discussed web-based identity management systems, namely Microsoft CardSpace, the Higgins project, the Liberty Alliance project, the Shibboleth project, and OpenID. These systems are discussed throughout the chapter; it also investigates certain security limitations shared by all these systems. The practicality of identity management systems is then discussed, as well as how their practicality can be enhanced by developing reliable integration and delegation schemes. The author also provides overviews of the Project Concordia integration framework, and the Shibboleth and OAuth delegation frameworks, as well as reviewing the related literature.

Security is one of the largest challenges facing the development of a Service-Oriented Architecture (SOA). This is due to the fact that SOA security is the responsibility of both the service consumer and service provider. In recent years, many solutions have been implemented, such as the Web Services Security Standards, including WS-Security and WS-SecurityPolicy. However, those standards are insufficient for the promising new generations of Web 2.0 applications. In this research, the authors describe an Intelligent SOA Security (ISOAS) framework and introduce four of its services: Authentication and Security Service (NSS), the Authorization Service (AS), the Privacy Service (PS), and the Service of Quality of Security Service (SQoSS). Furthermore, a case study is presented to examine the behavior of the described security services inside a market SOA environment.

This chapter presents R+DRC, an extension of the Role-based Access Control (RBAC) model. R+DRC allow for defining constraints, for example to enforce different forms of separation of duties, and the right of overriding a constraint. The model also defines delegations, and two forms of revocations. The model is discussed within the framework of modeling the access control of a hospital. Algorithms are provided for the more complex actions.

Internet banking has become the preferred channel for conducting banking activities across the globe and amongst all social demographics. Only a few other technological adoptions can compare with the recent trend of use of Internet banking facilities. Given the cost advantages and benefits it has to offer, it is widely touted as a win-win strategy for both banks and customers. However, with the growth in E-banking services and reliance on a public channel – Internet – to conduct business, it has been challenging for banks to ensure integrity and confidentiality of highly sensitive information. This chapter presents an overview of authentication issues and challenges in the online banking area with analysis on some of the better approaches. The chapter compares different authentication methods and discusses ensuing issues. The chapter will be invaluable for managers and professionals in understanding the current authentication landscape.

This chapter surveys the approaches for addressing privacy in open identity and access management systems that have been taken by a number of current systems. The chapter begins by listing important privacy requirements and discusses how three systems that are being incrementally deployed in the Internet, namely SAML 2.0, CardSpace, and eID, address these requirements. Subsequently, the findings of recent European research projects in the area of privacy for I&AM systems are discussed. Finally, the approach taken to address the identified privacy requirements by ongoing projects is described at a high level. The overall goal of this chapter is to provide the reader with an overview of the diversity of privacy issues and techniques in the context of I&AM.

In this chapter, the author provides overviews of the notion of identity and of identity management in Sections 1 and 2, respectively. In section 3, the author describes a conceptual identity management model as well as a number of practical models. The chapter also covers a number of related topics including Single Sign-On, Level of Assurance, identity source discovery, security policies, proof-of-rightful-possession, and the use of pseudonyms and temporary IDs. Section 4 concludes the chapter.

This chapter investigates how organizations can be supported in selecting and implementing Identity and Access Management (IAM) services. Due to the ever growing number of applications that are being used in organizations, stricter regulations and changing relationships between organizations, a new approach towards login- and password administration, security, and compliance is needed. IAM services claim to provide this new approach. Unfortunately, IAM selection projects have not been very successful in the recent past. Therefore, this chapter presents the IAM Services Assessment Model, which provides a useful and usable tool to support organizations in the selection and implementation of IAM services.

Preface

Digital identity and access management (DIAM) systems are widely believed to be one of the principal components of any good security framework for business processes, most of which are largely deployed online. Such systems assist with access control, specifically making sure that the right to use particular resources is approved provided that it is appropriately sanctioned. Their ability to rapidly and consistently confirm identities of individuals attempting to access specific services, and to tally that against their rights to do so, is a necessity from a business standpoint, in addition to being, in many cases, a basic regulatory condition that must be met. This book presents a collection of articles on a set of very significant and opportune issues in different fundamental and practical subjects connected to DIAM systems. The book aims to offer great academic value and inputs to the subject of information technology. The main purpose of this book is to activate a community-wide consciousness about the important and up-and-coming advancements in DIAM systems, and accordingly emphasize the vast promise of DIAM research to essentially transform and generate ground-breaking answers to an assortment of problems in the DIAM area.

PRIMARY CHALLENGES OF DIAM

Identity management systems control an individual's access to resources and services by managing his/her credentials by setting up, preserving, and in due course obliterating such identity, once its purpose has been served. Even though such systems are tightly incorporated with access control systems, their major purpose is to aid system managers and end users in carrying out maintenance procedures, such as managing access credentials (user roles, access rights), designating rights, and reviewing such rights on a routine basis, across different functional units, throughout the entire lifecycle of such credentials. Administering digital identities and system access rights can be challenging even under stable conditions. This is because DIAM systems affect practically all end-users and several business processes in addition to software applications and hardware infrastructure of an organization. Identity management is frequently perceived as largely a technical solution and consequently, a problem with such perception is that it may encourage a rather dedicated concentration on the technical plan and execution thereof, perhaps at the exclusion of softer organizational constraints. This can potentially result in solutions that fall short of the organizational expectations.

There are several added complexities that make for a number of interesting challenges in this discipline. Nowadays, organizational structures can alter fairly fast due to economic expansion and contractions. This, taken in conjunction with the reality of shifting technological dependencies, create still more hurdles for successful DIAM system deployment. With the increasing utilization of the cyberspace as a business platform, identity management is developing further and influencing our approach towards characterizing and stipulating identities online. Knowing the rewards of offering more services online and also the loss of market share that can result if such services are not made available in an effective manner for increasingly mobile consumers, it is not surprising that most firms are aggressively expanding their online presence. For certain sectors however, such as the financial or health and human services sectors, with the steadily increasing dependence on the Internet to carry out business, it means an increased pressure to guarantee the reliability and privacy of highly sensitive data.

The persistent employment of digital identities in the Internet these days has also directed greater attention towards the subject of identity management. Several interesting questions arise surrounding the issues of security, privacy, and system availability, in addition to the role of governance authorities for digital credentials. State-run identity projects in different countries which consolidate unique identification of their populace have also garnered some attention. Such governance programs present many apparent payoffs with regards to public administration and also several issues and roadblocks for effective implementations. There is also a tremendous amount of heterogeneity amongst users along several dimensions, which further exacerbates these challenges and generates more interesting research questions. Some users, while being highly conversant in browsing or shopping online, often show a naiveté when it comes to the frequently unregulated utilization of personally identifiable data that they supply on various websites. In spite of the fact that these websites candidly state their privacy procedures, generally, consumers either do not fully comprehend of the implications of such policies or simply choose to disregard them. Further, as IT becomes more pervasive in our daily lives, private and business affairs often unavoidably blend in. For any individual, it becomes vital to effectively manage private and business lives and accounts thereof, publicly available data, actions, and personas.

Along with the issues surrounding DIAM in the context of major organizational, economic, and market changes, there are several other facets of social and technical elements such as the challenges of separating personal and business identities, denial of service resilience of authentication systems, security issues surrounding service oriented architectures, and role based access control issues that the book covers in detail. The book offers readers an outstanding collection of related expert commentaries on the technology, processes, management, governance, research, and practices surrounding DIAM. This book has 16 innovative research contributions presented as chapters. We concisely delineate these contributions in the subsequent section.

OVERVIEW OF CHAPTERS IN THE BOOK

When enduring challenging financial crises, change happens in the form of insolvencies, resource curtailment, and comparable damaging events. Positive change inducing events can such as mergers and acquisitions can cause just as much upheavals. Regardless of the nature of the change, it is often essential for organizations to break apart, unite, halt, or otherwise adjust business units and their processes, in addition to the foundational computer and network systems. As a result, steps for identifying, validating, and approving rights to use system functions and data come under great pressure to react fast to organizational and system changes and withstand the effects of such changes with ideally negligible consequences on the general business operations. In Chapter1, "*IAM Risks during Organizational Change and Other Forms of Major Upheaval*," Dr. Warren Axelrod of the Delta Risk L.L.C., USA, appraises the different phases in the identity and access management (IAM) lifecycle specifically from the viewpoint of businesses experiencing considerable change from mergers and acquisitions, business expansions and contractions, and internal structural and technological changes. The effect on IAM of events initiated externally, for example natural disasters (earthquakes, deadly storms, volcanic eruptions, etc.) and manmade calamities (terrorist bombings, major oil spills, etc.) is also studied. The author tackles the problem of how one might get ready for and take action against such events by managing and controlling identification and authorization under dynamic, difficult-to-control circumstances.

Chapter 2, "*From Domain-Based Identity Management Systems to Open Identity Management Models*," focuses on the contradiction that open identity management models have been devised expressly to deal with the open nature of the Internet and yet conventional methods even now used to control these networks. The authors Ivonne Thomas and Dr. Christoph Meinel of the Hasso-Plattner Institute, Germany, find that one of the major causes for this is the difficulty of setting up trust relationships between independent parties, a dilemma which is intrinsic to open environments with numerous trust domains. In open environments members frequently are not acquainted enough with each other, yet they need an existing trust relationship to carry out vital transactions. Governments, business groups, and the academic world have tackled this subject by offering improved assurance guidelines for identity management. The result is a number of identity assurance frameworks that classify and group particular security factors into levels of trust or levels of assurance (LoA). These methodologies are explained, contrasted, and reviewed with reference to their role towards assuring dependable identity management across the Internet. Deficiencies of these approaches are provided and trust levels for attributes are suggested as possible areas for further research.

Chapter 3, "*Effective Guidelines for Facilitating Construction of Successful, Advanced, User-Centric IAM Frameworks*," suggests an effective method of approaching, planning, and putting into practice a practical, standards-based, centralized, and united IAM system, with which a trust relationship amongst the involved entities is set up in a protected and interoperable manner, allowing end-users to effortlessly get electronic and/or mobile (e/m) access to sophisticated business services, and Service Providers (SPs) to effectively improve their infrastructures by implementing it in their systems in a straightforward manner. The authors, Dr. Athanasios Karantjias and Dr. Nineta Polemi of the University of Piraeus, Greece, also share their collective knowledge in building IAM frameworks, delineating the key insights concerning the critical success factors for the integration of large-scale, user-centric, and federated IAM frameworks. It essentially presents a realistic guideline, intended for use by IAM practitioners, and has two prime target audiences, i.e. enterprises and their executing associates that search for help on planning IAM aware projects and enterprises and their cohorts that are now operationalizing IAM projects and who wish to ensure the efficacy of their tactic and consequent development.

The goal of Chapter 4, "*Feasibility and Sustainability Model for Identity Management*," is to identify the drivers and inhibitors for implementing a universal identity management system across different businesses for public administration, specifically national identity projects in different nations around the world that handle unique identification of citizens. The authors, Prof. Rajanish Dass and Sujoy Pal of Indian Institute of Management, Ahmedabad, India, propose a model for assessing the viability and sustainability of such a system. Different issues influencing successful implementation of the system and the likely effect of these aspects are also revealed. The recommended model would let public institutes and policy makers establish the critical factors for the implementation of comprehensive identity management systems.

Chapter 5, "*User-Centric Identity Management Architecture Using Credential Holding Identity Agents*," offers an identity management architecture that tries to resolve some of the security, privacy, and system availability problems associated with existing user-centric identity management systems. The system designed by the authors, Daisuke Mashima, David Bauer, Dr. Mustaque Ahmed, and Dr. Douglas Blough of Georgia Institute of Technology, U.S.A., depends on user-controlled identity agents. Identity agents achieve fine-grained influence over online identity disclosure by means of a minimal-disclosure identity credential plan and in addition advance users' consciousness about their credential usage through an identity-usage monitoring scheme that comprises of an instantaneous risk scoring instrument. A proof-of-concept implementation is demonstrated and assessed with regards to security, user-centricity, and performance.

The purpose of Chapter 6, "*Coming of Age or Just off the Boat: A Review of Contemporary Identity Management System*," is to put forward architecture and applications that will facilitate in setting up and examining the framework that Identity Management (IdM) systems abide by. The authors, Dr. Raj Sharman, Ryan Kendrick, and Dr. Manish Gupta of the State University of New York at Buffalo, U.S.A., describe the function of IdM systems nowadays, while investigating the difficulties that occur during implementation, management, and integration of the systems. The concluding part of this chapter scrutinizes eighteen commercial off-the-shelf IdM software solutions. The authors supply concise discussions on each of the solutions to emphasize dissimilarities and advantages. The deliberations in this chapter can support system managers and security professionals in their accurate perception of the present setting of IdM Solutions and Technologies. Their study can considerably ease such parties' decision making and risk management.

In Chapter 7, "*Separating Private and Business Identities*," the authors, Gábor György Gulyás, Róbert Schulcz, and Dr. Sándor Imre of Budapest University of Technology and Economics, Hungary, evaluate different aspects of employee privacy, and examine in depth two subjects of particular significance from the perspective of the disconnect between private and business records and personas: web and social network privacy. They discuss threats and solutions concerning these topics as well, and moreover, in addition to reviewing the pertinent literature, they enumerate existing Privacy Enhancing Technologies appropriate for each theme. Furthermore, they provide a concise assessment of additional ways of workplace surveillance, giving some glimpses of the world of smart phones, where the growth of new privacy-protecting technologies is predicted as these devices are getting proficient in assuming the tasks of personal computers.

Chapter 8, "*Identity and Access Management Architectures with a Focus on User Initiative*," puts forward the notion of Identity and Access Management Architectures encompassing a policy-oriented management system that facilitates the employment of user identity-related information. This policy-oriented management system persuades users to take the lead in supplying their own identity-related data and supports an understanding of the handling of such data by different entities. This architecture is intended to let users set up user policies for identity-related data security, just as entities have rules regarding their plan for using the data. The authors, Takao Kojima and Yukio Itakura of the Institute of Information Security, Japan, have created a Privacy Policy Matching Engine as a part of the Identity and Access Management Architecture. This engine permits the matching of a user's intent to make his/her identity-related data available with an entity's own guiding principles regarding privacy. Additionally, it automatically studies the guidelines with a spotlight on the categories and treatment techniques for identity-related data.

An Enterprise Architect who is endeavouring to produce an Identity Management (IdM) design may discover that the modern perception of an IdM enterprise framework relies to a greater extent upon a specific vendor's implementation as opposed to a clearly defined model. Even though nearly all major vendors offer complete IdM systems, Chapter 9, "*Starting the Revolution: Implementing an Identity Management Architecture*," contends that an enterprise should build its own Identity Management Architecture (IdMA) before trying any IdM implementation. It starts with a discussion on the growth of the Reference IdMA. In addition, it discusses the subject of integrating existing enterprise workflows and processes and other particular requirements of an enterprise into an IdMA. The author, Dr. Peter White of the Charles Sturt University, Australia, suggests the assimilation of existing information security controls into the IdMA by employing chokepoints to check on identified security hotspots. Privacy concerns regarding personal data along with the issues surrounding the defense of corporate data and assets are discussed, and it is shown how these matters may be adopted and incorporated in the Reference IdMA. Lastly, there is a discussion of how to incorporate federation with other enterprises as part of the enterprise's IdMA.

Single Sign-On (SSO) protocols form the keystone of Identity and Access Management systems as they allow companies to set up a federated environment in which users sign in once and gain the right to use services provided by diverse organizations. The OASIS *Security Assertion Markup Language* (SAML) 2.0 Web Browser SSO Profile (SAML SSO) is the emerging standard in this environment: it describes an XML-based format for programming security assertions in addition to numerous procedures and requirements that stipulate how assertions should be switched in a broad swath of applications and/or usage settings. This is accomplished to the smallest extent essential to assuring the interoperability amongst various implementations. As a result, SAML SSO includes several configuration options extending from optional fields in messages, usage of SSL 3.0 or TLS 1.0 channels (SSL channels) at the transport layer, application of encryption and/or digital signature on certain vulnerable message elements that require instantiation consistent with the conditions established by the circumstances of the application and the security systems on hand. The security recommendations that are accessible throughout the extensive SAML stipulations are helpful in evading the most common security pitfalls but are of little assistance in ensuring their absence in specific instances of the protocol. Leveraging an earlier work where a critical security defect in the SAML-based SSO for Google Apps was exposed, in Chapter 10, "*Automatic Security Analysis of SAML-Based Single Sign-On Protocols*," the authors, Drs. Alessandro Armando and Roberto Carbone of Fondazione Bruno Kessler, Italy, and Dr. Luca Compagna and Giancarlo Pellegrino of SAP Research Sophia-Antipolis, France, demonstrate that model inspection methods for security protocols can assist the development and analysis of SSO solutions, thereby aiding the designer in spotting severe security defects early in the development life-cycle and granting guarantees on the security of the solutions identified.

Cryptographic authentication systems provide improved security for interacting parties. However, they nevertheless have a susceptible spot corresponding to their vulnerability to denial of service (DoS) attacks. Chapter 11, "*Denial of Service Resilience of Authentication Systems*," concentrates on two vital facets connected to the security of authentication systems and their fight against intense DoS attacks, signified by attack detection and attack prevention. Towards that end, the authors, Valer Bocan and Mihai Fagadar-Cosma of Alcatel-Lucent, Romania, undertake a thorough examination of the techniques utilized to assess the attack state of an authentication system and the countermeasures that can be arranged to avert or deter a DoS attack.

Chapter 12, "*Identity Management Systems*," presents a summary of the concept of identity and of identity management. The author, Dr. Waleed Alrodhan of Imam Muhammed Ibn Saud University, Saudi Arabia, explains a theoretical identity management model in addition to numerous practical models. He also addresses many related issues including Single Sign-On, Level of Assurance, identity source discovery, security policies, proof-of-rightful-possession, and the exercise of pseudonyms and temporary IDs.

Security is one of the main issues confronting the development of a Service-Oriented Architecture (SOA). This is because both the service consumer and service provider is accountable for SOA security. This is an overarching item of interest, since it influences every advertisement, discovery and interaction of services and applications in an SOA ecosystem. In particular, SOA security usually necessitates authentication, privacy, auditing, and authorization. Currently, numerous solutions have been put into practice, for example Web Services Security Standards, together with WS-Security and WS-SecurityPolicy. However, those standards are inadequate for the promising new generations of Web 2.0 applications. In Chapter 13, "*Developing Proactive Security Dimensions for SOA*," the authors, Dr. Hany El Yamany of the Suez Canal University, Egypt and David S. Allison and Dr. Miriam A. M. Capretz of the University of Western Ontario, Canada, portray an Intelligent SOA Security (ISOAS) framework and present four of its services: Authentication and Security Service (NSS), the Authorization Service (AS), the Privacy Service (PS), and the Service of Quality of Security Service (SQoSS). A case study is also provided to observe the performance of the described security services in a market SOA setting.

Chapter 14, "*RBAC with Generic Rights, Delegation, Revocation, and Constraints*," puts forward R+DRC, an addition to the Role-based Access Control (RBAC) model. R+DRC permit the characterization of constraints, for instance, to implement various procedures for separation of duties, and the right of superseding a constraint. The model describes delegations and two types of revocations. The authors, Dr. Jacques Wainer, Fabio Negrello and Igor Ribeiro de Assis of the Instituto de Computação da UNICAMP, Brazil, discuss the model within the context of modeling access control for a hospital. Algorithms are provided for the more complex actions.

Few technological adoptions can measure up to the latest tendency of the general public to make greater use of Internet banking services. Based on the cost advantages and payoffs it tenders, it is broadly advertized as a win-win strategy for both banks and customers. Nevertheless, with the increase in E-banking services and dependence on a public network – the Internet – to carry out their trade, it has been difficult for banks to guarantee integrity and privacy of extremely sensitive data. Chapter 15, "*Who is Guarding the Doors: Review of Authentication in E-Banking*," portrays a summary of concerns and challenges pertaining to authentication in the online banking sphere with an examination of a few of the enhanced tactics. The authors, Pradeep Kumar KB of SRM University, India, Dr. Manish Gupta of M&T Bank, USA, and Dr. H. R. Rao of the State University of New York, Buffalo, USA, evaluate various authentication schemes and discuss resulting issues. The chapter is of particular value to executives and professionals wishing to familiarize themselves with the present authentication landscape.

Chapter 16, "*Privacy in Identity and Access Management Systems*," studies the tactics for assuring privacy in open identity and access management (I&AM) systems as used by several existing systems. The chapter commences by cataloging key prerequisites for privacy and discusses how three systems that are being increasingly deployed in the Internet (specifically SAML 2.0, CardSpace, and eID) deliver on these must-haves. Next, the authors, Dr. Andreas Pashalidis of the Katholieke Universiteit Leuven, Belgium and Dr. Chris J. Mitchell of Royal Holloway, University of London, UK, discuss the results of some of the latest European research projects in the field of privacy for I&AM systems. Lastly, the methodology applied to deal with the identified privacy requirements by current projects is explained at a high level. In general, the purpose of this chapter is to give the reader with an outline of the assortment of topics and methods related to privacy in the I&AM framework.

The majority of web-based identity management systems nowadays comply with one of the following practical identity management models: the isolated, Information Card-based or Federated identity management models. In Chapter 17, "*Identity Management*," the author, Dr. Waleed Alrodhan of Imam Muhammed Ibn Saud University, Saudi Arabia, gives a synopsis of five of the most extensively discussed web-based identity management systems: Microsoft CardSpace, the Higgins project, the Liberty Alliance project, the Shibboleth project, and OpenID. He also studies some security limitations common to all these systems and also discusses the feasibility of identity management systems, and reflects on how their practicality can be improved by developing robust integration and delegation schemes. Moreover the chapter offers a general idea of the Project Concordia integration framework, and the Shibboleth and OAuth delegation frameworks, in addition to examining the associated literature.

In recent years, quite a few big IT-suppliers such as Oracle, IBM, Sun Microsystems, Novell, and CA have launched Identity and Access Management (IAM) systems so as to help businesses manage their identification and access authentication processes. Even though the reality is that an increasing number of organizations are preparing to implement IAM tools, attempts to choose and implement the appropriate solutions are sometimes less than successful. Chapter 18, "*Selecting and Implementing Identity and Access Management Technologies: The IAM Services Assessment Model*," explores how organizations can be helped during the selection and implementation process for IAM services. Owing to the mounting number of applications that are being employed in organizations, stringent policies and evolving relationships between organizations, a novel method for login- and password management, security, and compliance is required. While IAM services generally claim to facilitate this new approach, the authors, Peter Haag and Dr. Marco Spruit of Utrecht University, The Netherlands, show the IAM Services Assessment Model which supplies a helpful and functional tool to assist organizations in the selection and implementation of IAM services.

The book is intended to serve a key audience of professionals, students, researchers, and educators operating in the swiftly developing discipline of digital identity management. Practitioners and managers functioning in the information technology or information security fields across all sectors of business would greatly advance their awareness and knowledge of myriad issues surrounding identity and access management.

Raj Sharman
State University of New York at Buffalo, USA

Sanjukta Das Smith
State University of New York at Buffalo, USA

Manish Gupta
State University of New York at Buffalo, USA

Chapter 1
IAM Risks during Organizational Change and Other Forms of Major Upheaval

C. Warren Axelrod
Delta Risk LLC, USA

ABSTRACT

Managing digital identities and computer and network access rights is difficult at the best of times. But today's rapidly changing organizational structures and technology dependencies make for even greater challenges. In this chapter, we review the various stages in the identity and access management (IAM) lifecycle from the particular perspective of organizations undergoing substantial change from mergers and acquisitions, business expansions and contractions, as well as internal structural and technological changes. We also look at the impact on IAM of incidents originating from outside organizations, such as natural disasters (earthquakes, hurricanes, volcanic eruptions, etc.) and manmade catastrophes (terrorist bombings, major oil spills, etc.). We address the question of how one might prepare for and respond to such events by managing and controlling identification and authorization in fast-moving, difficult-to-control situations.

INTRODUCTION

"It's very important that acquired companies are brought into the organization's safety culture." Colin Ive, Business Continuity Institute[1]

Change is on the short list of certainties (along with death and taxes).[2] In boom times, organizational change results from mergers, acquisitions, new businesses, expansion of current businesses and the like. When going through tough economic times, change arises from bankruptcies, cutbacks, and similar negative events. Whether one is experienc-

DOI: 10.4018/978-1-61350-498-7.ch001

ing the former virtuous circle or the latter vicious circle, it is necessary for both to break apart, combine, discontinue, or otherwise modify business units and their processes, as well as supporting computer and network systems. Consequently, procedures for identifying, authenticating and authorizing access to system functions and data come under intense pressure to respond rapidly to organizational and system changes and absorb the impact of such changes with minimal effect on the overall operation.

In this chapter, we examine IAM processes and systems, what they do, why they are needed, why automating IAM is generally a good idea, and how IAM systems can and should be implemented. We raise some of the many issues that relate to IAM implementation in "normal" times and describe how these issues are magnified and exacerbated when there are dramatic changes within and between organizational units. We then review some examples of successful and failed IAM implementations drawn from the author's extensive experience in this area and cull some lessons learned from them.

BACKGROUND

Information security professionals have long been in a quandary about Identity and Access Management (IAM) systems. It appears obvious that replacing largely manual computer-assisted systems with effective fully-automated IAM systems should lead to significant cost reductions and large increases in control by being able to more readily identify end users unambiguously and restrict them to access only functions and data appropriate to their roles. And yet, from personal experience and discussions with peers, the author has seen that even the largest IT shops are still burdened with labor-intensive, unresponsive, and inaccurate legacy access management systems. These IAM systems originated in the mainframe era of the 1960s and 1970s and, remarkably, many of them are still in use today.

Why is this so often the case? Given the huge advances in computer and network technologies over the past half-century, should it not have been possible to design, develop and implement IAMs that meet the needs of modern IT environments? What is it about these IAM systems, which apparently makes them so difficult to implement? And why have so many vendors seen their IAM offerings languish and fizzle in the marketplace?

As this chapter will show, there are valid reasons and strong arguments for the adoption of IAM systems not to have advanced to the extent one might have expected. Perhaps an important reason is that current identity and system access policy, processes and procedures are so tightly woven into the fabric of a typical organization's IT functionality that the effort to change the approach is considered too costly and overly demanding of resources. Consequently, few, if any, of those with the necessary knowledge and experience are given the time to devote to the enormous effort required to convert from manually-intensive to fully-automated IAM systems. Another possibility is that that the offerings of vendors do not measure up or are not designed to account for the myriad of situations found within and throughout typical organizations. Yet another complication comes from the typical unrelenting business and technology dynamics experienced in a typical modern organization in either the public or private sector. Or perhaps it is a combination of the above. Here we discuss the possible causes of the relatively low number of conversions and suggest what needs to be done to resolve them.

SOME ISSUES AND DEFINITIONS

One of the basic problems in complex areas, such as IAM, is that there is no generally-accepted commonality of definitions. We see the use of terms such as IAM (Identity and Access Management),

IdM (Identity Management), user provisioning,[3] entitlements[4], registration, identification, one-factor and two-factor authentication, validation, verification, federated systems, credentials, biometrics, behavior monitoring, authorization, entitlements, and so on. What do they all mean? How do they differ? Are they misused?

For the most part, when we discuss IAM, we are talking about authentication and authorization, where "authentication" is the verification of the identities of potential subjects, be they humans or computer applications, and "authorization" is permitting the use of certain application-based functions and rights to access and operate on specific data.

Many information security professionals assume that the person or computer application, which is seeking access, has been appropriately registered and in fact that they are who or what they claim to be. Generally, information security practitioners do not see the registration process as being part of their responsibility, which is a big mistake. The registration process is arguably the most important step in the whole process and yet, as shown in the ChoicePoint[5] case and others, information security professionals abdicate any responsibility for it.

We begin by defining the registration, identification, authentication, and authorization lifecycle, which is represented by the flow chart in Figure 1. As part of this section, we shall also examine how aspects of each lifecycle step affects, and is affected, by significant organizational and technological change. Such change also affects both business requirements and user assignments and entitlements, which is illustrated in Figure 2.

Registration

As mentioned above, the registration process is among the most important steps in the IAM lifecycle. It is the means by which it is established that you are who you claim to be. First and foremost, the persons or entities processing registrations and issuing credentials must be trustworthy.[6] Any failure at this initial step flows through the entire lifecycle. It is for this reason that the author believes that information security professionals ought to be intimately involved in the registration process and not delegate that responsibility to others.[7]

The registration process, also known as enrollment or identity proofing, normally involves a customer (also known as a user or subject) presenting acceptable registration information, such as a government-issued photo ID (e.g., driver's license, birth certificate, passport), to a duly-authorized registering agent. Additional information, relating to credit status and the like, may be obtained from credit agencies, such as TRW and Experian. These latter services provide "out of wallet" information, which the customer may have to verify by answering multiple choice questions, for example.

The main weakness with registration systems in general is that someone bent on criminal activity can readily obtain fake identifiers, such as a driver's license, and obtain specific information, such as social security number, date of birth, etc. from readily-available online sources. There is also the possibility that a registering agent might be personally involved in criminal activity and will provide a fake ID for monetary gain.[8]

Issuance of Credentials

Once someone had successfully registered and the registering agent is comfortable that the subject is fact who he or she claims to be, then the registrant will be given a credential in order to do what he or she has registered to do, whether it be driving a car, opening a bank account, entering a building, and the like. Often the issuance of credentials is an integral part of the registration process. In other cases, the processes might be separate.

The form of the credential will vary. It might be a physical token or card that a "guard" might check or the owner might swipe through a reader in

Figure 1. The identity and access management lifecycle

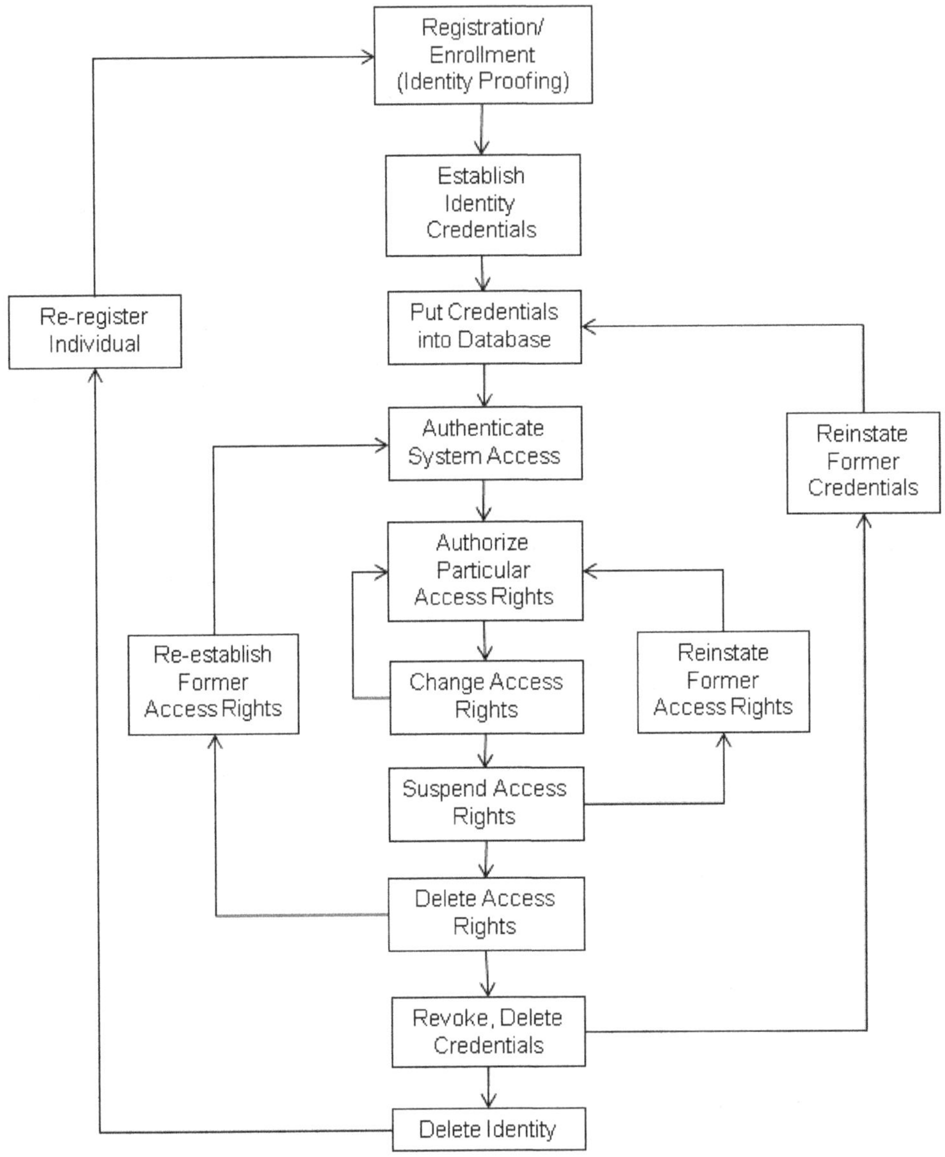

order to gain entry to physical space or a computer system, say. The credential could be something that a person must remember, such as a username and password, or an electronic certificate, such as is used for encryption. Also the issuer of the credential often, but not always, has control over the credential and may revoke it, change what the holder can do with it, determine how frequently it must be renewed, and so on.

Use of Credentials

The value of a credential is solely based on what a person is able do with it. The registering agent will verify who the person is, and the credential

Figure 2. Matching business requirements with system user assignments

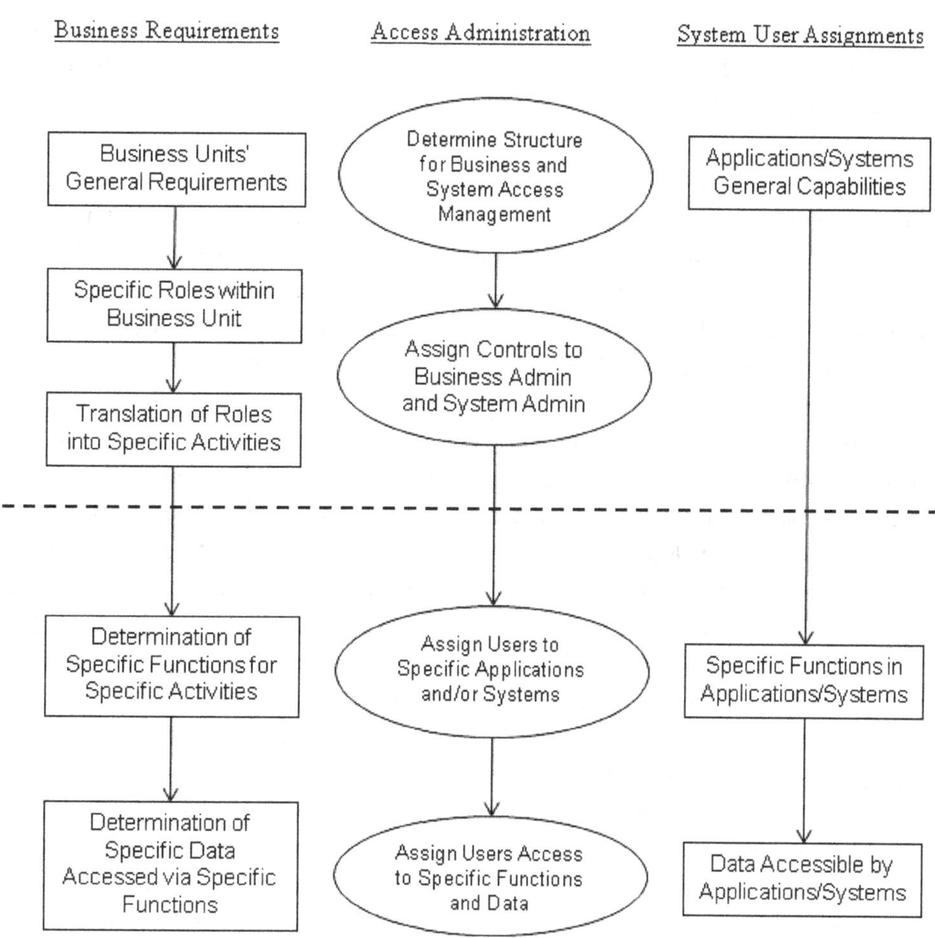

issuer (who may or may not be different from the registering agent) might know what the credential owner is permitted to do, although they may well not know. However, there is usually an additional step to determine which specific items or resources that the credential holder might access and use. For example, a passport is needed to travel abroad, but there may be certain countries that the holder of a U.S. passport may not be able to visit on that particular passport, such as Cuba.

The credential may or may not carry with it use restrictions, depending how specific the terms of use of the credential might be. For example, a driver's license will specify the type of vehicle the holder may drive, but not on which roads (although trucks may be prohibited from certain roads, bridges, tunnels, etc.). The same goes for computer systems. The initial credential may allow holders to log on to the corporate platform, but there are usually further restrictions to limit the applications, functions and data that can be used or accessed. The latter will often be tied to the credential, but not necessarily explicitly.

Change of Rights

A key capability of any access management system is its ability to change individuals' access rights rapidly in line with changes in their roles and responsibilities as well as changes in the objects to which they have access. It is this area that is often the Achilles heel of access management and where auditors almost always find deficiencies. It is generally not the fault of the access management systems themselves but rather it results from the inadequacy of the processes upon which the effectiveness of such systems depends. These changes often require some human intervention, such as a manager's reporting when employees' roles have been modified, and when they have moved to another department or left the organization. The last items will usually be picked up by the human resources system, although that is by no means a guarantee that the event will be reported to the system access administrators in a timely or complete fashion.

Another change management issue has to do with whether the manager or business unit head really understands how role changes affect access rights. This requires a keen knowledge of the business as well as of the access controls in the applications to which individuals have access.

We often see such systems being overridden in order to expedite a transaction or session. If, for example, a user has a specific one-time need to access a system, perhaps because the credential holder is on vacation, a manager may be able to approve a temporary access to someone not usually with those rights in order to enable the process to proceed in the absence of others. Such procedures are categorized as exceptions and as such they need to be well documented with a clear and complete audit trail.

Suspension of Rights

While many organizations are reasonably proficient at creating access rights for authorized individuals and systems, the removal or suspension of those rights, when roles and responsibilities change or are eliminated, is often deficient. This is to be expected since there is often much greater incentive to provide access fast so that individuals can become productive quicker than there is urgency to prevent someone from retaining previous access rights, although the latter is more important for cases of involuntary termination or when data breaches by known or unknown individuals are discovered.

The more common need for the suspension of access rights occurs when someone leaves an organization or, for consultants and contractors, when projects end. In such cases, it is necessary to suspend all related access rights. In many organizations, using outmoded access management tools, the administrator usually has to identify all the various systems to which a particular individual has been granted access and suspend access rights on each system individually.[9]

It should be noted that, in many organizations, the procedure is to suspend, rather than delete, access rights from the system and then, after a period of time (usually three months or so) actually delete the rights. This is because suspension might be instigated due to inactivity, but even inactivity over several months could be sue to extended leaves of absence, or the like. It is then much easier for an administrator to activate suspended rights than to recreate them from scratch.

Termination of Rights

If it can be determined it is highly unlikely that particular access rights will be needed for a given person, such as when the individual leaves the company, then those rights can be terminated without concern for having to reactivate them. This is more desirable from an IAM perspective than is suspension, since the latter can more readily lead to omissions and errors.

When rights have been terminated and the person subsequently requires those access rights, then he or she must go through the access rights procedure as if he or she had not previously had those rights.

Suspension of Identity Credentials

If, for example, someone is scheduled to go on an extended leave of absence, but is expected to return in a similar role at some future date, then it makes sense to suspend, rather than terminate the credentials of that person. In this way, the credentials can be reactivated on the persons return along with the prior set of access rights.

Again, this approach can lead to errors and vulnerabilities since the credentials and related rights are sitting on the system and can be compromised or inadvertently activated.

Sometimes, when someone is out unexpectedly for many months, such as a result of a serious accident or illness, there is a need to access that person's systems, such as their email account, on an emergency basis. In such cases, for example, the person who is out will not have gone through a procedure of formally transferring rights to someone else, as often is done when extended leaves are planned in advance. In such cases, one should follow formal documented procedure, with necessary approvals, whereby the administrator is able to grant temporary access to others approved by the appropriate levels of management.

Deletion of Credentials

Clearly, when someone leaves a position permanently, his or her credentials and all related access rights should be deleted from all the systems to which he or she had access. A major challenge here is ensuring that all access rights, including those for access to buildings, access to voicemail, and so on, are included in the deletion process.

Once credentials have been deleted, it should be required for the individual to go through the entire registration process again, as shown in Figure 1.

USER ATTITUDES IN GROWTH AND CONTRACTION SCENARIOS

Perhaps the most significant difference in user attitude between growth and contraction, from an information security professional's perspective, is that, during periods of growth, individuals, whether they are employees, part-timers, contract workers, consultants or workers associated with business partners, service providers, and overseers, see increasing opportunities for legitimate personal benefit. Therefore the majority of law-abiding citizens will more likely tend towards honest activities and will be less prone to trying to defraud or damage the organization, even when opportunities present themselves. On the other hand, during times of recession and contraction, mergers and acquisitions, and layoffs and reassignments, individuals may find themselves under greater financial pressure and/or be concerned about their losing their jobs or having their incomes reduced. Consequently they may more readily seek or take advantage of weaknesses in systems and business processes for their personal financial gain or to seek revenge against the organization.

During this author's career, which has been predominantly in the information technology and information security areas of financial services companies, he has experienced rapid change during both good times and bad. He has observed how such changes impact security, particularly in relation to lapses in restricting access to critical computer applications and data. This chapter will describe several actual experiences in order to derive some guidelines and preferred IAM practices.

Other changes, which can have significant impact on the viability of an organization, are those that are totally unanticipated.[10] In such cases, there is often neither time nor capability to plan an orderly transition from the prior state to the new one, as with such events as blackouts, hurricanes, terrorist attacks, and the like, with their impact on security and digital and physical identity and access management.

We shall now examine IAM issues under a variety of perturbing circumstances in which organizations are dislodged from their normal day-to-day access management procedures.

Authentication and Access Issues Relative to Structural Changes

During Stable Times

Even in times of relative stability, many organizations have difficulty managing digital identity credentials and computer and network access rights of individual employees, contractors and others. Two factors contribute to such problems, namely, ***complexity*** and ***inflexibility***.

As computer systems and networks evolve, they provide additional features that are often integrated with other systems for greater efficiency and for information sharing purposes. System designers seldom anticipate these enhancements and systems are frequently built for specific environments with little facility for changing to other contexts. This is because it is easier and faster to "hard code" features than to include the flexibility for unanticipated changes, such as might be gained through table-driven systems. Technological innovations, such as virtualization and cloud computing, further complicate matters as they introduce new challenges that were not considered when systems were first developed under prior architectures.

At the same time, user populations of employees, customers, business partners, and others, demand more features and greater flexibility and efficiency in their systems. Often such requests were not contemplated when the systems were originally designed, so that all manner of work-arounds will have been introduced to handle the inevitable series of urgent requests surrounding such changes. Furthermore, technological advances lead to opportunities for new features, efficiencies, and interconnections.

The holy grail of access management is the determination of role-based entitlements.[11] This requires knowledge of who has particular business roles and of their functional and data requirements. However, individuals' responsibilities change over time and with variations in responsibility come corresponding changes in end users systems' use requirements. As processes and operations naturally become more complex over time and as users demand greater flexibility in the use of these systems, so roles will change and diverge. Consequently, an initial assignment of the entire user population to, say, a dozen to two dozen roles, can rapidly grow into hundreds and even thousands of unique roles. Soon it becomes virtually impossible to provide effective role-based access controls (RBAC), with each individual's access rights having to be tailored to that person's specific requirements. On the flip side, it becomes increasingly difficult to shut people out of specific functions and data, since such restrictions were likely not contemplated in the original system design. Often, it is only with support from high-ranking management that RBAC gets implemented, since it often requires top-down mandated rules and strong enforcement to get individuals to acquiesce.

During Periods of Rapid Growth

When the economy is booming, one has additional issues that are specific to growth. It is likely that the changes described above will accelerate and that demands resulting from expansion, new systems and new business processes will grow rapidly. The demand for changes to identity and access management can grow exponentially as business expands, new businesses are developed or new and old businesses are integrated. These call into question the scalability, interconnection and compatibility of IAM systems.

During Economic Downturns

During recessions, many of the prior issues are carried forward as organizations merge, are phased out, or disappear. Issues in a downsizing exercise relate to whether or not systems can be scaled down or readily replaced with more effective, cheaper systems. The challenge here is to ensure that obsolete users and their access rights are rapidly removed. Also, if converting to another IAM system, a whole new access structure may have to be created. As systems are shrunk or replaced, interconnectivity and compatibility issues must be dealt with.

During Catastrophic Events

When a catastrophic event occurs, such as a major fire or flood, bombing, earthquake, hurricane, snow storm, the results can often be devastating. Responses will vary depending on whether facilities are intact and accessible, not accessible, or destroyed. Often it is a major challenge to maintain and enforce security policy and procedures in such circumstances, as described in (Axelrod, 2000). Each circumstance will be different, but well-conceived and tested contingency plans can be effective in a surprisingly high number of circumstances.[12]

IAM Scalability

IAM systems and processes need to be scalable to allow for changes in business volumes, new or discontinued products and services, etc. Scalability must be considered not only with respect to access to computer applications but also in terms of the administrative effort needed. Even if an IAM system can handle rapid and large increases in volumes of users and applications, it might take a considerable amount of time to train a team of administrators in the new IAM and/or to retain key administrators when contraction occurs.[13] Furthermore, during mergers and contractions, there is often a need for bulk transfers of individuals' accesses from one set of systems to another, which might also be subject to different access authorities. This type of change is particularly burdensome on administrators and opens up many opportunities for error.

IAM Interconnectivity and Compatibility

Systems

The authentication and authorization components of identity and access management systems can vary significantly from one COTS (commercial off-the-shelf) product or internally-developed system to another, both in terms of the inherent capabilities of IAM products as well as the way in which organizations have implemented them. It is quite common, for example, for organizations to develop their own custom-designed add-ons to COTS products due to specific requirements of their organizational structures and applications, particularly when those applications were developed in-house.

While IAM products will often have out-of-the-box interfaces with popular COTS software, they will often offer APIs, which organizations can use to adapt the IAM product for use with their proprietary applications. As a result, it can require significant effort to incorporate the custom applications of one organization with the IAM systems of another organization in order to achieve an integrated environment.

Operational Control Structure

Another aspect of combining disparate entities is the organizational structure that supports identity and access management function, which can be quite large. The author has had direct experience with transitioning the specific organizational structures of a number of large institutions and has found that, to a large extent, while functions are common across entities, the allocation of responsibilities and the nomenclature can vary significantly from one organization to another.

It is commonly recognized that knowledge as to which data and functions a particular person should be allowed to access and operate generally lies within the business units for which the applications were acquired or built. Therefore, it is usual to assign roles for determining who should access specific application functions and data to individuals from within divisions and departments of institutions since they understand appropriate business use of the applications and the roles and responsibilities of persons requesting access. Technically-oriented staff seldom knows business functions and user roles. Administrators also need to know the purposes for which applications are used and how they might be misused. Often administrators will have to obtain approval from both departmental managers and the "owners" of the application[14] in order to be able to allow particular access requests to be processed.

Once the business signoffs have been obtained, requests are usually handed over to an access management administrator familiar with both the business applications and the workings of the IAM system in operation (if any). In some organizations, once approval is obtained, the actual entering of the requisite data into the IAM system may be shared between departmental administrators and access management system administrators, with the former entering the business-oriented role and access requirements for the person, and the latter translating the requests into the technical form required for entry into the IAM system. The decision as to where to allocate tasks between business and IT staff will depend upon the size and structure of the organization, whether management runs the organization top-down versus delegating responsibility to lower levels of management, the ease-of-use and richness of functionality of the IAM system installed, and the availability of knowledgeable and/or trainable staff. We will examine each of these factors in turn.

Size and Structure of Organization

Large centralized companies will likely set up a single security administration group serving all divisions and departments, whereas large decentralized organizations might have satellite security administration teams, which are totally independent if the systems requiring access are all under the purview or control of the division, say, or whether divisions share central corporate systems.

Smaller organizations are more likely to have a dedicated unit, often comprising only a couple of individuals, who are responsible for granting access rights to employees, contractors, consultants, and perhaps vendors.

However, in organizations of all sizes, there are usually departmental and divisional administrators who understand the roles and responsibilities of the staff within their respective units and have a familiarity with the systems capabilities and access requirements. These business-oriented administrators tend to be key resources, bridging the gap between users who may understand or be in the process of learning their job functions but, initially at least, have no idea how they translate into the use of available computer systems, and the system administrators, who may have little understanding of business roles, but know how to handle the authorization tools.

Management Style

One of the key assignments in an access granting process is the final arbiter on what access privileges are granted to, or taken away from, specific individuals. In better organized organizations, with clear governance roles and recognition of the criticality of system access, the procedures will require the approvals of the "data owner" and the "business manager." That is to say, if someone in the marketing area requests access to the accounts payables system, for example, then the manager of the accounts payable department should sign off on such a request after a marketing manager had given his or her approval. A similar process should be followed when these access rights are removed.

The culture and management style of a particular organization has much to do with how successful and effective such a process might be. For example, it usually requires directives from above and strict auditing reviews for middle management to take their responsibilities seriously. In many cases, adherence to such procedures is perfunctory since oversight is often minimal. The "approvers" effectively sign off on requests without giving it much thought. It takes firm directives and detailed reviews to achieve an effective process, and even then, doing a good job might be stymied because, for example, the computer-generated reports on who has access to what are difficult to understand and may be replete with errors. Such problems are greatly exacerbated in the face of many significant organizational and technological changes.

One also has to take into account the different philosophies and management styles of organizations that are combined when there are mergers, acquisitions, and the like. Usually the culture and style of the dominant party takes over throughout, including in the IAM area, even though the less powerful entity may have had the better system.[15]

Ease-of-Use of IAM Systems

As alluded to above, an IAM system can be rendered ineffective if the process of authorizing users, reviewing access by user population and application, and deleting obsolete authorizations is complex, confusing and/or time-consuming. Many of the reports generated by access management systems are fraught with "computerize" and it can take a technical person with deep understanding and knowledge of the systems environment to interpret the reports. The result is that often mandated periodic reviews of access rights by business "owners" are inadequate, if not downright useless. They go through the process to meet an audit requirement, but the real controls in such cases are minimal.

IAM software vendors, to their credit, have attempted to simplify the reporting and change management processes. However, considerable effort is needed by key individuals in order to translate the hodge-podge of data feeds into a universal, easily understood and managed system, which integrates the data and presents results in a readable actionable form.

Major organizational and system upheavals greatly exacerbate management and control issues inherent in the IAM systems of different organizations and compatibility of such systems with new or modified systems. Again, in many situations, the selection of the method to use often depends upon which organization is dominant which systems are chosen, and which systems are phased out. Not only are there issues of relative usability of the IAM systems used by different organizations and computer systems that are being merged, terminated, and so on, but the transition process itself places a huge burden on IAM systems that may have functioned well in a more stable environment. The massive volumes of identity and access changes precipitated by major organizational and technology changes frequently overwhelm both the IAM systems and the individuals operating them. During such times, the risk of error by administrators and compromise by insiders becomes much greater than normal.

Availability and Retention of Quality Staff

A major issue in the real-world IAM space is the dearth of knowledgeable, experienced and qualified staff to perform the administrative functions. Often the work is delegated to lower-level inexperienced staff and it is viewed as somewhat menial. However, experience has shown that the work demands individuals with extensive knowledge of the business operations and the computer systems supporting them. Such people do exist in many organizations, but they generally are not interested in repetitive, day-to-day functions, such as those required for IAM systems. Furthermore, from the organization's perspective, it is wasteful to employ higher-paid professional staff for such administrative tasks. From the professional's viewpoint, such a role is boring and not likely to provide any career advancement opportunities, so these individuals will likely try to transfer to other functions or find another job as soon as they can. These attitudes and concerns are magnified during times of major organizational change.

This is a very good argument for implementing automated IAM systems that can be operated by lower-level staff because the systems themselves have the logic and intelligence built in. While it is true that the higher-level professionals are needed to implement such systems, they are more likely to be interested in a conversion project, which has a well-defined completion date, than day-to-day operations.

Periodic Reviews and Updates

In addition to the day-to-day operational requirements, many organizations also require periodic reviews (typically quarterly or annually), by data owners as to who has access to specific applications. The data owners must determine whether the level of functional access (e.g., read, write, change) and data access for everyone using particular applications is still appropriate. This type of review will generate requests to delete users from access lists or restrict the access rights to others on a need-to-know basis. These review cycles and the quality of the reviews varies considerably among organizations.

While the access management structures among organizations can be similar, the details of the process and the tools available to administrators will vary significantly among entities. Consequently the mapping of the structures of two or more different entities can be complex and difficult to implement.

ORGANIZATIONAL STRUCTURES AND IAM FUNCTIONS

As mentioned above, organizations go about authentication in a variety of ways, yet, taking a broader viewpoint, they are remarkably similar since the basic jobs to be done are they same. The main differences, which the author has seen, relate to the degree to which the responsibilities assigned between business and operational functions. This has major implications in regard to knowledge and training required.

If the access management process is viewed as a continuum from business requirements to operational implementation, we see a range of functions. The issue that arises is how to split those functions among staff in the business, operations and IT areas. It transpires that the split is highly dependent on the structure and culture of all entities involved. The division of responsibilities also depends on the level of IAM automation and the amount of information built into the IAM system, the degree of interconnectivity with other systems (such as the Human Resources system), and the like.

In Table 1, we show a list of the various functions that comprise a fully-implemented IAM system, and the assignments of roles and responsibilities to groups that vary as the functions change.

SOME CASES

In this section, we will examine several examples of actual or attempted implementations of IAM systems from the author's direct experience. The names of the individuals and companies involved will remain anonymous. The reader can also review the results of a detailed study of a fully disclosed conversion to RBAC in Chapter 11 of (Ferraiolo 2003).

Early access control products were developed for the IBM mainframe era in the 1960s and 1970s and included tools with names such as RACF, ACF2, and TopSecret. These systems were built to control data access down to the field level and generally operated in a contained environment. It might come as a surprise to some to learn that these systems are still in use today. They are available from IBM (RACF) and Computer Associates (ACF2 and TS) and still run on many legacy systems. Not only that, but they are frequently considered still to be the "authoritative source" for user authentication credentials and access entitlements for the many large organizations still running huge legacy systems, which many large financial institutions still do, for example.[16]

Subsequently, with minicomputers, personal computers, client-server architectures, and web applications, there arose the need for IAM systems able to handle much larger and more diverse user populations accessing networks of legacy and new systems.

Table 1. Responsibilities for each function in the IAM lifecycle

Function	Primary Responsibility	Additional Responsibility	Comments
Registration	Human Resources	External background checking companies	May not be economically feasible to maintain in-house expertise in all areas
Issuance of credentials and posting them to database	Information security administrators	Business units	Need to get confirmation from hiring manager that person is actually who he or she claims to be
Change in credentials	Human resources; business unit administrators	Information security administrators	For example, the earning of a professional certification may allow someone to perform additional tasks.
Issuance of system access rights	IT system administrators	Business unit administrators	Need to get confirmation from hiring manager that person is actually allowed to access the system/network.
Issuance of application access rights	Business unit administrators; Application owners	Information security administrators	In some cases, a business unit administrator can issue access rights, in other cases a request has to go to the information security administration team, depending on the structure and policy of the organization.
Change of system/application access rights	Business unit administrators; Application owners	Information security administrators	Changes have to be approved by business unit manager and the "owner" of the application when the change represents an increase in access rights.
Revocation (or suspension) of system/application access rights	Business unit administrators; Human Resources	Information security administrators	It is often the responsibility of the manager of business units to inform security administration that a user no longer needs access to a particular system. In the case of someone leaving the job, Human Resources will likely issue the order to revoke.
Deletion of system/application access rights	Information security administrators	Business unit administrators	Usually automatic after a certain period of time (say, 90 days) has elapsed without any requests for reconstituting rights.
Revocation (or suspension) of credentials	Information security administrators	Business units	May result from the observation, from a periodic review, say, that person no longer appears to be active.
Deletion of credentials from database	Human Resources; information security administrators		Need to get confirmation from hiring manager that person is actually gone. Deletion is also needed across other systems, such as those providing building access.

Good IAM Systems not Implemented

It was in the mid- to late-1990s when the author was introduced to a new breed of IAM system. The vendor had created a really impressive system with all the necessary workflow elements, reporting tools, agents running on most of the popular platforms, APIs (application program interfaces) to link to nonstandard platforms, and a host of tools for interfacing with Human Resources, synchronizing across systems, and so forth. In many ways, it appeared to be the ideal system. The main problem with it was that the system never seemed to get implemented in a production environment.

Next came a product with a very good workflow capability, but lacking a number of needed interfaces with legacy systems. Nevertheless, we went as far as getting a major consulting firm to propose a joint internal-external project for implementing this system, since it was very apparent that there were insufficient internal workers available to do the job. The multi-million dollar project did not get approved and the proposal languished.

There is an epilogue to this story. Several years later a review by the Internal Audit department discovered several major deficiencies related to the management and reporting the access management systems and procedures and demanded that remedial action be taken. In response, management assigned several senior information security specialists, along with a sizable number of administrative staff, for more than a year to the mind-numbing task of cleaning up the system and streamlining procedures. At least one member of the professional staff quit because the assignments provided little hope of career advancement, and was in fact seen as a detriment. It is quite likely that the cost of conducting the fire fighting exercise far exceeded what it would have cost to implement an automated IAM system in the first place.

Once Bitten, Twice Shy

A large financial company recognized the need for a company-wide IAM system and had actually purchased such a product from a large vendor. Unfortunately, the product did not live up to its claimed capabilities and the company was disappointed when it discovered that the system could only be implemented in one minor area and that, even then, functionality was limited.

Several years later, the company decided to revisit the subject, but this time in a more cautious way. They engaged a large consulting firm to perform an initial study on how an IAM system might be implemented across the organization, which had acquired several other companies in the interim, each of which had its own IAM approach.

The first phase was to get an understanding of the current environment in the parent company and its affiliates. The goal of the first phase of the project was to come up with a common IAM architecture driven from a single "authoritative source" of information about users, the systems that they could access, and the rights they would have within systems. This phase of the project was completely successfully.

Proposed subsequent phases, which would have covered the selection of one or more technologies and the implementation of the selected systems, were not approved and funded, so the initiative was abandoned and each subsidiary and affiliate continued along their current independent, and suboptimal, ways.

Not long afterwards, the parent organization merged with another company of comparable size, so that it is more than likely that the whole IAM issue had to be revisited and the analysis restarted from the beginning.[17]

We're Almost There! Oops!

A small-to-midsize financial firm had developed its own customized RBAC (role-based access control) system. The roles were defined, the procedures laid out, the systems to effect the procedures were written, tested and put into production, and a number of departments had already been converted. A plan for converting the remaining departments was in place.

And then a bombshell hit. The firm, which had been operating somewhat autonomously from its owner, was suddenly sold to a large bank with the philosophy of rolling in any acquisitions to its own systems. The acquiring institution did not have an advanced RBAC system in place, so all the effort of implementing such a system was thrown by the wayside.

It is unfortunate that, in the turmoil of transition, valuable nuggets of technology, such as an in-place RBAC, are abandoned and replaced with lesser technologies. Having lost much, if not all, of the experience gained from the initial implementation, subsequent RBAC initiatives within the merged venture will likely need to begin again from "square one."

LESSONS LEARNED

What is apparent time after time is that, while the managements of many organizations recognize the value of automating IAM functions at an intellectual level, they are seldom prepared to make the commitment and invest the resources to transition to such an automated environment. They seem to be more comfortable with spending at current levels on processes that are frequently criticized by auditors and complained about by business units.

While the justification for investing in automating the IAM process may be less convincing in relatively stable business environments, it becomes very evident during times of major upheaval, whether internally generated or the result of externalities, that it would have been very worthwhile to have such an automated process in place, but by then it is too late for the initiation of such a project to benefit the current chaos. Once the transition is completed, often at huge cost, it again becomes difficult to justify such a project since so much has been already spent on "fighting fires" through the prior upheaval. Since such major disruptions, as caused by mergers, acquisitions, changes in business direction and technology innovation, are difficult to forecast (although they are almost certain to occur), their economic impact may not be factored in to any proposal for an IAM project. As a result, we see the syndrome of recurring change being handled by inadequate processes continuing.

The quandary of it being difficult to justify large initial expenditures in order to reduce future expenses, improve control and avoid the high costs of compromise are common across the full range of security. They are perhaps greatest for IAM systems since the cost of implementation can be especially high when compared to other security measures and many of the savings are difficult to forecast. However, it is apparent from experience, that there will eventually be a high price to pay for not streamlining the IAM process.

The main lesson from this is that organizations must fully understand how the IAM lifecycle does, and should, operate within their particular environments and determine how automation fits into the structure and cultures of their own organization and any other organization with which they merge or do business, or which they acquire. It is desirable to implement IAM systems that have the flexibility and agility to adapt to many new and potential situations. For example, it is advantageous for them to handle most of the more popular operating systems and computer and network architectures, even if the organization itself operates only a few of them. In this way, transitioning in a new organization or operation will be much easier if not quite "plug and play."

Also, the very act of automating the processes means that the knowledge of experts on the legacy systems can be incorporated into the logic of the IAM system. In fact, one of the main arguments for justifying IAM systems is the fact that it is virtually impossible for one person, or even a small group, to be expert in every application, platform, etc. in all but the smallest and simplest of entities.

FUTURE RESEARCH DIRECTIONS

It is hoped that, as a result of describing the process and the issues in this chapter, researchers, vendors and practitioners will evolve methods and procedures, along with systems, that can make for orderly transitions within which there continues to be effective management of the identities and access rights of individuals within turbulent organizations and across different organizations, which are brought together in some fashion different from what existed previously.

CONCLUSION

It is clear that highly-disruptive organizational changes present particular challenges to the ability to control all the aspects of system access. Often, as a result of such changes, there is a need to merge perfectly good IAM processes and systems into lesser approaches, or even if the prior systems are not eliminated, the demands of huge movements and changes in the user population, and their management, can result in controlled (or sometimes uncontrolled) chaos.

In this article, we have examined the various stages in the IAM process and have related their importance to a variety of upheavals. We pointed out where the weaknesses are and what must be done in order to compensate for the loss of control. Since such disruptions are so common among modern organizations, one would think that there would be well-established procedures to manage the changes, yet time and again organizations founder in this area and expose their institutions to very high levels of risk and exposure. It is hoped that, by calling out IAM issues resulting from major changes, that organizations will address them proactively so as to avoid the misery that invariably occurs when such issues are neglected.

REFERENCES

AT&T and The Economist Intelligence Unit. (2006). Avoiding safety culture shock. *AT&T Networking Views, 5*. Retrieved August 12, 2010, from http://www.business.att.com/content/emailmessage/assets/NV-Issue_5.pdf

Axelrod, C. W. (2000). Systems and communications security during recovery and repair. In Doughty, K. (Ed.), *Business continuity planning: Protecting your organization's life*. Auerbach Best Practices Series. doi:10.1201/9780849390333.ch19

Ferraiolo, D. F., Kuhn, D. R., & Chandramouli, R. (2003). *Role-based access control*. Boston, MA: Artech House Publishers.

Smedinghoff, T. J. (2010). *Building an online identity legal framework: The proposed national strategy. Privacy & Security Law Report*. The Bureau of National Affairs, Inc.

KEY TERMS AND DEFINITIONS

Authentication: The process by means of which the identities of registered individuals are verified so that they might have access to systems.

Authorization: The process by means of which authenticated individuals are allowed to access specific functions and data within computer systems. *Also* entitlements, access rights.

Access Rights (Rights): Entitlements approved for users allowing them to gain access to certain functions and data contained within computer systems.

Credentials: Artifacts that are used by registered individuals to access systems and networks.

Entitlement: *See* User Entitlement.

IAM (Identity and Access Management): The management of the process of authenticating and authorizing users so that they might perform certain approved functions on computer systems. *Also* IdM (Identity Management), User Provisioning.

RBAC (Role-Based Access Control): An approach to access management whereby users are assigned roles based on their job responsibilities and access rights are attached to each role.

Registration: The process by which users identities are verified.

User Entitlement: Something, which describes a user's privileges or personalized environments, that a user needs in order to access specific systems and networks. *See* Access Rights.

User Provisioning: The creation, maintenance and deactivation of user objects and user attributes.

ENDNOTES

1. Quoted in (AT&T, 2006), pages 10-11.
2. This is derived from a quotation attributed to the Greek philosopher, Heraclitus of Ephesus. Retrieved August 12, 2010 from http://en.wikiquote.org/wiki/Heraclitus
3. The following definition of "user provisioning" was retrieved on August 12, 2010 from http://www.answers.com/topic/provisioning... "User provisioning refers to the creation, maintenance and deactivation of user objects and user attributes, as they exist in one or more systems, directories or applications, in response to automated or interactive business processes. User provisioning software may include one or more of the following processes: change propagation, self service workflow, consolidated user administration, delegated user administration, and federated change control. User objects may represent employees, contractors, vendors, partners, customers or other recipients of a service. Services may include electronic mail, inclusion in a published user directory, access to a database, access to a network or mainframe, etc. User provisioning is a type of identity management software, particularly useful within organizations, where users may be represented by multiple objects on multiple systems."
4. A discussion of the term "user entitlement" was retrieved on August 12, 2010 from http://www.outlookexchange.com/articles/richardwakeman/wakeman_c1p1.asp as follows "The term "user entitlements" is used to describe privileges or personalized environments on the network. Quite simply, a "user entitlement" is something that a user needs when they login to their network account. This can be a home directory located on a specific file share or provisioned access to a specific application..."
5. Details about and lessons learned from the ChoicePoint breach were retrieved on August 12, 2010 from http://www.pcworld.com/article/132795/choicepoint_details_data_breach_lessons.html
6. See (Smedinghoff, 2010).
7. In the ChoicePoint case, the breach occurred when the perpetrators were inappropriately registered as valid customers arguably as the result of an inadequate registration process. Then-CISO of ChoicePoint, Richard Baich, claimed that the failure to detect imposters during registrations was "not an information security problem." Retrieved on August 12, 2010 from http://searchsecurity.techtarget.com/news/article/0,289142,sid14_gci1062076,00.html
8. The author is reminded of the movie "Air Force One," starring Harrison Ford as the president, in which the bad guys were able to get on board the presidential plane because a malicious insider was able to preregister them into the hand recognition system used to gain entry to the plane.

9 Sometimes one can prevent access to all systems by suspending access to "the network." However, unless administrators are diligent in following up and suspending individual system access rights, there usually remains a number of open access rights that could be exploited by others with access to the network.

10 That is not to say that all organizational changes are predictable. Sometimes they are not. However, there is frequently the time and resources to plan for the specific transition of identities and access rights from the current state to the new one. This is not the case for external catastrophic events where the timing and scope are unknown in advance.

11 This is part of what is commonly known as RBAC, or role-based access control, see (Ferraiolo, 2003).

12 The author recalls how, when a major electrical blackout occurred in August 20xx, many firms dusted off their Year 2000 contingency plans (which fortunately were not yet obsolete) and used them to respond to the blackout.

13 The author was personally involved in such a transition. It took about a year to complete the project because of the organizational and systems changes needed by the combined entity.

14 There is much debate over the differences between "data owners" and "application owners' and who should be responsible for approving accesses. In large part, the problem derives from the fact that data, particularly critical or sensitive data, may originate in one department and will be used by many applications under the jurisdiction of other departments.

15 The author personally experienced a situation in which the smaller entity had implemented a superior role-based access structure to that of the much larger acquiring company. Many of the systems plus the well-designed RBAC approach were abandoned as a result of the takeover.

16 The Y2K remediation exercise highlighted the millions of lines of legacy code (often written in COBOL) that still are pervasive in large, longstanding organizations. These systems remain in place since, first, they still work, and second, they would be prohibitively expensive to replace.

17 The author had direct experience of the initial phases of this case, but is not familiar with subsequent activities.

Chapter 2
From Domain-Based Identity Management Systems to Open Identity Management Models

Ivonne Thomas
Hasso-Plattner-Institute, Germany

Christoph Meinel
Hasso-Plattner-Institute, Germany

ABSTRACT

With the change of the Internet from an information to a business platform, an evolution of identity management is ongoing, which affects the way in which we represent and provision identities in the digital world. Open identity management models are the result of this evolution and denote a shift from the traditional domain-based identity models to open models that represent identities as a set of claims (user attributes). Although open identity management models have been designed specifically to address the open nature of the Internet, traditional approaches are still pre-dominating in these networks. This chapter will focus on this contradiction and its reasons.

One of the main reasons is the problem of establishing trust relationships between independent parties—a problem inherent to open environments with multiple trust domains. In open environments, participants often do not know each other, but nevertheless require an existing trust relationship to perform critical transactions. Governments, commercial organizations, and academia alike have addressed this issue by providing better assurance guidelines for identity management. The outcome is a number of identity assurance frameworks that identify and cluster certain security criteria into levels of trust or levels of assurance (LoA). These approaches are described, compared, and assessed with regard to their role towards a reliable identity management across the Internet. Limitations are identified and trust levels for attributes are proposed as potential fields for further research.

DOI: 10.4018/978-1-61350-498-7.ch002

INTRODUCTION

Looking at the current online world, performing transactions as online banking, online shopping or communicating in social networks has become an inherent part of life. Hereby, personal, identity-related data plays a major role, since for many activities a service provider requires details about the identity of a user. Traditional approaches for identity management, like the application-centric or isolated model (cf. (Audun Jøsang, 2005)), require users to register with every single service and to re-authenticate each time they use a service in another trust domain. Over the time users register with several applications on the Internet and collect many digital identities together with their corresponding authentication credentials. This leads to a number of well-known problems. To name a few, users have for example difficulties to remember their passwords, and also bear a great burden to keep their account information up-to-date (cf. (Bertino, Martino, Paci, & Squicciarini, 2009), (Gail-Joon Ahn, Moo Nam Ko, & Mohamed Shehab, 2008)).

To overcome the limitations of the closed domain, open identity management models emerged as a way of sharing identity information across several trust domains in a controlled manner. The basic principle behind these new identity models is to manage and keep identity data in multiple trust domains, at so called *identity providers*, and to share this information with applications and services that are willing to rely on it. Hence, these applications and services are also called relying parties. Open protocols and standards as OpenID (The OpenId Foundation, 2007), Information Cards (OASIS, 2009) or WS-Federation (Lockhart, et al., 2006) already exist and form the backbone of the new models.

Nevertheless, the adoption of open identity management models has not set off tangibly, yet. The acceptance of the new models mainly depends on the willingness of services and applications to rely on information that they retrieve from foreign sources that are outside their own trust domain. Up to today, this willingness is very low. Each service provider usually forms an isolated identity domain. Looking at the reason, this development is little surprising. Organizations often have strict legal requirements and policies for the management and storage of user data. Moreover, a company's user database constitutes often one of the most valuable assets of a company. Therefore, it is not surprising that organizations find it hard to give up this control and to rely on user information from a partner.

However, especially, with regard to the Internet, we can find many use cases that do not require a strong trust relationship to rely on identity attributes from someone else. Often the user can enter information into his account that does not require any verification. It really depends on what a digital identity is used for. If the user logs on to a site to prove on repeat visits that it is the same user, it does not matter whether his digital identity matches with his "real- life identity" as long as it is always the same digital identity he uses to log on. Only if critical transactions are performed, as ordering an item or paying for a service, the integrity of provided user data is required to hold the user liable in case anything bad happens. Taking all these considerations into account, it becomes obvious that the willingness to believe in identity data from a foreign source is closely related to the trust level that is required by the transaction a user wants to perform. The more critical a transaction is, the more assurance into the identity of a user will be required by the relying party to accept identity data.

In order for relying parties to match the transaction requirements with those of their partners, proper assessment mechanisms for identity assurance are needed. In order to ease the process, identity assurance frameworks have been proposed and developed as a mean to define a global trust level that allows an immediate comparison between participants even though they might not know each other.

This chapter is divided into two parts. The first part focuses on the classification of identity management models. As suggested by Jøsang et al. (JøsangA., Fabre, Hay, Dalziel, & Pope, 2005), there are four models, which are the outcome of a development that is still ongoing. Accordingly, they are introduced in the chronological order given by this development. The four models are: *application-centric*, *centralized*, *user-centric* and *federated identity management*. Each model is described with its strengths and weaknesses, typical use cases, as well as the technologies to implement the model. Selected technologies for open identity management as OpenID, Information Cards and WS-Federation are described afterwards.

The second part of the chapter focuses on identity assurance and its role towards a reliable identity management in open networks. Existing identity assurance frameworks are presented and their shortcomings and limitations are discussed. To overcome the limitations, the final part of the chapter suggests trust levels for identity attributes as an emerging trend in future research.

BACKGROUND - IDENTITY MANAGEMENT: DEFINITION AND APPROACHES

Identity management is one of the most pervasive parts of IT systems. The reason is that almost all IT systems operate on assets such as personal data of customers and employees that need to be protected. Thus, in order to allow a person access to the system, the systems needs to know something about the identity of the subject. This knowledge is required to make access control decisions (cf. (Benantar, 2006)).

Identity management comprises the whole process of gathering information about a subject, storing this information in an account and distributing the information along the systems requesting parts of a user's digital identity. As described in (Windley, 2005), a digital identity follows a continuous lifecycle: An identity is created (provisioned) in the beginning, propagated and used for a certain time and destroyed once it is not needed anymore. Most works share the same or a similar definition of a *digital identity,* compare for instance (Windley, 2005), (Bertocci, Serack, & Baker, 2007), (Jøsang, Fabre, Hay, Dalziel, & Pope, 2005). A digital identity is a limited set of attributes represented by a unique identifier such as an account name or number, which is associated with a person's "real-life" identity. It is the task of *identity management* to control and facilitate this lifecycle.

Conceptual Evolution of Identity Management: From Domain-Based Identity Management Systems to Open Identity Management Models

Over the years, identity management has undergone a substantial change. In the beginning, computers were mostly isolated systems, hardly connected to the outside world, and mostly supporting the processes inside a company. Over the years, the IT system landscape has changed to a highly computerized and interconnected world, in which services are offered and consumed over the Internet. Naturally, this also had implications to the identity management. Caused by the change of system structures in IT, a number of identity management models emerged, each addressing the particularities of new IT system landscapes. Coming from the traditional, application-centric models, the centralized identity management model emerged to provide a more efficient identity management inside closed domains. Again, with the shift of IT systems from the closed to the open world of the Internet, new open identity management models emerged which were designed specifically to address the open nature of these environments. Some of the identity management sources, see for instance (Chappell, 2010), even state, that there is a major paradigm shift about to happen which leads from the traditional domain-based identity management approaches such as the isolated-/application-specific or the centralized identity management to open identity management systems. The shift affects in particular the basic conceptual approach how digital identities are represented in IT systems and shall be explained in the following.

Domain-Based Identity Management Systems

Domain-based Identity Management Systems are the traditional approach to manage users in applications. In the very early years of computing, application developers were in need for a way to recognize their application users in a reliable manner. The solution was mostly to augment applications with authentication and identity management features. In order to represent a user in the system, the notion of an *account* was created. An account is a unique identifier that is associated with an authentication secret, such as a password, to authenticate a user on subsequent visits.

As the application-specific identity management resulted in highly proprietary and isolated identity management solutions, centralized approaches were developed to take the burden of managing user accounts from the application developers. In the centralized approach, all users within a domain are managed by a single entity that provisions identity data to the applications. In particular with the advent of multi-user operating systems (e.g. Windows 95) centralized identity management was henceforth available with the platform and could be used directly in the applications. Later centralized identity management found widespread adoption inside the homogeneous networks of organizations.

Open Identity Management Systems

Domain-based identity management systems usually support a fixed identity model and use protocols that are only available inside closed domains. Beyond the borders of a closed domain, a world of heterogeneous networks emerges that does not know about identity attributes within closed domains. Also, many technologies, including for example Kerberos, usually reach only to the border of homogenous networks. Therefore, new technologies were needed to deal with the heterogeneous environment of the Internet and to allow applications to share identity information seamlessly across domains. Open identity management systems evolved as a way to connect existing identity management systems over the Internet. Besides interoperability between different technologies, open identity management models also feature an open identity model that allows any type of identity attribute (claim) to be included in a specific digital identity. Each attribute is named with an abstract identifier (e.g. a URI), which can be used by applications to access the attribute. The formats to exchange tokens are open and extensible to incorporate the identity model. In addition, the identity management system translates between different attribute/claim dialects, in order to provision applications with the attributes/claims they understand.

CLASSIFICATION OF IDENTITY MANAGEMENT

Today, mainly four different identity models can be found in the literature (Figure 1). See for instance (Jøsang A., Fabre, Hay, Dalziel, & Pope, 2005) or (Benantar, 2006).

A commonly used classification is the one in domain-based and open identity management models that has been introduced before. Looking at the typical area of usage, another vertical classification into end-user oriented and business-oriented models can be found (see figure). While the application-centric and user-centric identity management is often used in the private sector, the centralized as well as the federated identity management can be found predominately in the

Figure 1. Classification of identity management models

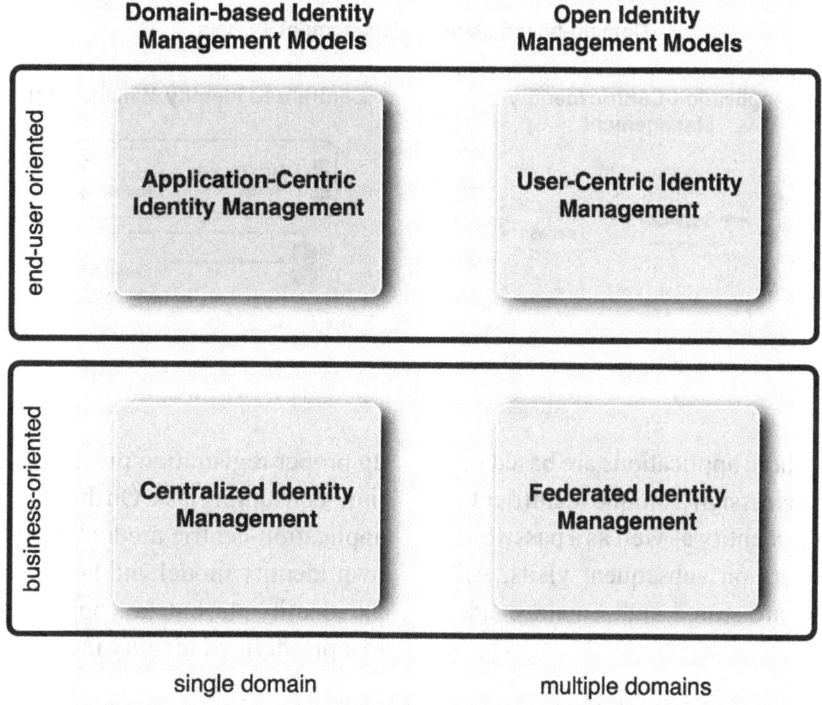

business context. The federated identity management in particular targets business-to-business scenarios and the centralized identity management is used by organizations to allow their employees and members to access various applications within a single domain.

In the end-user domain, the user-centric models targets end-users authentication on the Internet while the application-specific identity management is best suited for the domain of a single application. In the following, each of the four identity models shall be characterized in detail.

Application-Centric Identity Management

Definition

In the application-centric / isolated identity management, which is shown in Figure 2, each application takes care of its users itself. This implies that all users need to register with the application/service during a registration step before actually using the system.

Description

Since the beginnings of computing, application developers and designers are challenged with the need to identify users on subsequent uses of their applications. Examples include the need to personalize views and/or to ensure that the right users get access to the systems. The application-centric identity management was one of the very first approaches to add identity management features to applications. The way, it works is, that authentication and identity management features are directly built into the applications, resulting in highly proprietary, isolated identity management solutions. Each application has its own identity model containing a set of attributes appropriate for this specific application.

Figure 2. Domain-based identity management models

Domain-based Identity Management Models

Application-Centric Identity Management

Service

User Database

Centralized Identity Management

IDM

Central User Management

User Database

Service

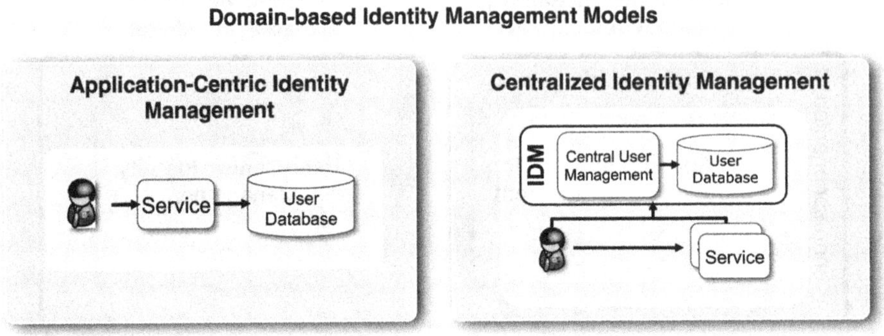

In most cases, these applications are based on user accounts, which assign a unique identifier to each managed user identity as well as a password to authenticate users on subsequent visits. All attributes of users are stored and remain inside the application.

Advantages and Disadvantages

While the application-centric model works well for single applications, it seriously lacks scalability when being applied to environments with multiple applications or services. Just consider a service-oriented architecture with a multitude of services. In such an environment, implementing identity management for each service is not recommended, as the possibilities to compose services to applications and to reuse services in various contexts would be lowered tremendously. Moreover users would need to register for each service separately. This does not only lead to an explosion of user accounts, but also bears significant security risks as users are overstrained with the sheer number of passwords they need to manage properly. A classical, but from the security point of view very dangerous, strategy is here for example to use the same easy-to-remember password for multiple accounts. Also when looking at the application provider side, the application-centric identity management is not always the best option. Setting up proper registration procedures is a costly and time-consuming task. On the other hand, using the application-centric model the application has its own identity model and hence full control over the identity attributes as opposed to being bound to a pre-defined identity model.

Usage Scenarios

While inside closed domains, as in most companies and organizations, the longing for single-sign-on features has widely replaced the application-specific model with more centralized solutions, one could observe its revival in the open world of the Internet in recent years.

Just think of some popular web applications as Facebook, Ebay or Amazon, that all require users to register. One of the reasons is its easy initial set up that does not require the establishment of strong trust relationships between identity providers and relying parties.

Technologies

Most applications have a built-in username and password database to store and manage its users.

Centralized Identity Management

Definition

In the centralized identity management model, which is shown in Figure 2, all users within a domain are managed by a central instance, which provides identity provisioning for multiple applications within the same domain.

Description

Multi-user operating systems (e.g. Windows 95) were among the first systems to offer a centralized identity management. All functionality to manage digital identities of users was built directly into the platform and therefore separated from the applications itself. As a result, application developers could concentrate on their actual business and did not need to care about developing a complete identity management for their applications. The only thing to care about was the integration of the identity management upon which they built. Today, a centralized identity management system is part of almost every company or unit that is in some way organizationally independent. As a result identity information about all members within the organization is hold at a central place and can be accessed by applications within the domain. This also leads to major benefits for the users of the system. Since identity management is centralized, users have to authenticate only once to access a multitude of applications. This feature is called single-sign-on. Also, user data is not stored redundantly in separate places and therefore easier to maintain.

Advantages and Disadvantages

Separating the business logic from the identity management systems and centralizing it yields significant advantages for developers and users alike. Application developers are relieved from implementing a whole identity management system. Their only task remains to integrate their application into the identity provider platform. The downside, however, is that these environments usually have a pre-defined identity model, which is fixed and most often not extensible. This means application developers are restricted to the capabilities of the underlying platform and can usually only use the identity attributes that are given by the used identity system.

On the user side, centralized identity management allows to implement a single-sign-on for multiple applications within the same domain. The direct benefit for the user is that they can logon to several applications using a single account and are relieved from remembering authentication credentials for every single application. However, caution has to be taken as a single centralized instance also bears risks for the users. Since all applications have access to the same database of users, trust is an important factor. While in the isolated identity management model, a user only needs to trust on a single application, in a centralized environment, he needs to have faith that all applications within a domain will use his identity data in the intended way. Usually this is easy in a closed environment of a single computer, it is also possible in the restricted environments of a company's network, in which the employee has no other choice but to trust on the company's network and applications. However, in an open environment as the Internet, each participant usually forms its own trust domain and it becomes increasingly difficult to believe that all participants act in the best interest of the users. Trust between domains does not come natural and requires a certain effort to be established. The more trust a transaction requires, the more effort it takes. Just imagine for example two companies establishing a partnership. As soon as transactions between the two involve a risk for either side, legally binding contracts are set up to balance the risk.

Another example showing how important it is that users have trust in the manager of their data is Microsoft's Passport (later.NET Passport, now

Windows Live ID). Microsoft Passport offered a centralized identity management for the Internet. Several applications on the Internet could make use of Passport to authenticate users by their MSN account. However, the user base never really exceeded the number of MSN users. As the system was not based on open standards and Microsoft was the only identity provider, many users and application developers choose not to use it (cf. also (Cameron, 2005)). Later Microsoft developed Information Cards and Cardspace as an identity management system for the Internet that allows having not only one, but multiple sources to manage identity data and that is based on open standards.

Usage Scenarios

Following up on the discussion of advantages and disadvantages, the centralized identity management is in particular suitable for centrally managed environments as the closed domain of an organization. Indeed, almost every organization, which forms an independent administrative domain, uses the centralized identity management to store information about users at a central place and foster a single-sign-on for various applications within the company's network.

Technologies

Within the closed domain of an organization, usually a centralized directory, such as Active Directory, is used to hold the identity data. For the authentication of users by the applications in the domain, several technologies can be used. One technology that is often used is Kerberos; other possibilities include SAML or public key infrastructures.

User-Centric Identity Management

Definition

In the user-centric identity management (cf. Figure 3), the digital identity of users is managed by various sources, the identity providers. The user is in the centre of all interaction and chooses upon request the digital identity he wants to use to authenticate with a certain application or service.

Description

The user-centric identity management uses an approach to identity management that is very similar to the way identities are used in the real world. In our daily life, every one of us possesses a number of identity cards to prove certain claims upon request. Just think of a driver's license to prove that one is eligible to drive a car, a passport to prove our citizenship or an ATM card to prove our ownership to a bank account. All these cards are issued by different authorities, our real-world identity providers. We carry them around and show them upon request. For example in order to retrieve a discount in the movie theater, our student card is requested by the ticket salesperson as a proof of us being a student.

User-centric identity management works exactly this way. Every user in the online world has his identity data stored with one or more identity providers. Instead of using one identity provider all the time, the user can choose which identity provider he wants to use for a certain application or service. This identity provider is contacted to assert a certain claim, such as "This user's name is Bob." This assertion, the counterpart of the real-world identity card, is given to the requesting application. As in the real world, the application provider now decides whether it trusts on assertions by this identity provider and either accepts the information or requests further proof for the same claim.

Figure 3. Open identity management models

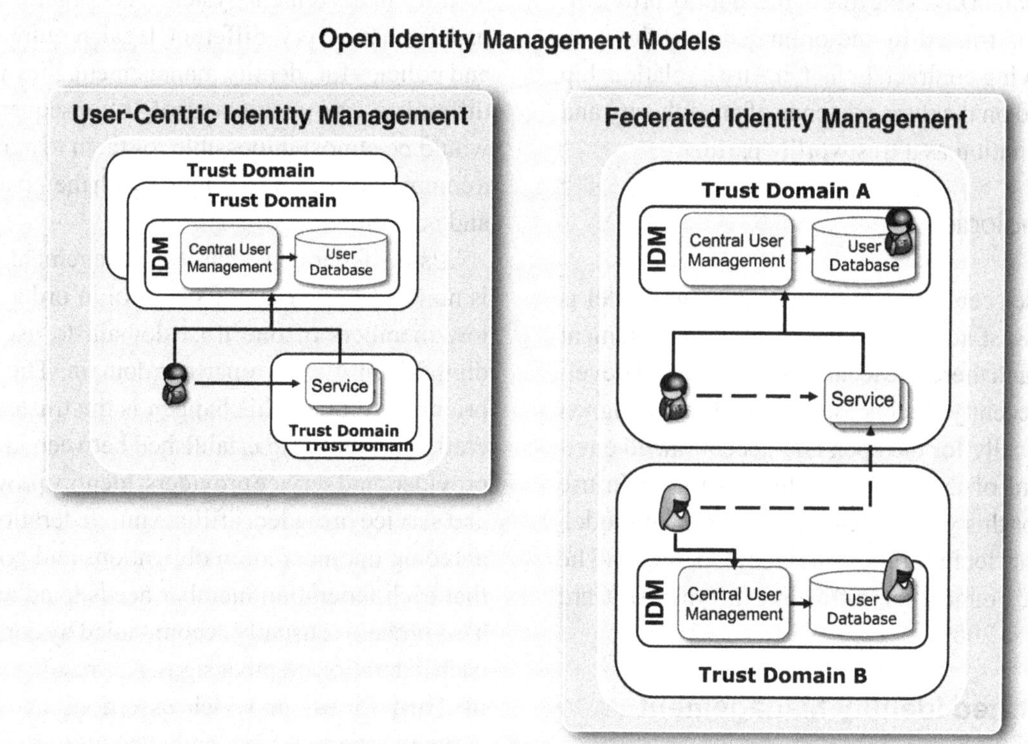

Advantages and Disadvantages

As the name suggests, the user-centric identity management puts the user into the heart of all decisions. The user decides with which identity provider(s) he wants to register an account with. The user also decides which of his identity providers he contacts to make assertions about his identity. And the user also decides which of his identity attributes are given to the requesting party. The clear benefit is, that the user enjoys more privacy and has full control over his data and knows who is using it and when. In fact, in the decentralized model the identity providers typically do not know where and what a user is using his identity for. Only the relying parties, such as a service or an application, know about the identity provider(s); otherwise they would have no basis for making a decision to trust an assertion.

Usage Scenarios

With the dynamic establishment of trust relationships and the relying parties deciding which identity providers to trust, the user-centric identity management fits best to non-business scenarios. Usually it is used in situations with a low demand for identity assurance, such as registering for social web sites as for example weblogs or forum discussions. In fact, it is often used as an alternative way for website users to fill in registration forms or as a way of identifying a user on repeat visits. In both cases, the web site might not be interested, whether the user's digital identity matches with his real-life identity, as long as it is always the same user it interacts with.

Furthermore the user-centric identity management is also beneficial in all scenarios in which the set up of contracts to establish trust is not feasible. This is for example the case between an

Online Shop and the government. In this case, the government takes the role of the identity provider, which is trusted by the online shop without an underlying contract. In fact, the trust relationship is based on the pure existence of an authority and its reputation as a trustworthy partner.

Technologies

The user-centric identity management model is the newest addition to the identity management world and therefore technologies have just developed recently. Technologies have been designed specifically for the open and decentralized environment of the Internet, which is the main use case for this young identity management model. Popular technologies include OpenID ((The OpenId Foundation, 2007)) and Information Card (OASIS, 2009).

Federated Identity Management

Definition

In the federated identity management (cf. Figure 3) several independent trust domains form a *Circle of Trust*, in which all participants agree on trusting each other's assertions about user authentication and attributes for the purpose of access control and single-sign-on.

Description

Similar to the user-centric identity management, federated identity management also is one of the new open identity management models that aim at providing user authentication and access control in the global context of the Internet. Looking at the Internet today, we mainly find an environment of independent trust domains formed by independent organizations. There is no central instance to manage identity data, but many isolated identity islands, each having its own identity management system. Isolation allows companies to retain control over their users and identity management systems. As organizations usually have very different legal requirements and policies for identity management, they find it difficult to give up this control. In consequence, it would be almost impossible for them to agree on a common centralized solution with their partners and customers.

Using federated identity management there is no need to give up this control in order to allow members of one trust domain to use their digital identities in a partner domain. The basic principle to make this happen is the trusted federation relationship established between identity providers and service providers. Identity providers and service providers affiliate into federations by agreeing upon common obligations and policies that each federation member needs to adhere to. This process is usually accompanied by contracts each federation member signs. As a result, a Circle of Trust forms, in which assertions about the authentication of users and attributes are shared among the federation members.

Technically, each federation member stays in control of its own identity management system, but augments this with additional federation features that allow users to link (federate) their digital identities between the federation members. Certain identity management functions like authentication or provision of identity attributes are then offloaded to the identity provider(s) in the federation. Identity consumers on the other side receive this identity and authentication information from the providers and use it as if it was coming from their own identity management system.

Advantages and Disadvantages

Federated identity management is primarily a way to allow single-sign-on (SSO) between partner organizations regardless of organizational borders. Members of one organization such as employees of a company can link their account with accounts they might have with other organizations in the same federation. Once linked, a member can access all connected accounts by authenticating just once, allowing him to sign in to a number of application at the same time. Of course, the more members the federation has, the more a user will benefit from SSO.

However, there is also a downside to the federated identity management concerning the privacy of the users. In a federation the identity provider "sees all"; that means it knows which relying parties a subject visits. Given this information and the identity data of the user, a malicious identity provider could track the users behavior and would hold a rather comprehensive profile of a user. Also, without proper protection mechanisms, identity providers and service providers are in the position to match different digital identities of the same user for the purpose of creating an even more comprehensive user profile that can be used to provide personalized offers.

Another threat arises from account linkage. Once the users password is compromised in any of the linked identity providers, an attacker has instant access to all applications and services that are connected with the user's account.

Usage Scenarios

Due to the federation agreements necessary to build up the Circle of Trust, federated identity management is mostly used in business-to-business scenarios. Typical use cases include the authentication of employees of one company in a partner company or the federation of companies offering complementary services for their customers. Using federation, employees can get easier access to shared project resources or can use services of the partner company, such as booking a business trip, without an additional authentication step. In the second case, customers are offered to link their accounts between the collaborating companies in order to create a better shopping experience.

Technologies

Technologies for federated identity management exist mainly in the field of service-oriented architectures. In the past, two initiatives have formed to develop a standard for the interoperable exchange of identity information across organizational borders on the basis of web services. As a result, we find today on one side the specifications of the Liberty Alliance (now Kantara Initiative (Kantara Initiative, 2010)) with SAML 2.0 (Cantor, Kemp, Maler, & Philpott, 2005) as a standard to describe identity information in an interoperable format and on the other side, WS-Federation (Lockhart, et al., 2006), a specification developed by IBM and Microsoft.

Originated as two separate specifications, latest efforts have driven a development towards interoperability between both specifications. (cf. (OASIS Cover Pages, 2008))

OPEN IDENTITY MANAGEMENT STANDARDS AND TECHNOLOGIES

Past experiences have revealed that traditional solutions as the application-specific and the centralized identity management work well in closed domains, but fail when they are applied to open environments containing multiple trust domains. Kim Cameron explains in his Laws of Identity (Cameron, The Laws of Identity, 2005) the successes and failures of digital identity systems. One of the main findings is that an identity management for the Internet needs multiple identity providers (Pluralism of Operators and Technologies). As the Internet was built without a central instance, there will also never be a central instance to manage identities. Instead we have several identity providers, either administrated by the government or big players as Google or Facebook. Nevertheless, potentially any application provider can take the role of an identity provider. Therefore, interoperability between different identity systems is one of the main requirements for an identity management for the Internet. Looking at the Internet, a number of technologies have been designed to address these needs.

OpenID

OpenID is a very light-wide protocol providing a single-sign-on for browser-based applications. It is built on top of HTTP. A digital identity in OpenID is represented as a unique URI, which contains besides the username of a subject also information of the identity provider. In order to authenticate with OpenID at a supporting web site, the user enters this unique URI instead of username and password. The website as the relying party redirects the user to his identity provider including a request for authentication. If the user is already logged in at his identity provider (a session already exists), the identity provider answers with an authentication assertion and the user can log on to the website without further authentication requests (direct single-sign-on). If the users has not authenticated at his identity provider previously, he is redirected to the login page of his identity provider and asked to log in, for example by means of a user name and password. Upon successful authentication, the identity provider sends an authentication assertion back to the requesting party, the web site.

The Identity Metasystem, Information Cards and CardSpace

The Identity Metasystem denotes an open architecture for the interoperable exchange of identity information between identity providers, relying parties and the user. As identity management solutions differ in the way identities are described and exchanged over protocols, the Identity Meta System aims at connecting different solution by adding an abstraction layer on top of existing solutions that hides the specifics of each identity system (as in the case of IP over Ethernet and Token Ring). The Identity Metasystem describes concepts that are equal in all identity solutions in an interoperable format and specifies how identity information can be translated between different systems.

Information Card is a concrete implementation of the abstract concept of the Identity Metasystem. It has been developed by Microsoft and implemented in several frameworks such as Suns Metro Web Service Stack or the.NET Framework.

Information Card uses unique URIs to describe identity attributes in a global context, so called claims. For example, if a relying party requires the name of a subject, it refers to this attribute as http://schemas.xmlsoap.org/ws/2005/05/identity/claims/givenname.

In order to request identity information from a user, the relying party sends a request based on the specifications for web services to a piece of software running on the computer of the user. This piece of software is called Identity Selector and holds the information about all identity providers a user has registered his identity with. Upon request from a relying party, such as a web site or a web service, the identity selector matches the requested attributes with the attributes each identity provider of the user can provide and presents the user with a set of matching providers. From this set, the user can choose the identity provider he wants to use and is requested to authenticate. Upon successful authentication, the identity provider asserts the requested identity attributes by writing them into an interoperable format and signing the values with its private key. Once the relying party retrieves the information, it can check its integrity and use the information for example for the purpose of access control.

CardSpace is an implementation of an identity selector that is installed per default in Windows Vista. Other implementations that can be used in the context of Information Card include Bandits DigitalMe (The Bandit Project) or various plug-ins for Safari and FireFox.

WS-Federation

WS-Federation is a specification in the field of service-oriented architectures. As a specification for federated identity management it sits on top of other web service specifications such as WS-Trust (Nadalin, Goodner, Gudgin, Barbir, & Granqvist, 2007), WS-MetadataExchange (Ballinger, et al., 2006) and others. WS-Federation provides mechanisms and protocols to establish a Circle of Trust, the federation, between trust domains with the intention to exchange identity information between the federation partners. Microsoft provides an implementation of the WS-Federation specification as part of their.NET Framework.

As part of the federation process, WS-Federation specifies the following mechanisms: exchange of federation metadata to create a federated relationship, account linking of accounts in different trust domains, management of pseudonyms to protect the user's privacy, as well as single-login and–logout.

TOWARDS IDENTITY ASSURANCE IN OPEN IDENTITY MANAGEMENT SYSTEMS

The Needs for Trust and Verified Identities

Past experiences with identity management solutions in open environments have shown that trust is a very crucial factor for the acceptance of identity and authentication information that is managed by someone else (cf. also (Kylau, Thomas, Menzel, & Meinel., 2009)). Looking at the Internet today, we still find an environment of mostly isolated domains formed by of our service providers. Most of these service providers require a portion of our identity in order to offer us personalized services or to hold us liable in case anything bad happens. Especially the second case requires that the service provider can rely on the information he has on the subject. Assurance of a subject's identity is required as soon as a transaction holds a risk for the service provider. To reduce the risk to an acceptable level, the service provider can increase identity assurance by setting up stronger registration processes. With stronger registration processes in place the service provider strengthens the binding between a person's real-life identity and its online identity. However, what works well for a single domain, does not automatically work well in an environment with multiple trust domains. In order to accept identity information from a different trust domain, the service provider needs to know whether the identity assurance procedures fulfill his own requirements. As organizations usually have different legal requirements and policies for identity management, aligning them with a third-party identity provider is not an easy task. Insights into the others systems and procedures are necessary, but often not possible, which leads to the current situation of isolated identity islands. One possible way to solve this situation is standardization. A common standard for identity assurance could provide a scale against which organizations can compare their haves and needs. Identity assurance frameworks are a step towards such a standardized view.

Existing Assurance Frameworks

People like to describe things in numbers. Numbers provide a mean for assessment and comparison as well as a way to create categories of similar things. In the field of security, assurance frameworks aim at categorizing and quantifying identity management processes, such as authentication or identity registration, in order to provide a better assessment. Over the past years, several initiatives around the world have formed with the goal to make authentication processes comparable by clustering different authentication requirement into categories and assign them a level of trust. What started as single initiatives of governments to provide common standards for electronic authentication within the country, has gained even more importance with regard to the number of business processes that are processed online today. In a world, in which organizational borders are crossed seamlessly in online transactions, the voices for common standards or levels of trust for identity management have become louder. A level of trust or level of assurance (LoA) reflects the degree of confidence that someone can assign to the assertions made by another party, such as an identity provider, with respect to the user's identity information.

UK Office of the e-Envoy

The United Kingdom was among the first countries that defined authentication trust levels. In 2002, the UK Office of the e-Envoy published a document called "Registration and Authentication -- E-Government Strategy Framework Policy and Guideline" (Office of the e-Envoy, UK, 2002) in order to provider clear authentication and registration guidelines for e-Government. For typical e-government transactions citizens could get involved in, such as filing a tax return electronically, these guidelines define the necessary registration steps to establish a secure digital identity as well as requirements for the authentication to identify a person in later transactions unambiguously. These requirements are clustered into four different levels—Level 0 being the level with the least requirements and Level 3 being the one with the highest requirements. For filing an income tax return electronically, an authentication trust level of two is needed, which is reached when the client can present a credential (preferable a digital certificate) and can proof his right to that credential, e.g. by signing it with his private key.

OMB M-04-04

Another initiative, the e-Authentication Initiative, has been started by the United States as part of the e-government program. The project involves the development of a federated architecture with multiple e-government applications and credential providers. In order to assist agencies in determining the appropriate level of identity assurance for electronic transactions, the initiative has published a policy called "E- Authentication Guidance for Federal Agencies" (OMB M-04-04 (e-Authentication Initiative, 2007). The document defines four assurance levels, which are based on the risks associated with an authentication error. The four assurance levels reach from "little or no confidence in the asserted identity" to "very high confidence in the asserted identity". In order to determine the required level of assurance, a risk assessment is accomplished for each transaction. Hereby, the potential harm and its likelihood of occurrence are identified.

NIST 800-63

NIST 800-63 is the name of a guideline that is accompanying the OMB-04-04 document and defines concrete technical requirements that apply for each assurance level. The US National Institute of Standards and Technologies (NIST) is the source of the guideline that is called "Electronic Authentication Guideline"(NIST 800-63) (National Institute of Standards and Technology, 2006).

While the OMB document suggests four assurance levels, this document specifies the processes and technologies to reach one of the suggested levels. These technologies concern aspects as identity proofing, security tokens, token and credential management, authentication protocols as well as the types of attacks that need to be prevented.

InCommon

A quite comprehensive approach that extends the OMB/NIST levels has been proposed by InCommon, a federation of more than 100 members from industry, government and the higher education sector (InCommon Federation, 2008). InCommon aims at providing a common standard between the members of the InCommon federation allowing them to assess and rely on identity information of a partner without further investigation. Their identity assurance assessment framework covers identity provisioning aspects as Registration and Identity Proofing, Digital Electronic Credential Technology, Credential Issuance and Management, Security and Management of Authentication Events, Identity Information Management, the Identity Assertion Content as well as the Technical Environment. In the end, two different profiles, Bronze and Silver, contain the requirements with respects to these aspects. Bronze defines a basic security level and Silver adds stricter requirements for more critical transactions. An audit conducted by independent authorities assigns each partner in the federation a corresponding level.

Limitations of Existing Assurance Frameworks

Current approaches for assurance frameworks as described in the previous section provide a comprehensive assessment for identity providers by defining (gathering) trust requirements with regard to all the processes, technologies, technical infrastructure and further protection in place that have an influence on the degree of confidence into the assertion's contents made by an identity provider. The result is a global trust semantics, which allows a classification of identity providers with respect to different levels of trust. Such a classification can serve as the input to policy frameworks as well as a base for contracts and inter-organizational agreements.

Although current approaches provide a quite comprehensive assessment, a number of limitations exists. Existing assurance frameworks mostly refer to the identity as a whole, but do not refer to trust requirements of specific attributes. It is for example not possible to distinguish between self-asserted attributes an identity provider might manage besides attributes that were verified. Especially with regard to platforms of non-institutional providers such as Facebook, users often prefer using pseudonyms when acting in these communities. In fact, in blogs and forum discussions, anonymity of users is a frequent requirement. Also for over-18-services, anonymity of the users often is in favor while at the same time a verified assertion of a user's age is required. For these purposes, an identity provider could manage self-asserted attributes besides verified attributes. When doing so, reflecting these differences in the assertions is a major requirement.

Also, using existing assurance frameworks, it is hard to reflect possible changes of a user's identity trust level over time. As identity proofing processes are cost-intensive and time-consuming due to the effort required to verify a user's identity attributes, a verification of an attribute might not be desired as long as a user is not involved in transactions that demand a higher trust level. Therefore a user might decide to register with an identity provider without proper identity proofing, having for example his/her name self-asserted and getting involved in the identity proofing only upon concrete requirement. This requires a different trust level per user and does not allow to rate an identity provider as a whole.

Furthermore, identity providers are inherently different due to their affiliation with an organization or institution and might be suitable for asserting certain identity attributes only to a limited extent. For example, a banking identity provider will be in particular suitable to assert that a user can pay for a certain service, but might have weak records of the user's status as a student while for a university's identity provider it would probably be the opposite.

In fact, such a diversity of identity provisioning sources is intended in the user-centric model that aims at reflecting the way identities are managed in the real world. (cf. (Thomas & Meinel, 2010)

FUTURE RESEARCH DIRECTIONS: TRUST LEVELS FOR ATTRIBUTES

The main purpose of an identity service is certainly the provisioning of identity attributes of registered users to parties that are willing to rely on it. For this reason, identity attributes are usually in the main focus of the provisioning process. Services can request certain identity attributes and will get the corresponding values if entitled to. This is the way claim-based identity in its core works. The unit of all transactions is the claim, which is an identity attribute that is subject to verification by an identity provider and is issued upon request to the relying party.

Trust and assurance frameworks on the other side put the identity providers and their processes, mechanisms and technologies to safeguard user identities in the middle of all considerations. An identity provider is assessed by basically all the mechanisms and technologies in place, such as credential and token management, legal aspects and storage of identity data that have an influence on the degree of confidence a relying party can put into the assertions of this identity provider.

Certainly, all these considerations are worthwhile. However, with regard to open identity management and its claim-based approach, an important part is missing to close the gap between the identity provider-centric view of identity assurance frameworks and the attribute- or claim-based view of open identity management models.

As has been stated in (Thomas & Meinel, 2009) trust should be defined on the same granular level as the identity values themselves. This means, that the decision to trust should not only be made between the issuing and the relying party on a all-comprising level–as this is also very difficult to achieve—but for each identity attribute, which is exchanged, separately. To give an example, we could consider a university that is trusted to make right assertions about whether a user is a student, but not about whether this user pays its telephone bills.

Work exists (Thomas & Meinel, 2010) which proposes a layered trust model that distinguishes between the overall trust into an identity provider and the trust into the identity of a user. The first layer, the trust into the identity provider, is defined as the degree of confidence that an identity provider has the proper mechanisms in place to makes right assertions. In particular, this also includes the legal situation as well as the adherence to governmental guidelines and laws. Based on this general trust relationship that is supposed to be relatively static, a second layer of trust is added. This layer, which is called identity trust, is defined as the degree of confidence a relying party can put into the identity of the subject of the assertion. This layer is based on the first layer and separates the static properties that are mainly related to the identity provider as a trusted entity from the properties that are subject to vary over the course of time. This includes for example attribute values, that are subject to expire after a certain time or which are entered into the system without verification and maybe verified later on if needed. The way an attribute has been verified and the source where it comes from make up the trust level of the attribute. Additional research is required to find out exactly which factors are relevant to assess the trust level for attributes and in which way the overall trust level of the identity provider relates to the trust levels of attributes.

CONCLUSION

Time has shown that the traditional centralized identity management does not work in open environments as the Internet and Service-oriented architectures and therefore new approaches to identity management are necessary to serve the needs of these networks. In this book chapter, we have drawn the conceptual evolution of identity management models from the classical domain-based approaches to the new open identity management models. We provided a classification of identity management models and discussed each of the four existing models, application-centric, centralized, user-centric and federated identity management with their advantages and disadvantages. A focus has been laid on the latter two, which belong to the category of open identity management models. Open identity management models support the management of identity data in multiple domains and facilitate identity information to be passed seamlessly across organizational borders. The basic idea is to share data between the entities holding identity information (the identity providers) and those consuming it (the relying parties) in a controlled manner. In addition to the conceptual background, technologies to implement user-centric and federated identity management have been described in this chapter.

Although all these technologies are available today, open identity management systems are still used very rarely. Instead we can observe that the Internet is still an environment of mostly isolated identity islands. As a possibly reason for this situation, we found out that the willingness to rely on information that comes from another than the own security domain is very low. Organizations find it hard to trust on identity management processes they have no insights into. Thus trust into identity assurance processes seams to be a major factor for the success of these new identity models.

In this chapter, we defined identity assurance and discussed several identity assurance frameworks that aim at providing a standard assessment for identity management processes. We further discussed their limitations. As an area for future research, we showed the benefits of having trust levels for attributes in addition to the trust levels for identity providers that are defined by existing assurance frameworks.

REFERENCES

Ahn, G.-J., Nam Ko, M., & Shehab, M. (2008). *Portable user-centric identity management*. International Information Security Conference. Boston, MA: Springer.

Audun Jøsang, J. F. (2005). *Trust requirements in identity management*. Newcastle, Australia: Australasian Information Security Workshop 2005.

Ballinger, K., Bissett, B., Box, D., Curbera, F., Ferguson, D., Graham, S., et al. (2006). *Web services metadata exchange* (WS-MetadataExchange). W3C.

Benantar, M. (2006). *Access control systems: Security, identity management and trust models*. Berlin, Germany: Springer.

Bertino, E., Martino, L., Paci, F., & Squicciarini, A. (2009). *Security for Web services and service-oriented architectures*. Berlin, Germany: Springer.

Bertocci, V., Serack, G., & Baker, C. (2007). *Understanding Windows CardSpace: An introduction to the concepts and challenges of digital identities (independent technology guides)* (*Vol. 1*). Amsterdam, The Netherlands: Addison-Wesley Longman.

Cameron, K. (2005). *Kim Cameron's identity weblog*. Retrieved 2010, from http://www.identityblog.com/stories/2004/12/09/thelaws.html

Cameron, K. (2005). *The laws of Identity*. Retrieved July 2010, from http://www.identityblog.com/stories/2005/05/13/TheLawsOfIdentity.pdf

Cantor, S., Kemp, J., Maler, E., & Philpott, R. (2005). *Assertions and protocols for the OASIS security assertion markup language (SAML) V2.0. Organization for the Advancement of Structured Information Standards*. OASIS.

Chappell, D. (2010). *Digital identity for. NET applications: A technology overview*. (C. &. Associates, Producer). Retrieved July 2010, from http://msdn2. microsoft.com/en-us/library/bb882216.aspx

Cover Pages, O. A. S. I. S. (2008, October). *Microsoft 'Geneva' framework supports SAML 2.0, WS-Federation, and WS-Trust*. Retrieved July 2010, from http://xml.coverpages.org/ni2008-10-29-a.html

e-Authentication Initiative. (2007). *E-authentication guidance for federal agencies*. US.

InCommon Federation. (2008). *Identity assurance assessment framework*. Retrieved 2010, from http://www.incommonfederation.org/docs/assurance/ InC IAAF 1.0 Final.pdf

Jøsang, A., Fabre, J., Hay, B., Dalziel, J., & Pope, S. (2005). *Trust requirements in identity management*. Newcastle, Australia: Australasian Information Security Workshop 2005.

Jøsang, A., Fabre, J., Hay, B., Dalziel, J., & Pope, S. (2005). Trust requirements in identity management. In Buyya, R., Coddington, P. D., Montague, P., Safavi-Naini, R., Sheppard, N. P., & Wendelborn, A. L. (Eds.), *ACSW Frontiers, 44* (pp. 99–108).

Kantara Initiative. (2010). *Website*. Retrieved 2010, from http://kantarainitiative.org/

Kylau, U., Thomas, I., Menzel, M., & Meinel, C. (2009). *Trust requirements in identity federation topologies*. International Conference on Advanced Information Networking and Applications (AINA-09). IEEE.

Lockhart, H., Andersen, S., Bohren, J., Sverdlov, Y., Hondo, M., Maruyama, H., et al. (2006, December). *Web services federation language* (WS-Federation), Version 1.1.

Nadalin, A., Goodner, M., Gudgin, M., Barbir, A., & Granqvist, H. (2007). *WS-Trust 1.3. Organization for the Advancement of Structured Information Standards*. OASIS.

National Institute of Standards and Technology. (2006). *Electronic authentication guideline*.

OASIS. (2009, July). *Identity metasystem interoperability,* version 1.0. OASIS Standards.

Office of the e-Envoy, UK. (2002). *Registration and authentication - e-Government strategy framework policy and guidelines*. Retrieved from http://www.cabinetoffice.gov.uk/csia/documents/pdf/ RegAndAuthentn0209v3.pdf

The Bandit Project. (n.d.). *Digital me identity selector*. Retrieved 2010, from http://code.bandit-project.org/trac/wiki/DigitalMe

The OpenId Foundation. (2007). *OpenID authentication 2.0 - Final specification*. Retrieved 2010, from http://openid.net/specs

Thomas, I., & Meinel, C. (2009). *Enhancing claim-based identity management by adding a credibility level to the notion of claims*. International Conference on Services Computing. Bangalore, India: IEEE.

Thomas, I., & Meinel, C. (2010). *An identity provider to manage reliable digital identities for SOA and the web*. 9th Symposium on Identity and Trust on the Internet. Gaithersburg, MD: ACM.

Vittorio Bertocci, G. S. (2007). *Understanding Windows CardSpace: An introduction to the concepts and challenges of digital identities (independent technology guides)* (*Vol. 1*). Amsterdam, The Netherlands: Addison-Wesley Longman.

Windley, P. J. (2005). *Digital identity*. O'Reilly Media.

ADDITIONAL READING

Baier, D., Bertocci, V., & Brown, K. (2010). *A Guide to Claims-Based Identity and Access Control: Authentication and Authorization for Services and the Web (Patterns & Practices)*. Microsoft Press.

Benantar, M. (2006). *Access Control Systems: Security, Identity Management and Trust Models*. Berlin: Springer.

Berger, A. (2008). *Identity Management Systems: Introducing yourself to the Internet*. Vdm Verlag Dr. Müller.

Bertino, E., Martino, L., Paci, F., & Squicciarini, A. (2009). *Security for Web Services and Service-Oriented Architectures*. Berlin: Springer.

Bertocci, V., Serack, G., & Baker, C. (2007). *Understanding Windows CardSpace: An Introduction to the Concepts and Challenges of Digital Identities*. Amsterdam: Addison-Wesley Longman.

Cameron, K. (2005, 05). *Microsoft's Vision for an Identity Metasystem*. Retrieved 08 2010, from Kim Cameron's Identity Weblog: http://www.identityblog.com/stories/2005/07/05/IdentityMetasystem.html

Cameron, K. (2005, 12 05). *The Laws of Identity*. Retrieved 08 2010, from Kim Cameron's Identity Weblog: http://www.identityblog.com/stories/2005/05/13/TheLawsOfIdentity.pdf

Chadwick, D. W., & Inman, G. (2009, May). Attribute Aggregation in Federated Identity Management. *Computer*, *42*(5), 33–40. doi:10.1109/MC.2009.143

El Maliki, T., & Seigneur, J.-M. (2007). A Survey of User-centric Identity Management Technologies. *The International Conference on Emerging Security Information, Systems, and Technologies (SECURWARE 2007)*. Valencia: IEEE.

Jones, M. B. (2006). The Identity Metasystem: A User-Centric, Inclusive Web Authentication Solution. *W3C Workshop on Transparency and Usability of Web Authentication*. New York City.

Josang, A., Maseng, T., & Knapskog, S. J. (2009). *Identity and Privacy in the Internet Age*. Berlin: Springer.

Jøsang, A., & Pope, S. (2005). User Centric Identity Management. In A. Clark, K. Kerr, & G. Mohay (Ed.), *AusCERT Asia Pacific Information Technology Security Conference*, (p. 77).

Kanneganti, R., & Chodavarapu, P. (2007). *SOA Security*. Manning Publications.

Leeuw, E. D., Fischer-Hubner, S., & Tseng, J. (2008). *Policies and Research in Identity Management: First IFIP WG11.6 Working Conference on Policies and Research in Identity Management (IDMAN'07), RSM... Federation for Information Processing)*. Berlin: Springer.

Madsen, P., & Itoh, H. (2009, May). Challenges to Supporting Federated Assurance. *Computer*, *42*(5), 42–49. doi:10.1109/MC.2009.149

Mercuri, M. (2007). *Beginning Information Cards and CardSpace: From Novice to Professional (Expert's Voice in. Net)*. Apress. doi:10.1007/978-1-4302-0204-2

Pacyna, P., Rutkowski, A., Sarma, A., & Takahashi, K. (2009, May). Trusted Identity for All: Toward Interoperable Trusted Identity Management Systems. *Computer*, *42*(5), 30–32. doi:10.1109/MC.2009.168

Paschoud, J. (2010). *Access and Identity Management: Controlling Access to Online Information*. Facet Publishing.

Recordon, D., Rae, L., & Messina, C. (2010). *The Definitive Guide*. Open, ID: O'Reilly Media.

Recordon, D., & Reed, D. (2006). OpenID 2.0: a platform for user-centric identity management. *Workshop on Digital identity management* (pp. 11-16). ACM.

Rieger, S. User-Centric Identity Management in Heterogeneous Federations. *International Conference on Internet and Web Applications and Services*. IEEE.

Seigneur, J.-M., & Jensen, C. D. (2007). User-Centric Identity, Trust and Privacy. In Song, R., Korba, L., & Yee, G. (Eds.), *Trust in E-Services: Technologies, Practices and Challenges*. IGI Global. doi:10.4018/978-1-59904-207-7.ch012

Sharoni, I., Williamson, G., & Yip, D. (2009). *Identity Management: A Primer*. Mc Pr Llc.

Steel, C. (2005). *Core Security Patterns: Best Practices and Strategies for J2EE(TM), Web Services, and Identity Management*. Prentice Hall International.

Surhone, L. M., Timpledon, M. T., & Marseken, S. F. (2009). *Authentication, Login, Service, Digital Identity, Password, User, Software System, List of OpenID Providers, Yadis, Shared Secret*. Open, ID: Betascript Publishing.

Surhone, L. M., Timpledon, M. T., & Marseken, S. F. (2009). *Security Assertion Markup Language: Security Domain, Single Sign-on, Identity Management, Access Control, OASIS, Liberty Alliance, SAML 1.1, SAML 2.0*. Betascript Publishing.

Thomas, E., Schittko, C., Chou, D., deVadoss, J., King, J., & Wilhelmsen, H. (2010). *SOA with. NET and Windows Azure: Realizing Service-orientation with the Microsoft Platform (Prentice Hall Service-Oriented Computing Series from Thomas ERL)*. Prentice Hall.

KEY TERMS AND DEFINITIONS

Digital Identity: A digital identity represents parts of a person's real-life identity in the digital world. A digital identity is usually comprised in an account that contains a limited set of attributes that characterizes this person.

Federation: A federation is a Circle of Trust across independent security domains.

Identity Assurance: A level of identity assurance (LoA) or level of trust reflects the degree of confidence that a relying party can assign to the assertions made by another identity provider with respect to a user's identity information.

Identity Management: Identity management refers to the process of establishing, representing and recognizing a person's identity as digital identities in computer networks.

Identity Trust Level: see Identity Assurance.

Security Domain: A security domain is a closed area that is administrated independently with regard to security. Often a security domain matches with the domain formed by organizational borders.

Service-Oriented: Architecture: Service-oriented architectures describe an architecture paradigm to build software systems from loosely coupled, self-contained components, the services. All services need to adhere to certain design principles and properties as being self-descriptive, re-usable and discoverable.

Single-Sign-On: Single-Sign-On is a concept that allows users by authenticating once in a certain security domain to gain seamless access to services and applications in other domains; synonym: single-logon.

Chapter 3
Effective Guidelines for Facilitating Construction of Successful, Advanced, User-Centric IAM Frameworks

Athanasios Karantjias
University of Piraeus, Greece

Nineta Polemi
University of Piraeus, Greece

ABSTRACT

Identity and Access Management (IAM) systems are considered as one of the core elements of any sound security electronic framework for electronic business processes. Their ability to quickly and reliably verify who is trying to access what service, and what they are authorized to do, is both a business enabler and a core requirement for meeting regulatory demands. However, IAM systems are difficult to implement since they touch virtually every end-user, numerous business processes, as well as every IT application and infrastructure component of an enterprise, and therefore most of the times IAM implementations fall short of expectations. This chapter proposes an effective way of approaching, designing, and implementing a constructive, user-centric, standards-based, centralized, and federated IAM system, with which a trust relationship among the involved entities is established in a secure and interoperable way, enabling end-users to easily gain electronic and/or mobile (e/m) access to advanced business services, and Service Providers (SPs) to effectively enhance their infrastructures by easily adopting it in their systems. In addition, a collective knowledge of IAM systems' implementation best practices is presented.

INTRODUCTION

Nowadays, enterprises are operating in a constantly shifting threat environment, where data breaches are all too common, identity theft is on the rise, and trust relationships are enforced in an inconsistent and hard-to understand manner. These threats are compounded by the increasing need for supporting electronic business at all levels of assurance, within the scope of the enterprise and with federal business partners (Forward Consortium, 2009).

DOI: 10.4018/978-1-61350-498-7.ch003

Enterprises themselves are experiencing a growing need to exchange information securely across network boundaries, and create digital representations of identities in order to enable system-specific processes, such as provisioning of access privileges. In addition, initiatives such as electronic health care records and transparency in electronic and mobile transactions are increasing the need to strongly authenticate all end-users in order to enable access to federal systems and frameworks. As a result, maintenance and protection of identities themselves is treated as secondary to the mission associated with the enterprise system itself.

The latest incarnation of a distributed computing framework is the Services Oriented Architectures (SOAs) that are most often implemented with Web Services, using open XML standards and focusing on reuse and loosely coupled integration. However, these objectives are often completely lost when advanced security is integrated. Until now, most SOA developments have relied on application or system level authentication and authorization for establishing simple trusted user identity features. Inert passwords remain the primary credential users employ to authenticate to enterprise systems and because of their nature it is simple to share a password amongst multiple individuals, which greatly increases the risks to an enterprise.

In general, current Identity and Access Management (IAM) solutions lack the following obstacles:

- Service Providers (SPs) have to implement multiple, different and separate authentication and authorization mechanisms for their applications and systems. According to statistics only 13 percent of companies surveyed by Ponemon Institute describe their company's approach to identity compliance as centralized (The Ponemon Institute, 2007) and only 10 percent of companies surveyed by Aberdeen have a single identity store, while 8 percent have more 100 (Aberdeen Group, 2007). This is rather expensive and difficult for an SP to manage and administer, while is inefficient for the end-users who have to manage multiple identities.
- Every attempt to interconnect separate applications in order to add value and build more advanced e/m-services often means linking separate user e/m-access security processes. This is rather complex and difficult to achieve from the technical point of view (Karantjias & Polemi, 2009). The usual solution is to lower the level of security and privacy to these systems and applications, while the end-users are not able to easily handle their identifiers and credentials.

The increasing regulatory compliance and audit requirements are additional burdens for the SPs. These oblige them to consider a higher assurance level for user identity in e/m-provision of services, which impose the implementation of proprietary IAM mechanisms with questionable levels of usability, manageability, and scalability.

Worldwide accepted and mature standards, specifications, and protocols lay the foundation for solutions and new security models that allow trusted user identity to be digitally and effectively managed across multiple and different security domains and enterprise systems (Karp, 2006). However, SOA implementations and architectures based on these do not actually gain the benefits of a truly parameterizable e/m-environment in which existing modules can be easily merged (Farahbod, Glasser, & Vajihollahi, 2007).

The uplift of the above mentioned obstacles requires more than basic web service communications protocols. What is needed is an efficient and practical way to use these standards and integrate a synchronous architecture, which will be able to introduce automation and system support of the identity management equally at the user and the SP sides. Based on it, enterprises should be able to easily build end-to-end identity infrastructures, supporting interoperable Web Services applications.

Especially when designing and building large-scale enterprise frameworks for both the public and private sectors, the vision behind the integration of advanced, user-centric, open, and federated IAM systems is ambitious and very attractive to any organization, interested in truly improving the effectiveness of its IT enterprise (Rieger & Neumair, 2007). This article aims at proposing an effective way of approaching, analyzing, and defining architectural practices for achieving a greater level of maturity and predictability when building synchronous IAM systems, which enhance the trust relationship among the involved entities and enable:

- End-users to adequately administrate and control their identities on their own, and easily e/m-access advanced business services
- SPs to harmonize their authentication/authorization procedures, enhance the majority of their infrastructures by easily plug-in them to core IAM system, and to effectively secure and manage their enterprise.

In order to achieve its aiming the article presents a novel IAM framework, the OpenIdAM, deployed for the IST European Project SWEB (SWEB Project, 2006), and partially integrated successfully in the LGAF framework (LGAF Project, 2009), deployed for the Central Union of Municipalities and Communities in Greece (Central Union of Municipalities and Communities in Greece, n.d.).

The article also reflects authors' collective experiences in building IAM frameworks, outlining the main insights regarding the critical success factors that need to be considered when integrating large-scale, user-centric and federated IAM frameworks. It actually offers a practical guideline, meant to be useful and used by IAM practitioners, and has two primary audiences:

- Enterprises and their implementing partners that seek guidance on preparing IAM aware projects
- Enterprises and their partners currently implementing IAM projects that want to check the effectiveness of their approach and progress

The rest of the article is organized as follows: Section 2 presents current traditional IAM models and reviews existing and related IAM work performed; Section 3 presents in detail our novel IAM framework; Section 4 identifies several critical success factors for successfully designing and integrating large-scale IAM frameworks, while Section 5 draws conclusions and suggests areas for further work and research to be performed.

DEFINITIONS, IAM MODELS AND RELATED WORK

Definitions

Before discussing the main concept of the article, some definitions and relevant parameters should be adequately clarified and defined in order to allow readers to better understand the main visions of an IAM system and therefore the main scope of the article.

Identity Management is the combination of technical systems, rules, and procedures that define the ownership, utilization, and safeguarding of personal identity information (NTSC, 2008). The primary scope of identity management is to establish a trustworthy process for assigning attributes to a digital identity and to connect this identity to an entity. Entity may be a person, group of persons, devices, enterprise, organization, service etc. Identity management includes the processes for maintaining and protecting the identity data of the entity over its lifecycle.

Credential is an object that authoritatively binds an identity to a token possessed and controlled by an entity (Burr, Dodson & Polk, 2006). Examples of credentials are smart cards, private and public cryptographic keys, digital certificates, the combination of a username and a password, and others. They are usually valid for a pre-defined period of time such as the digital certificates, which are issued to an entity and expire based on the issuer's Public Key Infrastructure (PKI) common Policy. Therefore, even if the identity of the entity does not change, the credentials associated with this entity can be revoked and newly issued. This does not have a bearing in the identity of the entity, as credentials are a tool for authentication that provide varying levels of assurance about its authentication.

Access Management is the management and control of the ways in which entities are granted access to resources. It ensures that the proper identity verification is made when an entity attempts to access security sensitive buildings, computer systems, or data. In this article we only consider the logical area of operation for access management, which is the access to an IT network, system, service, and/or application (Buhler & Wunder, 2010). Access management leverages identities, credentials, and privileges to determine access to resources by authenticating credentials. These processes allow agencies to obtain a level of assurance in the identity of the entity attempting to access to meet the following:

- Ensure that all entities attempting access are properly validated (Authentication)
- Ensure that all access to information is authorized (Authorization, Confidentiality)
- Protect information from unauthorized creation, modification, or deletion (Integrity)
- Ensure that authorized entities are able to access needed information (Reliability, Maintainability, Availability)
- Ensure the accountability of entities when gaining access and performing actions (Non-repudiation)

Identity and Access Management comprises of set of business processes, technologies, supporting infrastructure and policies to create, maintain and use digital identities within a legal framework (Burton Group Inc., n.d.). The main scope of IAM is to establish a scalable, extensible, interoperable and secure standards-based framework for identity data acquisition, storage and its access by the end-users, businesses and SPs to provide the following benefits:

- Reduction in the risk of unauthorized access to and modification of destruction of information assets
- Increase the value of data and make it more meaningful for decision making processes
- A single and comprehensive view of an identity
- Single-Sign-On features to different systems, modules and applications
- Elimination or significant reduction in storing duplicate identities.

Personally Identifiable Information (PII) refers to information (such as name, fingerprints, other biometric data, email address, street address, telephone number or social security number) that can be used to uniquely identify, contact, and/or locate a single person (Matthews & Esterline, 2010). It can be used with other sources to uniquely identify a single entity.

A **User Profile** is a set of PIIs (Matthews & Esterline, 2010). In synchronous IAM systems a user is able to create and have more than one profile, while each one of them identifies the user in a particular context.

Single Sign On (SSO) refers to an authentication process that enables a user to authenticate once and then gain access to the resources of multiple software systems (Elmufti et al., 2008). This process is actually a property of access control management of multiple, related, but independent software systems.

An **Identity Provider (IdP)** is a trusted entity that integrates advanced IAM mechanisms for verifying the authenticity of end-users or other entities. An IdP has the authority and responsibility to issue sets of different authentication and authorization credentials and provides identity management services of one or more relying parties (Matthews & Esterline, 2010), (Elmufti et al., 2008).

In general an IdP is responsible for the following:

- Managing end-users and their identities.
- Issuing credentials.
- Handling user administration.
- Authenticating end-users.
- Vouching for the user's identity with the SP.

A **Service Provider (SP)** refers to an entity that provides electronic and/or mobile services to other entities and individual end-users (Matthews & Esterline, 2010), (Elmufti et al., 2008). In the article this term refers to businesses that rely on a third party IdP for managing their identities. Such an entity may or may not have registered users.

A SP is responsible for the following:

- Controlling access to services.
- Validating the asserted identity information from IdPs.
- Providing access based on asserted identity.
- Managing only locally relevant user attributes, not an entire user profile.

Existing IAM Models

Followed in the field of identity management, this section assesses three traditional IAM models and practices followed on the field for managing user identities. Each model is depicted mainly from its usability and scalability perspective, describing how a user can request services from different SPs in each model. The explanation given for each one represents a very high level of abstraction, meaning that many implementation details of communication protocols and messages are omitted. However, the reader sufficiently gets the important aspects of the models from the user perspective.

Isolated IAM Systems

Even in our days the most common practice followed is for an SP to act as both credential and identifier provider to its users, controlling the name space for specific service domains and allocating users' identifiers (eMayor Project, 2004), (Ardagna et al., 2006), (The Ponemon Institute, 2007).

Isolated IAM systems (Figure 1), force users to get separate unique user profiles from each service/identity provider they transact with, and use separate credentials with each of their profiles and set of PIIs.

This approach surely provides a simple identity management for SPs, but is rapidly becoming unmanageable for users who are overloaded with identifiers and credentials that they need to remember, periodically change, and effectively manage.

In addition such IAM models constrict systems to interoperate on behalf of a user in order to provide more advanced e/m services, which is today a core requirement for both the public and the private sectors aiming at adding value on current.

Centralized IAM Systems

In centralized user identity models (Figure 2), a single authority undertakes the management of the namespaces, the issuance of the authorization tokens, and the authentication of all entities during each e/m-service access (Ardagna et al., 2006), (Koch & Moslein, 2005). This core IdP

Figure 1. Isolated IAM system model

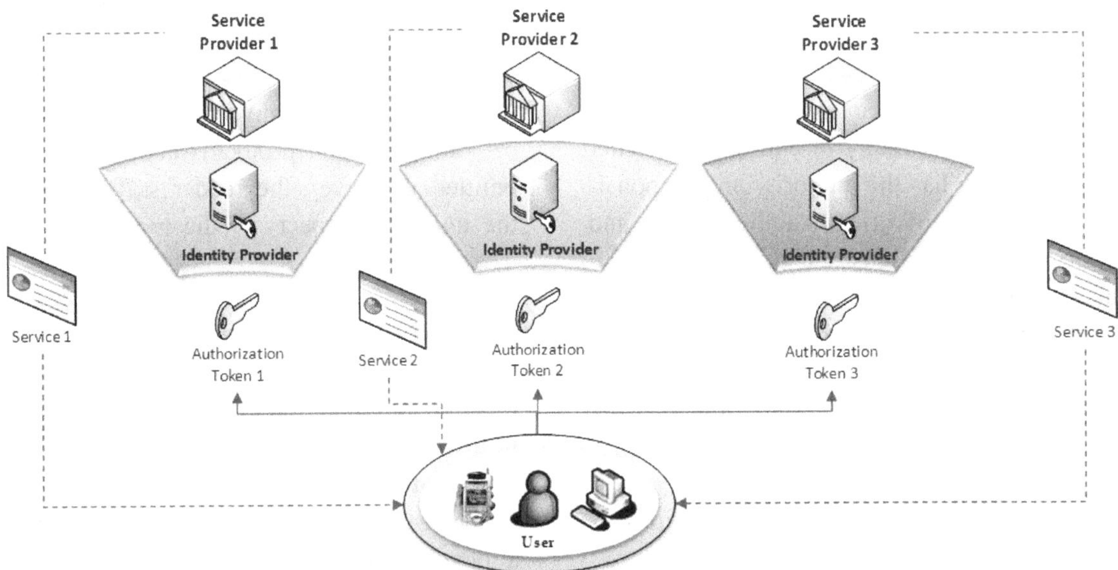

is used by many SPs or other identifiers and/or credential providers.

The centralized identity systems are an attempt to put the control back into user's hands. In this way users gain consent as to what information about them is disclosed to which systems and for what purpose. It provides loosely coupled relationships in which the relying party does not necessarily need to have a pre-existing trust relationship with the IdP. This arrangement allows for non-password-based account bootstrapping process, which is easier for both users and relying parties.

Current implementations, which adopt this model, are better suited for closed networks and frameworks, where multiple SPs are managed by the same enterprise such as governments and large companies, providing effective usability through SSO mechanisms. Usually this enterprise acts as Trusted Third Party (TTP) (SWEB Project, 2006).

The main difficulty for centralized IAM systems is caused mainly from the various SPs, which in open environments are not governed by a common policy and authority. In addition to this, current implementations do not clearly provide pluggable modules in order to connect with the majority of the applications and platforms on the SP.

Federated IAM Systems

Federated IAM systems are based on groups of SPs that enter into mutual security and authentication agreements in order to allow users SSO to their services. These agreements include policy and technology standards and result in a single virtual identity domain for the end-user, providing SSO in open environments. The federated model (Figure 3), is compatible with and can easily be retrofitted to the traditional isolated IAM model (Ahn & Lam, 2005), (Internet2, 2011), (PRIME Project, 2005).

One criticism of the federated systems is that they are enterprise-centric rather than user-centric. That is, the protocols are designed to meet the requirements of enterprises that need to federate with the control of information with IdP and SP. Users have less control than is desired over what information is required by the IdPs and SPs (PII),

Figure 2. Centralized IAM system model

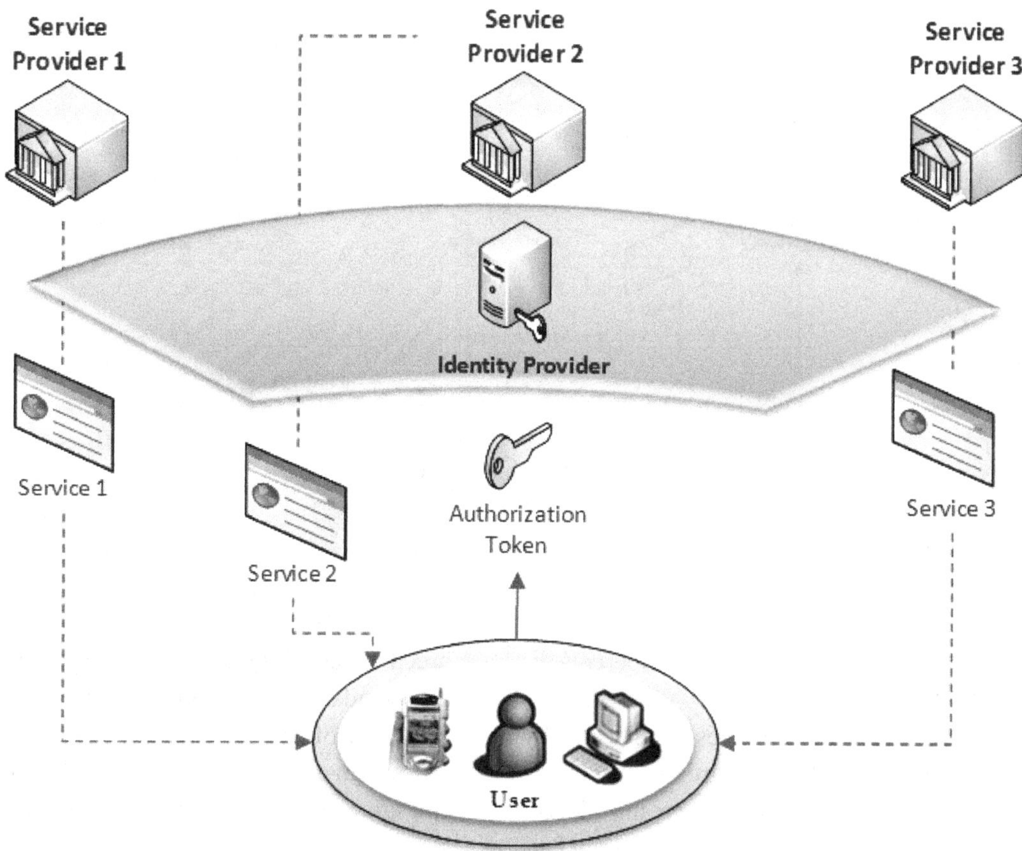

and often give over more information than is required for the type of transaction involved.

This model also creates legal and technological complexity since difficult strategies must be adopted in order for SPs to be able to distinguish between a security assertion that reflects a genuine user service request and one that represents an SP that acts on behalf of a user. Moreover, when dealing with multiple centralized identity domains, scalability problems for users cannot be avoided, since multiple federated IAM systems will exist in different domains.

Existing Implementations and Related Work

IAM is not a new concept in IT. Over the past fifteen years, companies have begun to address identity management through a variety of solutions that have focused on provision and web based SSO activities. Therefore, several solutions based on the above mentioned traditional IAM models, for managing and controlling end-user's access, permissions, PIIs, and allowed actions to electronic resources, have been already proposed by various projects and research initiatives (PRIME Project, 2005), (Internet2, 2011), (European Commission, 2006), (Papastergiou, Karantjias, & Polemi, 2007),

Figure 3. Federated IAM system model

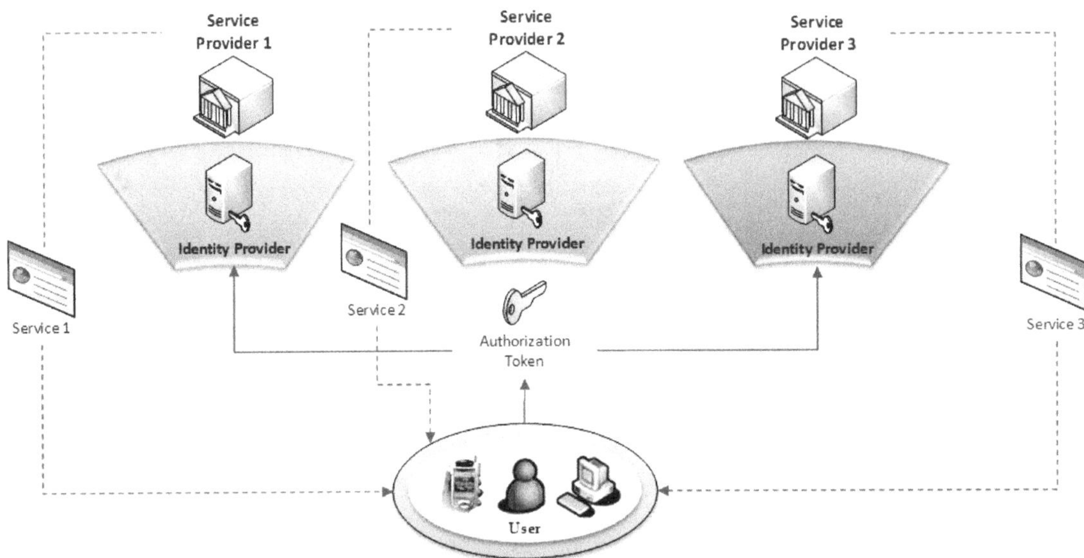

(Peyton, Doshi, & Seguin, 2007), (Liberty Alliance, 2003).

Often these tactical initiatives were driven by the need for cost reduction and greater efficiency. However, as regulatory mandates were introduced, compliance became a key catalyst (European Parliament, 1997), (European Parliament, 2001). On the other hand, our days mark a new beginning for ICT, since economic realities are moving faster than political realities (European Commission, 2011), as we have seen with the global impact of the financial crisis. Therefore, the focus is shifting back to cost and efficiency, although the need for compliance has certainly not diminished. These co-existing imperatives demand a solution that addresses as many as possible IAM issues with equal efficacy.

As enterprises deal with the IAM business drivers, it becomes immediately apparent that holistic, rather than piecemeal, approaches better address their needs. Thus, vendors shift in focus and now offer solutions that extend beyond the security organization and aim to improve efficiency and control costs for the entire enterprise. This new breed of identity management solution provides the foundation to support key areas, such as access control and certification, helping to reduce costs form overlapping compliance requirements and safeguard organizations form insider security breaches.

However, the fact that many initiatives (Liberty Alliance, n.d.), (Lockhart et al., 2007), (Goodner et al., 2007) are integrated in isolation affects significantly the integration of the current IAM systems, which become difficult to deploy and use, since they are seldom interoperable even though many have similar features and functionalities.

Besides, all these attempts aim to cover all possible cases and thus fall short of expectations, remaining in a generic level. The implementation of new IAM technology requires addressing of core underlying processes in order to avoid just implementing an automated flowed process. A privacy-aware process is actually an equally essential IAM component and access management processes must not be duplicative across the enterprise.

Moreover, existing user access management and audits are time-consuming and costly to execute, and often do not provide adequate assurance that the right users have the right access at the right time. As a result, many enterprises fail to effectively enhance and automate existing processes in order to reduce the time and overall complexity of managing user access that would result in greater adoption among end-users (The Ponemon Institute, 2007), (Aberdeen Group, 2007).

Very few of these solutions take into consideration the need for end-users to easily handle or even define their preferable PIIs and credentials. These solutions even if they provide automated systems to SPs for managing identities, authentication and authorization, they do not adopt the user perspective, who needs to simplify his/her entrance in a large scale enterprise framework.

On the other hand the seamless and straightforward integration of cross-organizational federated services conflicts with the need to secure and control the access to provided services. Traditional access control is based on dedicated models, such as role-based access control, access control lists, or task-based access control (Wolter, Kohler, & Schaad, 2007).

In a service federation, however, there might exist multiple models with different semantics or expressiveness for each federation member. Moreover, access control decisions in classical models are based on identities and permissions assigned to them, which cannot be exposed to all participants of the federation, in order to prevent information leakage of security policies or due to model inconsistencies (i.e. unknown attributes or even different role concepts). Thus, classical access control architectures provide a non-feasible approach in terms of the general independence of services in a SOA.

Even if these SOA and Web Services based solutions are properly designed and implemented in a way to satisfy the needs of end-users, they are unable to interconnect with existing, self sufficient applications and platforms, which do not necessarily conform to the assumptions of SOA's distributed application model (Karantjias, Stamati, & Martakos, 2010). Therefore most of the time an enterprise is obliged to change or exclude its legacy systems, even if they work fine, in order to adopt such unified (centralized, federated or hybrid) IAM systems.

A NOVEL IAM FRAMEWORK APPROACH

Given the benefits of IAM systems it is no surprise that their implementation is on the rise. In fact, IAM is among the highest areas of spending in the security budget today. Forrester predicts that the IAM market will grow from nearly $2.6 billion in 2006 to more than $12.3 billion in 2014 (Cser & Penn, 2008). Today enterprises should look beyond IAM's basic compliance and cost-saving benefits to harness more advanced capabilities such as automated user-access certification and role management. These systems assist in yielding a centralized and detailed view of end-users, roles, and privileges.

The authors believe that enterprises must adopt a holistic, centralized and federated strategy to create an IAM solution aligned with their IT platforms, systems, and applications, regulatory needs, and business goals. The successful IAM solution will create a series of centralized and federated services that empower organizations to effectively manage user access across their enterprises and serve as an enabler to lines of business and strategic partners.

This section introduces a high-level architecture of our novel user-centric approach, emphasizing in the core structure elements of an advanced IAM system, called OpenIdAM. This consists of two different main entities:

- The core centralized infrastructure, which issues privacy-aware identity tokens and manages the identities of all end-users.
- An advanced federated Integration Layer, which sits on top of the systems and applications on an SP, providing them advanced privacy-aware services in a unified manner.

The innovation of our approach consists on the standards-based integration of two different infrastructures, the provided functionality of the one is highly based on the mechanisms of the other. Specifically, in our approach the core centralized infrastructure, recognizes the benefits of the centralized IAM models, in which a single authority undertakes the management of the namespaces, the issuance of the authorization tokens, and the authentication of all entities during each e/m-service access.

On the other hand the advanced federated Integration Layer adopts the federated IAM model, in which groups of different systems and applications enter into mutual security and authentication agreements in order to allow users SSO to their services. A main difficulty that emerged the existence of this layer is to find a universal and standardized way to interoperate with all the different kinds of applications, systems, and tools that reside in a SP or even in different departments of an organization that provides internal or external e/m-services. In addition to this the interconnection of the core centralized infrastructure with existing, self-sufficient applications and systems (legacy systems), which do not necessarily conform to the assumptions of SOA's distributed system model, is also an emerging problem that requires a solid solution. The difficulties which arise from the above mentioned cases are summarized as follows:

- **Proprietary Interfaces:** Integration logic in terms of transformation rules, workflow services etc. cannot be ported between the different solutions that most governmental organizations host and operate. In their majority, these solutions are closely linked to different vendors, weakening the durability of integration-related developments
- **Limited communication protocols:** The end-to-end supervision of business processes, which are executed in more than one system, is very difficult. Although the use of SOAP/HTTP protocols provides a bridge between different solutions, it only tackles the rudimentary issue of the session-less RPC, overlooking other fundamental architecture services such as guaranteed delivery and limiting interoperability among them
- **Lack of scalability:** Deporting all or parts of a central integration logic to Web Services connectors has never been a trivial task and is something very complex to deploy and administer

Therefore the advanced federated Integration Layer is built on top of all enterprise solutions in an SP in order to allow further integration with other tools, applications, and services. It actually manages all interactions between the various components transparently, stipulating that different applications communicate through a common messaging bus, while it integrates policy and technology standards, acting as single virtual identity domain for all enterprise systems inside an SP.

Core Centralized Architecture

The core infrastructure of OpenIdAM integrates and ties service discovery, invocation, authentication and other necessary components, adding context and value to web services, required from every synchronous IAM system (Dabrowski & Pacyna, 2008).

This novel architecture aims to:

- Automatically compose advanced privacy-aware services based on a set of rules that check their composability.

- Develop cross-boundary privacy-aware information sharing. Several changes in organizational and technological IAM processes are proposed in order to better support enterprises' response capabilities. These changes are influenced by specific types of secured interactions, which take the form of group decision-making, learning, understanding, trust building, and conflict resolution, among others.
- Specify operational privacy policies. Rules and constrains are defined in order to govern the behavior of all IAM services for their successful interaction. These are machine-to-machine specifications that are expressed programmatically as assertions and grouped into various combinations.
- Integrate SOA Lifecycle Management mechanisms. Our proposition enables the monitoring and controlling of any change on a service, ensuring that the quality of the service remains consistent. Without it, policies may be violated resulting in non-compliant inefficient services.
- Preserve privacy. Credentials with filtering mechanisms are used to ensure that only authorized entities are able to access sensitive information and services.

The achievement of these features and goals required a highly secure, scalable and interoperable technology solution that will provide industry / de facto standard interfaces, ensuring the broadest support for end-users and SPs and integrating pick XML technologies that guarantee strong security and privacy.

In this context, the following core building blocks, among others, co-exist and collaborate in a multitier architecture (Figure 4):

- A Web Interactive Tier, which provides electronic and mobile secure access to all privacy-aware services of our novel IAM system as the central single-point of entry, aggregating all information and services in one place.
- A Business Process Management System (BPMS), which implements powerful new process modeling standards, adding advanced features in managing the business logic of all IAM services. It actually creates the required business rules based on workflow data.
- The Main Enterprise Tier, which enclosures and implements the core authorization mechanisms of the framework.
- The Middleware Tier, which integrates interoperable mechanisms through the use of an Enterprise Service Bus (ESB) framework.
- The Directory Tier, which provides a set of services, supporting the description and discovery of all business, enterprises, SPs, as well as the predefined policies, agreed between the OpenIdAM and each SP separately.

The use of the Web Interactive Tier as a single point of entry and delivery mechanism for privacy-aware services, standardizes all end-users' interactions with the OpenIdAM framework. It provides electronic and mobile based point of secure access to information and content, retrieved and processed from diverse sources, in a unified and user-friendly way, undertaking the establishment of communication with all external entities (i,e. e/m-users, the PKI, and the enterprises). This communication is mainly based on Web Services which are handled in the Web Services module (SWEB Project, 2008).

The quality of protection through message integrity, message confidentiality, and single message authentication, is provided through the use of Web Services Security (WSS) mechanisms, integrated in the Security module. This handles the security cryptographic credentials provided from the PKI, while it implements all the advanced security mechanisms on the OpenIdAM, such as

Figure 4. OpenIdAM architecture

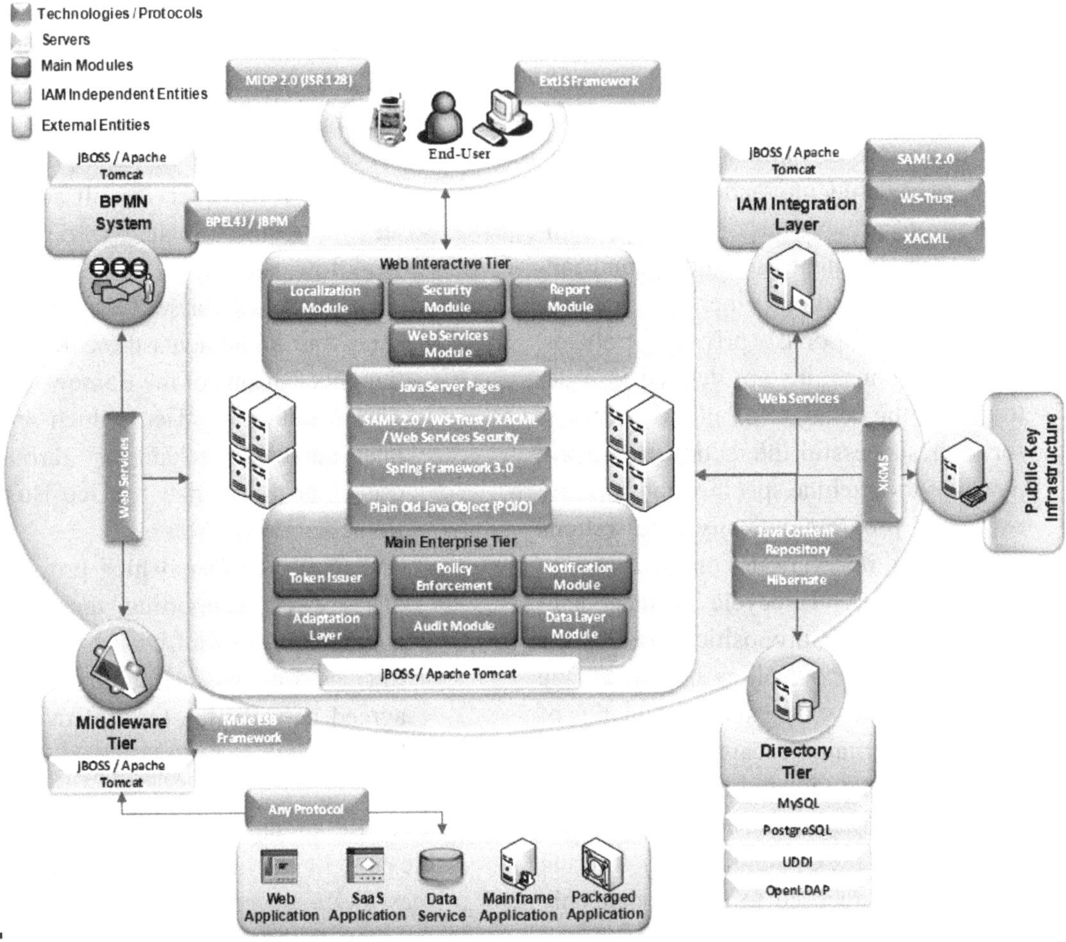

the creation/validation of XML digital signatures and XML encryption and decryption (Kaliontzoglou et al., 2005). In cases where the OpenIdAM is required to be configured for the public sector, this module already integrates long term validity (XAdES) e-signatures (Kaliontzoglou et al., 2005), since the authorization assertions for signed public documents may have to bear signatures lasting for a long time.

The use of strong, open source frameworks and rich User Interface (UI) technologies, such as Spring Web Flow - SWF, Java Server Faces–JSF, ExtJS, and Facelets, provides a user friendly web component based architecture, improving system performance (Karantjias & Polemi, 2009). Moreover, they offer the ability to easily build interactive interfaces and templates with basic form controls and efficient, reusable operations, while future architecturally developers will be able to separate the presentation logic (the "what") from the UI component's business logic (the "why" and "how").

The Main Enterprise Tier (Figure 4) enclosures and implements the core authorization mechanisms in the OpenIdAM. The XACML-based Policy Enforcement (Papastergiou, Karantjias, & Polemi, 2007), (SWEB Project, 2008) module specifies and enforces fine-grained, system-readable privacy policies, used to control access to Web Services, digital objects and services, enclosing users' PIIs and OpenIdAM's requirements. The enhancements, which the XACML 3.0 standard has gone through (OASIS, 2005), enhance our framework with the following significant features:

- **Multiple Decision Profile:** This is particularly useful in our novel proposition where decisions have to be reached for different parts of the framework within a given service for a given end-user.
- **Delegation of Administrative rights:** With this an administrator is capable of easily defining access control policies for an entire set of resources within an enterprise. In addition it enables the delegation of rights to other administrators to manage a set of resources. This is extremely useful in federation scenarios, cloud-based scenarios, and in environments where the domains to secure are so vast that they require local knowledge to define relevant policies (i.e. for every enterprise that participates in the framework).
- **Policy combination algorithms:** Policies are combined together to produce a single decision. Thus, each policy under specific circumstances can reach different decisions, which must be combined to return a single result.

Therefore, an initial policy matching of the SPs' requirements with the users' preferences (user profiles and PIIs) and capabilities and vice versa is achieved.

The externalization of end-users' authorization and the adoption of standards-based solutions requires a modular design and implementation. Therefore, every XACML module should be a component of a larger system and operate within the system independently in its operation, enabling:

- A scalable development, allowing the component to be naturally subdivided along the lines of its modules
- The built of robust XACML architectures, which are composed of smaller parts that can be easily managed and maintained.

The Token Issuer module (Figure 4) issues XML-based security tokens, integrating the WS-Trust standard (OASIS, 2007), providing strong authorization, and auditing mechanisms. It integrates the most effective way for managing, establishing and evaluating trust relations in order to enable Web Services to safely interoperate. WS-Trust introduces in our framework the Security Token Service (STS), a special Web Service that issues a set of security tokens for a given subject (SWEB Project, 2008). It defines standardized messages for obtaining, issuing, renewing, and validating security tokens and is built on the WS-S protocol.

To maximize interoperability with electronic and mobile clients and systems from multiple vendors, the OpenIdAM supports the WS-Federation and SAML 2.0 protocols (OASIS, 2007a). Moreover, for higher administrative efficiency, it automates federation trust configuration and management, using the harmonized federation metadata format (OASIS, 2008). This automation enables the OpenIdAM and SPs to publish their federation metadata in a standard format, which can be exchanged between potential enterprises. Consequently, using a single specification that can support both passive web application and active web service requestors is a key advantage for effectively using this framework in multiple and heterogeneous environments.

By making privacy-aware information assets available as reusable, independent services that better correspond to the business granularity and needs, our approach organizes the embedded logic of each service into district states in unified workflows, by means of a BPM System (Figure 4). It puts significant emphasis on the integrated processes both in terms of streamlining process logic to improve efficiency and also establishing processes that are adaptable and extensible so that they can be augmented in response to likely the OpenIdAM business changes (OMG, 2009). Specifically, the emergence of Business Process Execution Language (BPEL) and/or JBoss jBPM and their embracing by major vendors and IDE tools provide a higher-level description language to specify the behavior of Web Services' framework, orchestrating them into business privacy and identity-aware processes (Karantjias & Polemi, 2009).

Our primary goal in orienting the integrated privacy-aware services was to establish a highly agile automation environment, which will be realized by abstracting the logic of each process into its own tier, covering the following perspectives:

- **Functional:** The basic elements of privacy-aware processes are reusable activities that can either atomic or sub-processes, which are recursively refined by other activities.
- **Organizational:** The metadata model adopted is inspired by different enterprises, the role, the human, and the actual resource. Thus, the members of an enterprise may perform the selected activity. If a role is addressed, an activity is performed by a role or skill set. A role in this context is a function that a human has within an enterprise or the IAM framework itself (i.e. Administrators), while roles and enterprises represent a human in the overall OpenIdAM meta-model.
- **Behavioral:** Each data flow connects atomic activities with information resources and every other meta-data model element of this perspective is adopted from the workflow control patterns, performing through feedback loops, iteration, complex decision-making conditions, entry and exit criteria, and so forth.
- **Informational:** The basic elements of this perspective are resources and events, including data, artefacts, and objects. An event may trigger an activity, while a resource is an entity to be produced or consumed by an atomic activity.
- **Business Process Context:** It provides an overview of the process and describes major characteristics, such as goals and their measures, the process owner, its type, and the end-user at a glance. All process characteristics are integrated into the adopted meta-model, in order to better represent essential process theory that should be also made transparent in a process model.

The Middleware Tier (Figure 4) integrates all required interoperable mechanisms through the use of the open source Mule Enterprise Service Bus - ESB framework (Mule, 2008), (Karantjias & Polemi, 2009). This tier is actually a light weight messaging layer that uses disparate technologies, transports and protocols. An optimum IAM system must offer the ability to adopt and manage data structures from multiple and heterogeneous environments, while not changing the implemented services in the previously described tiers. Therefore, the middleware tier operates as a transformation layer for every possible data that have to be inserted or exported from the core OpenIdAM.

This tier operates as Web Service gateway for contacting external to IAM systems and application, which does not necessarily conform to SOAs' assumptions. Thus, all the processing related to the external communication is transparent and each service is consumed like any other service provided in the local domain at the middleware tier level.

In cases where the Directory Tier, which holds all the PIIs and profiles of end-users, as well as the negotiated predefined policies agreed with every SP, resides and is owned by an external party (i.e. in e/m-Government cases this data is usually owned by the Ministry of Interior or other Ministries), this tier undertakes to communicate with these Directories on behalf of the OpenIdAM.

Federated Integration Layer

Even if SOA and Web Services are being proposed as the best solution for integrating privacy-aware applications and IAM systems, they are not enough on their own. A synchronous IAM system works best when it links up newly built, pluggable modules across multiple domains to create distributed, composite applications. The enterprise integration problem is subtly different. It actually aims to connect together pre-existing, self sufficient applications, and platforms. A main difficulty that an implementer faces is to find a universal way to interoperate and standardize the provision of access to the legacy systems of a SP. However, most of the time an enterprise is obliged to change or exclude its legacy systems even if they work fine in order to adopt a unified IAM system.

In addition even when an XML or SOAP document arrives at an application or a SOA platform, there may exists semantic and process model differences that need to be harmonized. The problem may be as simple as the format being wrong or as complex as the incoming document being passed through a complete process before the application can accept it (i.e. when validating the sender, gathering secondary information from other systems and then transforming it into the appropriate request).

In order to fill such inconsistencies we adopted four typed of activities:

- **Validation against business definition:** Usually an invalid document has potentially disastrous consequences for any application.
- **Enrichment with additional information:** in order to ensure the completion of the data and involve other applications such as databases, and web services for example, as well as internal calculations such as aggregation, derivation, and analysis.
- **Transformation in the correct format:** before being mapped into main language domain. Usually there might be more information that must be filtered out or less information that must be augmented in some way, or even the information may be in a different format of order.
- **Exception handling:** which must be managed intelligently.

Consequently, validation, enrichment, transformation and exception handling are the first four attributes to be checked in any potential IAM solution. As web services moves into the area of application integration there is a need for an IAM system that will provide a new, independent and customizable federated integration layer.

This layer is built on top of all enterprise solutions in an SP in order to allow further integration with other tools, applications, and services. It actually manages all interactions between the various components transparently, stipulating that different applications communicate through a common messaging bus, while it integrates policy and technology standards, acting as single virtual identity domain for all enterprise systems inside an SP.

OpenIdAM's federated integration layer (Figure 5) navigates the differences in technology and information model of the applications that adopts it, undertaking the following:

- The communication and negotiation with the core OpenIdAM (through its Web Interactive Tier), for validating the received tokens, setting up the privacy policies, declaring electronically the provided services, the roles of the users who can access them, and the prerequisites for obtaining each one of these (roles) (Squicciarini, 2008).

Figure 5. OpenIdAM's federated integration layer architecture

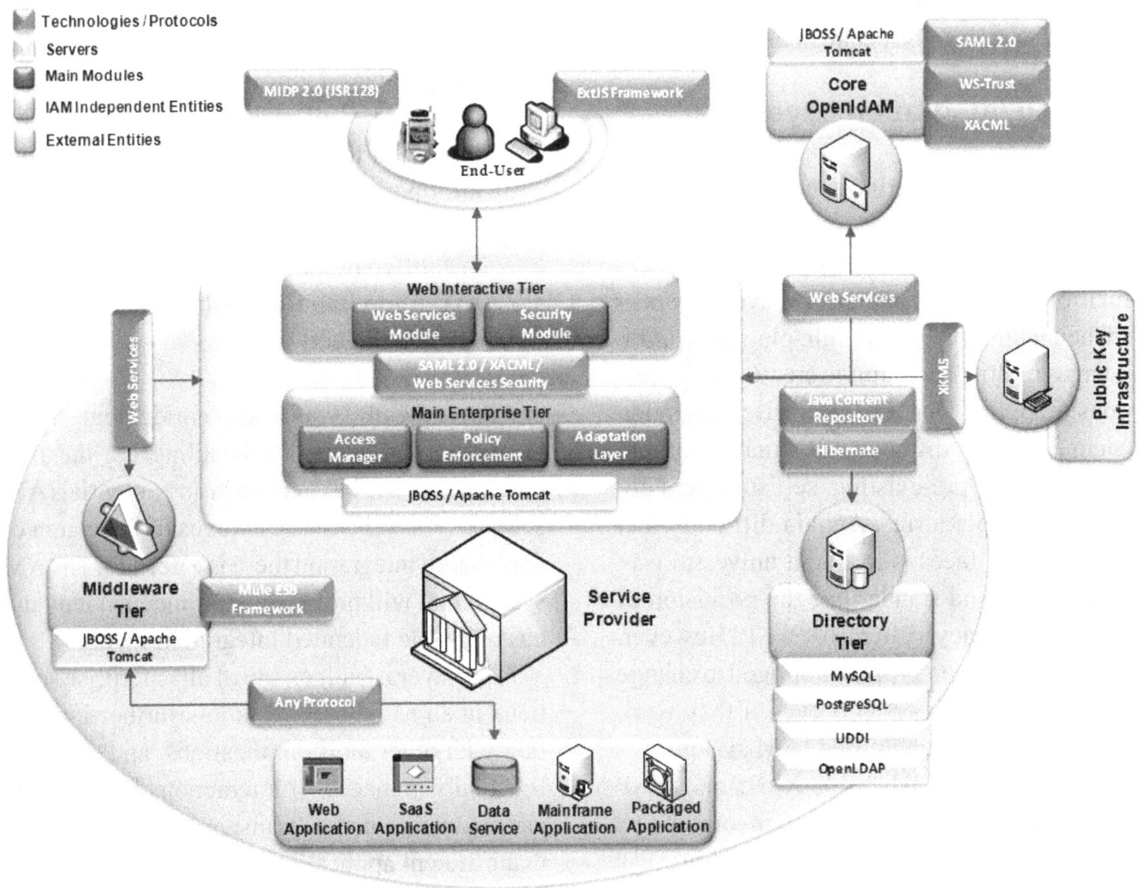

- The communication with end-users who wish to gain access to the systems and applications of an SP (through its Web Interactive Tier and/or its Middleware Tier).
- The communication with all internal to the SP applications and systems (through the Middleware Tier).
- The communication with every external to the SP enterprise system (through the Middleware Tier).

This layer involves the creation of privacy and access-aware service interfaces to existing or new functions, either directly or through the use of adaptors, by routing and delivering all service requests to the correct enterprise's application or system. It aims to support the substitution of one privacy and access-aware service implementation by another with no effect to the clients of this service. This requires not only the service interfaces to be appropriately specified according to SOA principles, but also for the core infrastructure to allow client code to invoke these services in an independent of the service location and the communication protocol involved manner.

In the Web Interactive Tier the Web Services module structures the requests sent to the core infrastructure of OpenIdAM, handling appropriately as well the responses from it. It uses the Security module to ensure the quality of protection through the message integrity, confidentiality and single message authentication.

The XACML-based Policy Enforcement module follows the design and implementation characteristics of the corresponding module integrated in the core OpenIdAM infrastructure, specifying and enforcing the privacy policies of the given enterprise. Although these policies are declared, integrated and enforced in the core OpenIdAM, this integration layer provides to the enterprise the ability to further validate and ensure that they are properly addressed. The actual validation of the received SAML tokens is performed from the Access Manager module, which validates the IdP's digital signature, the lifetime of the token, and the role assigned to the requestor.

The results of this validation process directly affect the behavior of the Middleware Tier, which allows the standardization of the communication messages with every external and internal to the SP entity. Consequently, when an SP wishes to adopt the OpenIdAM, it has only to properly build the custom internal communication channels of its legacy systems with the middleware tier and mainly with the ESB component. When receiving a privacy-aware request, the ESB relies on the gateway to handle the external communication. As the request must be sent in a domain or a Legacy to the enterprise system that may requires a different type of token (i.e. username-password) than the one used for the whole IAM framework, the gateway has to perform a token exchange before sending the request to it.

When adopting our novel architecture there are two important things that must be taken into consideration:

- A trust relationship must be established between the Access Manager module and the middleware tier itself. The return of a token implies that the Access Manager trusts the requesting Legacy System of the enterprise to authenticate end-users, and this is an organizational aspect. Therefore, a highly secure mechanism must be leveraged to guarantee that the token request is made by the requesting system (i.e. sign the token request using the middleware tier's private key).
- The identities in some cases (i.e. closed legacy systems) have to be propagated all over the information system (either by using the same user repository or by synchronizing the user repositories of the different systems)

The absence of this tier would oblige our novel IAM framework to integrate and support independent communication messages with every single SP. These messages would also have to be parameterized in every internal architectural change, affecting the general framework's operation. In a large scale federated framework where multiple and different kinds of SPs participate, wishing to communicate with each other on behalf of the user and provide advanced business services, this would have been very inefficient and therefore prohibitory. The existence of this layer offers the opportunity only to rebuild or reconfigure the connectors with the internal legacy applications and systems, while updating the flow of the processes in each involved component, included in this tier.

The Directory Tier is mainly used from the Middleware Tier to route all privacy and access-aware service requests, providing also a service catalog in order to achieve reuse of services across the legacy systems of the SP. The use of an internal UDDI could fulfill the vision of Web Services, enabling the dynamic discovery and invocation of these secure services. Such a directory could easily be viewed as part of the ESB component; however, until such solutions become common, it is likely to be separate from it.

CRITICAL SUCCESS FACTORS FOR BUILDING IAM FRAMEWORKS

Our involvement in designing and building large, national and international, cross border enterprise frameworks (SWEB Project, 2006), (LGAF Project, 2009), (eMayor Project, 2004), (Intelcities Project, 2006) convince us that the necessity for achieving the goal of building successful IAM systems, securing and modernizing processes and services for the private and public sector ought to come from the following different perspectives:

- Define a clear user-centered vision and priority areas
- Find experienced partners and find each one's strengths
- Implement Incrementally
- Overcome resistance from within the enterprises that will participate at the privacy-aware framework

The first step toward a successful IAM implementation is to understand the basics of IAM, which are sometimes misunderstood. Although potentially complex in application, the essence of IAM is fairly straightforward and that is to determine who should have access to what applications and resources according to business rules. However, someone must begin the planning of processes by establishing a broad vision of IAM that is shared by all stakeholders (end-users, enterprises, officials, society groups). The realization of security as a necessary evil, as most enterprises view it today, must be avoided, and instead it should be considered as business enabler, end-user-driven, and service-oriented.

This means that the vision of IAM implies providing greater access to information as well as better, more equal services and procedures for the public and the private sector. IAM is about a lot more than technology, which can help with resource provisioning and de-provisioning, making it a foundation for proper security and privacy, and can be an enabler for various business initiatives. The role IAM technology plays will vary greatly depending in end-users' and enterprises' requirements. Therefore, what is needed is to determine an IAM strategy that best fulfills the following:

- Enhance business value by improving security and privacy
- Strengthen legal system and law enforcement
- Reduce overall effort of IT administration
- Ease IT management and enhance overall Return Of Investment for business
- Provide scalable approach that enables IT expansion
- Improve productivity
- Provide more effective and secure end-user access mechanisms to services

Within each category different objectives might emerge. Given this, each vision should also be accompanied by a short list of priorities areas for the IAM, understanding and analyzing the current 'as-is' state of the security and privacy in the enterprises, and getting a grasp on what holes need to be filled and the steps that are required to be taken in order to reach the desired end-state. This analysis often leads to process re-engineering which is often a required initial step of an IAM project and requires organizational will. Behind every successful IAM project a visionary leader or leaders exist who push for change even through difficult challenges.

The design and implementation of effective IAM systems that will gain the adoption of enterprises and end-users requires expertise, resources and input from various sectors. Companies from the private sector can offer valuable lessons in customer service, responsiveness and adaptability to customer needs. Thus, the private sector should not be viewed as merely a place for 'outsourcing', but as a genuine partner. The finding of companies experienced not only in technology applications but also ICT project management in order for

IAM systems to be developed more quickly within given budget cycles, is necessary.

Since, centralized and federated IAM systems touch virtually many enterprises (from the private and/or the public sector), it is required to involve also representatives from all end-users communities (citizens, clients, employees, and others) as well as business experts from the enterprises themselves, and academia researchers who realize the roadmap of synchronous IAM systems, which ties together many advanced point security and privacy solutions. An initial diagnosis may reveal certain enterprise units that are more advanced, forward-thinking or capable than others. When deploying an IAM framework someone should start with the best enterprises and the necessary privacy-aware services, which are considered as the strongest links. For example, IAM involves creating roles for different functions in the organization as well as changes to the way people do things. Developers are not in the best position to define these roles or process changes, which means that this requires the involvement of the business personnel who are closest to those areas.

Fully integrating IAM solutions, taking into account existing applications and enterprises and making all the necessary process changes in order to effectively utilize its capabilities, requires a lot of time to complete. However, the vision and priorities aforementioned are not enough. A detailed work plan, with different rollout phases will make able developers, enterprises and end-users to realize value early on and incrementally adding more value as proceed to address the bigger strategic picture. Getting the business benefits out of IT investment as soon as possible and providing a rapid time to value will help to more effectively match the project to the vision obtained.

An effective scheduled rollout plan from small to larger groups will bring a degree of confidence on the implementation itself, it will provide the ability to take corrective actions required in an early phase, and will certainly help to overcome resistance from within the enterprises by involving in the project planning all the major participants. Indeed, very often end-users resist to changes and refuse to adopt new technologies and procedures. This problem is more severe in developing countries where human resources may be less robust, the economy less stable and other job opportunities less plentiful.

Since, it's the end users who will be most affected by the enforcement of an IAM system, the first step and need to be taken is for them to be well-presented in many phases of the project. The involvement from users in different enterprises, departments and boundaries will ensure the understanding of how they use their various systems and applications in their everyday life, giving a clearer picture for how they will have to deal with the changes the IAM solution will bring. In addition it will enable leaders to explain to end-users the goals of a synchronous IAM system, making clear that they are not the targets of reform.

Of course all of them should be trained on their new identity management tools before implementation begins. Only then they will be able to understand the fundamental underpinnings on the tools and concepts that will play into architectural designs.

Last but not least, the modernization of IAM processes and services comes from the effectiveness of the implemented technical solution itself. Effective guidelines, principles and policies should be established in order for the provided services to gain end-users' acceptance and allow the coordination and alignment of business processes and information architectures that span both intra- and inter- organizational boundaries.

Our proposition is that every IAM implementation should realize, like in OpenIdAM, the adoption of the following fundamental architectural principles (Karantjias, Papastergiou, & Polemi, 2009):

- Architectural Modularity
- Use of Open Standards and Specifications

- Interoperability of heterogeneous systems, applications and modules
- Scalability & Extensibility
- Strong Security
- Privacy and Trust
- Reusability

The main benefit of these is the consistent usage of standards-based architectures, which provide easily modified and expanded functionality and re-engineered privacy-aware services, ensuring that end-users perceive the quality of the services provided, and trust of these that being delivered.

CONCLUSION AND FURTHER WORK

As today's climate demands greater efficiency, security, privacy, and regulatory compliance, the need for effective IAM has never been more pressing. At the end of last decade IAM was tackled by relatively few leading-edge companies. Today it has become an imperative for almost all enterprises. Regulations now require that companies and their departments are accountable for lack of proper data security. Therefore, enterprises must implement comprehensive security controls to protect critical data and ensure privacy of sensitive information, and they are subject to material financial and legal liabilities if appropriate steps are not taken to protect relevant data. This applies more than just access to financial information. Actually it's also about who has access to what business information, a broad group that can include the majority of an enterprise's employees.

As business complexity is also increasing dramatically, the adoption of technologies and architectures such as SOA enable deeper lines of automation and integration, both within the enterprise and across inter- and intra- corporate boundaries. Compounding the IAM challenge is the constantly evolving and increasingly complex threat environment. Successful centralized and federated IAM represents a chance for fundamental change in the whole organizational structure, values, culture and the ways of conducting business by utilizing the potential of ICT as a useful tool. It fundamentally secures and very often alters the way services are delivered and managed. More and more enterprises around the world are introducing large scale, centralized and federated IAM frameworks as a means of reducing costs, improving services for end-users and increasing security and efficiency in the public and private sector. Therefore IAM has been identified as one of the top priorities for enterprises or group of them across the world.

However, just the idea of IAM can strike fear in the hearts of line-of-business and IT executives, since such projects have a reputation for being complex and expensive, and difficult to achieve their intended objectives, especially in a federated environment. Although, the engineering world appears today more mature than ever in providing stable technology premises in order to build real interoperable and secure systems, until now many IAM projects do not gain user acceptance, end up behind schedule and over budget, and deliver significant inefficient and cumbersome privacy aware services. While the reasons behind ineffective implementations are varied, most are not a result of failed technology but instead can be attributed to the following factors:

- No definition and adoption of a broad, clear, user-centralized vision
- Lack of experience and insight regarding the current state of IAM policies, procedures, standards, best practices and costs
- Limited understanding of IAM technologies
- Lack of experience to integrate IAM technologies with existing IT infrastructure
- Struggle to define principles, strategies and policies in designing large-scale, scalable, extensible and high-administrative IAM solutions.

Advanced SOAs are considered the most promising way to achieve complex communication among multiple actors across organizational domains. The deployment of an effective IAM framework requires a coherent design and implementation approach that considers fundamental design principles toward the provisioning of user-centric privacy-aware services. Essentially, this paper intends to provide practical and comprehensive coverage of a synchronous, user-centric, federated IAM framework, which consists of advanced enterprise systems that transform the delivery of privacy-aware services anytime, anywhere, by any means, and in interactive mode.

This framework addresses core electronic requirements of security, privacy, interoperability, transparency, scalability and high administration in the communications with end-users, enterprises and other similar frameworks.

Its adoption enables faster interaction among entities and minimizes effort to securely access electronic services from multiple domains, while at the same time provide privacy, integrity and confidentiality. This solution promotes the modeling procedure of future IAM architectures, and identifies all advanced modules, features and functions of an IAM system which aims to achieve the following benefits:

- Increased productivity–better output in terms of the quantity and quality of traditional results, or the performance of previously impossible tasks
- Cost effectiveness–due to reduction in time duration, complexity or possible repetition/duplication of tasks
- Improved service delivery–offering secure access to services, more and better information, choice of level/quality of service and guaranteed standards (including privacy), remedies for failures and, ultimately, value for money

Application knowledge by enterprises is not only creating more challenges within the organizations in trying to utilize the knowledge of their employees more productively, but the organizations are also pressured into changing their corporate strategies to encourage this utilization in order to remain competitive. In this process, competitive advantage in today's global and rapidly changing market requires organizations to build and continually replenish capabilities at both individual and organizational levels, to work effectively with uncertainty, especially considering digital gap in developing countries.

Despite the fact that this article describes a novel technological solution for providing cross-boundary, privacy-aware information and services through a centralized and federated IAM framework, it also outlines the main insights regarding the critical success factors that need to be considered and adopted when integrating such IAM solutions. It actually offers a practical guideline, meant to be useful and used by IAM practitioners, who need to effectively:

- Define a clear user-centered vision and priority areas
- Pick winners with adequate expertise
- Structure the clear and effective project plan with specified and rollout phases
- Overcome resistance from within the enterprises

The realization of our proposition assumes that all the interacting entities have agreed on several properties of the actual operation, such as the name of every possible PII labels and the corresponding data type for their values. In addition, it requires specified working rules that will govern how negotiation should be conducted and how an agreement can be reached, since the negotiation process details are out. The actual negotiation should take into account the risks, trust, necessities, and other factors that differ in heterogeneous environments (public or private sector) and probably in each country, when building cross-border scenarios. In addition, the fact that users can be anonymous in our federation (i.e. using blind certificates and/or session certificates) imposes the need to revoke this anonymity especially in a security breach investigation. A set of conditions need to be agreed among all involved parties to determine the circumstances under which user's anonymity can be revoked.

Moreover, even if WSS features are enforced in the transportation of all messages between the mobile device and the interacting entities (Karantjias & Polemi, 2009), (Karantjias, Papastergiou, & Polemi, 2009), the lack of conditions fulfillment enforcement may lead to the abuse of this capability, remaining a problem that its solution requires further research.

Last but not least, in order to have successful IAM implementations, it is necessary to establish their legitimacy, secure their efficiency and gain the trust between enterprises and end-users and also provide for the legal aspects to become part of their roadmap. Yet the legal frameworks are still in infancy. A cohesive legal framework is required for helping the facilitation of a better progress. For example, during our implementation, the main domains of concerns identified, included the 'Back-Office' re-organization, the inclusive access, the trust and confidence, and the better use of privacy-aware information. Therefore, four main sets of legislation are considered relevant: Personal data protection laws; Privacy and security laws; Information (provision) laws; and Administrative laws in National and International level.

ACKNOWLEDGMENT

The authors would like to thank the E.C. for its support in funding the SWEB project (SWEB Project, 2006), the Greek Ministry of Interior for the LGAF project (LGAF Project, 2009), and all the projects' partners.

REFERENCES

Aberdeen Group. (2007). *Identity and access management critical to operations and security: Users find ROI, increased user productivity, tighter security*. March.

Ahn, G., & Lam, J. (2005). Managing privacy preferences for federated identity management. In *Proceedings of the 2005 Workshop on Digital Identity Management,* DIM'05, ACM, Fairfax VA USA, (pp. 28-36).

Ardagna, C., Cremonini, M., Damiani, E., Capitani, S., Frati, F., & Samarati, P. (2006). *Privacy-enhanced identity management for e-services. Secure e-Government Web Services*. Idea Group Inc.

Buhler, J., & Wunder, G. (2010). Traffic-aware optimization of heterogeneous access management. *IEEE Transactions on Communications*, *58*(6), 1737–1747. doi:10.1109/TCOMM.2010.06.090182

Burr, W., Dodson, D., & Polk, T. (2006). *Electronic authentication guideline. National Institute of Standards and Technology (NIST), Special Publication 800-63, version 1.0.2*. Information Technology Laboratory.

Burton Group Inc. (n.d.). *Leading research and advisory services firm that focuses on providing practical, technically in-depth advice to front-line IT professionals*. Gartner Inc. Retrieved from http://www.burtongroup.com/

Central Union of Municipalities and Communities in Greece. (n.d.). *Index*. Retrieved from http://www.kedke.gr/index.asp

Cser, A., & Penn, J. (2008). *Identity management market forecast: 2007 to 2014.* Forrester Research, February. Retrieved from http://www.forrester.com/rb/Research/identity_management_market_forecast_2007_to_2014/q/id/43842/t/2

Dabrowski, M., & Pacyna, P. (2008). Modular reference framework architecture for identity management. In *Proceedings of the 11th IEEE International Conference on Communication Systems*, ICCS'08, Singapore, (pp. 743-749).

Elmufti, K., Weerasinghe, D., Rajarajan, M., & Rakocevic, V. (2008). Anonymous authentication for mobile Single Sign-On to protect user privacy. *International Journal of Mobile Communications, 6*(6), 760-769. ACM Press. eMayor Project. (2004). *Electronic and secure municipal administration for European Citizens*. IST-2004-507217, Sixth Framework Programme.

European Commission. (2006). *FIDIS Consortium: Structured overview on prototypes and concepts of identity management systems*. Retrieved from http://www.fidis.net/ fileadmin/fidis/deliverables/fidis-wp3-del3.1.overview_on_IMS.final.pdf

European Commission. (2011). *Europe 2020: A strategy for smart, sustainable and inclusive growth*. Communication from the European Commission, Brussels. Retrieved from http://ec.europa.eu/eu2020/index_en.htm

European Parliament. (1997). Directive 97/66/EC of the European Parliament and of the Council of 15th December 1997 concerning the processing of personal data and the protection of privacy in the telecommunications sector. *Official Journal, 24*, 1–8.

European Parliament. (2001). Directive 01/45/EC of the European Parliament and the Council of Ministers on the protection of individuals with regard to the processing of personal data by the Community institutions and bodies and on the free movement of such data. *Official Journal, 8*, 1–22.

Farahbod, R., Glasser, U., & Vajihollahi, M. (2007). An abstract machine architecture for web service based business process management. *International Journal of Business Process Integration and Management, 1*, 279–291. doi:10.1504/IJBPIM.2006.012626

Forward Consortium. (2009). *Managing emerging threats in ICT infrastructures*. Deliverable D3.1, FORWARD, 7th Framework Programme, Information & Communication Technologies Secure, dependable and trusted Infrastructures.

Goodner, M., Hondo, M., Nadalin, A., McIntosh, M., & Schmidt, D. (2007). *Understanding WS-Federation*, Version 1.0.

Intelcities Project. (2006). *Intelligent cities*. 6th Framework Programme, IST-2004-507860. Retrieved from http://intelcities.iti.gr/intelcities

Internet2. (2011). *Shibboleth Architecture*. Internet2 Middleware Iniative. Retrieved from http://shibboleth.internet2.edu

Kaliontzoglou, A., Sklavos, P., Karantjias, A., & Polemi, N. (2005). A secure e-government platform architecture for small to medium sized public organizations. [Elsevier.]. *Electronic Commerce Research and Applications, 4*(2), 174–186. doi:10.1016/j.elerap.2004.09.002

Karantjias, A., Papastergiou, S., & Polemi, N. (2009). Design principles of a secure federated e/m-government framework. *International Journal of Electronic Governance (IJEG)* [Inderscience Publishers.]. *Special Issue on Users and Uses of Electronic Governance, 2*(4), 402–423.

Karantjias, A., & Polemi, N. (2009). An innovative platform architecture for complex secure e/m government services. *International Journal of Electronic Security and Digital Forensics (IJESDF)* [Inderscience Publishers]. *Special Issue on Mobile Services Technological and Legal Issues, 2*(4), 338–354.

Karantjias, A., Stamati, T., & Martakos, D. (2010). Advanced e-government enterprise strategies & solutions. *International Journal of Electronic Governance (IJEG), Special Issue on Methodologies, Technologies and Tools Enabling e-Government, 3*(2), 170-188. Inderscience Publishers.

Karp, A. H. (2006). Authorization-based access control for the services oriented architecture. In: *Proceedings of the Fourth International Conference on Creating, Connecting and Collaborating through Computing* (C5'06), (pp. 160-167). IEEE Computer Society.

Koch, M., & Moslein, M. (2005). Identity management for e-commerce and collaborative applications. *International Journal of Electronic Commerce, 9*(3), 11–29.

LGAF Project. (2009). *Local government access framework*. Sixth Framework Programme. Retrieved from http://lgaf.kedke.org/wiki

Liberty Alliance. (2003). *Liberty Alliance & WS-Federation: A comparative overview*. Retrieved from http://www.projectliberty.org/resources / whitepapers/.

Liberty Alliance. (n.d.). *Liberty ID-WSF Web services framework overview*, version 2.0. Retrieved from http://www.projectliberty.org

Lockhart, H., Andersen, S., Bohren, J., Sverdlov, Y., Hondo, M., Maruyama, H., … Wilson, H. (2007). *Web services federation language (WS-Federation),* version 1.1, December.

Matthews, W., & Esterline, A. (2010). Personally identifiable information: Identifying unprotected PII using file-indexing search tools and quantitative analysis. In *Proceedings of the IEEE SoutheastCon 2010,* Concord, NC, (pp. 360-362).

Mule. (2008). *Technical Committee: Mule 2.0. release candidate 2*. Retrieved from http://mule.mulesource.org

NSTC. (2008). *Standards and conformity assessment working group: NSTC Subcommittee on biometrics and identity management*. Retrieved from http://www.biometrics.gov/Standards/default.aspx

OASIS. (2005). *XACML technical committee: eXtensible access control markup language (XACML) version 2.0*. OASIS Standard Specification, February. Retrieved from http://docs.oasis-open.org/xacml/2.0/access_control-xacml-2.0-core-spec-os.pdf

OASIS. (2007). *Web service secure exchange technical committee: OASIS WS-Trust 1.3*. OASIS Standard Specification. Retrieved from http://www.oasis-open.org

OASIS. (2007a). *Technical committee: Security assertion markup language v. 2.0 – Technical overview*. OASIS Standard Specification. Retrieved from http://www.oasis-open.org

OASIS. (2008). *WSFED technical committee: Web services federation language version 1.2*. OASIS Standard Specification, Working Draft. Retrieved from http://www.oasis-open.org

OMG. (2009). *Business process modeling notation (BPMN) version 1.2*. Object Management Group Specification. Retrieved from http://www.omg.org/spec/BPMN/1.2/

Papastergiou, S., Karantjias, A., & Polemi, D. (2007). A federated privacy-enhancing identity management system (FPE-IMS). In *Proceedings of the 18th Annual IEEE International Symposium on Personal, Indoor and Mobile Radio Communications*, PIMRC 07, Athens Greece, IEEE Digital Library.

Peyton, L., Doshi, Ch., & Seguin, P. (2007). An audit trail service to enhance privacy compliance in federated identity management. In *Proceedings of the 2007 Conference of the Center for Advanced Studies on Collaborative Research*, CASCON'07, ACM, Ontario Canada, (pp. 175-187).

PRIME Project. (2005). *Privacy and identity management for Europe*. European RTD Integrated Project under the FP6/IST Programme. Retrieved from http://www.prime-project.eu.org/

Rieger, S., & Neumair, B. (2007). Towards usable and reasonable identity management in heterogeneous IT infrastructures. In *Proceedings of the 10th IFIP/IEEE International Symposium on Integrated Network Management* (IM '07), Munich, (pp. 560-574).

Squicciarini, A., Trombetta, A., Bertino, E., & Braghin, S. (2008). Identity-based long running negotiations. In *Proceedings of the 4th ACM Workshop on Digital Identity Management*, Virginia USA, (pp. 97-106).

SWEB Project. (2006). *Secure, interoperable, cross border m-services contributing towards a trustful European cooperation with the non-EU member Western Balkan countries*. Sixth Framework Programme, IST-2006-2.6.5. Retrieved from www.sweb-project.org

SWEB Project. (2008). *D4.1: SWEB platform development report. Project Deliverable*. Brussels: European Commission.

The Ponemon Institute. (2007). *Survey on identity compliance*. March.

Wolter, C., Kohler, A., & Schaad, A. (2007). Classification model for access control constraints. In *WIA – Proceedings of the first International Workshop on Information Assurance*, (pp. 410-417).

Chapter 4
Feasibility and Sustainability Model for Identity Management

Rajanish Dass
Indian Institute of Management, India

Sujoy Pal
Indian Institute of Management, India

ABSTRACT

National identity projects in various countries around the globe, which manage unique identification of citizens, have captured attention of late. Although the perceived benefits in terms of public administration are numerous, the challenges and bottlenecks for a successful rollout are also many. The objective of this chapter is to identify the drivers and inhibitors for adopting a common identity management system across various organizations for public administration and to suggest a model for determining the feasibility and sustainability of such a system. We reveal the various factors affecting successful implementation of the system and the probable impact of these factors. The model suggested would allow public organizations and policy makers to determine the critical factors for the implementation of an identity management system on a large scale.

INTRODUCTION

Many countries have already implemented identity management by introducing national identity cards for their citizens, while others are still investigating the consequences of such an initiative from various angles, privacy and data security being the major concerns. There have been various motivators for governments to consider the option of issuing identification cards for citizens, ranging from protecting the country from terror attacks to achieving operational efficiency in providing services to citizens. However, there has been hardly any research on developing a model that could help a government analyze the feasibility and sustainability of an identity management system. This gap in the existing literature was the motivation for this study. We adopt case study

DOI: 10.4018/978-1-61350-498-7.ch004

based research methodology (Benbasat, Goldstein, & Mead, 1987) to design a model for determining the feasibility and sustainability of an identity management system.

Different countries have different perspectives on the various dimensions of identity management. The differences are visible in both motivators as well as inhibitors of the system. Considering these differences and the fact that the government of a country functions within an ecosystem of various organizations (namely, taxation department, electoral department, public distribution department etc.), similar differences would exist in the perspectives of these organizations as well. Hence, in determining the feasibility and sustainability of a common identity management system that could be used by each of these organizations, it is critical to understand and formulate the perspectives of each organization. Taking this into consideration, this study focuses on developing a model that would allow a government to understand the various factors acting as motivators and inhibitors for the adoption of an identity management system as perceived by the various organizations within the ecosystem.

BACKGROUND

Identity Management Initiatives by Various Nations

Though not much work has been published on the factors affecting the implementation of an identity management system, there are reports on the issuing of unique national identity cards for citizens in various countries. Many countries like Belgium, Finland, France, Germany, Greece, Hong Kong, Italy, the Netherlands, Malaysia, Portugal, Spain etc. have gone ahead with the implementation of national identity cards, some making the carrying of the cards mandatory for citizens, while countries like Australia and United States (US) have not (Beynon-Davies, 2006). Only after terror attacks on the US and United Kingdom (UK) have these countries started to seriously look into the implementing a national identity management system. In a country like Australia, the major motivators for the implementation of national identity card are national security, prevention of government fraud, anti-money laundering, replacement of existing cards with a single multipurpose card and improvement of efficiency of government services. Factors acting as inhibitors are privacy issues, political opposition and public opposition (Jackson & Ligertwood, December 2006). Canada, currently looking toward implementing a national identity card system, recognizes concerns for national security as the major motivating factor. In contrast to Australia, Canada enjoys strong support from its citizens for implementing national identity cards. Other major concerns for Canada are privacy issues, data security, possibility of function creep, technology gaps, risk of single point of failure and threat of racial discrimination. Existence of weak seed documents on which the cards would be issued is also a concern for Canada (Fontana, October 2003).

The US, which faces strong opposition statewide towards the implementation of national identity cards for its citizens, identifies national security as the only motivator for the implementation of such as system, with privacy issues, the possibility of function creep, technology gaps and high cost being the major inhibitors (Rotenberg & Ngo, May 2008). For countries like Belgium, Portugal and Spain, who have already implemented national identity cards for citizens, secured accessibility to e-government applications, social security, child safety, improvement of efficiency of government services, better accessibility to health care services and prevention of illegal immigration are the major motivators, while privacy issues, legal issues and data security are the major concerns(Fontana, October 2003; Mindrum, January 2008).

Most factors affecting identity management revealed in the existing literature are similar.

Table 1. Motivator and inhibitors for implementation of national identity cards

Motivators	Inhibitors
National security	Cost
Prevention of illegal immigration	Lack of cost benefit analysis
Public support	Legal issues
Anti-money laundering	Lack of public trust
Child safety	Political opposition
Commercial competitive advantage	Public opposition
Health care services	Technology gaps
Improvement of efficiency of government services	Data security issues
Prevention of fraud in government services	Privacy issues
Provision of secured access to e-government applications	Threat of racial discrimination
Replacement of multiple cards	Function creep
Security of internet transactions	Process gaps
Social security	Weak seed documents
	Risk of single point of failure

For example, the strongest motivating factor for countries like the UK, Australia and Canada is national security, followed by fraud detection, anti-money laundering and improvement of efficiency of government services. Privacy issues and political opposition are major factors acting as inhibitors for identity management for these nations. Other factors acting as barriers include high cost of implementation, lack of clarity on the benefits and unclear plans about accessibility of data to various departments. There are also issues regarding lack of clarity on policies of data protection and the period for which such data should be retained by any organization or the government. The reports suggest that the lack of clarity on the exact purpose and the multipurpose nature of the identity cards raise issues related to privacy and data protection. The factors acting as motivators and inhibitors for identity management in various countries are summarized in Table 1.

Technology Adoption and Diffusion Model

The various factors mentioned in Table 1 have different levels of impact on the implementation of an identity management system for different nations, according to the literature. For example, in the case of the US, the privacy issue is stronger compared to countries like Italy and Greece (Fontana, October 2003). Differences in the strength of factors in the adoption of technology by firms are also observed (Cragg & King, 1993). Effects of explanatory factors like perceived usefulness, organizational readiness and external pressure to adopt a system have been examined to determine the expected impact on technology adoption (Iacovou, Benbasat, & Dexter, 1995). The factors in Table 1 are mapped with five decision variables (i.e. explanatory factors) of technology adoption as shown in Table 2 according to the literature.

Perceived Usefulness

Perceived usefulness is defined as “the degree to which a person believes that using a particular

Table 2. Factors mapped with major decision variables of technology adoption

Explanatory Factors	Factors Identified from Reports
Perceived usefulness	Anti-money laundering
	Child safety
	Commercial competitive advantage
	Health care services
	Improvement of efficiency of government services
	Prevention of fraud in government services
	Provision of secured access to e-government applications
	Replacement of multiple cards
	Security of internet transactions
	Social security
Organizational readiness	Public support
	Cost
	Lack of cost benefit analysis
	Legal issues
	Lack of public trust
	Political opposition
	Public opposition
	Technology gaps
External pressure	National security
	Prevention of illegal immigration
Process complexity	Process gaps
	Weak seed documents
Perceived Barriers	Data protection and retention issues
	Privacy issues
	Racial discrimination
	Function creep
	Risk of single point of failure

system would enhance his or her job performance" (Davis, 1989). In the context of an organization or nation, perceived usefulness can be determined from the belief of the stakeholders about the ability of a system to help achieve its various goals and objectives. The degree and dimensions of perceived usefulness of an identity management system based on national identity cards varies from nation to nation. Studies suggest that factors such as child safety and replacement of multiple cards with a single card are considered more important in some countries compared to others. This suggests that even within the same country, different government and non-government organizations would have different dimensions and levels of perceived usefulness of the system. Hence, in determining the feasibility and sustainability of an identity management system to be used by these organizations, it is important to determine the dimensions and degree of usefulness of the dimensions as perceived by the various organizations who are the stakeholders of the system.

Organizational Readiness

Organizational readiness refers to the level of financial and technological resources of the firm (Iacovou, et al., 1995). Financial readiness indicates the availability of funds required for implementation as well as operation of the system. Lack of proper cost-benefit analysis often has a negative impact on the readiness of a nation to go ahead with the implementation of a common identity management system. The organization's technological resources for the implementation of the system also determine the organizational readiness. In addition to these two factors, for a nation to design a common identity management system, the amount of political opposition and public support are factors affecting the readiness of the nation. Moreover, the strengths and weakness of the nation such as corruption and black marketeering etc. also have an impact on organizational readiness.

External Pressure

External pressure refers to the environmental factors of the organization that affect the feasibility and sustainability of an identity management system. For instance, increases in terrorist activities and illegal immigration act as external pressure forcing national governments to implement an identity management system.

Process Complexity

Process can be defined according to four orientations as follows: (1) activity-oriented, i.e. a process as a set of partially ordered steps intended to reach a goal; (2) product-oriented, i.e. a process as a series of activities that cause successive product transformations to reach the desired product; (3) decision-oriented, i.e. a process as a set of related decisions conducted for the specific purpose of product definition; and (4) context-oriented, i.e. a process as a sequence of contexts causing successive product transformations under the influence of a decision taken in a context (Howard, Rolland, & Qusaibaty, 2004; Rolland, 1998). A high level of complexity involved in the process of implementation of an identity management system would have a negative impact on the feasibility and sustainability of the system. Reports suggest that the existing process gaps and weak seed documents based on which an identity card is issued contribute to process complexity.

Perceived Barriers

The types and intensity of perceived barriers of adoption of an identity management system vary from organization to organization. Moreover, high levels of perceived barriers negatively affect the adoption of technology (Chau & Tam, 1997). Existing reports on national identity cards also reveal similar facts. For most nations, privacy, data protection and retention issues in addition to other issues such as risk of single point of failure, function creep and risk of racial discrimination are the major factors negatively related to adoption of such a system.

In summary (Figure 1), of the five explanatory factors, three factors (perceived usefulness, organizational readiness and external pressure) are expected to have positive impact on the feasibility and sustainability of identity management, while the other two factors (process complexity and perceived barriers) are expected to have negative impact on the system.

MAIN FOCUS OF THE CHAPTER

To study the viability of a model for the implementation of an identity management system for a nation, we considered a real case of similar complexity. Self Employed Women's Association (SEWA), an NGO working in rural India with more than half a million members spread across the fifteen districts of Gujarat, was found to have many similarities with the nation of India when discussed in the context of identity management of its members. SEWA provides various services to its members through fifteen strategic business units (SBUs) managed independently. Each SBU provides different types of services to its members ranging from training to financial services such as banking and insurance. This structure is similar to various departments of a government providing different types of services to its citizens. An identity management system is required at SEWA to integrate activities conducted by the SBUs. This is similar to the case of most nations looking towards adoption of national identity cards. SEWA members work in eighty-four different trades, thus ensuring sufficient diversity within the sample. The fact that all the members as well as the management of SEWA are women, might pose a gender bias in the sample. However, the existing literature on technology adoption and diffusion models suggests gender to be an insignificant factor.

SEWA registered as a trade union in 1972 and evolved as an organization of poor, self-employed women workers who earn their living through their own labor or small businesses. These women, unlike workers in organized sectors, do not ob-

Figure 1. Feasibility and sustainability model for identity management

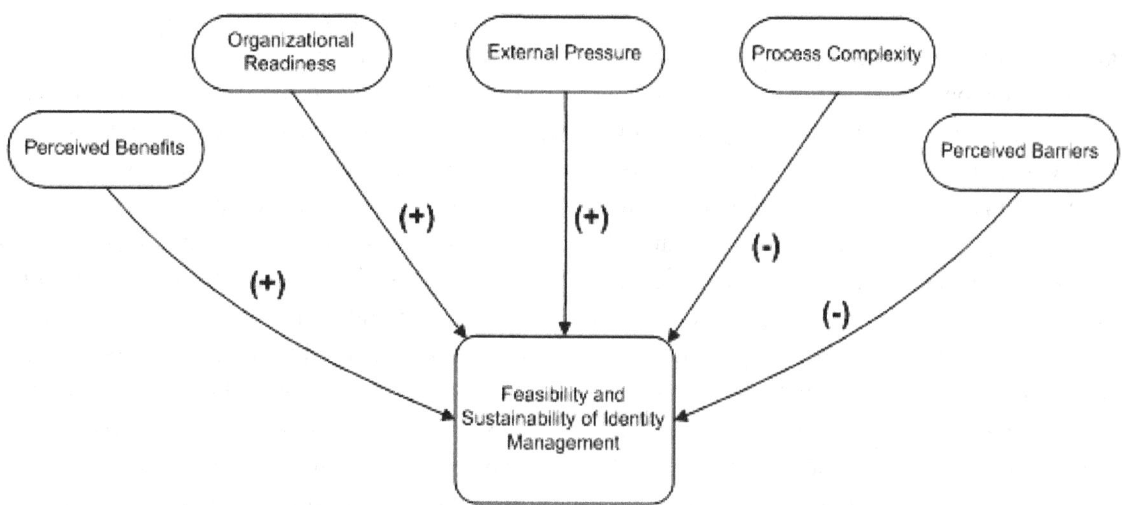

tain regular salaried employment with welfare benefits. According to estimates of the female labor force in India, more than ninety-four percent are in unorganized sectors, in jobs as diverse as hawkers, vendors, carrying of goods to markets, stitching of clothes at home, rolling bidis[1] and weaving cloth. SEWA's goal is to mobilize women workers to achieve their goals of full employment and self-reliance. For SEWA, full employment means employment whereby workers obtain work security, income security, food security and social security (at least health care, child care and shelter). Similarly, self-reliance means that the women are autonomous and self-reliant, individually and collectively, and economically and in terms of their decision-making ability.[2]

The disciplined and transparent electoral structure of SEWA has been the strength and inspiration for its rapid growth. The electoral structure provides equal opportunity for members to actively participate in the management of the organization. This helps the organization to keep its members and their interests at the center. The whole organization is bounded by and focused on its mission and goals. SEWA, being a trade union, mandates its members to renew their membership every year by paying a nominal membership fee of five rupees[3] (as of 2009). The aagewans (leaders)—members of SEWA selected as leaders within a village or locality by the members—are responsible for collecting the membership details and fees..

SEWA's mission is to make the lives of its members better by preparing women workers for full emploreliance[4]. SEWA empowers women to ensure that every family in the community obtains full employment. This is carried out through the joint action of the union and cooperatives. Various SBUs have evolved over the years to provide better services to the members. The services provided by SEWA are categorized into training/capacity building, social security, healthcare, childcare and housing. Each SBU is associated with a specific service. For example, the objective of SEWA Bank is to help the poor self-employed members in breaking out of the vicious cycle of poverty and guide them through the process of capital formation. Similarly, SEWA Insurance is focused on ensuring social security for its members. SEWA Academy, SEWA Manager's School and SEWA Life School provide education and training to the members. SEWA Trade Facilitation Center supports the marketing and production of various artesian products by the members.

Data Collection

Data was collected through in-depth interviews with the decision makers (top level management) and focused group discussions with the district coordinators, aagewans and spearhead team members of SEWA. Most of the interviews and focused group discussions were conducted in the local language to ensure full expression of the views and opinions of the respondents. Observations were carried out by conducting field visits in three districts (Ahemdabad, Anand and Surendranagar). These visits were to understand the reality and perspective of the organizers at the local level. Out of the three districts selected, Ahmedabad was the most advanced in terms of information and communications technology (ICT) infrastructure and other facilities. Anand was moderate in the same context. Surendranagar was the remotest of them all, being located near a salt desert with the majority of the members being salt farmers.

We reviewed the existing documents of the SEWA and its SBUs to understand the operation of and interrelationship within the organization. The documents included various reports as well as material published on the web. We also thoroughly studied the existing ICT systems implemented at SEWA to understand the technological readiness of the organization.

Empirical Findings

Analysis of the collected data revealed various factors affecting the feasibility and sustainability of an identity management system.

Perceived Usefulness

There was various perceived usefulness of implementation of an identity management system at SEWA. Some perceived usefulness was focused towards better management, while other was more inclined towards benefiting the members. Being a member-based organization, it is critical for SEWA to know exactly who its members are. Without an existing identity management system in place, SEWA and its SBUs cannot efficiently identify their members, nor determine how many members are new, existing or have dropped out.

In the absence of a proper identity management system, there exists a huge lag in various tasks performed at the organization. For example, membership slips filled out by members are supposed to reach the SEWA reception center (SRC) within three months from the date of issue at the latest. However, analysis of the existing data revealed that in some cases they take a year to reach the SRC. Further, there is a huge time lag in digitizing the membership data. Hence the top level management is not able to access the latest information about membership, hindering the proper planning of resources.

Each SBU handles various welfare activities for its members. Though these activities are conducted independently, better insight could be gained by looking at the participation of members in these activities more holistically, which cannot be done currently due to the lack of any unique identity for the members. This type of integration would help the SBUs to more efficiently coordinate their activities and better meet the needs of the members.

Many private companies, finding the urban markets saturated with their products, are looking towards rural markets to sell their products. But the needs of the rural population are quite different from the urban population. Hence, companies with no or very little experience in marketing in rural markets are finding it difficult to make their presence felt there. The decision makers of SEWA are very much aware of this and are eager to gear-up their efforts to obtain better products and services for their members at cheaper rates. This could be achieved by providing various companies information about the needs of their members.

Group discussions with the aagwans clearly revealed that they face criticism from the members for not being able to provide some kind of member identification. The members working in unorganized sectors face various challenges in dealing with the government and the police. The members believe a SEWA identity card would facilitate tackling such issues more effectively and efficiently, and provide them with a greater sense of social security.

The SBUs work independently to provide services to members. The district associations act as hubs for the SBUs to deliver services to members of the respective districts. In the absence of an identity management system, coordination among the SBUs in providing services to members is limited. Though the district associations and respective spearhead teams coordinate activities, there remains huge scope for improvement. The top level management of SEWA perceives that an efficient identity management system for its members would provide a means of better coordinating the activities of the SBUs.

Organizational Readiness

For any organization, economic factors are a critical dimension in the decision-making process for implementation of a new system. SEWA, being an NGO, primarily depends on donations and funds generated through its activities. Therefore, the high cost of implementation of an identity management system is a matter of concern for all SBUs. Further, as each SBU is concerned with different activities and works independently of others, the political landscape among the top level management of each SBU also plays a significant role in determining the course of such an initiative. Both the high cost of the system and the internal politics act as negative factors for determining the organizational readiness for adoption of an identity management system. When compared between these two factors, the cost of the system is a strong component for determining organizational readiness, while the political constraint is weak, which might be due to the fact that all the SBUs are bound by the common goals of SEWA.

Another dimension affecting organizational readiness is the availability of resources, including technological as well as manpower required to implement such a system. All SBUs have sufficient technological resources. Almost all the offices are equipped with basic hardware resources such as a computer, printer, scanner, webcam and telephone connection (in some cases broadband connection). In some remote districts, connectivity is an issue due to non-availability of adequate mobile or broadband connection. However, the lack of availability of skilled manpower is a limitation. Most aagewans involved in expanding SEWA's membership are illiterate. However, their level of motivation is very high, stimulating them to obtain training in technical skills such as computing to certain extent. The source of motivation is the electoral structure of SEWA that allows a capable and active member to climb up to top level management. Hence, the other factors affecting organizational readiness are the availability of technological, skill of personnel, motivation of personnel and organization structure. Here, the limited availability of skilled personnel and technology negatively affects the organizational readiness in the implementation of an identity management system, but is within the control of the organizations and indirectly related to cost. Motivation of personnel and the organization structure strongly supports organizational readiness.

External Pressure

SEWA together with its SBUs, being registered as a trade union, is mandated by the Labour Ministry of India to keep a record of all its members each year and charge the members an annual membership fee. The membership records are audited by the Ministry and any discrepancy is questioned. This obliges SEWA to maintain the records of all its members each year. Another external factor that motivates SEWA and its SBUs to look towards the implementation of an efficient identity management system is the growth of other NGOs who adopt various moral as well as immoral techniques to prevent the members from continuing their relationship with SEWA. These two external factors are the motivators for the implementation of an identity management system at SEWA. However, since there is not many NGOs with as strong an organizational structure as SEWA, both these factors were found to be very weak in impact. Further, no other NGO has an identity management system in place. Though the Labour Ministry mandates SEWA to maintain details of its members, it is not requiring implementation of an identity management system.

Process Complexity

Process complexity can be determined based on two dimensions: the complexity of the tasks involved and the size of the sample to be identified (i.e. the total number of members). The process of identity management typically involves enrollment, identification/verification, authentication, updating and deletion. For SEWA the process of enrollment includes collection of personal information of members such as name, residential address, trade, trade address, age, marital status and photograph. None of these dimensions are difficult to capture and, hence, the enrollment process would be low in complexity. In the case of verification/identification of a member, the member would be required to produce a valid ration card or voter identity card. The ration card would also act as a link for the member to her family. However, there exist some operational challenges in collecting these seed documents for verification. The discussions with the aagewans revealed that many of the members cannot produce these documents at the time of enrollment. Membership generation being one of the core processes for SEWA, the rule for producing the seed documents at the time of enrollment is not strictly enforced. Hence, the process of validation/identification remains an issue within these constraints.

SEWA members are supposed to renew their membership each year. Although this process is low in complexity, analysis of the existing data and interviews reveals a high degree of volatility in the captured dimensions. Even basic dimensions like first name, middle name and address were subject to change. Hence the process of updating membership details is moderately complex. The process of identity management discussed up till now remains common for all the SBUs of SEWA. The process of authentication is required at the time of service delivery and the risk of violating this process varies for different SBUs depending upon the type of service being delivered. For example, the services of the SEWA Bank involve financial transactions and, hence, would require more stringent authentication compared to an SBU providing training.

Perceived Barriers

The issue of data security and the right to access and retain information about various transactions made by the members is of major concern for the top level management of the majority of SBUs. SEWA considers information on the whereabouts of its members to be confidential. There are serious concerns about where the data should physically reside and how various SBUs are authorized to access the data. Setting up a data center at the premises of SEWA rather than hiring a space from any existing data centers is preferred. On the other hand, privacy is not found to be an issue either from the perspective of the top level management or from the members. Hence, in this context, the strength of perceived barriers on the feasibility and sustainability of an identity management system is low.

Discussion and Implications for Research

Perceived usefulness of an identity management system by SEWA's top level management as well as the members is strong and directly related to the goals and objectives of the organization. This provides a very strong basis for decision making on the implementation of an identity management system. Thus, perceived usefulness is a strong positive factor for the feasibility and sustainability of an identity management system. Four dimensions, namely, cost, non-availability of technological resources, lack of skill of the personnel and internal politics negatively affect organizational readiness. While the effect of cost as a dimension is strong, the remaining dimensions have weak impact on organizational readiness. Motivation of the personnel strongly affects organizational readiness in a positive way. Based on these dimensions, a moderate level of organizational readiness has a moderate level of impact on the feasibility and sustainability of an identity management system. However, since the dimensions negatively affecting organizational readiness are under the control of the organizations and, hence, under the influence of high perceived usefulness, organizational readiness may improve with time.

Process complexity has a strong negative impact on the feasibility and even more impact on the sustainability of an identity management system. Non-availability of seed documents for many members and high volatility of captured dimensions have a strong negative impact and increase the process complexity. Low complexity of the dimensions to be captured has weak positive impact. The fact that process complexity is not under the control of the organizations makes this a critical factor for determining the feasibility and sustainability of the system. Moreover, in the given case, SEWA is not in a position to strictly enforce each and every aspect of the process on its members. Hence, the only way through which the negative impact of this factor can be reduced is to increase the perceived usefulness for members.

While external factors such as terrorism and illegal immigration are strong factors affecting the implementation of an identity management system for various countries, the same is not found in the case of SEWA. Only two weak dimensions—namely, government regulations and competition from other NGOs—constitute external pressure factors. These positively affect the feasibility and sustainability of an identity management system. Perceived barriers are moderately negative impact on the feasibility and sustainability of an identity management system at SEWA. Though the concerns of privacy and data security are found to be strong negative dimensions for the majority of nations considering implementation of national identity cards, in the case of SEWA, these dimensions are weak determinants of perceived barriers. These dimensions and their effects on the factors of the model are shown is Figure 2. The thickness of the lines connecting the dimensions and the factors indicate the strength of the effect.

The model represented in Figure 2 demonstrates the effects of perceived usefulness, organizational readiness, external pressure, process complexity and perceived barriers on the feasibility and sustainability of an identity management system. In the study, we find that the dimensions and its effects on the factors of the model vary from organization to organization. Hence, for a system to be used in a multi-organization environment, all the factors and their related dimensions need to be examined from the perspective of each organization involved. A government intending to implement such a system would need to analyze these factors from the perspective of its different departments.

FUTURE RESEARCH DIRECTIONS

As the study was conducted under the context of a single umbrella organization, the diversity in the goals and objectives of the organization is limited. Further research needs to be conducted on organizations with more diverse and independent goals and objectives. Based on the model proposed in this study, a framework can be further that would help in determining the factors influencing the dimen-

Figure 2. Effect and strength of identified dimensions

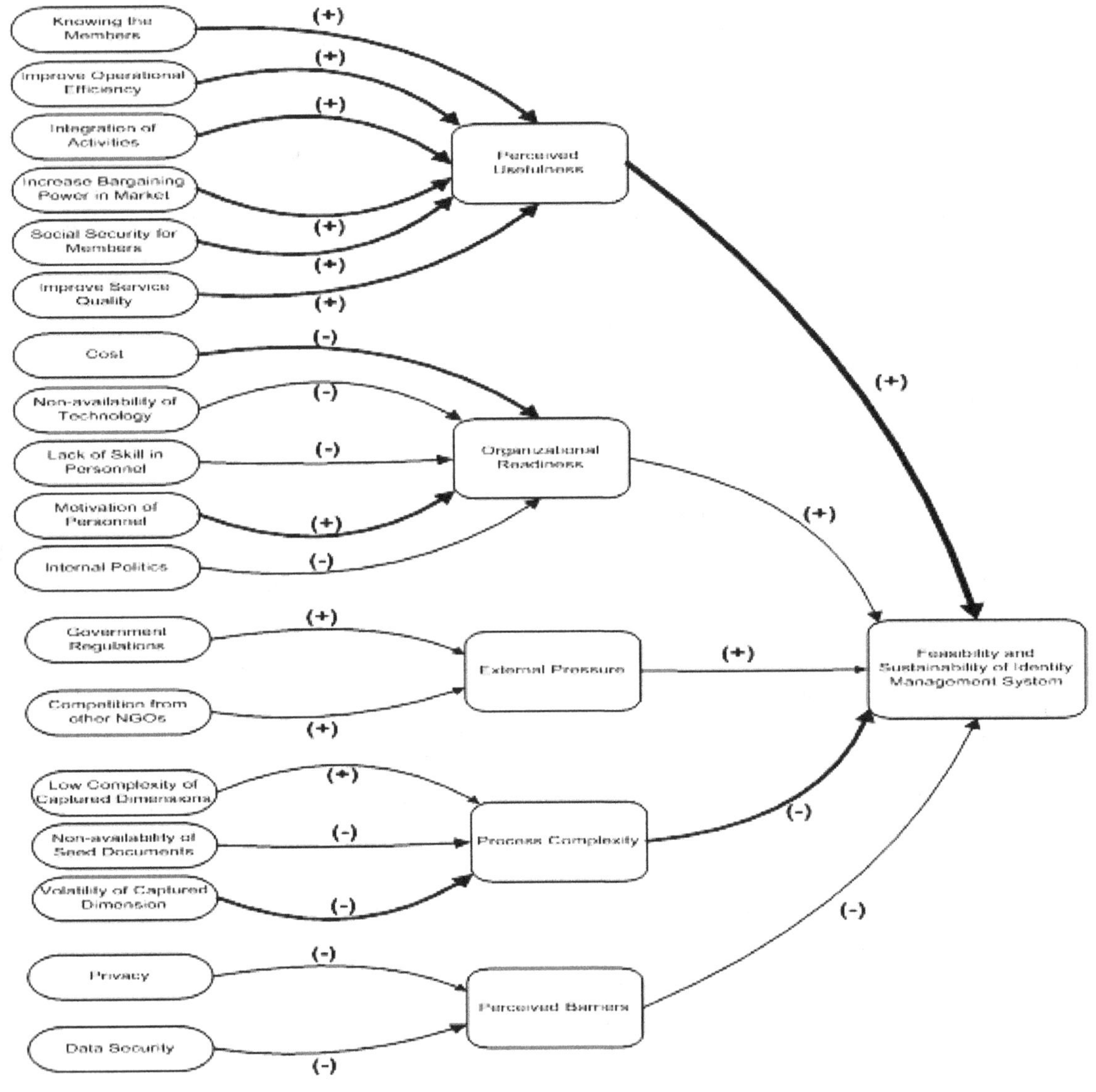

sions mentioned in the model. These factors may vary from organization to organization and differ in strength in their impact on the feasibility and sustainability of an identity management system.

CONCLUSION

This study reveals that though various factors affect the feasibility and sustainability of an identity management system, the intensity of the factors differ from organization to organization. In the case of SEWA, three dimensions, namely, perceived usefulness, organizational readiness and external pressure, positively affect the feasibility and sustainability of an identity management system. Two dimensions, namely, process complexity and perceived barriers, have a negative impact on the adoption and sustenance of the system. The effect of perceived usefulness and process complexity are stronger compared to the other dimensions. Various factors were identified as contributing to each of these dimensions. These factors also vary from organization to organization. Thus, it can be concluded that to determine the feasibility and sustainability of an integrated identity management system, it is necessary to identify the factors contributing to each of the five dimensions—perceived usefulness, organizational readiness, external pressure, process complexity and perceived barriers—and determine the intensity and impact of each on the system for each organization.

REFERENCES

Benbasat, I., Goldstein, D. K., & Mead, M. (1987). The case research strategy in studies of Information Systems. *Management Information Systems Quarterly*, *11*(3), 369–386. doi:10.2307/248684

Beynon-Davies, P. (2006). Personal identity management in the information polity: The case of the UK national identity card. *Information Polity*, *11*, 3–19.

Chau, P. Y. K., & Tam, K. Y. (1997). Factors affecting the adoption of open systems: An exploratory study. *Management Information Systems Quarterly*, *21*(1), 1–24. doi:10.2307/249740

Cragg, P. B., & King, M. (1993). Small firm computing: Motivators and inhibitors. *Management Information Systems Quarterly*, 47–60. doi:10.2307/249509

Davis, F. D. (1989). Perceived usefulness, perceived ease of use, and user acceptance of Information Technology. *Management Information Systems Quarterly*, *13*(3), 319–340. doi:10.2307/249008

Fontana, J. (October 2003). *A national identity card for Canada? Report of the Standing Committee on Citizenship and Immigration*. Ottawa, Canada: House of Commons, Canada.

Howard, N., Rolland, C., & Qusaibaty, A. (2004). *Process complexity: Towards a theory of intent-oriented process design*. Paper presented at the 2nd International Conference of Information and Systems.

Iacovou, C. L., Benbasat, I., & Dexter, A. S. (1995). Electronic data interchange and small organizations: Adoption and impact of technology. *Management Information Systems Quarterly*, 465–485. doi:10.2307/249629

Jackson, M., & Ligertwood, J. (2006, December). Identity management: Is an identity card the solution for Australia? *Prometheus*, *24*(4), 379–387. doi:10.1080/08109020601029953

Mindrum, C. (2008, January). It's in the cards. *Outlook*, 1.

Rolland, C. (1998). *A comprehensive view of process engineering*. Paper presented at the 10 International Conference CAISE'98, B. Lecture Notes in Computer Science.

Rotenberg, M., & Ngo, M. (May 2008). *Real ID implementation review: Few benefits, staggering costs*. Electornic Privacy Informatin Center.

ADDITIONAL READING

Agre, P. (1997). The architecture of identity: Embedding privacy in market institutions. *Information Communication and Society*, *2*(1), 1–25. doi:10.1080/136911899359736

Agre, P. E., & Harbs, C. A. (1994). Social choice about privacy: Intelligent vehicle-highway systems in the united states. Informaiton Technology & People, 7(4).

Al-Khouri, A. M. (2006). UAE National ID Programme Case Study. *International Journal of Social Sciences*, *1*(2), 62–69.

Besley, T., & Case, A. (1993)... *Modeling Technology Adoption in Developing Countries The American Economic Review*, *83*(2), 396–402.

Blume, P. (1990). The Personal Identity Number in Danish Law.

Chaum, D. (1985). Security without Identification: Card Computer to Make Big Brother Obsolete. *Communications of the ACM*, *28*(10), 1030–1044. doi:10.1145/4372.4373

Clarke, R. (1994). Human Identification in Information Systems: Management Challenges and Public Policy Issues. *Information Technology & People*, *7*(4), 6–37. doi:10.1108/09593849410076799

Clarke, R. A. (1988a). Information Technology and Dataveillance. *Communications of the ACM*, *31*(5). doi:10.1145/42411.42413

Clarke, R. A. (1988b). Just Another Piece of Plastic for Your Wallet: The Australia Card. *Computers & Society*, *18*(1). doi:10.1145/47649.47650

Clarke, R. A. (1991). The Tax File Number Scheme: A Case Study of Political Assurances and Function Creep. Policy, 7(4).

Davies, S. (1994). Touching Big Brother: How Biometric Technology Will Fuse Flesh and Machine. *Information Technology & People*, *7*(4). doi:10.1108/09593849410076807

Earl, M. J. (1993). *Experiences in Strategic Information Systems Planning MIS Quarterly*, *17*(1), 1–24.

FACFI. (1976). *The Criminal Use of False Identification: The Report of the Federal Advisory Committee on False Identification*. Washington, DC: US Department of Justice.

Fischer-Hubner, S., Duquenoy, P., Zuccato, A., & Martucci, L. (Eds.). (2008). *The future of identity in the information society*. New York: Springer. doi:10.1007/978-0-387-79026-8

Gupta, M., & Sharman, R. (2009). Emerging Frameworks in User-Focused Identity Management. In Gupta, J. N. D., Sharma, S., & Rashid, M. A. (Eds.), *Enterprise Systems* (pp. 362–377).

HEW. (1973). *Records, Computers and the Rights of Citizens: Report of the Secretary's Advisory Committee on Automated Personal Data Systems*. Boston, MA: US Department of Health, Education and Welfare.

Kuan, K. K. Y., & Chau, P. Y. K. (2001). A perception-based model for EDI adoption in small businesses using a technology–organization–environment framework. *Information & Management*, *38*(8), 507–521. doi:10.1016/S0378-7206(01)00073-8

Lederer, A. L., & Sethi, V. (1996). Key prescriptions for strategic information systems planning. *Journal of Management Information Systems*, *13*(1), 35–62.

NZCS. (1972). *Investigation of a Unique Identification System*. New Zealand Computer Society.

Parente, S. L., & Prescott, E. C. (1994). *Barriers to Technology Adoption and Development The Journal of Political Economy*, *102*(2), 298–321.

Premkumar, G., & King, W. R. (1994). Organizational Characteristics and Information Systems Planning: An Empirical Study. *Information Systems Research*, *5*(2), 75–109. doi:10.1287/isre.5.2.75

Raghunathan, B., & Raghunathan, T. S. (1994). Research Report—Adaptation of a Planning System Success Model to Information Systems Planning. *Information Systems Research*, *5*(3), 326–340. doi:10.1287/isre.5.3.326

Rotenberg, M. (1991). The Use of the Social Security Number as a National Identifier. *Computers & Society*, *21*, 13–19.

Rule, J. B. (1980). *The Politics ofprivacy: planning for personal data systems as powerful technologies*. New York: Elsevier.

Rule, J. B., McAdam, D., Steams, L., & Uglow, D. (1983). Documentary Identification and Mass Surveillance in the US. *Social Problems*, *31*, 222–234. doi:10.1525/sp.1983.31.2.03a00110

Segars, A. H., & Grover, V. (1998). Strategic Information Systems Planning Success: An Investigation of the Construct and Its Measurement. *Management Information Systems Quarterly*, *22*(2), 139–163. doi:10.2307/249393

Teo, T. S. H., & King, W. R. (1997). Integration between business planning and information systems planning: an evolutionary-contingency perspective. *Journal of Management Information Systems*, *14*(1), 185–214.

Thong, J. Y. L. (1999). An integrated model of information systems adoption in small businesses. *Journal of Management Information Systems*, *15*(4), 187–214.

Ward, J., & Griffiths, P. (1996). *Strategic planning for information systems* (2nd ed.). John Wiley & Sons.

Wigan, M. R. (1994). The Realizability of the Potential Benefits of Intelligent Vehicle-highway systems: The Influence of Public Acceptance. Informaiton Technology & People, 7(4).

KEY TERMS AND DEFINITIONS

Adoption Model: A conceptual model that mentions the factors contributing towards the adoption of technology within a system (e.g. nation, organization, etc.).

Citizen ID: An identification system that would provide unique identity to the citizens of a nation which can be further verified and authenticated.

Feasibility and Sustainability Model: A conceptual model that indicates the dimensions those contribute towards the feasibility and sustainability of an identity management system.

Identification: Association of data with a particular human being.

Identity Management: An administrative area that ensures unique identification of individuals within a system (e.g. a nation, organization, etc.) for different purposes including granting or denying of rights to access various resources within the system.

National Identity: An identification system that would provide unique identity to the citizens of a nation which can be further verified and authenticated.

Unique Identification: Mechanism to provide unique identity to individuals for a specific purpose.

ENDNOTES

1 "bidi": a type of cigarette made out of raw tobacco leaves.

2 http://www.sewaict.org/SEWA_Genesis.asp (accessed January 5, 2009).

3 1 rupee = US$0.022 (26th October, 2009).

4 Emploreliance: a term used by SEWA meaning full-employment and self-reliance.

Chapter 5
User-Centric Identity Management Architecture Using Credential-Holding Identity Agents

Daisuke Mashima
Georgia Institute of Technology, USA

David Bauer
Georgia Institute of Technology, USA

Mustaque Ahamad
Georgia Institute of Technology, USA

Douglas M. Blough
Georgia Institute of Technology, USA

ABSTRACT

The pervasive use of digital identities in today's cyberspace has led to an increasing interest in the area of identity management. Recently proposed user-centric identity management systems have accomplished higher-level of user control over online identity credentials. However, while the lack of a central authority that governs the entire system requires users to be responsible for their own digital identity credentials, the existing user-centric identity management systems still have problems in terms of security, privacy, and system availability. In this chapter, we present an identity management architecture that addresses these problems. Our scheme relies on user-controlled identity agents. Identity agents realize fine-grained control over online identity disclosure by using a minimal-disclosure identity credential scheme and also improve users' awareness over their credential usage via an identity-usage monitoring system that includes a real-time risk scoring mechanism. A proof-of-concept implementation is shown and evaluated in terms of security, user-centricity, and performance.

DOI: 10.4018/978-1-61350-498-7.ch005

INTRODUCTION

Digital identity credentials such as passwords, tokens and keys are used to ensure that only authorized users are able to access online services. Because of sensitive and valuable information managed by such services, they have become attractive targets of a variety of online attacks. For example, online financial services must use stronger credentials for authentication to avoid fraud. Because of serious threats and widespread theft and misuse of identity credentials, there is considerable interest in the area of identity management, which addresses secure use of identity credentials.

User-centric identity management, which allows users to flexibly choose what identity information is released to other entities in each transaction, offers better control over the use of identity credentials. For instance, users can choose an identity provider that they believe is the most appropriate for each transaction and control identity information to be disclosed to service providers. However, such user-centricity requires that disclosure of identity information be under user control and also expects users to assume more responsibility over their identity usage owing to the absence of a centralized authority (Hansen, 2004). Unfortunately, existing identity management schemes, such as OpenID and Windows CardSpace, have weaknesses against identity theft and misuse. For example, OpenID is susceptible to phishing attacks, and it does not offer effective protection after credentials are compromised. Moreover, at the high level, OpenID and Windows CardSpace heavily rely on online identity providers that issue context-scoped short-term identity credentials and thereby empower users to exercise flexible control over identity information. This fact implies that both schemes suffer from privacy issues because identity providers can potentially infer user's behavior. Additionally, unavailability of such online identity providers impacts the completion of transactions.

In this context, we propose a new identity management system architecture based on the concept of an identity agent that deals with identity credentials under user control. Identity agents are designed to offload many identity-related tasks from users. Through such identity agents and a minimal-disclosure identity credential scheme (Bauer, 2008), our system allows users to exercise flexible control over identity credential usage without relying on online identity providers. Furthermore, since disclosure of identity credentials is mediated by identity agents, it is possible to implement a user-centric identity usage monitoring mechanism (Mashima, 2008) to improve users' awareness of the use of their identity credentials, which reduces the risk and damage of online identity theft and misuse. We incorporate such a monitoring system with a real-time risk scoring mechanism into our architecture. In addition, we show how our architecture satisfies properties proposed in The Laws of Identity (Cameron, 2005) and how it addresses general drawbacks of two types of existing identity management schemes, which are credential-focused systems and relationship-focused systems (Bhargav-Spantzel, 2007). Our contribution also includes the implementation of a proof of concept prototype and its evaluation.

This chapter starts with enumerating requirements that our user-centric identity management system should meet and discusses our approach. Then, we discuss our architecture and its key components that address these requirements. After that, we present the prototype implementation of our identity management scheme, followed by its evaluation in terms of security, user-centricity, and performance. Finally, we conclude the chapter with a discussion of future work.

RELATED WORK AND DESIGN GOALS

In this section, we start by reviewing issues and threats against existing user-centric identity management schemes. We first discuss some of the related work in user-centric identity management area, and then identify the design goals that we pursue.

OpenID is a lightweight identity management system originally designed for relatively simple applications, such as blog services (Recordon, 2006). It involves three types of entities: users, service providers, which are also called relying parties or RPs, and identity providers. When a user wants to use a service provided by a service provider, the user contacts the service provider first. Then, if the user is not authenticated by an identity provider trusted by the service provider, it redirects the user to an online identity provider chosen by the user. The user authenticates herself to the identity provider and is redirected back to the service provider with an identity credential after the successful authentication process. OpenID suffers from phishing attacks by means of spoofed online identity provider sites, to which users could be deceived into disclosing their authentication credentials. Because a relatively weak authentication scheme relying on passwords is still widely used by online identity providers, stolen credentials can be misused.

Windows CardSpace (Chappell, 2006) is a user-centric identity metasystem designed based on The Laws of Identity. It provides a consistent user interface that enables users to select an appropriate identity provider for each context simply by selecting a "card". In terms of the architecture and protocol, it is similar to OpenID. By virtue of the use of client-side software called Identity Selector, which helps users notice something unexpected, CardSpace has stronger protection against phishing attacks than OpenID. However, there are still a number of security issues due to reliance on web browsers, which could be compromised by malware, and attacks such as DNS poisoning (Alrodham, 2009; Gajek, 2009). In addition, since metadata of user's identity credentials and private keys are stored on users' devices, physical theft of a device is more serious than with OpenID.

PRIME is a comprehensive identity management framework that emphasizes user privacy and control over user data including identity credentials (Camenisch, 2005; Leenes, 2008). It introduces a middleware layer in all participating entities and achieves secure and anonymous communication, a pseudonym mechanism, attribute-based authorization, and a policy negotiation and enforcement mechanism regarding user data handling even after data is released. While risks due to physical theft of user devices are not specifically addressed, device theft should be considered a serious threat because major software components and users' master credentials are stored on such devices, which could be abused by adversaries. Another problem with PRIME is that users' awareness over their identity credential usage relies solely on the transaction logging feature implemented at client side (PRIME Console). If the device is stolen or compromised, users will lose awareness of credential misuse. Auditing and fraud detection features could be implemented at service providers to improve the situation, but such features are not part of the PRIME architecture and therefore are out of users' control.

VeryIDX (Paci, 2009) is another type of user-centric identity management architecture that enables multi-factor identity verification. Service providers, when verifying a requester's identity credential, can challenge the requester to demonstrate possession of other identity credentials. By using a cryptographic commitment and an aggregate zero-knowledge proof of knowledge scheme (AgZKPK), users can prove such possession without disclosing actual values of the supporting identity credentials. This scheme has been applied to mobile devices as well as PCs. One potential issue with this system is, again, physical theft of user devices, because keys to open the cryptographic commitments of claims, which are used to prove the ownership of the identity, are usually stored on user devices. VeryIDX additionally proposes to split such keys into multiple shares and store one of the shares on a user-owned computer accessible via network. However, in such a case, users could have trouble when using their own identity in case the remote PC is not available.

Canard (2008) proposed a client-side identity federation mechanism using blind signatures. It aims at mitigating privacy issues inherent in Liberty and SAML approaches in which identity providers can potentially mass-correlate users' identities on multiple service providers. Canard's system allows users to have their identity providers authorize identity federation without disclosing their identities at service providers. However, like the Liberty protocol, identity providers need to be involved in each transaction, so system availability depends on the availability of such identity providers.

To prevent identity theft and misuse, an identity management system must be robust against security threats that could subvert the schemes described above. In addition, other types of attacks that could result in identity misuse even without compromise of identity credentials, such as session hijacking and replay attacks, should be reliably detected. However, the use of sophisticated techniques to prevent identity theft attacks cannot guarantee security against all possible attacks. An adversary could attack human users in an off-line manner using, for example, social engineering techniques, or zero-day malware could secretly steal identity credentials stored on user devices. Once compromised, such credentials can be misused, which could harm legitimate users legally and financially. To mitigate such risks, users should have robust awareness, in a user-centric manner, of how and when their identity credentials are used.

Another issue inherent in systems like CardSpace and OpenID is heavy reliance on online identity providers. Since context-scoped identity credentials need to be issued by online identity providers, it becomes necessary to involve them in every transaction. VeryIDX, when used in the "online mode," also relies on a trusted online entity called a "registrar," which stores commitments of users' identity claims so that service providers can retrieve them upon identity verification. The availability of the service largely depends on the availability of such identity providers or registrars, which are usually out of users' control. To mitigate the availability issue, some back-up mechanism to allow users to continue using services even when such online entities are disabled is desirable. In addition, reliance on online parties also leads to privacy issues. Specifically, online identity providers or registrars are potentially capable of compromising user's privacy by tracking and correlating user activities across multiple service providers. In order to mitigate such problems, involvement of entities that are not under users' control should be minimized.

According to Bhargav-Spantzel (2008), identity management systems can be categorized into two groups: relationship-focused systems and credential-focused systems. In general, the former relies on online identity providers and short-term identity credentials. OpenID and CardSpace belong to this group. On the other hand, credential-focused systems utilize long-term identity credentials, such as digital certificates. In this case, identity providers do not have to be online during transactions. Both have advantages and disadvantages. For instance, one of the drawbacks of credential-focused systems is lack of flexibility in terms of identity attributes to be disclosed. In other words, all information included in an identity credential must be disclosed as a whole, which violates the "Minimal Disclosure" principle in The Laws of Identity. On the other hand, relationship-focused systems suffer from availability and privacy issues as discussed above. It is desired to balance the advantages and disadvantages of the two.

Finally, it is desirable to meet a widely-accepted guideline for user-centric identity management systems discussed by Cameron (2005). For example, users should be able to choose identity providers that they can trust, instead of being forced to trust some specific provider. Furthermore, in each transaction, users should be aware of and be able to exercise control over which identity credentials are going to be released and by whom such identity information is consumed.

APPROACH

First, for the sake of user-centricity, it is desired that identity credentials are stored and managed under user control, and that disclosure of identity information is done with user consent. While user control is desirable, at the same time it poses extra burden on users. A typical design can be found in the architecture proposed by Eap (2007), where a user is required to decide whether to give consent or not for each transaction. While providing the desired user control, this is not necessarily a good approach in terms of usability and security. Specifically, human users could be deceived by phishers and then be misled to disclose their data to unintended parties. Thus, mitigation of such a negative impact on usability and a supporting mechanism for user's security decisions are important. For this purpose, we introduce the concept of identity agents that manage identity credentials under user control, which will be discussed in the next section.

Secondly, in order to allow users the flexibility to control information disclosed to service providers while avoiding privacy issues arising from involvement of online identity providers, we must achieve a reasonable middle ground between credential-focused systems and relationship-focused systems. To do this, we employ a novel credential scheme called minimal-disclosure identity credentials, which will be explained in the next section. By using this scheme with identity agents, a long-term identity credential can be used while retaining capability to disclose only a minimal number of identity attributes (Bauer, 2008). Thereby, we can reduce the reliance on online identity providers. Users will still have the flexibility to choose identity providers they can trust when obtaining their identity credentials.

Lastly, to enable users to be aware of when and how their identity credentials are used and thereby to minimize loss or damage caused by identity theft and resulting misuse, we incorporate an identity-usage monitoring system as part of our identity management architecture. Because, under user-centric identity management, there is no central authority governing the entire system, such monitoring mechanism needs to be implemented in a user-centric manner (Mashima, 2008). Anomaly detection mechanisms can then be built in conjunction with monitoring systems to raise alarms when suspicious identity usage is observed. An anomaly-based risk scoring algorithm that fits our architecture is discussed in the next section.

KEY COMPONENTS

User-Controlled Identity Agents

In our design, an identity agent is software installed on each user device or an online service that is designed to offload many identity-related tasks from users, aiming at flexible user control, usability, and security. Because its specific functionality can vary depending on underlying system architecture or contexts, in this section, we mainly focus on deployment options and generic requirements.

One objective of using identity agents is to allow users flexible control over their identity credentials, so identity agents must be accessible to users. Thus, it is natural to implement an agent as client-side software installed on a user's device, just like Identity Selector in Windows CardSpace. Another option is to implement an agent as a networked personal storage of identity credentials like Home Site in Sxip Identity. While the former option has an advantage in physical proximity and accessibility to users, the latter has higher security against device thefts. As a third option, we can combine both approaches. To be specific, we can store actual identity credentials on a networked agent and implement the functionality to exercise flexible and robust control over the agent on a user device. In our architecture proposed in the next section, we follow the third option.

Ideally, as discussed by Eap (2007), identity credentials should be released under users' security decision and consent. However, always requiring user participation could negatively impact usability. To reduce the burden on users, it is desirable to allow them to define credential disclosure policies in advance, which can be automatically enforced when credentials are required. Such policies must be enforced in a reliable and systematic way by identity agents. Furthermore, since human users could be misled by adversaries claiming identities that appear to be legitimate, robust verification of identities of relying parties is mandatory for the sake of accurate policy enforcement as well as prevention of phishing attacks. Such verification should also be supported by identity agents.

Management of credentials is another task expected from identity agents. Storing credentials in an organized way will reduce user burden. In addition, since some identity credential schemes, such as Bauer's minimal-disclosure credentials, U-Prove's credentials, and the proof-key mechanism in Windows CardSpace, rely on users' private keys, those keys need to be appropriately stored. Furthermore, some credential schemes require client-side processing. For instance, in the minimal-disclosure credential scheme, a verifiable credential is generated from a certified tree for each transaction (Bauer, 2008). Such a task must also be handled by identity agents.

Features described above must be executed under user consent. Thus, identity agents must have an ability to make sure that the requests are actually issued by the legitimate credential owner. This is especially important in case identity agents are deployed remotely. To do such verification, we can rely on a digital signature scheme using a user's key pair. So, associated cryptographic functionality should be incorporated.

Keeping audit trails for credential usage monitoring is also beneficial. When credential release is mediated by identity agents, it could be highly effective in enhancing user awareness and for detecting identity credential misuse. Identity credential usage logs can be pushed to the user periodically or on a real-time basis by means of SMS, etc. Enhancing users' awareness in this way will help users notice potential identity misuse cases with a shorter window of vulnerability. Identity agents can further utilize the data to detect suspicious identity usage that should be brought to users' attention. Such a scheme is discussed later in this section.

Minimal-Disclosure Identity Credentials

Identity information in our system is communicated through claims, where claims consist of attributes plus evidence that allow a third party to verify them. A simple form of evidence is an assertion by a third party that the claim is true, such as a digital signature. A credential is a set of claims held by an entity. This section presents a credential that efficiently allows a subset of its claims to be shown and linked to the entity holding the credential. The claims that are not shown remain safely hidden, protecting the privacy of the credential holder.

We achieve such selective disclosure by constructing credentials out of modified Merkle hash trees (Bauer, 2008) along with standard public key infrastructure certificates. As shown in Figure 1, the value of each node in the hash tree is a cryptographic hash over the values of its children; the leaf nodes of the tree contain the identity claims certified in the credential. The nature of the hash tree allows any attribute stored in a leaf node to be proven to be in the tree, where the tree is defined by the root hash. More importantly, proving the presence of an attribute does not require revealing any other attributes in the tree. The root node of the hash tree is placed in a certificate, which is

Figure 1. Merkle hash tree with leaf nodes holding hashes of claims

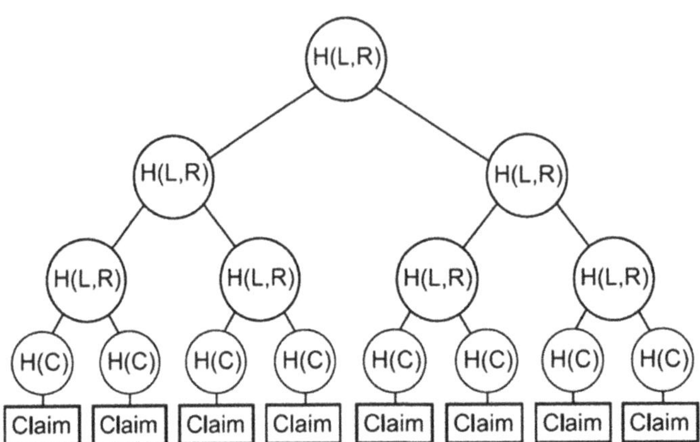

then signed by the certifying entity, i.e. an identity provider. The certificate ties the tree to a public key; the credential holder has the corresponding private key, which is used to prove rightful possession of the credential. In other words, a credential issued by an identity provider and this ownership proof presented by a credential owner together work as an "identity credential," following the concept of joint authority discussed by Lampson (1992). Such a mechanism is beneficial not only to make misuse of credentials more difficult by eliminating a single point of attack but also to facilitate revocation of compromised identity credentials even when we rely on long-term credentials issued by an off-line identity provider.

For efficiency and convenience, many simple credentials can be combined together into a single, composite credential. Combining credentials requires modifying the basic binary tree structure of the Merkle hash tree. A credential is embedded in another credential by making its root node a subnode in the tree of the outer credential (Figure 2). In addition, that new subtree root-node will have a third branch added to it, which will contain the certificate for the embedded node. When creating and checking the tree, the subnode is obviously a subtree root-node, because three branches are hashed to create it, instead of two.

To see the benefit of this style of credential, consider the simple act of buying a beer (or other age restricted item). Most often, the buyer will show a driver's license to prove that he is of legal age. However, the driver's license contains not just the age of the buyer, but also a full name, street address, full date of birth, and even other information such as social security number and medical restrictions. Our credential system allows the buyer to show the license, while covering up everything but the picture and year of birth. The buyer may use the same credential for other purposes, for example as ID for voting, in which case the full name and street address would be shown. Our system goes beyond the driver's license example by allowing the credential to hold, for example, credit card numbers, insurance information, a voter registration number, and more in the same credential.

User-Centric Monitoring and Identity Misuse Detection

For the sake of user-centric monitoring, a monitoring system should be deployed in a user's control domain, which is in general outside of service providers' domains, unlike typical fraud/intrusion detection mechanisms (Mashima, 2008). In this context, design implication for the identity

Figure 2. Modified Merkle hash tree with subtree

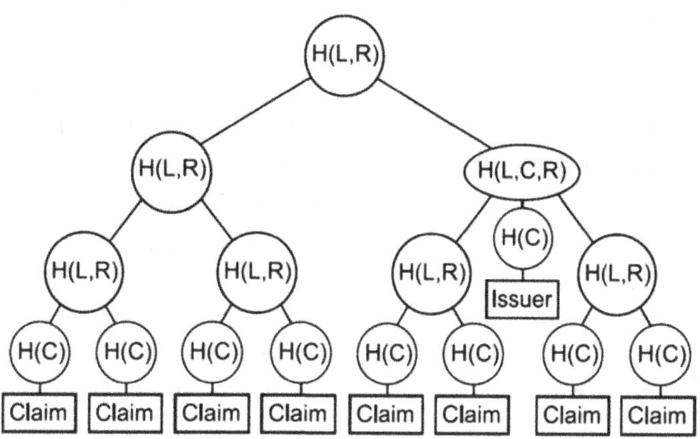

misuse detection algorithm is that the information available for computation is often very limited, compared to a situation where the monitoring is conducted at a service provider. In the extreme case, the external monitoring system could only know when and by whom an identity credential is consumed. We designed an algorithm to work with such limited data to compute risk scores, which quantify suspiciousness of observed credential usage (Mashima, 2009b). An overview of the algorithm is given below.

Assuming that a normal usage pattern shows some specific characteristics in terms of the frequency distribution over appropriately chosen categorical attributes, we use such frequency information for scoring. For instance, when a user uses a certain identity credential only on specific days of week, using "day of week" as an attribute to define a user's profile is reasonable. We consider only categorical parameters as input to the scoring algorithm. The primary reason for this is that many attributes can be represented as categorical values. For example, days of week and hours of day derived from timestamp and identifiers of relying parties, e.g., IP addresses or host names, are all categorical. Moreover, other types of data, such as ordinal measures, can be converted into categorical measures by appropriately defining bins. Thus, we believe this approach does not limit the applicability of our scheme.

In our risk scoring scheme, a user profile, which represents a user's normal identity usage pattern based on past observations, is built as a frequency distribution over categories of an attribute. Every time identity credential usage is observed, the frequency counts of corresponding categories are incremented by 1. For instance, if we choose "hour of day" as a profiling attribute, the corresponding user profile consists of 24 categories (bins). If identity usage is observed at 1:30 am, for example, the frequency count of the second category, which indicates 1-2am, is incremented. Multiple profiles can be defined for each user, such as an hour-of-day profile and a day-of-week profile. In this case, both profiles are updated simultaneously.

A *base score*, which is the primary part of our anomaly-based risk score, quantifies the deviation of an observed credential usage from the normal pattern. It is computed based on the relative frequency of a category corresponding to an observed attribute value. For instance, in the example mentioned above, the relative frequency of the second category is used for the score computation. Relative frequency of a category c can be computed as follows where C is the set of all categories in a profile.

$$RelFreq_c = \frac{FreqCount_c}{\sum_{i \in C} FreqCount_i}$$

From this relative frequency, a base score for an observed identity usage can be computed using the following equation:

$$BaseScore = -\log_2(RelFreq_c^A)$$

where c is the index of the category into which the observed attribute value is classified. A is an amplifying factor and can be equal to 1. In this way, identity usage records of categories that are infrequently observed in the past are scored high while records of frequently observed categories are scored lower.

In addition, when a user's normal usage pattern shows more distinctive traits, scores derived from such a profile should be considered more significant, compared to a case in which a user's identity usage does not exhibit any specific pattern. To quantify such "effectiveness" of each profiling attribute, we introduce a weight for a base score. Such a weight is calculated based on the "distance" between a user profile, which is a frequency distribution over the pre-defined categories, and a uniform distribution over the same categories. If the identity credential usage is frequent in some categories and is scarce in others, i.e. the shape of the frequency distribution is not flat, the weight becomes larger. On the other hand, if the pattern is nearly random, the frequency distribution of the profile is close to uniform. Thereby the resulting weight is small. There are multiple ways to compute such distance. A straightforward option is to use a distance measurement that can be used to compare the shape of discrete probability distributions (i.e. histograms), such as Bhattacharyya Distance (Cha, 2008). Bhattacharyya Distance (*BD*) can be computed as follows.

$$BD_{pu} = -\ln(\sum_{c \in C} \sqrt{p(c)u(c)})$$

where p is a profile distribution, u is a uniform distribution over the same categories, and C represents the set of all categories. This distance is 0 when the two distributions are exactly identical. On the other hand, when the two distributions disagree (i.e. $\sum_{c \in C} \sqrt{p(c)u(c)}$ is small), the resulting distance becomes larger.

As the final step of the score computation, we need to aggregate scores. We can have multiple profiles for each user, for instance an hour-of-day profile, day-of-week profile, and RP-identity profile. Then, three base scores and three weights are computed based on the three profiles. However, having a single overall score is often convenient. We call a product of a base score and the corresponding weight a *subscore*. We can compute an aggregated score in a number of ways, e.g., a weighted sum of subscores or the maximum of subscores. The best way to aggregate scores varies depending on context.

SYSTEM ARCHITECTURE AND PROTOCOL

In this section, we present our identity management system that integrates key components discussed in the previous section. We mainly focus on the architecture where there are both a local identity agent installed on a user's device and a network-resident remote identity agent, because the case in which only a local identity agent is involved can be explained as a variant of the more general case. Another reason is that a system with two types of identity agents has a higher level of protection against physical theft or compromise of a user device.

Entities in our Architecture

In our identity management architecture, there are three types of entities. Locally-installed identity agents (local IdAs) run on devices that are with users (e.g., smart phones and laptops), and remote identity agents (remote IdAs) reside in the network. The architecture also includes relying parties (RPs), which are various online service providers. These entities are elaborated in this section. In our architecture, identity providers issue long-term identity credentials to users. Thus, they do not have to be on-line and are not involved in identity-related transactions.

Local Identity Agent (Local IdA)

A local IdA is client-side agent software installed on a user's device, such as a laptop, PDA, or smart phone. To minimize the risk of identity theft and misuse resulting from a compromise of user's device, a local IdA does not hold actual identity credentials, which are stored instead on a user's remote IdA explained next. A local IdA stores index values of identity claims (attributes) included in the user's identity credentials. This is mainly because user devices could be compromised more easily by malware or physical theft since such devices are often managed by non-expert users. In case a remote IdA is not used, credentials need to be stored on a user's device or on a removable storage accessible to a local IdA upon initiating transactions. This setting will be discussed later in this section. A user's private key paired with identity credentials, which is used to create an ownership proof, is also stored on a local IdA. As mentioned earlier, RPs request users to demonstrate the knowledge of their private keys when verifying their credentials.

A local IdA also manages and enforces the user's policies for the disclosure of identity claims. A policy says, for example, "Age can be released to relying party X." Note that policies are defined based on pairs of user's identity attributes and identifiers of relying parties that consume the identity information. Our prototype relies on XACML (Extensible Access Control Markup Language), an OASIS standard that uses XML schema for representing authorization policies. In case any policy is not yet defined for a certain pair, a local IdA asks its user whether to add a new policy. As part of policies, users can also specify whether disclosure of each identity attribute requires verification of a password. When a password is required by the policy, a local IdA requires the user to input the password in advance of releasing identity information.

The other component stored on a local IdA is a certificate of the user's remote IdA. Such a certificate must be issued by a trusted certification authority or signed by the user's private key so that RPs can verify its authenticity. This certificate contains the location, such as an IP address or URL, of a remote IdA to let a RP know with whom it should interact when retrieving the actual identity credentials that belong to the user.

In the current implementation, a local IdA is implemented as an independent application on a user's device and works as follows. After the negotiation between a user (typically a web browser) and a service provider to determine required identity attributes to be verified, the service provider returns a signed text-based data, which is called an *IDM file*, to the user. The contents of this file will be explained later. Once the IDM file is downloaded, the local IdA is invoked via a MIME type configuration. Another thing to be noted here is that a local IdA opens a separate network connection to the service provider without relying on a web browser. After identity-related tasks are completed, a local IdA returns control to the user.

Remote Identity Agent (Remote IdA)

Remote IdAs, the second type of entity in the architecture, play an important role. They have their own public and private key pairs. They can be run by parties that naturally hold certain identity credentials for a user, such as an employer, a university, a bank, or any other entity that is trusted by the user. Alternatively, a user herself can set up a server in a cloud, such as Amazon EC2, and set up her own remote IdA on it. Remote IdAs store long-term minimal-disclosure identity credentials, which are issued originally by identity providers. Remote IdAs primary responsibility is to deal with these identity credentials. They create, based on authorizations from the user's local IdA, minimal-disclosure credentials that disclose the minimal identity attributes the user intends to release (Bauer, 2008).

The other important task of a remote IdA is enforcement of users' policies and verification of users' passwords as part of policy enforcement. A remote IdA works based on user-defined policies, which are synchronized with the user's local IdA. If a user defines a policy saying that disclosure of a certain identity attribute requires her password for the sake of additional security, a remote IdA is responsible for verifying that a correct password is provided. Note that a local IdA asks a user to input a password, and verification is done at a remote IdA to reduce the risk of password compromise, which could occur when a user's device is compromised.

The involvement of a remote IdA is not mandatory even though it is strongly recommended. The functionality mentioned above can be implemented as part of a local IdA module. However, in this case, identity credentials need to be stored with a user's device. While this feature is preferred in terms of availability by allowing users to continue using services even when a remote IdA is disabled for some reason, the credentials are more likely to be compromised or stolen. Also, when both the credential and the private key are compromised at the same time, the adversary can have full privilege to misuse the user's identity. Thus, some sort of additional protection against theft or compromise, such as use of encryption with a secret password, which should be strong enough and must not be stored on a user device, is required. It would be also effective to store such credentials in a removable storage physically separated from a local IdA. In order to balance system availability and security, we recommend involving a remote IdA for regular use while having an option to bypass it for the sake of an emergency situation.

An identity-usage monitoring system can be deployed either on a local IdA or remote IdA. But here is a trade-off. If the monitoring feature is implemented inside of a local IdA, like the transaction logging feature implemented in PRIME (Leenes, 2008), it could obtain richer information than a remote IdA can, because a remote IdA needs to obtain information remotely. However, in case the monitoring system is located with a local IdA, it could become totally useless once a user device is compromised or stolen. Thus, we recommend implementing it on a remote IdA as long as one is involved. Another option is to implement the monitoring system on a trusted third party. In this case, by separating the responsibility of identity credential management and monitoring between a remote IdA and a trusted third party, we can further improve the security and counter the risk of remote IdA compromise (Mashima, 2009a).

Relying Party (RP)

A relying party is a party with which a user intends to interact. A RP is typically an online service provider that offers services that are of interest to a user, so these two terms are often used interchangeably. However, in a peer-to-peer setting, a RP can be another user. Although our architecture is designed to support both cases, in this work we focus on the former setting.

Upon receiving a service request from a user, a RP negotiates with the requesting user for identity attributes to be verified and other details regarding identity credential verification. In our current system, this negotiation is abstracted as a single IDM file generated and signed by the RP. An IDM file

Figure 3. System architecture and communication sequence

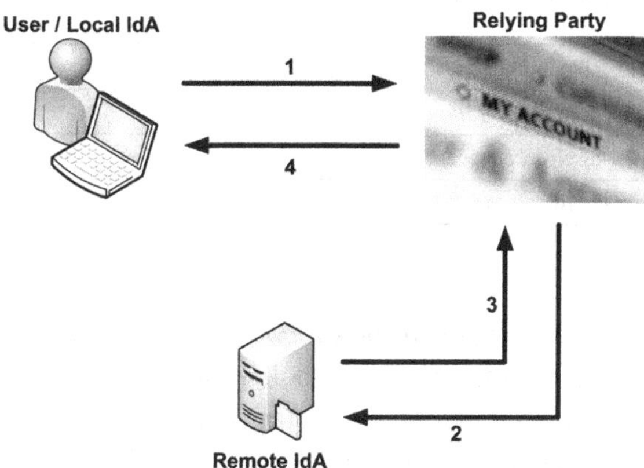

contains the RP's public key certificate, a nonce chosen by the RP for the corresponding transaction, and a list of identity claims to be verified by the RP. The exploration of negotiation protocols to determine the contents of the IDM file is outside the scope of this chapter.

Relying parties want to provide services only to legitimate users and hence need to make sure that requests for their services come from the users specified in the requests. Thus, they must verify, in addition to the identity provider's signatures on credentials, the ownership of users' identity credentials by checking users' signatures made with their private keys paired with the public keys tied to the identity credentials.

Protocol Description

The communication protocols used are relatively simple, due to the prototype nature of the system. In most cases, only a single message type is used in each direction of communication between two entities. Figure 3 shows the main messages in the system, with their order. Table 1 lists the main messages and their contents. We assume that users have obtained identity credentials in advance from identity providers they chose.

There is an additional message in the table not shown in the figure. This message (* in Table 1) is from a local IdA to a remote IdA. As noted in the Contents column of the table, it contains a token that is carried in another message (message 2 in the figure). The four entries in the table marked "Token" use a cryptographically signed and optionally encrypted message format and are sent over HTTP in our prototype (the token is implemented by directly sending a serialized Java object). Message 4 is implemented as a regular HTTP response. A local IdA and RP both generate session nonces, and the concatenation of the two nonces is used as a session identifier for connection tracking and for preventing replay attacks. Each of the three entities described above has a public certificate and public/private key pair used for signing, signature verification, and encryption.

In addition, in case identity credentials are provided by a local IdA instead of a remote IdA, "Remote IdA" in Table 1 is replaced with "Local IdA." Alternatively, it is also possible to simply piggyback credentials in message 1 and omit messages 2 and 3.

We chose to make a RP contact the specified remote IdA to retrieve the user's identity credential. The main reason for this is to enable a remote IdA to confirm that the identity credential is being disclosed to a party actually intended by the user. Since message 2 is signed by the RP and the token (* in Table 1) signed by a user contains the RP's public key, the remote IdA can perform such validation. Specifically, the remote IdA can be convinced when the RP's signature on message 2 can be successfully verified with the public key of a party intended by the user. Confirmed identity of the RP can be effective to counter phishing attacks and also can be used as an input parameter for the monitoring system described in the previous section.

An alternate protocol would make a local IdA retrieve credentials from a remote IdA in advance of contacting a RP. It is also possible that a local IdA simply asks a remote IdA to send credentials

Table 1. Messages used for communication between entities

No.	Message From	Message To	Type	Contents
1	Local IdA	RP	Token	Nonces, user and Remote IdA certificates, RP public key, token for Remote IdA
*	Local IdA	Remote IdA	Token	Nonces, user ID, RP public key, attributes requested, password
2	RP	Remote IdA	Token	Nonces, token for Remote IdA from Local IdA
3	Remote IdA	RP	Token	Nonces, minimal-disclosure credentials
4	RP	Local IdA	HTTP	Success or failure notification

to a RP. Neither of these schemes can achieve robust verification of a RP's identity. It might be argued that requiring modification of existing RPs is difficult. Although this could be a negative factor in large-scale deployment, we believe that its benefits outweigh such a disadvantage. In addition, by implementing a web server plug-in to handle this task in a transparent manner, the impact could be minimized.

EVALUATION

Security

The attacks that are the most relevant are replay attacks, session hijacking, and physical theft or compromise of a user device hosting a local IdA. We will consider these attacks one by one and then discuss how security vulnerabilities inherent in existing user-centric identity management systems are mitigated in our system.

Replay attacks are a particular concern for our system because of the authority given to a remote system, a remote IdA, which can act on behalf of a user. The authorization for the remote IdA is limited in scope by the nonces and a RP's public key. The two nonces (generated by a local IdA and a RP) form a session identifier. As long as either party correctly generates a non-repeating nonce, the session id will always be unique. The RP's public key is included in the authorization to limit the scope to just that RP.

Session hijacking here refers to any man-in-the-middle attack where the attacker can misdirect the session from its intended purpose. For example, an attacker can try to have the user authenticate to a different RP than expected or try to perform a classical man-in-the-middle attack, where an attacker tries to authenticate himself as a legitimate user to a service provider by intercepting and forwarding messages or credentials sent by the user. Our identity management architecture creates a chain of cryptographically secure connections, whereby the user's and RP's public keys are both tied to the session id and the user credentials by the signatures of the user and the identity provider. The connection of both parties' public (and therefore private) keys to the credentials prevents standard man-in-the-middle attacks. The keys can then be used for further secure communication (e.g., setting up an SSL session).

Physical theft of the user's local device is one of the main motivations for having a network-attached, remote IdA. By placing the bulk of credentials on the remote IdA, the damage is minimized when the local device is compromised. In addition, storing a private key and credentials on separate entities makes identity misuse more difficult since an attacker is required to compromise both of them. In case a remote IdA is not involved, compromise of user devices would directly give adversaries full privilege to misuse identity credentials. Thus, credentials should have extra protection. In addition, the risk of theft or compromise of devices is further mitigated by splitting and distributing users' private keys based on a threshold signature scheme at the expense of additional, but still acceptable, communication and computational cost (Mashima, 2009a).

Besides the threats discussed above, some issues regarding security of Windows CardSpace are identified (Alrodham, 2009; Gajek, 2009). One of them is the dependence on web browsers, through which an adversary could steal security tokens issued by identity providers. In our implementation, communication that sends signed tokens is not mediated by web browsers. Even if an IDM file is tampered by a man in the middle or man in the browser, a local IdA can detect it when verifying the RP's signature on it. Furthermore, vulnerabilities from reliance of DNS, including pharming and DNS cache poisoning, can be countered by specifying, during the negotiation, the RP's location by using an IP address, instead of a domain name that requires DNS lookup. In our current implementation, the negotiation result is conveyed via an IDM file. Recall that an IDM file is signed by the RP and that a local IdA independently opens network connection to the RP based on the information in the IDM file. In this way, a local IdA can communicate with a RP without relying on DNS services.

Identity usage monitoring by identity agents further reduces the risk of identity misuse and phishing attacks. Specifically, in case a user device hosting a local IdA and credentials is compromised or stolen, the usage pattern, for example in terms of time of use or relying parties accessed, could show a different pattern from the legitimate owner's usual pattern. Such anomaly can be detected by the monitoring system. Our previous work showed that the risk-scoring mechanism shown as one of the key components demonstrates decent accuracy even when only timestamp is available for monitoring (Mashima, 2008; Mashima 2009b). Moreover, as discussed in the previous section, robust verification of a RP's identity is effective in preventing credentials from being disclosed to unauthorized parties.

Assessment Against Laws of Identity

As a guideline for the design of identity systems, Kim Cameron's Laws of Identity (2005) are widely accepted, and a number of identity management systems follow them. Thus, we will evaluate our system in terms of these laws, and the summary is found in Table 2. As can be seen, our system meets all the laws presented.

Besides these laws, unlinkability and anonymity are sometimes emphasized in some settings, such as e-cash, to prevent identity providers and service providers from tracking a user's activity. In the current design, our system does not support these properties, which will be explored in our future work. Using an anonymous credential scheme such as the one proposed by Brands (2009), instead of the minimal-disclosure credential scheme, could improve unlinkability in our system, but there is a performance issue especially when the number of claims is large, according to Bauer (2008). Even under the minimal disclosure credential scheme we employed, allowing users to have multiple credentials under different pseudonyms and private keys could improve unlinkability. However, we believe that, in practical cases, it is not a major disadvantage of our architecture. For instance, in case of e-commerce and online banking services, RPs anyway need to know requesters' identities to provide services. Thus, even if complete unlinkability and anonymity are accomplished only in the identity management layer, compromise of user privacy due to collusion among RPs and identity providers could be possible. Furthermore, as discussed by Leenes (2008), other information, such as an IP address, could be used as a unique identifier that helps correlate user activities on multiple RPs, so complete unlinkability can be achieved only when an anonymization mechanism, such as TOR (Dingledine, 2004), is working in an underlying layer. We think that these are some of the reasons why unlinkability is not extensively pursued and accomplished by widely-used user-centric iden-

Table 2. Assessment based on laws of identity

Law	Satisfied?	Description
User Control and Consent	Yes	Trusted identity agents (local IdAs and remote IdAs) enforce user-defined policies, which are automatically applied once defined by users. These agents also interact with users when policies for a certain context do not exist. Thus, only identity information that users agree to release to a certain RP is disclosed, and identity agents help users be aware of to whom and which identity information is disclosed.
Minimal Disclosure	Yes	By the use of a minimal-disclosure identity credential scheme, only the minimal identity attributes required by relying parties (and a user agrees to release) are disclosed.
Justifiable Parties	Yes	During the initial negotiation phase to determine which identity attributes need to be released, users can reliably verify the identity of relying parties by means of their signatures and public key certificates. After that, users can determine whether the party requiring identity information is appropriate in the context or not. The verification of RP's identity is also done by identity agents in a systematic and reliable way.
Directed Identity	Yes	In our architecture, an omni-directional identity as a relying party is established by the public key. On the other hand, identity as an initiating party (i.e. a user) is unidirectional toward a specific party through session and entity scoping. Also, an identity credential that is created in each transaction is tailored to meet the demand of a specific RP and can be used only in a specific transaction.
Pluralism of Operators and Technologies	Yes	Our identity management system can be universally used as long as user-chosen identity providers issue identity credentials that can be integrated into the minimal-disclosure identity credential scheme. Then, users can use credentials issued by any identity provider by simply storing them on their identity agents as part of their minimal-disclosure credentials.
Human Integration	Yes	A user can control the system and obtain information from the system via a local IdA, which is installed on her own device physically carried by her. In addition, identity agents assist user decisions by means of robust verification of RP's identity etc. Illegal usage of identity information can be prevented by user-defined policies and password, and can be detected by the monitoring feature on an identity agent, which enhances users' awareness.
Consistent Experience	Yes	Identity agents in our system can provide users with consistent interface. Users are able to choose credentials and attributes from a list displayed by a local IdA upon each transaction. (See Figure 4.) Or, users can also define identity-disclosure policies in advance of actual service usage. In either case, user experience does not change depending on contexts.

tity management architectures. Also, note that in our system an identity provider is ignorant of users' identity usage and cannot compromise users' privacy without colluding with a number of service providers, which is not a likely situation in practice.

Response Time and Throughput

Since we added extra entities and additional communication and computation to the interaction between users and RPs, our architecture could have an impact on overall system performance. In this section, we see, through experiments with our prototype implementation, whether our system can provide acceptable performance. Before going into the results, we describe the experimental setup. We used separate PCs for a local IdA, a remote IdA, and a RP. The detailed information about them is shown in Figure 5. The client PC hosting a local IdA is located outside of the campus network, 13 hops away from the RP, to make the setting more realistic.

We first focus on response time as a key performance metric because it directly impacts user experience. We measured the response time 50

Figure 4. User interface of the prototype implementation (requesting user consent)

Requesting User Consent

Name of Party you are talking to:

SamTel Phones

The following are being released.

First name? IN Acme Credentials
Last name? IN Acme Credentials
Credit card? IN Acme Credentials

Password is required. Please input below.

OK CANCEL

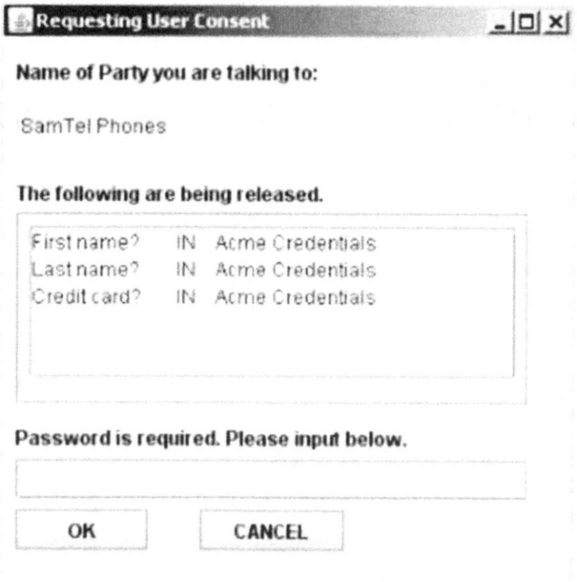

times and calculated the average of the recorded values. In this experiment, we configured a local IdA so that it did not require any user operations. The measured response time includes the initial negotiation to agree on the required identity claims between a RP and a user as well as token handling involving a remote IdA. Thus, time taken to complete two interactions (HTTP request/response) between a local IdA and a RP are included. The result we obtained is 1.3 seconds on average. In addition, our measurement also revealed that more than 0.7 seconds was actually consumed inside the local IdA. Thus, optimizing the implementation of a local IdA will further improve the response time. Recent research by Akamai Technologies (2006) shows that a response time of less than 4 seconds is acceptable for users in a retail website scenario. Therefore, we can consider that users will not be discouraged by this additional latency and can take advantage of the many benefits of our identity management approach.

Regarding the performance of a remote IdA and a RP, we also measured the processing time on each entity. Note that the processing time on a RP measures the duration from receiving the request message including an authorization token (message 1 in Table 1) to returning the result of the credential verification to the user (message 4). The processing time on a remote IdA is the duration from receiving an authorization token (message 2) to returning a message including an identity credential to the RP (message 3). The data in Table 3 are the average and standard deviation based on 30 measurements. Again, these times are acceptable for online services.

CONCLUSION AND FUTURE WORK

In this work, we proposed a user-centric identity management system architecture involving a minimal-disclosure credential scheme, user-centric identity usage monitoring system with a real-time risk scoring algorithm, and identity agents, which, under user control, manage and monitor user's identity credentials and control their disclosure. An identity agent can be locally-

Figure 5. Setting for response time measurement

Table 3. Throughput of RP and remote IdA

	RP	Remote IdA
Average Time per Request	0.06 sec	0.02 sec
Standard Deviation	0.004 sec	0.0005 sec
# of Request per Second	17	46

installed software running on a user's device, or its functionality can be split between a local entity and a networked entity for the sake of higher-level of security against compromise of a user device. We also showed that our architecture achieves a reasonable middle ground between credential-focused identity management mechanisms, such as a system using X.509 certificates as credentials, and relationship-focused systems, such as OpenID and Windows CardSpace, and that our approach addresses some drawbacks of both. In addition, our evaluation demonstrated that our architecture mitigates security, privacy, and availability problems inherent in existing user-centric identity management systems and how it meets the properties desired for user-centric identity management systems. We described a prototype implementation and used it to conduct experiments to measure the system's performance. The results of the experiments demonstrated that performance overheads are within acceptable limits.

Although our architecture satisfies the major properties desired in user-centric identity management, there are still some properties that need to be improved or additional ones to be implemented, such as unlinkability and anonymity. These will be explored in our future work. Another work will be improving the negotiation between users and service providers, which is currently implemented in a simplified form. We are also planning a user study to evaluate usability.

ACKNOWLEDGMENT

This research was supported in part by the National Science Foundation under Grant CNS-CT-0716252.

REFERENCES

Akamai Technologies. (2006). *Retail web site performance*. Retrieved from http://www.akamai.com/4seconds

Alrodham, W. A., & Mitchell, C. J. (2009). Improving the security of CardSpace. *EuRAsip Journal on Information Security, 9*.

Bauer, D., Blough, D., & Cash, D. (2008). Minimum information disclosure with efficiently verifiable credentials. *Proceedings of the Fourth ACM Workshop on Digital Identity Management*, Association for Computing Machinery.

Bhargav-Spantzel, A., Camenisch, J., Gross, A., & Sommer, D. (2007). User centricity: A taxonomy and open issues. *Journal of Computer Security, 15*(5). IOS Press.

Brands, S. (Ed.). (2009). *Rethinking public key infrastructures and digital certificates: Building in privacy*. MIT Press.

Camenisch, J., Shelat, A., Sommer, D., Fischer-Hübner, S., Hansen, M., & Krasemann, H. … Tseng, J. (2005). Privacy and identity management for everyone. *Proceedings of the First ACM Workshop on Digital Identity Management*, Association for Computing Machinery.

Cameron, K. (2005). *The laws of identity*. Identity Weblog. Retrieved from http://www.identityblog.com/stories/2004/12/09/thelaws.html

Canard, S., Malville, E., & Traoré, J. (2008). Identity federation and privacy: One step beyond. *Proceedings of the Fourth ACM Workshop on Digital Identity Management*, Association for Computing Machinery.

Cha, S. (2008). Taxonomy of nominal type histogram distance measures. *Proceedings of the American Conference on Applied Mathematics*.

Chappell, D. (2006). *Introducing Windows CardSpace*. MSDN Library. Retrieved from http://msdn.microsoft.com/enus/ library/aa480189.aspx

Dingledine, R., Mathewson, N., & Syverson, P. (2004). Tor: The second-generation onion router. *Proceedings of the 13th USENIX Security Symposium*, USENIX Association.

Eap, T. M., Hatala, M., & Gasevic, D. (2007). Enabling user control with personal identity management. *Proceedings of the 2007 IEEE International Conference on Services Computing*, Institute of Electrical and Electronics Engineers.

Gajek, S., Schwenk, J., Steiner, M., & Xuan, C. (2009). Risk of the CardSpace protocol. *Proceedings of the 12th International Conference on Information Security* (pp. 278–293), Springer.

Hansen, M., Berlich, B., Camenish, J., Claus, S., Pfitzmann, A., & Waidner, M. (2004). Privacy-enhancing identity management. [Elsevier.]. *Information Security Technical Report, 9*(1), 35–44. doi:10.1016/S1363-4127(04)00014-7

Lampson, B., Abadi, M., Burrows, M., & Wobber, E. (1992). Authentication in distributed systems: Theory and practice. *ACM Transactions on Computer Systems, 10*(4). Association for Computing Machinery.

Leenes, R., Schallabock, J., & Hansen, M. (2008). *PRIME White Paper – Third and final version*. Retrieved from https://www.prime-project.eu/prime_products/whitepaper/.

Mashima, D., & Ahamad, M. (2008) Towards a user-centric identity-usage monitoring system. *Proceedings of the Third International Conference on Internet Monitoring and Protection*, International Academic, Research, and Industry Association.

Mashima, D., & Ahamad, M. (2009b). Using identity credential usage logs to detect anomalous service accesses. *Proceedings of the Fifth ACM Workshop on Digital Identity Management,* Association for Computing Machinery.

Mashima, D., Ahamad, M., & Kannan, S. (2009a). User-centric handling of identity agent compromise. *Proceedings of the 14th European Symposium on Research in Computer Security* (pp. 19–36). Springer.

Paci, F., Bertino, E., Kerr, S., Squicciarini, A., & Woo, J. (2009). An overview of VeryIDX - A privacy-preserving digital identity management system for mobile devices. *Journal of Software*, *4*(7). doi:10.4304/jsw.4.7.696-706

Recordon, D., & Reed, D. (2006). OpenID 2.0: A platform for user-centric identity management. *Proceedings of the Second ACM Workshop on Digital Identity Management* (pp. 11–16). Association for Computing Machinery.

KEY TERMS AND DEFINITIONS

Identity Agents: Identity agents are software installed on users' devices or online services hosted on third parties trusted and selected by users. Identity agents work under user's control and authorization and typically are responsible for identity credential management and enforcement of user-defined security policies.

Identity Credential: In cyberspace, an identity credential is a set of identity-related claims whose integrity and authenticity can be verified by the recipients. A typical example is a digital certificate signed by a certification authority.

Identity Misuse Detection: This aims at detecting misuse of identity credential that are stolen or compromised by adversaries. Though it is part of a fraud detection mechanism, identity misuse detection relies typically only on observed credential usage, which implies that the available information is often limited.

Minimal-Disclosure Identity Credential: A novel identity credential scheme that allows users to flexibly select which identity attributes in the credential is disclosed. Even if some parts of the credential are hidden, the recipient of the credential can still verity the validity of the credential issuer's signature.

Risk Scoring System: Risk scoring systems are designed to quantify the risk of observed activities, such as login attempts, identity credential usage, and so forth. For example, such score can be computed based on deviation from normal patterns. An output of the risk scoring system can be further used by other security mechanisms.

User-Centric Identity Management: An identity management system architecture that allows users, i.e. owners of identity credentials, to flexibly control their own online identities. For example, users can select which identity information is disclosed as well as which identity providers they can trust.

User-Centric Identity-usage Monitoring: A user-centric identity-usage monitoring system keeps track of identity credential usage to help users be aware of when, where, and how their identity credentials are used. While its objective is similar to the one pursued by traditional fraud detection systems, which are typically run by service providers, a user-centric monitoring system works under users' control.

Chapter 6
Coming of Age or Just off the Boat? A Review of Contemporary Identity Management Systems

Raj Sharman
State University of New York at Buffalo, USA

Ryan Kendrick
State University of New York at Buffalo, USA

Manish Gupta
State University of New York at Buffalo, USA

ABSTRACT

Identity management (IdM) systems are information systems that help to manage an individual's credentials. This occurs through the establishment, description, maintenance, and eventual destruction of an identity. There are numerous IdM systems in place today that follow a general framework, yet provide users of the system with different solutions. This chapter will present architecture and applications that will help in establishing and analyzing the framework that IdM system follow. It will define the role of IdM systems in today's electronic age, while examining challenges that arise during implementation, management, and integration of the systems. The latter part of the chapter examines eighteen commercial off-the-shelf IdM software solutions. We provide brief discussion on each of the solutions to highlight differences and advantages. The discussions and presentations in the chapter can aid system managers and security professionals in understanding current landscape of Identity Management Solutions and Technologies and analyses we provide can significantly facilitate their decision making and risk management.

DOI: 10.4018/978-1-61350-498-7.ch006

INTRODUCTION

The term Identity management (IdM) refers to the process of being able to recognize and represent entities as digital entities in a computer network (Jøsang, et al., 2005). IdM systems are information systems which help to manage an individual's credentials. Much of the IdM software available today follows a general framework, yet provides users of the system with different solutions. With access requirements of users constantly changing, as well as laws being implemented that require stricter access permissions, it is evident that IdM implementation is still in a fairly young stage of development, but one that will mature quickly as it experiences growth in a wide range of applications. Enterprise digital identity management is a process of employing technologies and procedures to manage information about the identity of users and control access to enterprise resources. Identity management has shown to enhance employee efficiency and also bolster security posture while containing costs (Penn, 2002). Enterprises, including commercial corporations and government agencies, are increasingly relying on identities of customers and citizens to provide services and consummate transactions over Internet (Mont et al., 2000). While recent laws and legislations (S.761, 2006)(1999/93/EC, 1999) aim at speeding up the process of adoption of digital identities by recognizing the legal validity of digital signatures both on electronic documents and electronic transactions, Internet identity thefts, and related frauds (Arnold, 2000; Coates et al., 2000) are fast growing crimes that take advantage of poor security and privacy practices and the underestimation of the involved risks. The maintenance of security of IdM systems has become challenging due to the diversity of today's specifications concerning, for example, privacy, system integrity and distribution on the Web (Gaedke, Meinecke, & Nussbaumer, 2005). The contributions of this chapter are manifold. First it provides an overview of different architectures and applications of IdM systems. This will serve as an excellent primer for IT and security professionals in understanding what options available to them which can immensely help them in decision making. Second, it presents a rich discussion on challenges that corporations face today in management and operations of IdM systems. This provides an insightful discourse on issues that managers can avoid by effective planning and risk mitigation approached. Lastly, the chapter presents eighteen of most relevant commercial IdM systems that are available for purchase to meet the organizational security and compliance. This section is highly pertinent to most organizations who don't build a complex and comprehensive IdM system but buy it from software vendors. This is the most cost effective and widely used approach. The discussions of different IdM software products can cue them on features and advantages of specific implementations. The organization of the chapter is as follows: Section 2 and 3 present different IdM architectures and applications (where these IdM systems are deployed), respectively. Section 4 discusses some of the most common challenges and Section 5 details the eighteen commercial IdM products. Section 6 concludes the chapter with conclusions.

ARCHITECTURE

There is a general design that is used when integrating an IdM system. The system must first have a source of information which tells it which users should and should not exist, as well as what their access permissions should be. This is usually done through the use of an enterprise resource planner (ERP) such as SAP.

After these things have been established, the basic functions of the IdM server are to assign resources, remove resources, and disable resources. The IdM server creates user accounts and allocates resources based upon the information provided by the ERP system. This includes access to any of

Figure 1. Silo model

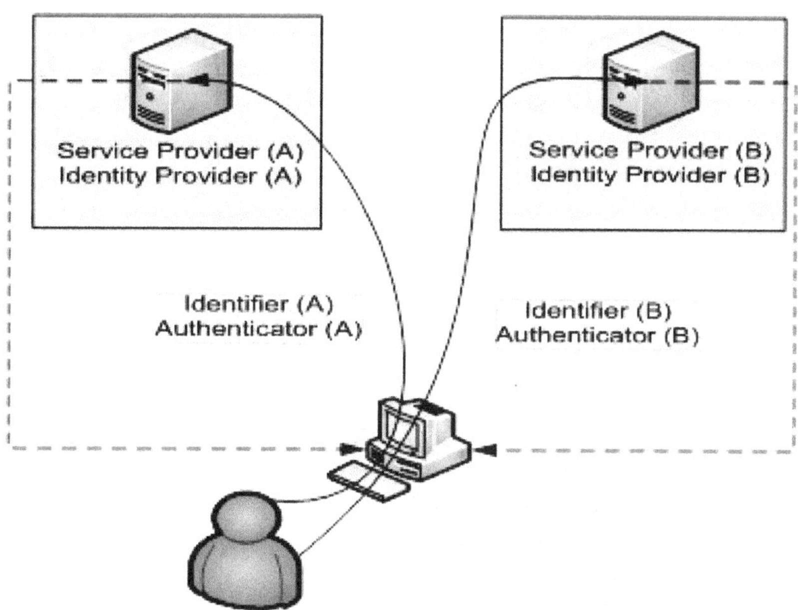

the various systems that the IdM system is intertwined with to allow for ease of access across all systems. With IdM in place a user may log in to an e-mail system and as a result of the credentials being checked, may also be granted access to their active directory without having to do anything else (Tracy, 2008). Even with a general architecture established, there is still room for variation. Some of the IdM models currently in existence will be described below.

Silo Model

In this model (Figure 1) the service provider manages both the name space and authentication for all of its users, making it the identity provider as well. A user is able to create his or her own identifier within the system as long as they are unique. The user is also able to set their own authentication password. This model is advantageous because of its simplicity to set up and personal information being exposed solely to the service provider. User account and password management has long been a major expense for organizations (Gupta and Sharman, 2008a).

A disadvantage to this model is that it used solely for access to one system, and thus a user must create their own identifier and authentication criteria for every service provider they encounter. It is not uncommon for users to forget the details to service providers they use infrequently, preventing the services from being used to their full potential (Jøsang et al., 2007).

Common Identity Domain Model

In the Common Identity Domain Model (Figure 2), there is only one common identity provider that encompasses each service provider. In this method a user could use the same identifying information for multiple services. A common authentication token in this model is to use a public-key certificate. This solution would be good for an organization that is able to assign a single, non changing identifier to a user. An advantage to this model is that it is simple to manage for both the service provider and user. Only one set of identifier and

Figure 2. Common identity domain model

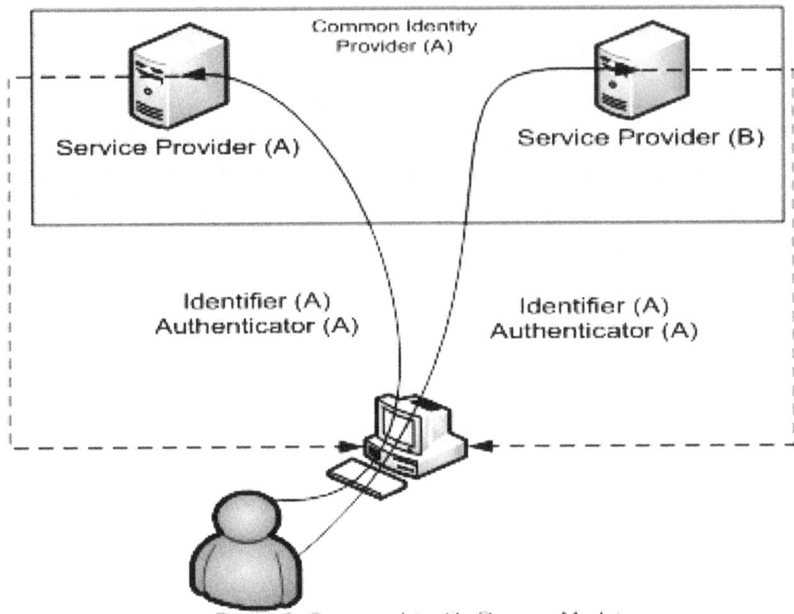

authentication information is needed, and thus it is easier to maintain.

A disadvantage is that it is not possible to manage a set of unique name spaces for all users worldwide that are considered to be both stable and without privacy implications. For example purposes, users are likely to have numerous e-mail addresses and as a result e-mail would not be a good identifier. Also using something such as social security number would be impractical for the previously given privacy example (Jøsang et al., 2007).

Centralized Single Sign-on Identity Model

This model allows for the use of a centralized identity provider (Figure 3). This centralized entity manages the name space, authentication tokens, and authentication of users. In sequence, a user sends their identifier and authentication information to the identity provider, the provider then sends a security assertion to the service provider(s); the service provider then grants the requested access. This model fits well into closed networks where multiple service providers are managed by a single organization. In such closed networks it is assumed that the identity and service providers are governed by the same authority with the same policies in place, making implementation a simpler process.

The disadvantage to this model is that it is considered to be unsuitable for environments where the service providers are not governed by a common authority. It is not that the model itself does not allow for easy implementation, but that it is unlikely that different service providers would accept an outside identity provider to manage and authenticate identities on their behalf. It would violate certain privacy protection principles regarding exposure of personal information (Jøsang et al., 2007).

Even with this disadvantage in place, it was attempted by Microsoft with their Passport authentication service in 1999. The purpose of this system was to "provide a standard authentication system that could be used by any site on the Internet." The reaction to such a service was quite negative

Figure 3. Centralized single sign-on model

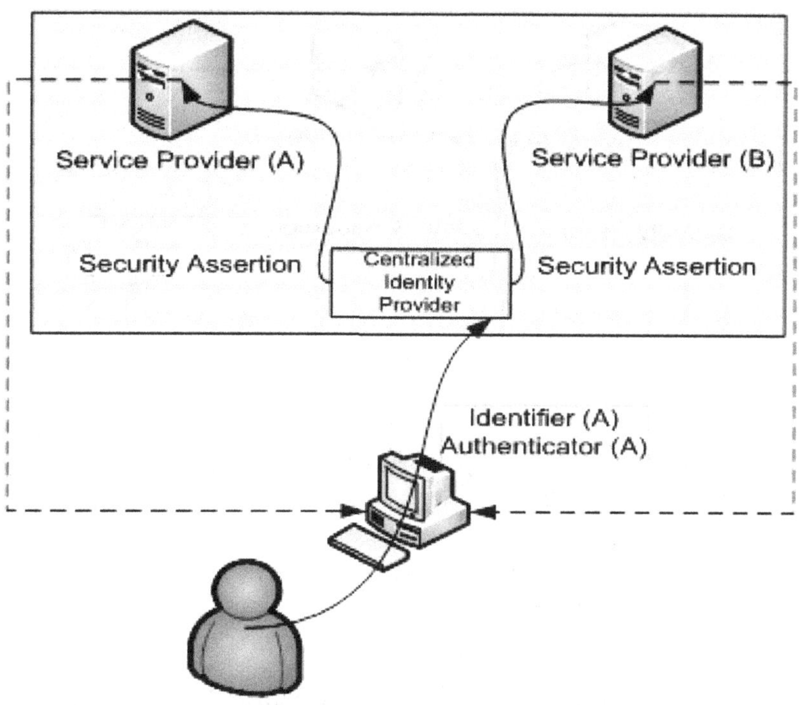

and Microsoft later stated that "no single organization, not even one as big as Microsoft, could act as the sole identity provider for everything on the Internet" (Chappell, 2006). The Passport service was later transformed into Windows Live, which focuses around Microsoft provided services, and is described further in the 'Where IdM is Used' section. Increased security and compliance, improved user productivity and convenience and real cost savings are few motivations that drive SSO implementation (Impravata, n.d). According to a Gartner report Single Sign-On system can save up to $300 per user per year which can account to huge amounts (Connelly, 2000). Single Sign-On (SSO) systems provide users the convenience of accessing multiple applications and systems while having to provide credentials only once (Gupta and Sharman, 2010).

Centralized Model with Browser Support

This model (Figure 4) could be described through a service that Microsoft is trying to leverage as a result of a modified Passport service. It essentially takes the centralized single sign on method they attempted to implement, with modifications so that multiple identity providers would be involved. The idea is that a user may want to use different identities for different situations. A user will have multiple 'InfoCards' stored on a computer contained in a 'CardSpace,' which do not contain any sensitive information. Each of these InfoCards points to a centralized identity provider where the sensitive information is stored. In this method a security assertion is first sent from an identity provider to the CardSpace module, and further forwarded to the service provider.

The advantage to this is that it improves upon centralized single sign on where service providers are not governed by a common authority. By

Figure 4. Centralized model with browser support

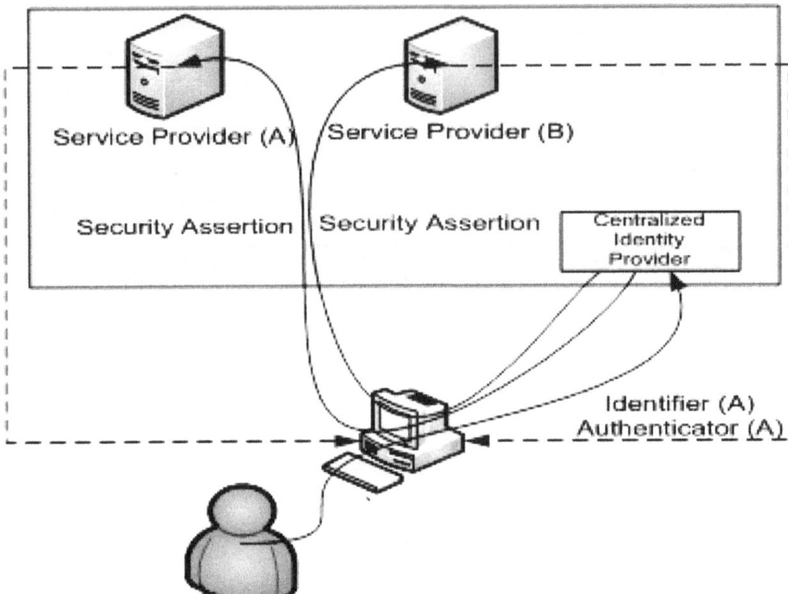

allowing for support of multiple identity providers and centralized domains, the problem of leaving personal information in the hands of one giant identity provider is no longer a problem.

When it comes to disadvantages it can be said that they are amplified over the previous centralized model. The same problem exists with a third party identity provider holding personal information, albeit it is multiple providers instead of just one. This model also brings back a problem seen in the silo model. A user will be responsible for remembering multiple sets of identifier and authentication information due to the likeliness that they will be interacting with multiple identity providers for the different services they are using. Finally, if someone with ill intentions finds a way to exploit the CardSpace system, they could use the InfoCards and pointers that they have to identity providers to utilize a person's identity without having to actually steal it (Jøsang et al., 2007).

Federated Single Sign-on Identity Model

This model (Figure 5) builds on single sign-on, with the idea that groups of service providers enter into a mutual security and authentication agreement. This agreement essentially enables service providers to recognize user identities from other service providers. Like in the silo model, each identity provider is also its own service provider. The difference is that the providers are linked. As an example, when logging in Provider A, a user will be identified as Identifier A. Provider A can send a security assertion to Provider B verifying the authenticity of the user that has Identifier A. The user will then be authenticated in the other providers system with its own unique Identifier B. The biggest advantage to this model is that it allows for single sign-on in environments where multiple entities are involved. It can also be retrofitted to an existing silo model, allowing for service providers to keep existing name space and authentication systems without the worry of conflict.

Figure 5. Federated single sign-on model

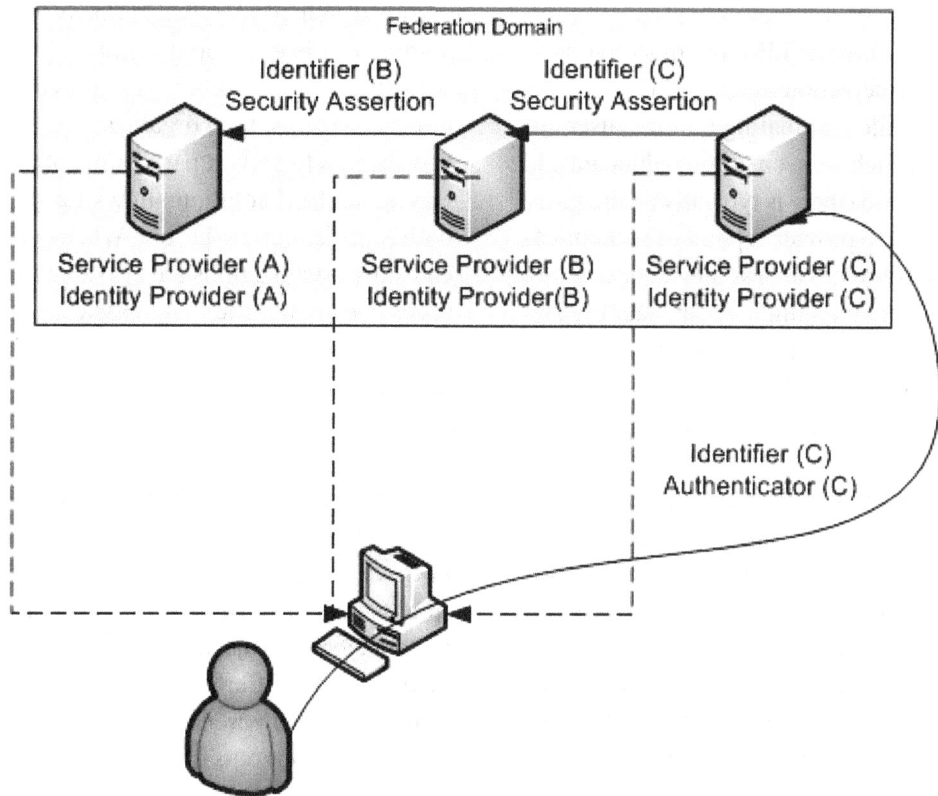

The main disadvantage to using this method is that it relies heavily on trust between multiple organizations. Service providers must be able to trust security assertions from each other and have confidence that another provider will not try to exploit this in any way. The link between service providers will also allow for information to be correlated about users, potentially creating a privacy threat. This type of thing can be prevented to a degree with a user's identity to a specific linked silo being anonymous. It all depends on privacy policies and what steps an organization feels are necessary or wants to have in place within the federation (Jøsang et al., 2007). This demands enterprises to enable convenient and secure business interactions with internal and external stakeholders, and create relationships to trust the electronic identities to access critical information resources. Federated identity management (FIM) is a system that enables individuals to use the same credentials or identification data to obtain access to the networks of multiple enterprises to conduct business transactions. FIM has demonstrated huge potential in providing reliable and scalable solutions to problems in systems security and access management. SAML (Security Assertion Markup Language) is the dominant web services standard for FIM (Gupta and Sharman, 2008b).

APPLICATIONS

A person's digital identity may not be limited to simply one instance. Identity management is used in various areas that include but are not limited to a person's personal documents, work connectivity, and attachment to social networks.

Consumer

In the consumer area of IdM, the objective is to enable smooth interactions between the consumer and services while eliminating multiple user authentications which are seen to be a redundant and a hassle. In this area there is typically a third party which is trusted to provide a point of authentication to the consumer to access the services while managing and maintaining the users identity and profile information (Casassa Mont, Bramhall, Gittler, Pato, & Rees, 2002). An example of where this is currently in wide use is with Microsoft's Windows Live platform.

Windows Live is a freely available service which allows a user to integrate their e-mail, Windows Live Messenger, online storage, Xbox gaming experience, and other Microsoft provided services. When a user logs in to one of these services and continues on to use another of the services included in Windows Live, they are automatically logged in and are able to continue on without any further proof of identification. When registering to create a Windows Live ID, it is marketed as something that "gets you in to all Windows Live services," and that is exactly what it does (MS-Live, 2010).

Commercial

In the commercial workspace, the administration of user accounts has, and will most likely continue to be a task that that consumes a large amount of an IT department's time. In most organizations that have the ability and means to do so, IdM solutions have been implemented which allow for easier modification of user roles across the entire organization as opposed to an individual basis. This does not remove the administration of individual users on a case by case basis, but does greatly simplify when a group of users needs access modification(s).

An important aspect of commercial based IdM which utilizes the technology to its fullest extent is when inter-organization shared space is involved. When two organizations collaborate on a project, it brings about a situation where both security and quick access is required. In a situation such as this, both organizations are likely to need access to certain parts of the others system. Having an IdM solution allows for the needs of both organizations to be met. When collaboration ends, the organizations are also able to easily cut access ties with little to no hassle.

Government

In the government realm there are a never-ending amount of identity related forms issued with a short list of more common ones including a driver's license, passport, and social security number. The management of identities within this realm is considered to be fragmented as citizens are identified by different government institutions through different credentials.

Implementation of IdM in the government sector involves strategies of exposing government services on the Internet and integrating mechanisms that allow for the proper identification of citizens. The recognition and definition of the legal validity of digital signatures would allow for steps to be taken that make this kind of implementation in government much easier. Leveraging the use of IdM use to the public is an area that the consumer and commercial areas need not worry about, but is of great importance to the government. In government usage, citizens would essentially have IdM forced upon them whereas in consumer uses it is by choice and in commercial uses it is as a result of employment. The government must weigh social and legislative aspects of implementation across an entire nation. Privacy and freedom that the government would both need to guarantee to the public, and follow through with law establishing all aspects of the system (Casassa et al., 2002).

Mobile

The mobile usage of IdM is an area that is currently expanding at a rate that can only be described as very fast. Not only are people drifting from desktop computers for everyday use to jump to laptops and netbooks, but the usage of smartphones is at an all time high and looking like it will only become more widespread. It is expected that smartphone penetration will grow from 19% to 54% between the time period of 2008 to 2012, with an actual growth of 193% already seen from 2009 to 2010 (AdMob, 2010).

With every operating system on a phone comes a different type of IdM that will connect the user to different services. A few of the more popular operating systems are Microsoft's Windows Mobile, Apple's iPhone OS, and Google's Android. As an example, on phones running the Android operating system, the screen a user encounters upon first boot of the phone asks for their Google Mail login information. Once a user does this, their phone syncs with their Google account and pulls mail, contacts, calendar events, and anything else they may use through Google. When the user updates or changes anything either through their phone or personal computer, the other is instantly updated.

CHALLENGES

Even though the overall concept of what an IdM architecture should include can be considered quite straightforward, there are four challenges that come into play when it comes time to set one up. These challenges are role definition, propagation of accounts, initializing the system, and integration with single sign-on.

Role Definition

When it comes to assigning different authorization levels it is almost without exception that certain people are going to share the exact same permissions as others. This is where the challenge of role definition comes in to play. Roles help to assign people into specific groups with predetermined permissions so that permissions can be added and changed on a group basis as opposed to an individual basis. A generalized example of this which applies to numerous situations is where customer and employee roles exist. A user within the customer role may have access to queries of certain information only, whereas the employee may be able to add, remove, update and have access to other information.

Propagation of Accounts

As a result of role definition, a need for quick and easy account propagation arises. There must be a system in place that is able to take the login information that is provided by user, verify their credentials, and apply permissions. No matter the specific method that is used for account propagation, it is imperative that the system is automatically and quickly able to make any required access or role changes.

Initializing the System

Upon a user's first access to the system there needs to be a method in place to verify that the user is indeed the correct person. A commonly used method is to take personal information about the user from the ERP system and to have them answer questions about themselves. After the user is successfully able to identify his or herself to the system, they are prompted to create a password that will be used in conjunction with their login to identify themselves in the future.

Integration with Single Sign-on

Far from a requirement, however highly desired is the integration of single sign-on. Single sign-on makes it so that once a user has logged in to one system which they have access to, they will access to all other areas defined by their user rights without having to log in to anything else during that session. Many access management solutions makes it easy deploy something such as this due to accounts and passwords being synchronized (Tracy, 2008). It has been discussed how single sign-on is easier to implement across models that contain a single entity, but quickly becomes more complex as moves on to other models such as the federated, and centralized with browser support models.

COMMERCIAL SOLUTIONS (OFF THE SHELF SOFTWARE)

In this section eighteen IdM software solutions will be evaluated. These evaluations will be based completely off of information found on the websites of said solutions. We feel it necessary to state that we have not personally used any of these solutions. The software will be listed in alphabetical order by company name in order to prevent any bias through the order in which they are listed.

Advanced Toolware: Identity Management Solution

Advanced Toolware lists different solutions on their site for people looking to manage different services. Their identity management solution is summed up as being "a reliable, fully automated solution… manages user accounts and resources in Active Directory and other directory services." They provide a single sign-on environment. Other services provided are server and workstation monitoring, disk quota management, detailed login reports, and a self service reset password management system which is used for remotely resetting Active Directory passwords. Pricing schemes for their identity management solution are available through requesting a price quote, with certain other services starting at $299 per administrative license or $999 per site license (Toolware, 2010).

AegisUSA: Identity Management Appliance Solutions

AegisUSA provides IdM systems for password management, single sign-on, federated identity, and provisioning. Within the different offerings Aegis provides, it is possible to bundle hardware, identity management software, and configuration services together for reduction of overall cost. There are three different pricing levels listed for identity management solutions. The first is for 'Identity Appliances' and is listed at a $25k fixed price. This involves a 30 day installation and allows for the use of open source, Oracle, or Sun solutions. It also allows for the organization to choose between hardware or virtualized implementation. Second is 'Identity and Access Management Assessments' which starts at $30k. This provides capability and maturity assessments and documentation deliverables with a roadmap, requirements, and architecture. Last is their 'Custom Deployment of Commercial IAM Toolset.' This solution is based upon the needs of the organization and typically ranges from $100k to $1M and between 3 and 12 months. It takes all needs into consideration and allows for a custom solution as the name implies (Aegis, 2009).

Atlassian: Crowd

Atlassian's Crowd is a single sign-on application that can be obtained for both small and large organizations alike. It allows for access changes to be made in applications and have them show up in the directories. Crowd's pricing scheme caters to both small and large. For $10 a 10 user license can be obtained with all proceeds going to charity. Licenses for 100, 500, and unlimited users can be obtained for $1200, $2200, and $8000 respectively (prices halved for academic use) and are good for a 12 month period (Crowd, 2010).

Avatier: Identity Management Suite

Avatier's solution provides the first Web Service Identity Management and development platform that automates certain daily processes such as user provisioning, account management, self-service password reset and strong password enforcement. Also, due to its web implementation, the solution can be deployed in most in environments in a single day with no client side programming required. Pricing is available through requesting a quote (Avatier, 2010).

Beta Systems: SAM Enterprise Identity Manager

The solution provided by Beta Systems allows for implementation across different platform boundaries. Solutions for Windows, UNIX and mainframe-based data centers are available. Self-service functions allow for employees to reset forgotten passwords on their own or even apply for new access rights over the Internet (Beta Systems, 2010). A pricing scheme is not available and no direct mention of obtaining a quote is listed. It can be assumed that pricing is obtainable through using contact information on the site.

BeyondTrust: Identity Management

BeyondTrust breaks their solution down in to five areas called Management Console, PowerBroker, PowerKeeper, PowerAdvantage, and Privilege Manager. Within these areas the comprehensive solution provides regulatory compliance, management of Windows permissions, strong password, and full implementation into Active Directory. Although no specific information is listed as to where to inquire about pricing, it can be assumed that this is obtained through the Contact Us tab on their website (BeyondTrust, 2010).

Computer Associates: Identity Manager

Within Computer Associates' Identity Manager comes automated user provisioning, user self-service, workflows for managing approvals, and delegated user administration. It supports common enterprise systems and applications such as CRM, ERP, Active Directory, and more through customization. Specific maintenance tiers and value-add offerings are listed; however, no pricing scheme is listed. Documentation states to contact Computer Associates' Account Team or Support (CA Identity Manager, 2010).

Courion: Enterprise Provisioning Suite

Courion's identity and access management solution provides user provisioning, password management, compliance management, and role management. The solution they provide allows for automation wherever possible and self-service in regards to password management. Their access compliance solutions fulfill regulatory requirements for things such as Sarbanes-Oxley, HIPAA, GLB and PCWe amongst others. Courion also provides two different types of single sign-on; a traditional solution and a web solution. Pricing and information regarding quotes is not available, however advisement is made to use Courion's Contact page for more information (Courion, 2010).

Cyber-Ark: Privileged Identity Management Suite

Cyber-Ark's solution is broken down in to three separate units. These are the Enterprise Password Vault, Privileged Session Manager, and Application Identity Manager. The Password Vault helps with securing managing, automating, storing, protecting and logging of activities associated with accounts. The Session Manager monitors and manages access to sensitive systems and devices while leveraging single sign-on capabilities. Lastly the Identity Manager takes steps to remove all passwords from scripts, encryption of passwords while at rest or in transit, as well as redundancy features for business continuity. Brochures for more information about the solutions provided are available through the site when personal information is provided (Cyberark, 2010).

HitachWe ID Systems: Identity and Access Management

The listing of services provided by HitachWe ID includes an identity manager, access certifier, group manager, privileged password manager, password manager, and login manager. The services are designed to manage identities and privileges on a variety of IT systems in order to help organizations reduce costs and improve efficiency through automation and self-service or assisted password resetting. HitachWe ID provides software licensing on a user basis and bases their maintenance cost on the annual contracts they form. Information to contact HitachWe ID for a price quote is listed on their site (HitachWe ID Systems, 2010).

HP: OpenView Identity Manager

HP's OpenView Identity Manager is broken up in to four sections. The first is Select Identity which allows for centralized management of users and their entitlements. Second is Select Access which provides centralized authorization management across web enabled tools and services. Third is Select Federation which enables sharing and management of user identities across business borders using the federated model of identity management. Last is Select Audit which helps with adherence to regulatory requirements and provides real-time alert handling. For information on pricing people are advised to contact their nearest HP reseller or sales office (OpenView, 2006).

IBM: TivolWe Identity Manager

A listing of the services offered by IBM's TivolWe Identity Manager includes self-service interfaces, closed loop user provisioning, access recertification, role management, group management and centralized web administration. Supported platforms for TivolWe include HP-UX, IBM AIX, Red Hat Enterprise Linux, Sun Solaris, SUSE Linux Enterprise Server, Microsoft Windows Server, and z/OS. The services are able to integrate with dozens of popular applications including databases, directories, access control systems, e-mail, service desks, and ERP systems. To implement these services, IBM also offers a variety solutions including but not limited to enterprise single sign-on, unified single-sign on, and a federated identity manager. Information regarding obtaining a quote is available on the IBM website (Tivoli, 2010).

Microsoft: Forefront Identity Manager

Microsoft breaks their Forefront Identity Manager down in to four feature areas. These are policy management, credential management, user management, and group management. Within policy management there is a SharePoint-based console for policy authoring and enforcement and heterogeneous identity synchronization and consistency. Credential management includes certificate management, management of credential types, self-service password reset, and integrated provisioning of identities, credentials, and resources. User management deals with user provisioning and de-provisioning as well as self-service user profile management. Lastly, group management includes Office-based self-service group management tools, offline approvals through Office and group and distribution list management including dynamic membership calculation. This solution by Microsoft is provided on a per server and per client basis with a list price of $15k per server and $18 per client. More in depth purchasing options are available upon contacting Microsoft (MS-Forefront, 2010).

Novell: Identity Manager

Novell's Identity Manager provides user provisioning, adjustable access, dynamic compliance for auditing, self-service password reset, and an extensive graphical interface to minimize any coding knowledge requirement for implementation. It provides integration modules for Active Directory, Windows NT, Novell GroupWise, Microsoft Exchange, Lotus Notes, Novell eDirectory, and other LDAP v3 directories. Numerous presentations, white papers, and brochures are available on the Novell site which include more specific information. Information to obtain a quote is available on Novell's website (Novell Identity Manager, 2010).

Oracle: Identity Management

Oracle has numerous different suites which can be licensed separately or together. These are Oracle Identity Manager, Oracle Identity Analytics, Oracle Access manager, Oracle Web Services Manager, Oracle Identity Federation, Security Token Service, Oracle Enterprise Single Sign-On, Oracle Entitlements Server, Oracle Adaptive Access manager, Oracle Directory Services, and Oracle Platform Security Services. Separately they do such things as manage privileges, deal with regulatory compliance, implement single-sign on, protection of web services access and dealing with security token issuance, validation, and exchange amongst other things. Pricing information can be obtained by contacting Oracle through means listed on their website (Oracle-IDM, 2010).

Passlogix: v-GO Access Accelerator Suite

Services provided by Passlogix include single sign-on, self-service password reset, universal authentication manager, provisioning manager, and shared accounts manager. Passlogix is able to implement these services in to existing legacy systems, lowering possible required replacement costs. Pricing is obtainable through contacting the Passlogix sales department (Passlogix, 2010).

Quest: One Identity Solution

Quest's One Identity Solution provides services that include single sign-on, directory consolidation, audit/compliance, strong authentication, self-service password reset, provisioning, and privileged account management. All of these provided services are different modules and can thus be implemented on their own according to functionality requirements of the project. Information to obtain a quote is available on Quest's website (Quest, 2010).

Sun Microsystems: Identity Management

It should be noted that Sun was acquired by Oracle in early 2010 and that these solutions may be incorporated in to the services Oracle now provides. Services provided by Sun include Sun Open SSO Enterprise, Sun Directory Server, Sun Identity Manager, Sun Role Manager, and Sun Identity Compliance Manager. These services help to provide a central repository for managing identities, allow for a comprehensive user provisioning and identity auditing system, and integration of automated enterprise-wide access certification. Due to the previously recent acquisition of Sun Microsystems by Oracle, products listed by Sun are currently under review and it is unclear whether Sun products are officially available. Interested parties may still contact Sun, although they may be redirected to Oracle (Sun-IDM, 2010).

CONCLUSION

Identity Management covers the spectrum of tools and processes that are used to represent and administer digital identities and manage access for those identities (Allan et al., 2008). Usually people use different digital identities in different contexts depending on association of different information with each identity (Gupta and Sharman, 2008c). The three main business drivers for identity management solutions are security efficiency (lower costs and improved service), security effectiveness (including regulatory compliance) and business agility and performance (including workforce effectiveness and customer convenience) (Allan et al., 2008). Identity Management is a means to reduce such risks, representing a vital part of a company's security and auditing infrastructure (Buell and Sandhu, 2003). The secure and efficient administration of numerous personal attributes that make up digital identities is one of the key requirements in open and closed networks. Especially in respect to confidentiality and integrity, the users themselves, rather than popular external threads like viruses, phishing, or pharming attacks represent the main risk (Stanton et al, 2005). As a result of incorrect account management and inadequately enforced security policies users accumulate a number of excessive rights within the organizations' IT systems over time, violating the principle of the least privilege (Ferraiolo et al., 2003). Moreover, people have a hectic life and cannot spend their time administering their digital identities (El Maliki and Seigneur, 2007). Identity Management in open networks like the Internet has received tremendous attention throughout the last years with researchers. Although considered important, Identity Management in closed networks, however, has not gained comparable significance within the research community.

IdM software and solutions are used in practically all digital interactions where a person must identify themselves whether people realize it or not. The current status of IdM is one where users have learned to jump from one method to the other in their everyday lives with little thought of the inefficiencies that still exist, purely because each advancement in this area is still one step in the direction of becoming more efficient. A user that at one point was required to have twenty sets of identifier and authentication information will certainly be happy with being able to lower it to ten; no complaints will be made about wanting to have only one. In the scheme of things IdM is fairly matured, at least in the product offerings and architectures given the current state of technologies. At the same time, with new threats emerging all the time, there are enough growth opportunities in this field for further improvement and innovation.

Through taking a quick outside look at all of the aforementioned companies, it can be said that many provide similar services. Almost all of the companies provide services such as single sign-on, self-service password reset, and 'easy' implementation in to commonly used services such as Active Directory. A quick Google search for the words 'Identity Management Software' brings up companies both large and small. We will not state which, but all of the companies that appear on the first page of the search appear above. It would be impossible to recommend any of these software solutions because certain solutions are better for certain situations. Hopefully this section gave anyone interested in implementing an IdM solution the information they can use when deciding upon a solution for their own project, or at the least a listing of companies they can use to begin a more in depth product evaluation.

REFERENCES

1999/93/EC – Directive. (1999). *1999/93/EC of the European Parliament and of the Council of 13, December 1999 on a Community framework for electronic signature*.

AdMob. (2010). *AdMob mobile metrics report*. Retrieved from http://metrics.admob.com/wp-content/uploads/2010/03/AdMob-Mobile-Metrics-Feb-10.pdf

Aegis. (2009). *Article on identity management software, identity management solutions, identity access management*. Retrieved from http://www.aegisusa.com/

Allan, A., Perkins, E., Carpenter, P., and Wagner, R. (2008). *What is identity 2.0? Key issues for identity and access management.* Gartner Research Report, ID Number: G00157012.

Arnold, T. (2000). *Internet identity theft: A tragedy for victims*. White Paper, SIIA.

Avatier. (2010). *Identity management, compliance management and password management software solutions at Avatier*. Retrieved from http://www.avatier.com/index.html

Beta Systems. (2010). *Beta Systems: SAM enterprise identity manager*. Retrieved from http://ww2.betasystems.com/en/

BeyondTrust. (2010). *Identity management, root access control, password management, privileged account management, UAC, Windows access control, admin rights control from BeyondTrust*. Retrieved from http://www.beyondtrust.com/

Buell, A. D., & Sandhu, R. (2003). Noevmber). Identity management. *IEEE Internet Computing*, 7(6), 26–28. doi:10.1109/MIC.2003.1250580

CA. (2010). *Identity manager*. Retrieved from http://www.ca.com/us/user-provisioning.aspx

Casassa, M., Bramhall, P., Gittler, M., Pato, J., & Rees, O. (2002). *Identity management: A key e-business enabler*. Presented at SSGR2002s, L'Aquila, Italy

Chappell, D. (2006, April). *Introducing Windows CardSpace*. Retrieved from http://msdn.microsoft.com/en-us/library/Aa480189

Coates, D., Adams, J., Dattilo, G., & Turner, M. (2000). *Identity theft and the Internet*. Colorado University.

Connolly, P. (2000, September 29). *Single sign-on dangles prospect of lower help desk costs.* Retrieved March 21, 2009, from http://www.infoworld.com/articles /es/xml/00/10/02/001002esnsso.html

Courion. (2010). *Courion identity and access management and compliance solutions*. Retrieved from http://www.courion.com/

Crowd. (2010). *Single sign-on (SSO) and identity management - Crowd*. Retrieved from http://www.atlassian.com/software/crowd/

Cyberark. (2010). *Privileged identity management Suite from Cyber-Ark software*. Retrieved from http://www.cyber-ark.com/digital-vault-products/privileged-identity-management/index.asp

El Maliki, T., & Seigneur, J.-M. (2007). A survey of user-centric identity management technologies. *The International Conference on Emerging Security Information, Systems, and Technologies*, SecureWare 2007, 14-20 Oct. 2007 (pp. 12-17).

Ferraiolo, D. F., Kuhn, R. D., & Chandramouli, R. (2003). *Role-based access control*. Artech House computer security series, ISBN 1-58053- 370-1

Gaedke, M., Meinecke, J., & Nussbaumer, M. (2005). *A modeling approach to federated identity and access management.* International World Wide Web Conference.

Gupta, M., & Sharman, R. (2008a). Security-efficient identity management using service provisioning (markup language). In Gupta, J. N. D., & Sharma, S. (Eds.), *Handbook of research on information security and assurance* (pp. 83–90). Hershey, PA: IGI Publishing. doi:10.4018/978-1-59904-855-0.ch040

Gupta, M., & Sharman, R. (2008b). Dimensions of identity federation: A case study in financial services. [Dynamic Publishers.]. *Journal of Information Assurance and Security*, *3*(4), 244–256.

Gupta, M., & Sharman, R. (2008c). Emerging frameworks in user-focused identity management. In Gupta, J. N. D., & Sharma, S. (Eds.), *Handbook of research on information security and assurance* (pp. 362–377). Hershey, PA: IGI Global Publishing. ISBN. doi:10.4018/978-1-59904-855-0

Gupta, M., & Sharman, R. (2010). Activity governance for managing risks in role design for SSO systems. *Journal of Information Assurance and Security, 5*(6). Dynamic Publishers.

HitachWe ID Systems. (2010). *HitachWe ID systems: Identity and access management*. Retrieved from http://hitachi-id.com/

Imprivata. (n.d.). *Benefits of single sign on*. Retrieved March 22, 2009, from http://www.imprivata.com/contentmgr/showdetails.php?id=1170

Jøsang, A., Al Zomai, M., & Suriadi, S. (2007). Usability and privacy in identity management architectures. In *The Proceedings of the Australasian Information Security Workshop* 2007, Ballarat, Australia.

Jøsang, A., Fabre, J., Hay, B., Dalziel, J., & Pope, S. (2005). *Trust requirements in identity management*. In Australasian Information Security Workshop 2005, Newcastle, Australia

Mont, M. C., Bramhall, P., Gittler, M., Pato, J., & Rees, O. (2000). *Identity management: A key e-business enabler*. Retrieved from hpl.hp.com

MS-Forefront. (2010). *Microsoft Forefront Identity Manager: Home page*. Retrieved from http://www.microsoft.com/forefront/identitymanager/en/us/default.aspx

MS-Live. (2010). *Home - Windows Live*. Retrieved April 14, 2010, from http://home.live.com/

Novell. (2010). *Identity manager*. Retrieved from http://www.novell.com/products/identity-manager/

OpenView. (2006). *HP OpenView select identity software*. Retrieved from http://www.hp.com/hpinfo/newsroom/press_kits/2006/rsa/ds_hires_select_identity.pdf

Oracle-IDM. (2010). *Identity management*. Oracle Identity Management. Retrieved from http://www.oracle.com/us/products/middleware/identity-management/index.htm

Passlogix. (2010). *Website*. Retrieved from http://www.passlogix.com/site/

Penn, J. (2002). *IT trends 2002: Directories and directory- enabled applications*. GIGA Report.

Quest. (2010). *Identity and access management software - Quest Software*. Retrieved from http://www.quest.com/identity-management/

S.761. (2006). *The electronic signature in global and national commerce act*. US - S.761.

Stanton, J. M., Stam, K. R., Mastrangelo, P., & Jolton, J. (2005). Analysis of end user security behaviors. *Computers & Security*, *24*(2), 124–133. doi:10.1016/j.cose.2004.07.001

Sun-IDM. (2010). *Identity management*. Sun Microsystems. Retrieved from http://developers.sun.com/identity/index.jsp

Tivoli. (2010). *IBM - Identity management software - TivolWe Identity Manager software*. Retrieved from http://www-01.ibm.com/software/tivoli/products/identity-mgr/

Toolware. (2010). *Identity management solutions by Advanced Toolware*. Retrieved from http://www.advtoolware.com/

Tracy, K. (2008). Identity management systems. [IEEE.]. *Potentials*, *27*(6), 34–37. doi:10.1109/MPOT.2008.929295

KEY TERMS AND DEFINITIONS

Authentication: Verifying user's assertion of its identification through credentials.

Authorization: Verifying user's privileges to a system.

Identity Management Architecture: Design of identity system for managing credentials and entitlements for users of covered system(s).

Identity Management System: A system for managing user identities.

Multiple Factor Authentication: An authentication system that is based on more than one factor of authentication such as something user knows (knowledge), something that user possesses (possession) and something user is (behavioral or physical trait).

Password Management: Managing users' passwords for purpose of authenticating users.

Role Management: Managing users' entitlements and rights to application(s).

Single Sign On: Use of single set of credentials to provide access to multiple applications and systems.

Chapter 7
Separating Private and Business Identities

Gábor György Gulyás
Budapest University of Technology and Economics, Hungary

Róbert Schulcz
Budapest University of Technology and Economics, Hungary

Sándor Imre
Budapest University of Technology and Economics, Hungary

ABSTRACT

As various information technologies are penetrating everyday life, private and business matters inevitably mingle. Separating private and business past records, public information, actions or identities may, however, be crucial for an employee in certain situations. In this chapter we review the interrelated areas of employee privacy, and analyze in detail two areas of special importance from the viewpoint of the separation: web and social network privacy. In relation to these areas we discuss threats and solutions in parallel, and besides surveying the relevant literature, we also present current Privacy Enhancing Technologies applicable in each area. Additionally, we briefly review other means of workplace surveillance, providing some insight into the world of smartphones, where we expect the rise of new privacy-protecting technologies as these devices are getting capable of taking over the functions of personal computers.

INTRODUCTION

The workplace is an area where the employee devotes his time and expertise to achieving goals designated by the employer; however, it is not possible to reach the total absence of private life in a workplace (Szabó & Székely, 2005). There are two typical cases where the employee's privacy may be violated by the employer; at labor recruitment and during employment, but there may be other cases as well (e.g. when the employee is forced to submit herself to personality tests). During these encounters the employer may collect information about the employee's private life, for instance, by searching for public records before conducting a job interview (Microsoft Research,

DOI: 10.4018/978-1-61350-498-7.ch007

2009), or pursuing surveillance during work time activities referring to security or other reasons.

Setting aside the legal aspects – as they vary in many countries (Privacy International, 2011) – we analyze how Privacy Enhancing Technologies (PETs) can be used to hide one's private life from the prying eyes of an employer. The purpose of the paper is to present possible technologies and techniques involving some theoretical solutions suitable for assembling a privacy protective portfolio that can be adjusted to the local legal aspects in any country. Therefore we intend to present a practical solutions with some theoretical background, focusing primarily on the technical side of the problem.

The outline of the paper is as follows. Since the selection of categories of breeching employees privacy is based on the work of Szabó & Székely (2005) we briefly present the relevant aspects of their analysis first. The focal point of our work is the discussion of three areas from the viewpoint of employee privacy. First, web privacy issues are discussed, including the analysis of the importance of information superpowers, but focusing on how privacy can be demolished by tracking user activities on the web and by using public Web 2.0 data sources. Then the significance of social networks is presented, and before concluding our work, other means of privacy violation are also briefly discussed.

BACKGROUND: ANALYSIS OF SCENARIOS IN HUNGARY

Szabó & Székely (2005) analyzed numerous complaints that were filed to the Hungarian Data Protection Commissioner from a non-technical, legal point of view in the context of Hungarian law. Their work includes a classification of the cases based on the purpose of the employer and determines four categories such as labor recruitment, work control and supervision, personality tests and other cases of unreasonable privacy violation.

During labor recruitment, the employer's goal is to learn about the applicants' personality, medical status and past records in order to choose the most adequate candidate for the job. This inevitably includes privacy-related issues, such as various kinds of (unnecessary) medical examinations, personality tests, using of lie detectors or exaggerated data inquiry. However, the internet can be also used as a data source for such investigations, since the purpose of many web services (e.g., social networks) is to gather and provide information on individuals.

Personality tests are usually conducted offline, and should be avoided by legal means if possible. Some of the issues reported in the work of Szabó & Székely, under the category of other cases of unreasonable privacy violation can be avoided by using PETs, but some do not even need them. For instance, the authors mentioned employers who were investigating the political background or the religious beliefs of applicants. These issues should be hindered by using PETs related to the first two categories, and if this is not possible, these issues need to be solved by other means, e.g. through legal redress or involving commissioners.

In case of successful recruitment, it is important for the employer to ensure that the employee devotes his time and expertise to the designated tasks. This can lead to work control and supervision over the concerned services, software or hardware provided by the employer, which does not necessarily imply the violation of the employee's privacy; however, some actions in the employee's personal life will inevitably take place during the working hours. This is even more likely to happen if corporate access is provided to public services like phone networks or the internet. Therefore, it is important to separate private and business actions in these cases as well.

In accordance with the work of Szabó & Székely, we selected web and social network privacy as these can be involved during the application process and employment alike. Besides, there are many less relevant, but existing problems, some of which are also analyzed – these are discussed under the category of other issues.

PRIVACY ON THE WEB

Tracking users on the web has a long history. At the beginning of the web it was possible to identify users by their IP addresses, later by the identifiers stored on their computers (Gulyás et al., 2008). Over time, these techniques became more and more sophisticated as the business value of uniquely identified users and profiling had been recognized. As companies with extensive service portfolios and services based on voluntarily submitted personal data appeared, new data sources became available. From the viewpoint of separating private identities from business ones, all areas should be considered, but probably the latter seems to be the most sensitive: companies can also search for previous blog posts, web pages, or other kinds of small pieces of information containing personal information about the applicant or the employee.

Information Superpowers

Today, there are several companies on the web offering a wide scale of services with single sign-on (e.g., search services, mail, and calendar). These companies usually offer their services for free, but in return they analyze the uploaded content and display advertisements. Besides allowing an insight into the uploaded private information, meta-data about the user are also revealed (e.g., first and last time of reading mails, daily routine, relaxation habits, interests) leading to extensive inter-application surveillance, as the content of different applications can be easily linked by the host.

These companies do not necessarily need to remain within the border of their services. For instance, by offering web analytic services, they can monitor how visitors browse across websites, and some of these tracked visitors can even be identified by their login name (Krishnamurthy & Wills, 2009). As the majority of web analytic services are provided by only a handful of companies that also serve a vast number of users with their applications, and therefore manage a huge amount of personal information, we call these information superpowers. Figure 1. illustrates the nature of information superpowers and some typical services they can access.

Usually, these services do not publish content by default, but some may have built-in social networking functionality. However, the related options should be revised from time to time, since new privacy settings may appear and new defaults can be set. The Privacy Policy changes committed over time by Facebook are good examples for that (McKeon, 2010). New functions or related services that publish private information can also appear, as was the case with Google Buzz (Wood, 2010). Therefore, an employee (or a job applicant) should consider managing the privacy settings carefully, and should avoid publishing sensitive material (e.g., via Google Reader) – self-consciousness might be even more important if the employer is the same company as the one running the concerned services.

Separating workflows is a powerful way of enhancing privacy. For services requiring logins, multiple unlinkable registrations can separate personal and business identities if they are accessed with anonymous web browsers (discussed in the next section). If logging in is not mandatory, then service specific PETs can be used to avoid profiling. For example, GoogleSharing is a Google-specific PET allowing access the public Google services anonymously (Marlinspike, 2010). As GoogleSharing provides anonymity, sequentially entered search queries sent by the same user are unlinkable for Google.

Open source alternatives can substitute some services of information superpowers. For example,

Figure 1. Information superpower inside the border of its services, and the outer world

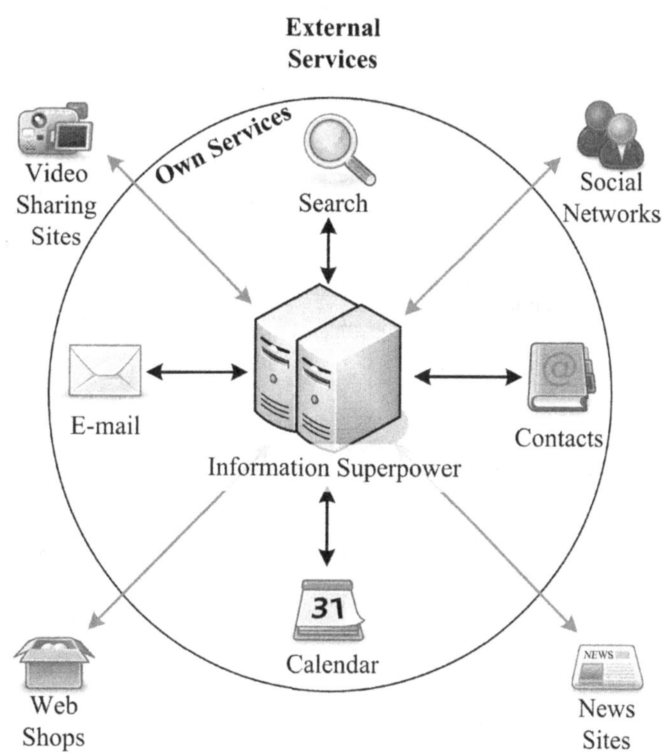

FengOffice (FengOffice, 2010) offers a web based calendar and task manager besides the regular web office suite (the latter can manage documents and presentations). As this is open source software, it can be freely installed on the employee's computer to allow her exercising total control over the uploaded data.

Tracking Users on the Web

The overall goal of tracking users on the web is to link user activity to a pseudonymous or a personal profile (Gulyás et al., 2008). Profiles can be created for various reasons, such as behavioral profiling, profiling for targeted advertising, or dynamic pricing. Large and complex profiles are more useful for these purposes, but creating such profiles requires users to be identified and recognized across websites. This kind of profiling is also relevant from the viewpoint of an employee who intends to separate her business and private life even if she is not working for a company, which is trying to track her activities. Local databases (e.g., cookies, history databases and cache, and other client-side storages) on her working computer can contain private information, which makes it possible to rebuild a complex behavioral profile on her.

Nowadays, there exist numerous techniques for online profiling and surveillance, and many of the leading web services are using them (What They Know, 2010). Initially IP addresses were used as user identifiers when IP changes and multiple users on personal computers were rare. As IP addresses became dynamic over time, this technique was not accurate enough anymore, and tracking cookies have replaced them. These identifiers are stored in the user's profile by the web browser application. Besides identifying returning visitors, tracking cookies can also be used to track user

Figure 2. The operation of Flash PIEs and cookie recreation

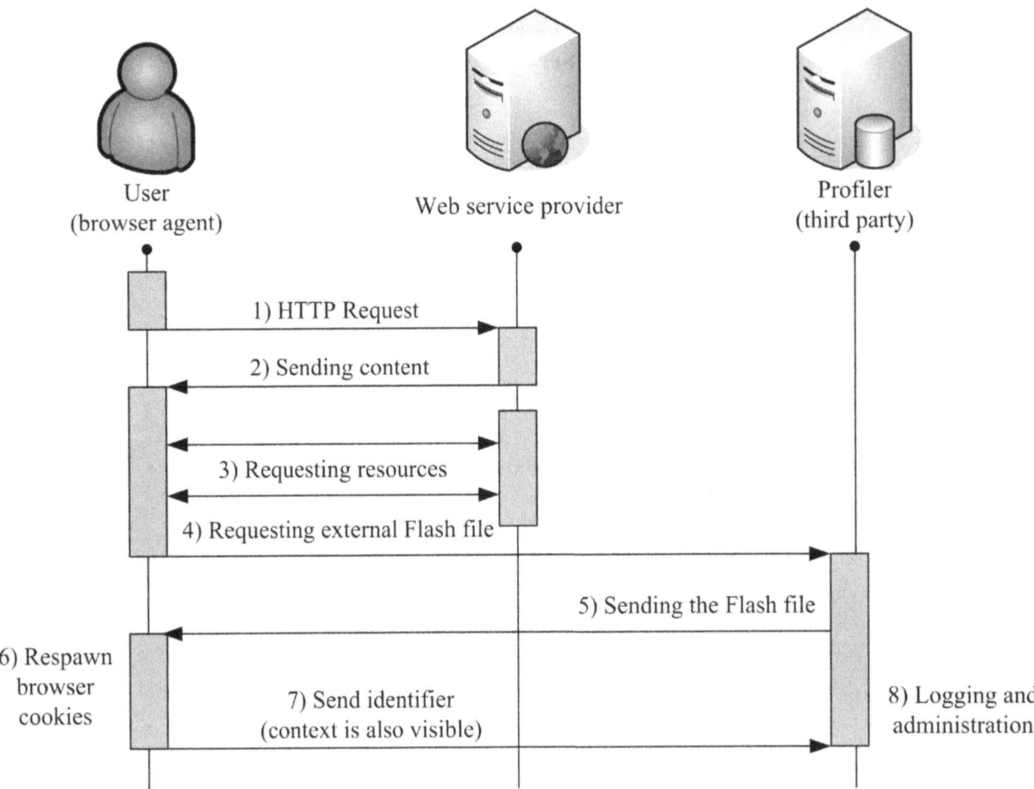

activities across different websites by embedding "detectors" into the content of the cooperating websites. For instance, web bugs (typically small 1x1 pixel transparent GIF images) specifically used for tracking, are still in use on many popular websites (Carver et al., 2009).

In addition to tracking cookies, "detectors" of other media types became also widespread for cross-domain user tracking. Adobe Flash (Adobe Systems Incorporated, 2010) is a popular extension for animation and interactive graphics used on many websites. Similarly to web browsers, the Flash player also provides its own cookies that can be used for storing identifiers. Soltani et al. (2009) found that a significant number of websites used Flash cookies to recreate deleted web browser tracking cookies. However, Flash cookies are also available as tracking cookies called Persistent Identification Elements, or PIEs for short (Gulyás et al., 2008). Figure 2. illustrates how Flash cookies can be used for tracking and restoring web browser cookies.

There are techniques that do not need to store additional data on the client-side: history stealing attacks aim to read the history of the web browser via web scripts. As browser history should be unique for most users, it can even be used to identify the user by determining her social networking profile (Wondracek et al., 2010). However, the fate of history stealing attacks is already sealed, as the API deficiency that allows history stealing attacks is going to be patched in Firefox 4 (Stamm, 2010), and other browsers are also expected to do the same in the near future. When direct monitoring of the local network is not possible, or for some reason the employee's computer is inaccessible for the company, history stealing can be used on the local corporate intranet to sniff what employees are browsing on the web.

There is a novel method combining all available local storage methods and flaws that can be exploited for storage, called evercookies (Kamkar, 2010). Evercookies use almost a dozen storage methods, and therefore they are quite resistant against attempts to clear browsing history and local storages. However, web browser vendors and plugin developers recognized these flaws, and the revision of local storage management can be expected as a response (Huang, 2011).

As a reaction to tracking issues, a novel feature called private mode has been implemented in modern browsers, aiming to provide protection against local observers (e.g., other users, administrator) by hiding traces of the user's activity, and also by making sessions unlinkable for service providers. Recent research has shown that private mode implementations failed their objectives in several browsers, and in addition, different plug-ins and extensions also allow the profiling of users (Aggarwal et al., 2010). Moreover, passive fingerprinting techniques can also be used to identify users (Eckersley, 2010). By comparing the fingerprints of modern web browsers in private mode, we found that the fingerprints were the same in normal and private mode (e.g., the font list, same settings, plug-ins are still visible to the visited site). According to Eckersley (2010), these fingerprinting techniques, together with IP addresses can also be used to restore tracking cookies; therefore, web browsers in private mode are also vulnerable to being tracked.

Although IP addresses allow imprecise identification only, hiding these addresses seems to be important, as the latter example emphasizes. For IP hiding, anonymous proxies are the simplest solutions; however, their architectural simplicity is also their weakness: the user has to place confidence in a single server (Gulyás et al., 2008). Mixes (Chaum, 1981) provide a better network level protection against both the unreliable servers in the network and the remote target. Additionally, MIXes provide extra protection against local observers. For example, in order to use the popular service called Tor (Dingledine et al., 2004), users need to install a local proxy on their computer that connects them to the anonymizing network. For employees, this is favorable: their connection is protected on the local company network against surveillance and censorship, and the visited websites cannot determine their IP addresses either.

The most complex PETs offering protection against all the aforementioned techniques of tracking user activities on the web are called anonymous web browsers (Gulyás et al., 2008). Modern anonymous web browsers, such as JondoFox (JonDos GmbH, 2010), are portable, offer tools for maintaining local databases (e.g., Flash cookie filtering), filter malicious content (e.g., web bugs, untrusted JavaScript) and apply network level anonymizing services for hiding the user's IP address. Considering their functionality, it can be stated that anonymous web browsers offer the most powerful privacy protection for users. The necessary level of protection is also guaranteed for privacy-aware employees for local databases and against possible network observers.

Profiling by Collecting Information from Public Sources

Numerous web services, especially Web 2.0 sites, are specialized in user contribution, and encourage their users to submit large amount of personal data, which often get published worldwide without any access control provided. These services include, but are not limited to social networking sites, content sharing sites, blogs, micro-blogs, forums, etc. Besides the lack of control over data publication, the evolution of search engines also played an important role in this process by organizing content and enhancing ease of access. For some Web 2.0 services, real time search is also provided (Singhal, 2009), which raises further privacy issues: as published data are immediately accessible via search engines, the revocation of information becomes very difficult or even impossible.

There are other, more alarming ways–completely disregarding the data subjects' approval–for service providers to access private data, which can also be used for abuses. For instance, tagging people on images is a popular feature on Facebook which allows tagging people either by their names and a link to their profiles or only by their names. The latter can be abused as it requires no confirmation from the tagged user, and removing such tags by others than their poster is not possible (Boutin, 2009). Allowing the website to access and search through one's email account is another popular feature that helps people build up their social network. However, as we pointed out earlier, even errors in privacy policies can lead to these kinds of breaches (Wood, 2010), and ownership issues or the difficulties around data revocation are just additional factors complicating the situation (Schroeder, 2009).

These issues should be considered both by applicants and employees. During the application process, a company can search for past records on the applicant (Microsoft Research, 2009), and, even during employment, the company can keep employees under control by collecting information from public sources (Matyszczyk, 2009). Therefore, besides raising the employees' own privacy-awareness on publishing content, it is important to technically separate sensitive information by means of access control. (Nevertheless, in cases where data publication is not voluntary, there is not much a user can do technically.)

There are several solutions for managing access control, but small, client-side applications using cryptography are the best practical choices (Paulik et al., 2010). These solutions provide strong confidentiality over the encrypted data due to strong encryption, and require no trust in the service provider or any third parties. However, Paulik et al. (2010) defined further requirements to be considered while choosing the proper software. Such an application should be gradually deployable for clients using the same service, and universal in order to be compatible with most popular services. The authors also emphasize usability without compromises and easy installation as the use of such software is intended for non-technically oriented people, too.

The FireGPG Firefox extension is a piece of generic encryption software allowing symmetric and public key encryption, also capable of encrypting messages posted on the web (Cuony, 2010). Although it is available as a Firefox extension, one of its main drawbacks is that it is not standalone: the user must have the GNU Privacy Guard installed to use it. This may be a convenient software for professional users, but the installation can be quite cumbersome for an average user, and its rich functionality can also be confusing.

The BlogCrypt Firefox extension allows only symmetric encryption, but it is more user-friendly, as it was specifically designed for web encryption (Paulik et al., 2010). The key management of BlogCrypt was designed for the structure of the web, since keys are identified by the domain name and a locally unique key identifier. Encrypted text appears on sites as a Base64 coded string, starting with a header tag including the related key identifier–the extension automatically tries to decrypt these content blocks if the key identifier is stored in its database. The operation of BlogCrypt is illustrated on Figure 3.

While BlogCrypt was primarily designed for regular web pages (though manual decryption works with AJAX-based software also), it is also possible to insert a cryptographic layer between the client-side software and the service provider in Web 2.0 applications. SeGoDoc is a client-side cryptographic solution designed this way: it demonstrates this functionality for Web 2.0 services using the AJAX technology by cooperating with Google Docs (D'Angelo et al., 2010). There are even further alternatives, and more software will be cited in the next section relating to social networking. Some of these tools can also be used for the web in general. For a more comprehensive

Figure 3. The operation of the BlogCrypt Firefox extension

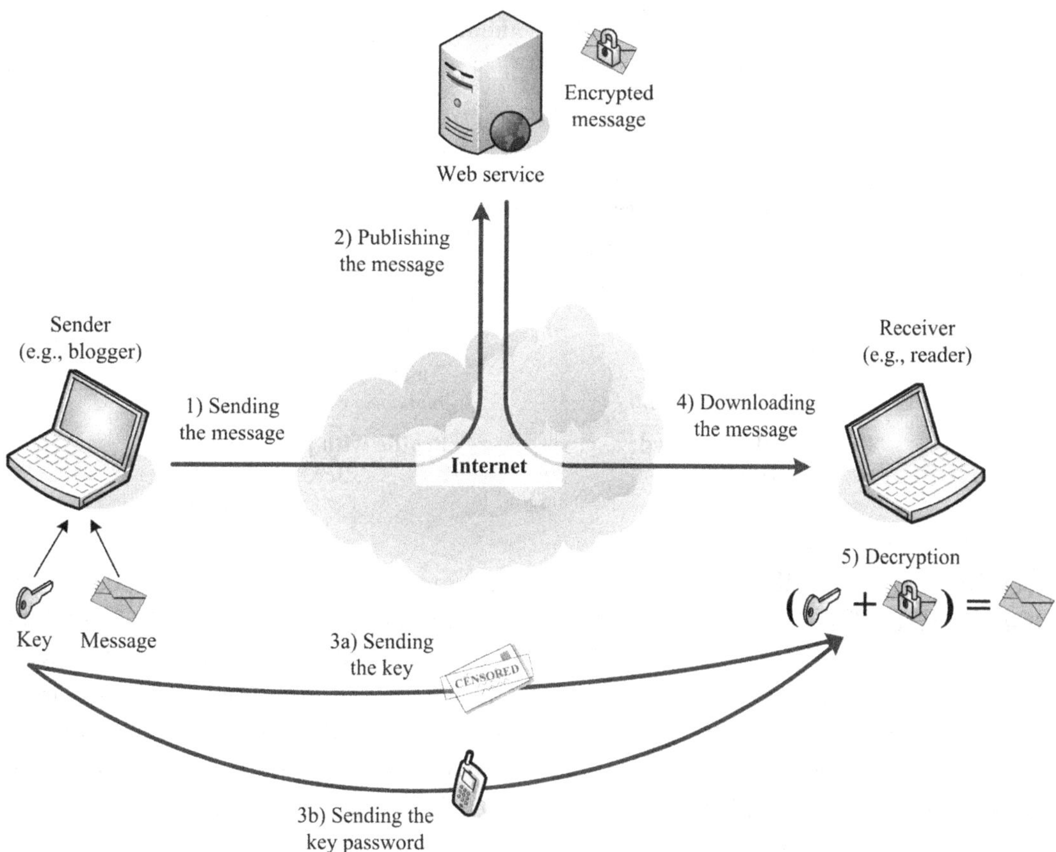

comparison of related software see the work of Paulik et al. (2010).

According to Paulik et al. (2010), the ideal PET for providing access control applies steganography. Here we give an insight into how such software could operate on social networking profiles–describing the generic solution in detail is beyond the scope of this article, and we leave that for future work. The core concept is as follows: after detecting that a password is assigned to the profile (e.g., after storing a local database of user ID and password pairs) the software retrieves real attributes by using the password and replaces them with the originals. This concept is visualized on Figure 4. by introducing an identity management-like scenario.

The retrieval can be realized by using random addresses identified by the password at an arbitrarily selected third party service (e.g., the hash value of the password can be used as the address identifier). Thus, different passwords would produce different address and content. As the content would be encrypted with the password, and the address would not contain the password itself, the third party service could not jeopardize revealing the real content, and backward linkability would not be possible. We note that as the retrieval process is based on the password, identity management can also be realized based on these principles (e.g., simply by assigning different passwords for distinct groups).

Figure 4. Different keys used to reveal different sets of data (i.e., profiles)

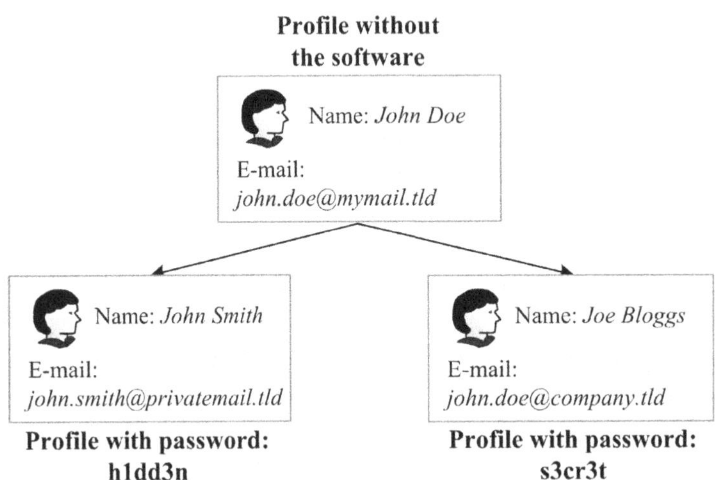

SEPARATING IDENTITIES IN SOCIAL NETWORKS

Social networks are getting more and more integrated into our private life, and therefore the use of these services at the workplace is nearly unavoidable. The result of the FaceTime (2008) survey shows that 51% of employees use these services every day; however, social networks raise several privacy issues concerning the relation of the employer and the employee, for instance, the separation of private and business identities (e.g., separation of registrations for the current and job seeking identities), separation of contacts (e.g., friends and colleagues), contact lists, group memberships, limiting access to events (e.g., personal activities) or hiding sensitive profile information (e.g., state of pregnancy). There are a few additional privacy issues derived from these, such as information flow control (Chew et al., 2008). These features are often unavailable or control possibilities are ineffective.

Due to the nature of social networking, these services involve several participating roles. Wang & Kobsa (2009) defined three roles representing privacy threat to employees: other users, the employer (represented by users) and the service operator. From the technical aspect of privacy protection, there are no differences between other users and employers (registration of bosses, managers, etc.), since all users are equal in regular social networking services. Company services are open only for employees (e.g., IBM Beehive; DiMicco et al., 2009), and since these services may fall under special regulations, the service provider being the company itself (e.g., use of PETs can be forbidden), these services should only be used with raised privacy awareness, or be avoided totally.

In addition to the work of Wang & Kobsa (2009), we note that third parties, as an additional role beside other users and the service provider, also pose a threat to user privacy. Structural analysis shows that social networks are vulnerable to active (Backstrom et al., 2007) and passive attacks (Narayanan & Shmatikov, 2009) aiming to re-identify nodes in anonymized data exports. As the latter algorithm only considers structural properties of the export, it can reveal hidden relationships between identities present in different networks; for example, this algorithm can reveal that a business and a private identity belong to the same user.

Cryptography-Based Access Control

Relating to web privacy, we have discussed several PETs that can be used to post encrypted messages on the web by allowing client-side access control. These access control techniques are useful for controlling other users' and the service provider's access to the uploaded content alike. Some of this software can also be used for social networks, such as FireGPG (Cuony, 2010) or BlogCrypt (Paulik et al., 2010), but there are other PETs specifically designed for social networking, providing similar functionality.

The main goal of these PETs is to hide profile attributes or to separate identities by presenting false names (Luo et al., 2009); however, link hiding can also be possible (Anderson et al., 2009). We emphasize that for proper identity separation, the use of anonymous web browsers is necessary, since the service provider can easily link profiles by identifying the user between different logins (e.g., using browser descriptor information and IP address for identification; see Eckersley, 2010).

We propose the use of client-side software for social networks, concerning that the same requirements apply here as to PETs that are used for access management of web content. Nevertheless, there is a significant number of software tools that have some unfortunate compromises while trying to achieve enhanced privacy in social networks. For example, FlyByNight (Lucas & Borisov, 2008) is a Facebook application offering symmetric and public key encryption, but stores data encrypted on Facebook servers and has the service provider involved in the key management as well. Although it is a browser and operating system independent solution (it uses JavaScript technology on the client-side), it works only for Facebook, and requires the permission of the service provider to operate.

Some PETs are more than applications created for a single social network; however, they still only work with a single service. NOYB (Guha et al., 2008) and FaceCloak (Luo et al., 2009) are both Firefox extensions, although they are implemented to work only with Facebook. Both applications replace fake data with the original to avoid the appearance of ciphertexts in profiles; due to the substitution, these methods resemble steganography. The most serious disadvantage of these solutions is that fake data are provided by the software, and the user cannot suggest alternatives: NOYB substitutes attributes by creating dictionaries compiled from real data sets where the key determines the secret assignment, while FaceCloak uses relatively small pre-compiled dictionaries. Both tools use third party servers: NOYB for storing dictionaries, FaceCloak for storing the original data in an encrypted form.

Beato et al. (2009) define their work as an extension to NOYB by allowing sophisticated access control management for Facebook users. Their Firefox extension uses an external binary for encryption that originates from FireGPG. In this application, users can define groups of users (called connection classes) and folders of documents (called content classes), and can set access rights respectively. An employee may find this useful for separating access of colleagues and friends easily, while this kind of separation is not possible with the previously analyzed software tools. We note that this access management resembles privacy-enhancing identity management (Clauß et al., 2005) discussed in the next section.

Furthermore, comparison of most of these solutions can be found in the work of Paulik et al. (2010). To sum it up, one should consider the following before choosing the proper software. A practical solution should not necessitate trust in the service provider, should nor reliance on third parties (if possible), and it should be service independent and should not require the collaboration of the service operator. Further requirements, such as browser and operating system independency, the comfort of use, external software independency, are mostly up to the user's decision (for instance, BlogCrypt meets these requirements). We also note that the concept of PETs using steganography suggested previously, could also be used here.

Using Privacy-Enhancing Identity Management

Gürses et al. (2008) put access control issues in a more generic context, and state the need for internal and external separation of digital identities. Internal separation means that users share different profile data with a selected group of their contacts, and external separation signifies that even the user herself runs under a different identifier (such as another registration). Both are quite useful functionalities for separating private and business life. For example, internal separation can allow an employee to share information on private and business events with her friends and boss respectively, and external separation can allow an employee to maintain different, unlinkable profiles for her private and business identities. Here, unlinkability should include the unlinkability of profile information.

For internal separation, the authors propose that the service providers should allow their users using group-based access control mechanisms, similarly to the techniques analyzed in the previous section. However, the client-sided cryptography-based solutions may not only provide more flexible access control management, but also protect the confidentiality of the data against the service provider. In addition, using these software tools does not require the consent of the service provider and can be changed any time, even by the user herself. Therefore, we propose using a client-side application providing the appropriate level of key management, supposing that it meets the presented requirements.

For external separation Gürses et al. propose the using of identity partitioning tools, for example partial identities, which is a privacy-enhancing identity management technique (Clauß et al., 2005). Other researchers have also concluded that current social networks are flat from an access control point of view, while real-life social networks have a partitioned structure (Adams, 2010). Since identity separation supports the partitioning of one's contacts, identity partitioning, in our opinion, is an excellent solution for internal separation.

The core concept of partial identities means that a user can partition her set of attributes (i.e., her profile) into smaller sets, which may be accessed under different pseudonyms. These pseudonyms with their attribute set are the partial identities. Sometimes it can also be important for a pseudonym to be unlinkable with the other pseudonyms of the users; therefore, random pseudonyms should be used with a client-side solution that fixes readability and management of identities (Borcea-Pfitzmann et al., 2005). Identities can be changed as the context or communication partners change (Brocea et al., 2005), thereby allowing the user to context-dependently present information on herself.

Both internal and external separation could be solved by introducing a novel model to social networks that applies the principles of privacy-enhancing identity management; for example, Nexus-Identity Networks (NIN) is such a model (Gulyás et al., 2009). Instead of offering a single profile, the NIN model allows users to have several profiles that are stored in a tree hierarchy, where leaves can refer to groups of users having access to that specific profile. An example for the comparison of regular and identity partitioning enabling social networks is provided on Figure 5.

Figure 5. Today's social networks with their flat structure (left), and social networks extended with identity partitioning (right) including a node that applies external separation

For providing identity separation, the NIN model allows three levels of anonymity. Pseudonymous identification refers to internal identity separation according to the terminology of Gürses et al. (2008). Identities running under pseudonymous identification are linkable for a global observer, but local observers (e.g., contacts) may receive different information. In case of unlinkable pseudonymity, the identities are not trivially linkable by a global or by a local observer (i.e., they have different pseudonyms, and unlinkability is further enhanced by profile attributes). The highest level is total anonymity, which means the total absence of identifiers for the identity.

Social networks providing these levels of anonymity and access control with high granularity are able to support internal and external identity separation. These services provide the strongest level of privacy if the service provider cannot act as a global observer and cannot access all user content. However, if profile crawling is permitted, it may be a threat.

Threats Posed by Large Datasets Exported from Social Networks

Datasets can be exported from a social network for various reasons. For example, it can be provided by the social network operator for business partners or researchers, or it can be crawled by other third parties. However, these copies can endanger user privacy, as third parties that can access anonymized network data are able to learn additional private information. Backstrom et al. (2007) showed that an attacker who can modify the structure prior to anonymization can execute targeted attacks in order to learn hidden profile information or hidden connections between some users. Narayanan & Shmatikov (2009) argued the viability of such active attacks, and showed that passive attacks can de-anonymize users by simply using data crawled from a public network as auxiliary source.

Companies do not need anonymized exports to pose a privacy threat to employees. For instance, the passive attack presented by Narayanan & Shmatikov, can also be run on two datasets crawled from a personal and a business-oriented social network to match private and official identities. Today there are no proven techniques to avoid such attacks, but using these networks with raised privacy awareness can still be useful. The employee should consider separating her contacts in these networks, and should carefully avoid business contacts on the personal social networking site and friends on the business social networking site (to achieve different neighborhood structure). Besides the separation, one should also use different names on these networks, and should access the services via anonymous web browsers.

Other Issues in Social Networks

We highlight, for the sake of the completeness, that a distributed network architecture is also a good solution for providing privacy against the service provider; although, this is not the user's choice. However, these types of services are yet to spread in the future. For example, Cutillo et al. (2009) propose a three-layered social networking service including a social networking, and a peer-to-peer layer, both above the internet layer. Their model also provides protection against mapping one's neighborhood due to the structure and encryption in the social networking system.

OTHER MEANS OF WORKPLACE SURVEILLANCE

The employer may provide hardware (e.g., computer, smartphone), software (e.g., operating system, utilities), or services (e.g., company email service, intranet) to the employee, and therefore perform further surveillance to ensure that these resources are used for the right purpose, and the employee is spending his time properly – not considering that private actions may also take place. There might be many services involved; here we just mention some of the most frequently used ones: web browsing (discussed previously), e-mailing, internet usage, telephone calls, smartphones.

Problems related to most of these areas are technically much less complicated than the ones discussed earlier, and therefore involving PETs is not always necessary. In most cases an agreement and a clear statement on the conditions of use are enough. For example, instead of asking for a detailed call list on a company phone, an employer may simply calculate with a slightly higher budget that includes a certain amount of private use (Szabó & Székely, 2005). Beyond the budget limit the employee should be responsible for the invoice. This kind of problem management can be used in many of these previously mentioned areas.

However, for some areas, there are PETs designed for solving these issues. There are application-related PETs like anonymous remailers providing e-mail sender anonymity (Danezis et al., 2003), but there are service specific PETs, too. For instance, to prevent network monitoring, anonymous VPNs (e.g., VPN Privacy, 2010) can be used, which hide all traffic and protect against traffic analysis attacks. The employer may also want to observe what the employee uses her computer for (including hardware and software-related issues). Malicious software, such as key loggers, can be removed by scanning the computer with regular security software, e.g., anti-malware applications that are the proper tools for removing key loggers and other malware.

If it is not possible to separate the hardware used both for work and free time activities, there exist other solutions. Many PETs are portable, meaning that it is possible to carry them on USB sticks, and to use them without leaving traces on the host computer. This is not possible for all programs, especially for regular software (e.g., some instant messaging software); therefore, it would be desirable instead to carry the digital workspace with all programs included (i.e., the operating system and applications). There are existing PETs that can run from a USB stick or drive, and, after being connected, they rebuild the user's private (or corporate) workspace, even allowing to install and remove programs, while the hosting system cannot access the hosted one. This kind of private computer-in-the-computer solution is supported by MojoPac (Rinocube, 2010).

This type of solution is more likely to be favorable for the employee who wants to build up a private workspace on a corporate computer. However, this may even work the other way around, when an employee wants to set up a corporate operating system on her own computer. For instance, the IronClad USB drive (Lockheed Martin, 2010) is such a solution including a standalone operating system. The IronClad drive offers enhanced control for the company: the employer can remotely observe what happens on the drive and can even control what the user may install or remove (e.g., the user cannot remove pre-installed spyware). Thus, this solution offers practically no privacy, but, by separating the disks via storing private content in an encrypted form with TrueCrypt (TrueCrypt, 2010), this solution can work well (even without the IronClad drive). The company can have the desired level of control, but the employee can switch to her private operating system any time, while her employer cannot access private information due to the encryption.

Today there are numerous brands of smartphones, which are taking over some of the functionalities of regular computers. These devices are equipped with applications that have been only used on personal computers before (e.g., web browsing, emailing, and even new apps can be installed on most of the phones), and as these accompany their user almost all the time, their integration into personal life is a serious threat to privacy. We expect the same or similar PETs to appear on these platforms in the near future, although a few are already available. For example, there are anonymous web browsers that use an implementation of the Tor anonymizing service adapted to smartphones (Gauld et al., 2009; The Guardian Project, 2010). There is also a software providing confidentiality for calls and text messages through encryption (Whisper Systems, 2010).

CONCLUSION

From the viewpoint of separating private and business life, our paper discussed numerous threats against user privacy due to the integration of online services into everyday life. By neglecting any legal support provided, we seek technical solutions for the separation. Based on the work of Szabó & Székely (2005) we focused on analyzing the privacy threats posed by the web and social networks, but also gave some insight into other means of workplace surveillance. Besides discussing the related literature, we have also proposed several PETs related to each of the areas; however, we drew the conclusion that it is not the technological solutions that are the most important, but awareness of data protection and privacy. We emphasize that with the necessary level of awareness, users are able to protect their privacy in the long run, by adjusting the set of chosen PETs to the local legal possibilities.

ACKNOWLEDGMENT

We are grateful for the comments, remarks and suggestions of Ádám Máté Földes, and we thank him for reviewing several versions of this article. We also thank Iván Székely for reviewing the final version, and for his useful comments.

REFERENCES

Adams, P. (2010). *Closing the gap between people's online and real life social network*. Paul Adams Presentations. Retrieved August 31, 2010, from http://www.slideshare.net/padday/the-real-life-social-network-v2

Adobe Systems Incorporated. (2010). *Adobe Flash player*. Retrieved August 31, 2010, from http://www.adobe.com/products/flashplayer/

Aggarwal, G., Burzstein, E., Jackson, C., & Boneh, D. (2010). *An analysis of private browsing modes in modern browsers*. Proc. of Usenix Security.

Anderson, J., Diaz, C., Bonneau, J., & Stajano, F. (2009). Privacy-enabling social networking over untrusted networks. In *Proc. of the 2nd ACM Workshop on Online Social Networks* (pp. 1-6). Barcelona, Spain: ACM Press. doi:10.1145/1592665.1592667

Backstrom, L., Dwork, C., & Kleinberg, J. (2007). Wherefore art thou R3579X? Anonymized social networks, hidden patterns, and structural steganography. In *Proc. of the 16th International Conference on World Wide Web* (pp. 181-190). Banff, Canada: ACM Press. doi:10.1145/1242572.1242598

Beato, F., Kohlweiss, M., & Wouters, K. (2009). *Enforcing access control in social network sites*. Paper presented at the HotPET section of the 9th PET Symposium.

Borcea, K., Donker, H., Franz, E., Liesebach, K., Pfitzmann, A., & Wahrig, H. (2005). Intra-application partitioning of personal data. In *Proc. of Workshop on Privacy-Enhanced Personalization*.

Borcea-Pfitzmann, K., Franz, E., & Pfitzmann, A. (2005). Usable presentation of secure pseudonyms. In *Proc. of the Workshop on Digital Identity Management, 2005* (pp. 70-76). Fairfax, VA: ACM Press. doi:10.1145/1102486.1102498

Boutin, P. (2009). How to block Facebook photos of yourself. *Gadgetwise Blog–NYTimes.com*. Retrieved August 31, 2010, from http://gadgetwise.blogs.nytimes.com/2009/05/05/how-to-block-facebook-photos-of-yourself/

Carver, B., Gomez, J., Pinnick, T., Soltani, A., Makker, S., & McCans, M. (2009). Know privacy, full report. *Know Privacy*. Retrieved August 31, 2010, from http://www.knowprivacy.org/report/KnowPrivacy_Final_Report.pdf

Chaum, D. (1981). Untraceable electronic mail, return addresses, and digital pseudonyms. *Communications of the ACM, 24*(2), 84–88. doi:10.1145/358549.358563

Chew, M., Balfanz, D., & Laurie, B. (2008). (Under)mining privacy in social networks. In *Proc. of Web 2.0 Security and Privacy 2008*.

Clauß, S., Kesgodan, D., & Kölsch, T. (2005). Privacy enhancing identity management: Protection against re-identification and profiling. In *Proc. of the Workshop on Digital Identity Management, 2005* (pp. 84-93). Fairfax, VA: ACM Press. doi:10.1.1.101.2196

Cuony, M. (2010). Install FireGPG. *FireGPG*. Retrieved August 31, 2010, from http://en.getfiregpg.org/s/install

Cutillo, L. A., Molva, R., & Strufe, T. (2009). Safebook: A privacy-preserving online social network leveraging on real-life trust. *IEEE Communications Magazine, 47*(12), 94–101. doi:10.1109/MCOM.2009.5350374

D'Angelo, G., Vitali, F., & Zacchiroli, S. (2010). Content cloaking: Preserving privacy with Google Docs and other web applications. In *Proc. of the 25th Annual ACM Symposium on Applied Computing* (pp. 826-830). Sierre, Switzerland: ACM Press. doi:10.1145/1774088.1774259

Danezis, G., Dingledine, R., & Mathewson, N. (2003). Mixminion: Design of a Type III anonymous remailer protocol. In *Proc. of Symposium on Security and Privacy, 2003* (pp. 2-15). Berkeley, CA: IEEE Computer Society.

DiMicco, J., Geyer, W., Millen, D., Dugan, C., & Brownholtz, B. (2009). People sensemaking and relationship building on an enterprise social network site. In *Proc. of the 42nd Hawaii International Conference on System Sciences* (pp. 1-10). Big Island, HI: IEEE Computer Society. doi:10.1109/HICSS.2009.343

Dingledine, R., Mathewson, N., & Syverson, P. (2004). Tor: the second-generation onion router. In *Proc. of the 13th USENIX Security Symposium.*

Eckersley, P. (2010). How unique is your web browser? *Panopticlick*. Retrieved August 31, 2010, from http://panopticlick.eff.org/browser-uniqueness.pdf

FaceTime. (2008). *The collaborative internet: Usage trends, end user attitudes and IT impact*. Security, Management & Compliance for Unified Communications, Web 2.0 and Social Networks. Retrieved August 31, 2010, from http://www3.facetime.com/forms/survey08_request.aspx

FengOffice. (2010). *Feng Office*. Retrieved August 31, 2010, from http://fengoffice.com/web/index.php

Gauld, C., Beresford, A., & Rice, A. (2009). *Shadow and TorProxy*. Computer Laboratory: Digital Technology Group. Retrieved August 31, 2010, from http://www.cl.cam.ac.uk/research/dtg/android/tor/

Guha, S., Tang, K., & Francis, P. (2008). NOYB: Privacy in online social networks. In *Proc. of the First Workshop on Online Social Networks* (pp. 49–54). Seattle, WA: ACM Press. doi:10.1145/1397735.1397747.

Gulyás, G. Gy., Schulcz, R., & Imre, S. (2008). Comprehensive analysis of web privacy and anonymous web browsers: Are next generation services based on collaborative filtering? In *Proceedings of the Joint SPACE and TIME Workshops 2008* (pp. 17-32). Trondheim, Norway: CEUR-WS.

Gulyás, G., Schulcz, R., & Imre, S. (2009). Modeling role-based privacy in social networking services. In *Proc. of Third International Conference on Emerging Security Information, Systems and Technologies, 2009, SECURWARE '09* (pp. 173-178). Athens, Greece: IEEE. *Computers & Society*. doi:.doi:10.1109/SECURWARE.2009.34

Gürses, S., Rizk, R., & Günther, O. (2008). Privacy design in online social networks: Learning from privacy breaches and community feedback. In *Proc of International Conference on Information Systems*.

Huang, E. (2011). On improving privacy: Managing local storage in Flash player. *Adobe Flash Platform Blog*. Retrieved February 15, 2011, from http://blogs.adobe.com/flashplatform/2011/01/on-improving-privacy-managing-local-storage-in-flash-player.html

JonDos GmbH. (2010). JondoFox. *JondoNym*. Retrieved August 31, 2010, from http://anonymous-proxy-servers.net/en/jondofox/

Krishnamurthy, B., & Wills, C. (2009). Privacy diffusion on the Web: A longitudinal perspective. In *Proc. of the 18th International Conference on World Wide Web* (pp. 541-550). Madrid, Spain: ACM Press. doi:10.1145/1526709.1526782

Lockheed Martin. (2010). *IronClads USB drive*. Lockheed Martin. Retrieved August 31, 2010, from http://lockheedmartinengineering.com/products/ironclad/index.html

Lucas, M. M., & Borisov, N. (2008). FlyByNight: Mitigating the privacy risks of social networking. In *Proc. of the 7th ACM Workshop on Privacy in the Electronic Society* (pp. 1-8). Mountain View, CA: ACM Press. doi:10.1145/1456403.1456405.

Luo, W., Xie, Q., & Hengartner, U. (2009). FaceCloak: An architecture for user privacy on social networking sites. In *Proc. International Conference on Computational Science and Engineering, 2009* (pp. 26-33). Washington, DC: IEEE Computer Society. doi:10.1109/CSE.2009.387.

Marlinspike, M. (2010). *GoogleSharing*. Retrieved August 31, 2010, from http://www.googlesharing.net

Matyszczyk, C. (2009). Facebook entry gets office worker fired. *CNet News*. Retrieved August 31, 2010, from http://news.cnet.com/8301-17852_3-10172931-71.html

McKeon, M. (2010). *The evolution of privacy on Facebook*. Matt McKeon. Retrieved August 31, 2010, from http://mattmckeon.com/facebook-privacy/

Microsoft Research. (2009). *Online reputation in a connected world*. Online Reputation Research. Retrieved August 31, 2010, from http://www.microsoft.com/privacy/dpd/research.aspx

Narayanan, A., & Shmatikov, V. (2009). De-anonymizing social networks. In *Proc. of the 30th IEEE Symposium on Security and Privacy, 2009* (pp. 173-187). Washington, DC: IEEE Computer Society. doi:10.1109/SP.2009.22

Paulik, T., Földes, Á. M., & Gulyás, G. (2010). BlogCrypt: Private content publishing on the Web. In *Proc. of the Fourth International Conference on Emerging Security Information, Systems and Technologies, SECURWARE 2010*, Venice, Italy.

Privacy, V. P. N. (2010). *VPN privacy*. VPN Privacy Service. Retrieved August 31, 2010, from http://vpnprivacy.com

Privacy International. (2011). *European privacy and human rights*. Privacy International. Retrieved February 15, 2011, from https://www.privacyinternational.org/ephr

Rinocube. (2010). *MojoPac*. Retrieved August 31, 2010, from http://www.mojopac.com

Samy Kamkar. (2010). Evercookie -- Never forget. *Evercookie - virtually irrevocable persistent cookies*. Retrieved February 15, 2011, from http://samy.pl/evercookie/

Schroeder, S. (2009). Are you sure those photos have really been deleted? *Mashable – The Social Media Guide*. Retrieved August 31, 2010, from http://mashable.com/2009/05/21/photos-deleted-facebook/

Singhal, A. (2009). Relevance meets the real-time web. *Official Google Blog.* Retrieved August 31, 2010, from http://googleblog.blogspot.com/2009/12/relevance-meets-real-time-web.html

Soltani, A., Canty, S., Mayo, Q., Thomas, L., & Hoofnagle, C. J. (2009). *Flash cookies and privacy.* Social Science Research Network. Retrieved August 31, 2010, from http://papers.ssrn.com/sol3/papers.cfm?abstract_id=1446862

Stamm, S. (2010). Plugging the CSS history leak. *The Mozilla Blog*. Retrieved August 31, 2010, from http://blog.mozilla.com/security/2010/03/31/plugging-the-css-history-leak/

Szabó, M. D., & Székely, I. (2005). Privacy and data protection at the workplace in Hungary. In Nouwt, S., & de Vries, B. R. (Eds.), *Reasonable expectations of privacy? Eleven country reports on camera surveillance and workplace privacy* (pp. 249–284). The Hague, The Netherlands: T. M. C. Asser Press, IT & Law Series. doi:10.1007/978-90-6704-589-6_10

The Guardian Project. (2010). Open-source mobile security. *The Guardian Project*. Retrieved February 15, 2011, from https://guardianproject.info

TrueCrypt Foundation. (2010). *TrueCrypt downloads*. TrueCrypt – Free Open-Source On-The-Fly Disk Encryption Software. Retrieved August 31, 2010, from http://www.truecrypt.org/downloads

Wang, Y., & Kobsa, A. (2009). Privacy in online social networking at workplace. In *Proc. of International Conference on Computational Science and Engineering, 2009, CSE '09* (pp. 975-978). Washington, DC: IEEE Computer Society. doi:10.1109/CSE.2009.438

What They Know. (2010). What They Know. *WSJ Blogs*. Retrieved February 15, 2011, from http://blogs.wsj.com/wtk/

Whisper Systems. (2010). *RedPhone, TextSecure*. Whisper Systems. Retrieved August 31, 2010, from http://whispersys.com

Wondracek, G., Holz, T., Kirda, E., & Kruegel, C. (2010). A practical attack to de-anonymize social network users. In *Proc. of IEEE Symposium on Security and Privacy, 2010* (pp. 223-238). Washington, DC: IEEE Computer Society.

Wood, M. (2010). Google Buzz: Privacy nightmare. *CNet News*. Retrieved August 31, 2010, from http://news.cnet.com/8301-31322_3-10451428-256.html

ADDITIONAL READING

Besmer, A., & Lipford, H. (2009). Tagged photos: concerns, perceptions, and protections. In *Proc. of the 27th international conference extended abstracts on Human factors in computing systems* (pp. 4585-4590), Boston, MA, USA: ACM Press.

Blacksheep (2010). BlackSheep – Firefox Add-on. *Zscaler Cloud Security*. Retrieved February 15, 2011, from http://www.zscaler.com/blacksheep.html

Bonneau, J., Anderson, J., & Danezis, G. (2009). Prying Data out of a Social Network. In *Proc. of the International Conference on Advances in Social Network Analysis and Mining, 2009* (pp. 249-254), Washington, DC, USA: IEEE Computer Society.

DiMicco, J. M., & Millen, D. R. (2007). Identity management: multiple presentations of self in facebook. In *Proc. of the International ACM conference on Supporting group work, 2007* (pp. 383-386), Sanibel Island, Florida, USA: ACM Press.

Duffy, M. K., Ganster, D. C., & Pagon, M. (2002). Social Undermining in the Workplace. *Academy of Management Journal*, *45*(2), 331–351. doi:10.2307/3069350

Firesheep (2010). Firesheep. *Firesheep*. Retrieved February 15, 2011, from http://codebutler.github.com/firesheep/

Franz, E., Groba, C., Springer, T., & Bergmann, M. (2008). A Comprehensive Approach for Context-dependent Privacy Management. In *Proc. of Third International Conference on Availability, Reliability and Security* (pp. 903-910), Washington, DC, USA: IEEE Computer Society.

Franz, E., & Liesebach, K. (2009). Supporting Local Aliases as Usable Presentation of Secure Pseudonyms. In *Proc. of the 6th International Conference on Trust, Privacy and Security in Digital Business TrustBus* (pp. 22-31), Linz, Austria: Springer-Verlag, 2009.

Goldberg, I. (2002). Privacy-enhancing technologies for the Internet, II: Five years later. In *Proc. of Privacy Enhancing Technologies workshop*.

Gross, R., & Acquisti, A. (2005). Information revelation and privacy in online social networks. In *Proc. of the ACM workshop on Privacy in the electronic society, 2005* (pp. 71-80), Alexandria, VA, USA: ACM Press.

Guha, S., Francis, P., & Tang, K. (2009). The NYOB official site. *NOYB: Posting Secret Messages on the Web*. Retrieved August 31, 2010, from http://adresearch.mpi-sws.org/noyb.html

Gulyás, G. Gy. (2009), Design of an Anonymous Instant Messaging Service. In *Proc. of the Fourth Privacy Enhancing Technologies Convention* (pp. 34-40), Dresden, Germany: Technical University of Dresden.

Hakkila, J., & Kansala, I. (2004). Role based privacy applied to context-aware mobile applications. In *Proc. of IEEE International Conference on Systems, Man and Cybernetics, 2004*, Washington, DC, USA: IEEE Computer Society.

Hansen, M., Schwartz, A., & Cooper, A. (2008). Privacy and Identity Management. *IEEE Security and Privacy*, *6*(2), 38–45. doi:10.1109/MSP.2008.41

Irani, D., Webb, S., Li, K., & Pu, C. (2009). Large Online Social Footprints – An Emerging Threat. In *Proc. of the International Conference on Computational Science and Engineering – Volume 03, 2009* (pp. 271-276), Washington, DC, USA: IEEE Computer Society.

Jendricke, U., & Gerd tom Markotten, D. (2000). Usability meets security – The Identity-Manager as your Personal Security Assistant for the Internet. In *Proc. of the 16th Annual Computer Security Applications Conference* (pp. 334-344), New Orleans, USA: IEEE Computer Society.

Nissenbaum, H. (2004). Privacy as Contextual Integrity. *Washington Law Review (Seattle, Wash.)*, *79*(1), 2004.

Oreilly, T. (2007). What is Web 2.0: Design Patterns and Business Models for the Next Generation of Software. *Communications & Strategies*, (1), 17-38.

Patil, S., & Kobsa, A. (2004). *Instant Messaging and Privacy* (pp. 85–88). Leeds, U.K.: Proc. of The Human-Computer Interaction.

Reichenbach, M., Damker, H., Federrath, H., & Rannenberg, K. (1997). Individual Management of Personal Reachability in Mobile Communication. In *Proc. of IFIP/SEC'97 13th International Information Security Conference*, Copenhagen, Denmark.

Rezgui, A., Bouguettaya, A., & Eltoweissy, M. Y. (2003). Privacy on the Web: Facts, Challenges, and Solutions. *IEEE Security and Privacy*, *6*(1), 40–49.

Sweeney, L. (2002). k-anonymity: a model for protecting privacy. *International Journal of Uncertainty. Fuzziness and Knowledge-Based Systems*, *10*(5), 557–570. doi:10.1142/S0218488502001648

Tootoonchian, A., Saroiu, S., Ganjali, Y., & Wolman, A. (2009). Lockr: better privacy for social networks. In *Proc. 5th International Conference on emerging Network Experiments and Technologies (CoNEXT)* (pp. 169–180). Rome, Italy: ACM Press. doi:10.1145/1658939.1658959

Zheleva, E., & Getoor, L. (2008). *How friendship links and group memberships affect the privacy of individuals in social networks*. Technical report.

Zheleva, E., & Getoor, L. (2009). To join or not to join: the illusion of privacy in social networks with mixed public and private user profiles. In *Proc. of the 18th international conference on World wide web* (pp. 531-540), Madrid, Spain: ACM Press.

KEY TERMS AND DEFINITIONS

Anonymizing Network: It works as a chain of proxies sitting between two communicating parties to provide anonymity for the sender, the receiver, or both. On the web, the purpose of these networks is to provide anonymity towards the service provider (or some other third parties) by hiding their users' IP addresses.

Anonymous Web Browser: A complex application or a web service that enables the user to access web pages anonymously. Anonymized users cannot be identified, tracked, profiled on web pages, and their presence cannot be linked to previous sessions.

Identity Separation: A single user creating two or more virtual identities with unlinkable attribute sets. In practice, the user relates her actions to these identities respectively by considering maintaining unlinkability.

Privacy-Enhancing Identity Management or PIDM: Its goal is to provide flexible control over the related data and meta data of the user's identities.

Privacy Enhancing Technologies or PETs: Computer applications, services or technologies that allow their users to protect their privacy, and provide access control and management on the data provided to the different actors they get involved with. PETs should especially provide protection over confidential and personally identifiable information.

Profiling: Collecting information on individuals. Its purpose is chiefly pursuing business benefits (e.g., through targeted advertising or dynamic pricing).

Pseudonymous Identification: An entity (i.e., a user) that has an identifier like a series of numbers, or a hexadecimal code is said to be identified with pseudonymous identifiers.

Social Network: An online service that allows individuals to build networks by creating relationship links toward each other, and also to interact with the community through these links.

Chapter 8
Identity and Access Management Architectures with a Focus on User Initiative

Takao Kojima
Institute of Information Security, Japan

Yukio Itakura
Institute of Information Security, Japan

ABSTRACT

Herein we propose the concept of "Identity and Access Management Architectures" comprising a policy-oriented management system that enables the utilization of user identity-related data. This policy-oriented management system encourages users to take the initiative in providing their own identity-related data and encourages awareness of the usage of such data by entities. This Architecture is designed to allow users to initiate "user policies" for identity-related data protection (user intention providing user data), just as entities have policies describing their intention to consume the data.

We have developed a "Privacy Policy Matching Engine" as a component of the Identity and Access Management Architectures. This engine enables the matching of a user's intention to provide his/her identity-related data with an entity's own privacy policy. Also, it automatically analyzes the policies with a focus on the types and handling method for identity-related data.

INTRODUCTION

With the recent explosion in the use of the Internet, many users now enjoy browsing corporate websites or online shopping in daily life. The majority of users, however, are unaware of the unfettered use of identity-related data that they provide to business entities. Despite business entities openly declaring their privacy policies, in most cases, users fail to understand of these privacy policies or just ignore them.

In this chapter, we propose the use of a new user support tool, "Privacy Policy Matching Engine".

DOI: 10.4018/978-1-61350-498-7.ch008

The aim of this engine is to encourage users to take the initiative in selecting business entities that users feel comfortable with. By, simply matching users' own policies with entitys' privacy policies. This 'engine' provides the user policy support feature and automatic collection and analysis feature. These two features give users "increased awareness" and "free choice of entities whom to connect with."

We describe the concept of the Privacy Policy Matching Engine and how it works as a component of the Identity and Access Management Architectures and examine the prototype for implementation.

BACKGROUND

Security and privacy issues in identity-related data management play an essential role in cloud computing. In particular, it is very important to define the right means for managing such data based on policies in order to comply with privacy-related standards and regulations. As a consequence, the identity management market—or identity and access management (IAM) market—is forecasted to grow from nearly $2.6 billion in 2006 to more than $12.3 billion in 2014 (including revenues from both products and implementation services) (Forrester, 2007). The cloud computing market which stood at $36 billion in 2008 is expected to reach $160.2 billion by 2015. Market growth is fuelled by the ease of information access made possible by the cloud (WinterGreen Research, Inc, 2009). The area of identity management has been addressed as part of the Seoul Declaration of the Future of the Internet Economy (2008/06) (OECD, 2008) and US President's Cyberspace Policy review (Whitehouse, 2009).

However, despite the fact that legal systems regarding privacy protection and personal information distribution, such as the OECD's Eight Principles (OECD, 1980), have been progressing on a global scale and the fact that most entities openly declare their privacy policies, the majority of users tend to just click the "I Agree" button without understanding the underlying details. Even though such policies are posted on websites where users can easily access them, the details are often too difficult for general users to comprehend and many contain technical jargon.

Therefore, we have developed the "Privacy Policy Matching Engine" as a component of the Identity and Access Management Architectures. The Privacy Policy Matching Engine enables users to provide their data as intended according to one's own policies.

MAIN FOCUS OF THE CHAPTER

Issues, Controversies, Problems

The majority of users tend to just click the "I agree" button when accessing entities' websites, with little or no regard to their own privacy protection.

Users' Unwareness for Identity-Related Data

Users can have "consciously provided information" and "unconsciously provided information." Although the information is recognized as being effective in some fields, such as behavior targeting advertisement (Hayashi, K., 2007; Oda, K., N. Takahiro, S. Suda, & T. Yukawa., 2007), users have extremely low awareness when it comes to explicitly managing their intentions to provide their information, and what's more, there is no tool to assist users in managing their intentions properly.

Usability of Privacy Policies

Entities' privacy policies are posted on websites where users can easily access them, however, these policies are often too difficult for general users to comprehend and many contain technical jargon.

Undeveloped Legal Framework for Users

"The Recommendation of the Council Concerning Guidelines Governing the Protection of Privacy and Transborder Flows of Personal Data," adopted by the Organization for Economic Cooperation and Development (OECD) in 1980, contains the OECD's Eight Principles. These include: Collection Limitation Principle, Use Limitation Principle and others. A legal notice, provided by an entity according to national laws complying with the OECD's Eight Principles, which describes the intention to consume identity-related data, represents a privacy policy. It describes information about the use of identity-related data, such as what identity-related data is collected and how the identity data may be used. However, such principles are entity focused. There is no framework to help users comprehend entitys' privacy policies.

Support Tools

As a guideline for policies with easy-to-understand and straight-to-the-point expressions, several systems exist which can help users analyze, investigate and evaluate policies; these include the TRUSTe Privacy Seal Program and the Privacy Ratings (Privacy Rating Jimukyoku & A.F. Westin, ed., 2006). The seal of trust, however, evaluates only the personal information handling systems. Thus, users cannot understand an entity's intention to consume based solely on the seal alone. In addition, the Privacy Ratings merely evaluates the privacy policies, which means it is impossible for users to understand "the intention to consume" via this service alone.

Solutions and Recommendations

"The Identity and Access Management Architectures" are distributed systems for the internet, which are constructed based on both consumers' (entitys') information policies and providers' (users') information policies for establishing confidence in the use of identity-related data. They include providing identity-related data, consuming identity-related data and a method of assurance level of identity-related data.

Design: Development Concept behind the Privacy Policy Matching Engine

Allowing Users to also have Policies

Allowing users to have their own policies, just as entities have their own privacy policies, enables users to clarify their intention to provide identity-related data, and to search entity policies from a user point of view. Also, allowing users to adopt their own policies depending on the situation and according to the purpose and or significance of services offered by entities, helping users enjoy a full range of services.

Enabling Automatic Collection and Analysis via a Program

The program automatically collects and analyzes privacy policies on the basis of user's policies.

User Experience

Raising Users' Awareness of Provision

Describing users' policies assists users to recognize and control their "consciously provided information" and "unconsciously provided information" (Figure 1).

Enabling Users to have Free Choice of Entities

Visualized matches and mismatches between the intention to provide and the intention to consume enables users to independently receive services after evaluating entities, without the threat of

Figure 1. Consciously or unconsciously provided identity-related data

Consciously Provided Information			Unconsciously Provided Information	
Name	**Actual Example**	**Provision Timing**	**Name**	**Provision Timing**
Attribute data	Address, name, email address	When submitted	IP Address Cookie	Collected by server from terminal at user access
Preference data	Search keyword		Access history	Created by server at user access
Authorization data	ID, Password		Purchase history Settlement history	Created by enterprise at user access

Figure 2. System architecture

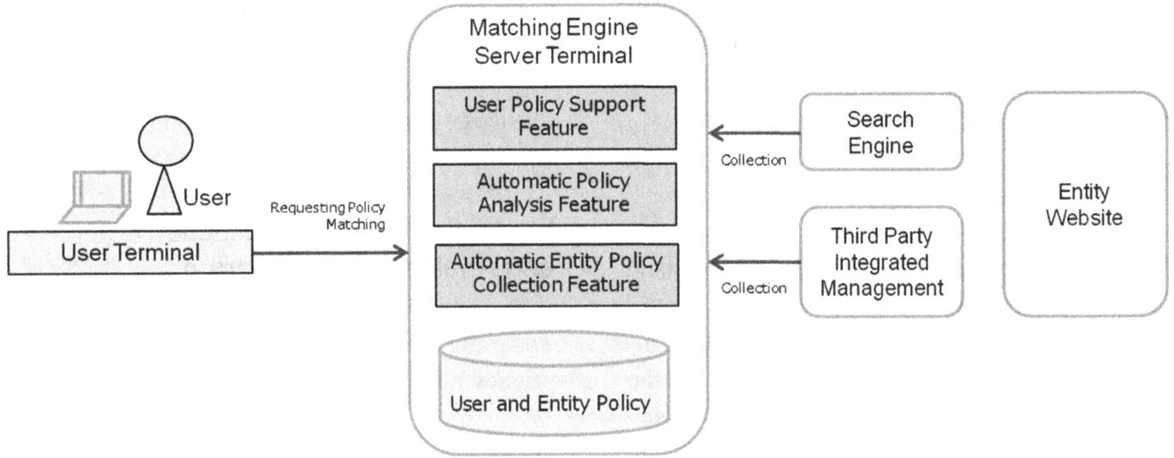

identity theft and exploitation of identity-related data. Using users' policies according to the purpose or significance of services offered by entities allows users to enjoy various services.

Concept

The concept of the system is shown in Figure 2. The Privacy Policy Matching Engine is a user support tool. The steps are as follows:

1. Inquiry regarding user policy.
2. Collect entity policy.
3. Automatic analysis.
4. Matching result response.

Features of the Privacy Policy Matching Engine are as follows:

- *User Policy Support Feature:* a feature that helps user develop user policy.
- *Automatic Entity Policy Collection Feature:*a feature that collect entity's privacy policy.

Figure 3. Physical layout

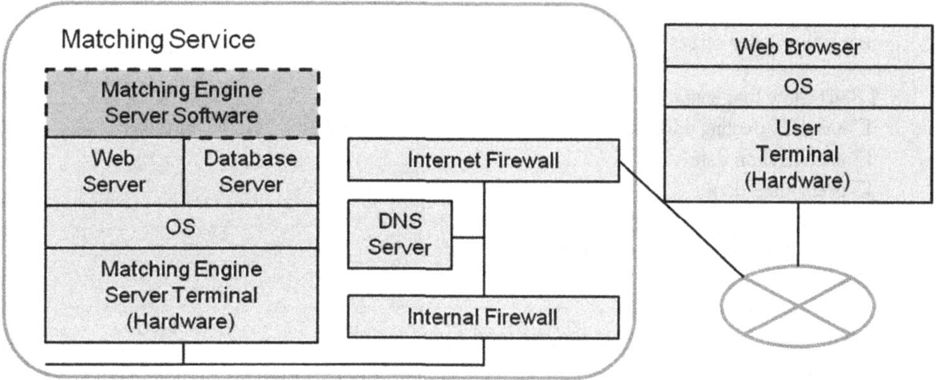

- *Automatic Policy Analysis Feature*: a feature that can analyze how to match user policy and entity's privacy policy.

Implementation

In this paper, the Japanese language is adopted as the natural language. For other languages, changing the morphological analysis environment and analytic function algorithm realizes the multilingualization.

Physical Layout

The physical layout of the system is shown in Figure 3.

- The Matching Engine, is connected to the Internet via Internet Firewall. User Terminal is connected directly. DNS Server is located on the DMZ segment between Internet Firewall and Internal Firewall.
- Hardware, related software (OS,Web Server,Database Server,Web Browser) are installed.
- Server Software is installed for the Matching Engine. The software is developed by Microsoft Visual Studio® 2005 with xdoc2txt (Hishida., 2007) and Unidic-chasen (DEN Yasuharu, YAMADA Atsushi, OGURA Hideki, KOISO Hanae, & OGISO Toshinobu., 2007) as a morphological analysis environment.
- Hardware and software work correctly and reliably.

User Policy Support Feature

User Policy Entry Screen

Figure 4 shows the entry screen. This screen is designed in the form of a questionnaire so that users can decide whether or not to provide their identity-related data (Figure 1) and select their intentions to provide the items in the user policy. The user checks checkboxes closest to his/her intention to provide the identity-related data. The created user policy is saved as a new file (named New user policy in Figure 4) when the selection is done. The user can create more than one provider's policy. The created user policies are stored in the policy analysis database.

Search Screen

In the Search screen (Figure 5), the user enters any given enterprise name in the text box, selects one of the user policies to apply from the policy pull-down list, and then click on the Search button. Users are allowed to change the user policy at will

Figure 4. User policy entry screen

user policy entry screen User policy name: My Shopping Policy Submit

I don't allow that entities collect:
☐ name ☐ posting address ☐ email address ☐ phone number ☐ sex ☐ birthday
☐ authorization data
☐ preference data
☐ ip address ☐ access log ☐ cookie / web beacon
☐ purchase history / settlement history
☐ sensitive data

I don't allow that entities collect and use for the purpose of:
☐ advertising ☐ questionare / survey ☐ enhance services and products
☐ providing services and products that I order ☐ customer support
☐ sharing/providing to the third party

I require that entities must have privacy policy:
☐ definition of identity-related data ☐ the purpose of collect and use
☐ sharing/providing to the third party ☐ management / data accuracy / security
☐ disclosure / correction ☐ contact ☐ improvement / confirmation

☐ collection content ☐ collection of information except identity-related data
☐ identity-related data of employee ☐ identity-related data of underage

☐ complied law ☐ qualified governing authority ☐ privacy seal
☐ policy change history ☐ exception

2010 Privacy Policy Matching Engine Ver.0.2

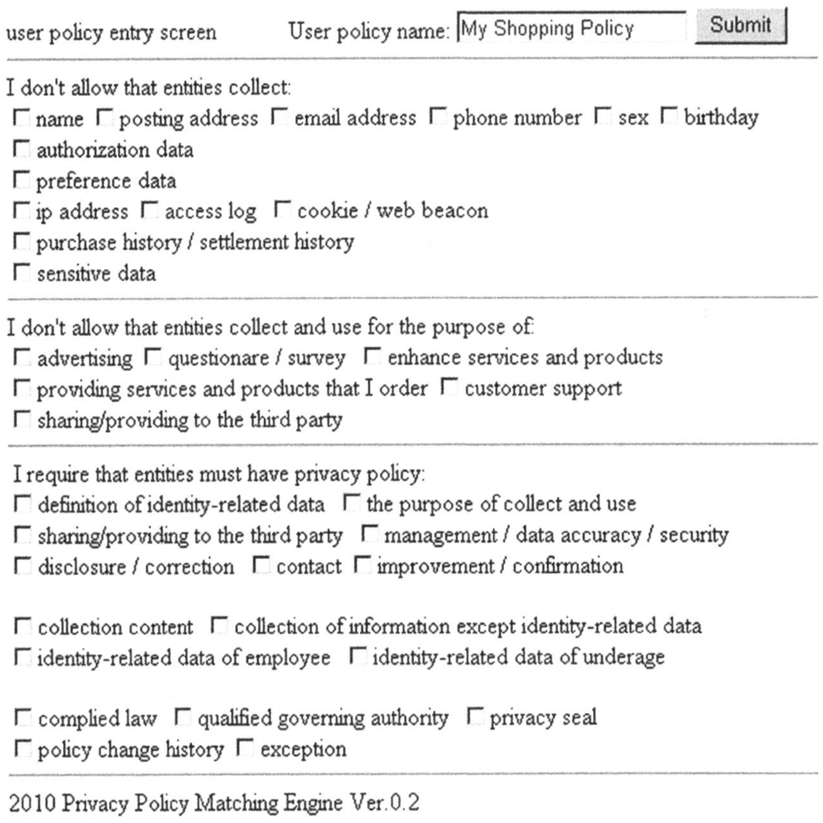

or find the most appropriate entity in accordance with the analysis results.

Automatic Entity Policy Collection Feature

The automatic entity policy collection feature enables to download and store entity policies in a policy analysis database through the entity policy download module.

- The module for the Internet web site (Natural Language Policy)

While the entity policy download module (which adopts the use of keywords specified to collect policies) is in operation, entity policies are downloaded from websites by using a search engine and the downloaded policies are inserted into the policy analysis database.We used ebot Lite (Goto., 2007) and Google Search Engine (http://www.google.com/) as an entity's policy download module. The downloaded privacy policies in PDF format are inserted into the policy analysis database.

- For third-party Integrated Management (Machine Readable Language Policy)

the module is based on Liberty Alliance Project IGF (Identity Governance Framework.) as a standard of Identity Federation. Machine readable language policy is based on AAPML and XACML (Moses, T., ed., 2005).

Figure 5. Search screen

Search Screen Sample Net Store Search Policy My Shopping Policy

Results **1** - **3** of **3** for **Sample Net Store**

Sample Store
gifts and accessories including nuts, chocolates, coffee, T-Shirts, sarongs and gift baskets.
www.sample-store.com/
Matching result: ■■■■■
Privacy Policy

Sample Net Shop
E-commerce store with built in shopping cart software within minutes just by pointing & clicking. With our secured shopping cart its easy and fast.
www.samplenetshop.com/
Matching result: ■■■□□
UnMatching Attribute: Purpose of Use(not found)
UnMatching Identity-related Data: Address(required)
Privacy Policy

Sample internetStore
Enjoy our European-style street market where the scents of gourmet ...
www.sampleinternetstore.com/
Matching result: ■■□□□
UnMatching Attribute: Purpose of Use(not found), Contact(not found)
UnMatching Identity-related Data: Address(required), Birthday(required)
Privacy Policy

2010 Privacy Policy Matchng Engine Ver.0.2

Automatic Policy Analysis Feature

The Automatic Analysis Feature has three phases, structuration, language analysis and evaluation.

Structuration Phase

Structuration phase for natural language policy: recognize the data file structure (format) of entity policies in order to extract a text portion which forms the main body. Using morphological analysis, natural language is structured applying rules of grammar. For Japanese, a sentence is segmented into separate words to recognize and extract various parameters related to word forms (Nagao, M. & M. Iri., 1981).

In this process, for example, a Japanese sentence in a privacy policy (which means "we will not provide the personal information to any third party") is segmented into 11 morphemes and the information about each token, including pronunciations, root forms, parts of speech, conjugation patterns and conjugated forms, is output, as shown in Figure 6.

1. Converts privacy policy PDF files to text files using xdoc2txt.
2. Strips newline characters and space characters from the converted text file.
3. Outputs the result into an XML file using Unidic-chasen.

Figure 6. Output example of morphological analysis

String	Pronunciation	Root form	Part of speech	Conjugation pattern	Conjugated form
個人 personal	kojin	個人	noun-common noun-general		
情報 information	jouhou	情報	noun-common noun-general		
を (Japanese particle)	wo	を	particle-case particle		
第三 third	daisan	第三	noun-common noun-general		
者 party	sya	者	suffix-noun-general		
に to	ni	に	particle-case particle		
提供 provide	teikyou	提供	noun-common noun-verbal noun		
いたし do kenjougo (humble)	itasu	致す	verb-ancil ary-verb	consonant-stem verb-sagyou type	conjugated form-general
ませ will	masu	ます	auxiliary verb	auxiliary verb-masu	imperfective form-general
ん not	zu	ず	auxiliary verb	auxiliary verb-nu	predicative form-N sound
. –		.	punctuation-full stop		

Figure 7. Analytic functions

Function	Action	Actual Example
`DoYesNo` function	Returns whether a declinable word of the sentence including the target word is affirmative or negative.	"manage" / "do not manage"
`CollectYesNo` function	Returns whether a declinable word of the sentence including the target word and the word "syutoku" (means "collect") is affirmative or negative.	"collect cookies" / "do not collect cookies"
`Exception` function	Returns a sentence that is an exception against the key clause including the target word.	"... not provide to any third party..." vs. "..., except for cases..."
`Subject` function	Returns a sentence that expresses the purpose of use against the key clause including the target word	"we will use the personal information..." vs. "...for the purpose of ..."
`Content` function	Returns the parts that expresses the content of the key clause including the target word	"Personal Information, as used herein,..." vs. "... refers to any information regarding..."

Language Analysis Phase

Language analysis phase for natural language policy: recognize and extract various parameters related to an entity's intention to consume data from the text portion, and then output the results as a combination of attributes and attribute values. Figure 7 shows analytic functions for language analysis. Key features of the analytic functions are:

- Detecting attributes and attribute values from natural language.
- Identifying a portion showing the conclusion of sentences.

The analytic functions analyze a target word in the text portion, for example, to determine whether it is affirmative or negative, and then returns the attribute value of the consumer's policy. Figure 7 shows the correspondence between attributes of consumer's policies and analytic functions.

The main function for language analysis opens the XML file created in the Structuration phase, and then calls an analytic function(s) which has one or more arguments and corresponds to each of the attribute keywords acting as arguments. (Figure 8) The main function outputs the results returned from the analytic function in the tables of Figure 10 and Figure 11 and inserts the results into the policy analysis database. Figure 9 shows the DoYesNo function algorithm among the analytic functions as an example. The algorism first searches for an attribute keyword specified as argument in the XML file. When the attribute keyword is found, it begins a search in the rest of the sentence for a word whose part of speech is a verb or an auxiliary verb and the conjugation pattern is a conjugated form. When the word is detected, it then searches for an auxiliary verb: "nu" or "nai" (means "not" or "never"). When a full stop is found, "affirmative" is returned as the return value if the detection count of auxiliary verb, "nu" or "nai", is 0 or 2. If the count is 1, "negative" is returned. If a full stop is found during the search, the process starts searching for the attribute keyword all over again. When a mark indicating the end of the XML file is found, "unknown" is returned as the return value.

Evaluation Phase

Evaluation phase for natural language policy and machine readable policy: evaluate the results of comparison between the entity policies and user policies and then present the results to the user. The main function for analysis opens provider's policy record and consumer's policy record in the policy analysis database and then compare with the attributes listed in Figure 7 as the arguments. The main function outputs the result returned from the comparative function. (Figure 5)

Figure 8. Correspondence between attributes and analytic functions

Attribute	Keyword Function	Keyword Search	CollectYesNo	DoYesNo	Exception	Subject	Content
Definition of identity-related data	"Personal information" refers to						✔
Purpose of use	purpose of use					✔	
Sharing/Providing to third party	share, provide			✔	✔		
Management/Data accuracy/Security	manage, personality, security			✔	✔		
Disclosure/Correction	disclose, correct			✔	✔		
Contact	contact			✔			
Collection content	(under discussion)						✔
Collection of information except identity-related data	except personal information		✔		✔		
Employee	employee information		✔				
Underage	underage		✔				
Improvement/Confirmation	improve, confirm			✔			
Questionnaire survey	questionnaire survey			✔		✔	
Cookie/Web beacon	Cookie, beacon		✔				
IP address	IP address		✔				
Access log	log		✔				
Complied law	Personal Information Protection Law, Safe Harbor Rule, Act on the Protection of Personal Information	✔					
Qualified governing authority	the Ministry of Economy, Trade and Industry, the Financial Services Agency, the Ministry of Health, Labour and Welfare	✔					
Privacy seal	Privacy seal		✔				
Policy change history	change history, revision	✔					
Exception	however, except				✔		

Figure 9. DoYesNo function

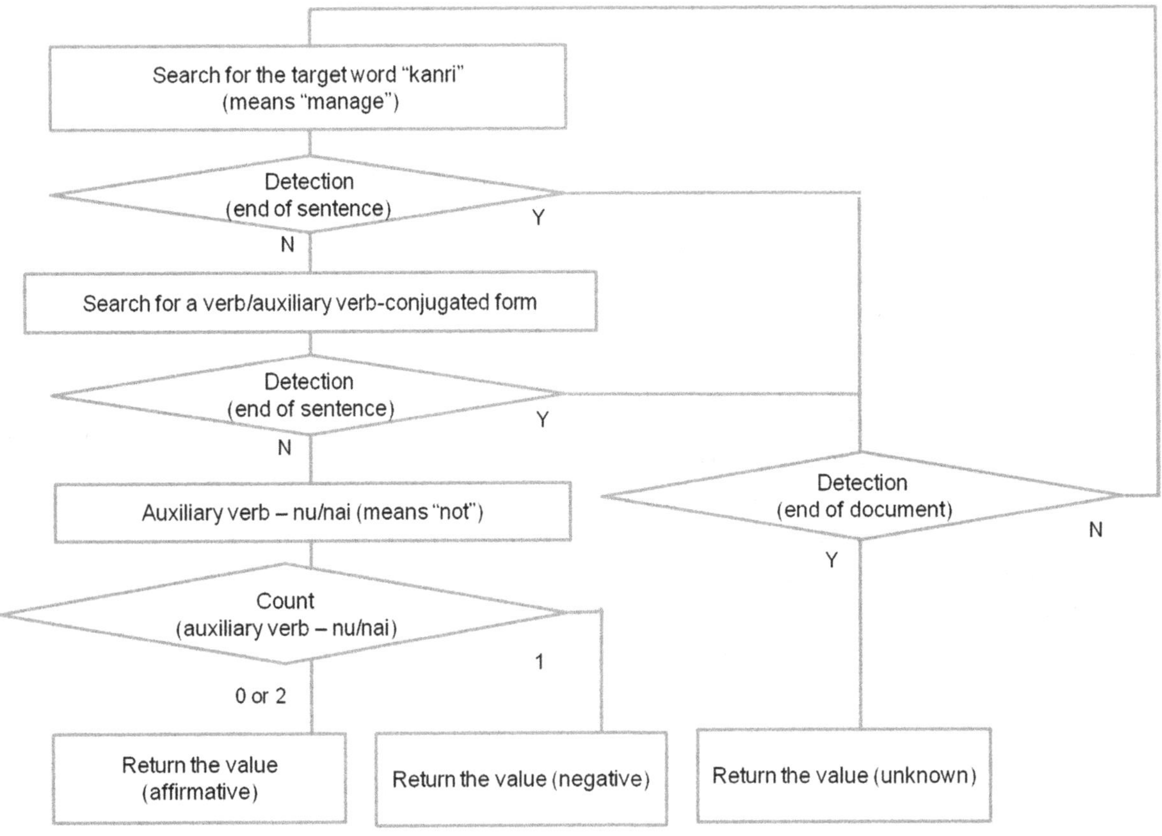

RELATED WORK

Policy in Computer Systems

In a computer system, policy is the basis for controlling the behavior of the system. Policy enforcement is to control the behavior of the system to comply with the policy. Policy enforcement consists of policy markup language and access control model.

Capability of Privacy Policy Markup Language

Policy markup languages in machine readable language which deals with identity-related information, are developed such as XACML (Access Control Markup Language) for policy enforcement (Moses, T., ed., 2005). and P3P (Platform for Privacy Preferences) for user agent (Wenning, R. & Cranor L., 2007).

Decision-Making Support System

As a protocol ,for decision-making of agent software according to privacy preferences that a user specified (Jensen, C. & Potts, C., 2004), by comparing privacy policies automatically collected and translated by a user agent.

Machine Readable Policy

Although a P3P-enabled search engine, called Privacy Finder (Cranor, L. F., Guduru, P., & Arjula, M., 2006), was proposed by L. Cranor, the penetration rate of P3P is only about 10% even in

Figure 10. Language analysis result (first part)

Attribute / Function	Keyword Search	CollectYesNo	DoYesNo
Definition of identity-related data	—	—	—
Purpose of use	—	—	—
Sharing/Providing to third party	—	—	do
Management/Data accuracy/ Security	—	—	do
Disclosure/Correction	—	—	do not
Contact	—	—	found
Collection content	—	—	—
Collection of information except identity related data	—	unknown	—
Employee	—	unknown	—
Underage	—	unknown	—
Improvement/confirmation	—	—	—
Questionnaire survey	—	—	unknown
Cookie /Web beacon	—	unknown	—
IP address	—	unknown	—
Access log	—	unknown	—
Complied law	found	—	—
Qualified governing authority	found	—	—
Privacy seal	—	unknown	—
Policy change history	not found	—	—
Exception	—	—	—

Figure 11. Language analysis result (latter part)

Attribute / Function	Exception	Subject	Content
Definition of identity-related data	—	—	not found
Purpose of use	—	data	—
Sharing/Providing to third party	data	—	—
Management/Data accuracy/Security	not found	—	—
Disclosure/Correction	data	—	—
Collection content	—	—	not found
Collection of information except identity-related data	not found	—	—
Questionnaire survey	—	not found	—
Exception	not found	—	—

the United States (Egelman, S., Cranor, L. F., & Chowdhury, A., 2006) and P3P privacy policies are infrequently used in comparison to natural language privacy policies. This situation makes it difficult to give users a sufficient number of search results. Publication of natural language privacy policies is required, whereas P3P privacy policies are not required to be released. Therefore, we cannot expect P3P will be widely used, and do not have any choice but to read the natural language privacy policies to understand entities' intention to consume.

FUTURE RESEARCH DIRECTIONS

Policy Negotiation

As an extension of the evaluation capability, there will be a growing demand for a user-support system that is able to provide compromise solutions even if the evaluation result does not satisfy the user's intention. For this to be feasible, we suggest a negotiation model incorporating the multi-agent system proposed in the artificial intelligence field (Babaguchi, N. & S. Yamada, 1999; Namatame, 1999). In this model, using the policy analysis database as a knowledge base, the agents equipped with inference mechanism conduct multiple negotiations to interactively propose an optimized compromise solution to the user. This realizes the match of consumer's policies and provider's policies with mismatched intentions in the environment that privacy policies are frequently updated (Itakura, Y., T. Kojima, & I. Miyaki, 2008).

The current system only evaluates whether a consumer's policy satisfies a user's intention to provide his/her identity-related data, not performs a search proposing compromise solutions to the user. A start has already been made at designing a system to give users compromise solutions, with the multi-agent system introduced in the evaluation phase to realize negotiations by the agents based on the contract net protocol.

Vendor Relationship Management

Allowing users to choose an appropriate enterprise entity as intended by making use of "Privacy Policy Matching Engine" will be able to be applied in realizing Vendor Relationship Management (VRM): the customer controls his or her relationship with vendors (Doc Searls, 2007).

CONCLUSION

The "Identity and Access Management Architectures" are designed to allow users to have policies like entities do. It is also designed to have users deposit their data and policies into the third party data storage organization, so that users can manage such data in exchange for cheque tickets.

The "Privacy Policy Matching Engine" is deployed as an operational support tool for data and policies according to user intention, as a component of "Identity and Access Management Architectures."

The Privacy Policy Matching Engine enhances unified management of user data and user policies by analyzing the user policies that are kept by the third party data storage organization.

Finally, the Privacy Policy Matching Engine analyzes the difficult policies of entities and provides matching results in order to help users select entity websites with minimum effort.

REFERENCES

Babaguchi, N., & Yamada, S. (1999). *Jinkou chinou no kiso* [Basic of Artificial Intelligence]. Shokodo Co., Ltd.

Cranor, L. F., Guduru, P., & Arjula, M. (2006). User interfaces for privacy agents. *ACM Trans. Comput.-Hum. Interact., 13*(2), 135-178. DOI=http://doi.acm.org/10.1145/1165734.1165735

Egelman, S., Cranor, L. F., & Chowdhury, A. (2006). An analysis of P3P-enabled web sites among top-20 search results. In *Proceedings of the 8th international Conference on Electronic Commerce: The New E-Commerce: innovations For Conquering Current Barriers, Obstacles and Limitations To Conducting Successful Business on the Internet, ICEC '06, vol. 156,* Fredericton, New Brunswick, Canada, August 13 - 16, 2006, (pp.197-207). New York, NY: ACM. DOI=http://doi.acm.org/10.1145/1151454.1151492

Forrester. (2007). *Identity management market forecast: 2007 to 2014*. Retrieved from http://www.forrester.com/rb/Research/identity_management_market_forecast_2007_to_2014/q/id/43842/t/2

Goto. (2007). *Ebot Lite*. Retrieved from http://www.listbrowser.com/

Hayashi, K. (2007). *Saishin netto koukoku no shikumi* [System of Latest Net Advertisement]. Nippon Jitsugyo Publishing.

Hishida. (2007). *xdoc2txt*. Retrieved from http://www31.ocn.ne.jp/~h_ishida/xdoc2txt.html

Itakura, Y., Kojima, T., & Miyaki, I. (2008). *A proposal of an architecture for effective utilization of personal information* (in Japanese). The 2008 Symposium on Cryptography and Information Security Miyazaki, Japan, Jan. 22-25, 2008, The Institute of Electronics, Information and Communication Engineers.

Jensen, C., & Potts, C. (2004). Privacy policies as decision-making tools: an evaluation of online privacy notices. In *Proceedings of the SIGCHI Conference on Human Factors in Computing Systems CHI '04*, Vienna, Austria, April 24 - 29, 2004 (pp. 471-478). New York, NY: ACM. DOI=http://doi.acm.org/10.1145/985692.985752

Moses, T. (Ed.). (2005). *eXtensible access control markup language* (XACML), version 2.0. OASIS Standard, February 1, 2005. Retrieved from http://www.oasisopen.org/committees/tc_home.php?wg_abbrev=xacml

Nagao, M., & Iri, M. (1981). *Iwanami jouhou kagaku 23 - Kazu to siki no bun no syori* [Iwanami Lecture of Information Sciences 23 - Processing of sentence of number and expression]. Iwanami Shoten.

Namatame. (1999). *A. Maruchi eijento to hukuzatukei* [Multiagent and Complex System]. Morikita Publishing Co., Ltd.

Oda, K., Takahiro, N., Suda, S., & Yukawa, T. (2007). *Jisedai koukoku tekunorozi* [Next-generation Advertising Technology]. SOFTBANK Creative.

OECD. (1980). *OECD guidelines on the protection of privacy and transborder flows of personal data.* http://www.oecd.org/document/18/0,3343,en_2649_34255_1815186_1_1_1_1,00.html

OECD. (2008). *The Seoul Declaration of the future of the internet economy*. Retrieved from http://www.oecd.org/dataoecd/49/28/40839436.pdf

Privacy Rating Jimukyoku & Westin. A. F. (Eds.). (2006). *White paper on the privacy in Japan 2007* (in Japanese). Yano Research Institute Ltd.

Searls, D. (2007). *ProjectVRM*. Retrieved from http://cyber.law.harvard.edu/projectvrm/Main_Page.Bowman

Wenning, R., & Cranor, L. (2007). *Platform for privacy preferences (P3P)*. Retrieved from http://www.w3c.org/P3P/

Whitehouse. (2009). *US President's cyberspace policy review*. Retrieved from http://www.whitehouse.gov/assets/documents/Cyberspace_Policy_Review_final.pdf

WinterGreen Research, Inc. (2009). *Worldwide Cloud Computing market opportunities and segment forecasts 2009 to 2015*. Retrieved from http://www.researchandmarkets.com/reportinfo.asp?report_id=1071781

Yasuharu, D., Atsushi, Y., Hideki, O., Hanae, K., & Toshinobu, O. (2007). *UniDic-chasen*. Retrieved from http://www.tokuteicorpus.jp/dist/

ADDITIONAL READING

AllianceL. http://projectliberty.org/liberty/specifications_1

Attribute Authority Policy Markup Language (AAPML). http://www.oracle.com/technology/tech/standards/idm/igf/pdf/IGFAAPML-spec-08.pdf

Client Attribute Requirements Markup Language (CARML). http://www.oracle.com/technology/tech/standards/idm/igf/pdf/IGFCARML-spec-03.pdf

Directive 95/46/ec of the European Parliament and of the council of 24 October 1995 on the protection of individuals with regard to the processing of personal data and on the free movement of such data, Official Journal L281 (23/11/1995), 031-050.

enonymous.com. Privacy Ratings; http://www.coyer.com/enonymous/privacyratings.htm

George, O. M. Yee and Larry Korba, Avoiding Pitfalls in Policy-Based Privacy Management; http://iitatlns2.iit.nrc.ca/publications/nrc-49848-print_e.html

Government of Canada. Directive on Privacy Impact Assessment (PIA); http://www.tbs-sct.gc.ca/pol/doc-eng.aspx?section=text&id=18308

Japanese Industrial Standards Committee. JIS Q 15001 Personal information protection management systems (PMS); http://www.jisc.go.jp/app/pager?id=4571

Liberty Alliance Identity Governance. http://www.projectliberty.org/index.php/liberty/strategic_initiatives/identity_governance

Microsoft CardSpace. http://msdn2.microsoft.com/enus/library/aa480189.aspx

OpenI. D.http://openid.net/

Oracle Identity Governance Framework (IGF); http://www.oracle.-com/technology/tech/standards/idm/igf/index.html

Privacy and Identity Management for Europe (PRIME). http://www.prime-project.eu.org/

Reay, I., Dick, S., & Miller, J. (2009). A large-scale empirical study of P3P privacy policies: Stated actions vs. legal obligations. ACM Trans. Web 3, 2 (Apr. 2009), 1-34. DOI= http://doi.acm.org/10.1145/1513876.1513878

the TRUSTe Privacy Seal Program. http://www.truste.com/

US Department of Commerce. the U.S.-EU & Swiss Safe Harbor Frameworks; http://www.export.gov/safeharbor/

U.S. Department of Homeland Security. Privacy Impact Accessments (PIA); http://www.dhs.gov/files/publications/editorial_0511.shtm

Wikipedia. Text segmentation; http://en.wikipedia.org/wiki/Text_segmentation

Wikipedia. Natural language processing; http://en.wikipedia.org/wiki/Natural_language_processing

KEY TERMS AND DEFINITIONS

Identity-Related Data: User's personal information and attributes.

Information Provider: A user who provides his/her Identity-related Data to entities.

Information Consumer: An entity which consumes Identity-related Data. It offers services and commodities to users as a provider of services.

Privacy Policy: (1) User's policy: the user intention setting of "consciously" or "unconsciously" provided identity-related data, and (2) Entity's policy: privacy policies on an entity's website indicating the intention to consume the information.

Third Party Integrated Management: An organization which keeps identity-related data and the user's policy information, transfers it to an entity.

User Policy Matching: Users can search entities from the user's point of view. Users can also recognize and control their "consciously providing information" and "unconsciously providing information". We develop the "Privacy Policy Matching Engine" as a support tool for users.

Chapter 9
Starting the Revolution:
Implementing an Identity Management Architecture

Peter White
Charles Sturt University, Australia

ABSTRACT

The chapter argues that an enterprise should develop its own Identity Management Architecture (IdMA) before attempting any Identity Management implementation. It begins with a discussion of the development of the Reference IdMA. It also discusses the issues of how to incorporate existing enterprise workflows and processes and other specific needs of an enterprise into an IdMA. It proposes the incorporation of existing information security controls into the IdMA by the use of chokepoints to monitor identified security hotspots. The issues surrounding the privacy of personal data as well as the protection of corporate data and assets are discussed and it is shown how these issues may be addressed and included in the Reference IdMA. Finally, there is a discussion of how to include federation with other enterprises as part of the enterprise's IdMA.

INTRODUCTION

Identity management (IdM) is often seen as a purely technical solution to a problem that exists in an enterprise. As a result, many enterprises tend to design and adopt IdM solutions that result in an almost single-minded focus on the technical design and implementation. This technical focus may result in the IdM solution ignoring the organizational ecosystem that surrounds it. The outcome often appears to end with an implemented solution that is not what the enterprise really needs. It only takes a few minutes of searching in some

DOI: 10.4018/978-1-61350-498-7.ch009

of the professional forums[1] to see that many IdM implementations fail to achieve their objectives.

But, an Enterprise Architect who is attempting an IdM design finds very quickly that the current understanding of an IdM enterprise framework really depends more upon a particular vendor's implementation than on a clearly defined model. Most major vendors offer complete IdM systems. But they often offer some components of those IdM systems as separate, stand-alone systems that can be installed and later linked together into a system that can provide some IdM services. Strictly speaking, this could be potentially recognized as an implementation of a framework that allows interoperability between the components (Gamma, Helm, Johnson, & Vlissides, 2000) but it does not define a formal model of an enterprise identity management system.

There are four basic models of IdM systems: Enterprise, Distributed, Internet and Federation (White, 2009). There appears to be some disagreement in the literature over the description of these models and their characteristics (White, 2009, pp. 35-40). The literature does not appear to agree upon a formal model, framework or architecture for an enterprise IdM model. This is possibly due to the fact that the literature tends to concentrate on each technical component to the virtual exclusion of all other components, except where they are either a pre-requisite or a dependency. The effect is that each component is viewed within a very restricted and narrow context and without the holistic view required for an enterprise system. There is also a considerable focus on the description of Internet and Federation modules in the literature (Cantor & Erdos, 2002; Cantor, Hodges, Kemp, & Thompson, 2003; Jones & Cameron, 2005; Josang & Pope, 2005; Meinecke, Nussbaumer, & Gaedke, 2005; Zhu, 2007).

But this lack of a formally described enterprise or base level framework leaves most enterprises without a foundation on which to base an adequate assessment of their needs or of any proposed system. It also means that an enterprise is left with no real guide to the design of an IdM system that will meet their requirements. It seems that the current view of an Enterprise model of an identity management system depends more upon an individual vendor's implementation than on a defined model.

This problem of a clearly defined model for the design of IdM solutions leaves both practitioners and researchers without a clear and consistent foundation on which to base a design.

It is further complicated by the fact that IdM is an area that is not clearly defined either in industry or in the literature. Many people claim to know what it means, but the definitions they use are often very different and address different aspects of the IdM ecosystem. The situation with Government IdM projects in Australia can be viewed as an example of problems that arise when there is not a clear definition of aims or ecosystem at the start of a project (White, 2008).

Is it any wonder that major projects continue to fail when we, as an industry, cannot provide practitioners with a basic agreed model to build on?

What is Identity Management?

Identity Management has been defined as "the administration of an entity's digital identity so as to provide secure and controlled access to the resources that the entity is entitled to use" (White, 2009, p. 5). This definition indicates that Identity Management covers a much wider scope than is initially realized. The '*administration of an entity's digital identity*' implies that all aspects of that administration, including identification of the entity and the issuing of credentials, are part of the identity management process. It also implies the continued maintenance of the identity and its credentials throughout their life-cycles. The need to provide '*secure and controlled access*' entails not only the use of a system of authentication to ensure that only the correct identities are allowed access, but it also includes access control of the enterprises resources. This ensures that the authenticated identity only has access to those resources that it is entitled to use. The use of the phrase '*entitled to use*' further implies that there must be a system of provisioning to ensure that an identity is granted access only to the resources that it is entitled to access. This leads to the implication that a system of governance must be in place to monitor the entire process of identity management.

This definition alone starts to outline the requirements for an enterprise architecture for IdM. Windley defined identity management architecture as

"...a coherent set of standards, policies, certifications and management activities. These are aimed at providing a context for implementing a digital identity infrastructure that meets the current goals and objectives of the business, and is capable of evolving to meet future goals and objectives"(Windley, 2005, p. 134).

It is interesting to note that this definition does not specify any form of implementation of systems or even technology generally. It is a definition that includes many of the activities that will surround any technical implementation. This definition states that identity management does not just consist of a technical implementation. It also consists of the process, workflows, policies and aims of the enterprise that is implementing the architecture. This view, and definition, is at odds with most of the literature, which tends to concentrate mainly on the technical aspects of authentication and access control.

Windley uses frameworks to define the processes and workflows that are an integral part of each IdM component. The literature indicates that there has been little real development in the area of internal frameworks. The Open Group (2002) stated that there is no standard enterprise IdMA and that enterprises need to define an individual architecture to meet their own needs. But, as White et al (2007) point out "...the increasing importance of compliance with standards, combined with the need to operate with procedures that can be verified and audited, means that this stance can no longer be adopted.". Enterprises may also be required to comply with a number of highly complex, and sometimes conflicting, sets of legislation or regulation. These requirements may also be in conflict with internal security controls and requirements. Pearsons (2007) recommended that enterprises "...should strongly consider the adoption of visionary security standards, such as ISO/IEC 27001 that provide a foundation and management system guidance...". The introduction and compliance with international standards, such as ISO/IEC 27001, ISO/IEC 17799, ISO/IEC 20000, or COBIT force enterprises to examine their existing processes and procedures and to then document them in order to meet their compliance targets.

This move to compliance with standards, with its insistence on the documentation of process, implies that some processes may be considered as generic processes that are common to many enterprises. Although the process may be implemented differently in similar enterprises, the general method, or framework, remains the same. A review of the literature, as seen above, indicates that there is no existing, generally agreed framework for IdM within an enterprise (Bertino, Khan, Sandhu, & Thuraisingham, 2006; Cao, Yang, Fu, & Yang, 2010; Casassa Mont, Bramhall, & Pato, 2003; Hu, Ferraiolo, & Kuhn, 2006; 2007). This is in line with The Open Group's (2002) assertion that enterprises need to define their own individual identity management architecture.

It is apparent that the implementation of an IdM solution will introduce a set of tasks and problems that will cost an enterprise a considerable amount of time and resources to resolve. It is proposed that the use of a Reference Architecture for Identity Management will provide enterprises with a set of tools and procedures that will reduce their effort in developing a solution to this set of problems. It will further ensure that the development of the

IdM solution does not take place in isolation, but rather as part of the organizational ecosystem.

WHAT IS AN IdMA?

The description of the IdMA is of some importance to both researchers and practitioners in the field of identity management. The IdMA is designed as a Reference Architecture. Windley defines a reference architecture as

"...a diagram or set of diagrams that shows the distribution of system functions among components in the identity infrastructure and provides a topographical map for how those functions relate to each other. Reference architectures do not give the design for an actual system or even a detailed diagram of how those systems interact, but rather provide architectural guidance and best practice information for practitioners" (Windley, 2005, pp. 211-212).

This is in accord with the IEEE standard for Architectural Description of Software-Intensive Systems 1471-2000 (IEEE, 2000, p. 3) which defines architecture as

"the fundamental organization of a system, embodied in its components, their relationships to each other and the environment, and the principles governing its design and evolution".

From these definitions, we can see that the essential criteria for an architecture are:

- Fundamental organization of a system;
- Components;
- Relationships between components;
- Relationships between components and the environment;
- Principles that govern design and evolution.

The literature tends to concentrate primarily on the technical aspects of security, authentication and access control to the virtual exclusion of all other aspects of identity management (Claub & Kohntopp, 2001; Hansen, et al., 2004; Koch & Worndl, 2001). It has often been proposed that the use of Public Key Infrastructure (PKI) is a possible solution to the issue of authenticating external users into an enterprise's resources. In some cases, this has also been claimed to be an IdMA. However, this is a very simplistic approach. PKI is really only an authentication mechanism that also addresses some issues of identity administration.

None of these proposed architectures (Bhargav-Spantzel et al., 2006; Claub & Kohntopp, 2001; Hansen et al., 2004; Koch & Worndl, 2001; Rouault & De Clercq, 2004; Taylor & Murty, 2003) meet the IEEE 1471-2000 standard for an architecture as they do not address the basic issues of the fundamental organization of the system nor do they properly define the relationships between the components, their environment and each other. Most do not also meet the minimum standards that have been proposed for identity management systems (National Institute of Standards and Technology, 2003; White, et al., 2007) as they do not address all of the major elements of identity management.

The Liberty Alliance project released in 2007 their specifications for an Identity Assurance Framework (Liberty Alliance Project, 2007a). This was followed by the release of an Identity Governance Framework (Liberty Alliance Project, 2007b). Oracle Corporation followed suit with its own release of an Identity Governance Framework (Chanliau, 2010) based on the Liberty Alliance specifications. Although these frameworks are quite detailed, they are still concerned primarily with the technical implementation of methods of creating and using digital identities. The Liberty Alliance frameworks are really attempting to define a standard approach for the technical implementation of an Identity Management System. The frameworks do not address the business requirements, needs or environment of an enterprise that may want to use it, and so cannot be considered to be an IdMA, even though they may possibly become a standard for technical implementation and deployment.

When we develop and deploy our enterprise's IdMA it must meet these criteria for it to be successful. It should be noted that the IEEE standard also requires us to look at the relationships that exist between any components and their environment.

The initial work on the development of a Reference IdMA found that the common elements of an IdMA were: Information & Data Management, Entity Management, Authentication Management, Access Control Management, Provisioning Management, Credential Management, Directory Services, Meta-Directories, Governance, and Privacy Management (White, 2009, pp. 65-66). It was also discovered that many of these elements had relationships with each other and that these were often described by an enterprise's workflows (White, 2009, pp. 86-87).

The Reference IdMA meets the IEEE criteria for a fundamental organization of a system. It starts with the enterprise need for a system of IdM and attempts to join all these enterprise requirements into a single architecture. It goes beyond the normal software solution approach that just attempts to implement software to solve a particular problem without necessarily trying to integrate it into the enterprise. The IdMA recognizes that IdM cannot just be implemented as a software solution. Instead, the Reference IdMA undertakes the integration of IdM completely into the enterprise by using a series of frameworks. Each of these frameworks groups some of the related elements of IdM and aims to integrate them into existing enterprise processes and workflow. In all cases, the frameworks work within the boundaries laid down by the enterprise's strategic aims and policies. Essentially, it can be said that the development of an IdMA is a revolutionary step as it attempts to fully integrate technical systems and enterprise process and workflow. This step fundamentally starts the enterprise on a process of re-organization.

The Reference IdMA is composed of a series of frameworks. Each framework contains a series of related components that addresses one aspect of the architecture. Each of these components represents, in most cases, an existing system or process. The Reference IdMA endeavors to show how each component fits into the overall architecture using existing workflows as a connector between different components as well as between frameworks.

However, one of the real strengths of the Reference IdMA is that it can show the relationships between components. Many of these relationships are well known to both researchers and practitioners. But the advantage of the Reference IdMA is that it can display these relationships graphically, as shown in Figure 1. This display will allow business unit managers to quickly grasp the relationships between systems, whether they are technical or non-technical. The Reference IdMA can also be used to test proposed changes in relationships or the addition of new components (systems). This use of the Reference IdMA for modeling new views of system relationships may prove to be useful for both researchers and practitioners alike.

The Reference IdMA ensures that the relationship between enterprise strategic policy, the governance environment and each component is always considered. The Policy & Governance framework has workflows that feed into every framework and ultimately into every component. The Reference IdMA ensures that the organizational environment cannot be ignored in any solution that is implemented.

What is the Reference Architecture?

The Reference Architecture is a high level view of the enterprise and does not specify what technology is to be used or how it is to be implemented. Instead, it provides an enterprise with the means to ensure that its strategic direction and policies are

Figure 1. The reference IdMA

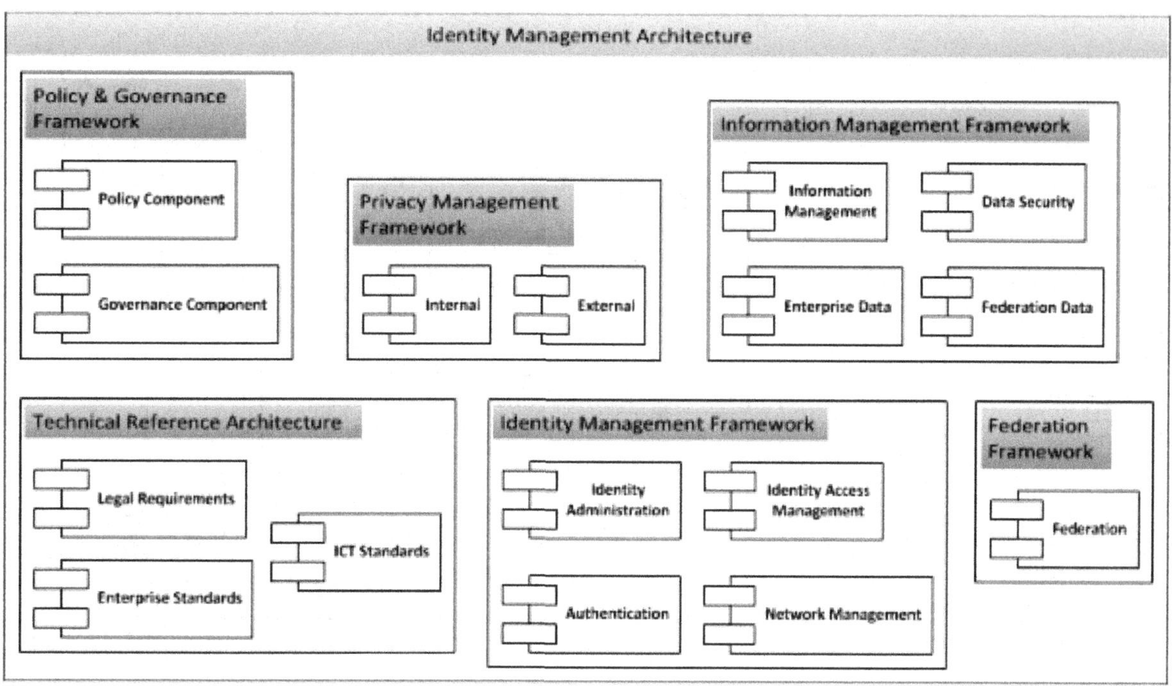

considered during the development of an IdMA that will suit its requirements.

The Reference IdMA is composed of a series of frameworks. Each framework in turn consists of a set of components, elements, constituents and functional modules. Functional modules are a process or workflow related function that joins two or more identity management elements. Each framework implements certain architectural elements of the IdMA (White, 2009, p. 94).

The use of frameworks allows the enterprise to concentrate on one aspect of the architecture at a time so that it does not become overwhelmed by complexity. The frameworks also interact with each other so that the entire architecture becomes a coordinated enterprise design. This architecture uses each of the frameworks to address different areas of integration into the existing enterprise infrastructure. It should be noted that an IdMA is not merely a technical implementation of an identity management system. The Reference IdMA also shows where information, process and workflows fit into each of the frameworks. These flows of information, process or work will be unique to each enterprise and the architect will need to identify these existing enterprise information, process and workflows and integrate them into the enterprise IdMA.

The Reference IdMA consists of six major frameworks: a Policy & Governance framework, a Technical Reference Architecture, a Privacy framework, an Identity Management framework, an Information Management framework, and a Federation framework. The workflows are represented as arrows in the diagram of the Reference IdMA and are shown in Figure 2.

The Frameworks

The Policy & Governance framework, shown in Figure 3, contains the enterprise's strategic policies as well as the Information Security policies contained in the Information Security Management System (ISMS). It also contains the governance

Figure 2. The reference IdMA with workflows

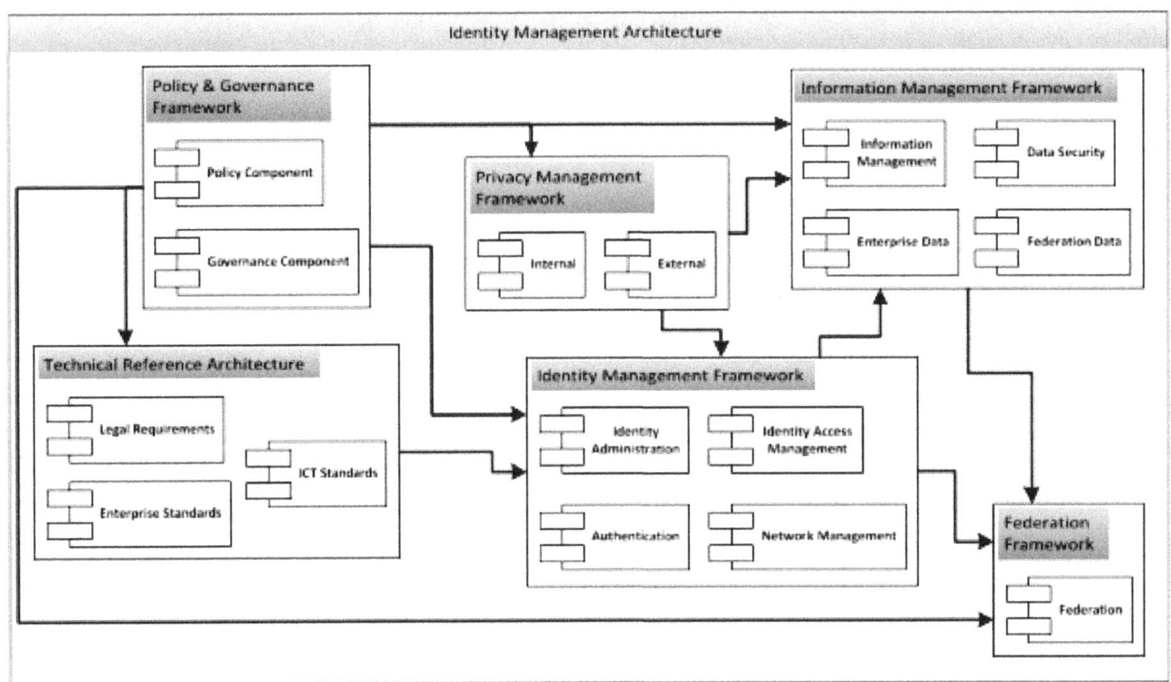

policies and procedures that provide oversight and monitoring throughout the IdMA. This framework provides the overall policy direction into each of the other frameworks. This allows each framework to ensure that all procedures, processes and workflows that are developed are in line with enterprise policy.

One of the major aims of this framework is to ensure that the operations of the other frameworks remain within the bounds of enterprise policy. The Security module in this component is where policy is applied and security chokepoints established, as shown in Figure 4. This framework approach to the application of security policies also allows for the workflows or other operations

Figure 3. Policy and governance framework

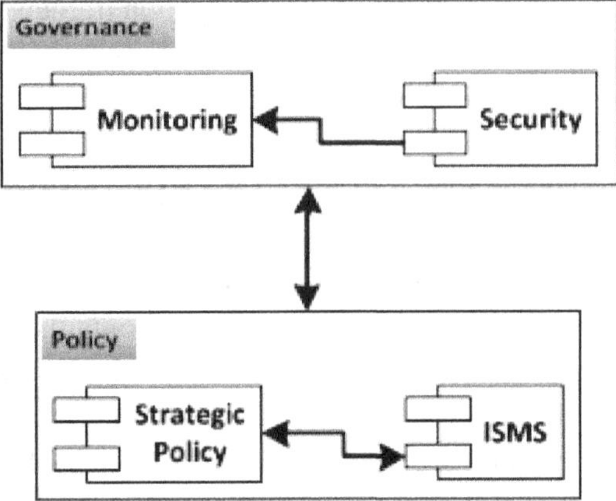

Figure 4. Security module

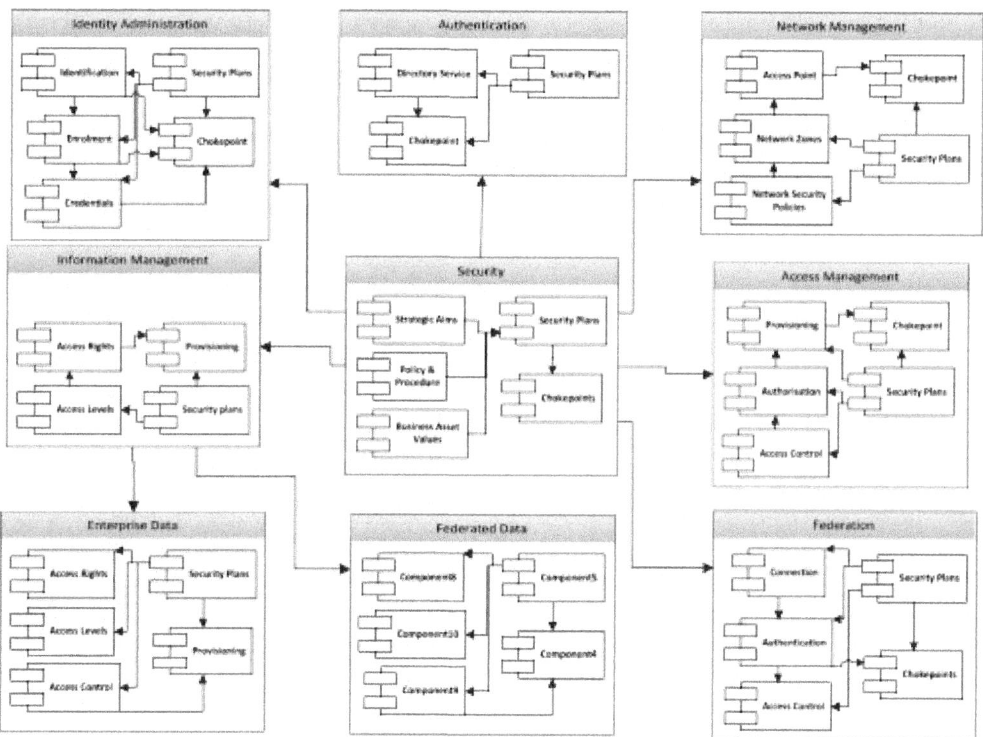

between modules, components and frameworks to be covered by a coordinated security policy. This provides the basis for the Monitor module to concentrate on the identified chokepoints within the architecture, while still being able to highlight and trap exceptions and other policy breaches as shown in Figure 5.

Workflows are an important element of the IdMA. These are shown as arrows in the diagram of the Reference IdMA, seen in Figure 2. It can be seen that the Policy & Governance framework has workflows that run from both the Policy & Governance components to the various frameworks of the IdMA. In all cases, the workflows show that there is a return of information back to these components in the form of operational feedback. This return flow of operational feedback is intended to provide the basis for further policy and governance development.

Each enterprise will need to define the workflows that exist within the enterprise ecosystem as these may well vary substantially from enterprise to enterprise. The workflows shown in the IdMA frameworks are to alert the enterprise architect to their existence.

The Technical Reference Architecture (TRA) is the technical base of the Reference IdMA (Figure 6). It contains those technical and security standards that the enterprise has decided to employ. The TRA should also include the standards and guidelines for interoperability within the enterprise. The decision as to what standards and guidelines are included in this framework needs to be guided by the decisions made in the Policy & Governance framework. As these standards are used, any modifications to the standards need to be fed back to the Policy & Governance framework.

The third framework of the Reference IdMA is the Privacy Management framework, shown in Figure 7. The enterprise's privacy policies and the details of any legal and regulatory requirements should be included in the Policy & Governance

Figure 5. Monitor module

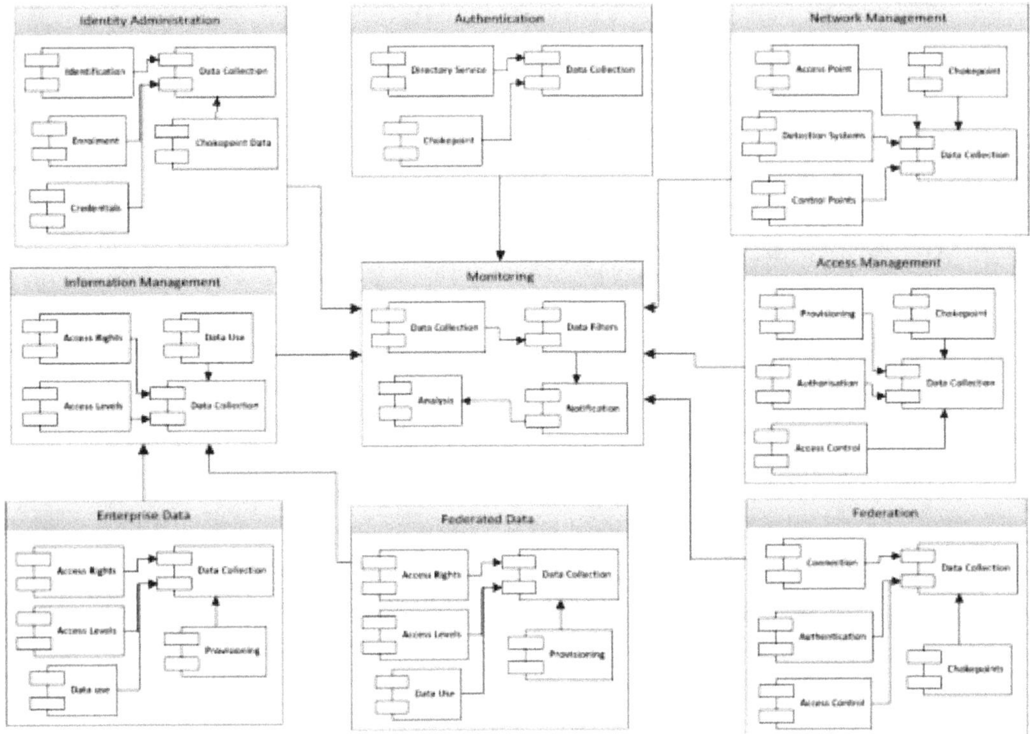

framework. This Privacy Management framework contains the processes employed to implement these policies and safeguard privacy within the enterprise. This framework should consider the privacy needs and issues that are likely to affect any internal entities or digital identities within the enterprise. It must also separately consider the privacy needs and issues for any external identities that may access the enterprise's resources and services as a result of federation or external access, for example, access through a web site or web service. The data held by the

Figure 6. Technical reference architecture

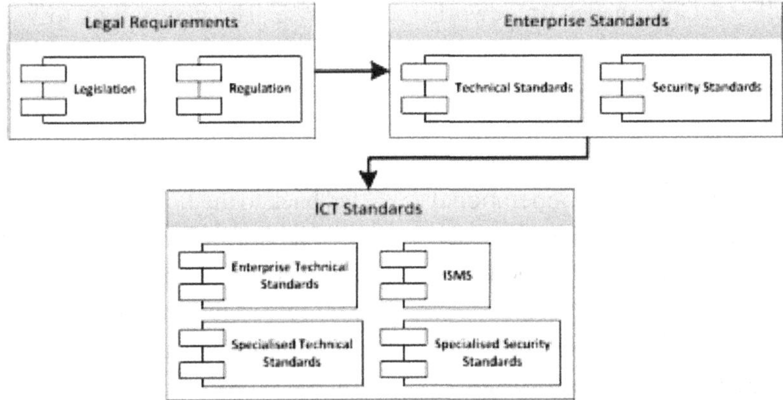

Figure 7. Privacy management framework

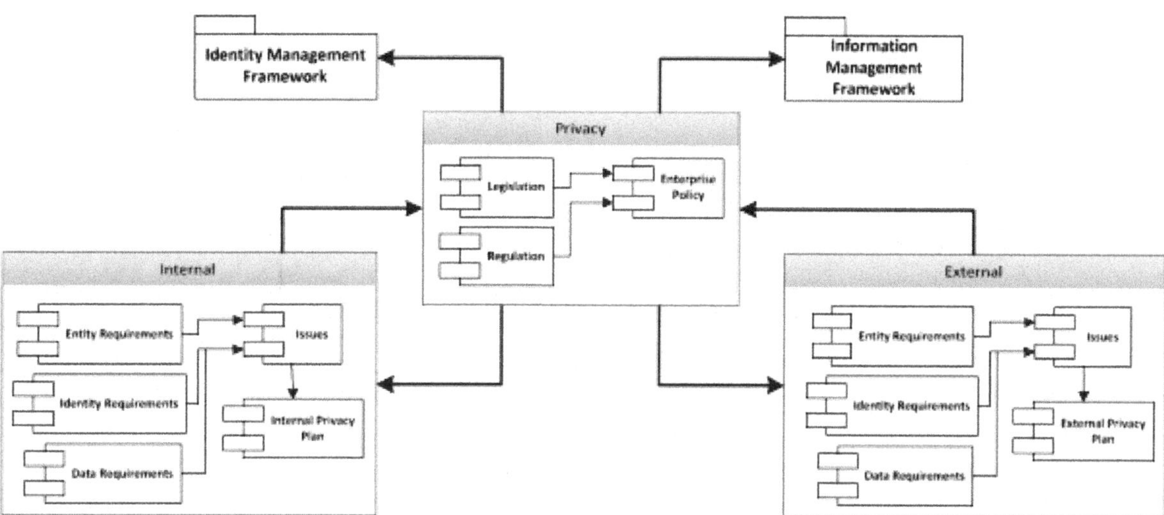

enterprise also needs to be considered to determine if any privacy issues may arise as a result of its use. It may be helpful to consider enterprise data in two conditions: Enterprise data which is data consumed solely within the enterprise, and Federation data which is the data that is consumed by external entities. The privacy conditions and requirements may be different for each type of data. The workflows from this framework feed these privacy requirements into the Identity Management framework and the Information Management framework.

The fourth framework is the Identity Management Framework, shown in Figure 8. This framework contains the components: Identity Administration, Identity Access Management, Authentication and Network Management. The Identity Administration component manages the lifecycle for both a digital identity and any credentials that it is issued. The Authentication component requires the mandatory use of a LDAP Directory Service to provide authentication services for the IdMA and is the essential binding between the other components. The Identity Access Management component manages the provisioning and authorization of a digital identity's access to data and resources. The Reference IdMA recommends that a Role based Access Control system be implemented rather than the usual Discretionary Access Control system that is implemented in most operating systems (White, 2009, pp. 120-121). The Network Management component manages a digital identity's access to the enterprise through one or more of the possible network access endpoints.

The Identity Management Framework has a workflow that feeds directly into the Information Management framework and provides the essential binding between identity management and the control and management of the enterprise's data and information. Without this link, the enterprise's data will be likely to remain in a series of isolated silos where authentication and access control are not linked to the enterprise architecture. Another workflow from this framework feeds directly into the Federation framework. This workflow provides the binding between any Federation that the enterprise may join and its identity management system.

The Information Management framework, shown in Figure 9, provides the basis for integrating enterprise data stores into the IdMA. The framework looks at differentiating Enterprise data and Federation data and then looks at the authen-

Figure 8. Identity management framework

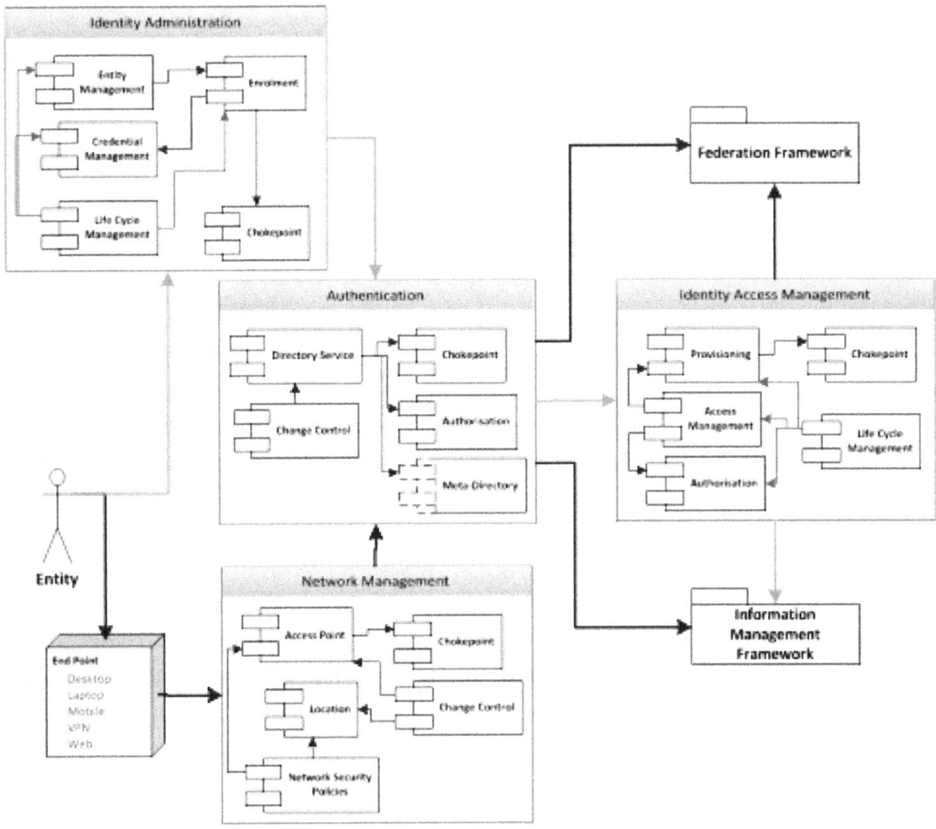

tication and access requirements for each type of data. In this context Enterprise data is defined as data that is consumed solely within the enterprise and Federation data is data that is available for consumption by external entities or enterprises. This allows the enterprise to adopt a more informed approach to how data is accessed. It also allows the enterprise to concentrate on the data sets that are to be accessed externally and that may require additional attention and security. This allows the enterprise to decide on access requirements for external federation clients. The workflows from this framework feed this information to both the Identity Management and Federation frameworks.

The Federation framework, shown in Figure 10, provides a method of specifying the requirements for federation with external partners. In this framework the Information Exchange Agreements with external enterprises and other providers are examined to determine the access and authentication requirements (Woodhouse & White, 2007). These requirements are examined against the requirements from the Privacy Management, Identity Management and the Information Management frameworks. The result is a set of decisions about the need for additional security controls and any other requirements. The workflows from this framework feed back to both the Identity Management and the Information Management frameworks.

This Reference IdMA allows an enterprise to design and implement an architecture that accords with existing enterprise policy. It builds on the use of the existing authentication and access control systems, but allows for improvement and the implementation of new technologies. The

Figure 9. Information management framework

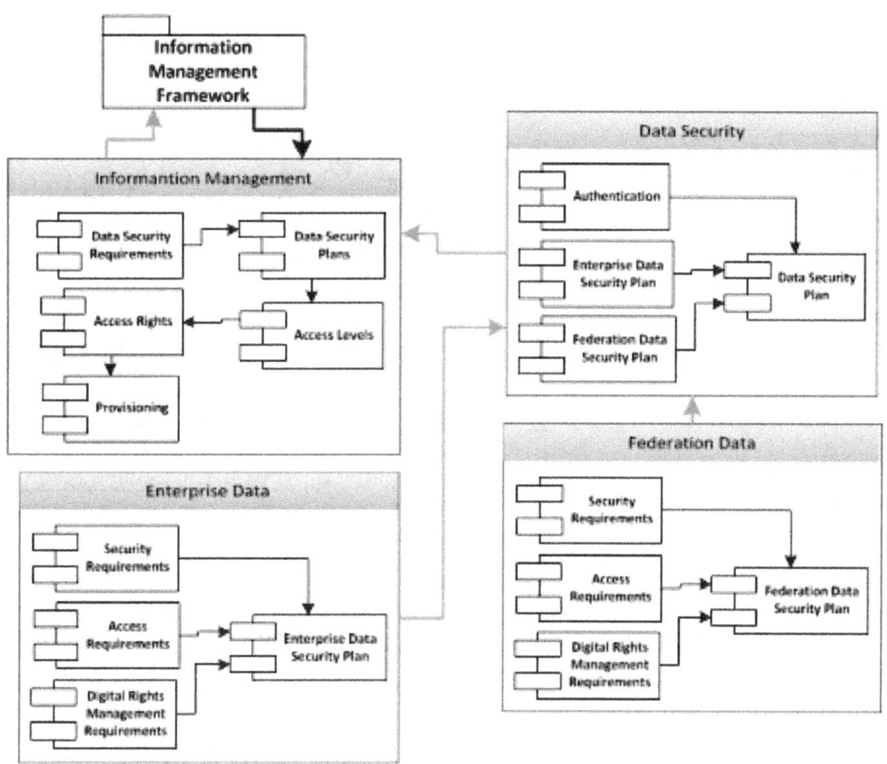

Reference IdMA is technology neutral and does not rely on any technology, other than an LDAP directory service, for implementation or operation. The use of the Reference IdMA also assures potential federation partners that the enterprise has an identity management system that can be verified and audited. This can only act to increase the level of trust between federation partners.

Chokepoints

The Reference IdMA also lends itself to the creation of security chokepoints. Day (2003) argues that a chokepoint enhances security by allowing a much closer security focus, control and monitoring on a particular point of security interest. Chokepoints have been used as a security solution for centuries. Ancient cities used chokepoints (we recognize them as the Gates in a city wall) to control and monitor access to the city. Networks are almost always protected from external attack by a chokepoint (a firewall) that controls and monitors access to the network. The use of a chokepoint allows the enterprise to concentrate its available resources on a known point of security interest in order to control and monitor that point more easily. This leads to an increase in the level of security that is provided, as the enterprise now maintains a focus on these areas of real concern instead of trying to cover every conceivable point of entry. The enterprise will also reduce the chance of exposure as a result of configuration errors if it can introduce a set of controls that address these areas of concern. This is a better solution than trying to enforce many security controls in many different areas simultaneously. The use of chokepoints also has the interesting side effect, from an enterprise point of view, of reducing security costs, while increasing security effectiveness.

Figure 10. Federation framework

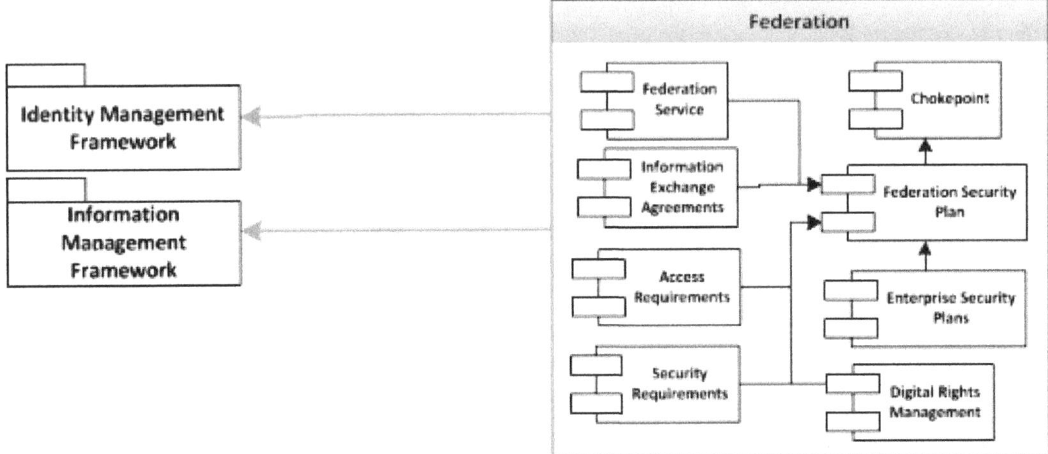

However, chokepoints can also introduce a new vulnerability for an enterprise. Many ancient cities found that even strong and imposing gates can also be a weak point if the invaders have the right equipment, or find a way to bypass them. Day (2003) makes the point that allowing both trusted partners and non-trusted external Internet users to filter through the same chokepoint can end up allowing some unexpected and undesirable results. The same applies if there is only one single chokepoint that can act as a single point of failure. For example, the Reference IdMA recommends that all authentication should occur through an LDAP directory service. However, if an enterprise decided to only deploy a single domain controller to control authentication, it would have introduced a single point of failure that would have catastrophic consequences on failure.

There are four Chokepoints to be found in the Reference IdMA. These are:

- The Enrolment process of Entity Management in Identity Administration. The point of interest here is to ensure that any digital identities that are created can be linked either to an identified and verified physical entity, or to a correctly authorized service account. This ensures that accounts are not created except to meet a specified and identified need.
- The Provisioning process of Identity Access Management is another chokepoint. Here, the aim is to ensure that all digital identities are provisioned only with the rights and permissions that they are entitled to hold. This ensures that digital identities cannot get additional rights or privileges that they are not entitled to hold.
- The Directory Service component of Authentication ensures that a consistent authentication policy is applied and that only authenticated digital identities can access resources.
- The Access point in Network Management provides a chokepoint where incoming digital identities are not only authenticated but their physical device is checked to ensure that it meets the criteria for network access.

These four chokepoints provide ideal places to monitor for unusual activity or security exceptions. The use of these chokepoints in the Reference IdMA enhances the enterprise's information security and effectively reduces the chance of "back door" access being available in strategic systems and resources.

CREATING THE ENTERPRISE IdMA

The Reference IdMA gives the Enterprise Architect a tool for designing an IdM system for the enterprise. The Reference IdMA is technology neutral, so it can be used with any software suite or a combination of software components. It allows the architect to map the relationships between processes, workflows and the systems that exist in the enterprise. This lets the architect consider the requirements of the enterprise when planning the integration of an IdM system with existing systems. This planning is independent of the considerations of individual software systems and their technical requirements.

Each of the frameworks in the Reference IdMA gives the architect an intuitive and natural method to approach the creation of the enterprise IdMA. Each framework displays the major related components and modules that must be considered in an IdMA. These components can then be adapted to suit the individual requirements of the enterprise while the linking workflows can be identified, described and added to the IdMA.

The process starts when the architect captures information about systems, process and workflow for each framework and begins planning the enterprise IdMA. As information is captured, each framework begins to display and document the different components, modules and workflows that exist within the enterprise. This process of framework description allows the enterprise to graphically display the relationships that exist within and between components and frameworks in the IdMA. This knowledge can be used to decide the priorities for implementation. It is often a necessity in an enterprise to get "quick runs on the board" in order to show senior management how effective a system is. The IdMA allows the CIO and the Enterprise Architect to decide the priorities of implementation in order to achieve their goals.

When the architect has finished describing the frameworks, the enterprise then has a repository of information that accurately describes the enterprise's processes and workflow. It further illustrates how the planned IdM system will integrate into the enterprise and the effects that it will have on the enterprise and its data. The IdMA will then form the baseline for all future plans and decisions on the evolution of enterprise architecture.

A further benefit is that the completed IdMA now gives the Enterprise Architect a tool to evaluate potential IdM solutions. The IdMA can be used to determine how a proposed vendor IdM solution could be integrated into the enterprise. It allows the architect to run a series of integration evaluations of IdM software against the requirements of the enterprise. This use of the IdMA allows the architect to assess how well a software solution will integrate into enterprise processes and workflows. This should result in IdM projects being tailored to fit the needs of the enterprise, rather than the ideas and desires of consultants or vendors.

WILL IT WORK? WALKTHROUGH AND ANALYSIS

So, where does our architect start to design the enterprise's IdMA?

The reference IdMA shows that the Policy & Governance framework (see Figure 3) underpins all other frameworks. In many enterprises, most, if not all, of the necessary policy and governance documents will already exist. These policies are examined in the Security module (see Figure 4) so that the different enterprise security, privacy and data requirements can be applied. The enterprise chokepoints should now be identified from the enterprise's Threat and Risk Assessment. The plans for monitoring the chokepoints should now be developed along with the response to be taken when an incident occurs in a chokepoint. This leads naturally to the development of the Monitoring module (see Figure 5) where the Governance policies are monitored to determine both effectiveness and compliance.

The Technical Reference Architecture (see Figure 6) will probably already exist for the enterprise, but it may not be current or complete. The TRA should contain a high-level architectural description of the existing systems and infrastructure of the enterprise. It should also provide the details of technical standards and references that are necessary for an understanding of this architecture. The TRA provides the architect with the details of the systems that will need to be integrated into the IdMA.

The Privacy framework (see Figure 7) should be the next to be considered. This framework will implement the enterprise's privacy policy which should be described in the Policy & Governance framework. The privacy requirements of both internal and external entities need to be considered as they are likely to have different privacy needs. It is also probable that there are separate legal requirements for internal and external entities which have to be met. The architect should also consider the need for privacy of both the enterprise and strategic data held by the enterprise. This consideration should include the privacy of entities that access particular pieces of data, as well as the privacy of entities that the data may refer to either explicitly or implicitly.

The Identity Management framework is the next framework to be adapted (see Figure 8). The architect should start with the Identity Administration component as this will then describe the identification, verification and lifecycle of entities, digital identities and their credentials. This description also allows the creation of a major chokepoint in the Enrolment module so that only identified and verified entities have a digital identity created. This module will probably include most of the existing Human Resource policies and functions that dictate the hiring of staff. However, the architect should also ensure that provision is made for the creation of digital identities for contractors, consultants, vendors and even the service accounts that are required to run various services in the production environment.

The Authentication component usually builds on the enterprise's existing Directory Service. The Reference IdMA requires all authentication to occur through an LDAP directory service. This means that a single and consistent authentication policy can be applied across the enterprise. The authentication strength can also be increased as there is now a single method of authentication employed at each system boundary (White, 2009, p. 122).

This centralized approach creates an authentication chokepoint. When the enterprise starts to implement provisioning through each of its individual systems, it creates a system of Simplified Sign On for digital identities where the authentication for all individual systems now occurs through the enterprise's LDAP Directory Service. This removes the requirement for individual systems to have their own sets of identities and authentication credentials and removes the possibility of "back door" access being available in strategic systems and resources. A Meta-Directory is shown in this component as an optional module. The use of a Meta-Directory may simplify the provisioning process into individual systems, but it is not a requirement of the Reference IdMA.

The Identity Access Management component is responsible for the maintenance of all roles in the enterprise, provisioning of identities into roles and the life-cycle maintenance of roles. The Access Management module maintains both the roles for the enterprise and the Access Control system. Roles are defined by the enterprise and include the essential job functions, application and data access requirements that an identity would require to carry out a specific job within the enterprise.

These definitions are then used to map each role to a specific set of application and data privileges. Digital identities can then be assigned to a role and will immediately receive the correct application and data entitlements required for the operation of that role (White, 2009, pp. 120-121). This can be achieved by using a role-by-role approach which maps one specific role for the business at a time. This approach allows the business to adapt and refine the approach as each role is completed.

The architect can use the Network Management component to control physical access to the network (see Figure 8). Most IdM systems have traditionally tended to ignore the network regarding it as just the underlying physical layer needed for access to systems. But, recent work on integrated network security (Johansson & Riley, 2005; Snyder, 2008) argues that the initial chokepoint for the architect to consider should be the access point where identities access the system. This may be any type of access point, such as a point on the enterprise LAN, a mobile device, a VPN or a Web portal. The chokepoint ensures that only authenticated users can get past the access point into the network. But Network Access policies can also be applied here so that the physical device that is connecting to the network must meet some essential criteria, such as patch level, current anti-virus application, etc, otherwise the device would be given restricted access to a quarantine zone or subnet within the LAN.

The Information Management framework provides the architect with the basis for integrating the enterprise's data stores into the IdMA as shown in Figure 9. In this framework, the authentication and access controls are used to bind access to enterprise data to the roles defined in the Identity Management Framework. This binding breaks down the use of separate silos of data that use different authentication and access control methods. Now the architect can ensure that enterprise authentication and access control policies apply to all data in the enterprise. It also ensures that data access can be audited and monitored in line with the enterprise security standards.

The architect should differentiate enterprise data from federation data so that their separate security needs can be correctly assessed. Both enterprise and federation data must then be assessed for any additional security or access requirements that it may have. Each type of data should be assessed separately to determine the level of access that each user role should have to that data. This approach gives the enterprise the opportunity to reassess the security needs of the data by classifying the data on who accesses the data sets and how they are accessed. It allows the enterprise to identify its own federation data and to decide if that data requires some additional attention and security. By changing the focus of how it views the data, the enterprise can make more informed decisions on the data access requirements for external federation clients. This could also include the need for stronger authentication or the use of secure access techniques, such as VPN, for access to particular sets of data from external clients (White, 2009).

The Federation framework is the last framework (see Figure 10) and is an optional framework to implement. This framework provides a method for an enterprise to consider how they are going to federate and to plan for that federation from the start of their IdM project. This framework allows the architect to consider the implications of federation particularly as it relates to access, authentication, authorization and access to data. It means that a plan to federate with another enterprise ensures that any access to the enterprises data by federation clients will occur through the enterprise chokepoints that have been already established.

Using the Reference IdMA frameworks allows the architect to clarify the scope of any IdM project. It allows the enterprise to design and then implement an IdM solution in a series of distinct phases rather than as a single whole of enterprise project. This should provide a minimal level of disruption to the enterprise's normal operations.

CONCLUSION

The problem that faces an architect at the start of an IdM project is that there is no accepted description of an IdMA that can be used to guide the design and development of the IdM project. The Reference IdMA provides a common starting point on which to base further research as well as design and implementation plans. Further, the Reference IdMA provides a basis for both researchers and practitioners to compare the application of different technologies in a structured and standard IdM architecture. The use of the Reference IdMA ensures that the technologies under test also comply with the standards and policies mandated by the enterprise in the architecture.

The IdMA uses a series of frameworks to ensure that an enterprise can concentrate on a single aspect of the architecture at a time. This reduces the chance of the project being overwhelmed by complexity. The frameworks in the IdMA are designed to use workflows to interact with each other so that the IdMA becomes a coordinated and integrated enterprise design. Each framework is designed to address an associated set of IdM elements. This allows them to be integrated into the existing enterprise infrastructure, its processes and workflows.

The IdMA frameworks are not designed to be a prescriptive solution. Each enterprise will have a different approach to each of the elements of the IdMA and may accord them differing levels of importance. The critical point for a practitioner is that the frameworks of the IdMA provide a series of reference points around which the integration of an IdM system can be planned for each individual enterprise. The frameworks can be used by a practitioner as part of an enterprise reference architecture to ensure the IdMA meets the requirements of the enterprise and is integrated into existing processes and workflows. This is a notable advance in the design of enterprise level IdM systems and architectures.

The IdMA frameworks allow the enterprise to consider all of the implications of an IdM system. They take the enterprise on a journey through its own aims, policies, processes, workflows, technologies and data. Each framework forces the enterprise to consider how those aims, policies, processes, workflows and technologies are to be integrated with its data and resources. The frameworks of the IdMA then show how the enterprise should provide the data and resources to both its internal users as well as any external users in a federation. This may well be a critical point for many enterprises, their business units, and their architects.

The Reference IdMA is technology neutral which allows it to be used in any enterprise with any suite of software. It allows the architect to map the relationships between processes, workflows and systems. This mapping allows the architect to consider the requirements of the enterprise and how they can be met in the plan for the integration of the IdM system. This planning is now independent of the considerations of individual software systems and their requirements. This represents another significant advance in the design of IdM systems.

The Reference IdMA provides a graphical representation of the enterprise and its policies, processes, workflows, technologies and data. Each of the diagrams of the Reference IdMA can be used to graphically model an aspect of the enterprise. They then display how the policies, processes and technology combine with a workflow to meet the enterprise requirements. This graphic representation of components, relationships and workflows provides a valuable tool for educating the enterprise about the IdMA and its implications.

The Reference IdMA provides enterprise architects with a tool to design an IdM system that is fully integrated into the enterprise. It can be used to evaluate potential IdM and federation technologies and solutions. This can take the form of investigating how proposed IdM solutions could be employed in an integrated IdMA. This allows an architect to assess a possible software solution for usability and integration into enterprise processes and workflows. It also becomes a reference tool for researchers as it can be used to evaluate how new IdM developments may integrate into an enterprise IdMA.

Finally the enterprise IdMA becomes the major repository of the enterprise's decisions, plans and information on the design of its IdM solution and its integration into the enterprise. It becomes the baseline for all future plans and decisions on the evolution of enterprise architecture.

REFERENCES

Bertino, E., Khan, L., Sandhu, R., & Thuraisingham, B. (2006). Secure knowledge management: Confidentiality, trust and privacy. *IEEE Transactions on Systems, Man, and Cybernetics. Part A, Systems and Humans*, *36*(3), 429–438. doi:10.1109/TSMCA.2006.871796

Cantor, S., & Erdos, M. (2002). *Shibboleth-Architecture DRAFT v05*. Retrieved from http://shibboleth.internet2.edu/docs/draft-internet2-shibboleth-arch-v05.pdf

Cantor, S., Hodges, J., Kemp, J., & Thompson, P. (2003). Liberty ID-FF architecture overview (T. Wason, Ed.). Retrieved from http://project-liberty.org/liberty/content/download/318/2366/file/draft-liberty-idff-arch-overview-1.2-errata-v1.0.pdf

Cao, Y., Yang, L., Fu, Z. B., & Yang, F. (2010). Identity management architecture: Paradigms and models. *Applied Mechanics and Materials*, *40-41*, 647–651. doi:10.4028/www.scientific.net/AMM.40-41.647

Casassa Mont, M., Bramhall, P., & Pato, J. (2003). *On adaptive identity management: The next generation of identity management technologies*. Retrieved from http://www.hpl.hp.com/techreports/2003/HPL-2003-149.pdf

Chanliau, M. (2010). *Oracle Identity Management 11G*. Retrieved from http://www.oracle.com/technetwork/middleware/id-mgmt/overview/idm-tech-wp-11g-r1-128261.pdf

Claub, S., & Kohntopp, M. (2001). Identity management and its support of multilateral security. *Computer Networks*, *37*(2), 205–219. doi:10.1016/S1389-1286(01)00217-1

Day, K. (2003). *Inside the security mind. Making the tough decisions*. Upper Saddle River, NJ: Prentice Hall.

Gamma, E., Helm, R., Johnson, R., & Vlissides, J. (2000). *Design patterns: Elements of reusable object-oriented software*. Reading, MA: Addison-Wesley Publishing Company.

Hansen, M., Berlich, P., Camenisch, J., Claub, S., Pfitzmann, A., & Waidner, M. (2004). Privacy-enhancing identity management. *Information Security Technical Report*, *9*(1), 35–44. doi:10.1016/S1363-4127(04)00014-7

Hu, V., Ferraiolo, D., & Kuhn, D. (2006). *Assessment of access control systems*. Retrieved from http://csrc.nist.gov/publications/nistir/7316/NISTIR-7316.pdf

IEEE. (2000). [Recommended practice for architectural description of software-intensive systems.]. *IEEE Standard*, *1471*, 2000.

Johansson, J., & Riley, S. (2005). *Protect your Windows network from perimeter to data*. Upper Saddle River, NJ: Addison-Wesley.

Jones, M., & Cameron, K. (2005). *Design rationale behind the identity metasystem architecture*. Retrieved from http://www.identityblog.com/wp-content/resources/design_rationale.pdf

Josang, A., & Pope, S. (2005). *User centric identity management*. AusCERT Conference 2005.

Koch, M., & Worndl, W. (2001). *Community support and identity management*. Paper presented at the Seventh European Conference on Computer-Supported Cooperative Work, Bonn, Germany.

Liberty Alliance Project. (2007a). *Liberty identity assurance framework*. Retrieved from http://www.projectliberty.org/liberty/content/download/4315/28869/file/liberty-identity-assurance-framework-v1.1.pdf

Liberty Alliance Project. (2007b). *An overview of the ID governance framework*. Retrieved from http://www.projectliberty.org/liberty/content/download/3500/23156/file/overview-id-governance-framework-v1.0.pdf

Meinecke, J., Nussbaumer, M., & Gaedke, M. (2005). Building blocks for identity federations. *Lecture Notes in Computer Science*, *3579*, 203–208. doi:10.1007/11531371_29

National Institute of Standards and Technology. (2003). *Electronic authentication: Guidance for selecting secure techniques*. Retrieved from http://www.itl.nist.gov/lab/bulletns/bltnaug04.htm

Pearsons, G. (2007). *Using international standards in your compliance program.* Retrieved 28 September, 2007, from http://www.securecomputing.net.au/feature/3759,using-international-standards-in-your-compliance-program.aspx

Snyder, J. (2008). *Refactoring networks: Five principles of integrated network security.* Paper presented at the SecurityPoint 2008, Sydney.

The Open Group. (2002). *Identity management business scenario*. Retrieved from http://www.opengroup.org/bookstore/catalog/k023.htm

White, P. (2008). *Identity management architecture in the Australian public sector.* Paper presented at the 5th International Conference on Information Technology and Applications ICITA 2008, Cairns, QLD.

White, P. (2009). *Managing enterprise complexity. The use of identity management architecture to control enterprise resources*. Saarbrucken, Germany: VDM Verlag.

White, P., Altas, I., Howarth, J., & Weckert, J. (2007). *An internal enterprise framework for identity based management*. Paper presented at the Australian Partnership for Advanced Computing Conference APAC07, Perth.

Windley, P. (2005). *Digital identity*. Sebastopol, CA: O'Reilly Media Inc.

Woodhouse, S., & White, P. (2007). *Identity based management: Extending the ISMS for federation.* Paper presented at the ISACA Oceania Computer Audit Control and Security Conference 2007, Auckland NZ.

Zhu, H. (2007). Strengthen access control with enterprise identity-management architecture. Retrieved 7 November, 2007, from http://msdn2.microsoft.com/en-us/library/bb447668.aspx

KEY TERMS AND DEFINITIONS

Authentication: The process of verifying the identity claim that is presented.

Chokepoint: A particular point of security interest where an enterprise maintains a close security focus through control and monitoring to reduce security exposure.

Digital Identity: The digital representation of a verified entity that is trusted to access enterprise resources.

Federation: A set of enterprises that share resources as a result of a trust relationship that regards any federated identity information as valid.

Identity: a set of characteristics, or identifiers, of an entity that uniquely identifies that entity within a specific context or system.

Identity Management Solution: A suite of software that is designed to provide identity management services for an enterprise.

Identity Management System: The implementation of a set of processes, workflows and software that provides identity management services for an enterprise.

IdM: Identity Management – The administration of an entity's digital identity so as to provide secure and controlled access to the resources that the entity is entitled to use.

IdMA: Identity Management Architecture - the set of processes, workflows, frameworks, standards and policies that defines and describes a system of Identity Management.

Provisioning: The process of granting of access to various resources based on the entity's role or position.

ENDNOTE

1 There is a continuing discussion in the LinkedIn Identity Management Specialists Group on "Why do Identity and Access Management Projects Fail?". See http://www.linkedin.com/groups?mostPopular=&gid=41311.

Chapter 10
Automatic Security Analysis of SAML-Based Single Sign-On Protocols

Alessandro Armando
University of Genova, Italy & Fondazione Bruno Kessler, Italy

Roberto Carbone
Fondazione Bruno Kessler, Italy

Luca Compagna
SAP Research Sophia-Antipolis, France

Giancarlo Pellegrino
SAP Research Sophia-Antipolis, France & Eurécom, France

ABSTRACT

Single-Sign-On (SSO) protocols enable companies to establish a federated environment in which clients sign in the system once and yet are able to access to services offered by different companies. The OASIS Security Assertion Markup Language (SAML) 2.0 Web Browser SSO Profile is the emerging standard in this context. In previous work a severe security flaw in the SAML-based SSO for Google Apps was discovered. By leveraging this experience, this chapter will show that model checking techniques for security protocols can support the development and analysis of SSO solutions helping the designer not only to detect serious security flaws early in the development life-cycle but also to provide assurance on the security of the solutions identified.

INTRODUCTION

Single Sign-On (SSO) protocols are the cornerstones of Identity and Access Management systems as they enable companies to establish a federated environment in which users sign in once and yet are able to access to services offered by different organizations.

The *Security Assertion Markup Language* (SAML) 2.0 Web Browser SSO Profile (SAML SSO, for short) (OASIS, 2005a) is the emerging standard in this context: it defines an XML-based format for encoding security assertions as well as

DOI: 10.4018/978-1-61350-498-7.ch010

a number of protocols and bindings that prescribe how assertions should be exchanged in a wide variety of applications and/or deployment scenarios. This is done to the minimum extent necessary to guarantee the interoperability among different implementations. As a consequence, SAML SSO features many configuration options ranging from optional fields in messages, usage of SSL 3.0 or TLS 1.0 channels (SSL channels from here on) at the transport layer, application of encryption and/or digital signature on specific sensitive message elements which need to be instantiated according to the requirements posed by the application scenario and the available security mechanisms.

The security recommendations that are available throughout the bulky SAML specifications (OASIS, 2005a, 2005b) are useful in avoiding the most common security pitfalls but are of little help in ensuring their absence in specific instances of the protocol. Indeed the designer of a SAML-based SSO solution, while striving to meet the requirements posed by the application scenario, may overlook the security implications associated with the choice of some optional elements or may even decide to deviate from the SAML standard. Needless to say, this may have dramatic consequences on the security of the SSO solution.

The situation is exemplified by the SAML-based SSO for Google Apps. The protocol is inspired by the SAML standard but the version in operation until June 2008 deviated from it in a few, seemingly minor aspects (see Section «The SAML Web Browser SSO Profile» for the details). In May 2008 a severe security flaw was discovered and reported to Google and US-CERT (Armando, Carbone, Compagna, Cuéllar, & Tobarra, 2008, US-CERT, 2008). The vulnerability allowed a dishonest service provider to impersonate a user at another service provider. In reaction to the finding, Google immediately asked their customers to implement counter-measures to mitigate potential exploits and then to migrate to a new, patched solution of their SSO solution. Interestingly, the vulnerability was found by using a model checker for security protocols.

By leveraging this experience, this chapter will show that model checking techniques for security protocols can support the development and analysis of SSO solutions helping designers not only to detect serious security flaws early in the development life-cycle but also to provide assurance on the security of the solutions identified. By using SAML-based SSO protocols as running examples it will be illustrated how the design space can be iteratively explored with the aid of a model checker leading to the identification of vulnerabilities and hence to more secure solutions.

This work is part of a wider project aimed at the development of automated verification technologies for security protocols and, more generally, for security-sensitive, distributed applications (Armando et al., 2005, The AVANTSSAR Team).

Structure of the Chapter

In the next section the scene is set by briefly describing the state-of-the-art in model checking of security protocols. In Section «The SAML Web Browser SSO Profile» a brief introduction of the SAML SSO is given. In Section «Formal Modeling of the SAML Web Browser SSO Profile» the specification formalism is given in order to model security protocols, the properties of the transport protocols as well as those that the protocols are expected to meet. Section «Security Analysis of SAML-based SSO Protocols» presents the results of the analysis of SAML-based SSO protocols. In Section «Future Research Directions» the future research direction is discussed and Section «Conclusion» concludes the chapter with some final remarks.

BACKGROUND

SSO protocols belong to the wider family of security protocols, i.e. communication protocols that, by means of cryptographic primitives, aim to provide security guarantees such as (mutual) authentication of the agents taking part in the protocol or secrecy of some information (e.g. a session key). In spite of their apparent simplicity, security protocols are notoriously error-prone. Many published protocols have been implemented and deployed in real applications only to be found flawed years later. For instance, the Needham-Schroeder authentication protocol (Needham & Schroeder, 1978) was found vulnerable to a serious attack 17 years after its publication (Lowe, 1996). Quite interestingly, many attacks can be carried out without breaking cryptography. These attacks exploit weaknesses in the protocol that are due to the complex and unexpected interleavings of different protocol sessions as well as to the possible interference of malicious agents. (The attack on the SAML-based SSO for Google Apps reported in (Armando et al., 2008) is of this kind.)

This is even more so for browser-based security protocols like the SAML SSO since, as pointed out in (Groß, Pfitzmann, & Sadeghi, 2005), browsers—unlike normal protocol principals—cannot be assumed to do nothing but execute the given security protocol. Moreover, browser-based security protocols normally assume for their proper functioning that communication between the browser and the server is carried over a unilateral SSL channel established through the exchange of a valid certificate. SSL channels provide a powerful mechanism for secure exchange of data in web-based applications, but the security guarantees they offer must not be overestimated. As it will be shown in the sequel, serious vulnerabilities are possible even when communication takes place of SSL channels. Indeed the security of a SAML SSO solution critically depends on several assumptions (e.g. the trust relationships among the involved parties) and security mechanisms (e.g. the secure transport protocols used to exchange messages) as well as on the options and decisions taken during the design, development and deployment of such a solution.

For this reason, SAML-based SSO protocols and, more in general, security protocols are considered a challenging and promising application domain for formal methods and model checking techniques in particular. Unlike traditional verification techniques (e.g. testing), model checking allows for the exhaustive exploration of the behaviors of the protocol when communication between honest principals is controlled by a Dolev-Yao intruder (Dolev & Yao, 1983), a malicious agent capable to overhear, divert, and fake messages. Notice that the problem of determining whether a security protocol meets the expected security properties is undecidable in the general case (Durgin, Lincoln, Mitchell, & Scedrov, 1999). However, a number of decidable subclasses of this general problem have been identified (Durgin et al., 1999, Rusinowitch & Turuani, 2001, Chevalier, Küsters, Rusinowitch, & Turuani, 2003). Moreover, even semi-decision techniques have proved very helpful in detecting flaws in security protocols. Thus, during the last decade it has been witnessed to the development of a new generation of model checking techniques specifically tailored for security protocols (Meadows, 1996, Basin, 1999, Jacquemard, Rusinowitch, & Vigneron, 2000, Millen & Shmatikov, 2001). As a result of this endeavor, a wide range of industrial strength security protocols can now be analyzed automatically by state-of-the-art tools (Armando et al., 2005, The AVANTSSAR Team).

The experiments reported in this chapter (see Section «Security Analysis of SAML-based SSO Protocols») have been conducted with the AVANTSSAR Validation Platform for security protocols (hereafter in the sequel referred to as the AVANTSSAR Platform). An architectural view of the platform is depicted in Figure 1.

The AVANTSSAR Platform takes as input a high-level specification of a security protocol, the expected security goals, as well as the scenario in which the protocol is employed and automatically evaluates its security. (A scenario is the parallel execution of a finite number of protocol

Figure 1. The AVANTSSAR platform

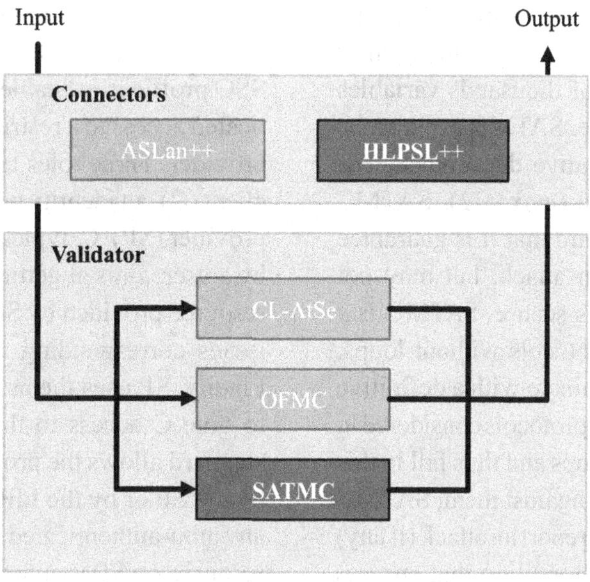

sessions, where a protocol session is a run of the protocol played by a given set of agents.) A key feature of the AVANTSSAR Platform is the support of several types of communication channels. This is a fundamental feature in the case study addressed, as—as Section «Introduction» has anticipated—SSO protocols heavily rely on the services offered by the transport protocols, namely SSL. The high-level specification is then translated by a connector into a security problem expressed in an intermediate specification language. The resulting specification, which is amenable to formal analysis, is fed to the validator which automatically checks—through the available back-ends—whether the protocol achieves its security goals. If this is not the case, then an attack trace is returned by the back-end and it is translated back into a user-friendly format. Currently the AVANTSSAR Platform supports three state-of-the-art model checker for security protocols as back-ends, namely CL-AtSe (Turuani, 2006), OFMC (Mödersheim & Viganò, 2009), and SATMC (Armando, Carbone, & Compagna, 2007). In the experiments reported in this chapter, the HLPSL++ connector and the SATMC back-end have been used.

The HLPSL++ connector takes as input a high-level specification written in HLPSL++ (see Section «Formal Modeling of the SAML Web Browser SSO Profile») and properly translates it so to instrument the formal analysis through the SATMC back-end. In addition, the HLPSL++ connector features a front-end that displays attacks (if any) as message sequence charts (MSC), a standardized notation commonly used in the protocol domain for the description of message exchanges between entities.

SATMC takes as input a formal specification of the protocol, a scenario to be considered for the analysis, a specification of the expected security property, and an integer *max* and tries to determine whether the protocol enjoys the expected security property in the scenario by considering up to *max* execution steps. At the core of SATMC lies a procedure that automatically generates a propositional formula whose satisfying assignments (if any) correspond to attack of length bounded by some integer $k \leq max$. Finding attacks (of length k) on the protocol therefore boils down to solving propositional satisfiability problems. SATMC relies on state-of-the-art SAT solvers for this task which can handle propositional satisfiability problems with hundreds of thousands variables and clauses and even more. SATMC can also be instructed to perform iterative deepening on k. By setting max to infinite ($max=-1$), SATMC is a semi-decision procedure that it is guarantee to terminate if there is an attack, but may not terminate if the protocol is secure. SATMC is a decision procedure for protocols without loops, i.e. it is guaranteed to terminate with a definitive sound answer. The security protocols considered in this chapter do not have loops and thus fall in this decidable class. When run against them, SATMC is thus guaranteed to either report an attack (if any) or to reach a termination condition that ensures that enough execution steps, say k_{safe}, have been explored proving the safety of the protocol (i.e., absence of attacks). More details on SATMC can be found in (Armando & Compagna, 2008, Armando et al., 2007).

AUTOMATED SECURITY ANALYSIS OF SAML-BASED SSO PROTOCOLS

The SAML Web Browser SSO Profile

The SAML specifications are based on the notions of assertions, protocols, bindings and profiles: A SAML *assertion* is an XML expression encoding a statement about a principal (also called subject). This chapter will consider a special type of assertions, called authentication assertions. Authentication assertion states, among other things, that a given subject was authenticated by a particular means at a particular time for the purpose to get access to the service provider. *Protocols* prescribe how assertions should be exchanged and *bindings* detail how assertions can be mapped into transport protocols, e.g. SOAP or HTTP. Finally, *profiles* define the use of SAML assertions, protocols and bindings so to meet some specific use case requirements (e.g. SSO).

The purpose of the Web Browser SAML 2.0 SSO profile is to enable a client to obtain authenticated access to a restricted resource on a service provider. Three roles take part in the protocol: a client (C), an identity provider (IdP) and a service provider (SP). C, typically a web browser guided by a user, aims at getting access to a service or a resource provided by SP. IdP authenticates C and issues corresponding authentication assertions. Finally, SP uses the assertions generated by IdP to give C access to the requested service. The standard allows the protocol to be initiated either by the SP or by the IdP. In the *SP-initiated SSO*, any non-authenticated client trying to access a resource on SP is automatically redirected to the IdP for authentication. In the IdP-initiated SSO, C starts the protocol by directly contacting to and authenticating at the IdP. This chapter focuses on the SP-initiated SSO using a Redirect Binding for the SP-to-IdP <AuthnRequest> message and a POST Binding for the IdP-to-SP <Response>. The protocol is depicted in Figure 2.

In step S1, C asks SP to provide the resource located at the address URI. SP then initiates the *SAML Authentication Protocol* by sending C a redirect response directed to IdP containing an authentication request of the form AuthReq(ID,SP)—where ID is a string uniquely identifying the request—and the address URI of the resource. IdP then challenges C to provide valid credentials and—if the authentication succeeds—IdP builds an authentication assertion *AA*=AuthAssert(SP,C,IdP,ID) and places it into a response message *Resp*=Response(ID,SP,IdP, $\{AA\}_{K_{IdP}^{-1}}$), where $\{AA\}_{K_{IdP}^{-1}}$ is the assertion digitally signed with K_{IdP}^{-1}, the private key of IdP. (As unnecessary for the analysis, it will not be modeled how the authentication between C and IdP is performed, but it is assumed it is successful.) IdP then places *Resp* into an HTML form as a hidden form control and sends it back to C. For

Figure 2. SP-initiated SSO with redirect/POST bindings

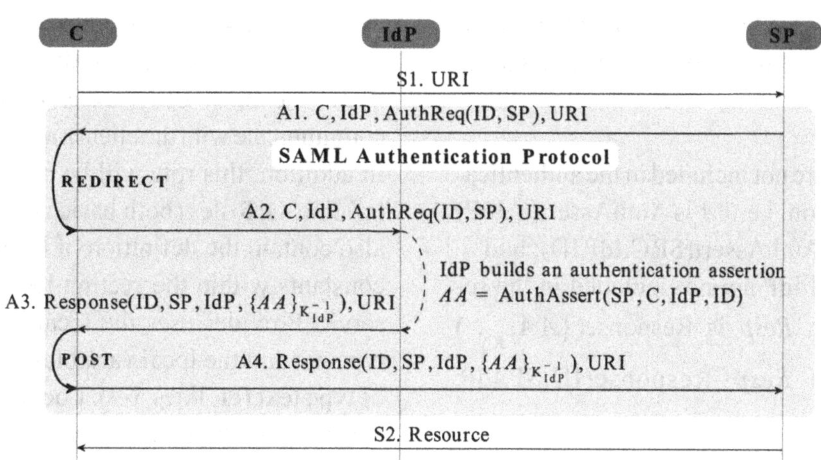

ease of use purposes, the HTML form is typically accompanied by script code that automatically posts the form to SP. This completes the protocol and SP can deliver the requested resource to C.

The security of the SAML SSO protocol relies on a number of assumptions about the trustworthiness of the principals involved as well as the security of the transport protocols employed. Below they are summarized.

Trust Assumptions

The protocol assumes that IdP is trustworthy for both C and SP, but SP is not assumed to be trustworthy. Indeed service providers do not necessarily trust each other e.g., a SP could have been compromised or simply act maliciously driven by own interests. In accordance with this the analysis will consider protocol sessions in which C and SP might be played by the intruder, while it is assumed that IdP is played by an honest agent. It is worth noticing that in the analysis of the SAML SSO v1.0 reported in (Hansen, Skriver, & Nielson, 2005) it is assumed that the SP is trustworthy. This assumption is not realistic as service providers do not necessarily trust each other and it would prevent the detection of the attack on the SAML-based SSO for Google Apps reported in (Armando et al., 2008).

Assumptions on the communication channels. Communications between the parties are subject to the following assumptions:

(A1) the communication between C and SP is carried over a unilateral SSL channel, established through the exchange of a valid certificate (from SP to C); and

(A2) the communication between C and IdP is carried over a unilateral SSL channel that becomes bilateral once C authenticates itself on IdP. This is established through the exchange of a valid certificate (from IdP to C) and of valid credentials (from C to IdP).

Under the above assumptions the protocol is expected to meet the following security properties:

(P1) SP authenticates C, i.e., at the end of its protocol run SP believes it has been talking with C; and

(P2) Resource must be kept secret between C and SP.

The SAML-based Single Sign-On for Google Apps used by Google until June 2008 shared the above assumptions and expected properties, but deviated from the SAML SSO protocol for a few, seemingly minor simplifications in the messages exchanged:

(G1) ID and SP are not included in the authentication assertion, i.e. *AA* is AuthAssert(C,IdP) instead of AuthAssert(SP,C,IdP,ID); and

(G2) ID, SP and IdP are not included in the response, i.e. *Resp* is Response($\{AA\}_{K^{-1}_{IdP}}$) instead of *Resp*=Response(ID,SP,IdP, $\{AA\}_{K^{-1}_{IdP}}$).

Formal Modeling of the SAML Web Browser SSO Profile

To formally specify SAML-based SSO protocols it has been used HLPSL++, a role-based specification language for security protocols developed in the context of the AVANTSSAR Project (The AVANTSSAR Team). Unlike its predecessor HLPSL (High-Level Protocol Specification Language) (Chevalier et al., 2004), HLPSL++ supports the specification of communication channels beyond the Dolev-Yao model. This includes confidential and authentic channels that are building blocks for capturing real world transport-level communications such as SSL. In HLPSL++, actions carried out by a protocol participant are grouped and specified in a *basic role*. Basic roles are then instantiated and glued together into *composed roles*. This section provides a brief introduction to the language through its application to the SAML SSO.

The definitions of the three basic roles participating in the SAML SSO, namely client, serviceProvider, and identityProvider, are given in the Figures 3, 4, and 5 respectively. The specification of a role includes a list of parameters and the agent playing that role. A basic role with parameters therefore corresponds to many possible instances of same role obtained by instantiating the parameters with terms of the appropriate type. For instance, the role serviceProvider—cf. lines 2-3 of Figure 4—has the following parameters: C, SP, and IdP of type agent, KIdP of type public_key, SP2C and C2SP of type channel (used by SP to communicate with the client), and URI of type text. In addition, this role will be played by agent SP (cf. line 4). Roles (both basic and composed) can also contain the definition of local variables and constants within the section local. For instance, serviceProvider uses the local variable State of type nat and the local variables ID and Resource of type text (cf. lines 5-7). Local variables can be assigned to initial values in the section init. For instance, State is initially assigned to the value 1 in the serviceProvider role (cf. line 9).

The behavior of roles is specified in the transition section. This comprises a collection of transitions of the form *Pre* =|>*Post*, where *Pre* is the conjunction (denoted by the $\wedge$ symbol) of preconditions for the applicability of the transition and *Post* is the conjunction of effects that result by the execution of the transition. For example, the first transition in Figure 4 (cf. lines 13-15) occurs only if State=1 and a message URI is received on channel C2SP from agent C—this is represented by rcv(C2SP, C, URI)—and its execution sets the value of State to 3, generates a fresh value for ID (cf. second conjunct in line 14), and makes SP (the player of the role) sending the message C.IdP.(ID'.SP).URI to C over channel SP2C. The primed variable ID' denotes the new value of ID. In general when a primed variable occurs in a received message, it means that the variable will be assigned to a new value, the one specified in the corresponding part of the message received. If the primed variable occurs in an outgoing message, then the value just assigned to that variable will be included in the message. In summary, unprimed variables denote message elements that the role is checking while receiving that message (as they are already stored somewhere in its state), while primed variables model those elements that are unknown to the receiver. For instance, the transition of identityProvider (see

Figure 3. HLPSL++ specification of the SAML SSO protocol: Role C

```
role client(
  C, IdP, SP : agent, KIdP : public_key,
  C2SP, SP2C, C2IdP, IdP2C : channel,
  URI : text
) played_by C def=
local
  State : nat,
  ID, Resource : text
init
  State:=0
transition
%% C asks for a resource to SP
S1.     State = 0 =|>
        State':=2 /\ snd(C2SP, SP, URI) /\ witness(C, SP,
sp_c_uri,URI)
%% C receives an AuthnReq(ID, SP) to be forwarded to IdP
A1_A2. State = 2 /\ rcv(SP2C, SP, C.IdP.(ID'.SP).URI) =|>
        State':=4 /\ snd(C2IdP, IdP, C.IdP.(ID'.SP).URI)
%% C receives a Response(SP, C, IdP, ID) for SP
A3_A4. State = 4 /\ rcv(IdP2C, IdP,
SP.{SP.C.IdP.ID'}_inv(KIdP).URI) =|>
        State':=6 /\ snd(C2SP, SP,
SP.{SP.C.IdP.ID'}_inv(KIdP).URI)
%% C receives a resource from SP
A4_S2. State = 6 /\ rcv(SP2C, SP, Resource') =|>
        State':=8
end role
```

Figure 4. HLPSL++ specification of the SAML SSO protocol: Role SP

```
role serviceProvider (
  C, IdP, SP : agent, KIdP : public_key,
  SP2C, C2SP : channel, URI : text
) played_by SP def=
local
  State : nat,
  ID, Resource : text
init
  State:=1
transition
%% SP receives a request for a resource and issues an
%% AuthReq(ID, SP)
S1_A1. State = 1 /\ rcv(C2SP, C, URI) =|>
       State':=3 /\ ID' := new()
                 /\ snd(SP2C, C, C.IdP.(ID'.SP).URI)
%% SP receives a Response(SP, C, IdP, ID) and serves the
%% resource to C
A4_S2. State = 3 /\ rcv(C2SP, C,
SP.{SP.C.IdP.ID}_inv(KIdP).URI) =|>
       State':=5 /\ Resource' := new()
                 /\ snd(SP2C, C, Resource')
                 /\ request(SP, C, sp_c_uri, URI)
```

Figure 5, lines 13-14) states that IdP checks whether the first two and the fourth element of the message received correspond to the (known) values of C, IdP and SP respectively, while it will not check the last and the third elements, namely ID' and URI'.

Once the basic roles are defined, their parallel composition is defined by means of the composed role session as shown in Figure 6. The parameters of the composed role can be related to those of the component roles so that when the composed role is instantiated its component roles are properly instantiated too. Parameters include the channels used by component basic roles to exchange messages. Each SSL channel (cf. assumptions (A1) and (A2)) is modeled by two unidirectional channels (see part (a) of Figure 7). C2SP and SP2C model the SSL channel between C and SP: the former carries messages from C to SP, the latter carries messages flowing in the opposite direction. They are assumed to enjoy the following properties (cf. lines 8-12):

- confidential(SP, C2SP), i.e. the output of C2SP is accessible to SP only, and weakly_authentic(C2SP), i.e. the input of C2SP is exclusively accessible to a single, yet unknown, sender;
- weakly_confidential(SP2C), i.e. the output of SP2C is exclusively accessible to a single, yet unknown, receiver and authentic(SP, SP2C), i.e. the input of SP2C is accessible to SP only; and
- link(C2SP, SP2C), i.e. the principal sending messages on C2SP is the same principal that receives messages from SP2C.

Channel C2IdP and IdP2C model the SSL channel between C and IdP. The former carries messages from C to IdP, the latter carries the messages flowing in the opposite direction. The properties enjoyed by C2IdP (IdP2C) are similar to those of C2SP (resp. SP2C), the only difference being that IdP2C is confidential to C and not simply weakly confidential thanks to the authentication of C on IdP (cf. lines 14-18). A precise definition of the properties of channels supported by HLPSL++ can be found in (Armando et al., 2008).

The HLPSL++ specification is concluded by the top-level role environment (see Figure 8). This role includes a const section (cf. lines 4-8) containing the declaration of global constants, the definition of the knowledge initially possessed by the intruder (cf. lines 9-11), and a composition section (cf. lines 13-14) that defines the parallel composition of the sessions. This specification

Figure 5. HLPSL++ specification of the SAML SSO protocol: Role IdP

```
1  role identityProvider (
2    C, IdP, SP : agent, KIdP : public_key,
3    IdP2C, C2IdP : channel
4    ) played_by IdP def=
5  Local
6    ID, URI : text,
7    State : nat
8  init
9    State:=7
10 transition
11 %% IdP receives an AuthReq(ID, SP) from C and issues a
12 %% Response(SP, C, IdP, ID)
13 A2_A3. State = 7 /\ rcv(C2IdP, C, C.IdP.(ID'.SP).URI') =|>
14          State':=9 /\ snd(IdP2C, C,
   SP.{SP.C.IdP.ID'}_inv(KIdP).URI')
15 end role
```

Figure 6. HLPSL++ specification of the SAML SSO protocol: Session

```
role session (
  C, IdP, SP : agent, KIdP : public_key,
  C2SP, SP2C, C2IdP, IdP2C : channel,
  URI : text
) def=
init
%% Assumption (A1): C <-> SP
     confidential(SP, C2SP)
  /\ weakly_authentic(C2SP)
  /\ weakly_confidential(SP2C)
  /\ authentic(SP, SP2C)
  /\ link(C2SP, SP2C)
%% Assumption (A2): C <-> IdP
  /\ confidential(IdP, C2IdP)
  /\ weakly_authentic(C2IdP)
  /\ confidential(C, IdP2C)
  /\ authentic(IdP, IdP2C)
  /\ link(C2IdP, IdP2C)
composition
     client(C, IdP, SP, KIdP, C2SP, SP2C, C2IdP, IdP2C,
URI)
  /\ serviceProvider(C, IdP, SP, KIdP, SP2C, C2SP, URI)
  /\ identityProvider(C, IdP, SP, KIdP, IdP2C, C2IdP)
end role
```

Figure 7. (a) Communication channels among basic roles; (b) Communication channels instantiated within the environment role

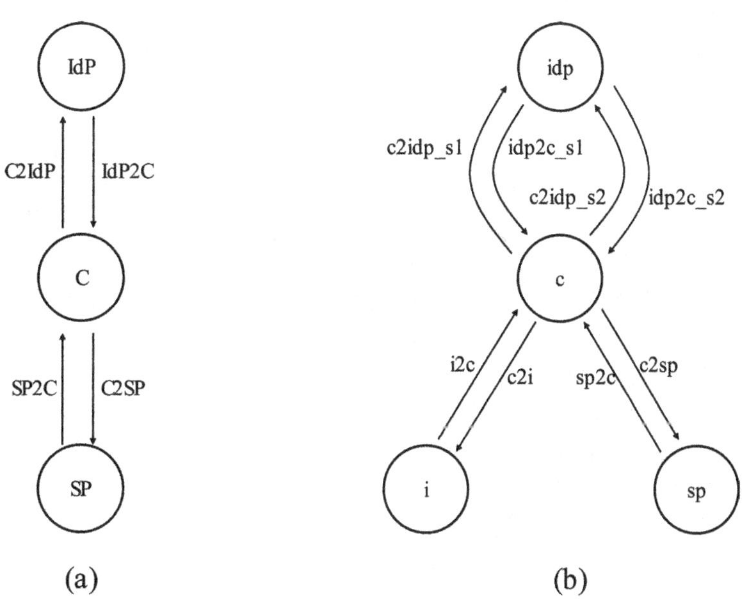

contains a session in which c and idp play the protocol with i (playing the role of SP) and a session in which c and idp play the protocol with sp by using proper communication channels to communicate (see part (b) of Figure 7). Notice that a constant i of type agent is implicitly declared and associated with the intruder.

The security properties that the protocol is expected to meet are stated in the goal section (cf. lines 17-22). These are the authentication property (P1) and the secrecy property (P2) described in Section «The SAML Web Browser SSO Profile». Hereafter more details will be provided about how these properties are modeled.

Authentication

The authentication property supported by the HLPSL++ language corresponds to the notion of agreement as defined in (Lowe, 1997). Thus, *SP authenticates C on URI* amounts to saying that whenever SP completes a run of the protocol apparently with C, then *(i)* C has previously been running the protocol apparently with SP, and *(ii)* the two agents agree on the value of URI (Lowe, 1997). To specify this property in HLPSL++ it suffices for SP to assert the fact request(SP, C, sp_c_uri, URI) in its last transition (cf. line 21 of Figure 4), and for C to assert the fact witness(C, SP, sp_c_uri, URI) as soon as it sends URI (cf. line 14 of Figure 3). The statement authentication_on sp_c_uri in the goal section (cf. line 19) states that if request(SP, C, sp_c_uri, URI) is asserted, then sometime in the past a corresponding witness(C, SP, sp_c_uri, URI) must have been asserted for the authentication property to hold. In fact, if a request is not matched by a corresponding witness, then the intruder must have been playing the protocol

Figure 8. HLPSL++ specification of the SAML SSO protocol: Environment and goals

```
1  role environment()
2  def=
3  Const
4    sp_c_uri, c_sp_resource, uri_i, uri_sp : protocol_id,
5    c, idp, sp : agent,
6    c2idp_s1,idp2c_s1,c2idp_s2,idp2c_s2,c2i,i2c,c2sp,sp2c:
   channel,
7    n : text,
8    kidp, ki : public_key,
9  intruder_knowledge={c, sp, idp, kidp, ki, inv(ki), uri_i,
   uri_sp, n,
10                     c2i, i2c, c2sp, sp2c, c2idp_s1, idp2c_s1,
11                     c2idp_s2, idp2c_s2}
12 Composition
13      session(c, idp, i, kidp, c2i, i2c, c2idp_s1, idp2c_s1,
   uri_i)
14   /\ session(c, idp, sp, kidp, c2sp, sp2c, c2idp_s2,
   idp2c_s2,uri_sp)
15 end role
16
17 Goal
18 %% property (P1)
19   authentication_on sp_c_uri
20 %% property (P2)
21   secrecy_of c_sp_resource
22 end goal
23
24 environment()
```

Table 1. Results of the experiments

Variant	Decisions				Property (P1)		
	Sign(AuthReq)	SP∈*AA*	ID∈*AA*	ID checked	Attack	Time (sec)	Steps
SAMLSSO	n	y	Y	y	n	15,2	21
GoogleSSO–Pre	n	n	N	-	y	3,7	13
SSOVariant1	y	n	N	-	y	3,3	13
SSOVariant2	n	n	Y	n	y	4,9	13
SSOVariant3	n	n	Y	y	y	11,3	17
SSOVariant4	n	y	N	-	n	3,7	15
GoogleSSO–Post	n	y	Y	n	n	8,4	18

run pretending to be the one that otherwise would have asserted the witness expression.

Secrecy

The secrecy property (P2) holds if and only if the resource at URI provided by SP to C is not learned by the intruder when the intruder is neither playing SP nor C in that protocol session. To specify this property in HLPSL++ it suffices for SP to assert the fact secret(Resource',c_sp_resource,{C,SP}) when sending the last message (cf. line 22 of Figure 4). (The identifier c_sp_resource serves as a label for this fact.) The statement secrecy_of c_sp_resource in the goal section (cf. line 21 in Figure 8) states that if secret(Resource',c_sp_resource,{C,SP}) is asserted, then i should not learn the secret value stored in Resource' unless i is the value of either C or SP.

Security Analysis of SAML-Based SSO Protocols

This section illustrates how the AVANTSSAR Platform can be used by software vendors and adopters of SAML SSO to evaluate the impact of their decisions (e.g., selected SAML SSO options and/or deviations from the SAML SSO standard) on the security of their SSO solutions. In doing so it focuses on a set of SAML-based SSO protocols ranging from that proposed by the OASIS standardization body (hereafter referred to as SAMLSSO) to the one currently in use by Google (GoogleSSO-Post) and considering in-between variants of the two, including the flawed version used by Google until June 2008 (GoogleSSO-Pre).

Table 1 presents an excerpt of the results obtained by running the AVANTSSAR Platform against all these SAML-based SSO variants that differ from each other for the decisions taken in their design, development, and/or deployment:

- **Sign(AuthReq):** it indicates whether the authentication request AuthReq is signed or not by the SP. (The SAML standard leaves this as optional.)
- **SP∈*AA*:** it indicates that the SP field is within the authentication assertion *AA* as required by the SAML standard.
- **ID∈*AA*:** it indicates that the ID field is within the authentication assertion *AA* as required by the SAML standard.
- **ID checked:** it indicates that SP checks that the ID value received in the authentication assertion is identical to the one it generated for the authentication request. (Stateless SPs may not be able to perform this check despite this is required by the SAML standard.)

Exhibit 1.

```
14        State':=9 /\ snd(IdP2C, C, SP.{C.IdP}_inv(KIdP).URI')
```

Exhibit 2.

```
19 A3_A4. State = 4 /\ rcv(IdP2C, IdP, SP.{C.IdP}_inv(KIdP).URI) =|>
20          State':=6 /\ snd(C2SP, SP, SP.{C.IdP}_inv(KIdP).URI)
```

Exhibit 3.

```
18 A4_S2. State = 3 /\ rcv(C2SP, C, SP.{C.IdP}_inv(KIdP).URI) =|>
```

For each variant, the table indicates the results of the analysis for the authentication property (P1): if there is an attack (Attack column), the time spent by the tool (Time column), and the number of steps required by SATMC to perform the analysis i.e., the number of steps necessary to either find the attack or prove the safety of the protocol (Steps column). (Experiments have been carried out on a laptop PC with an Intel Core 2 Duo 2.53 GHz CPU and 4 GB of RAM.) The results for the secrecy property (P2) are similar: when no attack is found on (P1), no attack is discovered on (P2) and whenever an attack is found on (P1), an attack on (P2) is found which contains an additional step in which the intruder receives the resource.

As shown in Table 1 the AVANTSSAR Platform does not find any attack on SAMLSSO. This means that the protocol is safe in the scenario considered.

GoogleSSO-Pre differs from SAMLSSO for the missing ID and SP fields in the authentication assertion. The reasons for not having used those fields are unknown. Maybe they were the consequence of internal requirements. For instance, a vendor may decide to not use ID as the advantages of handling it—from its generation in the authentication request to its check in the authentication response—are not evident when compared to potential drawbacks (e.g., additional communication between the server at the SP that generates the authentication request and the server at the SP that provides the final resources). To assess the implications of these decisions on the security of the protocol, the HLPSL++ specification for SAMLSSO has been modified by removing ID and SP from the authentication assertion. This amounts to carrying out the following changes in specification of the basic roles:

- **change for IdP:** Figure 5, line 14 becomes Exhibit 1
- **change for C:** Figure 3, lines 19-20 become Exhibit 2
- **change for SP:** Figure 4, lines 18 becomes Exhibit 3

By analyzing the resulting specification, the AVANTSSAR Platform reports violations on both authentication and secrecy in accordance with the discoveries outlined in (Armando et al., 2008). The attack shows that a compromised SP is able to impersonate a client at another SP. Figure 9 depicts the MSC returned by the AVANTSSAR Platform for the attack on the authentication property. The attack relies on the execution of two parallel protocol sessions where the intruder plays the man-in-the-middle by exploiting a weakness in the authentication assertion. In fact the authentication assertion no longer states that *C is authenticated at IdP for the request ID made at SP* as prescribed by the standard, but it simply

Figure 9. Attack on the SAML-based SSO for Google Apps

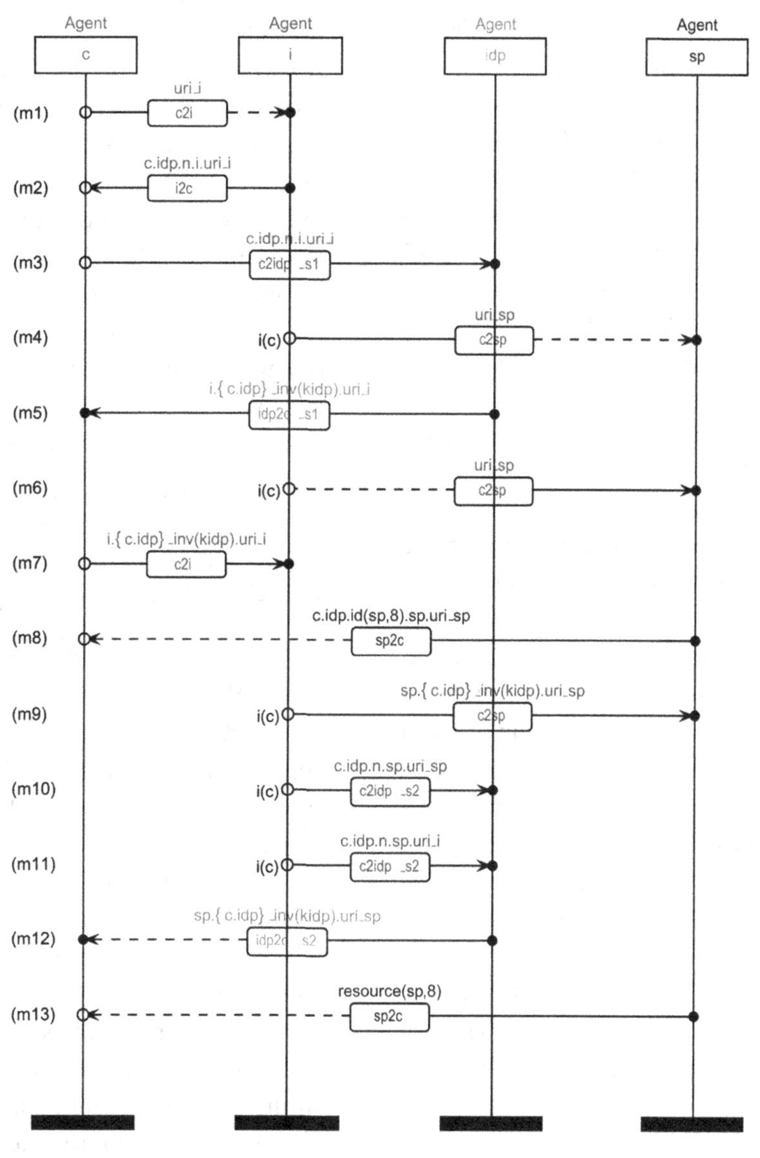

Legend:

A ∗—[ch]- -→⋆ B: A sends M to B over the channel ch

A ∗- -[ch]—→⋆ B: B receives M from the real sender A over the channel ch

A ∗—[ch]—→⋆ B: A sends M to B over the channel ch, and B receives it

Channel properties:

if $*$ = ○ then ch is weakly authentic

if $*$ = ● then ch is authentic for A

if $\star$ = ○ then ch is weakly confidential

if $\star$ = ● then ch is confidential to B

states that *C is authenticated to IdP*. This allows the intruder to misuse the assertion to get access to a different SP. More in detail:

- in message (m1) c initiates a session of the protocol to access a resource provided by the (malicious or compromised) service provider i. Notice that it is not necessary that the message is actually received by i because i already knows the content of the first message (uri_i).
- i sends to c a redirect response directed to idp containing an authentication request and the address uri_i of the resource (see messages (m2) and (m3)).
- The idp generates the authentication assertion which is posted by c to i (see messages (m5) and (m7)).
- In parallel i starts a new session of the protocol with sp pretending to be c (thus indicated as i(c)). This session is interleaved with the previous one. In message (m4) i sends the first message to sp, and in message (m6) this message is received by sp.
- The authentication request sent by sp to the official recipient c (see message (m8)) is neglected by i.
- The intruder mischievously reuses the assertion received by c (see message (m7)) to trick sp into believing he is c (see message (m9)).

In the MSC, different arrows are used to indicate if a particular message has been sent or received. The notation (*i*) $A \xrightarrow[ch]{M} B$ indicates that the message *M* has been sent by *A* over the channel *ch* to the agent *B* that has not received yet (pointed by the dotted arrow). With reference to the specification in Section «Formal Modeling of the SAML Web Browser SSO Profile», this corresponds to the execution of a transition of the basic role *A*, having as effect snd(*ch*,*B*,*M*). Notice that *M* will not be necessarily received by *B*. If this is the case, the notation (*ii*) $A \xrightarrow[ch]{M} B$ indicates that the message *M* sent by the sender *A* has been received by *B* (pointed by the solid arrow). With reference to the specification in Section «Formal Modeling of the SAML Web Browser SSO Profile», this corresponds to the execution of a transition of the basic role *B*, having as precondition rcv(*ch*,*B*,*M*). In order to increase the readability of the MSC, when the same message is sent and received by the same couple of agents in two contiguous steps, then (*i*) and (*ii*) are replaced by a single solid arrow, thus the resulting notation is as follows:

$$A \xrightarrow[ch]{M} B.$$

In the MSC, a bullet notation is used to display the properties of the channels defined in the HLPSL++ specification. For instance, the notation $A \xrightarrow[ch]{M} B$ indicates that the channel *ch* is weakly authentic and confidential to *B*, while $A \xrightarrow[ch]{M} B$ indicates that *ch* is authentic for *A* and confidential to *B*. A complete definition of these symbols is detailed in the legend of Figure 9.

Note that though SATMC is able to discover the shortest attack (if any), still this attack can comprise some spurious messages. This is the case for messages (m10), (m11), and (m12) that are not relevant for the attack.

As a possible countermeasure against this man-in-the-middle attack one may think to ask the SP to sign the authentication request. The corresponding HLPSL++ specification (SSOVariant1) is obtained by carrying out a few minor changes similarly to what it has been done above. By running the AVANTSSAR Platform against SSOVariant1, it has been discovered that the signature on the authentication assertion does not prevent the man-in-the-middle attack. The MSC of Figure 10 depicts the first four messages of this attack as the rest of the attack proceeds as in Figure 9, the only difference being the presence of the digitally signed authentication assertion in (m3) and (m4).

Figure 10. Attack on the SAML-based SSO for Google Apps despite signature on the authentication request

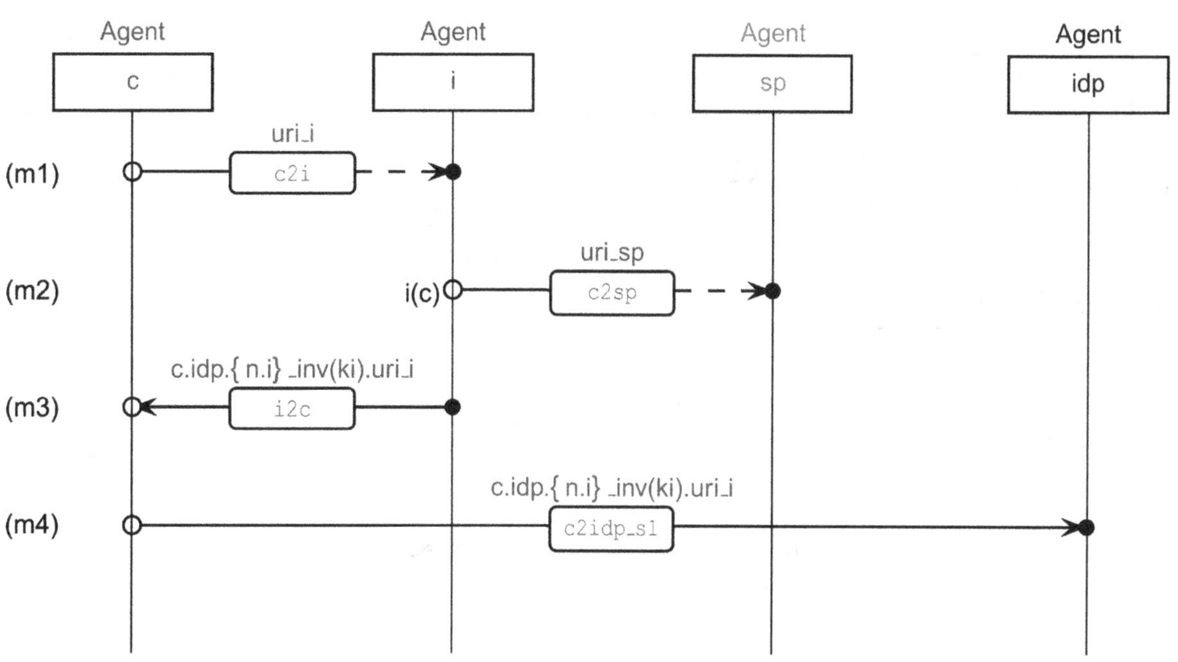

As shown above the lack of the SP field in the authentication assertion seems an insurmountable cause of the attack, but one may wonder whether the presence of the ID field in the authentication assertion could make the protocol secure. Two variants of the SAMLSSO protocol have been taken into account. Both of them do not contain the SP field in the authentication assertion but contain the ID field: SSOVariant2 and SSOVariant3. In the latter SP checks that the ID in the authentication assertion is identical to the one included in the authentication request, while in the former this check is omitted. Both variants are still vulnerable to the attack. Notice that the attack on SSOVariant3 requires a few more steps (cf. Table 1). In fact, differently from the previous attacks, the intruder cannot start the two sessions in parallel, because he needs to know the ID generated by sp before starting the session with c. The MSC of Figure 11 depicts the first messages of the attack, in which i starts a session of the protocol with sp in order to obtain the ID (cf. messages (m1) and (m2)). When i receives the request by c (cf. message (m3)), she sends to c message (m4) which contains the ID obtained in (m2). Thus, the authentication assertion produced by idp for i contains the ID expected by sp. The analysis of SSOVariant2 and SSOVariant3 thus confirms that the SP field is indeed necessary to prevent the man-in-the-middle attack of Figure 9.

One may now wonder whether the ID field, which is mandated by the standard, is necessary to achieve the expected security property. The specification SSOVariant4 models the variant of the protocol where the ID field is dropped from both the authentication request and the authentication assertion. No attack is found by the AVANTSSAR Platform in this case. This result questions the importance and need of the ID field: though this field is useful to link the authentication response with the corresponding authentication request (which seems a good practice to proceed with), it seems irrelevant for the authentication and secrecy properties that have been considered.

Figure 11. Excerpt of the attack on SSOVariant3

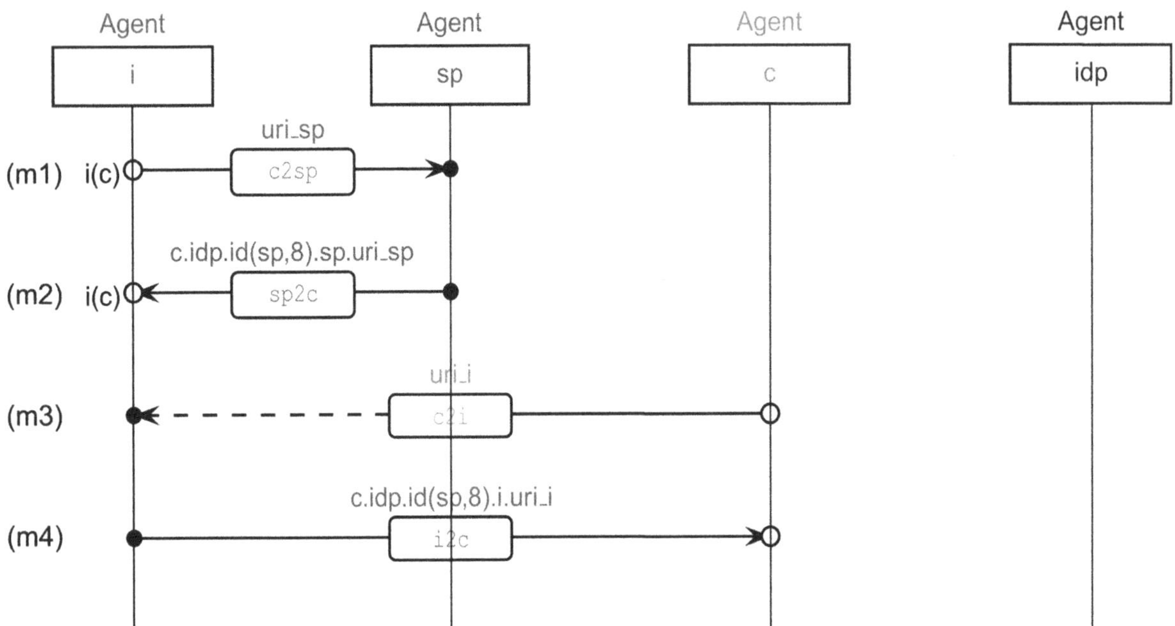

Finally it has been built a HLPSL++ specification of the current version of the SAML-based SSO for Google Apps which is in operation since August 2008. This specification (GoogleSSO-Post) comprises the ID field in both the authentication request and the authentication assertion but the correspondence of these values is not checked by the Google SP. As expected, by running the AVANTSSAR Platform on GoogleSSO-Post no attack is found.

FUTURE RESEARCH DIRECTIONS

As shown in the previous section, model checking is effective to automatically detect subtle flaws in the logic of distributed applications. Yet, it must be noted that the analysis is carried out on a formal model of the system (as opposed to the actual system) and therefore the applicability of model checking techniques is usually confined to the design phase.

Security testing, unlike model checking, can be used to check the behavior of the actual system. It has been successfully applied to authorization and similar application-level policies. A special form of security testing, namely penetration testing, is effective in finding low-level vulnerabilities in on-line applications (e.g., cross-site scripting), but heavily relies on the guidance and expertise of the user. Security testing is normally applied in later stages of the service life-cycle, i.e., during the deployment or even the consumption phase.

Both model checking and security testing are already routinely used to unveil serious vulnerabilities and are therefore going to play a central role in improving the security of SSO solutions, and more generally of web-based applications. However, there is an enormous potential in using these technologies in combination rather than in isolation. In fact, state-of-the-art security verification technologies, if used in isolation, do not provide automated support to the discovery of important vulnerabilities and of the associated exploits that are already plaguing complex, web-based, security-sensitive applications. On the one hand, while model checking is key to the discovery of subtle vulnerabilities due to unexpected interleavings of service executions, it provides no support to testing the actual services. On the other hand, penetration testing tools—by supporting the analysis of a single service at a time—lack the global view and the automated reasoning capabilities necessary to discover the kind of vulnerabilities found by model checkers, but provide both infrastructure and repertoires of testing techniques that are very useful to find exploits related to the high-level vulnerabilities found by model checkers.

The integration of model checking for security protocols and security testing can be achieved by automatically deriving test cases from counter-examples found through model checking. Preliminary work in this direction is proposed in (Armando, Carbone, Compagna, Li, & Pellegrino, 2010), where the feasibility of the approach is illustrated via its application to the SAML SSO.

CONCLUSION

Model checking is a verification technique that helps finding flaws in security-sensitive, distributed applications at the different phases of the service life-cycle. This chapter shows that model checking can be used by software vendors and adopters of SAML SSO to automatically assess the impact of their decisions (e.g., choice of options and/or deviations from the standard) on the security of their SSO solutions. The practical viability of the approach has been demonstrated through the application of a state-of-the-art model checker to support the security analysis of several variants of the SAML SSO. The analysis confirms the attack on the SAML-based SSO for Google Apps in operation until June 2008 as well as on variants thereof. The analysis also confirms the security of the SAML SSO 2.0 as well as of the SAML-based SSO for Google Apps in operation since August 2008, since no attack has been detected despite the several protocol scenarios considered. The analysis seems also to indicate that the presence of the ID field in authentication assertion—which is mandated by the standard—does not affect the security of the protocol.

ACKNOWLEDGMENT

This work was partially supported by the FP7-ICT-2009-5 Project no. 257876, "SPaCIoS: Secure Provision and Consumption in the Internet of Services" (www.spacios.eu) and by the "Automated Security Analysis of Identity and Access Management Systems (SIAM)" project funded by Provincia Autonoma di Trento in the context of the "Team 2009 – Incoming" COFUND action of the European Commission (FP7).

REFERENCES

Armando, A., Basin, D., Boichut, Y., Chevalier, Y., Compagna, L., Cuellar, J., et al. (2005). The AVISPA tool for the automated validation of internet security protocols and applications. In *Proceedings of the 17th International Conference on Computer Aided Verification (CAV'05)*. Springer-Verlag. Retrieved from www.avispa-project.org

Armando, A., Carbone, R., & Compagna, L. (2007, July). *LTL model checking for security protocols*. In 20th IEEE Computer Security Foundations Symposium (CSF20). Venice (Italy).

Armando, A., Carbone, R., Compagna, L., Cuéllar, J., & Tobarra, M. L. (2008, October). Formal analysis of SAML 2.0 Web browser single sign-on: Breaking the SAML-based single sign-on for Google Apps. In V. Shmatikov (Ed.), *Proceedings of the 6th ACM Workshop on Formal Methods in Security Engineering, FMSE 2008* (pp. 1–10). ACM.

Armando, A., Carbone, R., Compagna, L., Li, K., & Pellegrino, G. (2010, 6-10). Model-checking driven security testing of web-based applications. In *2010 Third International Conference on Software Testing, Verification, and Validation Workshops (ICSTW)* (pp. 361 -370).

Armando, A., & Compagna, L. (2008, January). SAT-based model-checking for security protocols analysis. *International Journal of Information Security*, *7*(1), 3–32. doi:10.1007/s10207-007-0041-y

Basin, D. (1999). Lazy infinite-state analysis of security protocols. In Baumgart, R. (Ed.), *Secure networking — CQRE (Secure)'99* (pp. 30–42). Springer-Verlag. doi:10.1007/3-540-46701-7_3

Chevalier, Y., Compagna, L., Cuellar, J., Hankes Drielsma, P., Mantovani, J., Mödersheim, S., et al. (2004). A high level protocol specification language for industrial security-sensitive protocols. In *Proc. SAPS'04.* Austrian Computer Society.

Chevalier, Y., Küsters, R., Rusinowitch, M., & Turuani, M. (2003). An NP decision procedure for protocol insecurity with XOR. In P. Kolaitis (Ed.), *Proceedings of LICS'2003.* IEEE.

Dolev, D., & Yao, A. (1983). On the security of public-key protocols. *IEEE Transactions on Information Theory*, *2*(29).

Durgin, N., Lincoln, P. D., Mitchell, J. C., & Scedrov, A. (1999). Undecidability of bounded security protocols. In *Proceedings of the FLOC'99 Workshop on Formal Methods and Security Protocols (FMSP'99).*

Groß, T., Pfitzmann, B., & Sadeghi, A.-R. (2005). Browser model for security analysis of browser-based protocols. In di Vimercati, S. D. C., Syverson, P. F., & Gollmann, D. (Eds.), *ESORICS* (*Vol. 3679*, pp. 489–508). Springer. doi:10.1007/11555827_28

Hansen, S. M., Skriver, J., & Nielson, H. R. (2005). Using static analysis to validate the SAML single sign-on protocol. In *WITS '05: Proceedings of the 2005 Workshop on Issues in the Theory of sEcurity* (pp. 27–40). New York, NY: ACM Press.

Jacquemard, F., Rusinowitch, M., & Vigneron, L. (2000). Compiling and verifying security protocols. In M. Parigot & A. Voronkov (Eds.), *Proceedings of LPAR 2000* (pp. 131–160). Springer-Verlag.

Lowe, G. (1996). Breaking and fixing the Needham-Schroeder public-key protocol using FDR. In T. Margaria & B. Steffen (Eds.), *Proceedings of TACAS'96* (pp. 147–166). Springer-Verlag.

Lowe, G. (1997). A hierarchy of authentication specifications. In *Proceedings of the 10th IEEE Computer Security Foundations Workshop (CSFW'97)* (pp. 31–43). IEEE Computer Society Press.

Meadows, C. (1996). The NRL protocol analyzer: An overview. *The Journal of Logic Programming*, *26*(2), 113–131. Retrieved from http://chacs.nrl.navy.mil/projects/crypto.html. doi:10.1016/0743-1066(95)00095-X

Millen, J. K., & Shmatikov, V. (2001). Constraint solving for bounded-process cryptographic protocol analysis. In *Proceedings of the ACM Conference on Computer and Communications Security CCS'01* (p. 166-175).

Mödersheim, S., & Viganò, L. (2009). The open-source fixed-point model checker for symbolic analysis of security protocols. In *Fosad 2007-2008-2009* (vol. 5705, pp. 166–194). Springer-Verlag.

Needham, R. M., & Schroeder, M. D. (1978). *Using encryption for authentication in large networks of computers* (Tech. Rep. No. CSL-78-4). Palo Alto, CA: Xerox Palo Alto Research Center.

OASIS. (2005a, April). *Security assertion markup language (SAML) v2.0.* Retrieved from http://www.oasis-open.org/committees/tc_home.php?wg_abbrev=security

OASIS. (2005b, July). *SSTC response to security analysis of the SAML single sign-on browser/artifact profile.* Retrieved from http://www.oasis-open.org/committees/tc_home.php?wg_abbrev=security

Rusinowitch, M., & Turuani, M. (2001). Protocol insecurity with finite number of sessions is NP-complete. In *Proceedings of the 14th IEEE Computer Security Foundations Workshop.* IEEE Computer Society Press.

The AVANTSSAR Team. (n.d.). *The AVANTSSAR project.* Retrieved from http://www.avantssar.eu/

Turuani, M. (2006). The CL-Atse protocol analyser. In *Term Rewriting and Applications (Proceedings of RTA'06)* (pp. 277-286).

US-CERT. (2008, Sep 2). *Vulnerability note VU#612636 - Google SAML single sign on vulnerability.* Retrieved from http://www.kb.cert.org/vuls/id/612636

Chapter 11
Denial of Service Resilience of Authentication Systems

Valer Bocan
Alcatel-Lucent, Romania

Mihai Fagadar-Cosma
Alcatel-Lucent, Romania

ABSTRACT

Cryptographic authentication systems are currently the de facto standard for securing clients access to network services. Although they offer enhanced security for the parties involved in the communication process, they still have a vulnerable point represented by their susceptibility to denial of service (DoS) attacks. The present chapter addresses two important aspects related to the security of authentication systems and their resistance against strong DoS attacks, represented by attack detection and attack prevention. In this respect, we present a detailed analysis of the methods used to evaluate the attack state of an authentication system as well as of the countermeasures that can be deployed to prevent or repel a DoS attack.

INTRODUCTION

Denial of service attacks on authentication systems can take two possible forms. On one hand, an attacker can prevent the network from sending the messages that it should normally transmit to its clients. On the other hand, it could force the network into sending messages it should not normally transmit. By far, the most popular DoS attack is server flooding that prevents legitimate clients from obtaining the services they request from that server.

One cause for the vulnerability to DoS in authentication systems is that the dialog between peers takes place before even a minimum pre-authentication is performed, which renders the server incapable of distinguishing legitimate from malicious traffic. Enforcing the authentication of all requests would represent a DoS attack by itself, since the server would be busy checking all

DOI: 10.4018/978-1-61350-498-7.ch011

digital signatures, no matter if these are valid or not. Such a method would be as dangerous as a TCP stack overflow is in case of TCP SYN attacks.

Another vulnerability is the lack of resource accounting. In this respect Spatscheck and Peterson (1999) consider that there are 3 key ingredients for protecting against DoS attacks: accounting all resources allocated to a client, detecting the moment when these resources rise above a predefined threshold and constraining the allocated resources by reducing them to a minimum level in case an attack has been detected and recovering the blocked resources.

The third vulnerability resides in the intrinsic design of the communication protocols, as described by Crosby and Wallach (2003). A new class of low-bandwidth attacks exploits the deficiencies of data structures employed in various applications. For example, hash tables and binary trees can degenerate into simple linked lists when input data is selected accordingly. Using the typical bandwidth of a dial-up modem, the authors have managed to bring a Bro server on the edge of collapsing: 6 minutes after the attack has begun, the server was ignoring 71% of traffic and was consuming its entire computational power.

Taking in consideration the global market tendency towards on-line availability, DoS attacks prove to be more dangerous than initially predicted therefore identifying them as soon as they take place is a decisive aspect. From the moment the attack has begun until it is detected and countermeasures are deployed, the targeted servers are blocked and all legitimate requests are ignored, which can result in significant financial losses. Chained attacks can occur if the communication protocol continues its dialogue with the attacker even after anomalies have been detected. The basic idea behind the so called fail-safe or fail-stop protocols is for the message-exchange to be discontinued with any client that does not follow the normal course of the protocol.

Considering the attack forms and characteristics described above, a resilient authentication system must fulfill two main requirements. First, the system must be able to detect an incoming attack as soon as possible in order to be able to respond accordingly and prevent any possible losses. Second, the system must be able to defend itself against an ongoing attack, either through its intrinsic characteristics or by deploying a set of countermeasures against the attacker. Given these requirements, we have structured this chapter into two main parts. In the first part we address the strategy and the techniques that enable an authentication system to efficiently detect DoS attacks, and their implementation into a detection engine called SSO-SENSE. In the second part we focus on the threshold puzzles concept as an a efficient way to protect against DoS attacks and analyze the case study of the SSL Handshake algorithm from both an implementation and a performance perspective.

BACKGROUND

The Client Puzzles Concept

An efficient measure for preventing DoS attacks during the authentication phase would be to ensure that the client allocates its resources proportionally with the resources allocated by the server. As a result, at any time during the execution of the authentication protocol, the computational cost for the client will be higher than that of the server. This can be achieved by asking the client to solve a puzzle with a difficulty established by the server. The solution to the client puzzle should be easily accessible to the server, in order to obtain a low resource usage, while the client should be forced to allocate computational resources into solving the puzzle according to the complexity requested by the server.

Merkle (1978) was the first to come up with the idea of using cryptographic puzzles, but he applied the concept only for key exchange and not for the authentication itself. Later, the client

Figure 1. The client puzzle concept

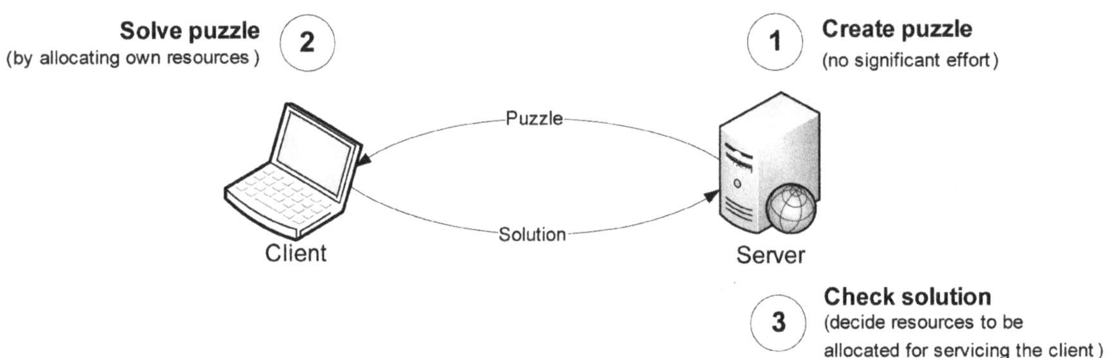

puzzles concept has been successfully applied against TCP SYN attacks by Juels and Brainard (1999), who also outline the vulnerability of SSL protocols against DoS attacks and provide a rigorous demonstration of their security characteristics. Aura, Nikander and Leiwo (2000) have applied the puzzles to authentication protocols in general while Dwork and Naor (1992) have proposed measures for regulating unsolicited messages within a protocol.

According to Aura, Nikander and Leiwo (2000) and to Harris (2001), the client puzzle must have a set of well-defined properties, as follows:

- Creating a puzzle and verifying the solution must not require significant resources on the server side;
- The cost of solving the puzzle should easily be changed from 0 to infinity;
- The puzzle should be solvable on most hardware platforms;
- Pre-calculating the solution to the puzzle must be impossible;
- While the client solves the puzzle, the server must not store the solution or other client-specific information; the same puzzle can be distributed to several clients, knowing that the solutions provided by one or more clients do not help in calculating a new solution;
- A client may reuse a puzzle by creating one or more of its instances.

The client puzzle concept is shown in Figure 1.

Client puzzles can take various forms, the most popular ones being the partial inversion of a hash function (Juels & Brainard, 1999; Aura, Nikkander & Leiwo, 2000), the discrete logarithm inversion applied by Waters, Juels, Halderman and Felten (2004), the time-locked puzzles proposed by Rivest, Shamir and Wagner (1996) and linked puzzles (Groza & Petrica, 2006; Ma, 2006).

Creating and Solving a Puzzle

Periodically (usually once every several minutes) the server generates a random 64 bit value N_S, enough to prevent the client from guessing the puzzle result. The server also attaches a value k to the puzzle, representing the puzzle complexity. In short, the puzzle which is sent by the server to its clients can be represented as a <Ns, k> pair.

In order to solve the puzzle, the client generates a random value N_C, with a double purpose: first, the client can generate a new puzzle by reusing the value N_S provided by the server to create the N_C value and second, it prevents an attacker from calculating the puzzle and sending it to the server before the legitimate client. A 24 bit size should be enough for this value, given the fact that it changes very often.

The client has to apply repeatedly a hash function to a quantity Y, and the puzzle is considered solved when the 1st k bits of the quantity Y are equal to 0, according to the equation

$$h(C, N_S, N_C, X) = Y,$$

where:

- h represents the hash function (e.g. MD5 or SHA),
- N_S is the random value generated by the server,
- N_C is the random value generated by the client,
- C represents the client identity and
- X is the solution to be sent to the server.

The server also maintains a list of the recently used $<N_S, N_C>$ pairs in order to prevent them from being reused.

Since there is no known way of determining X other than by brute-force, the client will be forced to use its computational power to reach the solution. The value k controls the puzzle complexity and thus the time needed for the client to reach the solution. The edge cases are k=0 which means no effort at all and k=128 for MD5 or 192 for the SHA function means a puzzle nearly impossible to solve.

Shortcomings of the Classical Puzzle Concept

Client puzzles make a good choice for securing authentication protocols, as long as the attack is not distributed (Schneier, 2000). One shortcoming is the fact that the computational power available to the client is ignored, since the puzzle difficulty is established using a metric that takes in consideration only the server engagement. As a result, an attacker which has access to significant computational power can unleash a so-called strong attack against the server, and can solve puzzles faster than a legitimate client.

During a strong attack, the server gradually increases the puzzle complexity up to levels which are very difficult for normal clients, which represents a DoS attack in itself. If the attacker has access to multiple computers and can solve the puzzle using parallel computing, it can reduce the solving time considerably. There are many real-life examples of such applications in literature, the SETI @home Program (2010) and the effort to break the RSA algorithm supported by the Distributed.net Organization (2010) being only two of them.

These considerations emphasize the necessity of adopting a puzzle mechanism which enables the server to assess the computational power of its clients and adapt the puzzle complexity accordingly, also taking in consideration the overall security status of the system. This requirement is even more complex given the variety of computational devices that can connect to a network service and the fact that the service must respond within an acceptable timeframe to all its legitimate clients, while at the same time keeping any possible attackers at bay.

DOS ATTACK DETECTION IN AUTHENTICATION SYSTEMS

Measurable Characteristics

The first step in being able to effectively protect against a DoS attack is to detect its presence. Thus, it is mandatory to determine if the server load is caused by a temporary and transitory aspect, by a peak in the network traffic, or by an attack. Deploying countermeasures induces a penalty experienced by clients as a drop in performance,

Figure 2. Detecting a possible DoS attack against a SSO authentication system by monitoring the protocol execution order

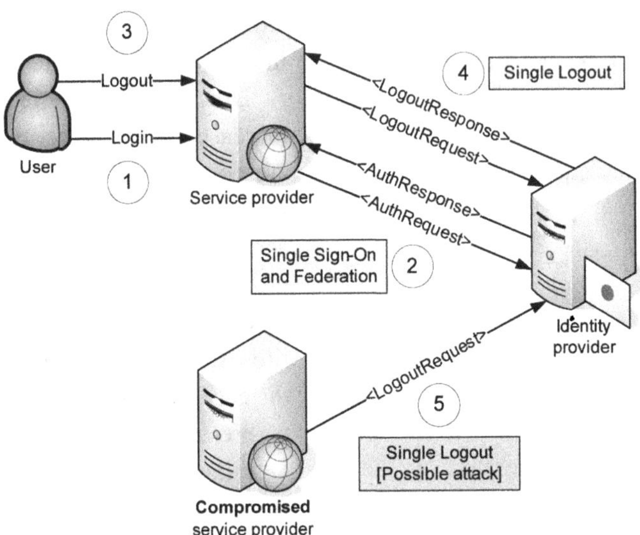

and this situation can become unpleasant as it appears more frequently.

Due to the complex nature of authentication systems and to the wide range of possible configurations into which they may be deployed, attack detection is an important challenge especially because of the lack of standard risk assessment metrics. In this section we propose three measurable characteristics that can be used as metrics in evaluating the system status and determining the threat level, and apply them as a case study to SSO systems based on the Liberty protocol suite (Liberty Alliance Project, 2010a, 2010b).

Protocol Discipline

The first aspect in this category is the order of protocol execution. The exchange of messages between server and clients must follow a certain order and any disturbance in this order can indicate a possible attack on the system. Given the example of the Liberty protocol suite, a Single Logout request should not be received by a service or identity provider if the Single Sign-On and Federation request has been previously received (Bocan & Fagadar, 2005b), as shown in *Figure 2*.

The request content is another characteristic to be considered. For each protocol, the request has a set of specific attributes which specify how the request should be processed by the receiving entity. A large variation of these attributes coming from a client may indicate a possible attack. For example, the AuthRequest message of the Single Sign-On and Federation protocol has an attribute which requests the identity provider to emit a temporary and anonymous identifier on behalf of the client, when data is exchanged among service providers. Too many requests of this kind received from the same client can indicate a DoS attack against the identity provider.

Network Health

Network health can be assessed by measuring traffic parameters on the server reception side and can be used to identify several aspects, such as:

- *network operation anomalies* represented by an abrupt increase in the measured values over a given time span;
- *flash crowd anomalies* due to the synergistic behavior of a group of users (e.g. when a new software product is available for download); this kind of anomaly can be detected in well-known points in the network such as download locations or mirror servers;
- *abuse anomalies* generated by ongoing DoS attacks or port scanning activities.

A software sensor can be placed in the system in order to monitor the anomalies and provide the relevant information—in raw or aggregated form—to the attack detection engine. According to several studies (Siaterlis & Maglaris, 2004; Kim, Lau, Chuah & Chao, 2004), reception parameters such as the time between two consecutive requests, request size, number of requests per second received from the same client can be used successfully to detect an ongoing DoS attack, but they must be incorporated into a more complex system for evaluating the health status of the authentication system.

System Health

System health is a crucial aspect which directly impacts the quality of service (QoS). If the system is functioning at nominal levels it can provide the QoS established by design. Altering these levels, either due to software or to hardware conditions, will lead to an immediate change in the QoS which will have as consequences delays in providing the response to the clients, intermittent responses or even a lack of response from the server.

System health can be characterized by several parameters, including processor load factor, available memory, frequency of I/O operations, resource reserve for virtual machines and the current state of system services, drivers or daemon processes.

Obtaining and Correlating the Threat Assessment Metrics

The information retrieved from the software sensors which measure the three main system characteristics presented above must be aggregated in order to reach a decision regarding the current threat level of the server.

The sensors which monitor the protocol discipline must be implemented directly into the SSO protocol, so that they have unrestricted access to the message exchange between peers. The sensors responsible of monitoring the network and system health can use the performance indicators built into the operating systems, such as *Simple Network Management Protocol* (SNMP), *Management Information Base* (MIB) indicators or *Windows Management Instrumentation* (WMI) specific to Microsoft Windows operating systems.

The threat level, at its simplest form, can be modeled as a real numerical value ranging between 0 and 1. A value of 0 indicates with the highest degree of certitude that the system is working properly and no attack is in progress, while a value of 1 represents a clear indication that the system is being affected by an ongoing attack which could lead to service failure. Any value in between can be considered as a degree of certitude associated to the detection of an ongoing attack.

As shown in one of our papers (Bocan & Fagadar, 2005b), Bayesian inference can be a good correlation mechanism for the information provided by the sensors, which generates as a direct output the probability that an attack has been identified, equal to the threat level.

CASE STUDY: THE SSO-SENSE RISK ASSESSMENT MODULE

System Overview

The SSO-SENSE is a specialized software module which relies on Bayesian inference theory in

Figure 3. Block diagram of the SSO-SENSE module

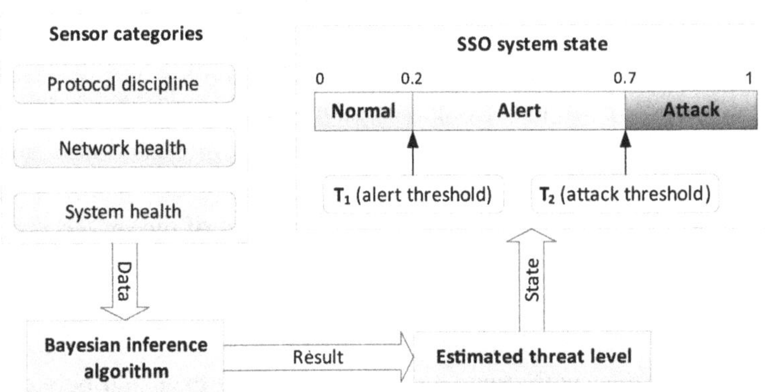

order to monitor network traffic and detect DoS attacks in Single Sign-On (SSO) environments. SSO-SENSE aims at providing better security for SSO systems, which are particularly vulnerable to DoS attacks since the protocols require every message to be signed.

As shown in *Figure 3*, SSO-SENSE gathers its input from a set of software sensors grouped across the three main categories mentioned earlier (protocol discipline, network health and system health) and applies Bayesian inference in order to estimate the threat level T of the system. Depending on this level, the system can be in one of the three states:

- *normal*, in which the system works within nominal parameters without being influenced by an attack;
- *alerted*, which indicates that the SSO system may be targeted by an attack and countermeasures like puzzle technology should be employed in order to reduce and control the rate of requests coming from the possible attacker;
- *attacked*, indicating a clearly identified DoS attack is in progress in which the server should forcibly close its connection with the attacker in order to save its resources for other legitimate clients.

In order to identify the current system state, SSO-SENSE compares the threat level with two thresholds, the alert threshold T_1 and the attack threshold T_2, with $0 < T_1 < T_2 < 1$, chosen in such a way as to efficiently delimit two adjacent states.

Evaluating the Threat Level using Bayesian Inference

When applying the Bayesian inference algorithm, SSO-SENSE considers a set of three mutually exclusive hypotheses H_1, H_2 and H_3, each associated with one of the system states. Initially, when system starts, a safe state is considered, for example $P(H_1) = 0.9$ for the normal state, $P(H_2) = 0.09$ for the alert state and $P(H_3) = 0.01$ for the attack state, where $P(H_i)$ represents the probability of hypothesis H_i being true.

When an event E is signaled by a software sensor which detects a cross-threshold condition within the measurable characteristics of the authentication system, that event will be used as evidence to compute the normalization factor Λ, as follows:

$\Lambda = P(E|H_1) \cdot P(H_1) + P(E|H_2) \cdot P(H_2) + P(E|H_3) \cdot P(H_3)$where, according to the Bayesian inference theory, $P(E \mid H_i)$ represents the conditional probability of seeing the evidence E if hypothesis H_i is true.

Next, SSO-SENSE evaluates the posterior probability of each hypothesis in the light of evidence E, according to Bayes' theorem:

$$P(H_i \mid E) = P(E \mid H_i) \cdot P(H_i) / \Lambda.$$

In the end, the current threat level T is determined, according to the following formula:

$$T = \max[P(H_1 \mid E), P(H_2 \mid E), P(H_3 \mid E)].$$

The event E which triggers the threat evaluation can be classified into one of the following categories:

- A break into the authentication protocol, such as message inversion, message loss or messages with incomplete parameters;
- Time between two successive requests coming from the same client;
- An authentication error;
- Sudden increase in CPU load for a short period of time;
- Sudden increase in network traffic, except for flash crowd anomalies;
- Port scanning activities.

Applying Heuristic Attack Detection to the Authentication Process

The various methods used to protect against DoS attacks in authentication systems can be enhanced in terms of behavior and efficiency by using the additional information provided by an attack detection engine. While a complex intrusion detection engine applied globally to the whole network may help in a general manner, attack detection on the authentication vector addresses a specific issue. In this case, the attacker does not aim to break into the system and steal valuable information but instead his goal is to compromise the authentication and to prevent legitimate clients from accessing a network service, an aspect which is not covered by the existing intrusion detection systems.

The SSO-SENSE has been specifically designed for monitoring the authentication process, which represents the gate into the system. Let us consider the simple case of an SSO system, illustrated in *Figure 4*.

A compromised service provider launches a DoS attack against two identity providers, which are both protected against attacks by their built-in client puzzle technology. The difference is that identity provider B benefits of the presence of the SSO-SENSE engine, which allows it to take efficient actions against the attacker with lesser impact on legitimate clients.

When using the classical client puzzle concept, the maximum puzzle difficulty k_{max} is calculated according to the formula:

$$k_{max} = \log_2(\max(1, Q \cdot t_S / t_C)) + 1,$$

where:

- Q represents the current size of the request queue on the server;
- t_S represents the average server time per puzzle solving operation;
- t_C represents the average client time per puzzle solving operation.

If no additional information is present regarding an imminent attack, identity provider A will choose the puzzle difficulty proportionally with the size of the request queue or according to a predefined variation rule. This will result in the same server behavior regardless of the presence of an attack.

If additional information is present, like in the case of identity provider B, the current state of the system can be used to decide on the variation rule of puzzle complexity k, as follows:

- In the *normal state*, the server does not reach its maximum load except for a few peak moments. As a consequence, lower

Figure 4. Heuristic attack detection on the authentication vector

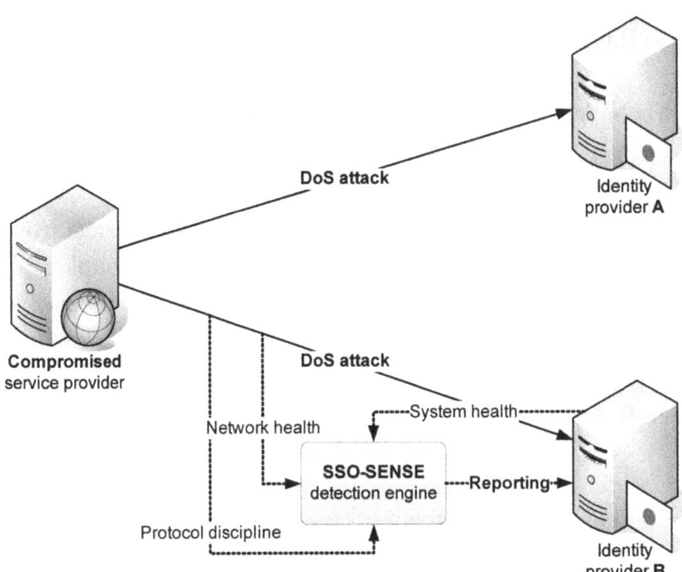

complexity puzzles can be chosen from the lower region of the [0, k_{max}) interval.

- In the *alerted state*, the server load constantly rises above the usual threshold, without necessarily indicating that an attack is in progress. However, as a precaution, medium complexity puzzles will be selected within the [0, k_{max}] range.
- For the *attacked state*, in which an attack has been identified with a reasonable certainty, the server will use k_{max} as difficulty level for all puzzles, even if it has not reached its maximum load.

Experimental Results

We have implemented SSO-SENSE on the Microsoft.NET 3.5 framework, using the C# language. In order to determine the behavior of the Bayesian inference module, the test scenario was composed of two real-life situations:

- Repeated failed authentication attempts, purposely generated by an attacker to increase the server load;
- Repeated breaks the normal flow of the protocol - by sending responses which do not comply with the protocol specification - which cause the server to keep waiting for a proper response until a timeout occurs.

During the simulation, the initial state of the SSO system was the *normal state*, with parameters Q = 400000, t_S = 0.003 and t_C = 0.5. As a result, k_{max} = 12.

Failed authentication attempts are low gravity events, therefore the transition from the normal to the attack state is done by passing through several alert states. As shown in the first series of *Figure 5*, after the first failed attempt the system maintains the normal state since such an event can be commonly generated by legitimate users. However, the following events will increase the system awareness by raising the threat level and forcing the system into a more defensive state,

Figure 5. SSO-SENSE simulation results

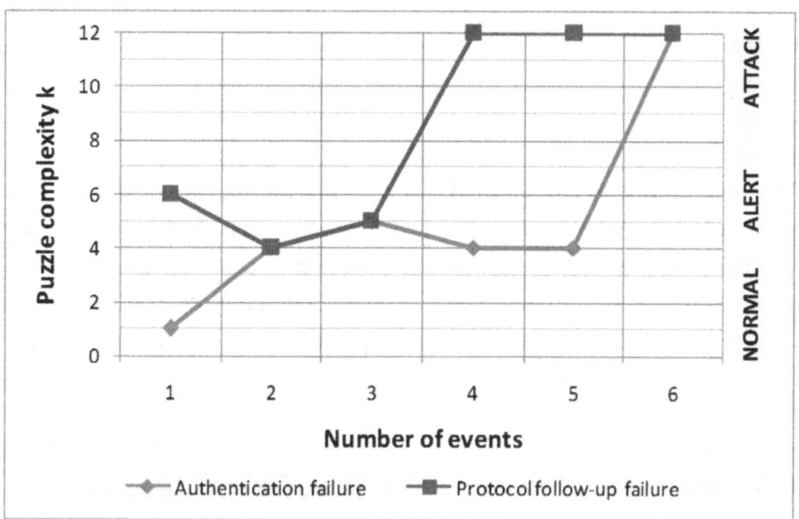

thereby signaling the system administrator that the gravity of the situation has been growing.

Protocol errors are more serious as established through the conditional probabilities associated to the hypotheses in the Bayesian inference engine. As a result, the system converges to the *attacked state* faster, as illustrated in the second series of *Figure 5*.

THRESHOLD PUZZLES AND ADAPTIVE THRESHOLD PUZZLES

The Need for Threshold Puzzles

The behavior of an authentication system protected by the current client puzzle technology can sometimes be suboptimal. There are two main reasons for this:

1. There is no upper limit to the puzzle complexity, which can result in clients spending too much time solving high complexity puzzles;
2. There is no minimum response time which could prevent an attacker from finding the puzzle solution too fast and overloading the server with a burst of requests.

Starting from these two limitations of client puzzles, we propose an improved solution which overcomes them by applying thresholds to both the puzzle complexity and the client response time. We will call the improved solution a *threshold puzzle* (Bocan, 2004).

Establishing an Upper Limit for the Puzzle Difficulty

The current client puzzle design specifies a difficulty range between 0 (no solving effort required) and 128 or 192 (theoretically impossible to solve, according to the employed hash function). Since this difficulty increases exponentially the current implementations of this mechanism are limited to using a narrow value range. High difficulty levels would result in DoS attacks targeted at legitimate clients, since these clients may spend a significant amount of time solving the puzzle.

In order to obtain an optimal perception of puzzle difficulty at client level, the solving time spent by the client must be lower than the time needed by the server to service a client request given the current load, which translates into the following inequality:

$$T_{client} \leq T_{server}.$$

Considering M to be the average number of operations required to solve the puzzle and t_C, the average time per operation at the client level, we can define the solving time at the client level as

$$T_{client} = M \cdot t_C$$

M can in turn be expressed in relation to the puzzle complexity k, since

$$M = 2^k \cdot (2^k + 1) / 2^{k+1} \approx 2^{k-1}$$

which leads to the approximation $M \approx 2^{k-1}$. As a result, we obtain the following equation:

$$T_{client} = 2^{k-1} \cdot t_C.$$

The time in which the server is able to respond to a request is proportional to the current size of the request waiting queue Q as well as to its average time per operation t_S, therefore the time spent by the server becomes

$$T_{server} = Q \cdot t_S.$$

The initial inequality can now be written as

$$2^{k-1} \cdot t_C \leq Q \cdot t_S$$

which gives us the upper limit for the puzzle complexity k, since

$$k \leq \log_2(Q \cdot t_S / t_C) + 1.$$

In case of a low server load, the logarithm quantity $Q \cdot t_S / t_C$ may be smaller than 1, which could result in a negative value for k. In order to avoid this situation, we will consider the following inequality which ensures that k has always a positive value

$$k \leq \log_2(\max(1, Q \cdot t_S / t_C)) + 1.$$

Figure 6 shows the comparative evolution between the difficulty of client puzzles and threshold puzzles for $t_S = 0.003$ and $t_C = 0.5$. It can be clearly seen that the client perception of performance degradation as server load increases is less significant when threshold puzzles are used.

Setting-Up a Minimum Response Time Threshold

For a DoS attack to be successful, the attacker must be capable of sending numerous requests to the server in a short time interval, despite the usage of client puzzles technology. To prevent the attacker from finding the solution too fast, the sever can associate to the puzzle a minimum time threshold necessary to find the solution, according to the puzzle difficulty. If the client response is received faster than this threshold, the server can interpret this as an attack and limit or terminate its communication with the client.

The basic idea consists of adding a timestamp T_S to the puzzle in order to mark the precise moment when the server has generated its random value N_S. When the puzzle solution is received, the server is able to calculate the exact time required by the client to find the solution. This time span should not be lower than a server estimation based on the difficulty level k. If it is, then the server can consider that it is under a strong DoS attack and should cease all communication with the client.

As shown in the previous paragraph, the average number of operations needed to solve a puzzle is 2^{k-1}, so the estimated time T_E for finding the solution, which is the minimum response time threshold, can be calculated with the following formula:

Figure 6. Comparative evolution of puzzle difficulty between client puzzles and threshold puzzles

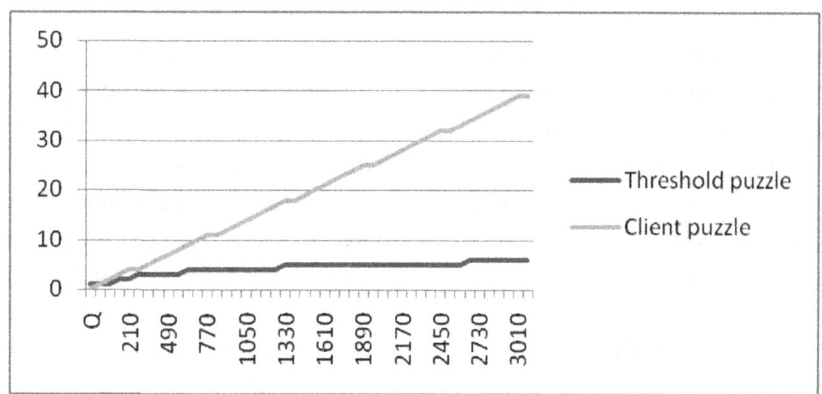

$T_E = 2^{k-1} \cdot T_{operation}$

where:

- k represents the puzzle difficulty;
- $T_{operation}$ is the average time needed to perform a cryptographic operation.

The Threshold Puzzles Algorithm

Given the theoretical considerations presented in the previous sections, we can now outline the complete threshold puzzles algorithm.

1. When a new communication channel is opened between the server and a client, the server checks the system state, using its own metric (for example, the one provided by the SSO-SENSE detection engine). If the server load does not exceed a critical threshold, the algorithm stops since no defense mechanism is required.
2. The server generates a unique random value N_S (also called a nonce), with a 64 bit entropy and records the timestamp T_S at which the value was generated.
3. The server sets the puzzle difficulty level k and estimates the minimum response time threshold T_E. The difficulty level k will be limited to an upper threshold so that an uncontrolled increase in difficulty will not have repercussions on clients with limited computational power.
4. The server creates a new puzzle, in the form of a tuple $<N_S, k, T_S>$, which is sent to the client.
5. When the puzzle is received, the client performs the following operations:
   a. Checks the timestamp T_S to ensure that the information is recent.
   b. Generates a random number N_C.
   c. Searches for the puzzle solution X, by applying repeatedly a hash function h to the arguments C, N_S, N_C and X, where C represents the client identity. Considering $Y = h(C, N_S, N_C, X)$ to be the output of the hash function, the puzzle is considered to be solved when the first k bits of Y are equal to 0.
   d. Sends back the solution to the server.
6. When the server receives the solution from the client, it executes the following steps:
   a. Calculates the time needed for the client to solve the puzzle, $T_{solve} = T_R - T_S$, where T_R represents the reception time. If T_{solve} is smaller than T_E, the client has a large computational power at its disposal and the server may choose to either terminate or to deliberately delay the communication with the client.

b. Checks if the client has previously submitted a solution with the same N_S and N_C parameters. If so, the server ceases all communication with the client.
c. Checks that solution X is correct.

7. If all the above requirements have been satisfied, the server can allocate resources for executing the authentication protocol with client C.

Adapting Threshold Puzzles to the Computational Power of the Client

Another aspect related to the threshold puzzle technology is the wide range of communication devices that can be used to access a certain network service and interact with an authentication system. Devices such as state-of-the-art desktop systems, laptops and notebooks, PDAs or smartphones can be used to connect to the same network service, and their computational power can range from very fast to medium or slow. In conjunction with the threshold puzzles technology, the user experience in relation to the server response time could vary greatly in similar load conditions. As a consequence, threshold puzzles need to be adapted to the computational power of each client in order to obtain a seamless user experience. We will call this concept *adaptive threshold puzzles* (Bocan & Fagadar, 2005a).

The main idea behind this approach is to enable the server to determine the computational power of the client and to adapt the puzzle difficulty accordingly. This assessment can take place during the first dialog between client and server, when the server sends an exploratory puzzle to the client and, based on the response time, identifies its computational power. The exploratory puzzle can either be a partial hash function inversion (similar to the client puzzles concept) or a completely different approach can be used depending on the implementation. A linear dependency between the difficulty and the solving time of the exploratory puzzle is desired.

The computational power P_C of the client can be calculated by the server based on the time it needed to solve the exploratory puzzle. It is possible though, for a malicious client to intentionally delay the response in order to hide the true value of P_C and to appear weaker in front of the server. If such a client launches an attack, it may lure the server into sending it lower complexity puzzles. Therefore, a method must be found in order to encourage the client to use its whole computational power when solving the exploratory puzzle. A solution to this problem is for the server to allocate a limited number of connections within a certain time span, according to the reported P_C value for a client. For example, a powerful client will be allocated a number N of connections within a time slot, while a slow client like a PDA or a smartphone will be allocated only N/2 or N/3 connections within the same time slot. As a result, the malicious client will receive a smaller number of connections than expected, and those connections that exceed this number will be ignored by the server. This way, clients who deliberately hide their true computational power will not be able to launch an attack to the full extent of their capabilities.

Once P_C is evaluated by the server, the adapted complexity k_C of the adaptive threshold puzzle can be calculated using the formula

$$k_C = \mathrm{round}(k \cdot \log_2(P_C / P_{ref}))$$

where:

- P_{ref} is the reference computational power defined at server level,
- P_C is the reported client computational power,
- k represents the reference puzzle difficulty, correlated with P_{ref}.

The reference puzzle difficulty k uses the same formula as it the case of threshold puzzles

$k \leq \log_2(\max(1, Q \cdot t_S / t_C)) + 1$

where:

- Q represents the current size of the request queue on the server,
- t_S represents the average server time per cryptographic operation,
- t_C represents the average client time per cryptographic operation.

The Adaptive Threshold Puzzles Algorithm

Based on the theoretical aspects described in the previous paragraph, we can now list the complete adaptive threshold puzzles algorithm as an evolution of the threshold puzzles algorithm presented before.

1. When a new communication channel is opened between the server and a client, the server checks the system state. If the server load does not exceed a critical threshold, the algorithm stops since no defense mechanism is required.
2. If it is the first time the client connects to the server, its computational power must be estimated. The server creates an exploratory puzzle, which is the simple partial inversion of a hash function, with a medium complexity (e.g. k = 6) and sends it to the client.
3. The client solves the exploratory puzzle and sends the solution back to the server.
4. The server checks the exploratory puzzle solution and estimates the computational power of the client, P_C. Depending on this quantity, the server will determine the maximum number of requests allowed for this client within a time slot.
5. The server generates a unique random value N_S (nonce), with a 64 bit entropy and records the timestamp T_S at which the value was generated.
6. The server calculates the adapted puzzle complexity k_C and estimates the minimum response time threshold T_E.
7. The server creates a new puzzle, in the form of a tuple $<N_S, k_C, T_S>$, which is sent to the client.
8. The client receives the puzzle, calculates the solution X as shown in the threshold puzzles algorithm and sends it back to the server.
9. The server checks the solution both in terms of correctness and in terms of solving time, according to the rules mentioned in the threshold puzzles algorithm.
10. If solution is correct, the server will apply a restriction on the maximum number of requests allowed for the client within a time unit, according to the P_C value determined in step 2.
11. If all the above requirements have been satisfied, the server can allocate resources for executing the authentication protocol with client C.

CASE STUDY: THE SSL HANDSHAKE PROTOCOL WITH ADAPTIVE EFFORT DISTRIBUTION

Overview of the SSL Handshake Algorithm

Given its wide-spread and popularity, we have chosen Secure Socket Layer (SSL) protocol to test the adaptive threshold puzzles technique. Before describing the changes made to the protocol in order to support the puzzle technology, we will present a short overview of its original, unmodified version.

Figure 7 illustrates the SSL Handshake protocol, which will be the target of our improvements. During this phase, the message exchange between peers contains information regarding the cryptographic capabilities of the client as well as

Figure 7. The original SSL Handshake protocol

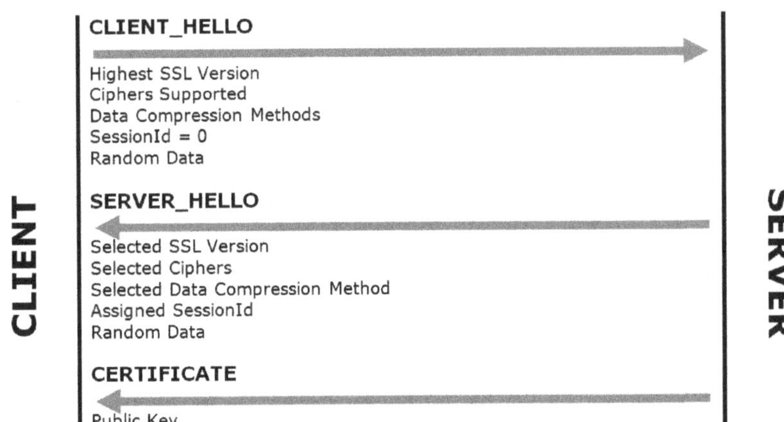

the configuration chosen by the server to enable the communication with the client.

It can be easily seen that the CERTIFICATE message contains the digital signature of the server, which represents the server engagement (and resource allocation) regardless of client identity and its true intentions. If the client does not intend to continue its dialog with the server but instead aims to overload it with useless requests that will end up being signed by the server, we are dealing with a typical DoS attack.

From the perspective of service availability, allocating server resources unconditionally is a major drawback. This is why we have focused on improving the mostly used authentication protocol, SSL, by using the adaptive threshold puzzle technology. The changes we brought are extensions to the original protocol, which provides it with the capability of balancing the authentication effort between peers without affecting its cryptographic validity.

Adding Adaptive Effort Distribution to the SSL Handshake Protocol

In order to extend the SSL Handshake protocol with support for adaptive threshold puzzles, we need to add additional messages to the information exchange between client and server.

First, the server must be able to assess the computational power of a new client, by introducing two new messages to the protocol: PUZZLE_EXPLORE_CHALLENGE and PUZZLE_EXPLORE_SOLUTION. Through the PUZZLE_EXPLORE_CHALLENGE message, the server asks the client to solve an exploratory puzzle of medium difficulty. The client will submit the puzzle solution via the PUZZLE_EXPLORE_SOLUTION message. If the server already knows the client (prior requests have been received from the client in the past), it may choose to skip this phase for a predetermined time frame or for an undetermined time frame, according to the application specifics.

Second, the authentication effort must be distributed between peers, instead of being unilaterally supported by the server. This is achieved by adding two new more message types: PUZZLE_CHALLENGE and PUZZLE_SOLUTION which represent the information exchange between the server and the client during the normal threshold puzzle solving process. During authentication, the server must keep its load under a critical threshold. If this threshold is crossed, the server must

Figure 8. The SSL Handshake protocol with adaptive effort distribution

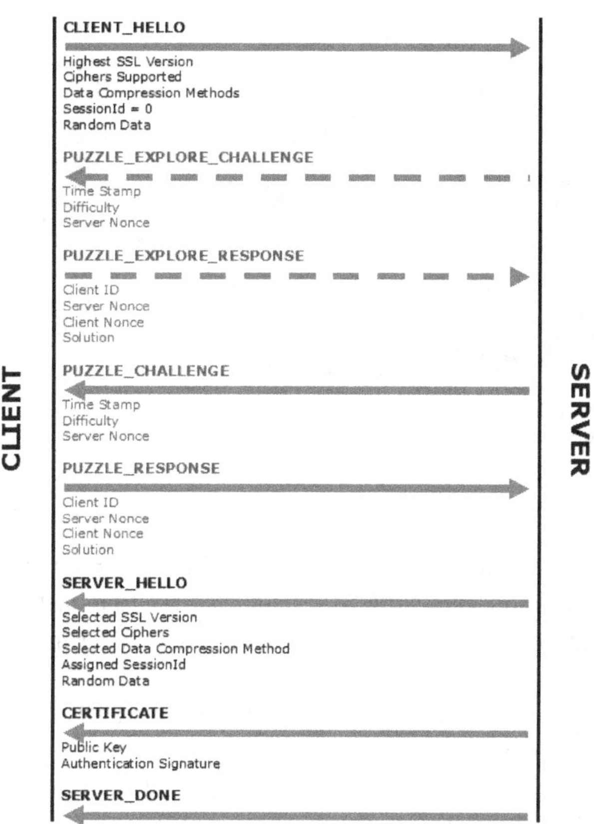

control the avalanche of authentication requests, and it achieves this goal by keeping the client busy with a puzzle proportional in complexity with the server load.

As shown in *Figure 8*, both the PUZZLE_EXPLORE_CHALLENGE and the PUZZLE_CHALLENGE messages contain the server timestamp (T_S), the puzzle difficulty (k and k_C respectively) and the server nonce (N_S). The client responds with the PUZZLE_EXPLORE_SOLUTION and PUZZLE_SOLUTION respectively, both containing its identity (C), the server nonce, the client-generated nonce (N_C) and the puzzle solution (X).

As it can be seen from the message exchange diagram, adding the new message types does not affect the cryptographic integrity of the protocol. Instead, the client is delayed with a duration proportional to the current server load and health state. Since the puzzle-related messages are exchanged before the CERTIFICATE and SERVER_DONE messages, the server does not commit to resource allocation until the client is validated. We call this adaptive effort distribution since the client delay and the resource allocation at server level are related to the computational power of the client.

A Test Prototype for the Threshold Puzzles Technology

In order to simulate the behavior of the threshold puzzle technology in a real context and to outline its benefits compared to the standard client puzzles, we have built the prototype illustrated in *Figure 9*.

The prototype contains the following modules:

Figure 9. Test prototype for the threshold puzzles technology

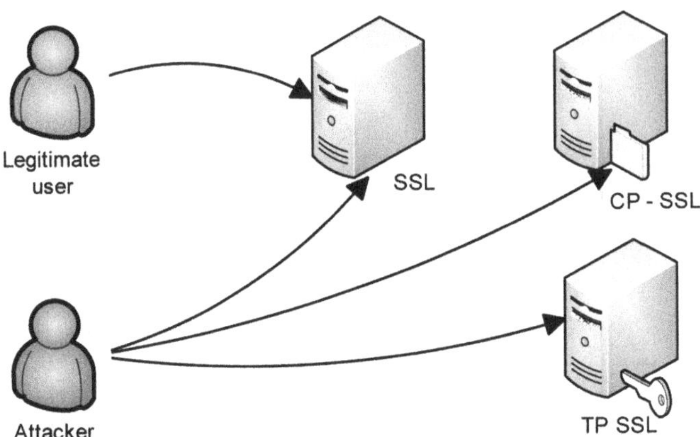

- *Legitimate user*: a normal client which attempts a SSL authentication according to the protocol specification.
- *Attacker*: a client with access to large computational power, able to make a large number of authentication requests within a short time frame.
- *SSL server*: a regular, unprotected SSL server.
- *CP SSL server*: a SSL server protected by standard Client Puzzles (CP) technology.
- *TP SSL server*: a SSL server protected by Threshold Puzzles (TP) technology.

Since in laboratory conditions it is hard to gather a really large computational power, in order to simulate this aspect we have configured the *Attacker* module to submit a random, incorrect, solution, while in the same time we have disabled the solution check at the server level. This way, the attacker appears to be solving the solution in a much shorter timeframe than the legitimate clients, without impacting in any other way the simulation results.

The simulation ran on two systems connected through a 100 Mbps local network with no disturbing traffic. The first system, representing the server, hosted the *SSL server*, *CP SSL server* and *TP SSL server* modules, while the second one hosted multiple instances of the *Legitimate user* and the *Attacker* modules.

Experimental Results

On the test environment described previously we have run several scenarios designed to determine the behavior of the Client Puzzles and Threshold Puzzles technologies, as follows:

- **Clients authenticated by a regular SSL server**–used as a reference when benchmarking the system performance, this scenario allowed us to measure the average time needed to completely execute the SSL protocol without any puzzle technology extensions. For a number of 100 authentications of 15 clients, the average server response time was 4545 milliseconds.
- **Clients and attacker authenticated by a regular SSL server**–the simulation contained 14 normal clients and an attacker. The attacker sends a burst of CLIENT_HELLO messages in order to trigger an equal number of responses signed by the server. The protocol execution is never finished by the attacker, who deliberately

Figure 10. Benchmark results for SSL Handshake protocol simulations

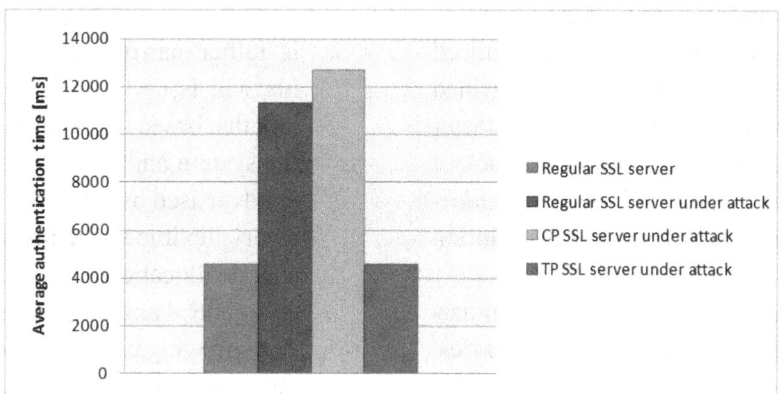

ignores the server response. The attacker has sent false requests with a rate of 30 requests / second, during which the server reached a 100% load. In this case, the average server response time for legitimate clients has increased to 11320 milliseconds.

- **Clients and attacker authenticated by the CP SSL server**–this scenario is the same as the previous one, with the exception that Client Puzzle technology has been activated at server level. Since we have simulated the availability of a large computational power at the attacker level and disabled the solution check at server level, for the same rate of 30 requests / second the server reached the 100% load and the average authentication time has increased again to 12730 milliseconds. This increase can be explained by the overhead introduced by the two additional protocol messages: PUZZLE_CHALLENGE and PUZZLE_RESPONSE.
- **Clients and attacker authenticated by the TP SSL server**–we have repeated the above scenario, using Threshold Puzzles technology. In this case, the average authentication time of legitimate clients has decreased significantly to 4553 milliseconds, almost the same as the one obtained when the server was not subject to any attack. This was due to the fact that the attacker solved the puzzles too fast, which lead to the server blocking its communication channels with the attacker.

Conclusion

Figure 10 summarizes the test results of the SSL Handshake protocol simulations.

During a so-called strong attack, the Client Puzzles technology did not have the expected results since the attacker was able to find the puzzle solution in a very short time frame and still send a large number of requests to the server. The average response time was similar to that of an unprotected server.

On the other hand, the server which employed Threshold Puzzles has systematically rejected the requests which were accompanied by solutions found too fast for their complexity level, so that the authentication time perceived by legitimate clients has not been altered.

FUTURE RESEARCH DIRECTIONS

Classic puzzle designs have two important drawbacks that make them less ideal for the purpose of thwarting Denial-of-Service attacks. The first and most serious drawback is *parallelizability*, i.e.

the possibility of computing the puzzle solution in parallel. In scenarios where a single adversary is in control of a large number of compromised machines, the huge computation power thus gained can be used to compute the solution much faster than the server expects. The second drawback of classic puzzle designs is the *lack of fine granularity*, i.e. the server is not able to adjust the solution time precisely.

Both non-parallelizability and fine granularity are important properties of good puzzles, but they are difficult to obtain. Therefore, new constructions have emerged as a solution to this problem and one such construction is the *puzzle chain* (Groza & Petrica, 2006; Ma, 2006). Instead of having one single puzzle of varying difficulty, one may use a chain of interdependent puzzles of smaller difficulty. This allows fine adjustments in time solving by altering the chain length with the added benefit that the intermediate or the final solution cannot be computed in parallel.

Puzzle chains come with a unique set of drawback themselves. One important issue is keeping and maintaining the chain state at the server level as well as transmitting it to the client. This requires important storage and high-bandwidth communication channels, but clever and judicious scheduling of resources alleviates this problem.

We intend to continue our research on increasing the availability of authentication protocols through the use of puzzle chains and provide a framework for general implementations in order to leverage our experimental findings. Though we are in the early stages of our research, we have already drawn the outlines of the augmented Adaptive Threshold Puzzles concept:

- As the puzzle chain solving time is driven by two factors—individual link difficulty and the chain length itself—we are in the position of integrating this into our earlier SSO-SENSE detection engine. While the server would be able to establish the desired puzzle difficulty based on the current system load—difficulty range which itself is rather narrow, the SSO-SENSE module will issue to clients chains of varying lengths, based on the threat level sensed by the system and on the computational power advertised by clients. This design allows a very flexible and democratic model or resource allocation and keeps under a natural self-control any client which misbehaves.
- The mapping process based on the computational power of the client corroborated with the sensed system threat level allows for a fine and judicious allocation of resources, where no resource livelock is possible. This means that clients are ordered by a democratic ranking where no single client is able to obtain entire or the majority of server resources.

CONCLUSION

DoS attacks represent a permanent threat to the present communication systems in general and to authentication systems in particular. In this chapter we have shown that authentication systems, including Single Sign-On (SSO) systems, are vulnerable to DoS attacks due to the lack of control over the resources allocated during the authentication process. This can result in severe performance degradation or even failure in delivering the authentication service to legitimate clients.

To overcome the vulnerability of authentication systems facing the threat of DoS attacks, we have brought several contributions meant to allow the early detection and prevention of such attacks. As a first step, the SSO-SENSE heuristic threat assessment engine was introduced, to facilitate the detection of DoS attacks at an early stage and to allow efficient deployment of countermeasures against the attacker. In the second stage, we have developed the Threshold Puzzles and Adaptive

Threshold Puzzles technologies, to address the scenarios which were not covered by classical client puzzles. In the last step, we have modified the widespread SSL Handshake protocol in order to support the Adaptive Threshold Puzzles technology for an efficient protection against DoS attacks. Based on the experimental results collected from a simulation platform, we can conclude that the proposed changes lead to a considerable increase in DoS resilience for an authentication system and that they prove to be a viable solution in securing authentication-based network services.

REFERENCES

Aura, T., Nikander, P., & Leiwo, J. (2000). DOS-resistant authentication with clientpuzzles. *Lecture Notes in Computer Science. Proceeding of the Cambridge Security Protocols Workshop 2000* (pp. 170-177). Cambridge, UK. doi: 10.1.1.106.9259

Bocan, V. (2004). Threshold puzzles. The evolution of DoS-resistant authentication. *Periodica Politehnica, Transaction on Automatic Control and Computer Science, 49*(63). Timisoara, Romania.

Bocan, V., & Fagadar-Cosma, M. (2005, November). Adaptive threshold puzzles. *Proceedings of EUROCON 2005. The International Conference on "Computer as a Tool"* (pp. 644-647). Belgrade, Serbia. doi: 10.1109/EURCON.2005.1630012

Bocan, V., & Fagadar-Cosma, M. (2005, November). Towards DoS-resistant single sign-on systems. *Proceedings of EUROCON 2005. The International Conference on "Computer as a Tool"* (pp. 668-671). Belgrade, Serbia. doi: 10.1109/EURCON.2005.1630018

Crosby, S. A., & Wallach, D. S. (2003, August). *Denial of service via algorithmic complexity attacks*. Paper presented at the 12th USENIX Security Symposium, Washington, DC.

Dwork, C., & Naor, M. (1992). Pricing via processing or combating junk mail. [Berlin, Germany: Springer-Verlag.]. *Proceedings of CRYPTO, 92*, 139–147.

Groza, B., & Petrica, D. (2006, May). On chained cryptographic puzzles. *Proceedings of 3rd Romanian-Hungarian Joint Symposium on Applied Computational Intelligence, SACI'06* (pp. 182-191).Timisoara, Romania.

Harris, S. (2001, September). DoS defense. *Information Security Magazine*.

Juels, A., & Brainard, J. (1999). Client puzzles: A Cryptographic countermeasure against connection depletion attacks. *Proceedings of the NDSS, 99*, 151–165.

Kim, Y., Lau, W. C., Chuah, M. C., & Chao, H. J. (2004). PacketScore: Statistics-based overload control against distributed denial-of-service attacks. *Proceedings of IEEE INFOCOM* (pp. 2594-2604). Hong Kong, SAR. doi: 10.1.1.137.6263

Liberty Alliance Project. (2010). *Liberty ID-FF protocols and schema specification 1.2*. Retrieved April 26, 2010, from http://www.projectliberty.org/liberty/content/view/full/179/(offset)/15/

Liberty Alliance Project. (2010). *Liberty specs tutorial*. Retrieved April 26, 2010, from http://www.projectliberty.org/liberty/specifications__1/

Ma, M. (2006, April). Mitigating denial of service attacks with password puzzles. *Proceedings of International Conference on Information Technology: Coding and Computing, Vol. 2* (pp. 621-626). Las Vegas, NV. doi: 10.1109/ITCC.2005.200

Merkle, R. C. (1978). Secure communications over insecure channels. *Communications of the ACM, 21*(4). doi:10.1145/359460.359473

Rivest, R. R., Shamir, A., & Wagner, D. A. (1996). Time-lock puzzles and timed-release cryptography. Retrieved April 26, 2010, from http://lcs.mit.edu/~rivest/RivestShamirWagnertimelock.pdf

Schneier, B. (2000, March). Distributed denial of service attacks. *Crypto-gram Newsletter*.

SETI @home Program. (2010). *Website*. Retrieved April 26, 2010, from http://setiathome.ssl.berkely.edu

Siaterlis, C., & Maglaris, B. (2004). Towards multisensor data fusion for DoS detection. *Proceedings of the 2004 ACM Symposium on Applied Computing* (pp. 439-446). ACM Press. doi: 10.1.1.9.8572

Spatscheck, O., & Peterson, L. (1999). Defending against denial of service attacks in Scout. *Proceedings of the 1999 USENIX/ACM Symposium on OSDI* (pp. 59-72). doi: 10.1.1.37.157

The Distributed.net Organization. (2010). *Website*. Retrieved April 26, 2010, from http://www.distributed.net

Waters, B., Juels, A., Halderman, J. A., & Felten, E. W. (2004). New client puzzle outsourcing techniques for DoS resistance. *Proceedings of 11th ACM Conference on Computer and Communications Security*. doi: 10.1.1.58.737

KEY TERMS AND DEFINITIONS

Adaptive Effort Distribution: A technique that adapts the threshold puzzle concept to the existing Secure Sockets Layer (SSL) protocol. This essentially means the addition of four new messages to the existing protocol design with the aim of gathering knowledge of the client computational power.

Adaptive Threshold Puzzle: A technology similar to the threshold puzzle that takes into account the computational power of the client. An adaptive threshold puzzle is able to discriminate its clients and ask puzzle solutions of varying difficulties.

Authentication System: A mechanism that establishes the identity of two parties either one way or both ways. Authentication systems usually employ cryptography and involve a secret quantity known by the parties.

Bayesian Inference: Is a method of statistical inference that calculates the probability of an event to be true based on observations of evidences.

Client Puzzle: A technology originally proposed as a way to increase the computational cost for the client in order to limit the request rate for the server. The technology most commonly involves the partial inversion of a cryptographic hash function.

Denial of Service: Usually abbreviated as DoS, is an attack targeted against a computer system which causes it to malfunction. The attacks “deny” access of the legitimate clients to the resources and services of the computer system by overwhelming it with false requests that are usually indistinguishable from legitimate ones.

Threshold Puzzle: A technology similar to the client puzzle which limits the puzzle difficulty level in order to avoid overloading legitimate clients with low computational power.

Chapter 12
Identity Management Systems

Waleed Alrodhan
Imam Muhammed Ibn Saud University, Saudi Arabia

ABSTRACT

In this chapter we provide an overview of five of the most widely discussed web-based identity management systems, namely Microsoft CardSpace, the Higgins project, the Liberty Alliance project, the Shibboleth project, and OpenID. These systems are discussed throughout the chapter; we also investigate certain security limitations shared by all these systems.

Next, we discuss the practicality of identity management systems, and consider how their practicality can be enhanced by developing reliable integration and delegation schemes. We also provide overviews of the Project Concordia integration framework, and the Shibboleth and OAuth delegation frameworks, as well as reviewing the related literature.

INTRODUCTION

An identity management system enables authoritative sources to perform identity management tasks via an operational framework. Most of today's web-based identity management systems adhere to one of the practical identity management models described in the previous chapter(i.e. the isolated, Information Card-based or Federated identity management models).

DOI: 10.4018/978-1-61350-498-7.ch012

The last few years have seen the development of a number of web-based identity management systems, including AOL OpenAuth[i], Yahoo BBAuth[ii], and Flickr Authentication API[iii]. Many of these systems are isolated, and they are largely not interoperable with one another.

After an open dialogue with a number of identity management experts, in 2005 Microsoft published its Laws of Identity (Cameron, 2005). These laws reflects Microsoft's vision of the requirements that should be met by any web-based identity management system. A list of these laws, with Microsoft's interpretation of them, is given below (note that we have changed the terminology slightly to use the term 'identity management system' instead of 'identity system').

1. **User control and consent:** The identity management system must only reveal information identifying a user with the user's consent.
2. **Minimal disclosure for a constrained use:** The solution which discloses the least amount of identifying information and best limits its use is the most stable long term solution.
3. **Justifiable parties:** The identity management system must be designed so that the disclosure of identifying information is limited to parties having a necessary and justifiable place in a given identity relationship.
4. **Directed identity:** The identity management system must support both 'omnidirectional' identifiers for use by public entities and 'unidirectional' identifiers for use by private entities.
5. **Pluralism of operators and technologies:** The identity management system must channel and enable the inter-working of multiple identity technologies run by multiple identity providers.
6. **Human integration:** The identity management system must define the human user to be a component of the distributed system, integrated through unambiguous human-machine communication mechanisms offering protection against identity attacks.
7. **Consistent experience across contexts:** The identity management system must guarantee its users a simple, consistent experience while enabling separation of contexts through multiple operators and technologies.

It seems reasonable to believe that, by following the laws stated above, identity management systems can reach an acceptable level of usability, reliability, flexibility, and privacy. We also observe that a number of these laws were derived from the OECD principles for personal data protection (OECD Guidelines on the Protection of Privacy and Transborder Flows of Personal Data, 1980).

In this chapter we describe five identity management systems and frameworks, namely Microsoft CardSpace, Higgins, the Liberty Alliance Project, Shibboleth, and OpendID. We also discuss enhancing the practicality of identity management systems by enhancing both their interoperability (using integration schemes) and their usability and flexibility (using delegation schemes).

Microsoft CardSpace

Back in 1999, Microsoft introduced.NET Passport, a ticket-based single sign-on system. Although. NET Passport was supported by a number of well-known service providers, such as eBay and Visa, it was not widely used for SSO. The single sign-on features have since been restricted to Microsoft web sites only, and Passport now functions simply as a means of logging-in to these web sites. In 2005, Microsoft published two white papers that discuss the 'failure' of.NET Passport (Cameron, 2005, Microsoft Corporation, 2005a), and this analysis has clearly influenced Microsoft's subsequent offerings in this area, including the development of Microsoft CardSpace.

Microsoft CardSpace (henceforth abbreviated to CardSpace) is the name for a Microsoft WinFX software component that is described by Microsoft as an 'identity metasystem'; using our terminology, it is an identity management system. It is designed to comply with the seven Laws of Identity, as promulgated by Microsoft. A new version of CardSpace, CardSpace 2.0, is expected to be officially released in 2010 (a Beta version has recently been released); however, Microsoft has stated that it will be compatible with the currently deployed version of CardSpace[iv].

The CardSpace Framework

CardSpace provides a way to represent identities using claims, and a means to bridge technology and organisational boundaries using claims transformations (Microsoft Corporation, 2005b). It is an ICIM system, and hence, as discussed in the previous chapter, is not an SSO system. It aims to reduce the reliance on passwords for Internet user authentication by service providers, and to improve the privacy of personal information.

The CardSpace identity management architecture is designed to provide the user with control over his/her digital identities in a user friendly manner, and to tackle identity management security problems, such as breaches of privacy and identity theft, with no single identity authority control. CardSpace works with Internet Explorer browsers (CardSpace plug-ins for browsers other than Microsoft Internet Explorer have also been developed, such as the Firefox Plug-in[v]).

Digital identities in CardSpace are represented as claims made by one digital subject (e.g. an Internet user) about itself or another digital subject. A claim is an assertion that certain identifying information (e.g. given name, social security number, credit card number, etc.) belongs to a given digital subject (or entity) (Cameron & Jones, 2006, Microsoft Corporation, 2005b). As in any ICIM system, user identifiers (e.g. a username) and attributes (e.g. user gender) are both treated as claims.

As in any ICIM system, The framework is based on the identification process we experience in the real world using physical ID cards. An IdP issues its users with virtual cards called Information Cards (InfoCards); such InfoCards are called managed cards. InfoCards can also be self-issued by the users themselves via the SIP, and such InfoCards are known as personal cards, or self-issued cards. Infocards are stored on the user machine as XML files with the extension '*.crd'. If the InfoCard is self-issued, then the values of the supported claims are stored in encrypted form by the SIP on the user machine.

A managed InfoCard is signed by the issuing IdP. An InfoCard (managed or self-issued) contains the following (relatively) non-sensitive meta-information:

- The image of the card that the user sees on his/her screen.
- The name of the card.
- A Uniform Resource Identifier (URI) (Berners-Lee, Fielding, & Masinter, 2005) from which the issuing IdP's policy can be obtained (managed cards only).
- One or more URIs which can be used to request security tokens from the IdP (managed cards only). For each URI the InfoCard must specify the authentication method that is used by the IdP as a prerequisite to supplying a token. If the authentication method is username/password, then the InfoCard must also contain the username.
- A list of the supported claims that can be asserted by the IdP (or the SIP). This allows the Identity Selector to match an SP's security policy to IdPs that are able to create security tokens meeting the SP requirements. Self-issued InfoCards can only contain 14 claim types, namely First Name, Last Name, Email Address, Street, City, State, Postal Code, Country/Region, Home Phone, Other Phone, Mobile Phone, Date of Birth, Gender, and Web Page.
- The types of security tokens that can be requested from this IdP (e.g. a SAML 2.0 assertion). These tokens will contain asserted claims, and must be encapsulated in a WS-Trust message (Nadalin, Goodner, Gudgin, Barbir, & Granqvist (editors), 2007b) and signed by the IdP. The only token type supported for a self-issued InfoCard is a SAML 1.1 assertion.

- The InfoCard creation and expiry times.
- The InfoCard's CardSpace reference, which is a globally unique URI (unique to the IdP). This identifier is created by the issuer IdP (or the SIP in the case of a self-issued InfoCard), and must be passed back to the IdP every time a security token is requested using this InfoCard.
- A flag to indicate whether or not the token requests must include information identifying the SP for which the token will be issued.
- An optional pointer to the privacy policy of the IdP.

When a user tries to log-in to an SP, the SP declares its security policy to the Identity Selector. The SP security policy can be retrieved using the WS-MetadataExchange protocol (Curbera, Parastatidis, & Schlimmer (editors), 2006), and is expressed using the WS-SecurityPolicy and WS-Trust protocols (Nadalin et al., 2007b, Nadalin, Goodner, Gudgin, Barbir, & Granqvist (editors), 2007a). The policy includes a variety of information, the most significant elements of which are as follows (Chadwick, 2008).

- **The issuer:** this field contains the WS-Addressing (Box & Curbera (editors), 2004) Endpoint References (URIs) of the IdPs that the SP trusts to issue the requested token (e.g. https://isg.rhul.ac.uk/idp). If this field is left blank, then the SP will accept a token from any IdP. If the SP is prepared to accept a self-issued token, then this field must contain the URI 'http://schemas.xmlsoap.org/ws/2005/05/identity/issuer/self'.
- **The claims that must be asserted:** this field contains a list of the claims to be asserted by the IdP. Each claim is flagged as mandatory or optional.
- **The security token type:** this field contains the security token type that the SP will accept (e.g. a SAML assertion). It is important to note that CardSpace identity metasystem itself does not restrict the type of security tokens, i.e. all types of token can be used within the framework as long as they are encapsulated in a WS-Trust message. As previously noted, in the case of a self-issued InfoCard, the only supported token type is a SAML 1.1 assertion.
- **The proof-of-rightful-possession method:** asymmetric, symmetric, or bearer.

The SP security policy can also specify other constraints on the security token (e.g. the maximum token age).

After processing the SP policy, the Identity Selector checks which InfoCards satisfy it and prompts the user to select one of them. Once an InfoCard has been selected, the Identity Selector retrieves the appropriate IdP security policy from the IdP. This policy is specified using WSDL (Christensen, Curbera, Meredith, & Weerawarana, 2001), and indicates the protocol messages that must be used to access the IdP-STS. The policy also contains details of how a security token must be retrieved from the IdP, and specifies the security measures that should be applied to the request token (e.g. whether the security token should be encrypted by the IdP using a short-term symmetric session key, or if the encryption provided by SSL/TLS is sufficient) (Chadwick, 2008). Additionally, the IdP security policy must contain the IdP's X.509 public key certificate ("X.509 Information technology—Open Systems Interconnection—The Directory: Public-key and attribute certificate frameworks", 2005).

The identity selector then requests the security token from the issuer IdP. After receiving the request, and prior to authenticating the user and generating the token, the IdP checks what claims it can assert for this user, whether its policy permits it to generate the requested security token, and how the user must be authenticated. If the IdP decides that it can generate the requested token, then it authenticates the user via the Identity Selector interface using the authentication method specified in the policy. Four authentication methods are supported, namely username/password, Kerberos V5 ticket, X.509 certificate (either software-based or using a smart card), and self-issued SAML 1.1 assertion (Nanda, 2007).

On receipt of the token from the IdP, the Identity Selector optionally shows its contents to the user; the displayed information is deleted from the system after the user has given consent to proceed. Finally, the Identity Selector forwards the security token to the SP, which will deem the user authenticated if the received token is valid and meets its requirements. Observe that, unlike the PID, in the case where the target scope information is present in the RST, the PPID must be handed to the IdP by the Identity Selector (within the RST), before the IdP can include it in the security token.

Figure 1 provides a simplified sketch of the CardSpace framework. In the figure it is assumed that the user has already been issued an InfoCard by an IdP, and has retrieved the SP web page that offers a CardSpace-based log-in. In step 1, the user clicks on the CardSpace icon in the SP web page using a CardSpace-Enabled User Agent (CEUA), also known as the Service Requester, which is essentially a CardSpace-enabled web browser. In step 2, the SP identifies itself using a public key certificate (e.g. a certificate used for SSL/TLS), and triggers the Identity Selector using XHTML code or HTML object tags. After the Identity Selector has been triggered, it retrieves the SP's security policy from the SP-STS in step 3 (Nanda, 2007).

In step 4 the Identity Selector matches the SP's security policy against the InfoCards possessed by the user in order to find one that satisfies it. If one or more suitable InfoCards are found, the user is prompted to select one of them. After the user has selected an InfoCard, the Identity Selector initiates a connection with the IdP that issued that InfoCard, and retrieves the IdP security policy in step 5. In step 6, the user performs an authentication process with the IdP via the Identity Selector. As stated above, the current version of the Identity Selector supports four authentication methods, namely: username/password, Kerberos V5 ticket, X.509 certificate (either software-based or using a smart card), and self-issued SAML 1.1 assertion (generated by the SIP).

Then, in step 7, the Identity Selector requests the IdP to provide a security token that asserts the truth of the claims whose types are listed in the selected InfoCard; this request is sent in a request security token (RST) message. The IdP then checks whether its security policy permits it to generate the requested security token. If so, the IdP replies by sending a security token within a request security token response (RSTR) message. Finally, the Identity Selector forwards the security token to the SP-STS in step 8 (after, optionally, showing its contents to the user) and, if the SP verifies it successfully, the service is granted in step 9.

As in any ICIM system, the SP will get an assertion from the IdP that the security token was issued to a particular PPID. The SP can verify whether or not the Identity Selector that forwarded the token is its rightful owner using one of the proof-of-rightful-possession methods described earlier, namely symmetric, asymmetric, and bearer. If the 'symmetric' proof-of-rightful-possession method is used, then the Identity Selector must inform the IdP which SP the user is trying to access; in CardSpace this approach is called 'auditing mode'. Alternatively, if the 'asymmetric' proof-of-rightful-possession method is used, then the Identity Selector does not need to inform the IdP which SP the user is trying to access; this is called 'non-auditing mode'.

We observe that there is some ambiguity regarding the default proof-of-rightful-possession method in CardSpace. In 2005, Microsoft published two documents (Microsoft Corporation, 2005b, Microsoft Corporation and Ping Identity Corporation, 2005) stating that if the SP does not specify the proof-of-rightful-possession method

Figure 1. CardSpace framework

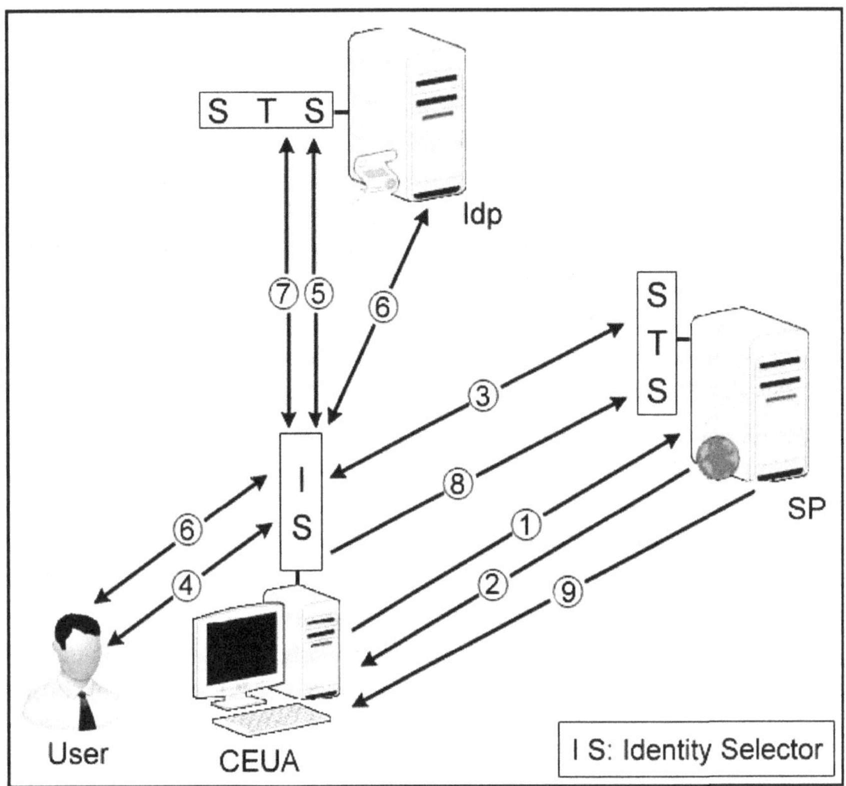

then the IdP will assume that the SP is requesting a 'symmetric' proof-of-rightful-possession method (i.e. the default is auditing mode). However, in 2008, Microsoft published a further document (Microsoft Corporation, 2008) stating that if the SP does not specify the proof-of-rightful-possession method, then the Identity Selector will request an 'asymmetric' proof-of-rightful-possession method (i.e. the default is non-auditing mode). In order for the Identity Selector to follow the latter approach, Windows operating system users must install the 'Microsoft.NET Framework 3.1 - Service Pack 1' optional update[vi].

The CardSpace identity metasystem relies on a number of Web Services protocols and SOAP. Most of these protocols require the SP to have an STS server in order to process the messages (Beznosov, Flinn, Kawamoto, & Hartman, 2005, M. B. Jones, 2006, Nadalin, Kaler, Monzillo, & Hallam-Baker (editors), 2006).

The CardSpace message flows are as follows:

1. **CEUA →SP:** User clicks on the CardSpace logo on the SP log-in web page
2. **SP →CEUA:** InfoCard Tags (XHTML or HTML object tags), to trigger the Identity Selector
3. **Identity Selector ↔SP–STS:** Identity Selector retrieves the SP security policy using WS-MetadataExchange
4. **Identity Selector ↔User:** User picks an InfoCard
5. **Identity Selector ↔IdP – STS:** Identity Selector retrieves the IdP security policy
6. **Identity Selector↔IdP:** User Authentication

7. **Identity Selector ↔IdP−STS:** Identity Selector retrieves security token using WS-MetadataExchange
8. **Identity Selector ↔SP − STS:** Identity Selector forwards the security token (after, optionally, showing its contents to the user)
9. **SP→CEUA:** Welcome, you are now logged in!

The messages in steps 3, 5, 7 and 8 are carried over SOAP (Mitra & Lafon (editors), 2007), and must be transmitted over an SSL/TLS channel to preserve their confidentiality. If the SP does employ an STS server, then the messages in steps 3 and 8 will be carried using HTTP over an SSL/TLS channel, since in this case the SP would not be capable of processing the WS-* envelopes that require an STS server to be processed. Moreover, such SPs accept only pure tokens (i.e. not encapsulated within XML envelopes) (Microsoft Corporation, 2008). The integrity of the security token is guaranteed using an XML-Signature, as part of the WS-Security protocol (Nadalin et al., 2006).

As in any ICIM system, IdP discovery is performed on the user machine. By selecting an InfoCard, the user locates the IdP to be asked to issue the token, since each InfoCard contains an IdP URI from where the security token can be obtained. As previously discussed, since discovery is performed on the user machine, a malicious SP cannot direct a user to a fake IdP, e.g. to steal the user's authentication credentials.

As discussed in the previous chapter, in an ICIM system the IdP (or the SIP) and the SP use the PPID as a 'secret' user pseudonym. These pseudonyms can be used for authentication purposes. Moreover, identifiers (e.g. PPIDs) are treated as claims, and the SP list of claims to be asserted by the IdP can include identifiers. Hence, since asserting an identifier uniquely identifies a user, and asserting user attributes can support service authorisation, then CardSpace can be used for both authentication and authorisation.

Limitations of CardSpace

CardSpace suffers from a number of limitations; some are shared by all web-based identity management systems, and some are specific to CardSpace. In this section we will discuss the CardSpace-specific limitations.

An obvious limitation of CardSpace is that, as mentioned earlier, the Identity Selector only supports four user authentication mechanisms, namely: username/password, Kerberos V5 ticket, X.509 certificate (either software-based or from smart cards), or self-issued SAML 1.1 assertion (generated by the SIP).

A further limitation of CardSpace is that the user is required to present her security credentials to the Identity Selector (e.g. a username/password) for transfer to the IdP every time. That is, even if the user chooses to use the same InfoCard/IdP to access multiple SPs, user authentication must be performed before a token is issued. This means that, as for any ICIM system, CardSpace does not support SSO. This feature also poses an obstacle to the development of delegation services.

Another limitation is that the CardSpace user-enabling components (such as the Identity Selector) only work with the Microsoft Windows operating systems. However, there are a number of other, very similar, ICIM systems that work on a variety of operating systems, such as Higgins[vii] (which works on Windows, Mac OS X, Linux, and Google Android), and DigitalMe[viii] (which works on Mac OS X).

Finally, one of the biggest limitations of CardSpace is that the user can only select one InfoCard to present to an SP within a single working session (Chadwick, 2008). This is a potentially difficulty since the user attributes for which the SP requests an assertion might not be covered by any one InfoCard. For example, if a user wants to pay his/her car road tax via an SP web site, the SP might ask for a number of attributes such as credit card information, the car insurance policy number, and the driving licence number. Since each of these attributes is issued by a different authoritative source, it is quite possible that no single IdP can provide an assertion for them all. It would thus be both more practical and more logical, if the user could present more than one InfoCard to the SP. An 'attribute-aggregation' solution such as that proposed by Chadwick (Chadwick & Inman, 2009) could address this issue, whilst also helping to preserve user privacy.

Higgins Project

Higgins is an open source ICIM system. The goals of its designers are to develop cross-platform Identity Selectors and to facilitate interoperability amongst web-based identity management systems. Higgins can integrate identity data from multiple, heterogeneous sources (e.g. LDAP directories, SQL data bases, social networking web sites, etc.) via a common Context Data Model (CDM). In the Higgins CDM, data sources are called 'contexts', and can be accessed using an Identity Attribute Service (IdAS) managed by IdPs (Clippinger, 2009). Another distinguishing feature of Higgins is that it can obtain security tokens from IdPs adhering to SAML SSO profiles.

The Higgins project started in the summer of 2003. In early 2005, Higgins was accepted into the Eclipse Foundation and, in 2006, IBM and Novell announced their participation in the project. Higgins has received contributions from Parity Communications Inc., IBM, Novell, Oracle, Computer Associates, Serena, and Google. Version 1.0 of Higgins was released in 2008, and the most recent version (Higgins 1.1) was partially released in 2009 (Higgins developers plan to release the complete version in 2010).

The Higgins Framework

The Higgins framework is quite similar to the CardSpace framework. The main difference is that Higgins provides an infrastructure to integrate identity data from multiple sources; by contrast, how identity data is obtained by the IdP is outside the scope of CardSpace, and the implementation details are left to the IdPs. Moreover, in Higgins it is assumed that the authentication service can be separated from the attribute service, which means that an IdP-STS can delegate the storage of user attributes to a separate Attribute Service.

As part of the attribute service separation, Higgins supports a third type of InfoCard called a 'relationship InfoCard' (or r-Card) (Trevithick, 2009), in addition to the two CardSpace InfoCard types (i.e. self-issued and managed InfoCards). A relationship InfoCard can be either self-issued or managed, and its main distinguishing feature is that it supports a special claim type called 'resource-UDR' (where UDR stands for Uniform Data Reference). A 'self-issued' relationship InfoCard contains both a resource-UDR claim reference and its value. However, in the case of a 'managed' relationship InfoCard, the value of the resource-UDR claim must be retrieved from the issuer IdP.

Unlike most claims, whose value is a literal that can be used directly, the resource-UDR claim value is a 'reference'. The value of the resource-UDR claim must include a Universal Data Identifier (UDI) (Sabadello, Trevithick, & Reed, 2009). A UDI contains the following two data fields:

1. **ContextId:** A URI reference identifying a data source (i.e. a network address for a context).
2. **EntityId:** A URI reference identifying a local object within the context (i.e. a network address for user identity data).

If an SP requests an assertion for the resource-UDR claim, then only relationship InfoCards can be selected by the user. The value of the resource-UDR claim can be used by the SP to discover the context that holds the user attributes, so that it can retrieve them directly. This is potentially useful if the IdP-STS has delegated the storage of the user attributes to a separate Attribute Service. Figure

2 shows how a relationship InfoCard can help SPs to locate a context that holds user attributes. As shown in the figure, a relationship InfoCard points to an IdP STS which can generate a token that points to an AS within a context.

Higgins 1.0 offers two types of Identity Selectors (known as Higgins Selectors):

1. **A web browser-embedded Selector.** This is a web-browser JavaScript plug-in that is capable of interacting with a 'stand-alone' Identity Selector installed on the user machine (e.g. the CardSpace Identity Selector, the Cocoa Higgins Selector (mentioned below), or the DigitalMe Identity Selector) to make use of its user interface. Only Firefox web browsers are supported by this selector (although Microsoft Internet Explorer web browsers are supported by Higgins 1.1).
2. **A stand-alone Selector.** This GTK C++ software is called the 'Cocoa Selector'[ix]. It works on the Windows, Linux, and Mac OS X operating systems. Figure 3 shows the interface of the Cocoa Higgins Selector on the Mac OS X operating system.

Higgins 1.1 offers an additional stand-alone Identity Selector called the 'AIR-Based Selector'[x]. This Selector has an interface built on Adobe AIR[xi], and, as previously stated, it works on the Windows, Mac OS X and Linux operating systems. Higgins developers hope that this selector will replace the current web browser-embedded Selectors that have a number of associated security concerns. Figure 4 shows the interface of the AIR-Based Higgins Selector on Windows.

Higgins 1.1 also offers an Identity Selector for iPhone mobiles[xii]. This selector works only with

Figure 2. Relationship InfoCard

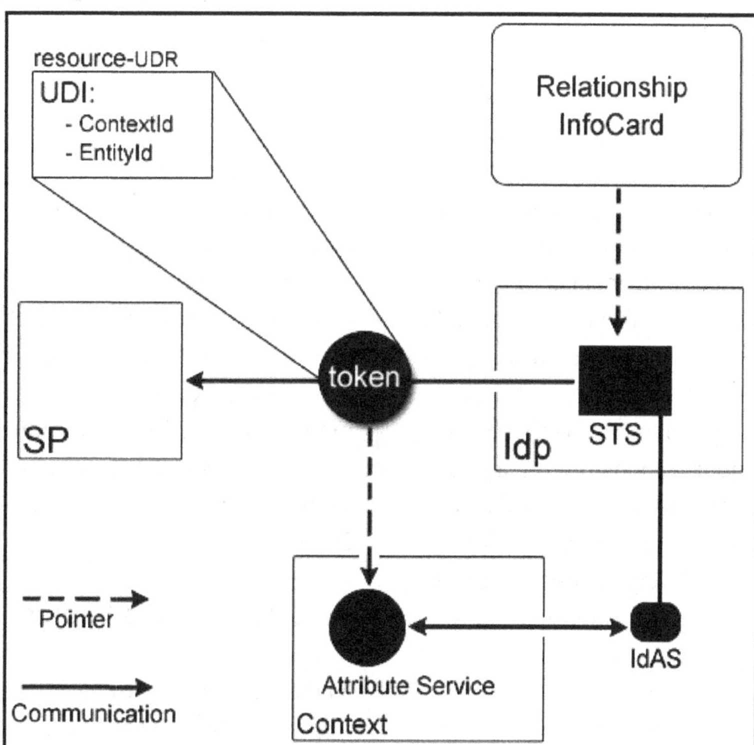

Figure 3. The interface of the Cocoa Higgins Selector on Mac OS X

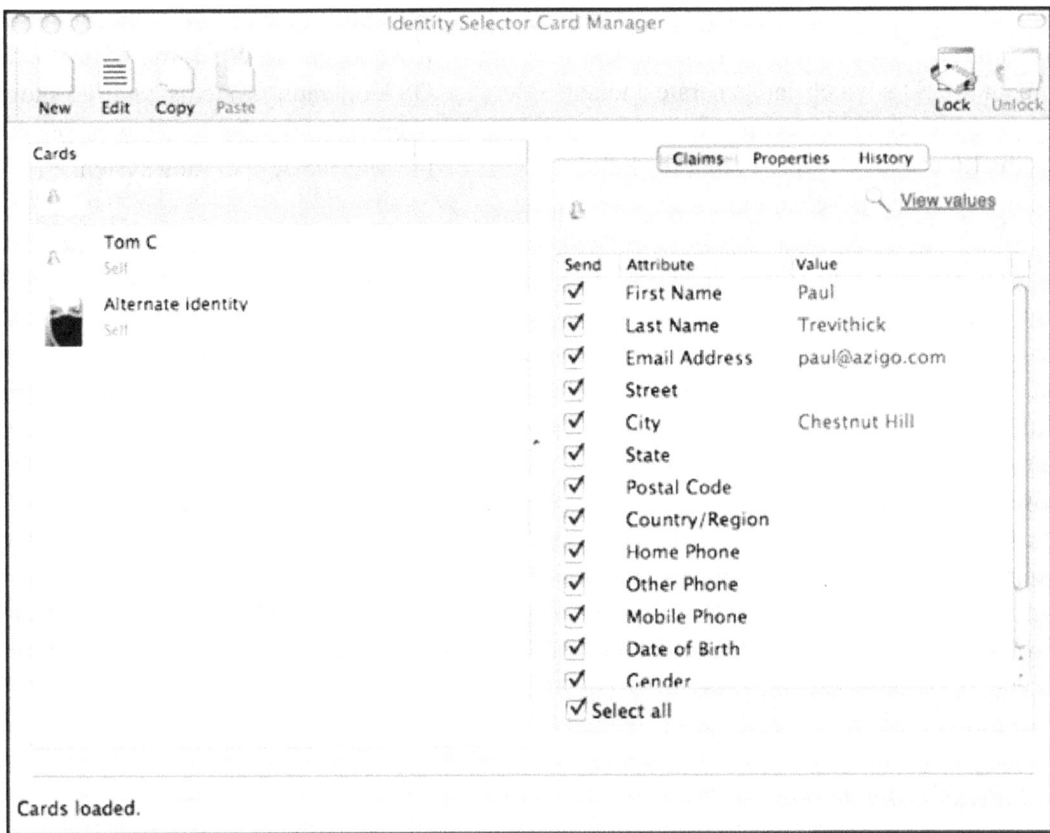

the iPhone operating system[xiii]. Figure 5 shows the interface of the iPhone Higgins Selector.

Finally, Higgins 1.1 introduced the concept of the Higgins Selector Switch (HSS), which provides an abstraction layer that decouples web browser-embedded Higgins Selectors from installed stand-alone Identity Selectors. As shown in Figure 6, the Higgins web browser-embedded Higgins Selector does not support a specific stand-alone Identity Selector; instead it interacts with the HSS, which is the component responsible for interactions with stand-alone Identity Selectors. The HSS is intended to make the task of developing and improving browser-embedded Higgins Selectors simpler and more consistent across identity selectors.

Limitations of Higgins

As in CardSpace (and all other ICIM systems), SSO is not supported. Moreover, a user can only select one InfoCard to present to an SP within a single working session.

A further limitation is that the Higgins web browser-embedded Selectors rely on the use of JavaScript web browser plug-ins, which have many associated security concerns even if they are digitally signed (Guide to Sun Microsystems Java Plug-in Security, report number C43-022R-2003, 2003).

Liberty Alliance Project

The Liberty Alliance project[xiv] (henceforth abbreviated to Liberty) is an industry collaboration first

Figure 4. The interface of the AIR-Based Higgins Selector on Windows

made public in 2001, at which time it involved 16 major companies including Sun, GM, United Airlines, and France Télécom. Liberty now involves more than 150 members, including government agencies, companies, banks and universities. In June 2009, the Liberty Alliance announced that its future activities will be taken forward under the umbrella of the Kantara Initiative[xv]. According to the project web site on 1st January 2010, there are more than one billion Liberty enabled identities and devices across the world[xvi].

Liberty aims to build open standard-based specifications for Federated identity management, provide interoperability testing, and to help provide solutions to identity theft. Liberty also aims to establish best practices and business guidelines for federated identity management systems. The Liberty specifications have been adopted by many identity management product vendors, including Sun[xvii] and Ping Identity[xviii].

Figure 7 shows the general Liberty model. In the example shown in the figure there are two distinct CoTs (see the previous chapter), and the principal (i.e. the user) has two IdP-issued identities, one for CoT A and one for CoT B, both federated with local identities within the same CoT. These two IdP-issued identities could also be

Figure 5. The interface of the iPhone Higgins Selector

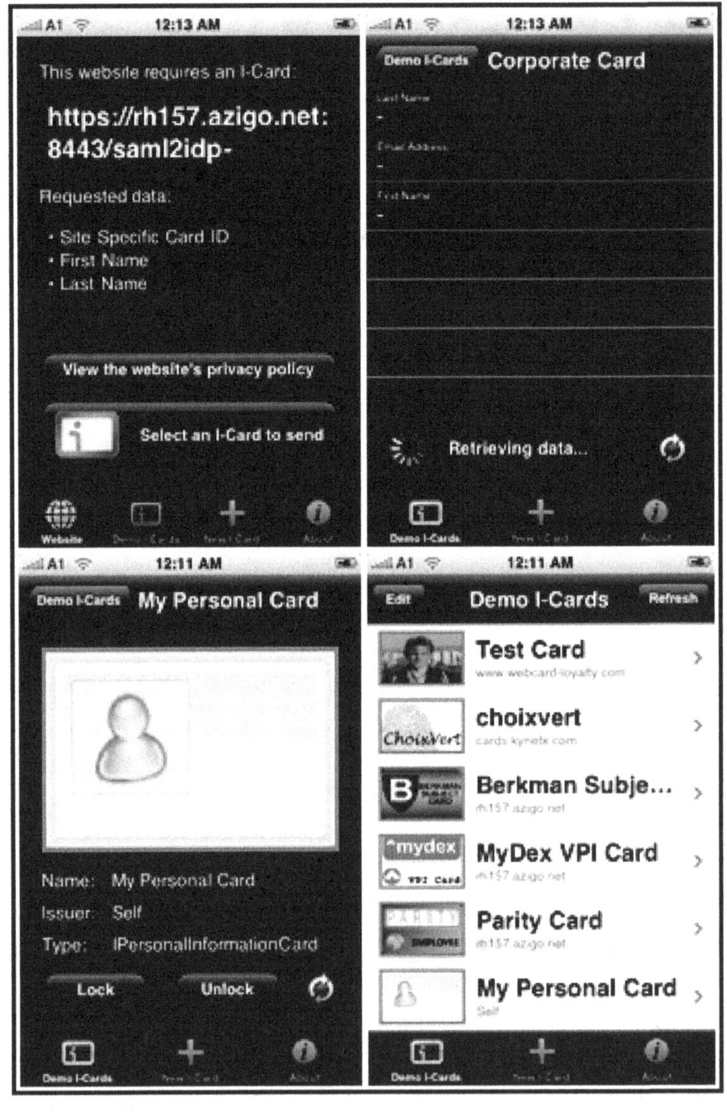

federated, but this would require a pre-established trust relationship between the IdPs.

The Liberty Framework

Liberty mandates 'identity federation', and supports the CDC technique for this purpose (see the previous chapter). The CDC name must contain the string '_liberty_idp', and a base-64 encoded list of the identifiers of all of the IdPs that have issued identities to the holding user. Liberty uses long-term pseudonyms, which are typically established between the IdP and the SP during the federation agreement process.

The Liberty specifications are divided into a number of frameworks. Currently, the most mature frameworks are the Identity Federation Framework (ID-FF) (Wason (editor), n.d.), and the Identity Web Services Framework (ID-WSF) (Tourzan & Koga (editors), n.d.). In Liberty, as in many federated identity management systems,

Figure 6. Higgins selector switch

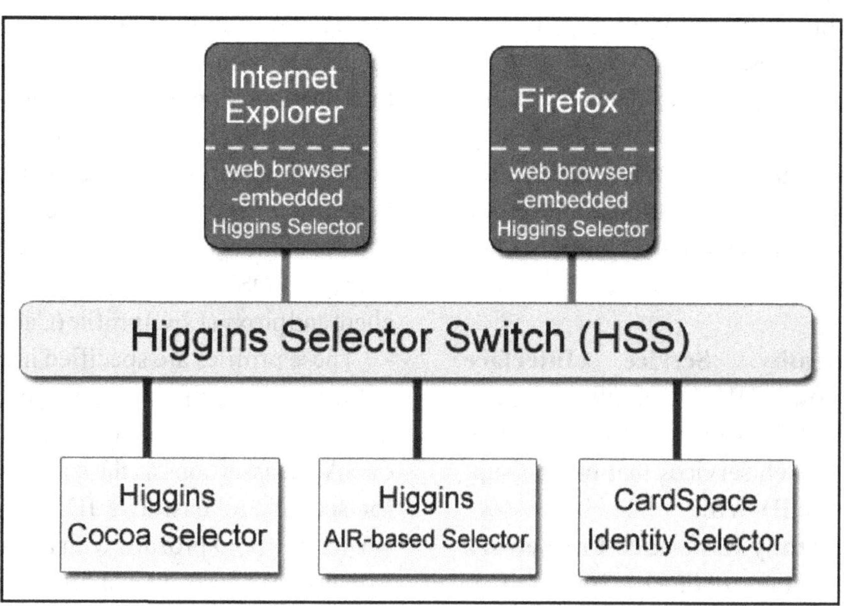

Figure 7. The Liberty model

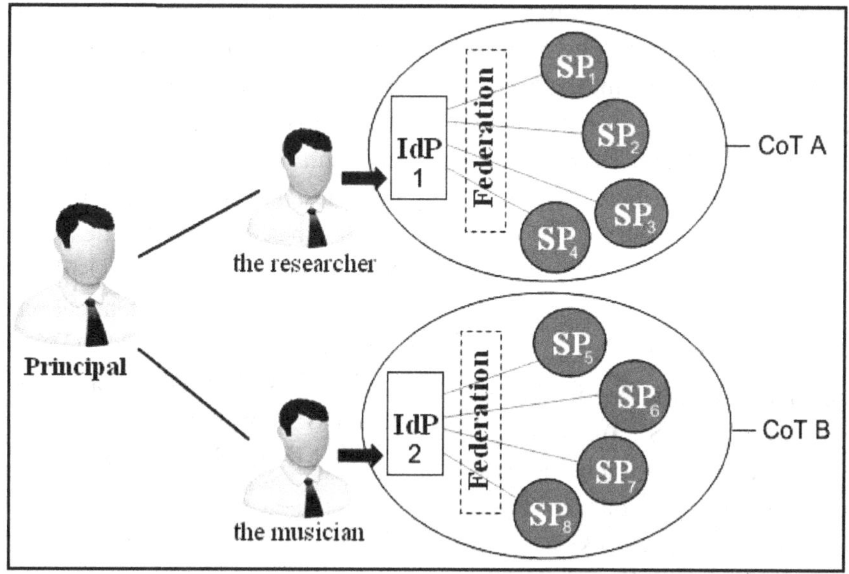

the authentication and authorisation frameworks are separate.

The ID-FF covers federation and authentication (and supports an SSO service). The main focus of the ID-WSF is the support of identity-based web services (e.g. Geo-location, Contact Book, blogs, calendars, photo sharing, etc.). Originally, the ID-WSF relied on the ID-FF to provide authentication services (and SSO) (Hodges & Aarts (editors), 2005); however, according to the latest specifications of the ID-WSF authentication SSO services, authentication services (and SSO) can be provided independently using the SAML 2.0 SSO profiles (Hodges, Aarts, Madsen, & Cantor (editors), 2006). Almost all the ID-WSF services are built on a user-attribute exchange scheme, which can be regarded as an authorisation framework. We provide here an overview of both the authentication and the authorisation frameworks.

Other Liberty frameworks include the following:

- **The Identity Service Interface Specifications (ID-SIS)** (Kellomai (editor), 2003). This provides detailed descriptions of the web services that can be supported by the ID-WSF.
- **Liberty Identity Assurance Framework (LIAF)** (Cutler (editor), 2008). This provides technical details on how to support the OMB/NIST LoA (see the previous chapter).
- **The Identity Governance Framework (IGF)** (Madsen (editor), 2008). This defines security polices for user attribute sharing using the Client Attribute Requirements Markup Language (CARML) (Hunt (editor), 2006), and the Attribute Authority Policy Markup Language (AAPML) (Mishra (editor), 2006).

The Authentication Framework

The ID-FF specifications support identity federation and authentication (with SSO). They also describe the required techniques, including session management and identity/account linkage.

In order to realise this framework, a set of profiles is required (so called ID-FF Liberty profiles). An ID-FF Liberty profile may best be defined as the combination of message content specifications and message transport mechanisms for a single type of client (that is, a user agent) (Cantor, Kemp, & Champagne (editors), 2004).

There are many types of ID-FF Liberty profile, including SSO and Federation Profiles, Register Name Identifier Profiles, Identity Federation Termination Notification Profiles, Single Logout (or Single Sign-out) Profiles, Identity Provider Introduction, NameIdentifier Mapping Profile and NameIdentifier Encryption Profile. In this chapter we are primarily concerned with the SSO and Federation Profiles. The currently defined SSO and Federation profiles are the Artifact profile, the Browser POST profile, and the Liberty-enabled client and proxy (LEC) profile (Cantor et al., 2004).

These profiles are specified in the version 1.2 of the ID-FF specifications (Cantor & Kemp (editors), 2004, Wason (editor), n.d.), and they rely on SAML assertions as the sole supported format for security tokens. The ID-FF is built on the SAML 1.1 SSO profiles with a number of added extensions. These extensions were later adopted by OASIS, and integrated into SAML 2.0. However, ID-FF is not completely compatible with the SAML 2.0 SSO profiles; there are a small number of technical differences. These differences have been listed on the SAML web site[xix]. The ID-FF SSO and Federation profiles adopt the SAML three proof-of-rightful-possession (or subject confirmation) methods, namely HoK, Sender-Vouches, and Bearer (see the previous chapter).

In Liberty, the authentication process is performed either using the ID-FF SSO profiles, or using the ID-WSF authentication service which is built in the SAML 2.0 SSO profiles.

In this section we describe each of the three ID-FF SSO profiles. These profiles are similar to the SAML 2.0 SSO profiles.

ID-FF Artifact Profile

This framework does not require an enabling software component to be installed on the user machine; it only requires the user to possess a user agent (i.e. a web browser). Figure 8 presents a sketch of the message flows within this profile in the case where the user has already been authenticated by the IdP. Note that the IdP can choose any authentication method in accordance with its security policy. The message flows within the ID-FF Artifact profile are as follows:

1. **User Agent →SP:** Log-in Request
2. **SP:** Obtains IdP (e.g. using CDC)
3. **SP →UserAgent →IdP:** Authentication Request (redirect – HTTP GET or POST)
4. **IdP →UserAgent →SP:** Authentication Response + SAMLart (redirect – HTTP GET or POST)
5. **SP →IdP:** SAMLart
6. **IdP →SP:** SAML-Assertion Response
7. **SP →UserAgent:** Log-in Granted!

As shown in the message flows above, in the first step the user tries to log-in to the SP. In step 2, the SP obtains the identity of the IdP. How the SP achieves this is not specified. However, the specifications suggest the use of the CDC technique described in the previous chapter. Alternatively, the SP could use the WAYF technique described in the previous chapter. In either case IdP discovery is implemented by the SP server.

In steps 3 and 4, the SP and the IdP communicate indirectly by redirecting the user agent (i.e. the web browser) from one party's web site to the other. This redirection is used to carry an Authentication Request message (containing a SAML authentication assertion request), from the SP to the IdP, and an Authentication Response message containing a SAMLart from the IdP to the SP. These messages are embedded within the HTTP GET or POST protocol text.

SAMLart is a SAML artifact that functions as a reference to a specific SAML assertion. This artifact is used later in steps 5 and 6, in which the SP communicates directly with the IdP to obtain the requested SAML assertion. If the SP finds this assertion acceptable, the user will be logged-in in step 7. Messages in steps 4 and 6 must be digitally signed by the IdP.

Steps 5 and 6 are bound to SOAP, which is carried over an SSL connection to provide confidentiality (integrity is preserved using an XML-Signature). Note that if the user has not been authenticated by the IdP prior to the SP log-in

Figure 8. The ID-FF Artifact profile message flow

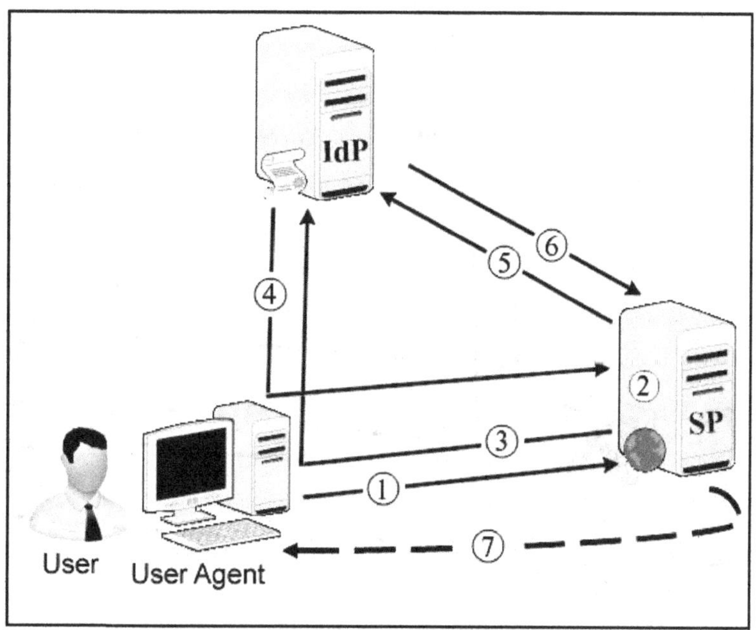

attempt, then the IdP must authenticate the user prior to step 3.

ID-FF Browser POST Profile

The ID-FF Browser POST profile, like the artifact profile, does not require an enabling software component to be installed on the user machine.

Figure 9 presents a sketch of the message flows within the ID-FF Browser POST profile in the case where the user has already been authenticated by the IdP. Note that the IdP can choose any authentication method according to its security policy. The message flows within the ID-FF Browser POST profile are as follows.

1. **User Agent→SP:** Log-in Request
2. **SP:** Obtains IdP (e.g. using CDC)
3. **SP →UserAgent →IdP:** Authentication Request (redirect – HTTP GET or POST)
4. **IdP →UserAgent →SP:** Authentication Response+SAML-Assertion (within HTML Form, Redirect – HTTP POST)
5. **SP →UserAgent:** Log-in Granted!

The message flows within this profile are similar to those within the ID-FF Artifact profile. The main difference is that, in this profile, the SAML messages (i.e. the SAML assertion request and response) are embedded within a hidden HTML form, so there is no need to use an artifact. Hence, there is no need for direct communication between the SP and IdP.

How the SP obtains the identity of the IdP in step 2 is up to the SP. However, the specifications suggest use of the CDC technique described in the previous chapter. Alternatively, the SP could use the WAYF technique described in the previous chapter. Again, in either case IdP discovery is implemented by the SP server.

Figure 9. The ID-FF Browser POST profile message flow

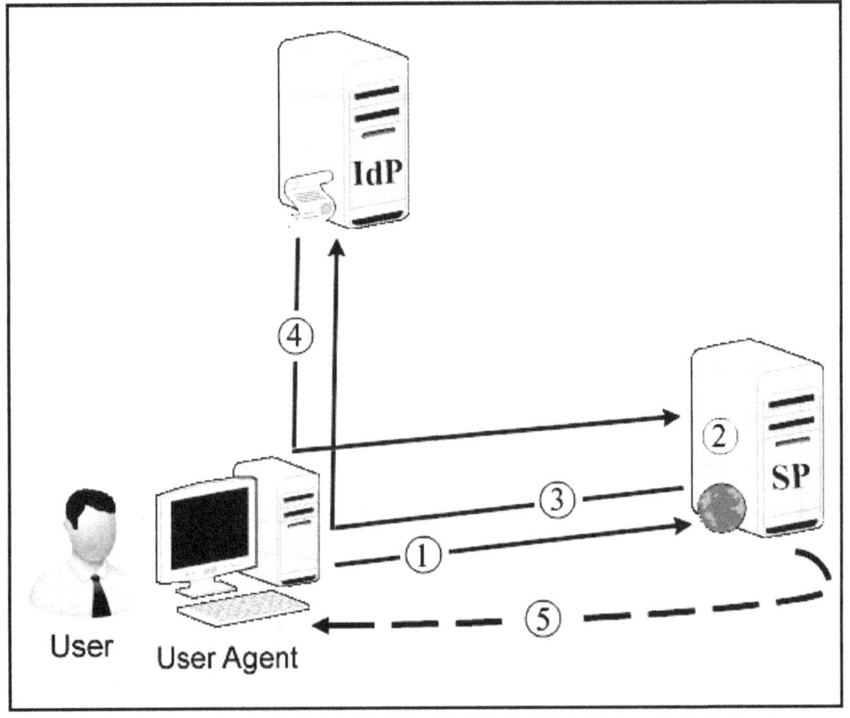

Figure 10. The ID-FF LEC profile message flow

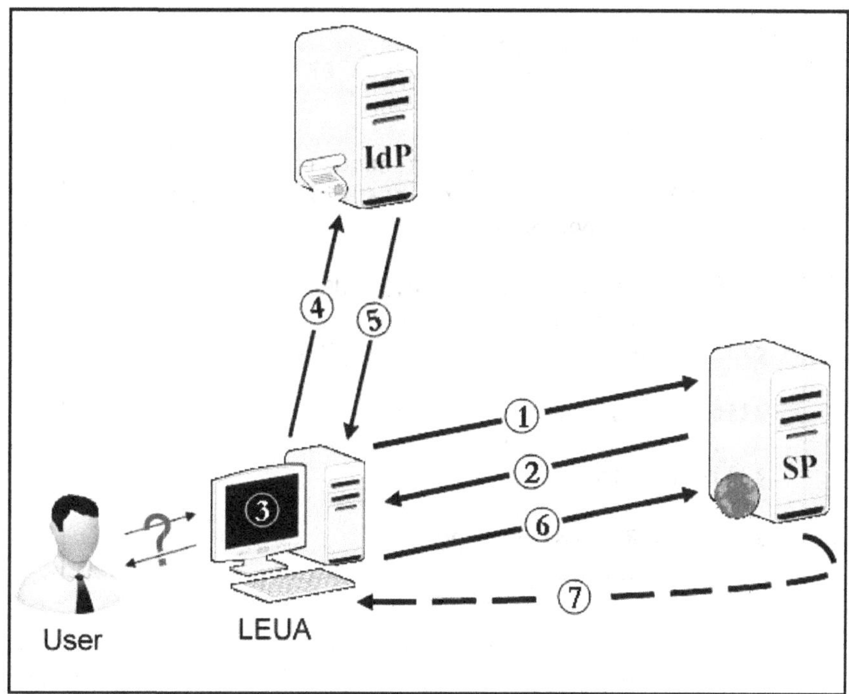

ID-FF LEC Profile

This profile requires the involvement of a Liberty-Enabled User Agent (LEUA) in order to act upon the messages sent and received during the federation and authentication processes. An LEUA is typically implemented as a web browser enhanced with JavaScript components installed on the user machine; such components can be downloaded freely from the Internet (e.g. the SecureID ID-FF 1.1 and ID-FF 1.2 Java Toolkits[xx], and the Sun FederationSPAdapter[xxi]).

Figure 10 presents a sketch of the message flows within the ID-FF LEC profile in the case where the user has already been authenticated by the IdP. Note that the IdP can choose any authentication method according to its security policy. The Liberty-Enabling component must be installed on the user machine prior to the steps shown in the figure.

The message flows within the ID-FF LEC profile are as follows.

1. **LEUA →SP:** Log-in Request (HTTP Request with Liberty Enabled Header)
2. **SP →LEUA:** Authentication Request + 'optionally' an IdP List
3. **LEUA or User**: Obtains IdP
4. **LEUA →IdP:** Authentication Request
5. **IdP →LEUA:** Authentication Response + SAML-Assertion
6. **LEUA →SP:** Authentication Response + SAML-Assertion
7. **SP →LEUA:** Log-in Granted!

In step 1, the Liberty-enabling components add a special Liberty Enabled header to the HTTP request, so that the SP knows that the requesting user agent is Liberty-enabled. In step 2, the SP replies with a special Authentication Request message, which may include a list of trusted IdPs in addition to the SAML authentication assertion request. A brief example of this message is given in Figure 11.

Figure 11. An authentication request message

```
<lib:AuthnRequestEnvelope
xmlns:lib="urn:liberty:iff:2003-08">

  <lib:AuthnRequest >
   . . . the authentication request
   + a SAML authentication assertion request . . .
  </lib:AuthnRequest>

  <lib:AssertionConsumerServiceURL>
    https://SP.com/LibertyLogin
  </lib:AssertionConsumerServiceURL>

  <lib:IDPList >
   . . . Optional IdP list goes here . . .
  </lib:IDPList>

</lib:AuthnRequestEnvelope>
```

The Liberty Specifications do not dictate how the user (or the LEUA) determines the identity of the IdP in step 3; this is left to the implementors of the Liberty-enabling components. However it is implemented, IdP discovery must be implemented on the user machine.

In step 4, the LEUA forwards the Authentication Request message to the IdP. Since the user has already been authenticated by the IdP, the IdP now sends a digitally signed Authentication Response message to the LEUA in step 5. This message is forwarded to the SP in step 6. Finally, the SP checks the forwarded Authentication Response message and, if it is acceptable, the user will be logged-in in step 7.

Messages in steps 4 and 5 must be carried over an SSL connection to provide confidentiality (integrity is guaranteed using an XML-Signature).

In Figure 12 we provide an example of a Liberty Authentication Response message. The message shown in the figure is tagged as <Lib:AuthResponse>, and it has a unique identifier (unique to the IdP). It also contains the unique identifier of the Liberty Authentication Request message (unique to the SP) to which it is a response. The issuer of the message is (http://IdP.com), i.e. the URL of the issuer IdP, and this functions as the identifier of the IdP. Similarly, the SP's URL is (http://SP.com), which functions as the identifier of the SP.

As stated above, this message contains a Liberty assertion (or <lib:Assertion>) which itself contains a Liberty authentication statement (or <lib:AuthenticationStatement>) which is an enhanced SAML authentication statement. The Liberty assertion has a unique identifier, and it also contains the unique identifier of the Liberty assertion request message to which it is a response. In addition it specifies the duration of its validity; in the example it is valid between 11:32:49 on the 1st of January 2010, and 12:00:00 on the 2nd of January 2010. Within the Liberty assertion is the <lib:Subject> element, which contains a shared pseudonym for the user. The assertion also contains the <SubjectConfirmation> element, which specifies the proof-of-rightful-possession method that has been used (in this case the Bearer method). Finally, the IdP's digital signature is included in the <ds:Signature> element.

Figure 12. Liberty authentication response message


```
<lib:AuthnResponse ResponseID="ihUj980QnjdbCsv43M099Rp"
 InResponseTo="nK665GfTRE39nmKsbnv" MajorVersion="1" MinorVersion="2"
 consent="urn:liberty:consent:obtained" IssueInstant="2010-01-01T23:50:41Z ">
      <samlp:Status>
            <samlp:StatusCode Value="samlp:Success"/>
      </samlp:Status>
 <lib:Assertion MajorVersion="1" MinorVersion="2"
 AssertionID="ref9393-fgvbvr-483jffhg0nfffoo9"
 Issuer="http://IdP.com" IssueInstant="2010-01-01T11:32:49Z"
 InResponseTo="vcbf76-urhhf8878-hgjuttee-1df34ghy">
      <saml:Conditions NotBefore="2010-01-01T11:32:49Z" -
      NotOnOrAfter="2010-01-02T12:00:00Z">
            <saml:AudienceRestrictionCondition >
                  <saml:Audience>http://SP.com</sam l:Audience>
            </saml:AudienceRestrictionCondition>
      </saml:Conditions>
       <lib:AuthenticationStatement AuthenticationInstant="2010-01-01T08:15:04Z"
            SessionIndex="3" ReauthenticateOnOrAfter="2010-01-01T10:25:17Z"
            AuthenticationMethod="urn:oasis :names:tc:SAML:1.0:am:pa ssword">
                  <lib:Subject>
                        <saml:NameIdentifier NameQualifier="http://SP.com"
                         Format="urn:liberty:iff:nam eid:federated">nbbhvg-uyjy5f9-bfg5658hj
                        </saml: NameIdentifier>
                              <saml:SubjectConfirmation>
                                    <saml:ConfirmationMethod>urn:oasis:names:tc:SAM
                                     L:1.0:cm:bearer</saml:Conf irmationMethod>
                              </saml:SubjectConfirmation>
                        <IDPProvidedNameIdentifier NameQualifier="http://SP.com"
                         Format="urn:liberty:iff:nam eid:federated">nbbhvg-uyjy5f9-bfg5658hj
                        </IDPPro videdNameIdentifier>
                  </lib:Subject>
      </lib:AuthenticationStatement>
 <ds:Signature>...</ds:Signature>
 </lib:Assertion>
 <lib:ProviderID>http://IdP.com</lib: ProviderID>
 <RelayState>nbhgjHhgpp764GGFHNVcfHgTjjdh9847JnHjKLDDGH184jN</ RelayState>
 </lib:AuthnResponse>
```


The Authorisation Framework

The ID-WSF builds upon the ID-FF to provide a framework for identity-based web services in a federated network identity environment. The ID-WSF originally relied on the ID-FF to provide authentication services (and SSO) (Hodges & Aarts (editors), 2005). However, according to the latest specifications of the ID-WSF authentication SSO services, authentication services (and SSO) can be provided independently using the SAML 2.0 SSO profiles (Hodges et al., 2006).

The People Service is one of the services offered by the ID-WSF (Madsen (editor), n.d.). This service provides a method by which a user can create an account with another user's SP to view pre-identified shared files. This gives a limited degree of support for functionality which might normally be supported by a delegation system, but it is not a full delegation service.

The ID-WSF supports user attribute sharing between SPs and/or between an IdP and SPs within the same CoT (Tourzan & Koga (editors), n.d.). Thus the ID-WSF can be regarded as an authorisation framework. In this section we provide a brief overview of the ID-WSF user attribute sharing model.

Before describing the attribute sharing model, we first consider the Discovery Service (DS) for the ID-WSF (Cahill & Hodges (editors), 2006). This service is typically managed by the IdP, and is designed to help SPs find a specific web service provider by providing them with a list of endpoint references (or EPRs), i.e. network resolvable addresses of web service providers. This is distinct from the IdP discovery service discussed in the previous chapter.

In order for an SP (or an IdP) to be able to share a given user attribute, it must first register this attribute with the DS. Figure 13 presents an example of the message flows for the user attribute registration process. In this example it is assumed that the user has federated his/her SP-issued identity with his/her IdP-issued identity, and that the user has already been successfully authenticated by the IdP. The user first logs-in to an SP (SP A), using the ID-WSF authentication service built on SAML 2.0 SSO profiles (or one of the ID-FF Federation and SSO profiles described in ?). The network resolvable address of the user's DS is included in the Liberty Authentication Response message, which means that SP A can now locate and communicate with the DS. The user then asks SP A, via the user agent, to share one (or more) attributes registered with SP A (attribute x, say) with other SPs in the same CoT. Finally, SP A sends a message to the DS asking it to associate specific metadata (in this example, the user attribute x) with a specific user. Subsequently, when other SPs in the same CoT query the DS about where to find a service that can provide the value of the user's attribute x to authorised consumers, they will receive EPRs pointing to SP A.

Figure 14 presents an example of message flows for user attribute sharing in the ID-WSF. In this example it is assumed that the user has federated his/her SP-issued identities with his/her

Figure 13. User attribute registration with the discovery service

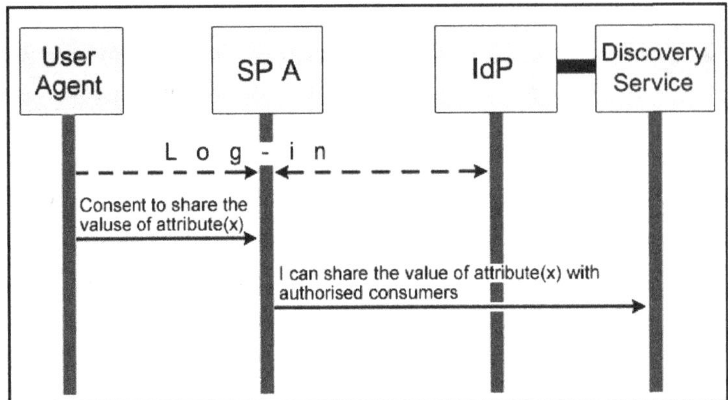

IdP-issued identity, the user has already been successfully authenticated by the IdP, and that the location of the service which can provide the value of the user's attribute x to authorised consumers has been already registered with the DS. The user first logs-in to an SP (SP B), using the ID-WSF authentication service built on the SAML 2.0 SSO profiles (or one of the ID-FF Federation and SSO profiles described earlier). The network resolvable address of the user's DS is included in the Liberty Authentication Response message, which means that SP B can now locate and communicate with the DS. The user then requests a service from SP B. SP B now discovers that it needs to obtain the value of the user attribute x in order to authorise access to the requested service. To achieve this, SP B sends a Discovery Query message to the DS asking whether or not the location of a service that can provide the value of the user's attribute x to authorised consumers has been registered.

Subsequently, the DS sends a Discovery query response message to SP B saying that user attribute x can be obtained from SP A, along with an EPR pointing to SP A. This EPR is conveyed within a signed SAML assertion (version 2 or 1.x). Moreover, the DS performs an automatic mapping of the user pseudonyms (i.e. PIDs), and includes an encrypted version of the user's PID (i.e. the pseudonym shared by the IdP and SP A) in the EPR so that SP A can identify the user. Note that the ID-WSF specifications do not dictate the choice of encryption scheme, so this assertion could, for example, be encrypted using a public key of SP A or a secret key shared by the IdP and SP A. After receiving the Discovery query response message, SP B forwards the received EPR to SP A. SP A then decrypts the user's PID, and identifies the user using the shared pseudonym. SP A now sends the value of the user attribute x to SP B, which, finally, grants the user access to the requested service.

Limitations of Liberty

One of the most significant limitations of Liberty is that, in the Artifact and Browser POST Profiles, IdP discovery is performed by the SP server. This means that a malicious SP could redirect a user to a fake IdP web site, which could then steal the user's security credentials. However, such an attack is not possible if the LEC profile is used.

Another limitation is that the IdP is made aware of all the SPs the user tries to access. This enables the IdP to track user activities, which could be a threat to user privacy (depending on the application scenario).

Finally, the fact that only one IdP can be queried in single working session (i.e. attribute-aggregation is not supported) is a major limitation of Liberty.

Shibboleth Project

The Shibboleth project[xxii] has overseen the development of an open source Federated identity management system. The system has been developed by the Internet2 consortium[xxiii], and offers standards-based authentication and authorisation frameworks (including an SSO service). In August 2008, Shibboleth superseded Athens[xxiv] as the JISC-preferred federated identity management system for use by UK educational establishments[xxv].

Development of Shibboleth started in 2000, and Shibboleth 1.0 was released in July 2003. Subsequently, Shibboleth 1.3 was released in August 2005, and Shibboleth 2.0 (the current version) in March 2008. Shibboleth 2.0 is backward compatible with Shibboleth 1.3.

Whilst the current version of Shibboleth does not support delegation, a draft specification supporting such functionality has been published.

The Shibboleth Framework

Shibboleth 1.x uses SAML 1.1 assertions as the syntax for security tokens (Cantor (editor), 2005b, Morgan, Cantor, Hoehn, & Klingenstein, 2004), whereas Shibboleth 2.0 supports both SAML 1.1 and SAML 2.0 assertions[xxvi].

Shibboleth mandates 'identity federation', in which the IdP and the SP exchange their public key certificates. Unlike in Liberty, the IdP and the SP do not have to establish long-term shared pseudonyms during the federation process (but they can if they wish) (Cantor, n.d.). Instead of long-term pseudonyms, the IdP and SP can use short-term random IDs to help preserve user privacy and maintain anonymity (Cantor, n.d.).

Although Shibboleth supports the SAML proof-of-rightful-possession methods (i.e. HoK, Sender-Vouches, and Bearer), implementing these methods is not mandatory (i.e. the SAML assertion is not required to contain a proof-of-rightful-possession field if the SP does not mandate it) (Cantor (editor), 2005b).

Unlike Liberty, the Shibboleth specifications do not include a stand-alone LoA framework. However, since Shibboleth 2.0 is built on SAML 2.0, an IdP can embed LoA information within a SAML 2.0 assertion[xxvii].

In Shibboleth 1.x, the authentication and authorisation frameworks are separate; however, in Shibboleth 2.0, they can be combined into single framework. We discuss these frameworks in greater detail below.

Figure 14. User attribute sharing in the ID-WSF

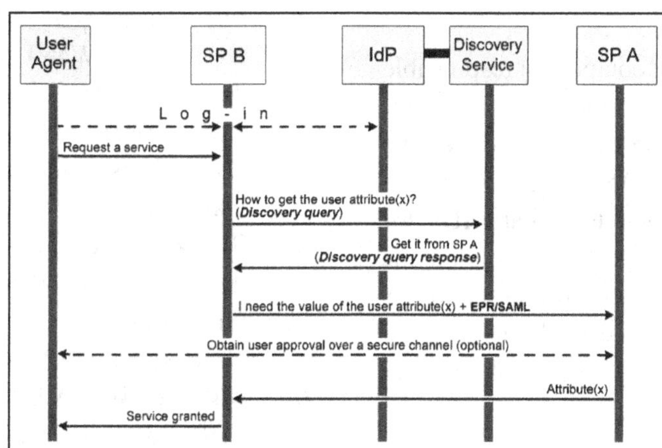

Figure 15. The message flows of the Shibboleth authentication framework

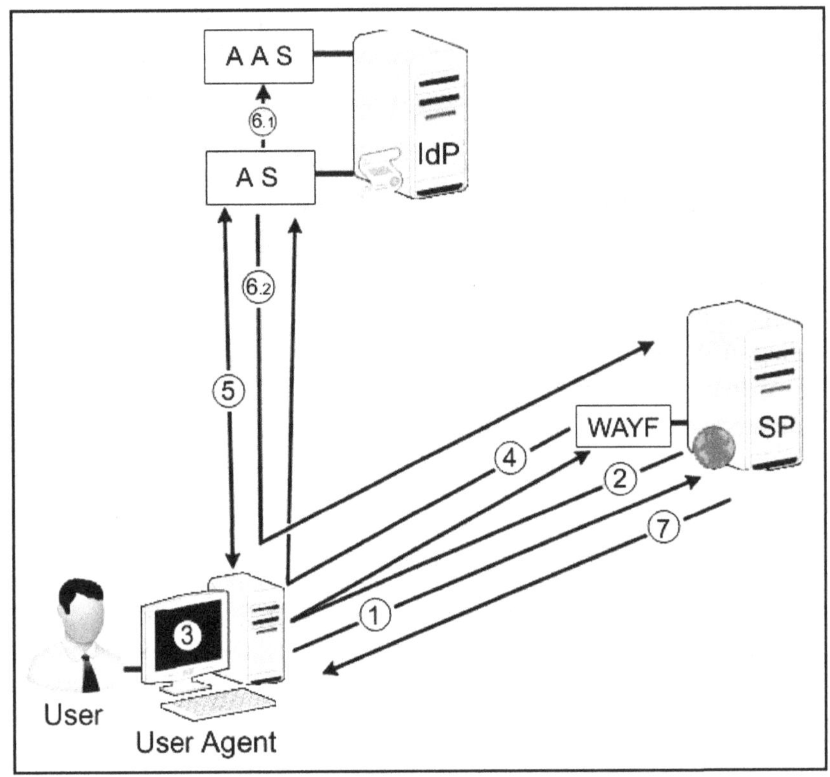

The Authentication Framework

The Shibboleth authentication framework is essentially an SSO framework, and is similar to the Liberty authentication framework discussed earlier in this chapter. Shibboleth 2.0 supports the Browser POST, Artifact, and ECP SAML SSO profiles, whereas Shibboleth 1.x only supports the SAML Browser POST profile (Hughes et al., 2005).

In Shibboleth, the IdP component responsible for authenticating the user and issuing authentication assertions for use by SPs, is called the Authentication Service (AS). The AS is also responsible for generating temporary IDs for users in the form of short-term pseudonyms or opaque handles (if long-term pseudonyms are not used). The Attribute Authority Service (AAS) is an IdP component responsible for user attribute management.

IdP discovery is performed by the SP server. It is typically achieved using the WAYF technique; however, the SP could use any IdP discovery technique (Cantor (editor), 2005b). The message flows within the Shibboleth authentication framework are as follows:

1. **User Agent →SP:** Service Request
2. **SP →UserAgent →SP – WAYFService:** GET the SP-WAYF Service web page (redirect–HTTP GET)
3. **User→UserAgent→SP–WAYFService:** User selects an IdP from the WAYF IdP list via the User Agent
4. **SP-WAYF Service →UserAgent →IdP – AS:** Authentication Request (redirect–HTTP GET or POST)
5. **UserAgent↔IdP–AS:** User Authentication
6. **IdP-AS→IdP–AAS+IdP-AS→UserAgent →SP:** IdP-AS shares the user temporary ID

Figure 16. An example of the user interface of a WAYF service web page

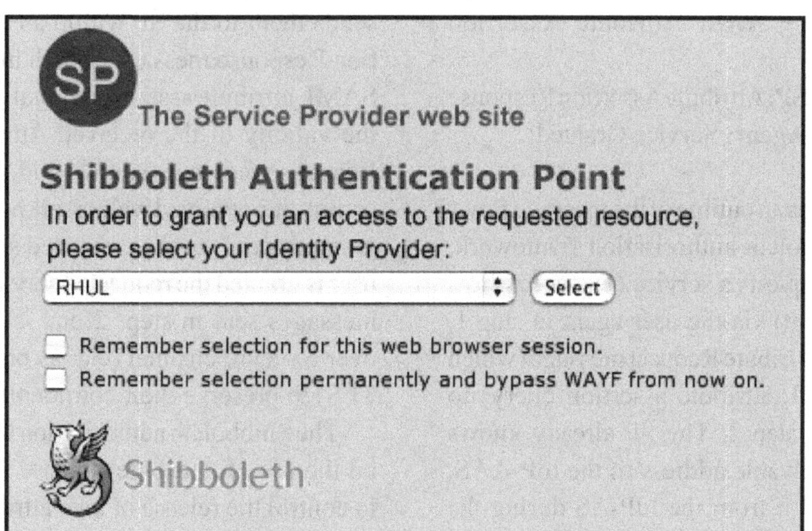

with the IdP-AAS and the SP, and sends an Authentication Response to the SP along with the IdP-AAS location (within HTML Form, redirect–HTTP POST)

7. **SP →UserAgent:** You have been authenticated!

Figure 15 gives an outline of the message flows within the Shibboleth authentication framework. In the first step, the user requests a service from the SP (e.g. access to a document) via the user agent; then, in step 2, the SP redirects the user agent to its WAYF service to determine the IdP. In step 3, the user selects an IdP from the list shown on the WAYF service web page (Figure 16 gives an example of such a WAYF service web page).

In step 4, the WAYF service redirects the user agent to the IdP-AS, simultaneously passing the IdP-AS an embedded Authentication Request message (which includes a SAML authentication assertion query). On receipt of the redirection, in step 5 the IdP-AS authenticates the user (if the user has not already been authenticated) using an authentication method of its choice. If the authentication is successful, the IdP-AS creates the requested SAML authentication assertion and a short-term random ID for the user. The IdP-AS shares this ID with the ID-AAS, and sends an Authentication Response message (which includes the created assertion) to the SP in step 6, embedded within a hidden HTML form. The message must be signed by the IdP and should contain the address of the IdP-AAS, so that the SP can request user attribute assertions from it when using the authorisation framework. If the IdP and the SP have shared pseudonyms for the user prior to the execution of the framework, then the SP-issued pseudonym is included in the authentication assertion; otherwise, a random ID is included. Finally, after receiving the Authentication Response message, the SP checks its contents and the validity of the signature. If the signature is valid, then the user is deemed to be authenticated by the SP.

The Authorisation Framework

As stated above, this framework can be optionally combined with the authentication framework in Shibboleth 2.0. If we assume that the authentication process has already been executed in the current working session, then the message flows of the authorisation framework are as follows:

1. **User Agent →SP:** Service Request
2. **SP →IdP – AAS:** Attribute Assertion Request
3. **Id-AAS→SP:** Attribute Assertion Response
4. **SP →UserAgent:** Service Granted!

Figure 17 gives an outline of the message flows within the Shibboleth authorisation framework. After the user requests a service (e.g. access to a specific document) via the user agent in step 1, the SP sends an Attribute Request message (which includes a SAML attribute assertion query) to the IdP-AAS in step 2. The SP already knows the network resolvable address of the IdP-AAS, since it obtained it from the IdP-AS during the authentication procedure. In addition to a list of the attributes for which the SP requires an assertion, the Attribute Request message includes the short-term random user ID that the SP received from the IdP-AS during the authentication procedure (note that the IdP-AAS also received this ID from the IdP-AS). In step 3, the IdP-AAS checks whether or not the Attribute Release Policies (discussed below) allow it to share the values of the requested attributes with the SP and, if so, it sends them to the SP within an Attribute Assertion Response message (which includes a signed SAML attribute assertion). Finally, the SP checks the validity of the received Attribute Assertion Response message, and if valid, checks whether or not the received values allow the user to be granted access to the requested service; if so, the user is granted the requested service in step 4. The messages sent in steps 2 and 4 must be carried over a secure channel (e.g. as provided by SSL/TLS) to preserve their confidentiality.

The Shibboleth authorisation framework relies on the use of Attribute Release Policies (ARPs) to control the release of user attributes. ARPs are written in XML, and are used by the IdP-AAS to express the user attribute release rules (i.e. an ARP indicates which user attributes can be released to which SP) (Cantor, 2008).

Typically, an ARP is created for each user by the IdP-AAS. An ARP contains a list of rules, where each rule consists of the following fields (Chadwick, 2008).

Figure 17. The message flows of the Shibboleth authorisation framework

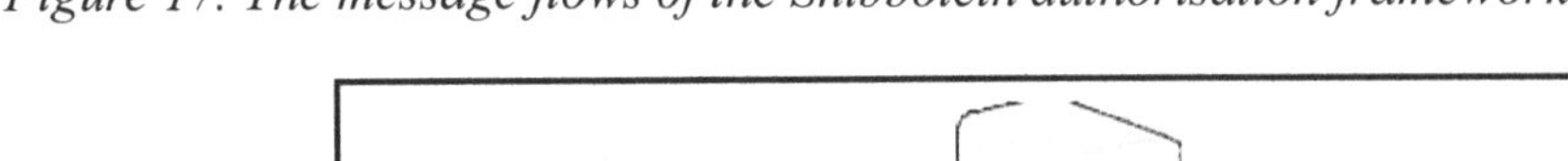

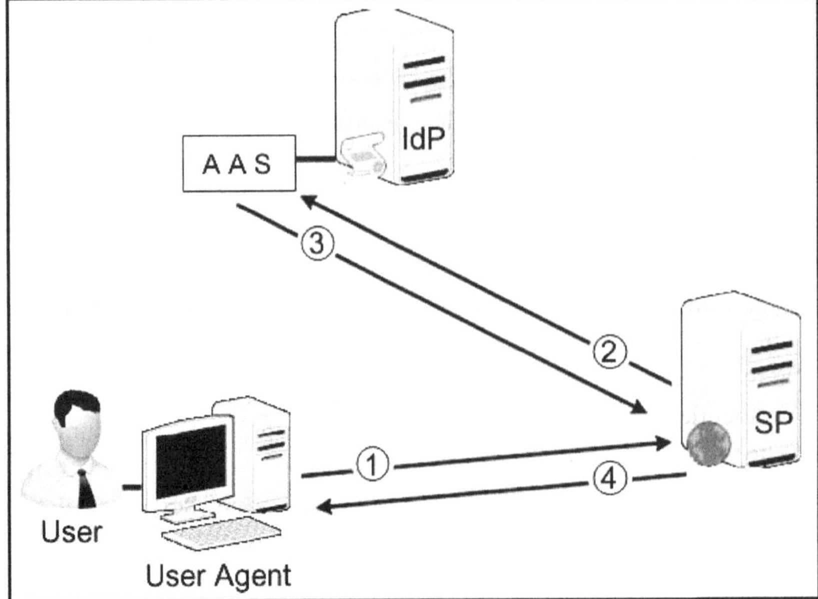

Figure 18. An example ARP

```
<?xml version="1.0" encoding="UTF-8"?>
<AttributeReleasePolicy xmlns:xsi="http://www.w3.org/2001/XMLSchema-instance"
xmlns="urn:mace:shibboleth:arp:1.0"
xsi:schemaLocation="urn:mace:shibboleth:arp:1.0 shibboleth-arp-1.0.xsd" >

    <Description>... A description of the ARP ...</Description>

    <Rule>
        <Target>
            <Requester
            matchFunction="urn:mace:shibboleth:arp:matchFunction:exactShar">
            https://SP1.com</Requester>
        </Target>
        <Attribute name="urn:mace:dir:attribute-def:eduPersonPrincipalName">
            <AnyValue release="permit"/>
        </Attribute>
    </Rule>

    <Rule>
        <Target>
            <AnyTarget/>
        </Target>
        <Attribute name="urn:mace:dir:attribute-def:eduPersonAffiliation">
            <Value release="permit">Waleed@isg.rhul.ac.uk</Value>
        </Attribute>
    </Rule>

</AttributeReleasePolicy>
```

- A destination SP identifier. This identifier is typically the SP's network resolvable address or URL (e.g. https://SP.com).
- A list of attribute types (and optionally specific attribute values). This specifies the attributes that can be released to the SP identified in the previous field.
- Other optional conditions. This is used to specify other conditions on release, e.g. the time of day, location of the user, etc.

When the IdP-AAS receives the Attribute Request message from an SP in step 2 of the authorisation framework, it extracts the SP's URL from the SAML attribute assertion query. Using this URL the IdP-AAS searches the relevant ARP to find the rules associated with this SP, and then checks whether or not the request attribute can be released.

Figure 18 presents an example of an ARP that includes two rules. The first rule permits the IdP-AAS to release the user attribute, PersonPrincipalName, to a specific SP, i.e. https://SP.com. The value of this attribute is not specified in the rule, so it can be any value chosen by the IdP-AAS. The second rule permits the IdP-AAS to release the user attribute, PersonAffiliation, to any SP. The released attribute value must be as specified in the rule, i.e. Waleed@isg.rhul.ac.uk.

As shown in Figure 18, the <Target> element has a single child element, either <Requester> or <AnyTarget/>. The <Requester> element must contain a matching function reference and the identifier of an SP to match against. Two matching function references are defined, namely regexMatch, indicating a regular expression, and exactShar, indicating that the rule applies only to the SP whose identifier exactly matches that specified. The <AnyTarget/> element indicates that the user attribute specified in the rule can be released to any SP.

The <Attribute> element specifies the user attribute for which the rule has been created, and whether or not the value of this attribute can be released to the SP specified in the <Target> element. Optionally, it can also contain a specific value for the attribute. If the default rule in the IdP-AAS is to deny the release of all user attributes, then the <Attribute> element will, if present, contain the word 'Permit' to indicate that the specified attribute can be released to the specified target (or targets). Similarly, if the default rule is to permit the release all of the user attributes, then the <Attribute> element will, if present, contain the word 'Deny' to indicate that the specified attribute cannot be released to the specified target (or targets).

There are two types of ARPs, namely site ARPs and user ARPs. A site ARP pertains to all the users of the IdP-AAS, whereas a user ARP applies only to an individual user. User ARPs can be maintained either by the IdP administrator or by the users themselves, according to the IdP local policy (Chadwick, 2008). If two ARPs apply to a particular user at the same time (i.e. the site ARP and a user ARP), then both ARPs must permit the release of a given user attribute to an SP before it can be released.

The Shibboleth Attribute Release Policy Editor (ShARPE)[xxviii] is an open source GUI ARP editor developed by the MAMS project[xxix]. This editor provides a user-friendly interface enabling both users and IdP administrators to construct ARPs.

ARPs are held in XML files (each file contains only one ARP), and the locations of these files must be specified in idp.xml, the Shibboleth IdP main configuration file, which must be located in the 'etc' folder of the Shibboleth IdP server. The <ArpRepository> element in the configuration file defines the type of ARP processing, and the path to the ARP directory (Cantor, 2008). The site ARP must be called arp.site.xml, and user ARPs must be called arp.user.$PRINCIPALNAME.xml, where $PRINCIPALNAME is the name of the relevant user.

Limitations of Shibboleth

One of the most significant security limitations of Shibboleth is that IdP discovery is performed on the SP server. This fact could be exploited by a malicious SP to redirect a user to a fake IdP web site, which could then obtain the user's security credentials.

Moreover, the use of proof-of-rightful-possession methods is optional (Cantor (editor), 2005b). Thus an IdP might not provide a user with the means to prove rightful possession of a security token to an SP. Such an approach increases the risk of an impostor using a stolen token to gain access to SP resources.

A further limitation of Shibboleth is that, for any given IdP, the authorisation framework only allows a single attribute authority (i.e. the AAS) to be queried for user attributes. It would enhance practicality if SPs were capable of obtaining user attributes from more than one independent attribute authority to be used in association with a particular IdP. In addition, attribute-aggregation is not supported.

Finally, the Shibboleth specifications do not support Single Sign-off. As a result, in order to terminate every open session, a user must sign-off from the IdP and from every SP to which the user signed on, adversely affecting Shibboleth's usability and security.

OpenID

OpenID is an open source identity management system in which IdPs issue their users with 'global' identifiers that can be used to log-in to any SP. Although OpenID fits the conceptual model described in the previous chapter, OpenID is neither a Federated nor an Information Card-based identity management system (using the terms as defined in the previous chapter), since it relies on a different model (described below).

The first version of OpenID was released in 2005, and the most recent version is 2.0 (Recordon, Bufu, & Hoyt (editors), 2007) (released in December 2007). OpenID is owned and managed by the OpenID Foundation[xxx], and is supported by many well-known organisations including Google, IBM, Microsoft, Yahoo!, PayPal, and VeriSign. According to the OpenID web site, there are currently over one billion OpenID-enabled identities, and approximately nine million OpenID-enabled SPs on the Internet[xxxi]. However, almost none of these SPs provide access to any information of any real value (although this may change in the future). In the remainder of this section we describe the OpenID framework in greater detail.

The OpenID Framework

In the OpenID framework, an IdP issues a user with a global identifier (or OpenID) that can be used to log-in to any OpenID-enabled SP. This identifier is usually a URI (e.g. a URL), and is used to discover the IdP that issued it. Obviously, there is no need for pseudonyms in this framework, since IdPs and the SPs can refer to a user using the OpenID global identifier.

There is no identity federation process in OpenID; however, if a user already holds an SP-issued identifier, then the SP may choose to 'locally' link this identifier with the user OpenID (i.e. the IdP-issued global identifier).

The OpenID specifications include an LoA framework that supports the OMB/NIST assurance levels (Bufu & Daugherty (editors), 2008). This LoA framework enables IdPs and SPs to define their own 'custom' assurance levels.

The OpenID authentication and authorisation frameworks are separate. We discuss these frameworks in greater detail below.

Finally, we observe that OpenID does not support any proof-of-rightful-possession methods (Hodges, 2009).

The Authentication Framework

The OpenID authentication framework is essentially an SSO framework; however, it is not built on SAML assertions or on the SAML SSO profiles (Recordon et al., 2007). Figure 19 sketches the message flows within the OpenID authentication framework. The message flows within this framework are as follows:

1. **UserAgent →SP:** Log-in Request (the user must enter her OpenID)
2. **SP:** Obtains IdP
3. **SP ↔IdP:** Optionally, the SP establishes a secret with the IdP using DHKE
4. **SP →UserAgent →IdP:** Authentication Request (redirect – HTTP GET)
5. **User Agent ↔IdP:** User Authentication
6. **IdP →UserAgent SP:** Authentication Response (within HTML Form, redirect – HTTP POST)
7. **SP ↔IdP:** Optionally, the SP checks the validity status of the token with the IdP
8. **SP →UserAgent:** Log-in Granted!

In the first step, the user tries to log-in to the SP web site via the user agent. The user must enter her OpenID as her identifier in the log-in form. The OpenID can be either a URL or an Extensible Resource Identifier (XRI) (Reed & McAlpin (editors), 2005), an abstract and domain-independent identifier. The URI and the Internationalized Resource Identifier (IRI) (Duerst & Suignard, 2005) standards are compatible with XRI.

The SP then obtains the identity of the IdP in step 2. The IdP discovery technique depends on the type of the user OpenID, as described below.

- If the OpenID is an XRI, then the SP performs the 'XRI Resolution' protocol (Wachob, Reed, Chasen, Tan, & Churchill (editors), 2008) via HTTP(S) URIs. The protocol execution should output an eXtensible Resource Descriptor Sequence

Figure 19. The message flows of the OpenID authentication framework

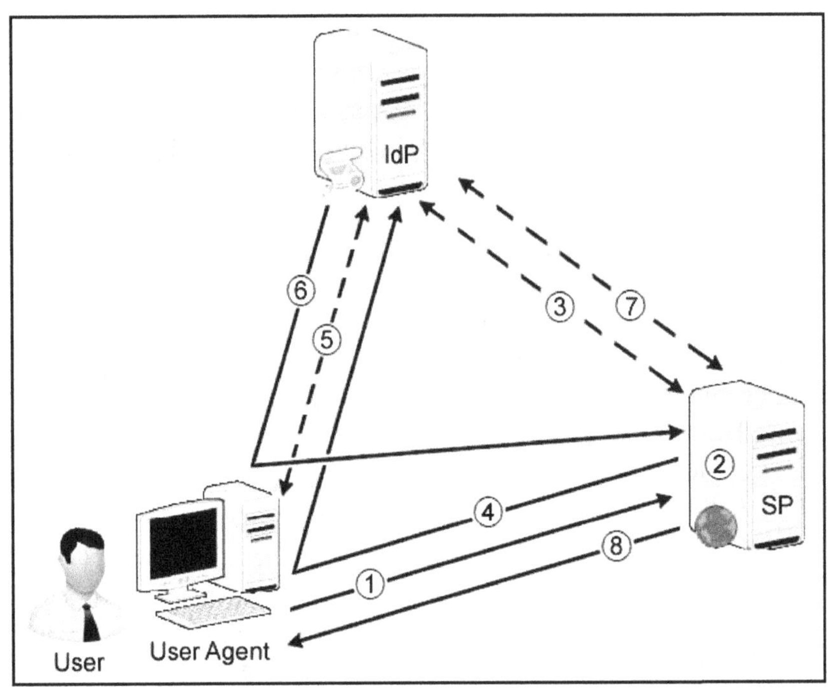

(XRDS) (Hammer-Lahav & Norris (editors), 2009) document that contains the IdP network resolvable address.

- If the OpenID is a URL, then:
  - the SP performs the Yadis protocol (Miller (editor), 2006), which uses the OpenID (i.e. the URL) to HTTP GET an XRDS document containing the IdP network resolvable address from a remote server. If the Yadis protocol does not find an XRDS document, then
  - the SP performs an HTML-based discovery, in which the SP fetches an HTML document stored at the same URL. The <HEAD> element of this HTML document must contain a <LINK> element with two attributes, rel set to 'openid2.provider', and href set to the IdP's URL.

In step 3, the SP optionally establishes a shared secret key with the IdP using the DHKE protocol (Diffie & Hellman, 1976). This process is called 'handle association' in the OpenID specifications. In step 4, the SP redirects the user agent to the IdP with an embedded Authentication Request message. If the user has not already been authenticated by the IdP during the current working session, then the IdP authenticates the user in step 5, using an authentication method of its choice.

After authenticating the user, the IdP extracts and processes the Authentication Request message. It then redirects the user agent to the SP with an Authentication Response message that contains a MACed authentication token, in step 6. If the SP has performed the 'optional' step 3, or has established a shared secret key with the IdP prior to the protocol run, then this MAC is computed using this secret key, so that the SP can verify the received token and skip step 7. Otherwise, i.e. if the SP has not performed the 'optional' step 3 and has not established a shared secret key with the IdP prior to the protocol run, then the SP must perform step 7, in which it directly sends the token back to the IdP, asking whether or not it is valid. SPs that choose to share a secret key with an IdP are called 'stateful' SPs, whereas SPs that choose not to are called 'stateless' SPs. If the token is valid, then in step 8 the SP permits the user to log-in.

The Authorisation Framework

OpenID supports an attribute exchange framework (Hardt, Bufu, & Hoyt, 2007), which functions as an authorisation framework. This framework can be used by the SP to retrieve specific user attributes (e.g. an email address) from the IdP, after obtaining the consent of the user to release the requested attributes. Retrieved attributes can be used by the SP to create a local account for the user (i.e. user registration), or to identify a registered user.

Two operations are defined: fetch and store. Fetch retrieves user attributes from an IdP, while store saves or updates user attributes at an IdP. These operations must be initiated by the SP, and they are passed to the IdP via the user agent as in the OpenID authentication framework. A demonstration of this framework can be found at the Sxip web site[xxxii].

Limitations of OpenID

OpenID suffers from a number of security limitations. Of particular concern is its reliance on the notion of global identifiers, which raises significant privacy concerns. According to the W3C P3P (Wenning & (editors), 2006), 'unique identifiers' should be treated as private information. However, in OpenID, user unique identifiers (i.e. OpenIDs) are global by definition, and releasing them to SPs is an essential part of the system. Malicious SPs could collude using the OpenID to trace user activities on the Internet, including the exchange of user preferences, interests and surfing behaviour, e.g. for targeted advertising.

Another limitation is that the IdP discovery is performed on the SP server. As discussed earlier, this could be exploited by a malicious SP to redirect users to a web site masquerading as the IdP, e.g. to obtain their credentials.

A further limitation of OpenID is the lack of attribute-aggregation support (i.e. only one IdP can be queried in single working session).

Finally, as previously mentioned, OpenID does not support any proof-of-rightful-possession methods, increasing the risk of an imposter using a stolen security token to log-in to an SP.

Shared Security Limitations

In this section, we investigate certain security limitations that are shared by all the identity management systems discussed in this chapter.

Reliance on DNS Names

The first security limitation we observe is a reliance on DNS names (i.e. URLs) as both identifiers and network addresses for IdPs and SPs. If an attacker is able to corrupt a DNS server, it could direct the user agent to a fake web site, which might then be able to obtain the user's security credentials. This problem is very difficult to address. Probably the only long term solution to this problem is to hope that the use of DNSSEC (Arends, Austein, Larson, Massey, & Rose, 2005), or some other secure address resolution solution, will become widespread.

Judgements of SP Authenticity

The user judgement regarding the authenticity of the SP is a security-critical task in all the identity management systems we have described.

- In a system in which IdP discovery is performed on the SP server (such as Federated identity management systems and OpenID), a malicious SP could redirect users to a web site masquerading as the IdP in order to steal their security credentials. Moreover, the SP will learn that there is a federation relationship between the user and the IdP (in a Federated identity management system), or will obtain the user's OpenID (in OpenID), which functions as a unique global identifier for the user. Unique identifiers can be regarded as private data, and hence this is an undesirable property.

- In an ICIM system, the SP obtains personal information belonging to the user in the form of claims asserted in a security token. Thus, if accepted by a user, a malicious SP could gather sensitive personal information about users. Thus any misjudgement of the authenticity of an SP could result in a serious privacy violation (Alrodhan & Mitchell, 2007, 2009, 2010).

In all web-based identity management systems, users are responsible for judging the authenticity of the SP. This typically involves either checking the validity of the SP's SSL/TLS certificate (if the SP has one), or just hoping that the visited SP is as intended, perhaps including a check that the expected URL appears in the address bar of the web browser.

CardSpace and Higgins possess the following user-friendly mechanism which helps to provide guidance to the user regarding the authenticity of the SP. When the user is prompted to provide consent to use a particular InfoCard with an SP for the first time, the user is shown a warning screen which helps in making a judgement regarding the authenticity of this SP. This judgement is based on one of:

1. a high-assurance public key certificate belonging to the SP,
2. an 'ordinary' public key certificate belonging to the SP (e.g. a certificate used for SSL/TLS), or
3. no certificate at all.

Obviously, in the third situation the user has no evidence of the honesty of the SP (Cameron & Jones, 2006). Microsoft recommends the first option, i.e. the use of a high assurance certificate (Bertocci et al., 2008, CA/Browser forum, 2008, Microsoft Corporation and Ping Identity Corporation, 2005) (also referred to as a 'higher-value', 'higher-assurance' or 'extended validation' certificate). This is an X.509 certificate that is only issued after a rigorous and well-defined registration process, unlike the CA-specific procedures used for issuing certificates commonly employed as the basis for SSL/TLS security (Nash, Duane, Joseph, & Brink, 2001). A high assurance certificate might include a digitally signed bitmap of the SP's company logo, in order to make it easier for the user to identify the certificate holder[xxxiii]. Figure 20 shows an example of a CardSpace message to the user describing a high assurance certificate issued by 'VeriSign' to a company called 'Overdue Media'. The 'check mark' beside a certificate's field is an indication that the certificate issuer has assurance of the veracity of that field.

In general, it would appear that a typical user is not qualified to make such a security critical decision. Many users do not pay much attention when they are asked to approve a digital certificate, either because they do not understand the importance of the approval decision, or because they know that they must approve the certificate in order to get access to a particular web site. SPs without any certificates at all can be used in web-based identity management systems (given user consent), and this leads to a serious risk of a privacy violation. If we consider the potentially large number of SPs, it is likely that (at least initially) many of them will not possess a high assurance certificate. Even in the case where an SP does have a high assurance certificate and the user is careful, the user may be deceived by a company name or logo that is similar to that used by a legitimate SP (although in principle this

Figure 20. An example of a higher-value certificate (Cameron & Jones, 2006)

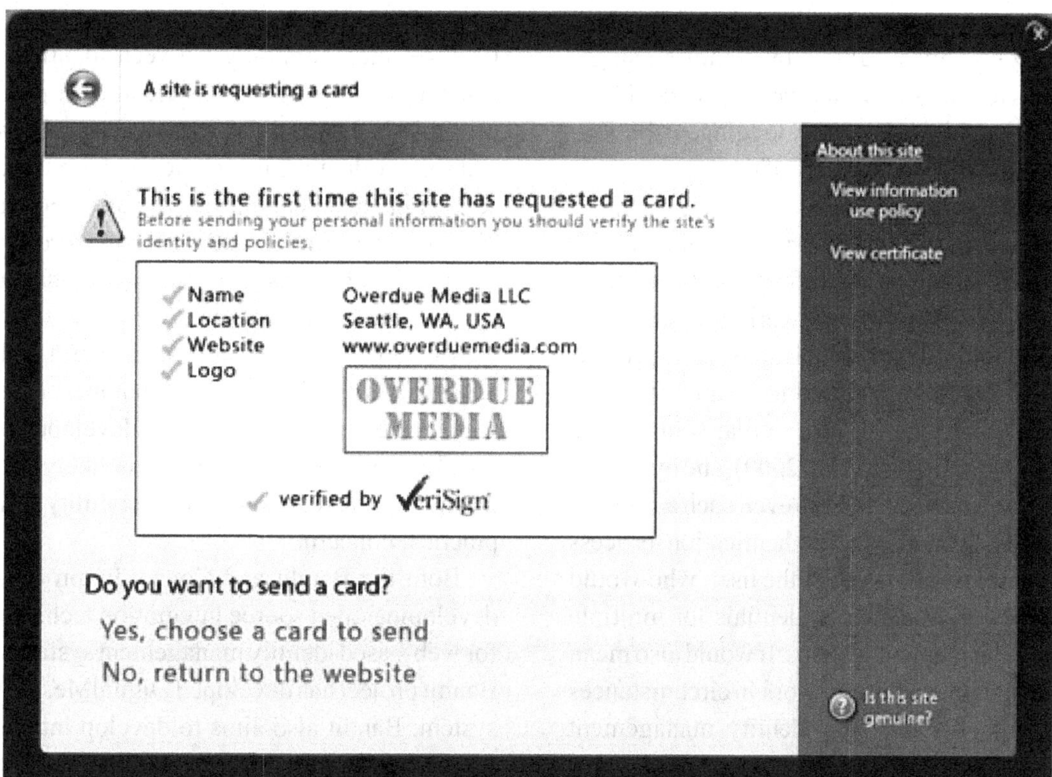

should be prevented by the registration process for a high assurance certificate).

Finally, we observe that, as discussed above, the Identity Selector in an ICIM system warns the user when accessing an SP for the first time. Although this warning might help the user to detect a false SP, it is not a complete solution. One reason for this is that the identities of visited SPs are stored locally on the user machine. Thus every time a user accesses an SP for the first time via a particular machine a warning will be provided. Thus if a user employs more than one PC[xxxiv](e.g. a personal laptop and an office desktop), then repeated warnings will be received for the same SP. Such repetition may result in the user becoming desensitised to the warnings. Also, once an SP has successfully deceived a user, then no warning will be provided on subsequent accesses to the same fraudulent SP.

Alrodhan and Mitchell proposed a scheme that aims to mitigate the risk of this problem (Alrodhan & Mitchell, 2007, 2009).

Reliance on a Single Layer of Authentication

All the identity management systems we have considered rely on authentication of the user by the IdP. In the case where a single IdP and multiple SPs are involved in a single working session, which seems likely to be a typical scenario, the security of the system within that working session will rely on a single layer of authentication, i.e. the authentication of the user to the IdP.

This user authentication can be achieved in a variety of ways (e.g. username/password, X.509 certificate, Kerberos v5 ticket, self-issued token, one-time password, etc.); however, it seems likely that in many cases a simple username/password authentication technique will be used. If a working session is hijacked (e.g. by compromising a Kerberos token), or the password is cracked (e.g. via guessing, brute-force, key logging, or dictionary attacks), then the security of the entire system will be compromised.

One approach to mitigating this vulnerability involves combining two different authentication frameworks during the same working session. For example, before a user agent is able to use an ICIM system, it could be required to be authenticated by OpenID, or vice versa (a similar solution has been proposed in (Kim et al., 2009), and by others, including Cameron[xxxv]). However, such a solution would clearly make the authentication process more complex, not least for the user, who would be required to maintain credentials for multiple identity management systems. It would also mean that the system would only work in circumstances where both the required identity management systems are available.

Alrodhan and Mitchell proposed two schemes in (Alrodhan & Mitchell, 2007, 2009, 2010) by which an additional layer of authentication is introduced.

Practicality of Identity Management Systems

A variety of approaches can be pursued to enhance practicality; we focus here on two particular directions. The first involves developing integration schemes to enable interoperation between identity management systems. The second is to develop means of delegation, so that a user can delegate to a third party all or subset of its access rights at an SP.

In this section we review prior work on integration and delegation for identity management systems.

Integration

Lack of interoperability between identity management systems is an obstacle to their practical use; this is especially the case since almost all web-based identity management solutions require several independent entities to participate in the identification and/or authentication process. If the user's IdP uses one identity management system, and an SP that the user wishes to access uses another incompatible system, then a problem arises. Given the relatively large number of identity management systems that have developed in the last few years, such a scenario is likely to arise frequently; thus system interoperability is a key practical concern.

Both the Bandit and Concordia projects are developing open source integration technologies for web-based identity management systems. The Bandit project has developed DigitalMe, an ICIM system. Bandit also aims to develop integration techniques supporting interoperation between ICIM systems. Bandit and Higgins have ensured that the DigitalMe Identity Selector is seamlessly interoperable with the Higgins Identity Selector.

Project Concordia is a global initiative intended to promote interoperability between web-based identity management systems; recently it joined the Kantara Initiative[xxxvi]. Concordia has proposed an interoperation framework for Federated and Information Card-based identity management systems[xxxvii]. The scheme covers two types of Federated identity management systems, namely systems built on SAML SSO profiles (or SAML-enabled systems), and systems built on WS-Federation (or WS-Federation-enabled systems). The framework enables users to access SAML-enabled (or WS-Federation-enabled) SPs, even if their IdP is ICIM-enabled. In the case of a SAML-enabled SP, the main parties involved are as follows:

1. A user.
2. An ICIM-enabled user agent.

Figure 21. ICIM and SAML-enabled systems integration framework

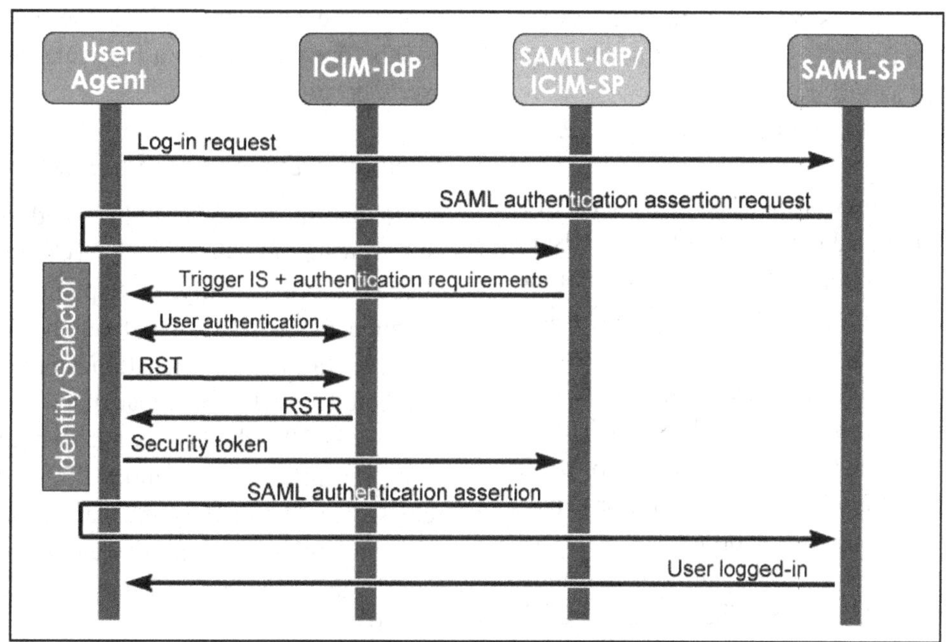

3. A SAML-enabled SP (e.g. a Liberty-enabled SP); such a party is referred to below as a SAML-SP.
4. A SAML-enabled IdP (e.g. a Liberty-enabled IdP) that must simultaneously act as an ICIM-SP (e.g. a CardSpace-enabled SP); such a party is referred to below as a SAML-IdP/ICIM-SP.
5. An ICIM-enabled IdP (e.g. a CardSpace-enabled IdP); such a party is referred to below as a ICIM-IdP.

Figure 21 provides a sketch of the framework message flows. User authentication involves the following steps:

1. The user tries to log-in to a SAML-SP via a user agent.
2. The SAML-SP redirects the user agent to a SAML-IdP with a SAML authentication assertion request message. This message contains the authentication method that the SAML-SP wants the IdP to use, which must be one of the methods supported by the ICIM system in use.
3. The SAML-IdP/ICIM-SP authenticates the user via an ICIM system and WS-Trust, as required by the SAML-SP. The SAML-IdP converts the attribute requirements specified by the SAML-SP into the corresponding claim type(s) in order to enable the selection of an appropriate card. If the specified authentication mechanism requires a managed card to be used, then an appropriate managed Infocard must be selected.
4. If a managed Infocard is used, then the Identity Selector sends an RST to the ICIM-IdP, which authenticates the user and responds to the Identity Sector with an RSTR.
5. The Identity Selector sends the RSTR to the SAML-IdP/ICIM-SP.
6. The SAML-IdP/ICIM-SP redirects the user agent back to the SAML-SP, specifying the authentication context extracted from the RSTR token. (If the token is a SAML

2.0 assertion, the SAML-IdP/ICIM-SP can simply copy the saml:AuthenticationContext element from the token into a newly constructed assertion).

7. The user is logged-in to the SAML-SP.

A similar framework is used in the case of a WS-Federation-enabled SP. Further details of this integration framework, and examples of the framework messages, can be found at the Project Concordia web site[xxxviii].

A scheme for integrating CardSpace and Liberty has also been proposed by Jørstada, Thuan, Jønvikc and Thanh (Jørstada, Thuan, Jønvikc, & Thanh, 2007). This scheme requires the user to possess a mobile phone with Short Message Service (SMS) support. The concept is simple; the IdP must support both CardSpace and Liberty, so that a CS-E user agent will be able to access any SP supporting either Liberty or CardSpace, without requiring an identity management adapter to be installed on the user machine. Moreover, the IdP must perform the same user authentication technique, regardless of the identity management system the user is trying to use. The IdP simply sends an SMS to the user, and, in order to be authenticated, the user must confirm receiving that SMS. This confirmation is also an implicit user approval for the IdP to send a security token (or assertion) to the SP. Another scheme for integrating CardSpace and Liberty has been proposed in (Alrodhan & Mitchell, 2008a, Al-Sinani, Alrodhan, & Mitchell, 2010). This scheme is built on a client-side model in which an 'Identity Management Adaptor' is installed to map the messages between the two systems.

Delegation

Providing support for delegation services in an identity management system enhances its practicality by improving its flexibility and scalability. Delegation enables an SP to perform tasks on behalf of its users (e.g. obtaining user information from another SP in order to create a new user account). Delegation must be bound to user consent; i.e. an SP must obtain the consent of the user before performing a particular task on the user's behalf.

Shibboleth Delegation Framework

Draft specifications for a Shibboleth delegation system were published in 2005 (Cantor (editor), 2005a). More recently, in September 2008 an announcement[xxxix] appeared on the Shibboleth web site stating that delegation support is on the Shibboleth development road map. At the time of writing, the 2005 drafts have not been superseded. Most recently, in November 2009 Shibboleth released a software plug-in[xl] that can be installed with Shibboleth to support delegation for web portals; this plug-in conforms to the 2005 draft specifications.

The Shibboleth delegation framework is essentially a SAML authentication assertion delegation framework, and it can be built on either the Browser POST or the ECP SSO profile (Hughes et al., 2005). Figure 22 provides a sketch of the Shibboleth delegation system message flows (for the Browser POST profile case).

As shown in the figure, the authentication process described earlier must be performed prior to performing the delegation procedure. The main steps in the delegation procedure are as follows.

1. The user is authenticated by an SP, A, using the authentication procedure described earlier. This results in A obtaining a SAML authentication assertion signed by the IdP. This assertion is referred to below as assertion-1.
2. Subsequently, suppose the user requests a service from A that requires certain user information to be obtained from another SP, B.
3. In order to obtain the required information, A must log-in to B on behalf of the user. This

Figure 22. Shibboleth delegation framework (Browser POST)

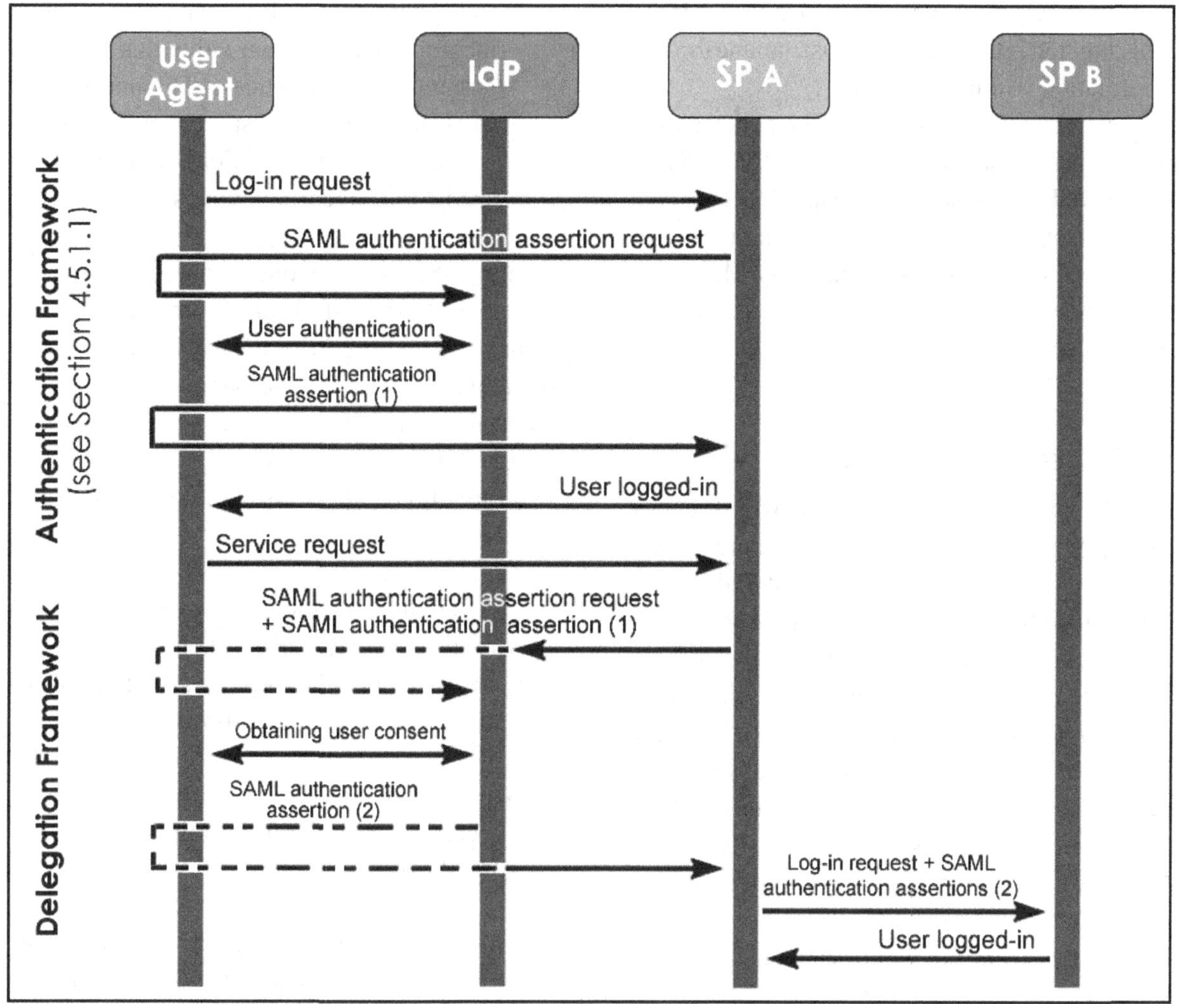

involves A sending a new SAML authentication assertion request to the IdP along with assertion-1. The inclusion of assertion-1 proves to the IdP that the user has recently accessed A. This message can be sent either by redirecting the user agent to the IdP web site, or directly from A to the IdP.

4. The IdP asks the user for her consent via the user agent.
5. After the user has provided her consent, the IdP checks the validity of assertion-1. If assertion-1 is valid, then the IdP generates a new SAML authentication assertion to be presented to B (in which the subject is the user). This assertion is referred to below as assertion-2. The IdP then sends assertion-2 to A either by redirecting the user agent to A's web site, or directly to A.
6. A then forwards assertion-2 to B.
7. Finally, after checking the validity of assertion-2, B grants A access to the required information on behalf of the user.

The 2005 draft specification (Cantor (editor), 2005a) recommends that the SAML proof-of-rightful-possession (or subject confirmation) method specified within assertion-2 is HoK; however, Bearer assertion can also be used. If the HoK method is used, the IdP must include the key information within assertion-2.

This framework is not really a delegation framework; instead it is essentially a 'user-masquerading' framework, in which SPs are able to impersonate users, which raises a number of concerns regarding user accountability. Moreover, the framework does not offer a reliable means to ensure that the delegation assertion will be used for a specific privilege or role.

OAuth Delegation Framework

OAuth[xli] is an open delegation framework designed to enable users to share private resources (e.g. photos, videos, contact lists, etc.) stored by one SP with another SP without having to reveal the security credentials associated with the first SP to the second. The OAuth 1.0 specifications were released in 2007 (Atwood et al., 2007); a revised version of these specifications was subsequently released in 2009 (Hammer-Lahav (editors), 2009).

Figure 23 provides a sketch of the OAuth framework message flows. Prior to execution of the framework, the two SPs involved must establish an identifier and a secret called a consumer key and a consumer secret, respectively. The main steps in the delegation framework are as follows (given that the exchanged messages in this framework are very short, we also provide examples of the main messages).

1. The user requests an SP, A say, via the user agent, to perform a task that requires certain information belongs to the user to be obtained from another SP, B say.
2. A first tries to access the necessary information stored on B's server. However, we suppose that it receives an HTTP 401 error message, indicating that the required information is private and can not be accessed without authorisation.
3. A then sends an HTTP POST request message to B containing a 'Request-Token', which incorporates a random value that acts as a reference for the request. This message is MACed using the consumer key. The MAC is held in the signature field. An example of such a message is as follows.

https://SP-B.com/request_token?oauth_consumer_key=evb1234rd9&oauth_signature_method=PLAINTEXT&oauth_signature=k93k4268kf54&oauth_timestamp=31012010&oauth_nonce=8485hbf75b330&oauth_version=1.0&oauth_callback=http://SP-A.com/token_request

4. After checking the validity of the MAC, B replies with a Request-Token message in the body of an HTTP response. An example of such a message is as follows.

oauth_token=ynk56vcck98&oauth_token_secret=kc244456ao03&oauth_callback_confirmed=true

5. After receiving the Request-Token, A redirects the user agent to B, and attaches the received Request-Token to B's URL, as in the following example.

http://SP-B.com/authorize?oauth_token=ynk56vcck98

6. B authenticates the user (e.g. using username and password). The user must be authenticated every time the framework is used. The authentication method by which B authenticates the user is beyond the scope of OAuth. After the user has successfully been authenticated, he/she is asked whether or not A should be granted access to the requested information.

Figure 23. The OAuth delegation framework

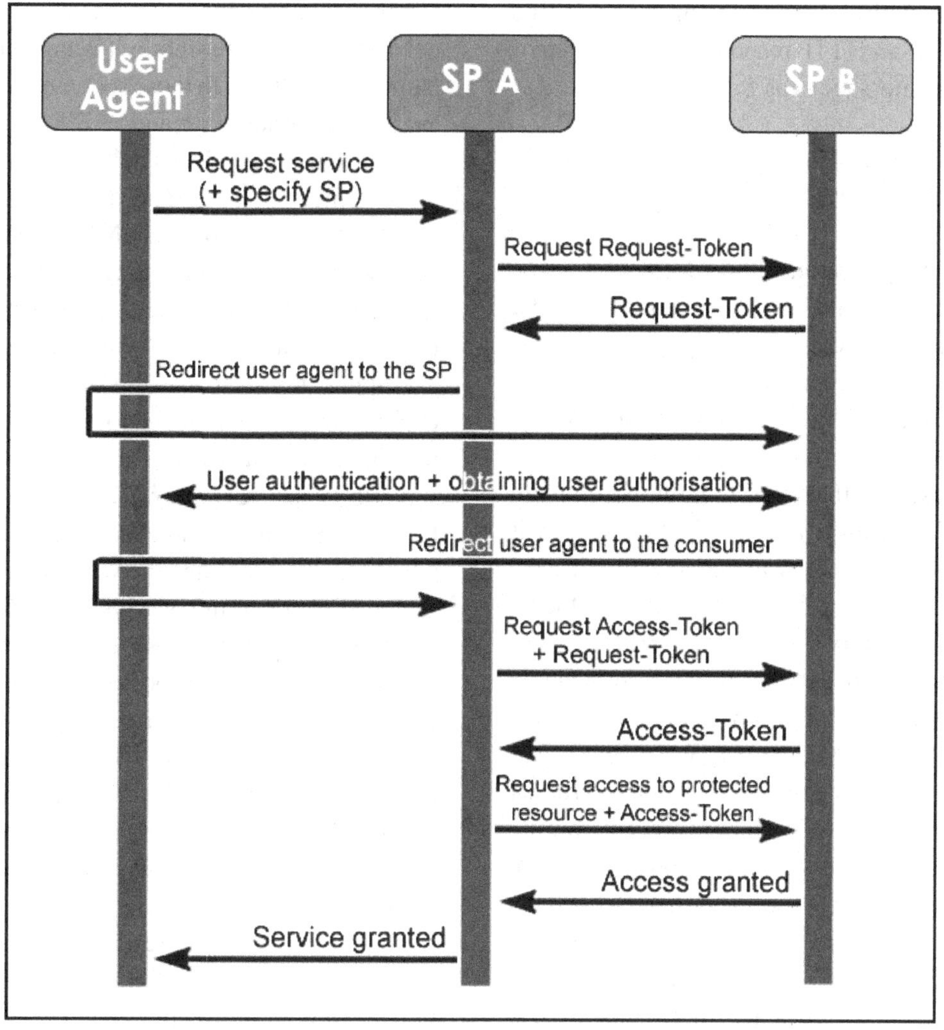

7. If the user approves the request, B redirects the user agent back to A with a verification code attached to A's URL, as in the following example.

http://SP-A.com/token_request?oauth_token=ynk56vcck98&oauth_verifier=bgh758204nft

8. A then sends an HTTP POST request message to B to request an 'Access-Token', which can later be used to access the private resources stored by B. This message is also MACed using the consumer key. An example of such a message is as follows.

https://SP-B.com/access_token?oauth_consumer_key=evb1234rd9&oauth_token=ynk56vcck98&oauth_signature_method=PLAINTEXT&oauth_signature=k93k4268kf54hg67320ge4v&oauth_timestamp=31012010&oauth_nonce=bvhgf657494932yfhbf&oauth_version=1.0&oauth_verifier=bgh758204nft

9. After checking the validity of the MAC, B replies with an Access-Token in the message body of an HTTP response. An example of such a message is as follows.

oauth_token=rtra6456484j56&oauth_token_secret=pfnvbr4s0er

10. Finally, A presents the received Access-Token to B, and, after checking its validity, B grants A access to the requested information. The Access-Token can be used more than once within a single working session.

We observe that the OAuth delegation framework is simple and efficient; however, it has a number of security and practicality issues. One shortcoming is that most of the protocols used are proprietary (i.e. non-standardised). The framework would potentially be more reliable and interoperable if it was built on standardised protocols (e.g. SAML, SOAP, WS-*, etc.). Additionally, the framework does not support robust authentication means for a user to authenticate the SP (e.g. using high-assurance certificates) before giving it permission to access her/his private data. Judging the reliability of an SP based on an SSL/TLS certificate (or weaker mechanisms) is risky, and leaves users open to attack from malicious SPs. Finally, we observe that the framework does not protect the user from being deceived by a malicious SP which redirects the user agent to a fake web site in order to steal the user's credentials.

Related Work

One of the most widely discussed techniques to support delegation in a web-based identity management system is to extend SAML attribute assertions to carry delegation information. Such techniques have been discussed by a number of authors (see, for example, Alrodhan and Mitchell (Alrodhan & Mitchell, 2008b), Gomi et al. (Gomi, Hatakeyama, Hosono, & Fujita, 2005) and Wang, del Vecchio and Humphrey (Wang, Vecchio, & Humphrey, 2005)). In these schemes, the IdP acts as a delegation authority, and SAML attribute statements are used by SPs as delegation assertions.

A number of other approaches to providing support for delegation via XML-based protocols have been discussed, including the grid delegation protocol of Ahsant, Basney and Mulmo (Ahsant, Basney, & Mulmo, 2004), which is designed for grid applications and uses the WS-Trust protocol. Other examples include the approaches described in (Chadwick, Otenko, & Nguyen, 2009, Sánchez, Reverte, López, & Gómez-Skarmeta, 2008, Seitz, Rissanen, Sandholm, Firozabadi, & Mulmo, 2005) which use XACML, and the Wohlgemuth-Müller scheme (Wohlgemuth & Müller, 2006) which is built on proxy-based PKI services. Chadwick (Chadwick, 2005), proposes extensions to the X.509 ("X.509 Information technology—Open Systems Interconnection—The Directory: Public-key and attribute certificate frameworks", 2000) that can be used to implement a 'delegation issuing service'; this service issues X.509 attribute certificates on behalf of an attribute authority. These latter extensions are defined using Abstract Syntax Notation One (ASN.1) ("X.680 Information technology—Abstract Syntax Notation One (ASN.1): Specification of basic notation", 2002).

Finally, we mention the work of Austel et al. (Austel et al., 2008), who investigated the feasibility of using the CardSpace, Higgins, and OAuth frameworks to support delegation for Mashup[xlii] web sites. For CardSpace and Higgins they propose a 'user-masquerading' technique similar to that used in the Shibboleth delegation framework; this enables SPs to use security tokens issued to users by the IdP to access other SPs.

REFERENCES

Ahn, G. J., Ko, M., & Shehab, M. (2008). Portable user-centric identity management. In Proceedings of the IFIP TC-11 23rd International Information Security Conference, IFIP 20th World Computer Congress, IFIP SEC 2008, Milano, Italy (pp. 573-587). Springer-Verlag.

Ahsant, M., Basney, J., & Mulmo, O. (2004, July). Grid delegation protocol (Technical Report No. YCS-2004-380). University of York, Department of Computer Science.

Al-Sinani, H. S., Alrodhan, W. A., & Mitchell, C. J. (2010). CardSpace-Liberty integration for CardSpace users. In Proceedings of the 9th Symposium on Identity and Trust on the Internet, IDTrust 2010, Gaithersburg, Maryland, USA, April 13-15, 2010 (pp. 12-25). ACM.

Alrodhan, W. A., & Mitchell, C. J. (2007). Addressing privacy issues in CardSpace. In Proceedings of the Third International Symposium on Information Assurance and Security, IAS 2007, Manchester, UK (pp. 285–291). IEEE Computer Society.

Alrodhan, W. A., & Mitchell, C. J. (2008a). A client-side CardSpace-Liberty integration architecture. In Proceedings of the Seventh Symposium on Identity and Trust on the Internet, IDTrust 2008, NIST, Gaithersburg, USA (vol. 283, pp. 1-7). ACM International Conference Proceeding Series.

Alrodhan, W. A., & Mitchell, C. J. (2008b). A delegation framework for Liberty. In Proceedings of the Third Conference on Advances in Computer Security and Forensics, ACSF 2008, Liverpool, UK (pp. 67–73). Liverpool John Moores University.

Alrodhan, W. A., & Mitchell, C. J. (2009). Improving the security of CardSpace. *EURASIP Journal on Information Security*, *9*, 167216. doi:10.1186/1687-417X-2009-167216

Alrodhan, W. A., & Mitchell, C. J. (2010). Enhancing user authentication in claim-based identity management. In Proceedings of the 2010 International Symposium on Collaborative Technologies and Systems, CTS 2010, Chicago, Illinois, USA (pp. 75–83). IEEE.

Arends, R., Austein, R., Larson, M., Massey, D., & Rose, S. (2005, March). DNS security introduction and requirements. RFC 4033, Internet Engineering Task Force.

Atwood, M., Conlan, R. M., Cook, B., Culver, L., Elliott-McCrea, K., & Halff, L. (2007, December). OAuth Core 1.0. OAuth Core Workgroup. Retrieved from http://oauth.net/core/1.0

Austel, P., Bhola, S., Chari, S., Koved, L., McIntosh, M., & Steiner, M. (2008). Secure delegation for Web 2.0 and mashups. A Position Statement for the 2008 Workshop on Web 2.0 Security and Privacy (W2SP). IBM Corporation.

Berners-Lee, T., Fielding, R., & Masinter, L. (2005, January). Uniform resource identifier (URI): Generic syntax. RFC 3986, Internet Engineering Task Force.

Bertocci, V., Serack, G., & Baker, C. (2008). *Understanding Windows CardSpace*. Addison-Wesley.

Beznosov, K., Flinn, D. J., Kawamoto, S., & Hartman, B. (2005). Introduction to Web services and their security. *Information Security Technical Report*, *10*, 2–14. doi:10.1016/j.istr.2005.02.001

Bolten (director), J. B. (2003, December). E-authentication guidance for federal agencies — M-04-04. Office of Management and Budget (OMB), Executive Office of the President, The White House, Washington DC, USA.

Booth, D., Haas, H., McCabe, F., Newcomer, E., Champion, M., Ferris, C. (2004, February). Web services architecture. The World Wide Web Consortium (W3C).

Box, D., & Curbera, F. (Eds.). (2004, August). Web services addressing (ws-addressing). The World Wide Web Consortium (W3C).

Bramhall, P., Hansen, M., Rannenberg, K., & Roessler, T. (2007, July/August). User-centric identity management: New trends in standardization and regulation. *IEEE Security & Privacy*, *5*(4), 84–87. doi:10.1109/MSP.2007.99

Bufu, J., & Daugherty, J. (Eds.). (2008, December). OpenID provider authentication policy extension 1.0.The OpenID Foundation. Retrieved from http://openid.net/specs/openid-provider-authentication-policy-extension-1_0.html

Burr, W. E., Dodson, D. F., & Polk, W. T. (2006, April). Electronic authentication guideline — Special Publication 800-63 — Version 1.0.2. Recommendations of the National Institute of Standards and Technology (NIST), USA.

CA/Browser forum. (2008, April). Guidelines for the issuance and management of extended validation certificates — version 1.1.

Cahill, C., & Hodges, J. (Eds.). (2006). *Liberty ID-WSF web services discovery service specification — Version 2.0*. Liberty Alliance Project.

Camenisch, J., Shelat, A., Sommer, D., Fischer-Hübner, S., Hansen, M., & Krasemann, H. (2005, November). Privacy and identity management for everyone. In Proceedings of the 2005 Workshop on Digital Identity Management (pp. 20-27). Fairfax, VA: ACM.

Cameron, K. (2005, May). The laws of identity. (Microsoft Corporation)

Cameron, K., & Jones, M. B. (2006, February). Design rationale behind the identity metasystem architecture. Microsoft Corporation.

Cantor, S. (Ed.). (2005a, October). SAML 2.0 single sign-on with constrained delegation. Internet2. Retrieved from http://shibboleth.internet2.edu/shibboleth-documents.html

Cantor, S. (Ed.). (2005b, September). Shibboleth architecture — Protocols and profiles. Internet2. Rerieved from http://shibboleth.internet2.edu/docs/internet2-mace-shibboleth-arch-protocols-200509.pdf

Cantor, S. (2008, January). Attribute release policies. Internet2. Retrieved from https://spaces.internet2.edu/display/SHIB/IdPARPConfig

Cantor, S. (n.d.). User authentication and subject identifiers in Shibboleth. Retrieved from https://spaces.internet2.edu/display/SHIB/IdPUserAuthnConfig

Cantor, S., Hirsch, F., Kemp, J., Philpott, R., & Maler, E. (Eds.). (2005, March). *Bindings for the OASIS security assertion markup language (SAML) V2.0. OASIS Standard Specification*. OASIS Open.

Cantor, S., & Kemp, J. (Eds.). (2004). *Liberty ID-FF protocols and schema specification — 1.2-errata-v3.0*. Liberty Alliance Project.

Cantor, S., Kemp, J., & Champagne, D. (Eds.). (2004). *Liberty ID-FF bindings and profiles specification — 1.2-errata-v2.0*. Liberty Alliance Project.

Cantor, S., Kemp, J., Philpott, R., & Maler, E. (Eds.). (2005, March). *Assertions and protocols for the OASIS security assertion markup language (SAML) V2.0. OASIS Standard Specification*. OASIS Open.

Chadwick, D. W. (2005, April). Delegation issuing service for x.509. In Proceedings of the 4th Annual PKI R&D Workshop, USA (Vol. IR 7224, pp. 66-77). NIST Technical Publication.

Chadwick, D. W. (2008). Federated identity management. In Aldini, A., Barthe, G., & Gorrieri, R. (Eds.), *Foundations of security analysis and design v, FOSAD 2007/2008/2009 Tutorial Lectures* (*Vol. 5705*, pp. 96–120). Springer. doi:10.1007/978-3-642-03829-7_3

Chadwick, D. W., & Inman, G. (2009). Attribute aggregation in federated identity management. *IEEE Computer, 42*(5), 33–40. doi:10.1109/MC.2009.143

Chadwick, D. W., Otenko, S., & Nguyen, T. A. (2009). Adding support to XACML for multi-domain user to user dynamic delegation of authority. *International Journal of Information Security, 8*, 137–152. doi:10.1007/s10207-008-0073-y

Christensen, E., Curbera, F., Meredith, G., & Weerawarana, S. (2001, March). Web services description language (WSDL)—Version 1.1. The World Wide Web Consortium (W3C).

Claubeta, S., Kesdogan, D., & Kölsch, T. (2005). Privacy enhancing identity management: protection against re-identification and profiling. In Proceedings of the the 2005 Workshop on Digital Identity Management, Fairfax, Va, USA (pp. 84-93). ACM.

Clippinger, J. H. (2009, December). Higgins towards a foundation layer for the social Web. Higgins — Working draft.

Curbera, F., Parastatidis, S., & Schlimmer, J. (Eds.). (2006, August). Web services metadata exchange (WS-MetadataExchange) — Version 1.1. BEA Systems, Computer Associates, IBM, Microsoft, SAP AG, Sun Microsystems, and webmethods.

Cutler, R. (Ed.). (2008). *Liberty identity assurance framework — Version 1.1*. Liberty Alliance Project.

Diffie, W., & Hellman, M. E. (1976, November). New directions in cryptograph. *IEEE Transactions on Information Theory, IT-22*(6), 644–654. doi:10.1109/TIT.1976.1055638

Duerst, M., & Suignard, M. (2005, January). Internationalized resource identifiers (iris). RFC 3987, Internet Engineering Task Force.

Gollmann, D. (2004). *Computer security*. John Wiley & Sons.

Gomi, H., Hatakeyama, M., Hosono, S., & Fujita, S. (2005). A delegation framework for federated identity management. In Proceedings of the Workshop on Digital Identity Management (DIM '05) (pp. 94–103). New York, NY: ACM Press.

Graux, H., & Majava, J. (2007, December). eID Interoperability for PEGS — Proposal for a multi-level authentication mechanism and a mapping of existing authentication mechanisms. The Interoperable Delivery of European eGovernment Services to public Administrations, Businesses and Citizens (IDABC).

Hammer-Lahav, E. (Ed.). (2009, June). OAuth Core 1.0 revision A. OAuth Core Workgroup. Retrieved from http://oauth.net/core/1.0a

Hammer-Lahav, E., & Norris, W. (Eds.). (2009, November). Extensible resource descriptor (XRD) version 1.0 — Working draft 10. OASIS Open.

Hardt, D., Bufu, J., & Hoyt, J. (2007, December). OpenID attribute exchange 1.0 — Final. The OpenID Foundation. Retrieved from http://openid.net/specs/openid-attribute-exchange-1_0.html

Hodges, J. (2009, July). Technical comparison: OpenID and SAML — Draft 07a. White paper. Retrieved from http://identitymeme.org/doc/draft-hodges-saml-openid-compare-05.html

Hodges, J., & Aarts, R. (Eds.). (2005). *Liberty ID-WSF authentication service and single sign-on service specification — Version 1.1*. Liberty Alliance Project.

Hodges, J., Aarts, R., Madsen, P., & Cantor, S. (Eds.). (2006). *Liberty ID-WSF authentication, single sign-on, and identity mapping services specification — Version 2.0*. Liberty Alliance Project.

Hughes, J., Cantor, S., Hodges, J., Hirsch, F., Mishra, P., & Philpott, R. (2005, March). Profiles for the OASIS security assertion markup language (SAML) V2.0. OASIS Standard Specification, OASIS Open.

Hunt, P. (Ed.). (2006). *Client attribute requirements markup language (CARML) specification — Working draft 03*. Oracle.

ISO/IEC. (2010, January). Second CD 24760 — Information Technology — Security techniques —A framework for identity management. [Manuel de logiciel].

ITU-T X.1250. (2009, February). X.idmreq, Baseline capabilities for enhanced global identity management trust and interoperability — Draft new recommendation [Manuel de logiciel].

Jones, M., MacIntyre, R., Morrow, T., Nenadi?, A., Pickles, S., & Zhang, N. (2006, November). E-infrastructure security: Levels of assurance. The Joint Information Systems Committee (JISC).

Jones, M. B. (2006, March). A guide to supporting InfoCard v1.0 within web applications and browsers. Microsoft Corporation.

Jørstada, I., van Thuan, D., Jønvikc, T., & van Thanh, D. (2007). Bridging CardSpace and Liberty Alliance with SIM authentication. In Proceedings of the 10th International Conference on Intelligence in Next Generation Networks, ICIN 2007, Bordeaux, France (pp. 8-13). ADERA.

Jøsang, A., & Pope, S. (2005). User centric identity management. In Proceedings of Australian Computer Emergency Response Team Conference (AUSCERT 2005).

Jøsang, A., Zomai, M. A., & Suriadi, S. (2007). Usability and privacy in identity management architectures. In Proceedings of the Fifth Australasian Information Security Workshop (Privacy Enhancing Technologies) (AISW 2007), Victoria, Australia (pp. 143-152). Australian Computer Society.

Kellomai, S. (Ed.). (2003). *Liberty ID-SIS employee profile service specification — Version 1.0*. Liberty Alliance Project.

Kemp, J., Cantor, S., Mishra, P., Philpott, R., & Maler, E. (Eds.). (2005, March). *Authentication context for the OASIS security assertion markup language (SAML) V2.0*. OASIS Open.

Kim, S. H., Choi, D. S., Kim, D. J., Kim, S. H., Noh, J. H., & Jung, K. S. (2009, October). OpenID authentication method using identity selector. United States Patent. (US 2009/0249078 A1).

Madsen, P. (Ed.). (2008). Liberty IGF privacy constraints specification — Version 1.0-04. Liberty Alliance Project.

Madsen, P. (Ed.). (n.d.). Liberty ID-WSF people service — Federated social identity.

Maler, E., Mishra, P., & Philpott, R. (Eds.). (2003, September). Bindings and profiles for the OASIS security assertion markup language (SAML) V1.1. OASIS Standard Specification. OASIS Open.

Microsoft Corporation. (2005a, May). Microsoft's vision for an identity metasystem.

Microsoft Corporation. (2005b, August). A technical reference for InfoCard v1.0 in Windows.

Microsoft Corporation. (2008, July). A guide to using the identity selector interoperability profile V1.5 within Web applications and browsers.

Microsoft Corporation and Ping Identity Corporation. (2005, August). A guide to integrating with InfoCard v1.0.

Miller, J. (Ed.). (2006, March). Yadis 1.0 (HTML). The Identity and Accountability Foundation for Web 2.0. Retrieved from http://yadis.org/wiki/Yadis_1.0_%28HTML%29.

Mishra, P. (Ed.). (2006). *AAPML: Attribute authority policy markup language — Working draft 08*. Oracle.

Mitra, N., & Lafon, Y. (Eds.). (2007, April). SOAP — Version 1.2. The World Wide Web Consortium (W3C).

Monzillo, R., Kaler, C., Nadalin, A., & Hallem-Baker, P. (Eds.). (2006, February). Web services security: SAML token profile 1.1. OASIS Standard Specification. OASIS Open.

Morgan, B., Cantor, S., Hoehn, S. C. W., & Klingenstein, K. (2004). Federated security: The Shibboleth approach. *EDUCAUSE Quarterly*, *27*(4), 12–17.

Nadalin, A., Goodner, M., Gudgin, M., Barbir, A., & Granqvist, H. (Eds.). (2007a, July). *WS-Security policy — Version 1.2*. OASIS Standard.

Nadalin, A., Goodner, M., Gudgin, M., Barbir, A., & Granqvist, H. (Eds.). (2007b, March). *WS-Trust — Version 1.3*. OASIS Standard.

Nadalin, A., & Kaler, C. (Eds.). (2006, December). Web services federation language WS-Federation, version 1.1. BEA Systems, BMC Software, CA, IBM, Layer 7 Technologies, Microsoft, Novell, and VeriSign.

Nadalin, A., Kaler, C., Monzillo, R., & Hallam-Baker, P. (Eds.). (2006, February). Web services security: SOAP message security — Version 1.1. OASIS Standard Specification.

Nanda, A. (2007, April). Identity selector interoperability profile v1.0. Microsoft Corporation.

Nash, A., Duane, W., Joseph, C., & Brink, D. (2001). Pki: Implementing and managing e-security. Osborne/McGraw-Hill.

NIST. (2001, May). Security requirements for cryptographic modules [Manuel de logiciel]. Gaithersburg, MD: NIST.

Noor, A. (2008). Identity protection factor (IPF). In The 7th Symposium on Identity and Trust on the Internet (IDTrust 2008) (vol. 283, pp. 8-18). ACM.

NSA. (2003, December). Guide to Sun Microsystems Java plug-in security, report number C43-022R-2003. Network Applications Team of the Systems and Network Attack Center (SNAC), National Security Agency (NSA), USA.

OECD. (1980, September). Guidelines on the protection of privacy and transborder flows of personal data. Organisation for Economic Co-operation and Development.

OECD. (2008, February). At a crossroads: "Personhood" and digital identity in the information society. Organisation for Economic Co-operation and Development.

Recordon, D., Bufu, J., & Hoyt, J. (Eds.). (2007, December). OpenID authentication 2.0. The OpenID Foundation. Retrieved from http://openid.net/specs/openid-authentication-2_0.html.

Reed, D., & McAlpin, D. (Eds.). (2005, November). Extensible resource identifier (XRI) syntax V2.0. OASIS Open.

ENISA Report. (2008, November). Mapping IDABC authentication assurance levels to SAML v2.0 — Gap analysis and recommendations.

Sabadello, M., Trevithick, P., & Reed, D. (2009, April). Universal data identifiers. Parity Communications Inc.

Sánchez, M., Reverte, Ó. C., López, G., & Gómez-Skarmeta, A. F. (2008). Managing the lifecycle of XACML delegation policies in federated environments. In Proceedings of the IFIP TC-11 23rd International Information Security Conference, IFIP 20th World Computer Congress, IFIP SEC 2008, Milano, Italy (pp. 717-721). Springer-Verlag.

Scavo, T. (Ed.). (2009, November). SAML V2.0 holder-of-key assertion profile — Version 1.0 — Committee draft 3. OASIS Open.

Seitz, L., Rissanen, E., Sandholm, T., Firozabadi, B. S., & Mulmo, O. (2005). Policy administration control and delegation using XACML and delegent. In Proceedings of the 6th IEEE/ACM International Conference on Grid Computing, Grid 2005, Seattle, Washington, USA (pp. 49-54). IEEE.

Suriadi, S., Foo, E., & Jøsang, A. (2009). A user-centric federated single sign-on system. *Journal of Network and Computer Applications*, *32*, 388–401. doi:10.1016/j.jnca.2008.02.016

Taylor, J. A., Lips, M., & Organ, J. (2009). *Identification practices in government: Citizen surveillance and the quest for public service improvement. Identity in the Information Society*. Springer-Verlag.

Tiffany, E., Madsen, P., & Cantor, S. (Eds.). (2009, May). *Level of assurance authentication context profile for SAML 2.0 — Working Draft 03*. OASIS Open.

Tourzan, J., & Koga, Y. (Eds.), *(n.d.). Liberty ID-WSF web services framework overview — Version: 1.1*. Liberty Alliance Project.

Trevithick, P. (2009, September). Relationship cards. Higgins Report 19 — Draft 0.46.

Wachob, G., Reed, D., Chasen, L., Tan, W., & Churchill, S. (Eds.). (2008, February). Extensible resource identifier (XRI) resolution version 2.0 — Committee draft 03. OASIS Open.

Wang, J., Vecchio, D. D., & Humphrey, M. (2005). Extending the security assertion markup language to support delegation for web services and grid services. In Ieee International Conference on Web Services (ICWS 2005) (vol. 1, pp. 67-74). IEEE Computer Society.

Wason, T. (Ed.), *(n.d.). Liberty ID-FF architecture overview — Version: 1.2*. Liberty Alliance Project.

Wenning, R., et al. (Eds.). (2006, November). The platform for privacy preferences — version 1.1. W3C Working Group Note.

Widdowson, R., & Cantor, S. (Eds.). (2008, March). *Identity provider discovery service protocol and profile — Committee specification 01. OASIS Standard Specification*. OASIS Open.

Windley, P. (2005). *Digital identity*. O'Reilly Media.

Wohlgemuth, S., & Müller, G. (2006). Privacy with delegation of rights by identity management. In Proceedings of the Emerging Trends in Information and Communication Security, International Conference (ETRICS 2006) (vol. 3995, pp. 175-190). Springer-Verlag.

X.509. (2000). Information Technology — Open systems interconnection — The directory: Public-key and attribute certificate frameworks [Manuel de logiciel].

X.509. (2005). Information Technology — Open systems interconnection — The directory: Public-key and attribute certificate frameworks [Manuel de logiciel].

X.680. (2002). Information Technology — Abstract syntax notation one (ASN.1): Specification of basic notation [Manuel de logiciel].

Y.2720. (2008, September). NGN identity management framework — Draft recommendation [Manuel de logiciel].

ENDNOTES

i http://dev.aol.com/api/openauth

ii http://developer.yahoo.com/auth

iii http://www.flickr.com/services/api/misc.userauth.html

iv http://technet.microsoft.com/en-us/library/dd996657(WS.10).aspx

v https://addons.mozilla.org/en-US/_refox/addon/51667

vi http://www.microsoft.com/downloads/details.aspx?FamilyID=AB99342F-5D1A-413D-8319-81DA479AB0D7

vii http://www.eclipse.org/higgins

viii http://code.bandit-project.org/trac/wiki/DigitalMe/Installation/MacSafari

ix http://wiki.eclipse.org/GTK_and_Cocoa_Selector_1.0

x http://wiki.eclipse.org/Adobe_AIR_Selector

xi http://www.adobe.com/products/air

xii http://www.apple.com/iphone

xiii http://wiki.eclipse.org/IPhone Selector

xiv http://www.projectliberty.org

xv http://kantarainitiative.org

xvi http://www.projectliberty.org/liberty/resource_center/faq/adoption__1

xvii http://www.sun.com/software/products/identity/standards/liberty.xml

xviii http://www.pingidentity.com

xix http://saml.xml.org/differences-between-saml-v2-0-and-liberty-id-ff-1-2

xx http://www.sourceid.org

xxi http://docs.sun.com/source/819-4682

xxii http://shibboleth.internet2.edu

xxiii http://www.internet2.org

xxiv http://www.athens.ac.uk

xxv http://www.jisc.ac.uk/whatwedo/programmes/amtransition/iamsp.aspx

xxvi http://shibboleth.internet2.edu/shib-v2.0.html

xxvii https://spaces.internet2.edu/display/SHIB/LevelOfAssurance

xxviii http://www.federation.org.au/twiki/bin/view/Federation/ShARPE

xxix https://mams.melcoe.mq.edu.au/zope/mams

xxx http://openid.net/foundation

xxxi http://openid.net/2009/12/16/openid-2009-year-in-review

xxxii https://verify.sxip.com/demorp

xxxiii The inclusion of a logo is discussed in a number of documents circulated by Microsoft (Cameron & Jones, 2006, Microsoft Corporation and Ping Identity Corporation, 2005), although the latest version of the draft standard for extended validation certificates (CA/Browser forum, 2008), as published by the CA/Browser Forum, does not mandate the inclusion of a logo. Whether or not such a requirement will be included in the standard at a later date remains unclear.

xxxiv Indeed, the user should be careful when downloading InfoCards onto multiple PCs. Downloading InfoCards on shared PCs (e.g. in an Internet Café) is clearly unwise.

xxxv http://www.identityblog.com/?p=659

xxxvi http://kantarainitiative.org/confluence/display/concordia/Home

xxxvii http://projectconcordia.org/index.php/Infocard_Authentication_Scenario_Details

xxxviii http://projectconcordia.org/index.php/Infocard_Authentication_Scenario_Details

xxxix https://spaces.internet2.edu/display/SHIB2/Shibboleth+Roadmap

xl https://spaces.internet2.edu/display/ShibuPortal/Configuring+Shibboleth+Delegation+for+a+Portal

xli http://oauth.net

xlii http://en.wikipedia.org/wiki/Open_Mashup_Alliance

Chapter 13
Developing Proactive Security Dimensions for SOA

Hany F. EL Yamany
Suez Canal University, Egypt

David S. Allison
The University of Western Ontario, Canada

Miriam A. M. Capretz
The University of Western Ontario, Canada

ABSTRACT

Security is one of the largest challenges facing the development of a Service-Oriented Architecture (SOA). This is due to the fact that SOA security is the responsibility of both the service consumer and service provider. In recent years, many solutions have been implemented, such as the Web Services Security Standards, including WS-Security and WS-SecurityPolicy. However, those standards are insufficient for the promising new generations of Web 2.0 applications. In this research, we describe an Intelligent SOA Security (ISOAS) framework and introduce four of its services: Authentication and Security Service (NSS), the Authorization Service (AS), the Privacy Service (PS) and the Service of Quality of Security Service (SQoSS). Furthermore, a case study is presented to examine the behavior of the described security services inside a market SOA environment.

INTRODUCTION

Service-Oriented Architecture (SOA) is a software architecture that is based on the key concepts of an application front end, a service, a service repository, and a service bus. SOA includes three main components: the service provider, who offers a service, the service consumer, who seeks to access the provider's service, and the service repository, where the provider can publish his/her services for discovery by the consumer (Erl, 2005).

One of the major challenges in designing SOA involves developing its security requirements. SOA security is an overarching concern, as it affects every advertisement, discovery and interaction of services and applications in an SOA environment. Specifically, SOA security generally requires authentication, privacy, auditing and

DOI: 10.4018/978-1-61350-498-7.ch013

authorization. Authentication entails the validation of identity, while privacy guarantees the nondisclosure of an individual's data. Moreover, auditing makes a user accountable for the messages that they send, while authorization establishes the actions that a user is allowed to perform (Erl, 2005). SOA security is the responsibility of both the service provider and consumer, since they share much of the same resources and data. Organizing SOA security is an intensive endeavor, which involves coordinating different security requirements for the service provider and consumer.

Another challenge of SOA security requirements involves an increase in flexibility for incorporating Quality of Service (QoS) terms, such as reliability and security, which fulfill the various requirements of customers. QoS requirements entail a commitment to a certain level of service, which is based on a measurable set of parameters. According to these parameters, the level of service can indicate the amount of security in terms of variables such as assurance and mechanical strength.

This chapter aims to describe and design an intelligent framework for SOA security. The suggested SOA security framework includes five services that incorporate the most important security aspects: authentication, authorization, Quality of Security Service, privacy, and auditing. Each service encapsulates its own security logic, which can be consequently published, discovered, and reused. Moreover, almost all of the services embed an intelligent core in order to automate the security processes.

The chapter begins with an investigation into related work in the field of SOA security. Following this review, four of the described services are discussed in detail, through an introduction of their objectives, structures, intelligent core and implementation; these services include the Authentication and Security Service (NSS), the Authorization Service (AS), the Privacy Service (PS) and the Service of Quality of Security Service (SQoSS). The Intelligent SOA Security (ISOAS) framework is shown in Figure 1.

At the end of this chapter, a case study is introduced to establish the interactions among the services within the SOA security framework in order to provide the sufficient and necessary security dimensions for an SOA environment.

BACKGROUND

Researchers in educational institutions as well as in companies such as Microsoft, Oracle and IBM, are devoting time and effort to developing and maintaining security solutions for SOA. One of the most remarkable industrial studies has been introduced by IBM, who has announced its proposal for a complete security model of SOA applications, especially those within banking systems (Buecker et al., 2007). The suggested IBM model consists of three basic levels: Business Security Services, Security Policy Infrastructure and IT Security Service. Overall, the framework discusses most of the security issues involved in an SOA environment, and it is primarily designed based on the Web Services Standards.

Both similarities and differences exist between the IBM SOA security model (Buecker et al., 2007) and the ISOAS framework discussed in this chapter. In terms of similarities, both frameworks manage most of the SOA security aspects, including authentication and authorization. Also, both frameworks follow the SOA security approaches, such as Security as a Service, for managing the SOA security aspects and the required security levels, including the Message and Services Levels. Finally, the authentication service in each framework can utilize several security tokens in order to authenticate the different service consumers.

On the other hand, there are several differences between the two frameworks; for example, the ISOAS framework contains many intelligent engines in order to automatically manage the security activities, such as the prediction of Web attacks,

Figure 1. Intelligent SOA security (ISOAS) framework

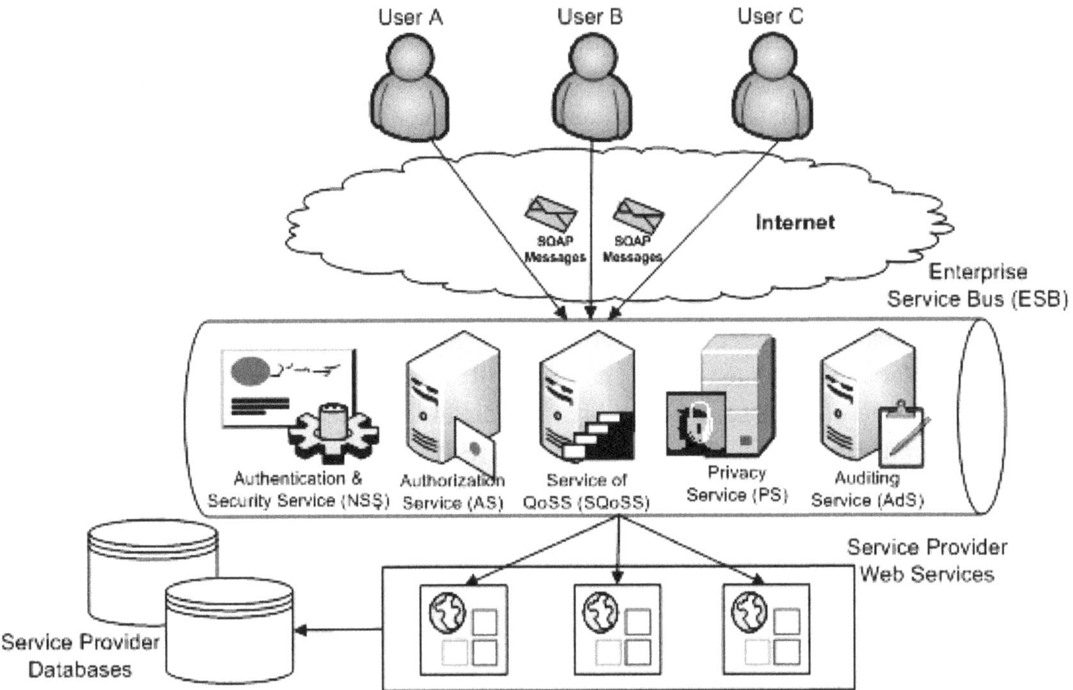

and consequently, to improve the performance of the security process. Also, the Authorization Service (AS) in the ISOAS framework depends on a unique 4-Attribute Vectors Authorization Structure, which enables the AS to handle all of the known authorization roles; while the corresponding IBM framework utilizes eXtensible Access Control Markup Language (XACML) (Moses, 2005), which only incorporates three dimensions for managing the authorization roles.

Another difference between IBM's solution and the ISOAS framework is the handling of privacy. IBM combines the task of providing authorization and privacy into one group of services. Authorization in this case is determining if a consumer has the right to access information. Privacy is considered an extension of this definition, determining if a consumer has the right to access Personally Identifiable Information (PII). This differs from the approach taken by the ISOAS framework as authorization and privacy are considered tasks for two separate services. IBM's approach for determining privacy authorization is done through the use of privacy policies. IBM relies on the standard WS-Privacy to describe how service consumers and providers state their privacy preferences within a policy and XACML (Moses, 2005). This reliance on WS-Privacy is ultimately the weakness of the IBM approach, as no such standard currently exists. WS-Privacy has been long discussed, with an anticipated completion date of 2004 (Cover, 2003), however as of 2011 it has still yet to be released. With the absence of WS-Privacy, the security framework given by IBM lacks the vocabulary required to provide a proper privacy solution.

In terms of academia, there are several ideas, suggestions and solutions for securing SOA. The most intensive research focuses on guaranteeing that the services can stop a single attack or a certain category of attacks. For example, Rahaman and Schaad (2007) have attached a new section to a SOAP message, which is called the SOAP account. The function of this section is to record the structure of a SOAP message's elements, such as the number of header elements and the number of signed elements. The main role of the SOAP account is to protect the messages from rewrite attacks. Since the SOAP account is vulnerable on its own, the authors have suggested that additional routine checks are performed on both the account and on the message in order to guarantee the absence of attacks.

Loh, Yau, Wong and Ho (2006) have suggested an XML Firewall to protect Web Services by filtering their incoming SOAP messages. They have proposed three different filters: message size filtering, syntax parsing and XML schema validation. This approach has achieved success in blocking some Web attacks, such as oversized payloads, recursive payloads and SQL injections.

Bertino and Martino (2007) not only discusses authentication but also examines access control and identity management in terms of the service level. Specifically, these authors have proposed an architectural reference framework for those services which are founded on the event-based approach. In this approach, an event is considered an authentication performed on a subject.

There are currently several works that focus on authorization techniques. For instance, XACML (Moses, 2005) is a popular standard language used to describe the architecture of an authorization policy based on the attributes of the subject, the resource and the environment. Despite its status as an established language, XACML is still undergoing extensive research in both the academic and industrial sectors. For example, Priebe, Dobmeier, Schlager and Kamprath (2007) suggest extending XACML by adding an inference engine for collecting additional attributes that a specific Web Service may require.

Security Assertion Markup Language (SAML) (Madsen & Maler, 2005) is another authentication and authorization language. It is designed solely for solving the problem of Web Browser Single Sign-On (SSO), and is therefore not suitable for all authorization situations. The authorization model, Role-Based Access Control (RBAC) is defined by Sandhu, Coyne, Feinstein and Youman (1996). Its main structure is designed for the task of coordinating users, objects and permissions. However, this model was rendered obsolete with the advent of modern Web technologies, as it could not handle complex authorization tasks.

Subsequently, an Attribute-Based Access Control (ABAC) model was suggested by Shen and Hong (2006). ABAC was designed to overcome the disadvantages of RBAC and to correspond with the architecture of Web Services. ABAC is based mainly on defining the attributes of the entities in the authorization process, and it grants or denies access based on those attributes. An Attribute Role-Based Access Control (ARBAC) model, a model created as a hybrid of RBAC and ABAC, is defined and explained by Liu, Guo and Su (2005). The work by Emig, Brandt, Abeck, Biermann and Klarl (2007) suggests a hybrid Access Control Metamodel, which enhances the combination of RBAC and ABAC.

As an intelligent security feature, data mining has been used intensively in the field of network and application security, particularly as an analytical tool for Web applications. In this role, it is capable of processing a massive amount of data to detect any possible intrusions and block potential security breaches. Data mining has already experienced some success in predicting dangerous scenarios that could damage a computerized system or even threaten a whole country, such as in the case of terrorism (Seifert, 2007).

The capabilities of data mining extend beyond anticipating security threats, as it can also be used to improve existing security methodologies. In improving these processes, data mining strives to create a robust defense that prevents any unexpected fraud or inappropriate action that a system is incapable of handling. Accordingly, the framework presented here utilizes data mining techniques to enhance the construction of Web Service security and its related policies in an SOA environment.

The ISOAS framework presented in this chapter is unique and required due to the completeness of its security coverage. The ISOAS provides complete SOA security aspects, similar to IBM's approach (Buecker et al., 2007), as well as protection from attacks and Quality of Security Service (QoSS) (Irvine & Levin, 2001). In addition, this model will maintain all of the SOA security characteristics, such as autonomy and reusability. Finally, it will work with all or most of the SOA security approaches, such as the Security as a Service approach. Hence, our ISOAS framework is a uniquely fine-grained solution for SOA security.

THE AUTHENTICATON AND SECURITY SERVICE (NSS)

In the following section, the NSS is described by exploring the main structure for handling the incoming request SOAP messages. Subsequently, the role of the Association Rules mining algorithm in predicting Web attacks is explained.

The Authentication and Security Service (NSS) Structure

The NSS is divided into two basic parts: authentication and intelligent security. The authentication is responsible for authenticating the service consumers that may use several types of tokens, such as a username token, to identify themselves to the service provider. Primarily, the intelligent security part accepts or rejects the incoming request SOAP message as it is managing the security message layer. The main functionalities for the NSS therefore include authenticating the service consumers, and the parsing, analysis, and filtering of a SOAP request message that can be sealed within an operation called ***CheckSOAPStatus***. This operation can then be utilized for publishing and reusability purposes. The main structure of the suggested processes for NSS can be divided into smaller steps, as illustrated in Figure 2.

1. The service consumer sends a SOAP message to request access to a service on the provider side.
2. The authentication part of the NSS, which is located at the front of the provider side, authenticates the service consumer, validates his/her credentials and then forwards the SOAP message request to the intelligent part once the authentication process has been completed and verified.
3. The intelligent security part of the NSS processes the incoming SOAP message request and performs the following functions:
    a. Parse the SOAP message. The intelligent part contains an internal SOAP parser to capture the incoming SOAP message requests and to extract the embedded message's security features, such as the security tokens and the encryption algorithms.
    b. Store the security features inside the security database (SDB) which is attached to the NSS. These features include the deployed security tokens, which range from a simple username/password token to a complex binary token such as X.509, and the utilized encryption algorithms from the SOAP message. The message attributes, such as parsing time, are then saved.
    c. Predict the attacks that might arise from the SOAP message by using the Association Rules mining model.
    d. Classify the service consumers and accordingly determine his/her degree of the trust level based on the number of the suspicious SOAP messages he/she sends.
4. A report is generated for the service provider and a SOAP message response is forwarded

Figure 2. The authentication and security service (NSS) for SOA

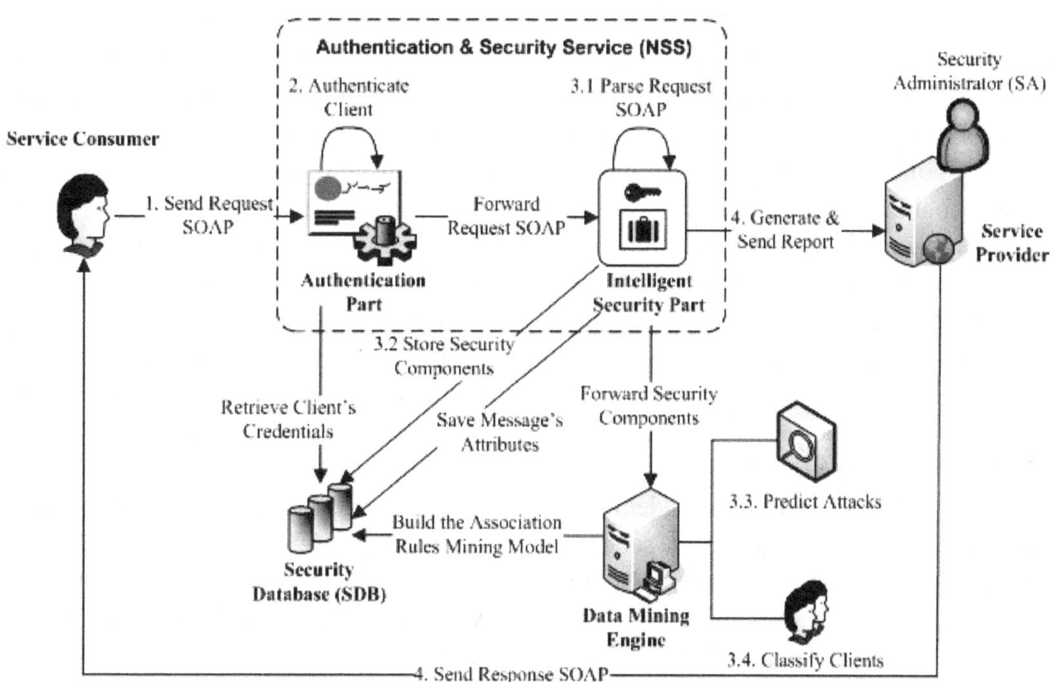

to the consumer, informing whether his/her request is accepted or denied.

The SDB consists of many tables that are intended to save the security features within the policies. Also, it is designed to store the various attacks that have historically compromised the services. Finally, it contains a classification of service consumers, demonstrating the number of breaches from each consumer, and thus assisting the service provider in establishing each consumer's degree of trust.

The potential service attacks on the SDB are classified into two main categories. The first category defines the attacks that arise due to a weakness in the security tokens, including dictionary password attacks. This weakness can threaten the service when the security policy utilizes a username/password token for authenticating the service consumers. The second category specifies the attacks that result from a weakness in the digital signature and encryption algorithms, such as the compromising of a symmetric key that is shared among multiple recipients (Eastlake & Reagle, 2002).

The Association Rules Mining Model

The Association Rules mining technique is applied to find interesting correlations among particular items within a large volume of data (Tang & Meclennan, 2005). This technique is a suitable method for finding the required relationships between the possible Web attacks and the embedded security features inside the exchanged transactions. First, there is a substantial amount of transactions that may occur between the service provider and his/her consumers. Also, a significant number of the embedded security features may be applied inside of these transactions. Lastly, there are a large number of possible attacks that may violate the security of the service provider. In this project, the association rules technique is used to extend the security features described in WS-Security, that provide techniques for securing the SOAP message exchange among Web Services. The model will examine the correlations among the violations, security features and policies in order to produce a new strategy that improves upon the preceding policies. For instance, the mining model will recognize the relationship between an authentication token, such as username/password, and a potential security threat that results from that token, which may cause security violations due to its weakness. In recognizing the relationship between the violation and the applied token, the mining model will produce a rule. The resulting rule will illustrate the security challenge for the administrator on the service provider side. Consequently, the administrator will alter the security policy to deploy a stronger token or a hybrid token for the authentication task, thereby guaranteeing an increased level of security. Some of the produced rules will be structured as follows:

Security Token Type, SOAP Parsing Time → Web Attack Specification

Encryption Algorithm Type, SOAP Payload Size → Web Attack Specification

The Association Rules Mining Model in SQL Server 2005 Data Mining (SSDM) (Tang & Meclennan, 2005) has been used to construct the required prototype models. The classification used for the Web attacks are utilized again; however, the type of embedded security features inside a SOAP message are classified, thus building two different mining models. The first mining model deals with the security tokens and their related attacks, while the second mining model manages the digital signature, encryption algorithms and any resulting attacks from these components.

The main mining model consists of a case table, RequestSOAPAnlsys, and two nested tables, RequestSOAPTokens and ReqTokenAttackSolun. The RequestSOAPAnlsys table includes information about the request SOAP messages, such as their policy, their message size, their parsing time, their starting timestamp and their expiring timestamp. While the RequestSOAPTokens table includes the name of the tokens embedded inside the SOAP messages. Finally, the ReqTokenAttackSolun table includes the Web attacks that have arisen from some of the SOAP messages.

Once the required data is collected, it is used as a test for the mining model to generate the association rules containing SOAP message attributes, such as parsing time and size. The rules are produced using the security tokens, such as username/password, in order to predict when an attack may damage the services. Various association rules are generated as a result of processing the mining model, as depicted in Table 1.

In order to demonstrate the prediction process, Association rules have been extracted from Table 1:

1. Username = Existing, Parsing Time = 393 - 1034 -> Username = Message Alteration
2. X.509 = Existing, Req SOAP Size = 7221 - 8431 -> X.509 = Message Eavesdropping

The first rule outlines a scenario where a username/password token was used as a security token in order to validate the service requestor. The parsing time of the SOAP message embedded in this token falls within the designated range of 393 to 1034 milliseconds, as measured by the processor clock. An XML Document Object Model (DOM) parser has been used to analyze the incoming request SOAP message. The parsing time is measured by recording the time taken to examine the entire SOAP message and store any embedded security features it contains into the special security database. Both the embedded security token inside the SOAP message and its recorded parsing time prompt the rule to indicate that the Web Service may face a "Message Alteration" Web attack. The second rule outlines a scenario where an X.509 token was utilized as a security token inside a SOAP message; the size of

Table 1. A group of the association rules resulting from the suggested mining model

Probability	Importance	Token Name	SOAP Size & Parsing Time	Possible Web Attack
1	2.17801718	Username = Existing	Parsing Time = 1272 - 1676	Username = Weak Password
1	2.17801718	Username = Existing	Parsing Time = 587 - 1272	Username = Message Alteration
1	1.876987184	Username = Existing	Parsing Time >= 1676	Username = Replay Attack
1	2.001925921	X.509 = Existing	SOAP Size = 6465 - 7877	X.509 = Message Alteration
0.75	2.175125086	Username = Existing	Req SOAP Size >= 8980	Username = Replay Attack
0.667	2.431363764	X.509 = Existing	Parsing Time >= 1676	X.509 = Man-In-The-Middle
0.6	2.10720997	Username = Existing	Parsing Time < 288	Username = Replay Attack
0.5	1.874095091	X.509 = Existing	Req SOAP Size >= 8980	X.509 = Message Eavesdropping
0.5	2.052116551	Username = Existing	Req SOAP Size = 6465 - 7877	Username = Message Eavesdropping
0.6	*1.8140951*	*Username = Existing*	*Parsing Time = 393 - 1034*	*Username = Message Alteration*
0.75	*2.4331166*	*X.509 = Existing*	*Req SOAP Size = 7221 - 8431*	*X.509 = Message Eavesdropping*

that message is in between 7221 and 8431 bytes. In this second case, the Web Service may face a "Message Eavesdropping" attack.

Each rule is identified by two important factors: the probability of the attack occurring and the importance of the produced rule. The probability is a confidence value that shows the extent to which the NSS may depend on the rule for attack prediction.

For example, the first rule has a probability of 60% and an importance of 1.81. Both values were automatically calculated inside the mining model application. These values indicate that the rule has a relatively high probability as well as a considerable degree of importance, and thus, it will greatly affect the prediction process of the mining engine inside the NSS. The Security Administrator (SA) working on the service provider side also determines a security probability threshold value that will be used as a gauge for allowing or denying the request SOAP messages. If the predicted probability for a Web attack is greater than the pre-defined threshold value, the security part of the NSS triggers an alarm, warning that this message may breach security. Consequently, the NSS consults the consumer profile and identifies the level at which he/she belongs, classifying the consumer as clean, suspect or prohibited based on the number of the suspicious messages that he/she sends. The NSS then may ask for more credentials if the consumer is at the clean or suspect levels, or it will drop the message if he/she is at the prohibited level. Any false positives in this process will initially block the SOAP message, but the message can later be delivered successfully if the consumer provides additional credentials. Since it takes a number of suspicious messages to change the classification level of a consumer, a single false positive will not have any lasting effect on a consumer. If a consumer repeatedly produces false positive results, the changing of a consumer classification will alert an SA. The SA can determine if the changing was warranted and take the necessary steps to prevent further false positives from that consumer if required.

THE AUTHORIZATION SERVICE (AS)

The AS is another intelligent service for the ISOAS framework, as shown in Figure 1. In this section, a 4-attribute vector structure embedded inside of the AS is presented. The interaction between the authorization roles and the vector framework manages the access control requirements for the Web Services in an SOA environment. The authorization structure is mainly constructed based on the definition of Attribute Role-Based Access Control (ARBAC) suggested by Liu et al. (2005). The following subsections describe the 4-attribute vector framework.

The main functionalities of the AS are to authorize the various service consumers, determine the appropriate access for each consumer, and help the Security Administrator (SA) assign authorization roles to the new consumers and objects when they join the SOA enterprise. As is the case with the NSS, these functionalities can be stored inside service operations for future publishing and reusability purposes. The recommended operations are specified as follows:

AuthorizationDecision: It determines whether an access request to an object located inside an SOA enterprise is granted or denied.

GetAuthRolesForCase: It elects the possible authorization roles that might be assigned to a new user or object when it is added to an SOA business.

The 4-Attribute Vectors Authorization Structure

The 4-attribute vectors defined in this section are described below:

1. The *Users Vector* handles the attributes of the diverse users who access the Web Services or other objects in the SOA environment. Since the nature of the users varies according to the SOA environments they will access, each user has several different attributes. In a business environment for example, the users may be individuals such as customers and employees, whose attributes include first name, last name, email, and phone number.
2. The *Objects Vector* includes the attributes of objects located within an SOA environment that the users are attempting to access. Each object and its attributes also differ depending on the SOA environment within which they are situated. In the business environment, for instance, the object might be a purchase order whose attributes could include product names and the invoice.
3. The *Environments Vector* depicts the attributes of two specific environmental dimensions: time and geography. Time is determined by several attributes such as month, year and quarter. On the other hand, geography is established by location, which varies based on the nature of the SOA environment. For a business environment, the location might be a city and a province. The consumer geography could be verified, for instance, through verifying the location he/she introduces in his/her signed digital certificate such as the Certificate X.509.
4. The *Conditions Vector* is an innovative addition to the authorization service, as it has not been discussed in previous models. Although it was defined by Shen and Hong (2006), no further details of this vector were examined. The Conditions Vector presented here describes the attributes of the required circumstances that must be met in order to establish a reliable and verifiable authorization process. The conditions can be simple, such as a business promotion, whose attributes include the start date, end date and discount amount; however, they can also be complex, such as a calculated condition derived from an OLAP cube.

Figure 3. An Illustrated Diagram for Data Flow within the Authorization Service (AS)

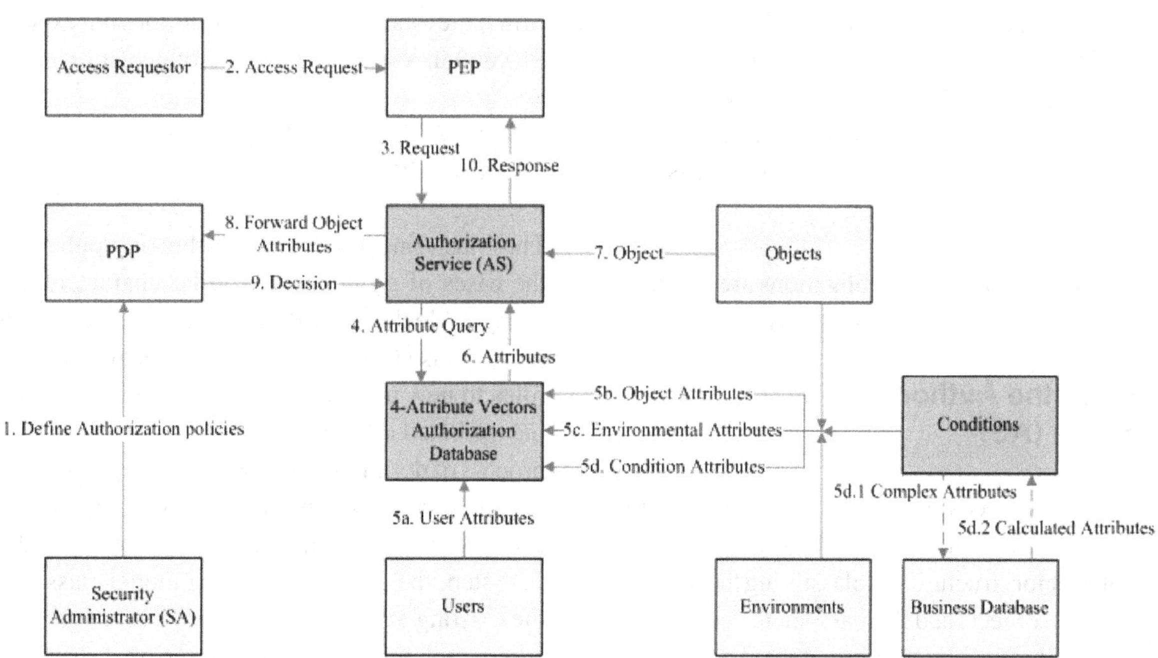

The 4-Attribute Vectors Authorization Flow

The data flow for the model, depicted in Figure 3, will be described in this section. The access control decision and the enforcement procedure are performed according to the following steps:

1. The security system administrator defines the suitable authorization policies and access enforcement requirements, such as the necessary environment and condition attributes that allow a user to retrieve an object. This enforcement procedure also allows the user and the object to be available for evaluation by the Policy Decision Point (PDP).
2. The user sends an access request for an object by using a SOAP message.
3. The Policy Enforcement Point (PEP) forwards the authenticated user request to the Authorization Service (AS). Specifically, the request includes the user attributes, the target object, the environmental attributes and the condition attributes.
4. Using the Attribute Vectors Authorization Structure Database, the Authorization Service (AS) begins to collect the required attributes for all of the participating elements related to the target object.
5. Depending on the role that is assigned to the target object, the attributes for the user, object, environment and condition are gathered and calculated. Occasionally, the AS requests a calculated attribute, such as a purchase order quota. In these cases, it collects the necessary data in order to obtain a value for the calculated attributes.
6. The AS receives the necessary attributes from the user, object, environment and condition dimensions.
7. In some cases, the AS attaches the object itself to the request.
8. The AS forwards all of the collected attributes to the PDP, which then compares those at-

tributes with the predefined attributes that have been specified by the SA.

9. The PDP sends the result of the modified attributes back to the AS.
10. The AS formulates the decision in a SOAP message response format and forwards it to the PEP.

If all of the preceding obligations are verified, access is granted; otherwise access is denied.

Mining the Authorization Service (AS)

The mining process inside the AS is divided into two main tasks: representing the suggested 4-attribute vector structure and classifying the users as well as the objects and their associated authorization roles through the common attributes that they share. In the ensuing sections, the mining process of the AS is explained, especially with regards to the role of the algorithms inside of it.

The OLAP Cube Algorithm and the Mining Process

The OLAP Cube mining algorithm is used to build a structure consisting of 4-attribute vectors or dimensions, including the attributes of users, objects, environments and conditions within a physical space. These four vectors are connected to a fact table, which handles all types of authorization roles, including both regular roles and business roles. Regular roles consist of situations where a user has the right to access an object without any environmental or conditional requirements, while in business roles users can only access an object in a certain environment and under restricted conditions. The conditions attributes are classified as either simple or complex; in the case where aggregation calculations are required to determine the value of a specified condition's attribute, the condition would be complex. For example, in an enterprise SOA environment, a retailer could purchase the products he/she needs from a large firm if the total amount of the sale does not exceed $10,000 in a specified quarter of a year.

The Clustering Algorithm and the Mining Process

The clustering mining algorithm is applied in the cases of groups with similar characteristics (Tang & Meclennan, 2005). The clustering mining model is used here to assign dynamically defined roles to new users or objects when they become incorporated into an SOA environment. Since the process of defining roles for a new user and a new object is identical, our example of how to add a user also applies in the case of an object. In the first step, the clustering mining model classifies the existing authorized users into a set of groups, where each group consists of users that share the same attributes. Subsequently, the new user is then assigned to the group that best matches his/her attributes. Next, the mining model suggests the authorization roles that may be assigned to the new user based on the roles that are already assigned to the other group members. The new user can be assigned any or all of the authorization roles held by other members. There are two different modes for determining which of the discovered authorization roles will be assigned to the new user: automatic or semi-automatic. In the first instance, the discovered roles are assigned directly to the new user without the supervision of a human being, whereas in the semi-automatic mode, the SA assigns the discovered roles. This project utilizes the semi-automatic style in order to prevent any mistakes that may occur in the process of discovering the roles or in assigning the discovered roles directly to the new user.

The Mining Process

In order to facilitate the mining process that dynamically assigns roles to a new user or object, the AS is built based on the authorization cube

Figure 4. An illustrated diagram for mining the authorization service (AS)

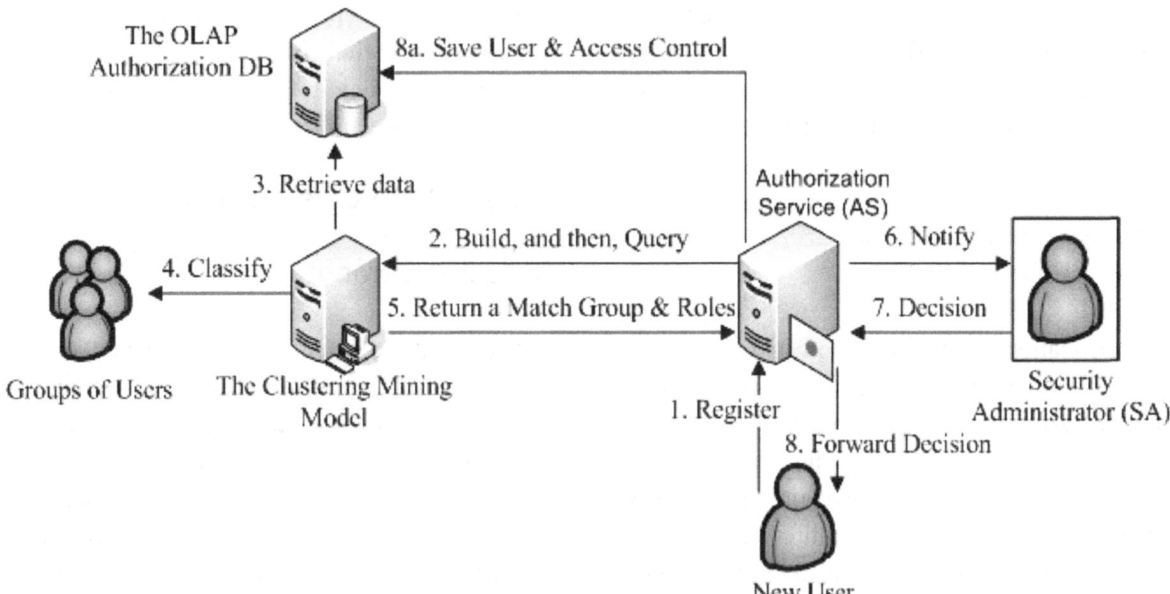

structure; Figure 4 depicts the authorization mining process.

Mining the authorization service is summarized in the following steps:

1. New users are registered within the AS and inquire about the objects they can access. It is assumed that these users are already authenticated and trusted.
2. The AS starts to build a clustering mining model based on the available attributes inside the users' dimensions. With this data, the AS then clusters the roles that belong to each group of users. After the building process is completed, the AS then forwards the attributes of the new user to the mining model for discerning the group to which he/she belongs.
3. The clustering mining model is constructed based on the authorization cube. This model is updated periodically based on the changes in both the users and roles.
4. The expected result of the clustering model shows segments of users sharing the same attributes.
5. The clustering model matches the user with a group that best suits his/her attributes and potentially assigns him/her authorization roles that are owned by the elected group.
6. The AS forwards the elected roles that the new user may access to the SA.
7. The SA sends his/her final decision to the AS, determining which of the elected roles will be assigned to the new user.
8. The AS notifies the new user of his/her right to access certain roles or objects by creating and sending a report through his/her email account. The AS then updates the authorization cube with the new data.

THE PRIVACY SERVICE (PS)

The Privacy Service (PS) uses privacy policies to determine how interactions should take place between a service consumer and service provider.

A privacy policy consists of privacy rules, which are in turn created from a set of privacy elements. Each of these items will be explained, starting from the most basic concept, the privacy element, to the most complex concept, the privacy contract agreement process.

Privacy Elements from OECD Principles

A justification for the selection of the privacy elements will first be outlined. These privacy elements are designed to build privacy rules that can be general enough to function in many environments that use services, while retaining the ability to be specific to one case if required. This ability will allow the privacy elements to form rules that thoroughly protect privacy in either the general or specific case. The elements to be created will be based on the Fair Information Practices (FIP) developed by the Organisation for Economic Co-operation and Development (OECD, 1980). The FIP created by the OECD were selected as the basis for the privacy elements presented here because these guidelines have been used as the model for most of the privacy legislation throughout the world (Cavoukian & Hamilton, 2002). Using the guidelines of the OECD, it has been found that six elements are required (Allison, EL Yamany, & Capretz, 2009):

- **Collector:** The collector of the data.
- **What:** What type of data will be collected.
- **Retention:** The length of time the collected data can be stored.
- **Purpose:** The reasons for which the data is collected.
- **Recipient:** Which parties, if any, the data is allowed to be disclosed.
- **Trust:** The level of trust of a PS.

Together, the six elements form a single privacy rule. A privacy policy is created by combining one-to-many privacy rules together with an identifying owner tag. The privacy policy of a consumer contains no actual private information about that consumer, only their preferences for protection. As such, the policy itself is unclassified and can be passed between Privacy Services as required.

Privacy Elements for SOA

Collector Element

The collector element states the name of the organization or party who will be collecting the data. As the provider is the one collecting the information, this element on the provider side will simply consist of the name of the provider. The consumer will use this element to list the collectors they are willing to have gather their information. Therefore, the element on the consumer side will consist of a set of names, or the general term "Any". If "Any" is selected by the consumer, no comparison will be made between the fields. If a set of one or more names is specified by the consumer, this consumer set must contain the name specified by the provider in order for the comparison to be successful.

What Element

The what element allows the privacy policy to outline what types of private information will be collected. It is impossible to universally declare one piece of information more private than another since what is considered private information varies greatly between different individuals. Instead, individuals are allowed to rank their information according to four ordered levels, based on the levels of classification used by the government of the United States of America (Office of Security Management and Safeguards, 2003). Though these levels are the same as the Bell-La Padula (BLP) model (Bell & La Padula, 1973), they do not share the same properties as BLP, such as no write-down. This scheme of classification was selected because it is in use throughout the world and the vocabulary used is such that a layperson could easily discern the order in which the levels are ranked.

An individual acting as a service consumer would be required to sort a list of the most common types of private information into the four levels according to their own preferences. These four levels are Top Secret, Secret, Confidential, and Unclassified. This information would be saved on the consumer side in a document called a What Element Ranking (WER). This requirement does place some responsibility on the individual, which should regularly be minimized. Due to the subjective nature of private information, this responsibility is unavoidable.

The set of values specified by the provider will be compared to the level selected by the consumer and their corresponding WER. In order for this element to be compared successfully, each of the values mentioned by the provider must be less than or equal to the level selected by the consumer. If any piece of information asked for by the provider is missing from the consumer's WER, the consumer will be informed and given the opportunity to add it.

Purpose Element

Purpose can be interpreted in two different ways. The first is to consider the purpose to be the goal of the service, such as for "Identification". The second interpretation is for purpose to outline the operational reasons for needing data access, and will consist of four possibilities, ordered from the most to least secure: "No Collection and No Distribution", "Collection and No Distribution", "Collection and Limited Distribution", and "Collection and Distribution". In order to fulfill both of these interpretations, a purpose element that consists of two parts, a goal and an operation, will be created. The goal is required from the service provider in order to inform the consumer and to satisfy the OECD guidelines. If the consumer wishes to limit their data to a particular goal they have that option, or they can choose "Any" and allow any purpose as long as it satisfies the second criterion. This second criterion is the operation, which will consist of four ordered levels outlining the possible operational uses of data.

The creation of a hierarchy allows for the comparison of two privacy policies even if the specific goal of the provider has not been outlined by the consumer. As long as the consumer has defined a rule with the value "Any" selected in the goal portion of the purpose element, a valid comparison can be made if the consumer's corresponding operation level is less than or equal to the provider's operation level. This greatly reduces the total number of rules required in the privacy policy of a consumer. If the consumer has specified any other value in the goal portion of the purpose element, two comparisons must be done in order to successfully compare the element. First, the goal portion of the purpose element of the consumer must equal the goal portion of the purpose element of the provider. Second, the level of operation selected by the consumer must be less than or equal to the level of operation selected by the provider.

Retention Element

Retention is an element that outlines how long a consumer's data may be stored by a provider. For the consumer, the retention element is an integer -1 or greater, used to state how many days data can be held by a provider. The selection of -1 signifies an unlimited amount of time, and is useful when a consumer is not concerned with how long a piece of information is retained. On the provider side, the retention element is used to state how long they wish to retain a consumer's data. The value of zero is used to signify that any information gathered is deleted immediately upon completion of the service.

Recipient Element

The recipient element outlines who is permitted to have the data passed to them. Since the consumer specifies who may receive their data with the collector element, the recipient element does not need to list any provider names. For the provider, recipient will consist of a set of names, listing each third party service provider who could possibly receive data from the original service provider. The recipient element is only compared if the "Collection and Limited Distribution" level is specified in the operation portion of the consumer's purpose element. If this level is specified by the consumer, they must select from one of two options: "Delivery" or "Approved". If "C&LD" is not selected by the consumer, Recipient may be left blank and is ignored. "Delivery" is selected by the consumer if they will allow for any third party to be involved as long as it is required in order to deliver the original service. "Approved" allows for the consumer to specify a list of approved providers who are then allowed to have the consumer's data passed to them. In this second case, the names listed in the provider's recipient element must be a subset of the names listed in the consumer's collector element in order for a successful comparison.

Trust Element

The trust element gives the consumer a degree of control over what PS can be used to negotiate the privacy contract. Without this ability, the consumer would have no assurance that the policy comparison is being done without bias. The provider in this element provides the name of the PS it wishes to use. There are four levels of trust a consumer can select for a PS to have: "High", "Moderate", "Low" and "Not Required/Not Ranked".

For the comparison of this element to be successful, the trust level of the PS the provider supplies must be at least as high as the level chosen by the consumer. Ratings are given to each PS by consumer or provider services that have previous experience using the PS. These ratings can be used to develop a trust metric. Trust metrics are algorithms that are able to predict the trustworthiness of an unknown user (Massa & Avesani, 2007), or in the case of SOA, an unknown service. Trust classification can be carried out either internally by the company or party that provides the PS, or externally by an outside body.

QUALITY OF SECURITY SERVICE (QoSS)

In this section, novel QoSS metadata for SOA is described by adding to the traditional authentication specifications, created more attributes describing the authorization and introduced a complete description for the privacy principles. The QoSS metadata will be encapsulated inside an agreement running as an enforced policy between the service provider and consumer. To the best of our knowledge, the privacy principles have never been discussed in terms of QoSS. Also, some attributes of the QoSS metadata have been constructed based on the suggested hypotheses in our ISOAS framework. The metadata is fully described in Extensible Markup Language (XML) format which makes it easy to encapsulate in a service for secure SOA. Table 2 provides a full description for each element involved in the suggested QoSS metadata for SOA.

The QoSS Metadata Levels

Four different levels for each section of the QoSS metadata are defined: High, Moderate, Low and Guest. These four levels were selected as they provide the customization required without becoming too complex.

Figure 5 shows that each element in the QoSS metadata has a different value according to the suggested four levels. This amount of customization provides the QoSS metadata with the flexibility to meet many situations.

Table 2. QoSS metadata description

Element Name	Description	Example
Authentication		
Certificate	The authentication token	X.509 certificate
Digital Signature Algorithm	The algorithm used to sign the SOAP messages	Digital Signature Algorithm (DSA)
Encryption Method	The algorithm used to encrypt the SOAP messages	Advanced Encryption Standard (AES)
Web Attack Prediction	It indicates whether the deployed security framework can predict the Web attacks or not	The NSS in this chapter
Authorization		
Technique	The deployed access control type	Role-Based Access Control (RBAC)
Roles Types	The types of the roles that SOA access control technique can handle	The business roles
Object • Class • Location • Access Time	• The classification of the existing objects based on its importance for the service provider • The localization of the object that the consumer would like to access • The determined time in which the consumer can access the target object	• Class A • Business Enterprise SOA • All day
Condition	Determine who is placing the required conditions to have the consumer access the object	Local
Roles Assign Process Type	Specify how the roles are assigned to the consumers	Partially dynamic as within AS
Privacy		
Collector	Establish who can obtain and collect the consumer attributes	Trusted
Data Category (What)	Classify which side should specify which consumer attributes are considered sensitive	User-specified
Purpose	The operation that the provider can perform on the consumer attributes	Read only
Retention Time	How long the provider is going to keep the consumer attributes	Short

The Service of Quality of Security Service (SQoSS)

The suggested QoSS metadata needs to be placed inside an SOA application to gain all the benefits SOA provides, including autonomy, loose-coupling, discoverability and reusability. Since the ISOAS framework works at the service layer, the QoSS metadata will be encapsulated inside an autonomous service to manage the security requirements between the service provider and consumer. The main functionality beyond building the Service of Quality Security Service (SQoSS) is producing a QoSS agreement establishing the security requirements that the service provider and consumer should follow. The security services working inside the ISOAS framework such as the Authentication and Security, and Authorization Services, will organize their activities in authenticating and authorizing the consumers based on that QoSS agreement. The SQoSS has four main operations to handle the QoSS metadata. The following is a description of each of those operations:

- **ShowQoSSDetails:** The SQoSS is being accessed as an object. Therefore the service consumer should be authenticated and authorized first to call this operation in order to be able to load the details of the SQoSS.

Figure 5. The QoSS metadata levels

Level	Certificate	Digital Sign	Encryption	W-Attack Pred.
High	X.509	DSA	AES	Yes
Moderate	Kerberos	RSA_Sha1	3DES	Yes
Low	Username/Password	Any Hash Algo.	128-bit key	No
Guest	not required	not required	not required	No

Figure 5a. The QoSS Authentication Levels

Level	Technique	Roles	Class	Location	Time	Condition	Assign Process
High	ARBAC	All	A	Enterprise	All the day	Enterprise	Dynamic
Moderate	ABAC	All	B	Local	Most of the day	Provider	Semi-Dynamic
Low	RBAC	Regular	C	Local	Portion of the day	Object	Static
Guest	RBAC	Regular	D	Not specified	Not specified	Not specified	Not specified

Figure 5b. The QoSS Authorization Levels

Level	Collector	Data Category	Purpose	Ret. Time
High	Local	User Specified	Read Only	Short
Moderate	Trusted	User Specified	Read/Copy	Medium
Low	Enterprise	Provider Specified	Read/Write	Long
Guest	Anyone	Not Specified	All	Not Specified

Figure 5c. The QoSS Privacy Levels

- **ShowQoSSConfiguration:** It is responsible for illustrating the general configuration of the abstract QoSS metadata that the service provider can offer for its consumer.
- **ReviewAgreement:** The negotiation process between the service provider and consumer about the QoSS metadata is done through this operation. Once the service provider and consumer establish an agreement, a QoSS agreement is produced and saved in the database belonging to the SQoSS.
- **RetrieveAgreement:** The service consumer can review his/her QoSS agreement through this operation. The operation works automatically as the service consumer is permitted the access to the SQoSS.

CASE STUDY AND IMPLEMENTATION

In this section, the behavior of the security services working inside the ISOAS framework is examined. For the case study, the service consumer, Jon, needs to ensure that his security requirements are considered by the service provider. Hence, he may need to check the Quality of Security Service (QoSS) terms that the service provider offers. In this case, Jon is concerned with the authorization and privacy terms. For example, he needs to ascertain the availability of the objects that he seeks to access as well as the duration of time that the service provider will maintain his credentials, which are used to authenticate and authorize him. On the other hand, the service provider is concerned with all of the SOA security aspects, including authentication, authorization, and privacy. Specifically, the service provider needs to ensure that he grants access rights to the correct service consumer, so he may apply strong security policies, which include forcing the service consumer to utilize robust security tokens, such as the X.509 Certificate, restricting the access time, and collecting and maintaining the service consumer's credentials for as long as necessary.

Often, there is a conflict between the security requirements of the service provider and those of the consumer. Thus, the service provider offers his/her SQoSS as an intermediary for resolving this conflict. Remarkably, the SQoSS is considered one of the provider assets that the service consumer, Jon, should be authenticated and authorized in order to access, as previously examined when discussing the behavior of the NSS and AS. After Jon is authenticated and authorized, he is able to access the four main Web operations that are applied in order to establish an XML contract containing the approved security requirements for authentication, authorization, and privacy. These four operations are identified as *ShowQoSSDetails, ShowQoSSConfiguration, ReviewContract, and RetrieveContract*. Jon accesses the SQoSS operations to submit his desired security requirements by performing the following steps:

1. He explores the QoSS details by sending a SOAP message requesting to use the operation *ShowQoSSDetails*, and he checks to see if the service provider applies the security terms in which he is interested; otherwise, he searches for another service provider that offers the necessary security requirements. However, Jon must be authenticated and authorized to access SQoSS.
2. He investigates the security levels that the service provider reveals by using the operation *ShowQoSSConfiguration*. However, if Jon does not find the QoSS details he requires, the following steps can be omitted and in this case, Jon may look for another service provider offering the security requirements he desires.
3. He selects the security levels that meet his requirements and then asks the service provider to review these levels by using the operation *ReviewContract*.
4. The service provider will review Jon's selected security requirements and validate them against his security policies. If there is no conflict, the provider will approve Jon's requirements; otherwise, the provider informs Jon that his requirements are not approved. Subsequently, the negotiation process is expected to continue until they reach an acceptable XML contract that states the approved security items. If the negotiation process fails, Jon searches for another service provider that can satisfy his security requirements. However, the complete negotiation process exceeds the scope of this chapter.
5. By using the operation *RetrieveContract*, Jon has the ability to retrieve and review his QoSS contract within the timeframe specified by the contract. If the contract has already been established, this operation works automatically when Jon accesses the SQoSS.

In this case study, an SOA business environment is examined, where a service consumer, Jon, needs to access a business Web Service (e.g. a Web Service handling a particular purchase order), defined and published by a specific service provider. First, the behavior of the Authentication and Security Service (NSS) is studied, which authenticates the service consumer and analyzes his request SOAP messages in order to detect whether or not it would create a Web attack to harm the services on the service provider's side. Specifically, the incoming SOAP message is processed by the mining core encapsulated inside of the NSS. In detecting possible Web attacks, the NSS informs the service provider of the strength of his/her deployed security policies; with an increasing in the number of detected attacks, the service provider is alerted to check his/her security policies and possibly replace them.

Secondly, the Authorization Service (AS) functions to manage the authorization process by means of the suggested 4-Attribute Vectors structure, which is connected to the authorization roles. The service consumer is required to satisfy all of the needed attributes that correlate with the particular authorization role, in this case, the "sales" role, which allows him to access the target object, which is the purchase order. Moreover, the mining process for the authorization roles facilitates the addition of a new consumer, the "ABC" company, to the SOA market environment.

Thirdly, the Privacy Service (PS) releases the attributes that could be used to authenticate and authorize the service consumer, Jon, according to the agreement between Jon and the service provider. The PS reaches this agreement by acting as a third party and negotiating the contract between the service consumer and service provider. If and when conflicts arise between the service consumer and provider, the PS will attempt to negotiate with the parties in order to come to an agreement.

Finally, the Service of the Quality of Security Service (SQoSS) manages and builds an XML QoSS contract, which aims to satisfy the security requirements of both the service provider and consumer in terms of authentication, authorization, and privacy.

FUTURE RESEARCH DIRECTIONS

The future work for this framework can be summarized in three basic directions. The first new direction involves extending the SOA security framework by adding new services that are capable of handling the remainder of the SOA security aspects, such auditing. In addition, there are plans to enhance the capabilities and performance of the services suggested in this chapter. For example, in federated SOA enterprises, many objects and services are added, deleted, or composed from other objects or services over a given period of time, thus requiring an adaptive authorization structure. Therefore, the AS should be structured to consider the objects originating from the trusted and federated partners and correlate them with the defined authorization roles.

Moreover, the second direction will be to design and construct a special ESB, which also functions as a service. This ESB service is intended to act as an intermediary interface between the service consumers and the suggested intelligent SOA security framework as well as among the various security services. In particular, it will contain specific routing mechanisms in order to organize the processing of the SOAP request messages, which might be sent as synchronous or asynchronous. Also, this service may encapsulate an intelligent engine, whose main functionality is to replicate the security services based on the volume and size of the incoming SOAP messages. For example, the ESB may replicate the NSS and create several copies of it; in one situation, it may make three copies in order to handle a large volume of oversized SOAP messages that have been intercepted over a short period of time. This dynamic replication can achieve many goals; first, it guarantees that all messages will be processed within an acceptable period of time. Secondly, it will enhance the performance of the intelligent SOA security framework and increase the availability of exposed assets that the consumers seek to access. Finally, it improves the impact of the intelligent SOA security framework.

Lastly, the final piece of research incorporates this framework in a business environment in order to determine its accuracy and performance as well as to optimize its features and functionalities.

CONCLUSION

In this chapter, an intelligent SOA security framework is described and the first four services that it involves are examined. Two of these services, the Authentication and Security Service and the Authorization Service, both include an intelligent mining core that helps to predict attacks that may be hidden within a request SOAP message. Furthermore, they also enhance the configuration of existing authorization techniques by introducing a new OLAP structure that can manage all of the authorization role types, consisting of regular roles and business roles. The OLAP structure also enables the new feature of data mining for the Security Administrator as well as the advantage of dynamically assigning the authorization roles when a new user or object is added. The Privacy Service uses elements generated from widely accepted fair information practices to create privacy contracts that allow service consumers and providers to express their privacy preferences. The Privacy Service will then act as a trusted third party to negotiate the terms of a privacy agreement using the contract of each party.

Quality of Security Service (QoSS) metadata for SOA was described which included several elements representing the three main aspects of SOA security: Authentication, Authorization and Privacy. This QoSS metadata is flexible and editable and is divided into four basic levels. These levels allow the varied security requirements of the service provider and consumer to be satisfied. The QoSS metadata has also been encapsulated inside an abstracted and reusable service. This helps the service provider publish its QoSS configuration as well as help the consumer find a suitable QoSS. The Service of QoSS also assists in establishing an agreed upon QoSS agreement between the service provider and consumer that will act as an enforced policy to manage the interactions between the two sides.

Finally this chapter discussed a case study in a business SOA environment in order to demonstrate the operation of the suggested security framework.

REFERENCES

Allison, D., El Yamany, H., & Capretz, M. (2009). Metamodel for privacy policies within SOA. *Proc. of the 5th IEEE International Workshop on Software Engineering for Secure Systems in conjunction with the 31st IEEE International Conference of Software Engineering*, Vancouver, Canada, May 19, (pp. 40-46).

Bell, D., & La Padula, L. (1973). Secure computer systems: Mathematical foundations. *MITRE Technical Report, 2547*, 1.

Bertino, E., & Martino, L. (2007). A service-oriented approach to security - Concepts and issues. *Proc. of the 8th International Symposium on Autonomous Decentralized Systems*, Sedona, AZ, USA, Mar. 21-23, (pp. 31-40).

Buecker, A., Ashley, P., Borrett, M., Lu, M., Muppidi, S., & Readshaw, N. (2007). Understanding SOA security design and implementation (2nd edition). Retrieved February 11, 2011, from http://www.redbooks.ibm.com/redbooks/pdfs/sg247310.pdf

Cavoukian, A., & Hamilton, T. (2002). *The privacy payoff: How successful businesses build customer trust.* Whitby, Canada: McGraw-Hill Ryerson Limited.

Cover, R. (2003). *IBM releases updated enterprise privacy authorization language (EPAL) specification.* Retrieved February 11, 2011, from http://xml.coverpages.org/ni2003-07-09-a.html

Eastlake, D., & Reagle, J. (2002). *XML encryption syntax and processing.* Retrieved February 11, 2011, from http://www.w3.org/TR/xmlenc-core

Emig, C., Brandt, F., Abeck, S., Biermann, J., & Klarl, H. (2007). An access control metamodel for web service-oriented architecture. *Proc. of the 2nd IEEE International Conference on Software Engineering Advances*. Cap Esterel, France, Aug. 25-31, (pp. 57-64).

Erl, T. (2005). *Service-oriented architecture: Concepts, technology, and design.* Upper Saddle River, NJ: Pearson Education, Inc.

Irvine, C., & Levin, T. (2001). Quality of security service. *Proc. of the 2000 Workshop on New Security Paradigms*. Ballycotton, County Cork, Ireland, Sept. 18-21, (pp. 91-99).

Liu, M., Guo, H., & Su, J. (2005). An attribute and role-based access control model for web services. *Proc. of the 4th International Conference on Machine Learning and Cybernetics*, Guangzhou, China, Aug. 18-21, (pp. 1302-1306).

Loh, Y., Yau, W., Wong, C., & Ho, W. (2006). Design and implementation of an XML-Firewall, *Proc. of the International Conference on Computational Intelligence and Security*, Guangzhou, China, Nov. 3-6, (pp. 1147-1150).

Madsen, P., & Maler, E. (2005). SAML V2.0 Executive Overview, Retrieved Feb. 11, 2011, from http://www.oasis-open.org/committees/download.php/13525/sstc-saml-exec-overview-2.0-cd-01-2col.pdf.

Massa, P., & Avesani, P. (2007). Trust-aware recommender systems. *Proc. of the 2007 ACM Conference on Recommender Systems*, Minneapolis, MN, USA, Oct. 19-20, (pp. 17-24).

Moses, T. (2005). eXtensible access control markup language (XACML) version 2.0. Retrieved February 11, 2011, from http://docs.oasis-open.org/xacml/2.0/access_control-xacml-2.0-core-spec-os.pdf

Office of Security Management and Safeguards. (2003). *Further amendment to EO 12958, as amended, classified national security information.* Retrieved February 11, 2011, from http://nodis3.gsfc.nasa.gov/displayEO.cfm?id=EO_13292_

Organisation for Economic Co-operation and Development. (1980). *OECD guidelines on the protection of privacy and transborder flows of personal data.* Retrieved February 11, 2011, from http://www.oecd.org/document/18/0,3343,en_2649_34255_1815186_1_1_1_1,00.html

Priebe, T., Dobmeier, W., Schlager, C., & Kamprath, N. (2007). Supporting attribute-based access control in authorization and authentication infrastructures with ontologies. *Journal of Software*, *2*(1), 27–38. doi:10.4304/jsw.2.1.27-38

Rahaman, M., & Schaad, A. (2007). SOAP-based secure conversation and collaboration. *Proc. of the International Conference on Web Services*, Salt Lake City, UT, USA, Jul. 9-13, (pp. 471-480).

Sandhu, R., Coyne, E., Feinstein, H., & Youman, C. (1996). Role-based access control models. *IEEE Computer*, *29*(2), 38–47. doi:10.1109/2.485845

Seifert, J. (2007). *Data mining and homeland security: An overview*. Retrieved February 11, 2011, from http://www.fas.org/sgp/crs/intel/RL31798.pdf

Shen, H., & Hong, F. (2006). An attribute-based access control model for Web services. *Proc. of the 7th IEEE International Conference on Parallel and Distributed Computing, Applications and Technologies*, Taipei, Taiwan, Dec. 4-7, (pp. 74-79).

Tang, Z., & Meclennan, J. (2005). *Data mining with SQL server 2005*. Hoboken, NJ: Wiley Publishing, Inc.

ADDITIONAL READING

Allison, D., & Yamany, E. L. H., & Capretz, M. (2009). Privacy and Trust Policies within SOA, *Proc. of the 4th International Conference for Internet Technology and Secured Transactions*, London, UK, Nov. 9–12, 382-387.

Ashley, P., Hada, S., Karjoth, G., Powers, C., & Schunter, M. (2003). Enterprise Privacy Architecture Language (EPAL 1.2). Retrieved Feb. 11, 2011, from http://www.w3.org/Submission/2003/SUBM-EPAL-20031110/.

Atkinson, B., Della-Libera, G., Hada, S., Hondo, M., Hallam-Baker, P., Kaler, C., et al. (2002). Web Services Security (WS-Security). Retrieved Feb. 11, 2011 from http://msdn.microsoft.com/en-us/library/ms951257.

Bennett, C. (1997). Arguments for the Standardization of Privacy Protection Policy: Canadian Initiatives and American and International Responses. *Government Information Quarterly*, *1*(4), 351–362. doi:10.1016/S0740-624X(97)90032-0

Canadian Standards Association. (1996). Model Code for the Protection of Personal Information (Q830-96). Retrieved Feb. 11, 2011, from http://www.csa.ca/cm/ca/en/privacy-code/publications/view-privacy-code.

Cheng, V., Hung, P., & Chiu, D. (2007). Enabling Web Services Policy Negotiation with Privacy preserved using XACML, *Proc. of the 40th Hawaii International Conference on System Sciences*, Waikoloa, HI, Jan. 3-6, 33a.

Cranor, L., Langheinrich, M., Marchiori, M., Presler-Marshall, M., & Reagle, J. (2002). The Platform for Privacy Preferences 1.0 Specification. Retrieved Feb. 11, 2011, from http://www.w3.org/TR/P3P/.

Epstein, J., Matsumoto, S., & McGraw, G. (2006). Software Security and SOA: Danger, Will Robinson. *IEEE Security & Privacy*, *4*(1), 80–83. doi:10.1109/MSP.2006.23

Garcia, D., & de Toledo, M. (2008). A Web Service Privacy Framework Based on a Policy Approach Enhanced with Ontologies, *Proc. of the 11th IEEE International Conference on Computational Science and Engineering - Workshops*, São Paulo, Brazil, July, 209-214.

Guermouche, N., Benbernou, S., Coquery, E., & Hacid, M. S. (2007). Privacy-Aware Web Service Protocol Replaceability, *Proc. of the IEEE International Conference on Web Services*, Salt Lake City, Utah, USA, Jul. 9-13, 1048-1055.

Kanneganti, R., & Chodavarapu, P. (2008). *SOA Security*. Greenwich, CT: Manning Pub. Co.

Malek, M., & Harmantzis, F. (2004). Security Management of Web Services, *Proceeding of the IEEE/IFIP Network Operations & Management Symposium*. Seoul. *Korea & World Affairs*, (Apr): 19–23, 175–189.

Nakamura, Y., Tatsubori, M., Imamura, T., & Ono, K. (2005). Model-Driven Security Based on a Web Services Security Architecture, *Proc. of the 2005 IEEE International Conference on Services Computing*, Orlando, Florida, USA, Jul. 11-15, 7-15.

Patel-Schneider, P., Hayes, P., & Horrocks, I. (2004). OWL Web Ontology Language Semantics and Abstract Syntax. Retrieved Feb. 11, 2011, from http://www.w3.org/TR/owl-semantics/.

Schneier, B. (2000). *Secrets & Lies*. Toronto, ON, Canada: Wiley Publishing.

Shan, T., & Hua, W. (2006). Service-Oriented Solution Framework for Internet Banking. *International Journal of Web Services Research*, *3*(1), 29–48. doi:10.4018/jwsr.2006010102

Siebenlist, F., Welch, V., Tuecke, S., Foster, I., Nagaratnam, N., Janson, P., et al. (2002). OGSA Security Roadmap. Retrieved Feb. 11, 2011, from http://www.globus.org/toolkit/security/ogsa/draft-ggf-ogsa-sec-roadmap-01.doc.

Viega, J., & Epsten, J. (2006). Why Applying Standards to Web Services is Not Enough. *IEEE Security & Privacy*, *4*(4), 25–31. doi:10.1109/MSP.2006.110

Vitvar, T., Moran, M., Zaremba, M., Haller, A., & Kotinurmi, P. (2007). Semantic SOA to Promote Integration of Heterogeneous B2B Services, *Proc. of the 4th IEEE Conference on Enterprise Computing, E-Commerce and E-Services*, Tokyo, Japan, Jul. 23-26, 451-456.

Yamany, E. L. H., & Capretz, M. (2008a). An Authorization Model for Web Services within SOA, *Proc. of the 3rd IEEE International Conference on Digital Management*, London, UK, Nov. 13-16, 75-80.

Yamany, E. L. H., & Capretz, M. (2008b). Use of Data Mining to Enhance Security for SOA, *Proc. of the 3rd IEEE International Conference on Convergence and Hybrid Information Technology*, Busan, Korea, Nov. 11-13, 551-558.

Yamany, EL, H., Capretz, M., & Allison, D. (2010). Intelligent Security and Access Control Framework for Service-Oriented Architecture. *Journal of Information and Software Technology*, *52*(2), 220–236. doi:10.1016/j.infsof.2009.10.005

Yee, G. (2009). Estimating the Privacy Protection Capability of a Web Service Provider. *International Journal of Web Services Research*, *6*(2), 20–41. doi:10.4018/jwsr.2009092202

Yee, G., & Korba, L. (2005). Semi-Automated Derivation and Use of Personal Privacy Policies in E-Business. *International Journal of E-Business Research*, *1*(1), 54–69. doi:10.4018/jebr.2005010104

Yu, W., Doddapaneni, S., & Murthy, S. (2006). A Privacy Assessment Approach for Serviced Oriented Architecture Applications, *Proc. of the 2nd IEEE International Symposium on Service-Oriented System Engineering*, Shanghai, China, Oct. 25-26, 67-75.

KEY TERMS AND DEFINITIONS

Authentication: The determination of whether a consumer is who they claim to be, through a verification of the consumer's identity.

Authorization: The determination of whether a consumer has the right to access a piece of software or information through the establishment of what actions that consumer may perform.

Data Mining: The ability and processes involved in extracting patterns from large amounts of data.

Privacy: The ability to control information about oneself that has not been released, and to also retain some measure of control over the information that has been released.

Quality of Service (QoS): A set of measurable requirements which must be met to provide a satisfactory level of service.

Security: An overarching concern of software to keep it safe from danger. Security includes topics such as authorization, authentication, auditing and privacy.

Service-Oriented Architecture (SOA): SOA is a growing paradigm in the world of IT that uses services as the basis for building enterprise applications. Services act as an application front-end and encapsulate the logic required to accomplish a specific task. Services, together with a directory to locate them, known as a service repository, and a means for services to communicate, known as a service bus, form the foundation of SOA.

Web Service: An autonomous software system which allows for networked, machine-to-machine interaction.

Chapter 14
RBAC with Generic Rights, Delegation, Revocation, and Constraints

Jacques Wainer
University of Campinas, Brazil

Fabio Negrello
University of Campinas, Brazil

Igor Ribeiro de Assis
University of Campinas, Brazil

ABSTRACT

This chapter presents R+DRC, an extension of the Role-based Access Control (RBAC) model. R+DRC allow for defining constraints, for example to enforce different forms of separation of duties, and the right of overriding a constraint. The model also defines delegations, and two forms of revocations. The model is discussed within the framework of modeling the access control of an hospital. Algorithms are provided for the more complex actions.

INTRODUCTION

Consider the following description of some of the rights in a hospital. The doctor who admits a patient can prescribe drugs, ask for exams, schedule procedures, and discharge the patient in the non emergency ward of the hospital. A doctor may have a team to whom he delegates some or all the rights regarding the patients he admitted. The doctor may also delegate different rights to different members of the team, so some team member may have the right to prescribe medication to the patients but not to discharge them. The doctor may also assemble an ad hoc team of other physicians to deal with a particular patient, and delegate different rights regarding that patient to different physicians in the ad hoc team.

If the patient dismisses his doctor, or if no one who has the right to discharge the patient can be reached after some reasonable effort, then the chief medical officer of the hospital may discharge the patient. The chief medical officer may also del-

DOI: 10.4018/978-1-61350-498-7.ch014

egate this right to exceptionally discharge a patient to a few other trusted colleagues, if he knows he will be unavailable for some time.

This scenario presents some challenges to a standard ANSI-RBAC modeling (ans, 2004). Most of the rights discussed above are not rights that are attached to roles such as the right to admit a patient which is attached to the role of physician. The right to prescribe drugs to patient *x* is not attached to the role of a physician but to the specific members of the medical team responsible for the patient *x*. Furthermore, some of the rights discussed above are not attached to a particular patient, but are in fact generic - the chief medical officer has the right to discharge *any* patient (and has the right to delegate this right). In ANSI-RBAC, rights are necessarily attached to objects in what is called *permissions*. Thus, in standard RBAC, for each new patient admitted, a new permission of discharging him or her should be created and associated to the chief medical officer role.

The other scenario involves a clinical reviewing board. If there are any questions regarding a patient's treatment, a reviewing board of senior physicians may be called for. The reviewing board analyzes the actions taken on behalf of a patient, and thus no one that acted in the patient's treatment can be a member of the reviewing board. This is an example of a *separation of duties* constraint. Furthermore, if reviewing boards are infrequent, the hospital may impose a further restriction that if physician A served on a reviewing board of a patient's case in which physician B was involved, then B cannot serve in the reviewing board of a patient's case in which A was involved. We call this *mutual separation of duties*. But if it becomes hard to select physicians given the mutual separation of duties policy, the chief medical officer can assign physicians to a review board so that it violates the mutual separation of duties, but not the separation of duties rule.

This example illustrates that violating constraints is also a right that some particular roles may have, in order to guarantee that the work should proceed. Violations of constraints is particularly important in business processes, where some constraints represent desirable but not necessarily required rules.

Finally, let us consider the following scenario in a large engineering company. In this company, people are added to projects as it becomes clear during the project development that their particular expertise is needed.

Now let us consider the situation in which engineer A invites B to work in a part of the project because B is one of the specialists in radiation calculations. Or in the terms of this chapter, A delegates to B not only the access to the project, but also the right to delegate it further, that is, B also has the right to invite other engineers to the project. B delegates access to C which is one of the specialists in radiation safety regulations. Some weeks later, D also delegates to C access to the project, because C is also a specialist in fire safety regulations. Now let us suppose that A leaves the company, and thus all delegations made by A must be evaluated by his substitute, and the safest way to proceed is to revoke all delegations made by A and add new delegations as the substitute approve them. But it is desirable that the revocation of the delegations causes the least changes as possible as not to totally halt the project. In particular, the standard, time-stamp based algorithm for delegation would revoke A's delegation to B, and B's delegation to C, but a more careful algorithm could realize that C's access can be justified by D's independent delegation.

The three scenarios above illustrate the issues we will tackle in this chapter. The first hospital scenario raises the issues of:

- **generic rights:** rights that apply to any object of a class
- **direct rights:** rights that are directly associated to users, and are not mediated through roles. Usually these rights come about from delegations but there are other forms.

The second hospital scenario, the review board, raises the issues of:

- **complex constrains:** that limit who can exercise which right in particular cases
- rights to violate some of the constraints.

Finally the engineering scenario raises the issues of

- complex chains of delegation of rights
- forms of revocation of delegations that causes less disturbance.

Some of the issues discussed above have been dealt with in the RBAC literature. Generic rights as far as we know have not been discussed in the literature, but the solutions are somewhat trivial, and probably it has been re-invented many times. There is a large literature in adding constraints to RBAC ((Ahn and Sandhu, 1999, Kuhn, 1997, Nyanchama and Osborn, 1999, Simon and Zurko, 1997) among others), beyond the capabilities of expressing constraints in ANSI-RBAC (see section 2). Some also propose the use of logic programming expressions to represent constraints, as we propose in this chapter (Jajodia et al., 1997, Becker and Sewell, 2004) (including our own research (Wainer et al., 2003, Wainer et al., 2007)), but (Wainer et al., 2003) was the only one to propose a controlled violation of constraints. The solution proposed in this chapter is an improvement on the one in (Wainer et al., 2003). Similarly, there is an extensive literature regarding adding delegation to RBAC ((Barka and Sandhu, 2000a, Barka and Sandhu, 2000b, Zhang et al., 2003a, Ruan and Varadharajan, 2002, Bacon et al., 2002) among others), and some of these proposals allow rights assigned to people without the mediation of roles, as proposed in this chapter. But research on revocation of these delegations is less common (Griffiths and Wade, 1976, Fagin, 1978, Hagstrom et al., 2001), and in particular, the idea of a least disturbance revocation, or a downgrade revocation as we call in this chapter, has only been discussed in (Wainer et al., 2007). The downgrade revocation proposed in this chapter is an extension of the one proposed in (Wainer et al., 2007). Related Work presents an in depth comparison of this work with the different models presented in the literature.

Thus, although some of the issues have been addressed in some form by other research, this is the first model that puts all these concepts into a single unified framework, in which the interaction between them is correctly addressed. In particular, we prove some correctness properties of the whole framework.

This chapter is organized as follows. Section RBAC below briefly reviews the concepts of RBAC. Our Solution: R+DRC discusses the central concepts of our model. Definitions and Algorithms formally states the main definitions and algorithms, while the section Properties lists and proves some of the important proprieties of the R+DRC framework (after RBAC plus Delegations, Revocations, and Constraints). The section Implementation discusses a Prolog implementation of the R+DRC system, including execution time figures for some randomly created evaluation cases. Related Work discusses the related literature, and the section titled Discussion discusses some limitation and extensions of the model.

RBAC

The core component of ANSI RBAC (ans, 2004) is constructed based on the concepts of *users*, *roles*, *operations*, and *protected object*. Operations are "an executable image of a program which upon evocation executes some function for the user" (Ferraiolo et al., 2001, p.233) and intuitively corresponds to verbs or verb phrases such as "admit" or "prescribe a drug" in our hospital example. The protected objects are the resources under control of the access control system. The combination of a operation and an object is called a *permission*. An example of permission is "prescribe a drug to patient Aaron Aardvark". In this chapter we will use the word "right" as an alternative to permission.

Users are associated to roles through the user assignment (UA) relation, and permission are associated to roles through the permission assignment (PA) relation.

Not relevant to this chapter is the core RBAC concept of *session* which is a mapping of a user and an activated subset of roles that are assigned to the user. Also not relevant are the other components of the RBAC model: the hierarchical RBAC and the static and dynamic separation of duties relations (SSD and DSD respectively). The Hierarchical RBAC extend the core RBAC by adding an inheritance hierarchy on roles; SSD creates relations between users and role assignments, and DSD creates relations between roles and sessions. The hierarchical RBAC allows one to create roles such as "senior engineer" which inherits all permissions of an "engineer" plus some extra permissions. SSD allows one to restrict the assignments users can have with respect to roles, for example, one can state that no user can be assigned to both the "requester" and "approver" roles. DSD allows one to restrict a user as using at the same time (in the same session) the roles of "requester" and "approver".

All component of the RBAC model have associated *administrative functions* which allow the creation of new users, roles, permissions, and the creation of new instances of the relations defined.

OUR SOLUTION: R+DRC

Hierarchy on Operations, Objects, and Permissions

An important relation for this chapter is the *imply* partial order relation among operations, which we will denote as $\supseteq_{op}$. O_1 **implies** O_2, or $O_1 \supseteq_{op} O_2$, if someone that executes O_1 can do at least as much as someone who executes O_2. Thus for example, the operation of prescribing any drug implies the operation of prescribing orally taken drugs.

Similarly we will define a *contains* partial order relation among objects, denoted as $\supseteq_o$. Object $X_1 \supseteq_o$ object X_2 if any operation in X_2 would also affect X_1. We will also define the object **-class* as a representation of a generic object of that class, and we will stipulate that the *-class object contains any instance of the class. Thus *-patient $\supseteq_o x$ if x is any patient.

Finally we define the partial relation among permissions $\supseteq$. If $P_1=\langle O_1,X_1\rangle$ and $P_2=\langle O_2,X_2\rangle$, then $P_1 \supseteq P_2$ iff $O_1 \supseteq_{op} O_2$ and $X_1 \supseteq_o X_2$.

The intuition on the partial relation $\supseteq$ is that if a user makes a requests to perform an operation O on an object X and he has a stronger permission, that his request should be accepted. Thus, the *-class objects allow us to define generic permissions. The permission ⟨**discharge**,*-patient⟩ is a generic permission that can be applied to any particular patient. If the chief medical officer holds ⟨**discharge**,*-patient⟩, when he attempts to discharge the patient "Aaron Aardvark", he will succeed, since his permission is stronger than the potential permission ⟨**discharge**,"Aaron Aardvark"⟩ needed.

In this chapter, permissions will be represented as ⟨Operation,Object⟩. Operations that need to be made explicit will be represented **in bold**.

Object Subclasses

Beside the standard protected objects in core RBAC which refer to the *external* or *domain* objects under control of the access control system, we define *control* objects, which are objects of the access control system itself. Control objects include:

- direct rights (Non Role-Mediated Rights)
- trace objects (Traces and Requests)
- delegations (Delegation)
- constraints (Constraints)

Non Role-Mediated Rights

The R+DRC allows for users to have rights (or permissions) that are not mediated by the roles, such as the rights of the physician team members in the hospital example. Rights not mediated by roles may arise by two different ways. Delegation and direct rights creation rules. Delegation will be discussed in section Delegation. *Direct rights* are permissions associated with a user that are not derived from delegation. They are created by rules, the *direct rights creation rules* or DRCR.

A direct right is represented as

inst(U,Per)

where U is a user and Per is a permission.

A direct right creation rule is represented as

trigger⇒direct right$_1$,direct right$_2$,...direct right$_n$

Conceptually DRCR are event-condition-action rules (ECA rules) without the conditions - when the event/trigger happens, the direct rights will be created. The trigger of the DRCR are mainly two kinds:

- timer events
- the creation of a control object in the system.

We will discuss an example of DRCR in the section below.

Traces and Requests

We assume the following architecture for the R+DRC. A user or a system makes a *request* to the system, which is accepted or not. The request lists the user, an operation, and an object, with the meaning that the user intends to perform the operation upon the object. The R+DRC system either denies the request or accepts it. The request is denied if the user does not have the appropriate permission to do execute the operation on the object, or if executing it would violate any constraint. Otherwise the request is accepted, that is informed to the system or user that made the request, and a record of the operation on the object is created.

The object created is called a *trace*, and its representation is:

trace(U,O,X)

where U is the user, O is the operation executed, and X is the object.

A trace is not a audit log but an object that is represented in the system and may be used as part of constraints (see section Constraints) and as part of direct rights creation rules.

From a conceptual point of view, each request granted should be represented as a trace, but from a practical point of view, not all of them will. Otherwise the set of trace objects would grew indefinitely when the system is in operation. Trace objects are only needed if they are part of constraints and rules. Even when traces take part in constraints and rules they may have a time-bounded usefulness and may be erased if no longer useful. The section on implementation discusses some of the heuristics regarding the creation and destruction of traces objects. Exactly because not all trace objects need to be created, and they may be destroyed in the future, they should not be though as an alternative of an audit trail.

We will express that a user U made a request to perform the operation O onto object X as

O(U,X)

We will also refer to the request O(U,X) as "the user U issue the action O on object X".

Requests can be aggregated into a single *combined request*. The requests that make up the combined request are called *components*. The combined request are treated as a single atomic action. If a single component of a combined request is denied, the whole request is denied. On the other hand, if all components are granted, the whole request is treated as atomic, and will not be interleaved with other user requests. A combined request is represented as:

$$O_1(U_1,X_1)+O_2(U_2,X_2)+\ldots+O_n(U_n,X_n)$$

Usually, the user in all components of a combined request are the same.

All operations may have two separate effects. The *immediate effect* is executed immediately, before the next operation in the combined request. The *delayed* effect is postponed until the end of the combined request. In the example above, the immediate effect of O_1 will become true before the execution of the next operation in the request (O_2). The delayed effect of O_1 will only become true after the immediate effect of O_n becomes true. Combined requests and delayed effects are particular relevant when we discuss overriding constrains (see section Active Constraints and Overriding) - the scope of an overriding operation is just the combined request to which it belongs.

With the concept of traces, we can also illustrate an example of a DRCR. In the first hospital scenario, once a physician admits a patient, he or she has permission to prescribe drugs, request exams, operate, and discharge the patient (and permission to delegate these permissions). This is accomplished by a DRCR of the form

trace(*U*,***admit***,*P*)⇒***inst***(*U*,⟨***opera te***,*P*⟩), ***inst***(*U*,⟨***prescribedrug***,*P*⟩), **inst**(U,⟨**discharge**,P⟩), …

where the the … would contain also direct rights regarding delegation of the permissions ⟨**operate**,P⟩, ⟨**prescribedrug**,P⟩, and so on. (see next section on delegations and permission to delegate.

Delegation

If the user A has the appropriate rights, he can issue a delegation, or more precisely, he can perform an operation for the creation of a delegation object. If there is no risk of confusion we will say that "A delegated a right to B" or "A created a delegation of the right to B", instead of "user A executed the operation of creating a delegation object which states that there is a delegation of said right to user B."

Right to Delegate

Delegation requires that the user that is delegating should have the appropriate permission to delegate. The permission to delegate is the association of the operation **cd** (after create delegation) and another permission (P). The permission ⟨**cd**,P⟩ allow the delegation of the permission P.

This extends our definition of permission, which was a relation between an operation and an object. A permission is a relation between an operation and an object or a permission. The permission to delegate the right to delegate the permission P is ⟨**cd**,⟨**cd**,P⟩⟩.

Regarding the $\supseteq$ relation among delegation permissions, we define: ⟨**cd**,P1⟩ $\supseteq$ ⟨**cd**,P2⟩ if P1 $\supseteq$ P2. That is, the permission to delegate a stronger permission is itself stronger than the permission to delegate a weaker permission.

We also define that ⟨**cd**,⟨**cd**,P1⟩⟩ $\supseteq$ ⟨**cd**,P1⟩. That is, the permission to delegate a delegation permission (of P) implies the permission to delegate P. There is a clear intuition here, if A has the right to delegate the right to delegate P, than A can delegate P.

Let us define the abbreviation ⟨cd^n,P⟩ recursively as

- ⟨cd^1,P⟩ = ⟨**cd**,P⟩
- ⟨cd^n,P⟩ = ⟨**cd**,⟨cd^{n-1},P⟩⟩

That is, $\langle cd^1,P\rangle$ is the right to delegate the permission P, $\langle cd^2,P\rangle$ is the right to delegate the right to delegate P, and so on.

A delegation request that is accepted will create the corresponding trace object and the delegation object

$\mathbf{del}(G,R,P)$

where G is the *grantor* of the delegation, R is the *receiver* of the delegation and P is the permission delegated.

Finally, the representation of the delegation request is

$\mathbf{cd}(G,\mathbf{del}(G,R,P)$

that is, the request is to create (**cd**) the delegation object. Unfortunately, the representation is redundant regarding the grantor, but to maintain the syntax uniform, we will accept this small inelegance.

Revocation of Delegations

Revocation is the operation of canceling a delegation. There are two forms of revocations, with different effects. The standard revocation **srk** removes a delegation and all other delegations that depend on it - please see Effects of Revocation for the precise definition of "dependency" we are using. The downgrade revocation **drk** will remove a delegation and downgrade, or reduce the strength of the delegations that depend on it so it will no longer depend of on the revoked delegation, if that is possible.

Constraints

Constraint is an expression that refers to an action and that describes a situation that is **not acceptable**. In other words, constraint is an expression that when evaluated for a particular action should return **true** or **false**. If it returns **true**, than the action *violates* the constraint; if it returns **false** then the action is *allowed* by the constraint.

Constraints will be denoted as:

$\text{violation}(c_j,U,O,X)\leftarrow\Phi.$

where c_j is the constraint identity, U is the user that issued the request, O is the operation, and X the object. Φ the constraint expression. Constraints are themselves control objects of the R+DRC system, identified by the constraint identity.

The constraint expression Φ is expressed in a full logical programming language, that is, it may make reference to recursive predicates, mathematical operators and relations, and may use conjunction, disjunction and negation as failure to connect these predicates. The section titled Discussion discusses the consequences of using a full logic language to define constraints and section ? discusses alternatives of less powerful and thus less expressive languages proposed in the literature.

The following constraints on delegation:

$\text{violation}(c_1,G,\mathbf{cd},\mathbf{del}(G,R,\langle O,X\rangle))\supseteq\mathbf{design}\wedge R/\in\mathbf{engineer}$

defines a constraint that states that it is a violation if a delegation for any permission that contains an operation that is stronger than **design** is given to a recipient that is not a member of the role **engineer**.

$\text{violation}(c_4,G,\mathbf{cd},\mathbf{del}(G,R,\langle O,X\rangle)) \leftarrow \mathbf{clearance}(R)\geq\mathbf{security{-}level}(X)$

is a constraint that implements a MAC controlled delegation - only recipients with clearance above the object's security level can receive the delegation.

We can also define the constraint regarding the separation and mutual separation of duties discussed above (Box 1).

The separation of duties example, where we translated "being involved in the patient's treat-

Box 1.

```
violation(c11,A,review,Pat) ← trace(A,prescribedrug,Pat)∨
trace(A,request-exam,Pat)∨trace(A,operate,Pat)
```

ment", as either having prescribed drugs, requested exams, or operated on the patient. In this example, we treated the **trace** object as a predicate with the semantics that the predicate is true if the corresponding object exists.

The expression would be simpler if we define an auxiliary predicate as in Box 2.

Then, the constraint would be

violation(c_{11},A,**review**,Pat)←treated(A,Pat)

With the auxiliary predicate, the constraint of mutual separation of duties would be represented as:

violation(c_{12},A,**review**,Pat)←treated(B,Pat),treated(A,Qat),**trace**(B,**review**,Qat)

Active Constraints and Overriding

Constraints can be *active* or *inactive*. Active is the default state for a constraint and it means that the constraint will be checked when an action is being verified.

The only relevant permission related to constraint is the permission to override it. If c_j is a constraint, ⟨**ov**,c_j⟩ is the permission to override it. The immediate effect of**ov** is to set a constraint to inactive, and the delayed effect is to set it back to active. Overriding operations are only relevant as part of a complex requests, to "turn off" a constraint for the following components - by itself an **ov** will set the constraint inactive and then immediately active again.

DEFINITIONS AND ALGORITHMS

Has-Right

Has-right is an auxiliary relation between users and permissions that is true if the user has that permission (or a stronger one) through some of the means allowed by our model: through the role, through delegation, or through a direct permission.

Definition 1 *User A**has-right**to P iff*

- there is a role R and a permission P^+, such that ⟨A,R⟩ ∈ **UA** and ⟨R,P^+⟩ ∈ **PA** and $P^+ \supseteq P$ or
- there is an user U and an object **del**(U,A,P^+) and $P^+ \supseteq P$ or
- there is an object **inst**(A,P^+) and $P^+ \supseteq P$

Allowing Single Requests

Definition 2 *The request O(U,X) is allowed iff*

- the user **has-right** for ⟨O,X⟩

Box 2.

```
treated(U,Pat)←     trace(A,prescribedrug,Pat)∨
                         trace(A,requestexam,Pat)∨trace(A,operate,Pat)
```

- the query **violation**(C,A,O,X) is not true for any of the active constraints.

If a request is allowed, then its immediate effects take effect and the trace object for the request is created.

Allowing Combined Requests

Definition 3 *The request $O_1(U_1,X_1)+O_2(U_2,X_2)+\ldots+O_n(U_n,X_n)$ is allowed iff each $O_i(U_i,X_i)$ are allowed sequentially (which includes carrying out the immediate effects of each component request). If the combined request is not allowed, then the immediate effects of the component requests that were allowed must be undone. If a combined request is allowed, then the delayed effects of all its component requests are executed.*

Effect of Overriding

Definition 4 *The immediate effect of the operation* **ov** *on object c_i is that the constraint object c_i is set as inactive. The delayed effect is that c_i is set back to active.*

Effect of Delegation

Definition 5 *The immediate effect of the operation* **cd** *on object d_i in a combined request is that the delegation object d_i is created. There is no delayed effect.*

Effects of Revocation

To understand the effects of the two forms of revocations, we need a few definitions:

- The *decrement* (denoted by *dec*) of the permission $\langle cd^n, P\rangle$ is $\langle cd^{n-1}, P\rangle$. We will say that $dec(\langle \mathbf{cd}, P\rangle) = P$.
- A delegation **del**(A,X,*P*) is *grounded* if there is a role *R* and a permission P^+, such that $\langle A,R\rangle \in \boldsymbol{UA}$ and $\langle R,P^+\rangle \in \boldsymbol{PA}$ and $P^+ \sqsupseteq P$ or there is an object **inst**(A,P^+) and $P^+ \sqsupseteq P$
- A delegation **del**(A,X,*P*) is *supported by* a delegation **del**(Y,A,P^+) if $dec(P^+) \sqsupseteq P$.
- A *downgrade* of the delegation **del**(G,D,*P*) is any delegation **del**(G,D,P^-) where $P \sqsupseteq P^-$.

That is, a delegation is grounded if the grantor had the right to execute the operation of delegation through some role he can assume or if there is a direct right that assigns the proper permission to the grantor. A delegation d_a is supported by another delegation d_b if the user that issued d_a *could* have received the right to execute d_a from the delegation d_b.

A *support chain* of a delegation d_n is a sequence of delegations $\langle d_1, d_2, \ldots d_{n-1}, d_n\rangle$, where d_1 is grounded, none of the d_i $i>0$ are grounded, and d_i is supported by d_{i-1}. A delegation is *supported* if it has at least one support chain.

Definition 6 *The* immediate *effect of the action* **srk** *on object d_x, where d_x is a delegation is that the object d_x is deleted.*

The delayed *effect of the action is that all delegations that are unsupported are deleted.*

Definition 7 *The* immediate *effect of the operation* **drk** *on d_x where d_x is a delegation is that d_x is deleted.*

The delayed *effect of the action that all delegations d that became unsupported are downgraded into the stronger possible delegations so they become again supported. If a delegation cannot be supported regardless of how much it can be downgraded, it is deleted.*

Examples of Revocation

Let us suppose that *y* and *x* are permissions and that $y \sqsupseteq x$. Given the sequence of delegations in Table 1.

Table 1.

1. **del**(A,C, $\langle cd^7,y\rangle$)	2. **del**(C,D, $\langle cd^6,y\rangle$)
3. **del**(D,G, $\langle cd^5,x\rangle$)	4. **del**(D,E, $\langle cd^4,y\rangle$)
5. **del**(B,D, $\langle cd^4,y\rangle$)	6. **del**(D,I, $\langle cd^1,x\rangle$)
7. **del**(G,H, $\langle cd^4,x\rangle$)	8. **del**(A,D, $\langle cd^5,x\rangle$)

The result of the sequence of delegations is represented in Figure 1, where the two solid circles represent users A and B which had the rights to start the chains of delegations. The lines indicate the right delegated and the exponent.

The effect of the standard revocation of the delegation from C to D is depicted in the left pane of Figure 2. The delegations from D to E, from D to G, and form G to H all loose support and must be deleted.

The effect of the downgrade revocation of the delegation from C to D is depicted in right pane of Figure 3. The central aspect is that the delegation from D to E is downgraded into two delegations, a delegation of $\langle cd^4,x\rangle$, which is supported by the delegation from A to D, and a delegation of $\langle cd^3,y\rangle$, which is supported by the delegation from B to D. The delegation from D to G is downgraded to $\langle cd^4,x\rangle$, and G to H, to $\langle cd^3,x\rangle$.

Algorithm for Standard Revocation

The algorithm for standard revocation is based on considering the set of delegations as a set of vertices and the **supports** relation between two delegations as a direct edge between the two corresponding vertices. The resulting graph will be called a *delegation graph*, denoted as *DG*. In the delegation graph, let us create a new vertex d_0 and edges from d_0 to each grounded delegation. In this graph, a delegation is supported if and only if there is a path from d_0 to it.

If *n* is the number of delegations, constructing the delegation graph is $O(n^2)$, because there may be as many as $O(n^2)$ edges between the nodes in the delegation graph.

Figure 1. The result of the sequence of delegations. The first letter on the arcs indicates the permission being delegated and the second the exponent of the delegation.

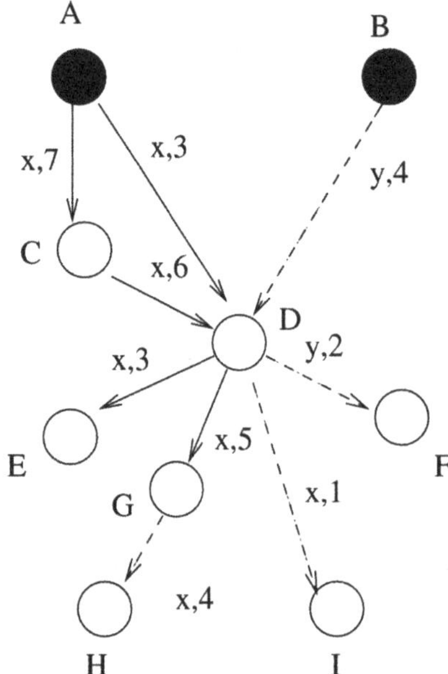

Let us assume a function reach(d) which returns the set of delegations reachable from the delegation *d*. This can be computed in $O(n)$ by any graph search algorithm.

Algorithm 1 computes the effect of the standard revocation of the delegation *d* as a change on the set *D* of all delegations. Thus the total cost of revoking a delegation is $O(n^2)$.

Algorithm for the Downgrade Revocation

Greatest Lower Bound of Two Rights

Given two permissions *R* and *S*, we will define the *greatest lower bound* of *R* and *S* (denoted as meet(*R*,*S*)) as the permission *x* such that $R \sqsupseteq x$ and $S \sqsupseteq x$ and there is no such that $x' \sqsupset x$ and $R \sqsupseteq x'$ and $S \sqsupseteq x'$.

Figure 2. The resulting delegations after the standard revocation

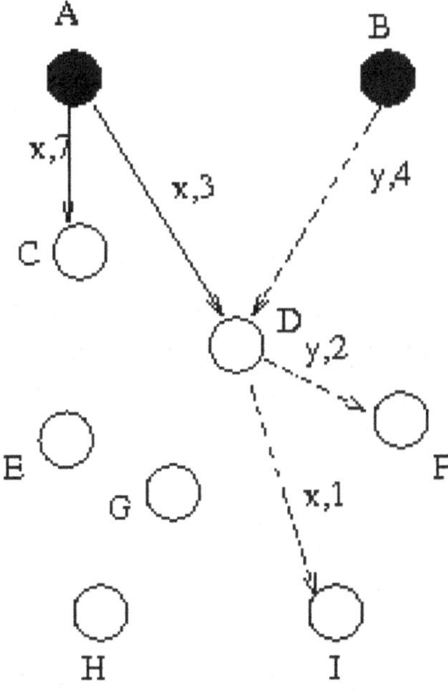

Figure 3. The resulting delegations after the downgrade revocation

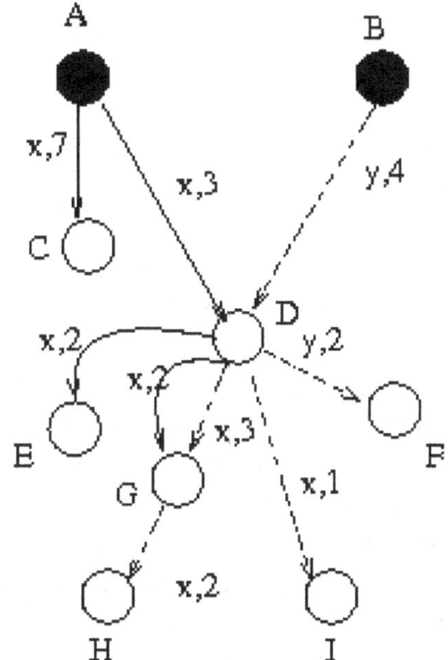

Theorem 1 *The following defines the* meet *action for delegations rights:*

$$\text{meet}(\langle \mathbf{cd}^n, R\rangle, \langle \mathbf{cd}^m, S\rangle) = \langle \mathbf{cd}^{\min(m,n)}, \text{meet}(R,S)\rangle$$

The proof sketch is as follows. Clearly $\langle cd^n, R\rangle \supseteq \langle cd^{\min(m,n)}, \text{meet}(R,S)\rangle$ and similarly for $\langle cd^m, S\rangle$. Let us assume that there is a right $\langle cd^k, Z\rangle$ such that $\langle cd^n, R\rangle \supseteq \langle cd^k, Z\rangle$ and $\langle cd^m, S\rangle \supseteq \langle cd^k, Z\rangle$ and $\langle cd^k, Z\rangle \supseteq \langle cd^{\min(m,n)}, \text{meet}(R,S)\rangle$. Clearly $k \leq m$ and $k \leq n$, thus $k \leq min(n,m)$ and since $k \geq min(n,m)$ by the assumption, then $k = min(n,m)$. Similarly, $R \supseteq Z$ and $S \supseteq Z$ and thus, $\text{meet}(R,S) \supseteq Z$. By the assumption $Z \supseteq \text{meet}(R,S)$, and thus $Z = \text{meet}(R,S)$. Therefore $\langle cd^k, Z\rangle = \langle cd^{\min(m,n)}, \text{meet}(R,S)\rangle$.

The theorem shows that computing the meet of two delegation permissions is only as complex as computing the meet of two permissions in the RBAC permission structure. In simpler structures, for example if the lattice of permissions is join-irreducible[1] the computation is trivial. Since we do not make any requirements on the structure of the permission lattice, we will consider that computing the meet takes time *meet*.

D-Support

A delegation **del**(A,X,*R*) *d-supports* a delegation **del**(Y,A,*S*) if there exists the permission meet(*dec*(*R*),*S*)). That is, a delegation d_a d-supports

Algorithm 1. Compute the effect of the standard revocation of d

```
Construct the delegation graph DG
D←D-{d}
X←reach(d0) is the set of all delegations reachable from d0
Remove the delegations in D-X
```

Algorithm 2. The down function

```
z← •
The condition that verify if x d-supports d
if (d=del(a,b,r) andx=del(X,a,s)) then
     z←del(a,b,meet(r,dec(s)))
end if
returnz
```

d_b if there is a downgrade of d_b that can be supported by d_a.

Let us define in algorithm 2 the auxiliary function down(d,x) that computes the delegation that d should be downgraded to so it is supported by the delegation x. The function returns • if x does not d-support d.

Let us also define the function find_max(D), which given a set of delegations D, returns a delegation $x \in D$, such that, there is no $y \in D$ such that $y \sqsupset x$. That is, find_max return a maximal element in D.

The Algorithm

Algorithm 3 implements the downgrade revocation. The set D_x are the delegations that may be downgraded. The set Q are delegations that are supported, and thus that can support a downgrade of the delegations in D_x. The algorithm is a slight modification of the Dijkstra algorithm. Line 6 pick x a maximal element in Q. All elements in $d_j \in D_x$ that are d-supported by x are downgraded (to d'_i). The set R is the set of new downgraded delegations. If there is no stronger element to d_j'already in R, then not only d_j will be added as a new downgraded delegation (line 1), but it will also be added to Q (line 12), since now d'_j is supported and can now d-support some delegation in D_x.

The complexity of the algorithm 3 is dominated by the loop stating in line 5, but different than Dijkstra's algorithm, the set Q grows during the computation. Thus the complexity of the algorithm is then $O(|Q| \times n \times meet)$ where *meet* is the cost of the meet action executed in the down function. The set Q can grow to at most $O(n^2)$ elements since a single delegation can be downgraded into $O(n)$ other delegations. Therefore the complexity is $O(n^3 \times meet)$.

PROPERTIES

Since delegations are the only actions whose effect persists for a long time, there is the need to prove some properties about them.

Theorem 2 *After any accepted request all delegations objects are supported.*

This theorem is trivial for the delegate and the standard revocation actions - a delegation is only accepted if it is supported, and the standard revocation removes all unsupported delegations. Regarding the downgrade revocation, the proof is as follows. First, let us define that if d'_i is a downgrade of d_i (line 9 of algorithm ?), we will say that d_i is the parent of d'_i. Let us assume that all delegations are supported before a downgrade revocation. By induction we will prove that all delegations remaining are also supported. The induction is in the number of times the loop starting in line 5 is executed. At the first time, Q only contain supported delegations (by construction), and thus x is supported and thus each d'_i added to Q are supported (which are the d'_i added to R. By the induction assumption, all delegations added to Q up to interaction $j-1$ are supported, and thus the d'_i added in interaction j are also supported. Thus all delegations in R are supported. □

Now let us consider the interplay between delegations and constraints. A constraint c is *monotonic* if whenever the request $O(U,X)$ is allowed by c then $O'(U,X)$ will be also allowed, where O' is a weaker operation than O. The RBAC structure is *static* for a particular period, if there was no change in the **UA** and the **PA** relations. That is, the RBAC structure is static if no user changed roles, and no role changed the rights it hold.

Theorem 3 *If the RBAC structure is static, and the constraints for delegations are monotonic and do not make references to traces or other delegations, then given a set of delegations D, it is possible to remove D and issue a set of delegations $d_1, d_2, \ldots d_n$ such that D is restored.*

This theorem is a roundabout way of stating that at any time, and given the conditions listed, the set of delegations do not violate any constraint. The problem is that constraints do not apply to objects (like delegations) but to requests. The proof is as follows. From theorem 2 we know that all delegations $d_i \in D$ are supported, and thus any order in which d_i is issued before d_j if d_i supports d_j will guarantee that each action of delegation d_j can be accepted because

- if d_j is grounded then, since the RBAC is static, the grantor still has the right to issue the delegation,
- if d_j is not grounded then the grantor received the right to issue the delegation by its supporting delegation d_i, which was issued before.
- in either case, the delegation d_j does not violate any constraint, because by the conditions of the theorem, the constraints on delegations makes no reference to traces or other delegations. New traces and a different set of delegations are the only objects that may have changed since d_j was first issued, or when its parent was issued (if d_j was downgraded). Since d_j did not violate any constraint then, it does not violate any now. If d_j was downgraded, that its parent dP_j did not violate any constraint then, and since all constraints regarding delegations are monotonic, then $dP_j \supseteq d_j$, then d_j does not violate any constraint. □

IMPLEMENTATION

A prototype of the R+DRC was implemented in Prolog. Prolog is well suited as the language to implement the system because all definitions are straight forwardly implemented as predicates. For example, definitions 1, 2, and 3 are implemented as the predicates in Algorithm 4.

We experimented with two alternatives for the storage of the objects and relations in R+DRC. The standard alternative is to store them in a data base which is consulted and altered by the Prolog program. We call this the database version of the program. But Prolog allows for a second alternative. All objects and relations can be represented in Prolog as facts that are kept in memory. Current Prolog implementations can store millions of facts in memory in relatively modest desktop hardware (Wielemaker et al., 2003). We call this the in-memory version of the program.

The in-memory version would load the whole set of objects and relations into memory at start. As the program executes objects are created and destroyed all in memory. Of course the system must keep a journal of the initial state and posterior changes of the memory state, so that it can be recovered in case of system crash.

If one considers that in steady state the number of domain objects should remain approximately constant, the main problem for the in-memory architecture are the trace objects. Since there is one trace objects for each allowed request, that number will grow without bounds the longer the system runs. Delegations are also a potential problem - each new domain object will likely spawn new delegations. But it is much more likely that a user will let a delegation "lose its usefulness" than to explicitly revoke it. For example, the delega-

Algorithm 3. Compute the effect of the downgrade revocation of d

```
let D be the set of delegations
compute the set of delegations D_x that would be removed by the standard revoca-
tion of d.
Q←D−D_x R←∅
while(Q≠∅)
    x←find_max(Q)
    Q←Q−{x}
     forall d_i∈D_x d'_i←down(d_i,x)
        if(d'_i≠ • and there is no r∈R such that r⊐d'_i)
            R←R∪{d'_i}
            Q←Q∪{d'_i}
         end if
    end for
end while
remove the delegations D_x
```

Algorithm 4.

```
hasright(U,P):-
        ua(U,Role),
        pa(Role,Pplus),
        greater(Pplus,P).
hasright(U,P):-
        del(_,U,Pplus),
        greater(Pplus,P).
hasright(U,P):-
        inst(U,Pplus),
        greater(Pplus,P).
allow(U,O,X):-
     Per = perm(O,X),
     hasright(U,Per),
     findall(C,violation(C,U,O,X),L),
     suspendedconstraints(Sup),
     subset(L,Sup).
dispatch(U,ov,C):-
    generatetrace(U,ov,C),
    asserta(suspended(C)).
dispatch(U,cd,D):-
    gentrace(U,cd,D),
    asserta(del(A,D)).
...
```

tions from the responsible physician to its team for each patient will loose its usefulness once the patient is discharged.

We devised some strategies to remove the trace and delegation objects once it is clear that they are no longer useful for the functioning of system. For delegations, as soon as an domain object is removed, which could be associated with some domain operation, like discharging a patient, all delegations of permissions that involve that object and sub-objects contained in it can be removed. This strategy also work for traces if all constraints are “intra-object”, that is, if all constraints refer to a single object. This is clearly the most common form of constraint discussed in the literature. The exception are the mutual separation of duties and the famous Chinese Wall (Brewer and Nash, 1989) constraints.

An orthogonal alternative for traces is the conditional creation of traces. Not all operations leave traces that are useful to the system - if there in no constraint or DRCR that depends on the operation **readexam** for example, there is no need to create the corresponding trace[2]. The conditional creation can be automatically set up by processing all DRCR, constraints and their auxiliary predicates - the program discovers the list of all operations involved in the DRCR and constraints, and only traces of these operations are created. Finally, as a last resource, trace objects may be stored in a database and not in memory.

The System

The implemented system receives a request in XML, through an SSL (or TLS) channel. The SSL guarantees authenticity of both the request and the system's response. The system assumes that the user identity has been verified appropriately and that if the request is allowed, the operation will be performed on to the object. If the request is about a control operation such as delegation, revocation, overriding, and so on, if granted, the system itself will execute the operation.

In terms of the XACML reference model (xac, 2005), the systems implements the PDP (policy decision points), it receives a request context and returns a response. The format of the request and of the response is in accordance to the XACML specification, for requests that refer to external operations. For control operations, we extended the XACML syntax to allow for the appropriate attributes.

Performance Evaluation

Since there is no standard benchmark for access control system, we exercised the system using artificially created, random cases. We evaluated the system using only the RBAC concepts of user, role, and permissions, which we call the RBAC test, and using the concepts of delegation and revocation of R+DRC, the simplified R+DRC. The RBAC test serves as a baseline, that is it shows what is the computational cost of using the basic computational infrastructure (such as Prolog, data bases, XML parsing, etc). The difference between the RBAC test and simplified R+DRC shows the cost of the extensions we proposed on RBAC.

The tests involved the creation of a random model (users, roles, permissions, and their corresponding relations) and random requests. The random model is parametrized on the number of users (NU). The role structure has a inheritance hierarchy (the role hierarchy of ANSI-RBAC, not discussed in this chapter). NU/20 role hierarchies are created, and each hierarchy has around 15 roles. Permissions also have a structure with NU of those hierarchies, each one with two permissions, a stronger and a weaker hierarchy. All permissions are generic rights, that is, their corresponding object is *.

Each user is associated to a random number (between 1 and 10) of roles (chosen randomly). Each role is associated with a random number (between 1 and 10) permissions (chosen randomly).

The RBAC requests are simply a random user, operation, and object from the set of available users, operations and objects.

The simplified R+DRC requests are more complex. Each block of 100 requests would contains 81 domain requests, 12 randomly created delegations (from a random user to another random user of a random permission), and 7 random downgrade revocations.

In all cases, the request were generated at the rate of 1 per second a process, and the answer was send to a different process who measure the response time. All tests were executed in a computer with a Intel Core Duo CPU, 1.8 GHz CPU and 2GBytes of memory, running Linux. The program was developed using SWI Prolog version 5.6.38, and in the database version of the program, the DBMS used was SQLite 3.4.1.

Figure 4 displays the response time of the RBAC and the R+DRC tests for five model sizes, and for the in-memory and database versions. Each data point is the average response time for at least ten thousand requests for 3 random models with the appropriate number of users. For the in-memory version, the inversion of the RBAC and R+DRC for models of twenty thousand users is not statistically significant. The database version tests do not cover the whole range of model

Figure 4. Response time of the RBAC and R+DRC test

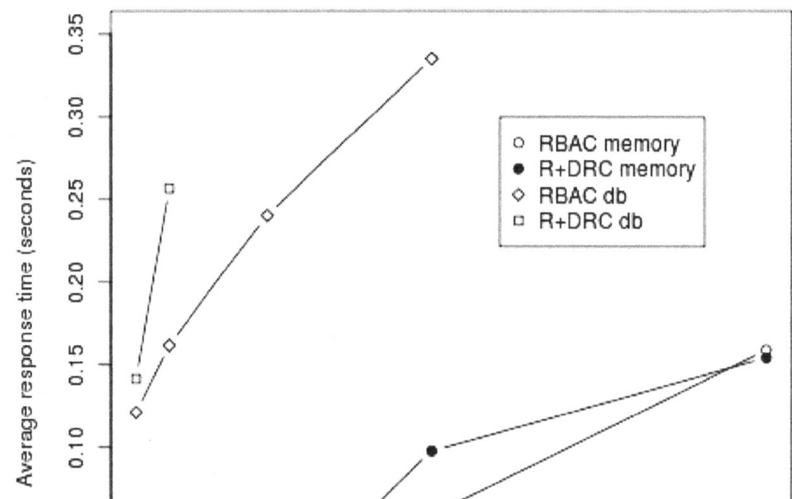

sizes because their average response time for those model sizes was above 1.0 seconds. Since the request rate was 1 per second, an average response time above 1.0 indicates that the queues were growing as the system operation continued.

The sharp differences in response time for the RBAC and R+DRC cases in the data base version are probably due to the fact that our implementation of the downgrade revocation was particularly ill-fitted to the database structure. The downgrade operation has to calculate transitive chains of delegations, which is a costly operation in a databases.

The figures indicate that the in-memory architecture is very interesting for such an implementation. Although storing the relations and objects in memory can be done in any programming language, Prolog is particularly suitable for it because of a efficient storage and indexing of these relations and objects.

RELATED WORK

As we discussed, some of the ideas and issues proposed in this work have been discussed in the literature.

Order among permissions was part of the earlier RBAC model (Sandhu et al., 1996, Ferraiolo et al., 1995) but the idea was dropped in more recent RBAC models and articles (with some exceptions, for example (Belsis et al., 2006, Naumenko and Luostarinen,) and our own work (Wainer et al., 2003, Wainer et al., 2007)) in favor of the hierarchy of roles. The two concepts are not contradictory, but somewhat redundant (specially to what is called the “permission hierarchy interpretation” of the role hierarchy (Bertino, 2003)).

Constraints have been in the RBAC literature since it started. As mentioned in section 2, the current RBAC model includes the possibility of expressing some constrains. In some way each research decides on a particular families of constraints it wants to model, and defines the set of concepts and language needed to model that families. For example, (Simon and Zurko, 1997) not only provide a taxonomy of different forms of separation of duties, but shows how they were addressed in the Adage system. They define a language in which constraints are expressed as Box 3.

which states that users in role Teller must not perform the operation in the set TellerActions on objects in the set TellerTargets if they had already performed operations from the set AuditorActions on those objects.

Other research proposes a less powerful language, and thus can express less complex constraints. (Ahn and Sandhu, 1999, Kuhn, 1997, Nyanchama and Osborn, 1999) are examples of such proposals. Our solution is to use logic programming to define constraints. Together with the trace object, which can capture some of the past history of the system, our language is powerful enough to capture the constraints we described in the introduction, and others we encountered in the same hospital scenario. Other research such as (Jajodia et al., 1997, Becker and Sewell, 2004) also find that logical languages have the correct expressiveness to represent real life constraints.

Delegations in RBAC have been proposed by many researchers. (Barka and Sandhu, 2000a, Barka and Sandhu, 2000b) present a framework to classify different alternatives for role delegation models in RBAC. In their classification, our model of delegation is temporary (in the sense that a delegation can be revoked, but not in the sense that it has a predefined validity), monotonic (because the grantor does not loses the rights delegated), partial (because not all rights assigned to a role are delegated), self-acted (because the grantor issues the delegation action), multi-step (because with the appropriate rights delegations can be further delegated), multiple-delegation (because the same grantor can delegate the same right to more than one delegate), unilateral agreement (because the delegate does not need to agree to accept the delegation), with a version of cascading revocation (based on our definition of dependency).

In (Barka and Sandhu, 2000b), the RBDM0 model (Role-based Delegation Model Zero) is proposed as an extension of RBAC (more specifically RBAC0 model of the RBAC96 family) to include delegation. Being derived from RBAC0, it is restricted to flat roles and does not allow hierarchies. Moreover, RBDM0 is based on one step, total delegation (of all rights attached to a role); revocation is either by an expiration mechanism or by any member of the same role as the grantor. Some extensions are discussed: grant-dependent revocation, delegatable and non-delegatable permissions, and two-step delegation, as well as delegation in hierarchical roles. This work is further extended in (Zhang et al., 2003b) to a Permission Based Delegation Model (PBDM). The role-based delegation model of Zhang, et al. (Zhang et al., 2003a) sees delegation as both user and role centered - a delegation is issued by a User1 who holds Role1 and delegates his role to User2 who holds Role2. Moreover, the model

Box 3.

```
Users in Team <Teller> may perform Action <TellerActions>
                      on Targets in Scope <TellerTargets>
if <THIS USER NEVERDID <AuditorActions> TO THIS TARGET>
```

also allow for constraints on delegations, and grant dependent and grant independent revocations.

In (Bacon et al., 2002), delegation is achieved by the notion of an appointment. A user acting in the appointer role grants another user called the appointee a credential which may be used to activate one or more roles. Role activation takes places based on rules. Thus, it is possible for an appointer to give access to privileges that she does not possess. Still other related work on role hierarchy supporting restricted permission inheritance may be found in (Park et al., 2003). This approach is based on dividing a single role hierarchy into inter-related hierarchies for controlling permission inheritance behavior. Approaches for delegation in the context of trust management systems are discussed in (Tamassia et al., 2004, Yao, 2003). Another method of delegation that can constrain "the shape of delegation chains" through regular expressions is discussed in (Bandmann et al., 2002).

In another work on delegation (Ruan and Varadharajan, 2002), the authors present a graph based approach where a delegation from A to B is shown as a link between nodes A and B on a graph. The line joining A and B can be of three types depending upon whether the delegation of the right is positive, negative, or delegatable (i.e., the right can be further delegated). The authors give various rules for correctness and consistency of delegation, along with algorithms. This work, like ours, follows the idea that delegation is a relation between two users and a permission.

Generally speaking, delegation of roles, instead of rights, results in an "all or nothing" situation, i.e., either the grantor must delegate all the privileges of his or her role or none. In practice, a grantor may wish to delegate only certain privileges. A company CEO may wish to delegate her privilege to sign checks, approve expenses, and authorize capital expenditures, but not the privilege to hire new employees. This would be impossible if the entire role is being delegated, unless one artificially divides the CEO role into a subrole which holds the rights to sign checks, and so on, and a different subrole which holds the right to hire new employees.

Regarding revocation, our proposal for revocation also differs from the well known Griffiths-Wade revocation mechanism (Griffiths and Wade, 1976, Fagin, 1978), where the issue centers around multiple chains of delegation. The Griffiths-Wade revocation mechanism uses a time stamp to identify which delegations causally derive from others. An alternative revocation framework is given in (Hagstrom et al., 2001). That work takes into account negative permissions (i.e. denials), in addition to positive permissions. The revocations are based on three dimensions: resilience, propagation, and dominance. Since we do not allow negative permissions, the resilience aspect is not relevant to our approach. However, our approach addresses the latter two aspects. In particular, our algorithm for revocation performs global propagation and strong dominance.

Finally regarding our own work (Wainer et al., 2003, Wainer and Kumar, 2005, Wainer et al., 2007), the R+DRC can be considered a generalization of the WRBAC and DW-RBAC models described in those papers, with some simplifications. In WRBAC (Wainer et al., 2003) we developed the concept of object and constraints, but only within the scope of workflow systems, where the objects were instances of processes (or *cases* in workflow language). Regarding constraints, they were similar to the ones presented here, but the overriding mechanism was less clean - we considered that constraints were totally ordered by levels of severity, and roles would have rights to override constraints up to a level of severity. We find that having the right to override particular constraints, as proposed here, is simpler and more practical. In DW-RBAC we developed the concepts of delegation and revocation, although downgrade revocation was only mentioned there as a future work. In DW-RBAC we added the concept of conditions on delegations, one can delegate a delegation right to a user provided all delegates in the delegation chain satisfy the condition attached to the delegation. We found that such idea was impractical and would make the downgrade algorithm too complex.

DISCUSSION

This chapter has presented a extension of RBAC systems which includes a set of concepts:

- generic rights
- constraints
- overriding of constraints
- delegation
- two forms of revocation

We feel that R+DRC achieves a good balance between the organizational level non-discretionary requirements (from RBAC) with a discretionary component that allow users to delegate rights, to override constraints, and so on.

It is not an accident that we devised R+DRC when examining the access control requirements of an hospital. Most hospitals have in common that physicians have a lot of autonomy to deal with their patients; they can bring in new physicians, they can violate certain organizational rules, and so on, but only when dealing with *their* patients. On the other hand, hospitals will also like to enforce organizational rules, that set up limits to the physicians autonomy. Finally, hospitals also need standard RBAC concepts, for example any ultrasound operator can perform an ultrasound exam in any patient and cannot delegate that right.

This chapter has not dealt with administrative operations and permission - that is the permission to create roles and rights, and to create associations of permission and roles, and so on. More specific to R+DRC, the administrative operations would allow the creation of DRCR, of constraints, and so on.

Finally, in relation to the safety of the R+DRC, theorem 3 requires that all constraints regarding delegations do not make reference to traces and other delegations, which seems reasonable. But the requirement that the RBAC structure be static is clearly not acceptable. An important extension of this work is to deal with a dynamic RBAC structure and propose efficient algorithms to review the relevant delegations for constraint violation when the RBAC structure changes in any way. An added complexity is that the user may have overridden a constraint to issue a delegation, and in the RBAC structure, he may no longer have the right to override it, although he may still have the right to issue the delegation - thus potentially all delegations must be reviewed in case the RBAC structure changes.

This work, of course, is not exhaustive in listing extensions to RBAC that are useful or necessary to model real life situations. For example the role hierarchy concept of ANSI-RBAC can and should be added to this framework. From the hospital scenario above, we see that two other concepts would be useful - automatic delegations and groups of users. It would be useful to a physician to set up automatic delegations, so that once he admits a patient, the system would automatically issue (on his behalf) the delegations to his team (a group of users but not really a role). We have not added such concepts because it would lengthen the chapter too much, but mainly because we feel that they can be added to R+DRC without any concern for unexpected interactions.

Also, not all concepts presented in this chapter are needed to model a hospital domain. In the introduction, the third scenario was not hospital related exactly because chains of delegation are not common in hospital situation, and our ideas on revocation are only relevant on long chains of delegation. But clearly delegation is relevant in the hospital scenario, and we decided not to present a model in which chaining was not an option.

Finally there was some design choices in creating the R+DRC model that we would like to make explicit. The first choice was regarding the generic permissions. In a previous version of this chapter we had two different forms of permission, the standard one - a combination of operation and object, and one that was only the operation. Thus the permission to admit a patient was really just the

admit operation. This solution not only required to double all definitions to take into consideration the two forms of permissions, but was further apart from the current RBAC model. We opted then on using the *-class solution for both these reasons.

A second important choice was that we feel that delegations should be fully discretionary, that is, the delegation of a permission from a user to another user. As discussed in the related works section, that is not the most common direction used in RBAC delegations.

Finally the stronger design choice was the use of logic programming as the representation language for constraints, combined with the choices on the trace object. Logic programming is the most expressive language to express constraints - in fact it is as expressive as writing the constraints as code in any programming language. There are two consequences to this expressiveness - it may take too long to verify if a constraint is violated and (administrator) users may find the language less user-friendly. Regarding the first issue, (Becker and Sewell, 2004) uses Datalog, a restriction of logic programming in which recursive data structures such as lists, etc are not allowed, as representation language, since it has better worse-case complexity (Dantsin et al., 2001). Such restriction seems to us reasonable - all the examples of constraints we encountered in practice could be represented using Datalog. But to arbitrarily restrict the language in which to express the constraint seems to us similar to making design decisions like "since WHILE can create infinite loops, let's only allow Fortran/Pascal style FOR statements in our language". If constraints are so complex that they need to be expressed in powerful languages, there is little point in restricting the constraint language because of concerns regarding the computational complexity of evaluating the expressions. Regarding user-friendliness, until experimentation with real users is carried out, it is too soon to make judgments on whether users will accept writing the constraint using logic programming, or whether some syntactic sugaring would be needed.

On one hand, we defended that the most expressive language should be used to represent constrains, but on the other hand our choices for the trace object limits them. For example we cannot express constraint such as "the physician cannot schedule a new X-ray if the patient had an X-ray in less than a week" or constraints that refer to which role the user was playing when he performed a request. The trace object, which is where history data is recorded, does not contain a time argument, and thus, although it is possible to know that the patient had an X-ray, it is not possible to know when. Similarly, the trace object does not record the role the user is playing when performing an operation. This decision was derived from our experience in the target field in which temporal constraint and role information are not that important (for access control). But, or course, the format of the requests and the trace object can be easily changed if other information must be recorded and used in the constraints.

REFERENCES

Ahn, G.-J., & Sandhu, R. S. (1999). The RSL99 language for role-based separation of duty constraints. In *Proceedings of the 4th ACM Workshop on Role-Based Access Control*, (pp. 43–54).

ANS. (2004). *Role based access control*. ANSI/INCITS 359.

Bacon, J., Moody, K., & Yao, W. (2002). A model of OASIS role-based access control and its support for active security. *ACM Transactions on Information and System Security*, *5*(4), 492–540. doi:10.1145/581271.581276

Bandmann, O. L., Firozabadi, B. S., & Dam, M. (2002). Constrained delegation. In *IEEE Symposium on Security and Privacy*, (pp. 131–142).

Barka, E. S., & Sandhu, R. (2000a). *Framework for role-based delegation models*. In 16th Annual Computer Security Applications Conference. Retrieved from http://www.acsac.org/2000/abstracts/34.html

Barka, E. S., & Sandhu, R. (2000b). *A role-based delegation model and some extensions*. In 23rd National Information Systems Security Conference. Retrieved from http://csrc.nist.gov/nissc/2000/proceedings/papers/021.pdf

Becker, M. Y., & Sewell, P. (2004). Cassandra: Flexible trust management, applied to electronic health records. In *Proceedings of the 17th IEEE Computer Security Foundations Workshop (CSFW04)*, (pp. 139–154).

Belsis, P., Gritzalis, S., & Katsikas, S. K. (2006). Optimized multi-domain secure interoperation using soft constraints. In *Artificial Intelligence Applications and Innovations*, vol. 204, (pp. 78–85). IFIP International Federation for Information Processing, Springer.

Bertino, E. (2003). RBAC models – Concepts and trends. *Computers & Security*, *22*(6), 511–514. doi:10.1016/S0167-4048(03)00609-6

Brewer, D., & Nash, M. (1989). The Chinese Wall security policy. In *Proceedings of the 1989 IEEE Symposium on Security and Privacy*, (pp. 206–214).

Dantsin, E., Eiter, T., Gottlob, G., & Voronkov, A. (2001). Complexity and expressive power of logic programming. *ACM Computing Surveys*, *33*(3), 374–425. doi:10.1145/502807.502810

Fagin, R. (1978). On an authorization mechanism. *ACM Transactions on Database Systems*, *3*(3), 310–319. doi:10.1145/320263.320288

Ferraiolo, D. F., Cugini, J. A., & Kuhn, D. R. (1995). Role-based access control (RBAC): Features and motivations. In *Proceedings 11th Annual Computer Security Applications Conference*.

Ferraiolo, D. F., Sandhu, R., Gavrila, S., Kuhn, D. R., & Chandramouli, R. (2001). Proposed NIST standard for role-based access control. *ACM Transactions on Information and System Security*, *4*(3). doi:10.1145/501978.501980

Griffiths, P. P., & Wade, B. W. (1976). An authorization mechanism for a relational database system. [TODS]. *ACM Transactions on Database Systems*, *1*(3), 242–255. doi:10.1145/320473.320482

Hagstrom, A., Jajodia, S., Parisi-Presicce, F., & Wijesekera, D. (2001). Revocations: A classification. In *CSFW '01: Proceedings of the 14th IEEE Workshop on Computer Security Foundations*, (p. 44). IEEE Computer Society.

Jajodia, S., Samarati, P., & Subrahmanian, V. S. (1997). A logical language for expressing authorizations. In *SP '97: Proceedings of the 1997 IEEE Symposium on Security and Privacy*, (p. 31). Washington, DC: IEEE Computer Society.

Kuhn, D. R. (1997). Mutual exclusion of roles as a means of implementing separation of duty in role-based access control systems. In *Proc. of the Second ACM Workshop on Role-based Access Control*.

Naumenko, A., & Luostarinen, K. (2006). Access control policies in (semantic) service-oriented architecture. *Proceedings of the Semantics 2006 Conference, Austrian Computing Society (OCG)*, (pp. 28–30).

Nyanchama, M., & Osborn, S. (1999). The role graph model and conflict of interest. *ACM Transactions on Information and System Security*, *2*(1), 3–33. doi:10.1145/300830.300832

Park, J., Lee, Y., Lee, H., & Noh, B. (2003). A role-based delegation model using role hierarchy supporting restricted permission inheritance. In *Proceedings of the International Conference on Security and Management, SAM '03*, (pp. 294–302). CSREA Press.

Ruan, C., & Varadharajan, V. (2002). Resolving conflicts in authorization delegations. In *7th Australian Conference on Information Security and Privacy*, volume 2384 of *Lecture Notes in Computer Science*, (pp. 271–285). Springer.

Sandhu, R., Coyne, E., Feinstein, H., & Youman, C. (1996). Role-based access control models. *IEEE Computer*, *29*(2), 38–47. doi:10.1109/2.485845

Simon, R., & Zurko, M. E. (1997). Separation of duty in role-based environments. In *Proc. of the 10th Computer Security Foundations Workshop (CSFW '97).*

Tamassia, R., Yao, D., & Winsborough, W. H. (2004). Role-based cascaded delegation. In *Proceedings of the 9th ACM Symposium on Access Control Models and Technologies*, (pp. 146–155). ACM.

Wainer, J., & Kumar, A. (2005). A fine-grained, controllable, user-to-user delegation method in RBAC. In *SACMAT '05: Proceedings of the Tenth ACM Symposium on Access Control Models and Technologies*, (pp. 59–66). New York, NY: ACM Press.

Wainer, J., Kumar, A., & Barthelmess, P. (2003). WRBAC - A workflow security model incorporating controlled overriding of constraints. *International Journal of Cooperative Information Systems*, *12*(4), 455–486. doi:10.1142/S0218843003000814

Wainer, J., Kumar, A., & Barthelmess, P. (2007). DW-RBAC: A formal security model of delegation and revocation in workflow systems. *Information Systems*, *32*, 365–384. doi:10.1016/j.is.2005.11.008

Wielemaker, J., Schreiber, G., & Wielinga, B. (2003). Prolog-based infrastructure for RDF: Scalability and performance. In *The Semantic Web - Proceedings ISWC'03, LNCS 2870* (pp. 644–658). Springer.

Wikipedia. (2006). *Lattice (order)*. Retrieved from http://en.wikipedia.org/wiki/Lattice_%28order%29

XAC. (2005). *eXtensible access control markup language (XACML)*. OASIS, version 2.0. Retrieved from http://docs.oasis-open.org/xacml/2.0/access_control-xacml-2.0-core-spec-os.pdf

Yao, W. (2003). Fidelis: A policy-driven trust management framework. In *Trust Management, First International Conference, iTrust, Lecture Notes in Computer Science 2692* (pp. 301–317). Springer.

Zhang, L., Ahn, G.-J., & Chu, B.-T. (2003a). A rule-based framework for role-based delegation and revocation. *ACM Transactions on Information and System Security*, *6*(3), 404–441. doi:10.1145/937527.937530

Zhang, X., Oh, S., & Sandhu, R. (2003b). PBDM: A flexible delegation model in RBAC. In *SACMAT '03: Proceedings of the Eighth ACM Symposium on Access Control Models and Technologies*, (pp. 149–157). ACM Press.

ENDNOTES

1. If x=meet(a,b) then either x=a or x=b [Wikipedia, 2006]
2. Again we must point out that traces cannot substitute and do not play the role of audit trails entries.

Chapter 15
Who is Guarding the Doors: Review of Authentication in E-Banking

Manish Gupta
State University of New York at Buffalo, USA

Pradeep Kumar KB
SRM University, India

H. R. Rao
State University of New York at Buffalo, USA

ABSTRACT

Internet banking has become the preferred channel for conducting banking activities across globe and amongst all social demographics. Only a few other technological adoptions can compare with the recent trend of use of Internet banking facilities. Given the cost advantages and benefits it has to offer, it is widely touted as a win-win strategy for both banks and customers. However, with the growth in E-banking services and reliance on a public channel–Internet–to conduct business, it has been challenging for banks to ensure integrity and confidentiality of highly sensitive information. This chapter presents an overview of authentication issues and challenges in the online banking area with analysis on some of the better approaches. The chapter compares different authentication methods and discusses ensuing issues. The chapter will be invaluable for managers and professionals in understanding the current authentication landscape.

INTRODUCTION

The online banking is a service provided by many banks to their customers to access their account from anywhere with a computer and Internet connection with them (Online Banking, 2010). The users prefer this service as they can save time by accessing their bank transaction through the Internet from home or any place. With increase in fraud and identity theft, the banking sector is constantly on its toes and is struggling a lot with the authentication issues. The authentication of the user is of utmost importance as fraud should be avoided on this service and bank should also ensure that only authorized person accesses the account. Though the banks have taken keen interest

DOI: 10.4018/978-1-61350-498-7.ch015

in developing secure authentication mechanisms for the users, the fraud is still growing and the improvement in the authentication processes are much needed. At present banks follow different methods to secure their service.

Authentication is a process of verifying that the right person is provided access when requested (Authentication, 2007). Using the authentication we can ensure that the right person is provided with exact identity such as driving license, passport etc to show that he/she is the authorized person to hold those identity cards. There are different types of authentication methods available to authorize a person. The person once verified using those methods are permitted to access the particular resource where the authentication is required. The access control is a term where the authorized person is provided with authorization to access particular factor in the web resources which can be granted or declined as per the service provider (control, 2010).

The authentication can be provided through many methods and authentication is an essential factor in banking sectors to provide complete security to the online banking service. The banks are investing more in providing security to their online banking services, but securing the services without proper authentication will never provide a complete secure to online banking and so authentication plays an important role. For a really long time, passwords were the most common and a de-facto standard for authentication. With recent changes in the stakes and increasing value of underlying information, users are required to remember longer and more complex passwords while also requiring them to change them frequently. This has led to more insecurity and inconvenience (see for example, Bunnell et al., 1997; Furnell et al, 2000; Pond et al, 2000, Bishop and Klein, 1995); and alternative and more secure methods of authentication have made their way in the mainstream. There are different types of authentication methods and each had their unique qualities in providing authentication. There many different issues that are faced by the banking sectors in the online banking and are described in detail in this paper.

AUTHENTICATION: BACKGROUND

Authentication is a process where one has to prove his identity. The authentication can be provided in general using a user name and a password as a primary term and may be enhanced with other methods to strengthen the authentication process. Reliable customer authentication is imperative for financial institutions engaging in electronic banking (Gupta et al,, 2004). In today's online financial services environment, authentication is the bedrock of information security. Simple password authentication is the prevailing paradigm, but its weaknesses are all too evident in today's context (Gupta et al, 2008). The authorization is a term which is provided to identify whether the identified person is authorized to enjoy the service. This is verified based on the records that are maintained in the database and it should match the identification provided by the person. Authorization is like the boarding pass that is used to board airplanes. The access control is another term where the authorized user is provided with the limit in the accessing of the service. The service provider has the full rights to grant or denied the access level to the user. In general, means controlling the full access of the user (control, 2010). There are many different methods are used to provide a secure authentication.

Need for Authentication

The delivery of the services through the publicly accessible infrastructure (i.e Internet) has increased to a great level. The users are expecting the e-commerce business methodologies and the banking sectors follow by entering into the online banking to satisfy their users. The transactions in the e-commerce are done using the Internet as medium and the provider cannot see the user as he/she may be from anywhere in the world. So the service providers should ensure that only the right person is accessing the right account. To identify that, the authentication of the users is essential to perform the transactions through Internet as it's an open network and anyone can access it. The security is very much essential as the user needs the good security for the services that are provided by the providers (Liang and Wang, 2005).

The authentication is provided by the concept of cryptography using the encryption and decryption technique. The basic authentication can be provided by the user's password. The authentication can be created only when the user submits any authentication code like passwords when requested (Liang and Wang, 2005).

The corporate world has now started to use the web technology to improve their operations and they use the Internet as the medium. The corporations have also started to share confidential information to their users through the Internet. Some organizations are even operating their servers from one place to another using the remote accessing technique and which needs a high secure authentication so that the data can be transferred within the certain authenticated groups. Most of the organizations use the intranet and hence they need to secure their web server and only the authorized persons can access the server and authentication method provides a good security (Byron, 2003). "In an April 2002 report, the FBI/Computer Security Institute (CSI) noted that ninety percent of respondents (primarily large corporations and government agencies) detected computer security breaches within the last twelve months. As in previous years, the most serious financial losses occurred through theft of proprietary information and financial fraud. (Byron, 2003)".

Many organizations struggled due to the intruders in the Internet and those unauthorized persons started to collect the confidential information and the level of the fraud increased. To overcome this issue the authentication process is created and using this process the right person alone is allowed to access the right resources. A secret code (passwords, PINS etc) are provided to the users and so they can access only using those access codes and so that the organization can have only the authorized persons accessing their intranet and this reduces the fraud to a higher extent (Byron, 2003).

Types of Authentication

The authentication is provided differently by different web servers and all servers have their own authentication methodology and properties for authentication. The authentication in general can be classified into eight types and are as follows,

- Basic authentication
- Client certificates and Server certificates
- Digest authentication
- Integrated authentication
- Customized authentication with HTTP module
- Pass through authentication
- Windows integrated authentication
- URL authentication

Basic Authentication

The basic authentication type means where the user name and passwords are requested and when entered data are sent in a format with the full document as normal text and only the user name and password are encoded. The passwords are encoded and this provides the basic authentication to the user's data. It's the user's responsibility to remember the password and also its properties like case sensitive etc. The user will enter the data to the application when requested by the servers and the entered data are stored in the server. Later when the user access the application, the data that are requested by the server and when the user enters the data are being matched by the saved data and finally the user is allowed to access the application only if the data matches the stored data in the server. This is the method followed in the basic authentication technique (Magalhaes, 2001).

Client Certificates and Server Certificates

- **Client certificates:** The authentication in this type is performed such that the server requests the client to provide the client certificate before the client request to connect to the service provider. After the client sends the certificate the server checks with the earlier stored details about the client and matches it. If the details provided matched, then it request the service provider the details about the client and it provides the certificates that are supplies earlier from the service provider to the client. After the client accepts that certificate and ensures that he is getting the response from the correct service provider and not a fraud, he/she provides the details and then after matching with those details it allows the client to connect the service provider (Magalhaes, 2001).
- **Server certificates:** The service providers have to register their server certificates with the ISA servers when they obtain the server. The client when trying to connect to the service provider will be provided with the certificate that will be used for verifying the client. The client accepts the certificate means the ISA server will link the client and the service provider. Thus authentication is made and both the client and server can ensure that they are working with the authorized persons (Magalhaes, 2001).

Digest Authentication

This is advanced version of the basic authentication where the user's data is sent in the encrypted form using the hashing methodology whereas in the basic methodology the data is transferred unencrypted. In the digest authentication it provides more security as the encryption and also hash (message digest) makes the data more secure so that intruders cannot decipher the text that are transferred in the Internet. The hash strings added will easily locate the place, computer's details, username and domain. More security is available than to the basic authentication methodology (Magalhaes, 2001).

Integrated Authentication

This is another type where we are able to get more security as the exchange of the username and passwords among the service provider and the client is not done and so the intruders can't trace any details. This scenario is very similar to federation identity management where Identity and access management systems are used by online service providers (SP) to authenticate and authorize users to services based on access policies (Gupta and Sharman, 2008). The verification in this authentication type is provided in such a way that use of the inbuilt challenge/response authentication protocol. The IE 5.5 (and above) that comes with Microsoft Windows operating system has the inbuilt authentication protocol which verifies the certificate and provides a reliable authentication to transaction (Magalhaes, 2001).

Customized Authentication with HTTP Module

The authentication is provided faster than the web method in this type. The ASP.NET will create series of events and all the events perform their operation till the verification is made and this will be complete in a quick manner than that of the web method. The data can be edited even after the request is on progress and this helps the users more easier and convenient way to get accessed (Liu, 2004).

Pass through Authentication

This type of authentication occurs when the ISA server passes the clients information to the server and this is provided for both the incoming and outgoing web requests. The following are the steps involved in pass-through authentication:

1. The request to the server from the client is made through the web server
2. The web server request for the authentication code and type the server supports.
3. The client provides the required authentication code and it will be directed by the web servers to the appropriate service providers.
4. The response from the service providers will be taken into account and then the client is made to communicate with the service providers directly.

Windows Integrated Authentication

This is another type which is similar to basic authentication but also an advanced version of it. In this type the authentication is provided based on the hashing algorithm. This type is used in most organizations where the intranet is used and they want to control the access. This authentication helps in providing good access control inside the organization (Liu, 2004).

URL Authentication

This is another type of authentication such that it based on the verification done using the ASP.NET. Here when the client provides the authentication code the server checks for the occurrence of the username in the database. It will scroll top-down the database till it obtain the username in the database and then it checks for authentication code and then provide access to the client (Liu, 2004).

Methods of Authentication

The authentication can be provided by means of three different methods based on the authentication technique and the human nature and are as follows,

- What you have: The physical cards that the user has and use it to prove his identity. This includes the tokens, smart cards, pass cards etc.
- What you know: These are known to the user only. This can be obtained only by forcing the user and only if the user wishes can be provided. This includes passwords, PIN, pass phrases etc.
- What you are: This can be obtained only from the user's physical appearance and characteristics. This term differs from all the individuals. This includes all Biometrics, DNA etc (Kay, 2005).

Authentication Techniques

The authentication which is provided to obtain more security for accessing certain services through Internet had follows various methods of authentication technique. Each authentication technique had its own unique properties and each provide authentication in different forms. There are many different techniques in the authentication and some techniques are as follows,

- Usernames and passwords
- PIN
- Identifiable picture
- One-time password
- Swipe card
- Token
- Biometric
- Keyboard rhythm
- OTP Scratch card

Usernames and Passwords

The usernames and passwords authentication technique is the first and old technique where the user will be provided with unique username and a secret phrase known as the passwords. These data's are stored in the database and are verified all times when the user enters the information. The password can be numeric, alphabetic, symbols etc based on the service provider's terms and conditions. This is the basic, common technique but a weak technique to provide authentication. The user provides the username and then the existence of the username in database is to be verified and if available the password is requested from the user. The user then enters the secret phrase and then after checking with the database it allows the user to access and hence the authentication is provided. This technique is weak because the possibility to remember the password is low and since the passwords are to be typed and the possibility of others to identify the passwords is easy hence the confidential level of this authentication technique is very low (Thigpen, 2005).

PIN (Personal Identification Number)

The PIN is another technique which is similar to that of passwords but contains only numeric terms and it should be kept in secret. The PIN is a four digit number and it's used mostly in the Automated Teller Machine (ATM) to identify the personal identification. If the user enters the wrong PIN a certain number of times, his/her account gets locked automatically. The number of combinations for guessing the PIN number are high so it is not easy to guess and so a safer method and its used as the authentication method in ATMs at present (Thigpen, 2005).

Identifiable Picture

This is another technique of authentication which is provided by means of using the picture. This system is used as a subsidiary term for entering passwords and personal identification numbers. The user is provided with a picture when he registers his account and so that the user can easily remember the picture. When the user needs to access the account many pictures are provided as choice and the user has to select the appropriate picture and after that access will be granted only if the correct picture is identified (Thigpen, 2005). This technique has matured a lot in today's technological environment (see for example: Renaud, 2009; Komanduri and Hutchings, 2008; Wiedenbeck et al., 2005; Chiasson et al., 2008).

One-Time Password

This is the advanced form of the passwords that overcome the vulnerable that are in the basic authentication techniques. The user enters the password once and they are associated with many hashing techniques and the data are then exchanged with the server and will be stored. So when user tries to connect multiple times the hash technique helps to identify the password and so it will be more secure and the user can avoid changing the passwords many times (Thigpen, 2005).

Swipe Card

The swipe card is a card that is provided with a magnetic strip and the data's are encrypted in it. The best example for the swipe cards are credit and debit cards. The user can swipe this card and transactions are made based on the information provided in the magnetic strips. The possibility of fraud is more in this card as the card can be theft and duplication of the magnetic strip can be made this result in misuse of the card (Thigpen, 2005).

Token

The token is the device that is provided to the user and the user will physically submit the device which provides authentication. The tokens can be classified into three types:

- **USB Token:** The device can be connected to the system directly and the software is not needed. The device requests for a password upon connecting to the machine which gives it a double authentication (Authentication Techniques, 2006).
- **Smart card:** This is another device, which is of similar form factor as of a credit card and contains small microprocessor. The user inserts the card into the appropriate reader and the inbuilt identity provides the basic information about the user and after checking the details the user provides a password to authenticate (Authentication Techniques, 2006).
- **Password Generating Token:** This is a token where the token itself generates a new password after every use of the old password. The token generates the OTP (One Time Password) or the unique pass code each time and ensures that the password is not used consequently. The generated password is provided by the token and the user will enter his existing username and password and then enters the newly generated OTP. This provides a higher degree of strength to the authentication process. This technique is more secure than other token (Authentication Techniques, 2006).

Biometric

Another attractive method of authorization or identification is using the biometrics. "Biometrics are automated methods of identifying a person or verifying the identity of a person based on a physiological or behavioral characteristic (Podio and Dunn, 2001)". A *biometric* typically refers to a feature or characteristic measured from a biological body. Biometric authentication systems use these features to distinguish users and for establishing an identity. Some of the most common biometrics used include fingerprints, retina, iris, voice, face, hand, etc (Jain et al., 1998).

The biometrics will be compared between the enrolled data and the currently captured data. The identification mode of this technique will search for the captured data with the central database and finally the exact data of the user that has been enrolled earlier will be matched and provided using the "One-to-Many Matching" technique. The verification mode is that when the user provides the data the captured data is identified using the "One-to-One technique" matching. There are many different forms of biometric test forms available like fingerprint recognition, face recognition, voice recognition, retinal scan, signatures, Iris feature etc.

- **Fingerprint recognition:** This is an interesting method of authentication where the user's finger print is recognized. Each and every individual had their unique finger print and this technique had followed earlier by the law and order of the government. At present they are stored using the finger print reader machines and stored electronically and used when ever needed. Each finger had different form of prints and even the difference can be found among twins and so the individual can be identified easily. This is a good replacing technique than entering the passwords (Podio and Dunn, 2001).
- **Face recognition:** In this technique the facial image of the user is identified and accordingly the identification is obtained. The user's face has been recognized using some inexpensive cameras where the image of the face in the visible spectrum is captured. It can be done using the IR (Infrared) of facial heat image. Even though the user changed his appearance the user's hair properties and facial expressions will never change and this provides

the proper identification of the user (Podio and Dunn, 2001).

- **Voice recognition:** This is another technique to authenticate such that the user's voice is used as the identification code for verification. The user had to register the voice to the service providers while the authentication is initially made and when ever needed the user has to speak (ex: the user can say his/her name) and the voice will be matched with the voice in the database. The requirement for this system to execute is need of the system and voice recognizing software. The software calculates the user's vocal track and the characteristics that are present in the user's voice and finally it will be matched when the user used them finally. The main drawback of this process is that if the user affected with any throat related problem, the system cannot able to recognize the voice and the access cannot be provided until the reset in done.
- **Iris Recognition:** This feature provides identification using the featured iris of the eyes which is a colored portion that covers the pupil in the eyes. Each and every individual had their unique difference in their iris and this is recognized by the system and can able to identify the exact match for that iris. Both the verification and identification is done easily using this method and the increase in this type of technique is increasing at recent trends. Nowadays many users are using contact lens and eyeglasses and at present the teat of the iris can be done even with that. This system also provides good identification of the users.
- **Hand and Finger Geometry:** This is an old method for more than about twenty years and in this method the user's hand characteristics are analyzed. The characteristic includes the length, width, surface, thickness etc. The distance among the fingers are calculated and used to later identification. This system is tough to handle and need more space when compared to other biometrics technique and so the usage of this technique is reducing (Podio and Dunn, 2001).

Digital Signature

This is a process where the user's signature is used to identify the person. The user can enroll the signature digitally and the pressure, angle and modes used to create that signature is calculated and stored. So when the user need to authenticate using the signature the characters of the signature is analyzed with the enrolled one and matched and finally the access will be provided if it matched with the existed signature.

Keyboard Rhythm

This technique is followed in some workplaces where the user's usage of the keyboard is calculated and accordingly the authentication is provided to the user. The pressure the user uses the keyboard, the time needed to strike between the keys used by the user is calculated and accordingly the authentication is provided. This is also a different technique that is used in some workplace to reduce unauthorized access of the system (Thigpen, 2005).

OTP Scratch Card

The scratch card is a low expensive card that contains the numbers arranged in rows and column format like grids. The number of the grids in the card is recognized. The user when use this card will enter the username and password first time and then will enter the randomly generated passwords that are created by the scratch card with the numbers in it. This is easy for the user to carry as he can place it in wallets and the drawback of this method is that the physical misuse and theft of the product (Authentication Techniques, 2006).

ROLE OF AUTHENTICATION IN ONLINE BANKING

Nowadays the usage of the Internet banking has increased a lot and the possibility of fraud also increased. Since many users started to use the online banking and also the intruders increased in order to hack the users details and to steal the money from others account without their knowledge. Because of this problem many users stopped using these services from the banks. It's bank's responsibility to provide users the account security and so banks prefer to authenticate the user so that they can ensure that only the right person is using the appropriate account. Attacking the banks server had started to occur often and the banks are pushed to authenticate their users (CEPIS, 2007).

Some banks provide authentication based on the 'Two Factor Authentication' which has two basic authentication factors. The security is more essential factor in banks and they depend only on the two factor authentication and are as follows,

- What the user knows (PIN, Password, Pass phrases)
- What the user has (Smart cards, Tokens, etc)

Most of the banks use only the username and password or pass phrase as their authentication factor over the Internet. The users are requested to provide the PIN/Passwords/Passphrase when they try to access the online banking. These are used as the basic authentication term in online banking. If the security provided to be more means then the bank will provide with extra hardware security devices like tokens along with the password provided to the users. The authentication factor provided are implemented in the following ways and are as follows,

- One-time password approach
- Certificate based approach
- Time based password approach

Certificate Based Approach

In this approach a certificate is provided along with the password to the user. The certificates are software token that is installed inside a USB or any Smart card device and it should be provided by the user. The bank server will execute the card along with the passwords provided and will be used for the authentication purpose.

One-Time Password Approach

This is another method where the passwords are provided to the user by the server and can be used only once for a transaction and after single use, it expires. The user will have to request new password for next attempt to login. The passwords that are created temporarily are termed as TAN's (Transaction Authorization Numbers). There are three types of TAN's and are iTAN (TAN's distributed in lists), eTAN (TAN's created using special hardware devices) and mTAN (Tan created through mobile phones). The operation of the TAN's are represented in Figure 1. The iTAN process is also described in the figure which is done using the lists for each TAN request. The same approach is followed in the eTAN and mTAN where the SMS messages and other media devices are used as the medium of transaction.

Time-Based Password Approach

This is another method which is more secure than the one-time password approach. The operation is similar to that of one-time password approach but there will be certain time limit provided to it such that after the password is generated it will be there only for certain time after that it will expire. This is created with a design that the hackers cannot have sufficient time to calculate the codes and so it will be more secure (CEPIS, 2007).

Figure 1. Authentication–TAN approach (CEPIS, 2007)

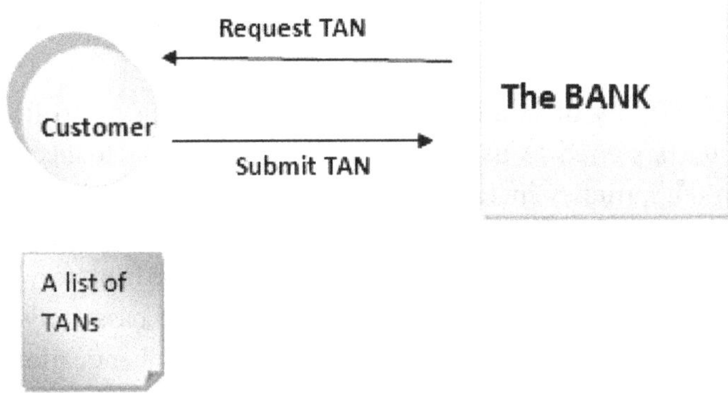

INTERNET BANKING – ISSUES

In recent trends, the use of the Internet in the organization had increased to higher extend and many organizations follow Internet as their major business medium. Similarly the banking sector also introduces the Internet banking to their customers as an easier method to perform their transactions. Since most of the public are involved in the Internet the usage of the information of the user are more important and this becomes the major issue in the Internet banking (OCC, 1999). Some of the issues in the Internet banking are, Authentication, Trust, Non-repudiation, Privacy, and Availability.

- **Authentication:** Another issue in the Internet banking is the Authentication. The banking operations performed through Internet must be well authenticated with the provider and the user. The bank should provide more care for authenticate their users. In general, the bank uses the encryption and decryption technique to transfer the authentication code where the public key and private key are used for the authentication. Later on the passwords used as codes are transferred and now they are using biometric identification codes are used as latest form of authentication codes.
- **Trust:** This is another issue in Internet banking. Since the transactions are made through the Internet, authentication service provider for Internet i.e, Certificate Authority is essential and it's a trust oriented part that the bank relies on the third party for their security. The certificate authorities provide the "Digital Signatures" which helps in providing good security with good mix of the preventive, detective and corrective controls to provide authentications.
- **Non-repudiation:** The participation by both the sender and receiver in transferring their authentication codes are undeniable proof and this is one of the issues in the Internet banking.
- **Privacy:** This is consumer issue in the Internet banking. Consumers in the Internet banking should be provided more security and their privacy in more essential such that the customer should rely on their security services.
- **Availability:** This is a major part that user expects from the service providers. The service should be provided all times and no inconvenient should be faced by the customers from the bank's service. The service should be provided to the customers twenty hours a day and seven days a week.

The customer should be comfortable with all sort of service provided by the Internet banking service providers.

Authentication Issues in Online Banking

The banking is a sector where many users are investing their money and they act as a member of the bank. The banks had now provided the online banking facility and so transferring the confidential information through Internet to their users is essential. The bank must be more particular about the security as attacks to their servers will be more as the hackers will try to access the information and so the banks should take necessary precautions to well secure their servers. The bank should ensure that before providing access to this service to a user the authentication of the user should be done. The user should be requested to submit the proof about his identity and so that in future can identify who is trying to authenticate their server. If the user provides the provided passwords correctly then bank can ensure that right person is accessing and who is accessing by getting answers to the questions that are provided to the user during the initial authentication (Weigold, 2006). The attack to the website may be done in many forms and some of them are provided below,

- Online Channel Breaking Attacks
- Offline Credential Stealing Attack
- Software based Attacks
- Phishing
- Data Breaches

Online Channel Breaking Attacks

This is a system where the intruders attack the online banking sector of the banks. The intruders will never aim to obtain the user's credential instead they try to hijack the information that was transferred between the user and the bank. The intruders will watch the transactions and also will intercept the messages from the client and the server and will record the authentication codes used by the user. The intruders will make use of those codes and may access that account as an authenticated user. This is one way of attacking the authentication of the online banking. Most of the intruders are using this methodology to attack the bank servers (Weigold, 2006).

Offline Credential Stealing Attacks

This is another type of attack that is faced by the banking sector. This attack is performed when the system is placed in offline mode. The system is hacked by means of miscellaneous software that contains viruses and Trojan horses. This viruses and Trojan horses will get rooted into the system and will be used to store the confidential data is processed by the system and is then provided to the attackers. The hackers install software through un-trusted sites and downloads from the Internet. Sometimes the users are forced to provide the data by means of phishing. The authentication codes are provided by the users to the intruders by these phishing websites. Phishing is a method where the hackers will create a fake website of some top financial organization and the users will provide the details and it will be easy for the hackers to create fraud (Weigold, 2006).

Software Based Attacks

Usually, banks use software based protection for their servers. Banks use software protection rather than the hardware-based protection because former is cheaper (Yang, 1997). There are many drawbacks in this system and are as follows,

1. The encryption algorithm used to encrypt the data in these software based protection system can be attacked by the attackers.
2. Direct approach of trying the combination of the possible occurrence of the PIN can be calculated by the attackers.

3. Hacking the bank's server and accessing all the confidential data.
4. Hacking client's personal computers through miscellaneous programs.

Phishing

This is a process where the fake websites like bank's website, financial institution website or government websites are created to and fraud users into revealing confidential data such as passwords and access codes; and then to access their accounts to indulge in fraud. There are many organizations that are affected by phishing websites created by the attackers. Many e-commerce organizations are still trying to reduce the effect of these phishing websites attacks. "There are several different types of phishing attacks including misleading e-mails, man-in-the-middle, URL obfuscation, page content overriding, malware phishing, key loggers and screen grabbers, session hijackers, web Trojans, IP address manipulation, and system reconfiguration attacks (Williamson, 2006)". While organizations try to track and bring down these fake websites creation, the perpetrators continuously invent new ways to phish. In year 2005 alone, the number of phishing sites almost quadrupled (Williamson, 2006).

Data Breaches

This is another type of attack that is used to obtain users confidential information. The Internet is used as the medium and the users are provided with names of famous organizations to provide different offers and terms. The users are lured into entering Credit Card details, Social Security Number, Date of Birth etc that is stolen by the attackers. The users tend to provide the information as the links seem to be coming from banks, high level financial organizations, big organizations etc. After the trap is successful, the stolen information is used to launch fraudulent activities (Williamson, 2006).

FRAUD PREVENTION STRATEGIES

The fraud in the Internet banking has become common and prevention has become more essential and banks have to take precautionary steps to perform the process without fraud (BITS, 2003). There are three different stages where strategies are followed to prevent the fraud and some are provided below,

- Application process
- Application Authentication
- After application approval

Application Process

- **Limit timeframes:** This process is implemented when the application is filled up by the customers and it is provided with time limit so that it will be closed before the provided time and application should be finished by the user within the provided time.
- **Provide a secure channel:** This is provided to the user immediately so that the user can verify provided details and also check for any intruders or intercept of the data.
- **Create an audit trail:** This feature will automatically record the user's IP address and time for the further references.

Application Authentication

- **Use a real time process:** This is created to verify whether the provided details by the user are accurate. It also verifies the details provided by the user during applying through online and the user should register to the concern authority before applying.
- **Ask "in wallet" Question:** The wallet questions are the one of the confidential question where the user can provide like social security number, driving license number and date of birth etc where the

intruders can hack these wallets but don't know whether they are applying for a new application or an existing application.

- **Use "Out-of wallet" Questions:** This is automatically generated questions asked to the user about the exact value of the monthly chargers to be paid. So that the intruders can be avoided if wrong details are provided.
- **Use of "Out-of credit" questions:** These are about the personal questions about the user apart from the credit of the account. This also secures the server from the intruders.
- **Provide standard field variation:** This is to ensure that whether the user is using the application correctly.
- **Verify application data:** The user details are verified with the central database and the information provided is correct and to ensure the user also that he/ she enters only the correct information.

After Application Approval

- **Wait for funding prior to opening an account:** The waiting time is provided by the financial institutions for the user to enter the PIN numbers in ATM centers so that criminals cannot able to identify the code within the provided time.
- **Require that a signed application on file:** The user's signature is verified with the signature recorded in the database and so that unauthorized users cannot misuse the user's checks or any other transactions.
- **Require customer authentication to be completed in the branch or through customer call centers:** The information about the user are to be recorded earlier in the particular branch where the user operates the accounts. If not the information should be registered either through the customer call centers.
- **Implementing Manual fraud screening on initial deposits:** The image that is captured when the check is dropped and the machine also captures the image of the person who deposits the initial amount and it can be helpful to avoid unauthorized access to the account.

SYSTEMS AND SOLUTIONS TO ATTACKS IN ONLINE BANKING

The online banking should be provided with high security so that the attacks in the authentication of the Internet banking can be stopped and the server can be secured (Yang, 1997). The solutions are provided by means of the two terms namely,

- Software based security system
- Hardware based security system

Software Based Security System

In this system the authentication is based on the software programs. Encryption is the main method used to encrypt the code. Encryption is a technique where the data is jumbled and can be retrieved using some shared secret. This process needs both the public key and private key. In one method only one key is used by both the client and server where both for encryption and decryption the key is used (symmetric encryption). The second method is that using a private key and public key (asymmetric encryption). The public key should be made available to both the client and the server. The data can be transferred using the public key in the public domain but retrieved by means of the private key. This method is more secure than that of first encryption method. The encryption methodology can be classified in to four classifications such as Digital signatures, Secure Electronic Transactions, Pretty good privacy and Kerberos (Yang, 1997).

- **Digital Signatures:** A digital signature is used to identify the sender by the receiver using the signature placed along with the messages. The private key is used to encrypt and the public key to decrypt. The user's signature is used as the private key in this case. Only the user can create the signature and it is difficult to copy the signature.
- **Secure Electronic Transactions (SET):** This is another method based on the software to create a secure card which can be used to do the payments in Internet. These cards are provided with the world wide accessible terms such as Visa Master Card, IBM, Microsoft, Netscape communication corp, Verisign. The online bank transaction can be done securely using the SET technology. RSA public key encryption technique is used in this method. The digital signature is created using a unique public and private key. A digital signature is provided with the data and it encrypted using some hashing techniques. The encrypted data will be sent along with the user's private key which helps to provide users identity to the bank so that the receiver can get the details of the sender. The receiver uses the hashing algorithm to generate the messages and should match the old one.
- **Pretty Good Privacy (PGP):** This is another method where its functions are based on the combination of the public key algorithm and private key algorithm. No transmitted channel medium is required for this technique. The received public key can be decrypted with the user's private key and so the identity of the sender can be verified. This method also provides more security for the data transfer.
- **Kerberos:** This is a private key encryption technique. It creates an encrypted data packet called ticket and it will be transferred through Internet. The tickets are used to identify the user and the tickets can be transferred only between Kerberos servers. The private keys are shared between the two systems.

Hardware Based System

It is another more secure form of exchanging data over Internet and comprises physical devices which are expensive and difficult to handle. There are many hardware based systems and most common is the Smart card and MeChip (Yang, 1997).

- **Smart Card:** This card is mechanically designed with the programs and chips are inbuilt and it can store data related to the user's personal identification terms. The user can use this card when needed to retrieve the information. The virus can affect this card but this will be used mostly in outdoors and the Internet usage cannot be made in this card.
- **MeChip:** This is a device that is connected using the USB port of a personal computer. The information that needed to be sent in a secure manner is added to the device, which transfers the data and checks the status of the transmission.

Comparison of Authentication Techniques

In this section, we present a comparison of different authentication methods that are most commonly used. Table 1 presents a summary of the comparison based on handling (support and maintenance from user standpoint), cost (to the company) and security of the solution. As we can see, tokens and OTP scratch pads are the most difficult methods for support and for handling (more from a convenience standpoint). Biometrics has the most costs in terms of implementing a solution and on-going maintenance. However, there are several methods that score "*High*" on security or

Table 1. Comparison of authentication techniques

S.NO	TECHNIQUE	HANDLING	COST	SECURITY
1	Username & Passwords	Easy	Nil	Average
2	PIN	Easy	Nil	Average
3	Identifiable picture	Easy	Nil	Moderate
4	One-Time Password	Moderate	Nil	Moderate
5	Swipe Card	Easy	Low	Average
6	Tokens	Hard	Medium	High
7	Biometric	Easy	High	Very High
8	Keyboard Rhythm	Moderate	Medium	Moderate
9	OTP Scratch Card	Hard	Medium	Moderate
10	Digital Signatures	Easy	Medium	High
11	Secure Electronic Transactions (SET)	Easy	Medium	High
12	Pretty Good Privacy (PGP)	Moderate	Medium	High
13	Kerberos	Easy	Medium	High
14	Smart Cards	Easy	Low	Moderate
15	MeChip	Moderate	Medium	Moderate

on authentication strength including biometrics, which has the highest score.

CONCLUSION

The security of the bank operations is essential, more so when the intensity and frequency of attacks is higher than ever. So, the need of authentication in a secure manner is more essential than ever. There are many different authentication techniques available and each has its own unique properties in providing authentication. The online banking which is now used worldwide has more useful functions, but the growth in fraud and identity theft shows failure in securing the information. Authentication has emerged to be the one of the most vital pieces of strengthening security. The chapter presented several authentication methods and the solutions to some potential types of attacks. We discussed our survey of different authentication issues, some of the most important factors in selecting an authentication mechanism. The discussions and conclusions in the chapter can be used by managers and security professionals in understanding different approaches to authentication and will aid them during the decision making process.

REFERENCES

Bankers' Ideanet. (2006, January 10). *Authentication techniques*. Retrieved April 2010, from http://www.sheshunoff.com/ideanet/index.php?itemid=204&catid=4

Bishop, M., & Klein, D. V. (1995). Improving system security via proactive password checking. *Computers & Security*, *14*(3), 233–249. doi:10.1016/0167-4048(95)00003-Q

BITS. (2003, April). *Fraud prevention strategies for internet banking*. Retrieved April 2010, from http://www.bits.org/downloads/Publications%20Page/mointernetwp.pdf

Bunnell, J., Podd, J., Henderson, R., Napier, R., & Kennedy-Moffat, J. (1997). Cognitive, associative, and conventional passwords: Recall and guessing rates. *Computers & Security*, *16*(7), 645–657. doi:10.1016/S0167-4048(97)00008-4

Byron, B. (2003, August 1). *The need for authentication and authorization*. Retrieved April 2010, from http://www.redbooks.ibm.com/abstracts/tips0266.html?Open

CEPIS. (2007, October 27). *Authentication approach for online banking*. Retrieved April 2010, from http://www.cepis.org/files/cepis/20090901104203_Authentication%20approaches%20for%20.pdf

Chiasson, S., van Oorschot, P. C., & Biddle, R. (2008). Graphical password authentication using cued click points. *Lecture Notes in Computer Science*, *4734*, 359–374. doi:10.1007/978-3-540-74835-9_24

French Government. (2010). *Authentication, authorization and access control*. Retrieved April 2010, from http://eregie.premier-ministre.gouv.fr/manual/howto/auth.html

Furnell, S. M., Dowland, P. S., Illingworth, H. M., & Reynolds, P. L. (2000). Authentication and supervision: A survey of user attitudes. *Computers & Security*, *19*(6), 529–539. doi:10.1016/S0167-4048(00)06027-2

Gupta, M., Lee, J., & Rao, H. R. (2008). Implications of FFIEC guidance on authentication in electronic banking. In Gupta, J. N. D., & Sharma, S. (Eds.), *Handbook of research on information security and assurance*. Hershey, PA: IGI Publishing. doi:10.4018/978-1-59904-855-0.ch022

Gupta, M., Rao, H. R., & Upadhyaya, S. (2004). Electronic banking and information assurance issues: survey and synthesis. *Journal of Organizational and End User Computing*, *16*(3), 1–21. doi:10.4018/joeuc.2004070101

Gupta, M., & Sharman, R. (2008). Dimensions of identity federation: A case study in financial services. [Dynamic Publishers.]. *Journal of Information Assurance and Security*, *3*(4), 244–256.

Investor Glossary. (2010). *Online banking*. Retrieved April 2010, from http://www.investorglossary.com/online-banking.htm

Jain, A., Bolle, R., & Pankanti, S. (Eds.). (1998). *Biometrics: Personal identification in networked society*. Dordrecht, The Netherlands: Kluwer.

Kay, R. (2005, April 04). *Biometric authentication*. Retrieved April 2010, from http://www.computerworld.com/s/article/100772/Biometric_Authentication?taxonomyId=17&pageNumber=1

Komanduri, S., & Hutchings, D. (2008). Order and entropy in picture passwords. Proceedings of Graphics Interface 2008

Liang, W., & Wang, W. (2005). *A quatitative study of authentication & QoS in wirless IP network*. Retrieved April 2010, from http://www.ece.ncsu.edu/netwis/papers/05LW-INFOCOM

Liu, S. (2004, February). *Authentication in ASP.NET web servers*. Retrieved April 2010, from http://progtutorials.tripod.com/Authen.htm

Magalhaes, R. M. (2001, November 19). *Understanding ISA's different types of authentication*. Retrieved April 2010, from http://www.isaserver.org/tutorials/Understanding_ISAs_different_Authentication_types.html

OCC. (1999, October). *Internet banking*. Retrieved April 2010, from http://www.occ.treas.gov/handbook/intbank.pdf

Podio, F. L., & Dunn, J. S. (2001). *Biometric authentication technology*. Retrieved April 2010, from http://www.itl.nist.gov/div893/biometrics/Biometricsfromthemovies.pdf

Pond, R., Podd, J., Bunnell, J., & Henderson, R. (2000). Word association computer passwords: The effect of formulation techniques on recall and guessing rates. *Computers & Security, 19*(7), 645–656. doi:10.1016/S0167-4048(00)07023-1

Renaud, K. (2009). On user involvement in production of images used in visual authentication. *Journal of Visual Languages and Computing, 20*(1), 1–15. doi:10.1016/j.jvlc.2008.04.001

SearchSecurity. (2007, June 4). *Authentication.* Retrieved April 2010, from http://searchsecurity.techtarget.com/sDefinition/0,sid14_gci211621,00.html

Thigpen, S. (2005, July 17). *Banking authentication methods.* Retrieved April 2010, from http://www.infosecwriters.com/text_resources/pdf/Authentication_Methods_For_Banking.pdf

Weigold, T. K. (2006, March/April). *Secure internet banking and authentication.* Retrieved April 2010, from http://www.zurich.ibm.com/pdf/csc/SecureInternetBankingAuthentication.pdf

Wiedenbeck, S., Waters, J., Birget, J., Brodskiy, A., & Memon, N. (2005). PassPoints: Design and longitudinal evaluation of a graphical password system. *International Journal of Human-Computer Studies, 63*(1-2), 102–127. doi:10.1016/j.ijhcs.2005.04.010

Williamson, G. D. (2006). Enhanced authentication in online banking. *Journal of Economic Crime Management, 4*(2).

Yang, Y.-J. (1997). *The security of electronic banking.* Retrieved April 2010, from http://csrc.nist.gov/nissc/1997/proceedings/041.pdf

KEY TERMS AND DEFINITIONS

Authentication: Verifying user's assertion of its identification through credentials.

Authorization: Verifying user's privileges to a system.

Identity Management Architecture: Design of identity system for managing credentials and entitlements for users of covered system(s).

Identity Management System: A system for managing user identities.

Multiple Factor Authentication: An authentication system that is based on more than one factor of authentication such as something user knows (knowledge), something that user possesses (possession) and something user is (behavioral or physical trait).

Password Management: Managing users' passwords for purpose of authenticating users.

Role Management: Managing users' entitlements and rights to application(s).

Single Sign On: Use of single set of credentials to provide access to multiple applications and systems.

Chapter 16
Privacy in Identity and Access Management Systems

Andreas Pashalidis
Katholieke Universiteit Leuven, Belgium

Chris J. Mitchell
Royal Holloway, University of London, UK

ABSTRACT

This chapter surveys the approaches for addressing privacy in open identity and access management systems that have been taken by a number of current systems. The chapter begins by listing important privacy requirements and discusses how three systems that are being incrementally deployed in the Internet, namely SAML 2.0, CardSpace, and eID, address these requirements. Subsequently, the findings of recent European research projects in the area of privacy for I&AM systems are discussed. Finally, the approach taken to address the identified privacy requirements by ongoing projects is described at a high level. The overall goal of this chapter is to provide the reader with an overview of the diversity of privacy issues and techniques in the context of I&AM.

INTRODUCTION

Identity and Access Management (I&AM) systems support *access control*, namely ensuring that access to certain resources is granted only if the requestor is properly authorized. For example, a company employee that accesses a company VPN (Virtual Private Network) while working from abroad is likely to be granted access by an access control system. Although I&AM systems are closely integrated with access control systems, their main function is to support the system administrators and the end users in performing maintenance procedures, such as managing access credentials, user roles, access rights, rights delegation, auditing, and relationships between organizational units, throughout the lifetime of the system.

Over the last fifty years, many I&AM systems with a wide range of functions have been devel-

DOI: 10.4018/978-1-61350-498-7.ch016

oped. Such systems are typically composed of a number of modules, each with a specific task. Some I&AM systems are as simple as a database with authorized username/password pairs, while others are complex distributed systems that could include sophisticated policy decision points, interconnection with business process engines, accounting and billing infrastructures, credential negotiation agents, customer relationship management systems, administrative interfaces for the lifetime management of comprehensive user profiles, and provisions for auditing. Many I&AM systems are *closed*, i.e. they are designed for environments where there is a single system provider, such as a company or government organization, that has a very strong relationship with the prospective users.

The focus of this chapter is *open* I&AM systems, i.e. systems that cover multiple organizations. In the context of such systems, users interact with a range of different organizations using one or more credentials. New users may be introduced into the system by multiple parties, or users may be able to independently create new accounts for themselves. In open systems there is clearly a need for interoperability, and thus standardization is probably more important than in closed systems; privacy also plays a central role. Users should, for example, be able to control the degree of dissemination of their personal information to organizations and other users. The particular focus of this chapter is the various degrees of privacy achieved by current open I&AM systems, and what issues need to be addressed in future such systems.

PRIVACY REQUIREMENTS FOR I&AM SYSTEMS

The need for user privacy in open I&AM system arises from the need to reduce the risks of unnecessary or otherwise unwanted disclosure of personal information. In recent years, legislation in Europe, both at EU and at national levels, has become an important driver for the introduction of privacy and transparency enhancing techniques within I&AM systems. This is because many of these laws require businesses to follow the principles of data minimization, data protection, and, in some cases, data retention. The data minimization principle requires that personal data is not disclosed to a transacting partner unless that information is strictly needed in order to carry out the transaction. In order to establish such strict necessity, the purpose of disclosure must be specified for each data item to be disclosed. Data protection and retention require that users have access to, and can update, their personal information when it is stored at an organization, but also that organizations have to keep records in a way that facilitates effective investigation of past transactions. In this context, 'personal data' is any data that could potentially lead to the identification of an individual, even if this is only possible in combination with additional information.

The following more concrete requirements arise from the requirement to minimize the personal data that is transferred between parties. We say that a privacy-preserving I&AM system should enable its users to:

- selectively disclose personal data to organizations and other users;
- create multiple identities or pseudonyms;
- attach different pieces of personal information to different identities;
- review data disclosed in the past;
- maintain different identities towards different organizations;
- formulate 'sticky' policies that follow personal data and that govern under which conditions the data may be disclosed and used;
- minimize the amount of trust users are required to place in third parties and infrastructural components in general; and

- provide explicit consent for sharing personal information, and enable users to revoke previously given consent.

Of course, achieving all the above in a usable manner, i.e. without placing too great a burden on users and system administrators, is very challenging.

The above requirements can be roughly captured by the following criteria. They can be used to evaluate I&AM systems with respect to their privacy-friendliness.

Trust Model

Some I&AM systems are designed so that a remote entity, typically called the 'Identity Provider' (IdP), stores and manages the user's personal information. Users are typically authenticated by an IdP, and are then able to access their own information and forward it to requesting parties. While this has the advantage of mobility–users may use the system from any computer and any location–this model also raises significant privacy issues. This is because the trusted party not only learns the personal data of the user, but will also gain information about the behaviour and relationships of the user, since other parties will refer to the trusted party every time they require user data and or assurances about user authenticity. Moreover, the trusted party must be relied upon not to assert that a user has been authenticated when this has not occurred, and/or to assert false information about the personal attributes of a user (as discussed in (Alrodhan & Mitchell, 2010)).

Of course, the privacy issues arising from the use of a third party IdP can to some extent be mitigated if the user is able to choose which IdP to use. This issue of choice arose starkly in the case of Passport, Microsoft's initial attempt to solve the identity management problem by making itself the IdP for everyone. As has been widely documented, the notion of trusting Microsoft with large quantities of personal data gave rise to a widespread and violent negative reaction, which clearly took Microsoft by surprise (Kormann & Rubin, 2000). Indeed, this informed Microsoft's subsequent effort in this space, the CardSpace system, discussed later in this chapter. Of course to be effective, choice requires a rich ecosystem of entities prepared to act as IdPs, and this ecosystem is still at an early stage of evolution. Moreover, even as and when such an ecosystem develops, not all users will be equipped with the means to decide which IdPs they can trust with mission-critical personal data.

An approach in which personal data, such as attributes and certificates, are stored on the user's own computer and are then disclosed directly to the parties that require it, is likely to be more privacy-friendly. Such an approach, however, is less convenient, since mobility is no longer guaranteed and the users may have to perform a greater number of administrative tasks. It also increases the importance of security management of the platform on which the user information is stored.

Ultimately it all comes down to trust. Users will have to make a trust decision with regard to the handling of personal data, either in terms of the use of a trusted third party (e.g. an IdP) or a personal platform. Sadly, recent history suggests that this is a highly problematic issue, since users are known to make poor trust decisions with regard to the handling of personal data, as the many issues identified with social networking sites have proved (Hogben, 2007).

Multiple Unlinkable Identities

The notion of a user identity is commonly defined as the set of personal information for that user (attributes, certificates, credentials, and other statements concerning the individual). The user may 'compose' one or more personal identities by grouping relevant pieces of personal information. Identities do not need to be consistent; for example, one identity may include the user's real name and address, whereas a pseudonym (e.g. a nickname) and address (or no address at all) may be included in another. The grouping of data into identities makes it easier for a user to switch between contexts or roles. Note that the literature sometime uses the term 'virtual identity' in order to refer to such a composed identity (see, e.g. (Aguiar, 2010)).

In closed systems users are typically restricted to a single identity, whereas open systems typically do not have such a restriction. In particular, if the I&AM system interacts with multiple organizations that can each identify users, it may be desirable for users to be able to use different identities with different organizations. Moreover, in order to achieve data minimization, mechanisms should be provided to prevent collaborating organizations from linking a given user's profile at one organization with the same user's profile at another. While it is relatively easy to let users create and maintain multiple identities for themselves, ensuring that these identities remain unlinkable is not straightforward. In particular, there is always a risk that usage patterns and attribute values leak enough information to link the identities of a given user. The system itself, however, should not prevent privacy-conscious users from maintaining identities that are effectively unlinkable (up to certain inherent limits, discussed in (Pashalidis & Meyer, 2006) and (Pashalidis & Mitchell, 2004)).

Selective Disclosure

Selective disclosure requires that it is both possible and simple for a user to disclose only part of an identity to a given requestor. If, for example, the system has registered the user's date of birth, it should be possible to disclose only the user's age or even age group (e.g. 18–25) without having to install a separate identity or undergo a lengthy registration process.

Consent

Personal data can be used for a wide range of purposes. If, for example, a user wishes to buy electronic goods that are shipped via email, then the user must disclose his email address. However, an online shop may wish to employ a user's email address for other purposes, such as research or marketing. A privacy-preserving I&AM system should enable a user to be asked for explicit consent for such secondary uses of personal information. Similar provisions should be implemented regarding data retention times where input is needed from the user. The system should also support the revocation of consent, for example if the user no longer wishes to be contacted by the other party.

Privacy Respecting Sharing of Personal Information

Sometimes it is necessary for a piece of personal information to be transferred from one organization to another. If, for example, a user orders a book from an online shop, the shop must be able to forward the user's address to the shipping company in order for the book to be delivered. In such situations it should be possible for the user to define a policy that tells the shop for which purposes and to which recipients the data is permitted to be forwarded. The notion of a 'sticky policy' is similar to consent solicitation in that they both enable the user to define acceptable retention periods, purposes, and authorized recipients. The difference, however, is that while consent only applies to the first recipient of personal information, a sticky policy is 'stuck' to the data. This means that the policy is visible and applies to all 'downstream' data processors, i.e. everyone to whom the data is disclosed in the context of a process of the I&AM system. Note that there is an interplay between privacy-respecting sharing of personal information and revocation of consent: if personal data has been already shared, then effective revocation of consent becomes very challenging; effectively revoking consent would, for example, require dynamic updates to sticky policies. To the best of our knowledge, to date no deployed I&AM has tackled this problem.

SOME COMMON SYSTEMS

We next examine some widely discussed protocols used by open I&AM systems. It is important to observe that products offer a variety of user interfaces and varying degrees of usability and functionality. Moreover, as open I&AM systems are developing rapidly both in the technical and legal dimensions, so are the interfaces and functionality of individual products. Hence it is of limited use to evaluate current implementations at a very fine level of detail. It is more valuable to examine the *protocols* that are used to support I&AM systems. Because these protocols are standardized, they are more likely to be stable than user interfaces and software functionality sets, which change much more frequently.

In particular, we examine the privacy properties of SAML 2.0, CardSpace, and electronic ID. The reader should keep in mind that these systems focus more on identity management rather than access management. Access management infrastructures, typically located in the backend of an organization's infrastructure, are largely orthogonal to the processes that affect the systems below. Nevertheless, much current research, as outlined later in this chapter, is aimed at achieving a tighter integration between identity and access management, for example by enabling policy evaluations to be distributed over multiple domains.

SAML 2.0

SAML, which stands for 'Security Assertions Markup Language', is a set of web services protocols used in web services, and is standardized by OASIS. SAML versions 1.0 (Haller-Baker & Maler, 2002) and 1.1 (Maler, Mishra & Philpott, 2003) were published in 2002 and 2005, respectively. SAML 2.0 (Cantor, Kemp, Philpott & Maler, 2005), specifies protocols enabling organizations to exchange data about users. The typical use case involves a user that is authenticated by an organization called an Identity Provider (IdP), who maintains an account for the user.

The IdP can authenticate users by a variety of methods (Kemp et. al., 2005). The scheme is not restricted to a single IdP, and users may choose their preferred IdP from a list that contains all IdPs that are recognized by the website which they wish to access. The specifications also provide data structures which enable the IdP to send attributes it stores about a user to other websites in a manner that enables the receiving websites to verify the validity of the attributes. It is up to the IdP to provide user interfaces through which users can compose identities and exercise selective disclosure. Selective disclosure can be exercised if the user is given the opportunity to specify policies that tell the IdP which potential recipients are allowed to see which attributes, or by explicitly asking the user to confirm attribute disclosures every time they are about to take place. Both approaches have usability disadvantages.

SAML 2.0 and Access Management

XACML (Extensible Access Control Markup Language), another OASIS standard (Moses, 2005), specifies a format for access control policies as well as formats for messages that can be used by a Policy Enforcement Point (PEP) to request a policy decision from a Policy Decision Point (PDP). The XACML SAML profile (Anderson & Lockhart, 2005) specifies how XACML messages can be sent inside SAML 2.0 messages. This specification involves a close integration of Identity and Access Management technologies. In a typical use case, some of the XACML-enhanced SAML 2.0 messages, typically exchanged between a PEP and a PDP, will carry personal data, such as attributes. This standard enables more elaborate access management because it enables one domain to outsource policy decisions to another domain. However, use of the standard is also likely to increase the risk of privacy breaches because the exchanged messages may contain personal user information (e.g. attributes) and, while this information may be necessary to reach an access control decision, the messages are forwarded across domain boundaries The particular risk level, however, depends on the details of the deployment.

CardSpace

CardSpace is a software product produced by Microsoft that enables users to manage their identities on their own computer. In Microsoft terminology it is an 'identity metasystem', i.e. a system that aims to accommodate multiple, ideally all, Identity Management systems and offer a unified user experience towards the user. Cardspace offers suitable abstractions for processes such as the creation of identities (i.e. grouping together attributes), authentication of remote websites, and remembering histories of disclosed personal information. Cardspace has been designed to promote adoption of Identity Management systems by presenting these abstractions to the user in a self-explanatory and easy to use manner, namely in the form of 'Information Cards'. Each such card can contain a range of different types of personal information, and part or all of the contexts of such a card can be selected for disclosure to a remote website.

CardSpace conforms to the Identity Metasystem Interoperability Standard (Jones & McIntosh, 2009) and supports "U-Prove" anonymous credentials (Brands, 2000). According to (Jones & McIntosh, 2009), 'Information Cards can be used both at applications hosted on Web sites accessed through Web browser and rich client applications directly employing Web services'. In a typical use case, however, while composition and selection of cards is done at the user's computer, the personal information itself may be stored at a variety of providers on the Internet. CardSpace can handle different types and formats of credentials, claims and attributes including SAML 2.0 and the recently specified protocol for U-Prove credentials (Paquin, 2010). Even though it is envisaged that Information Cards reside on the user's computer, most use cases require a wider infrastructure, with IdPs that authenticate users and provide assertions containing personal data. That is, the IdP and potentially other parties such as attribute and storage providers, are likely to be actively involved whenever the user chooses to show a card to a remote website.

As we have discussed, in CardSpace an IdP provides interested parties with statements about the attributes of a user. The system allows the recipient of such statements to be confident that the user with which it is communicating is the rightful holder of such attributes. If the attributes include a unique identifier, then the system thereby provides a means for a party to (indirectly) authenticate a user. That is, in some sense CardSpace combines attribute management with the provision of user authentication services. This property is shared by a number of other identity management systems. However, other identity management systems, such as Liberty[1], deal only with the issue of authentication. By restricting scope in this way, the privacy implications are much reduced, since in Liberty the IdP solely provides statements about whether a user (identified by a pseudonym) has been authenticated.

Finally we observe that CardSpace has the capability to reduce the trust requirement on IdPs not to monitor user activity (as discussed under Trust model above). A CardSpace IdP provides statements about user attributes, but, depending on which cryptographic options are in use, may not be required to know to which party this statement is being provided.

eID

eID, which stands for electronic IDentity, refers to efforts inside the European Union to introduce the electronic equivalent of national identity cards to its citizens. An eID solution typically takes the form of a smart card embedded into a credit-card-sized plastic card. An eID card can be used to authenticate a citizen, and to share information about the citizen that has been verified by the issuer of the card, i.e. the government. One rationale for the introduction of eID is an expected reduction of costs in the public sector resulting from its role in enabling citizens to interact electronically with government services. However, eID applications are not necessarily restricted to government applications; any business could decide to accept eID cards in order to identify or collect information about its customers. In some countries, e.g. in Germany, eID cards are likely to be able to generate so-called 'qualified signatures'. These signatures can be used to sign legally binding contracts, and, because of special technical protection measures, are exoected to have greater legal weight than non-qualified signatures.

A number of countries have introduced eID cards, for example Estonia and Belgium, and other countries are planning such a deployment; indeed, only a minority of EU member states do not have plans to roll out an eID in the future (Naumann & Hogben, 2009). Unfortunately, the eID systems of different countries differ to such an extent that future interoperability may be hindered (Naumann & Hogben, 2009). In order to prevent this from happening, efforts are underway to harmonize the eID landscape and to introduce more stringent privacy measures[2]. It is important to keep in mind that many of the differences are due to differing national legal frameworks (Naumann & Hogben 2009, Jentzsch 2010).

Given the diversity of national legal frameworks, it is no surprise that different eID systems have different properties with respect to protecting citizen privacy. Apart from the the German eID system, all deployed systems of which we aware produce a signature in order to authenticate the citizen. This is a violation of the data minimization principle since, when used for authentication only, the signature reveals more information about the citizen than is strictly necessary (Naumann & Hogben, 2009). The protocol used by the German eID card, called PACE (shown to be secure in Bender, Fischlin & Kügler 2009), circumvents this problem.

The type of data that is stored on different national eID cards, as well as the conditions under which access to this data is granted, also differs greatly from one system to the other. For example, currently the chips used in Belgium, the Netherlands, Portugal and Germany store a picture of a citizen's face, but only the German system restricts access to governmental services, whereas those used in Belgium, the Netherlands and Portugal impose no such access restrictions. Similarly, currently only the Austrian and the German cards support pseudonymous transactions, in the sense that different organizations get to see different identifiers for the citizen/card; other schemes reuse the same identifier for the citizen and/or card across contexts, thereby enabling colluding organizations to breach privacy by linking the transaction histories of any given citizen. It should be mentioned, however, that certain countries, e.g. Belgium, legally prohibit organizations from storing any long-term identifiers that are retrieved from the card, thereby reducing the risk level. For more information on the differences of eID approaches, the reader is referred to (Naumann & Hogben, 2009) and (Modinis-IDM consortium, 2006). A European eID card, called the European Citizen Card (ECC) is currently being specified; this specification supports unlinkable pseudonyms, and the different possibilities to integrate ECC with SAML 2.0 are investigated in (Eichholz, Hühnlein & Schwenk, 2009).

Other Systems

SAML 2.0, CardSpace and eID are certainly not the only I&AM systems. We conclude this discussion on existing systems by briefly mentioning some other widely discussed examples of such systems.

The Liberty Alliance Project (usually abbreviated to Liberty), which went public in 2001, is one of the most prominent collaborative efforts aiming at building open standard-based specifications for identity federation systems. The Liberty model is essentially that of an Internet single sign-on (SSO) system. In this scheme, a principal (or a user) can federate its various identities to a single identity issued by an identity provider, so that the user can access services provided by service providers belonging to the same circle of trust by authenticating just once to the identity provider. This relies on a pre-established relationship between the identity provider and every service provider in the circle of trust. As stated above, Liberty does not support the management of personal information, and provide only authentication services.

Shibboleth is an open source federated identity management system that has been developed by the Internet2 consortium. It offers standards-based authentication and authorization systems. Shibboleth mandates identity federation, in which the IdP and the service provider systems consuming user information exchange public key certificates. Unlike in Liberty, the IdP and the serve provider do not have to establish long-term shared pseudonyms during the federation process (but they can if they wish). Instead of long-term pseudonyms, the IdP and SP can use short-term random IDs to help preserve user privacy and maintain anonymity. The latest version of Shibboleth, version 2.0, is based on SAML 2.0.

OpenID is an open source identity management system in which IdPs issue their users with 'global' identifiers that can be used to log-in to any service provider. OpenID is somewhat different in nature to SAML 2.0, CardSpace, Liberty and Shibboleth, and relies on a rather different model. In OpenID, an IdP issues a user with a global identifier (or OpenID) that can be used to log-in to any OpenID-enabled service provider. This identifier is typically a URL, and identifies the IdP that issued it. Obviously, there is no need for pseudonyms in this system, since IdPs and the SPs can refer to a user using the OpenID global identifier. There is no identity federation process in OpenID; however, if a user already holds an service provider-issued identifier, then the service provider may choose to 'locally' link this identifier with the user OpenID (i.e. the IdP-issued global identifier). Of course, since everything is based on a global identifier, OpenID does not support any degree of anonymity or pseudonymity, and hence is much less privacy-friendly than the other systems we have discussed.

PREVIOUS RESEARCH PROJECTS

We briefly discuss some of the approaches taken by three recently finished European research projects in the area of I&AM, namely DAIDALOS, SWIFT, and PRIME. The European projects discussed here are all large scale research collaborations involving a significant number, typically between 15 and 40, of partners representing both industry and academia. The lengths of the projects discussed range from 30 months to four years.

DAIDALOS[3], a project with nearly 40 partners, involved two consecutive phases that ran from 2003 to 2008, involved a number of mobile phone operators including Deutsche Telekom, France Telecom, Telekom India, and Telefonica (Spain). According to the project website, its overall goal was to 'design, prototype and validate the necessary infrastructure and components for efficient distribution of services over diverse network technologies' and to 'integrate complementary network technologies to provide pervasive and user-centred access to these services'. As a result of the broad scope of the project, it would be unfair to say that its focus was on I&AM. However, a significant part of the project was dedicated to I&AM and the related privacy issues. In this context, DAIDALOS (in its second phase) introduced the concept of virtual identities. A virtual identity is an index of pointers to personal information that may reside at various places in the network. According to the project vision, users should be free to construct as many virtual identities for themselves as they wish, and choose where different items of personal information are stored. The index would be stored at an IdP (perhaps the user's network operator), and would itself be identified by a random-looking pseudonym.

DAIDALOS virtual identities are cross-layer in nature. This is because it was recognized that lower communication layers trivially enable an adversary to link transactions, even if these transactions are made unlinkable at the application layer. To this end, the adversary simply has to observe the user's Internet Protocol (IP) address; if the same IP address is used, with high probability the same user is behind the transaction. The project introduced mechanisms that trigger a switch of all identifiers across the stack, namely MAC address, IP address and, if applicable, SIP address, whenever the user switches his VID at the application layer. Moreover, multiple VIDs can be simultaneously active, with the consequence that the user's device will have an equal number of concurrently active MAC addresses and IP addresses (Aguiar, 2010).

Whether or not the results of the DAIDALOS project with respect to privacy-enhancing I&AM will be taken up by industry and deployed in real mobile networks remains to be seen. Certainly many practical obstacles will have to be overcome, most importantly the introduction of the new infrastructure that enables different operators to interoperate. Moreover, the replication of the entire communication stack whenever the user switches a VID is likely to introduce potentially unacceptable performance degradation.

The SWIFT (Secure Widespread Identities for Federated Telecommunications), was a 30-month project that built on the concept of DAIDALOS virtual identities. The main focus of the project was the integration of virtual identities into the authentication infrastructure of telecommunication operators, enterprises and ISPs. One important driver was the desire to support flexible charging and billing schemes as well as a form of single sign-on in which the user's ISP acts as an IdP, causing the user to be automatically logged into services on the Internet without further interaction (Azevedo 2008).

One goal of the PRIME (Privacy and Identity Management for Europe) project was to develop a privacy-preserving identity management system. The approach it adopts makes use of cryptographic tools called 'anonymous credentials'. Such credentials enable a level of data minimization that is not possible with conventional public key cryptography. In particular, an anonymous credential enables a user to demonstrate possession of a certified attribute to third parties, while at the same time avoiding the disclosure of any unique identifiers that would enable different demonstrations of the same credential to be linked. The project also developed an architecture that acts as a middleware component between an application and the repository that holds the user's personal information. The architecture combines access control policies that support obligations, negotiation and trust management; for further detail, the reader is referred to (Sommer, Cassasa Mont & Pearson 2008).

While DAIDALOS and SWIFT seem to assume that the user's data will be primarily stored by services (e.g. IdPs) in the network, PRIME's default mode of operation appears to assume that user data is managed on the user's own computer. It should be emphasized that these two approaches are very different, because the former requires third parties to be entrusted with user data while the latter does not. The distinction is, however, a superficial one since, in principle, both modes of operation are possible. Meta-identity systems like Higgins[4] and Cardspace (Brands, 2000) make this degree of flexibility explicit.

ONGOING RESEARCH PROJECTS

This section presents currently running European research projects that, amongst other things, aim to improve privacy in open I&AM.

PrimeLife

PrimeLife[5] (Privacy and Identity Management throughout Life) is a European project that aims to develop mechanisms that prevent the collection of the massive amounts of personal data that individuals leave behind in their online transactions. The project takes a somewhat holistic approach, looking at the problem not only in specific domains, but in a range of domains and throughout an individual's lifetime. PrimeLife builds on the work done in PRIME[6], but also aims at addressing the requirements listed earlier in this chapter. To this end, a number of mechanisms are being developed within the project. These can be roughly divided into cryptographic primitives, transparency support tools, privacy enhancing technologies, mechanisms for access control, and user interface development.

The cryptographic mechanisms build on previous work on anonymous credentials and related types of cryptosystem. In this area, the project has developed more efficient mechanisms for the encoding of attributes and the revocation of anonymous credentials, as well as protocols that allow users to retrieve information from a server without the server learning which exactly item of information was disclosed. Research topics also include enforcement mechanisms to prevent excessive data sharing in the context of social networks, and a 'trusted wallet' i.e. a software module that can manage sensitive information for multiple security modules.

Transparency support tools are, in the view of the project, tools that enable the user to access data that is stored about the user at third parties, the purposes of data collection, and the risks involved in divulging further information. First results aim to obtain an overview of technologies in this area, but also results on measuring privacy properties such as anonymity and unlinkability have been produced. It should be noted here that the topic of how to obtain and communicate reliable privacy measurements to end users is very challenging and still in its infancy.

Privacy enhancing technologies considered within PrimeLife include mechanisms suitable for the establishment of collaborative groups, the management of trust for privacy-preserving reputation systems, and for querying large collections of personal information without compromising the privacy of the individuals that are represented in the data set. In the area of access control, the project concentrates on how to capture the purpose for which personal data may be requested within access control policies, as well as the confidentiality of the policies themselves, and how users can define access control for data that is stored at external parties. These external parties do not necessarily have to be trusted with the data, but only with encrypted versions of the data. The project also aims to examine how such approaches can lead to better protection of biometric traits.

Finally, the project aims to increase end user awareness about privacy issues and to provide useful controls to users. This is to be achieved by implementing a variety of prototype user interfaces and subsequently conducting user studies in order to gain understanding of what abstractions and metaphors work in practice. For more information, the reader is referred to (Camenisch & Samarati 2009) and (Fischer-Hübner, Wästlund & Raggett 2009), as well as the project website.

TAS3

TAS3 (Trusted Architecture for Securely Shared Services) is a project related to I&AM which aims to develop an architecture that deals with authentication of users and organizations, credential management, the establishment of trust between users and organizations, compliance considerations such as data protection policies, and a seamless integration into established business processes.

One of the main differences between PrimeLife and TAS3 is that, while the former project focuses on improving different privacy-preserving techniques, TAS3 focuses on the specification and development of a concrete architecture that integrates such techniques, while addressing the challenges that arise from this integration. Like PrimeLife, TAS3 also introduces mechanisms for the specification and management of policies that govern access to personal information. In particular, the project specifies a comprehensive authorization infrastructure that takes into account the requirements from different stakeholders: the user's privacy preferences in the form of explicit consent and sticky policies, policies from multiple organizations, and input from a business process engine.

Although the TAS3 architecture is generic and is designed to handle any type of information and personal data, the main scenarios targeted by the project are e-health and employability. In the e-health scenario, sensitive medical data about patients must be made available to doctors, while it must also be ensured that non-authorized persons cannot access a patient's medical data. Moreover, it must be guaranteed that the system can be audited, and hence a trustworthy log file of who accessed which files must be constructed. Emergency situations must also be addressed, where a doctor may need to access a patient's file even if the doctor could not do so in the absence of the emergency.

The employability scenario, on the other hand, focuses on the situation where a user uploads CV data to a special server in order to support a search for a job; instead of the user manually filling out cumbersome forms at every potential employer's site, the system enables potential employers to see the required data from the user's uploaded CV. This scenario highlights the need for the system to be able to handle complex structures in personal data, and to handle complex policies regarding the handling of data with respect to consent, purpose, and forwarding to third parties.

Both the e-health and the employability scenarios provide a motivation for introducing a business process engine that orchestrates the overall information flows and that enables changes to the process to be introduced in a structured manner.

Organizations may not only use different policy formats, but also use different vocabularies when formulating their policies. For example, while one organization might use the term 'manager', another may use the term 'supervisor' to refer to the same concept. In order to address the resulting semantic interoperability issues, TAS3 is also developing modeling tools that capture the diversity of naming. A dedicated TAS3 component is planned that will translate the affected policies into a common format at runtime. More details of the TAS3 architecture are given in (Kellomäki 2009).

SUMMARY AND CONCLUSION

In this chapter we have discussed privacy issues that arise in the context of I&AM, and provided a high level overview of how certain systems that are currently being used or developed address these issues. We have found that privacy protection plays a major role in the current I&AM landscape, and that most protocols are designed with at least some of the privacy requirements in mind. Whilst privacy-protecting protocols and mechanisms are a necessity in order to achieve an overall system that is privacy friendly, their mere presence is not sufficient. Assuming that privacy-protecting protocols are in place, the user interfaces of the system, as well as the degree to which the system enables users to exercise fine-grained control over the dissemination of their personal information, will to a large extent determine the level of privacy that can actually be obtained. That is, the mode of operation imposed by the I&AM infrastructure, including the underlying trust assumptions, determine whether or not it is possible for users to retain their privacy.

Finally, the usage of the system also affects privacy; if only one user is using the system then clearly there cannot be any privacy. That is, whether or not the design and assumptions regarding future usage of the system matches the actual usage when it takes place, is also important. Hence, the issue of privacy protection in the context of I&AM is likely to remain an important and active research area for the foreseeable future.

REFERENCES

Aguiar, R. L. (2010). *Deliverable DII-122.* Updated Daidalos II global architecture. Retrieved August 23rd, 2010, from http://www.ist-daidalos.org/

Alrodhan, W. A., & Mitchell, C. J. (2010). Enhancing user authentication in claim-based identity management. In *Proceedings of CTS 2010, the 2010 International Symposium on Collaborative Technologies and Systems* (pp.75-83). 17-21 May 2010, Chicago, Illinois, USA. Piscataway, NJ: IEEE.

Anderson, A., & Lockhart, H. (2005). *SAML2.0 profile of XACML v2.0.* OASIS Standard, 1 February 2005; Retrieved August 23rd, 2010, from http://docs.oasis-open.org/xacml/2.0

Azevedo, R. (2008). *SWIFT deliverable D.402 – Specification of identity-based service architecture with AAA function.* December 2008. Retrieved August 23rd, 2010, from http://www.ist-swift.org/

Bender, J., Fischlin, M., & Kügler, D. (2009). *Security analysis of the PACE key agreement protocol.* Paper presented at the Twelfth International Conference on Information Security (ISC 2009), Pisa, Italy.

Brands, S. (2000). *Rethinking public key infrastructure and digital certificates: Building in privacy.* MIT Press.

Camenisch, J., & Saramati, P. (2009). *PrimeLife deliverable D2.1.1, first report on mechanisms.* Retrieved August 23rd, 2010, from http://www.primelife.eu

Cantor, S., Kemp, J., Philpott, R., & Maler, E. (2005). *Assertions and protocol for the OASIS security assertion markup language (SAML) V.2.* OASIS Standard, 15 March 2005. Retrieved August 23rd, 2010, from http://saml.xml.org/saml-specifications

Chadwick, D. W., Zhao, G., Otenko, S., Laborde, R., Su, L., & Nguyen, T. A. (2008). PERMIS: A modular authorization infrastructure. *Concurrency and Computation, 20*(11), 1341–1357. doi:10.1002/cpe.1313

Eichholz, J., Hühnlein, D., & Schwenk, J. (2009). *SAMLizing the European Citizen Card.* Paper presented at BIOSIG 2009 Special Interest Group on Biometrics and Electronic Signatures, September 2009, Darmstadt, Germany.

Fischer-Hübner, S., Wästlund, E., & Raggett, D. (2009). *PrimeLife deliverable D4.3.1, UI prototypes, administration and presentation version 1.* Retrieved August 23rd, 2010, from http://www.primelife.eu

Hallam-Baker, P., & Maler, E. (2002). *Assertions and protocol for the OASIS security assertion markup language (SAML).* OASIS Standard, 5 November 2002. Retrieved August 23rd, 2010, from http://saml.xml.org/saml-specifications

Hogben, G. (2007). *Security issues and recommendations for online social networks*. ENISA Position Paper 1. Retrieved August 23rd, 2010, from http://www.enisa.europa.eu/act/res/other-areas/social-networks/security-issues-and-recommendations-for-online-social-networks

Jentzsch, N. (2010, May). *Welfare analysis of secondary use of personal data.* Paper presented at the Ninth Workshop on the Economics of Information Security (WEIS 2010), Harvard University, USA.

Jones, M. B., & McIntosh, M. (2009). *Identity metasystem interoperability version 1.0.* OASIS Standard, 1 July 2009. Retrieved August 23rd, 2010, from http://docs.oasis-open.org/imi/identity/v1.0/identity.html

Kellomäki, S. (2009). *TAS3 deliverable 2.1 – TAS3 architecture*. Retrieved August 23rd, 2010, from http://www.tas3.eu

Kemp, J., Cantor, S., Mishra, P., Philpott, R., & Maler, E. (2005). *Authentication context for the OASIS security assertion markup language (SAML) V2.0.* OASIS Standard, 15 March 2005. Retrieved August 23rd, 2010, from http://saml.xml.org/saml-specifications

Kormann, D. P., & Rubin, A. D. (2000). Risks of the passport single SignOn protocol. *Computer Networks, 33*(1-6), 51-58.

Maler, E., Mishra, P., & Philpott, R. (2003). *Assertions and protocol for the OASIS security assertion markup language (SAML) V.1.1.* OASIS Standard, 2 September 2003. Retrieved August 23rd, 2010, from http://saml.xml.org/saml-specifications

Modinis-IDM Consortium. (2006). *D3.5 identity management initiative report 1 IIR1.* Deliverable of Modinis Project. Retrieved August 2nd, 2010, from https://www.cosic.esat.kuleuven.be/modinis-idm/twiki/pub/Main/ProjectDocs/modinis.D3.5_Identity_Management_Initiative_Report_1_IIR1.pdf

Moses, T. (2005). *eXtensible access control markup language (XACML) version 2.0.* OASIS Standard, 1 February 2005. Retrieved August 23rd, 2010, from http://docs.oasis-open.org/xacml/2.0

Naumann, I., & Hogben, G. (2009). *Privacy features of European eID card specifications.* ENISA Position Paper. Retrieved August 23rd, 2010, from http://www.enisa.europa.eu/act/it/eid/eid-cards-en

Paquin, C. (2010). *U-Prove technology integration into the identity metasystem V1.0.* Retrieved August 23rd, 2010, from http://connect.microsoft.com/site642/Downloads/DownloadDetails.aspx?DownloadID=26953

Pashalidis, A., & Meyer, B. (2006). Linking anonymous transactions: The consistent view attack. In G. Danezis & P. Golle (Eds.), *Privacy Enhancing Technologies, 6th International Workshop, PET 2006, LNCS 4258,* Cambridge, UK, June 28–30, 2006, Revised Selected Papers (pp. 384-392). Berlin, Germany: Springer Verlag.

Pashalidis, A., & Mitchell, C. J. (2004). Limits to anonymity when using credentials. in: *Security Protocols, 12th International Workshop, LNCS 3957,* Cambridge, U.K., April 26-28. 2004, Revised Selected Papers (pp. 4-12). Berlin, Germany: Springer Verlag.

Sommer, D., Cassasa Mont, M., & Pearson, S. (2008). *PRIME deliverable D.14.2d – PRIME Architecture V3.* July 2008, Retrieved August 23rd, 2010, from https://www.prime-project.eu

ENDNOTES

1. http://www.projectliberty.org
2. See, for example, the STORK project at https://www.eid-stork.eu/
3. http://www.ist-daidalos.org/
4. http://www.eclipse.org/higgins/
5. http://www.primelife.eu/
6. https://www.prime-project.eu/

Chapter 17
Identity Management

Waleed A. Alrodhan
Imam Muhammed Ibn Saud University, Saudi Arabia

ABSTRACT

In this chapter we provide overviews of the notion of identity and of identity management in Sections 1 and 2, respectively. In section 3 we describe a conceptual identity management model as well as a number of practical models. We also cover a number of related topics including Single Sign-On, Level of Assurance, identity source discovery, security policies, proof-of-rightful-possession, and the use of pseudonyms and temporary IDs. Section 4 concludes the chapter.

IDENTITIES

The term *Identity* is used here to mean the representation of an entity in a given context, where an *entity* is something that has a distinct existence and can be uniquely identified (e.g. a person or an organisation). This representation takes the form of a defined collection of entity attributes or distinctive characteristics (ISO/IEC Second CD 24760, 2010). These attributes and characteristics are also collectively referred to as personally identifiable information (PII).

In line with this use of the term, a recent draft of ITU-T X.1250 (ITU-T X.1250 (X.idmreq), 2009) defines identity as the "*Representation of an entity (or group of entities) in the form of one or more information elements which allow the entity(s) to be uniquely recognised within a context to the extent that is necessary (for the relevant applications).*"

Whilst, in principle, every entity has a 'whole' identity that consists of all its distinctive attributes, subsets of these attributes can form different 'partial' identities in different contexts. An *identifier* is a unique label for an object, that can be used to refer to an entity in a specific context (e.g. a username that refers to a user's digital account) (ISO/IEC Second CD 24760, 2010). We can consider an identifier as a special attribute of an entity that must be unique within its context of use.

DOI: 10.4018/978-1-61350-498-7.ch017

Figure 1. Relationship between entities, identities and identifiers

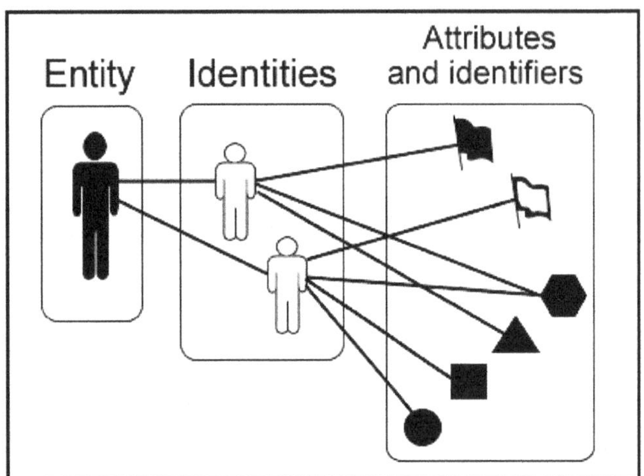

Figure 1 shows the relationship between entities, identities and identifiers. As shown in the figure, an identity is a representation of a subset of all possible attributes of a given entity. Attributes can be shared by different identities of a given entity.

Identification can be defined as a "*process to determine that presented identity information associated with a particular entity is sufficient for the entity to be recognised in a particular domain*" (ISO/IEC Second CD 24760, 2010). A representation of an identity in a digital system is called a *digital identity*. Henceforth, 'identity' is used to mean 'digital identity' unless we explicitly state otherwise.

Figure 2 shows a possible identity lifecycle which includes five steps, namely: provision, propagate, use, maintain, and deprovision (Windley, 2005). In the *provision* step, an identity is created by defining an identity record that includes the correct attributes. This step involves identity *registration* to allow an entity to be known within a particular domain of applicability. This requires an initial entity authentication to be performed, i.e. a particular form of authentication based on identity evidence, performing which is a necessary condition for the identity record to be created (ISO/IEC Second CD 24760, 2010). This identity record can be propagated to other systems or subsystems (e.g. a database system) in the *propagate* step. After being provisioned and propagated, the identity record can be used by authorised entities in the *use* step. The identity record can be updated and its information can be changed in the *maintain* step, where the identity record must be repropagated after being updated. Finally, the identity record is deleted in the *deprovision* step.

In 2008, the Organisation for Economic Cooperation and Development (OECD) published a document specifying certain *Properties of Identity* (OECD, *At a Crossroads: "Personhood" and Digital Identity in the Information Society*, 2008). These properties apply to 'personal identities' (i.e. identities that belong to individual humans), and for each property the OECD (*OECD Guidelines on the Protection of Privacy and Transborder Flows of Personal Data*, 1980) describes how the OECD privacy guidelines apply to it. We list below these identity properties, along with their OECD descriptions.

1. **Identity is social.** Humans are naturally social, and to engage in social interactions requires that people be able to connect the past to the present, and the present to the future. People need, in other words, something

Figure 2. Digital identity lifecycle

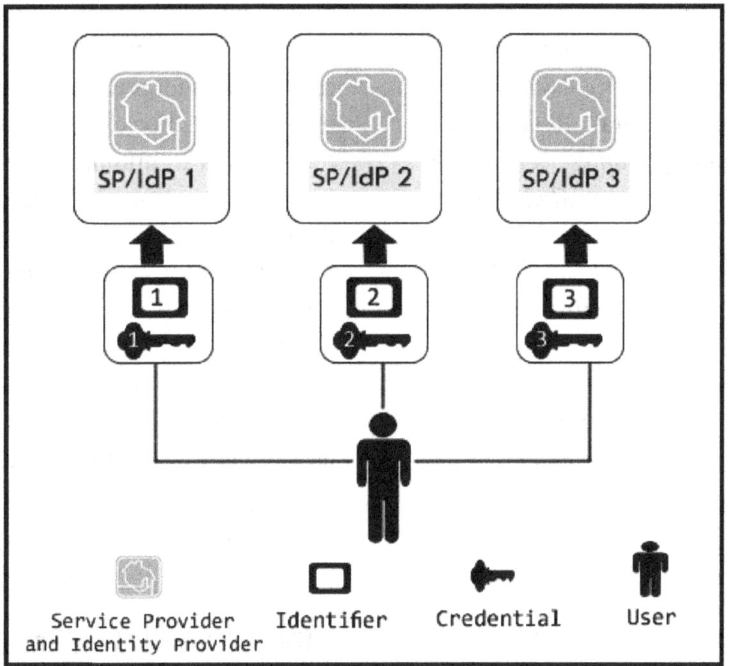

that persists and that can be used as a basis for recognition of persons—an 'identity'.

2. **Identity is subjective**. Different people have different experiences with the same individual and therefore attribute different characteristics to that individual; that is, they will construct different identities for him.
3. **Identity is valuable**. By building a history of a person's past actions, an exchange of identity information creates social capital and enables transactions that would not be possible without identity. In other words, identity lends predictability to afford a comfortable level of confidence for people making decisions.
4. **Identity is referential**. An identity is not a person; it is only a reference to a person.
5. **Identity is composite**. Some information about a person arises from the person himself; he volunteers it. But much information about him is developed by other actors without his involvement.
6. **Identity is consequential**. Because identity tells of a person's past actions, the decision to exchange identity information carries consequences. Disclosure of identity information in a certain context can cause harm; failure to disclose identity information in another context can create risk.
7. **Identity is dynamic**. Identity information is always changing; any particular identity dossier might be inaccurate at any given moment.
8. **Identity is contextual**. People have different identities that they may wish to keep entirely separate. Information can be harmful in the wrong context, or it can simply be irrelevant. Keeping identities separate allows a person to have more autonomy.
9. **Identity is equivocal**. The process of identification is inherently error-prone.

IDENTITY MANAGEMENT

A recent draft of ITU-T recommendation Y.2720 (Y.2720 (Y.ngnIdMframework), NGN Identity management framework—Draft Recommendation, 2008) defines *identity management* as a "*set of functions and capabilities (e.g. administration, management and maintenance, discovery, communication exchanges, correlation and binding, policy enforcement, authentication and assertions) used for:*

- *assurance of identity information (e.g. identifiers, credentials, attributes);*
- *assurance of the identity of an entity (e.g. users/subscribers, groups, user devices, organisations, network and service providers, network elements and objects, and virtual objects); and*
- *enabling business and security applications*".

A similar definition of identity management can be found in the first committee draft of ISO/IEC 24760 (ISO/IEC Second CD 24760, 2010); identity management is defined there as a set of processes, policies and technologies that help authoritative sources as well as individual entities to manage and use identity information. An *authoritative source* (or *identity authority*) of identity information is a place from which a relying party can obtain reliable information about the attributes of a given entity (ISO/IEC Second CD 24760, 2010).

Identity management processes include: management of the identity lifecycle, management of identity information, and management of entity authentication as a preparatory step for authorisation. Identity management is an essential part of many security services, since it provides assurance of user legitimacy. As a result, identity management is an integral part of any access management system (ISO/IEC Second CD 24760, 2010).

Since identity management requires storing, processing, and transforming identity information, it raises many privacy concerns. Moreover, requirements for privacy and identity management may conflict. For example, while it is a privacy requirement to minimise the amount of identity information collected about a person (according to the first of the OECD principles for personal data protection (*OECD Guidelines on the Protection of Privacy and Transborder Flows of Personal Data*, 1980), this may effect the level of assurance that can be obtained regarding the correctness of the claimed identity of a person. Hence protecting user privacy in identity management systems is a challenging issue (Claubeta, Kesdogan, & Kölsch, 2005, Taylor, Lips, & Organ, 2009).

IDENTITY MANAGEMENT MODELS

In this section we give a conceptual model for identity management; we then provide an introduction to the concept of Single Sign-On. Finally, we define three categories of identity management systems which cover most of the widely discussed schemes, namely isolated, Information Card-based, and Federated identity management systems.

Conceptual Model

Although a variety of identity management schemes have been proposed, these schemes have similar primary goals and share many technical features. Here, we focus on 'web-based' identity management schemes. Such schemes are of considerable practical significance because of the growing use of web applications.

It has become common, or even necessary, for Internet users to possess multiple digital identities. Managing these identities and protecting the corresponding credentials are difficult problems. This is because of the need for growing numbers of such identities, and the major security threats posed by criminal activities such as identity theft. Web-based identity management aim to address the growing range of security threats and to simplify identity management for both Internet users and service providers.

Web-based identity management systems use the World Wide Web[1] and Web Services (WS) (Booth et al., 2004) protocols as the communication means between parties. These schemes have been primarily developed to manage Internet users' digital identities.

Three main parties can be identified within the web-based identity management model:

1. **The Identity Provider or Identity Issuer** (IdP) issues an identity to the user, and is trusted by the other parties for the purposes of identity management. The IdP is essentially an 'identity authority' (see Section 2).
2. **The Service Provider** (SP) (or Relying Party (RP) in Microsoft[2] terminology), needs to identify the user before providing services to him/her.
3. **The User** needs to use the SP services. Typically, the user employs a *user agent* (e.g. a web browser) as the means by which she/he interacts with the IdPs and SPs.

All web-based identity management systems adhere to the same conceptual model, shown in Figure 3. In order for the user to use the services offered by a specific SP, it must first be authenticated by an IdP that is trusted by the target SP. Subsequently, the SP asks the IdP for cryptographically-protected statements (or assertions) about the authenticity and/or attributes of the user. The SP then uses the provided statements to help decide whether or not the user should be permitted to use its services.

Both the IdP and the SP have their own *security polices*. The IdP security policy includes information specific to individual users, including: how the user should be authenticated, which SPs it can send assertions about that user to, and which user attributes can be asserted. The SP security policy specifies which IdPs it trusts, how users must be authenticated by a specific IdP, and what types of attributes must be asserted by a specific IdP in order for a user to be granted the requested services.

A process called *discovery of identity source* (or simply *discovery*) (ISO/IEC Second CD 24760, 2010) must take place during the user authentication process. This step enables the system to locate the IdP which is to be asked for an assertion. This step could be performed by either the user machine or the SP server; however, performing it on the user machine has the advantage of giving some protection against phishing attacks. Specifically, if a malicious SP performs discovery, then it could direct the user client to a fake IdP.

If there is a need for direct communication between the IdP and the SP, e.g. in order to exchange information about a user, then, depending on the identity management system in use, they may use a pseudonym or a temporary ID to refer to the user instead of the registered user identity. Such a procedure helps to preserve user anonymity.

If assertions are passed from the IdP to the SP via the user agent, then some identity management systems allow the user agent to prove its rightful possession of the assertion to the SP. This mitigates the risk of attacks in which an attacker uses an assertion issued to another user to impersonate that user. Such services are known variously as *proof-of-rightful-possession*, *subject confirmation* or *proof-key* methods. A variety of techniques for providing such proof have been proposed, and specific examples are described in Section 3.4.2 and 3.4.3. Before proceeding we observe that the so-called *Bearer* technique does not provide the SP with any cryptographic evidence that the user who forwarded a security token has the right to possess it. Use of this technique therefore increases this risk of an imposter using a stolen security token to gain access to an SP.

Identity management frameworks can be classified into the following three main classes,

Figure 3. An identity management conceptual model

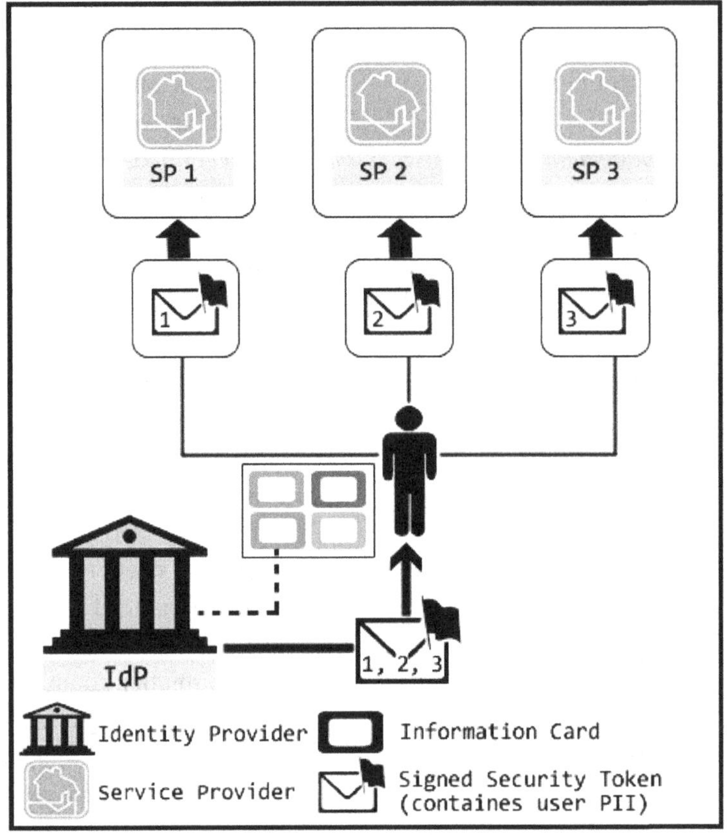

depending on the nature of the IdP/IdP and IdP/SP relationships (Ahn, Ko, & Shehab, 2008).

1. **Isolated framework**. In such a framework there is no co-operation between parties to support user authentication. The SP trusts only itself, and also plays the role of the IdP.
2. **Centralised framework**. A framework of this type has a single IdP that provides identity services to other participating SPs within a closed domain or 'circle of trust'.
3. **Distributed framework**. In such a framework each party within a given group trusts some or all of the parties within this group. This means that every party within a group is either an IdP that is trusted by some or all members of this group, or an SP that trusts some or all of the IdPs within the group.

In this chapter we are concerned with centralised and distributed identity management frameworks.

Single Sign-On

Single Sign-on (SSO) is an access control feature which allows a user to access multiple SPs during a session, after being authenticated only once by a trusted authentication authority (e.g. an IdP). Obviously, all accessed SPs must trust this authority's decision regarding the legitimacy of the user. A system that supports SSO typically also provides support for 'Single Sign-off' (where a user signs-off just once and is then automatically signed-off from all accessed SPs).

One important property of SSO, as we define it, is that it must work without the need for the user to participate interactively (in real time) in the authentication process, or in any other identification relevant process, more than once in a single working session. That is the SSO feature should work transparently to the user, since one of the main reasons for deploying an SSO system is user convenience.

Although SSO potentially enhances both system usability and user convenience, its use also raises significant security concerns. This is because, in many SSO systems, if an attacker breaks the authentication process with the authentication authority (e.g. by cracking the user password) then she/he can readily access all the participating SPs (Gollmann, 2004).

Level of Assurance

A widely used definition of the term *Level of Assurance* (LoA) in the context of identity management, states (Bolten, 2003) that LoA is:

1. the degree of confidence in the vetting process used to establish the identity of the individual to whom the credential was issued (i.e. the degree of confidence in the registration process); and
2. the degree of confidence that the individual who uses the credential is the individual to whom the credential was issued (i.e. the degree of confidence in the authentication process).

The concept of LoA is also referred to in the literature as Personal Identity Verification (PIV) Authentication Level, PIV Assurance Level, Identity Assurance Level, Authentication Profile, Authentication Context, and Authentication Assurance Level.

It is clear that an SP's level of assurance that a user is truly who he/she claims to be depends on both the authentication process used by the IdP and the IdP's initial identity registration process (Chadwick, 2008). Accordingly, an SP could define an access control system that gives the same user different access rights and privileges depending on the SP's level of confidence in the IdP's registration and authentication processes.

In 2006, the US National Institute of Standards and Technology[3] (NIST) published its *Electronic Authentication Guideline* (Burr, Dodson, & Polk, 2006), which adopted Office of Management and Budget[4] (OMB) guidance originally published in 2003 under the title *E-Authentication Guidance for Federal Agencies* (Bolten, 2003). According to these two documents, LoA can be classified into 4 levels, where Level 1 is lowest and 4 is highest. The main features of the OMB/NIST levels are as follows.

- **Level 1**: This level does not require any proof of identity during the registration process. However, it provides a range of methods to be used in the authentication process. Although a simple username/password authentication method is permitted at this level, plaintext passwords must not be transmitted across a network. However, this level does not require the use of cryptographic methods that block offline attacks by an eavesdropper. At Level 1, long-term shared authentication secrets may be revealed to verifiers. Assertions issued about users as a result of a successful authentication by the IdP must be either cryptographically authenticated by the SP or obtained directly from the IdP via a secure authentication protocol.
- **Level 2**: This level mandates a single factor authentication process. At Level 2, identity proof requirements are introduced, requiring presentation of identifying materials or information during the registration process. Eavesdropper, replay, and on-line guessing attacks are prevented. Long-term shared authentication secrets, if used, are never revealed to any party except the claimant and verifiers operated by the Credentials

Service Provider (CSP); however, session (temporary) shared secrets may be provided to independent verifiers by the CSP. Assertions issued about users as a result of a successful authentication by the IdP must be either cryptographically authenticated by the SP or obtained directly from the IdP via a secure authentication protocol.

- **Level 3**: This level mandates a multi-factor authentication process. A minimum of two authentication factors is required. At this level, identity proof procedures require verification of identifying materials and information. Level 3 authentication is based on 'proof of possession' of a key or a 'one-time password' through a cryptographic protocol. Level 3 authentication requires the use of cryptographically strong mechanisms to protect the primary authentication token (secret key, private key or one-time password) against compromise by protocol threats including: eavesdropper, replay, on-line guessing, verifier impersonation and man-in-the-middle attacks. Long-term shared authentication secrets, if used, are never revealed to any party except the claimant and verifiers operated directly by the Credentials Service Provider (CSP); however, session (temporary) shared secrets may be provided to independent verifiers by the CSP. Approved cryptographic techniques are used for all operations. Assertions issued about users as a result of a successful authentication by the IdP must be either cryptographically authenticated by the SP or obtained directly from the IdP via a secure authentication protocol.
- **Level 4**: This level is intended to provide the highest practical authentication assurance. Level 4 authentication is based on proof of possession of a key through a cryptographic protocol. The user token shall be a hardware cryptographic module validated at FIPS 140-2 Level 2 ("Security Requirements for Cryptographic Modules", 2001) or higher, with at least FIPS 140-2 Level 3 physical security. By requiring a physical token which cannot readily be copied, and since FIPS 140-2 requires operator authentication at Level 2 and higher, this level ensures robust, two-factor, remote authentication. Eavesdropper, replay, on-line guessing, verifier impersonation and man-in-the-middle attacks are prevented. Long-term shared authentication secrets, if used, are never revealed to any party except the claimant and verifiers operated directly by the Credentials Service Provider (CSP); however, session (temporary) shared secrets may be provided to independent verifiers by the CSP. All sensitive data transfers are cryptographically authenticated using keys bound to the authentication process.

In 2007, the Interoperable Delivery of European eGovernment Services to Public Administrations, Businesses and Citizens[5] organisation (IDABC) published a document entitled '*Proposal for a multi-level authentication mechanism and a mapping of existing authentication mechanisms*' (Graux & Majava, 2007), in which four levels of assurance are proposed: minimal assurance, low assurance, substantial assurance, and high assurance. These levels are similar to the OMB/NIST levels, and cover both registration and authentication processes.

It would potentially be helpful if the concept of LoA could be integrated into the currently used assertion exchange protocols (e.g. SAML), so that the IdP could specify the LoA of every assertion it provides. According to a survey conducted by the Joint Information Systems Committee[6] (JISC) (M. Jones et al., 2006), 83% of surveyed IdPs would be willing to follow technical guidance on the use of LoA if such guidance was available. Fortunately, SAML 2.0 provides the means to express the LoA of assertions (Kemp, Cantor, Mishra, Philpott, &

Maler, 2005, Tiffany, Madsen, & Cantor, 2009). A recent European Network and Information Security Agency[7] (ENISA) report (*Mapping IDABC Authentication Assurance Levels to SAML v2.0—Gap analysis and recommendations*, 2008) proposes a model for mapping the IDABC levels to SAML 2.0.

Both the OMB/NIST and the IDABC levels have been criticised for the fact that they focus only on the user authentication process, and do not cover user identity attributes (as used for authorisation) (Chadwick, 2008). Moreover, even though the OMB/NIST and IDABC LoA metrics combine the registration and the authentication processes, Chadwick (Chadwick, 2008) suggests that "*it is more useful if the LOA is split into two separate metrics, one for registration of the identity attributes, and one for the authentication method being used in the current session*". A further limitation of the OMB/NIST and IDABC levels of assurance is that they combine both symmetric and asymmetric cryptography within the same level, which can be confusing for implementers (Noor, 2008).

Practical Models

In this section we describe three categories of identity management systems which cover most widely discussed schemes. These categories are defined in terms of the techniques used for user authentication and identification. We refer to these three categories as *practical models*.

Isolated Identity Management

An *isolated* identity management scheme is one in which there is no cooperation between parties for the purposes of user authentication (Jøsang & Pope, 2005). Historically, most Internet service providers operated isolated identity management systems. As a result, users were, and often still are, required to maintain a distinct identifier for each service provider. As shown in Figure 4, in the isolated model the service provider is also an identity provider (i.e. the service provider issues identities to its users).

Isolated identity management schemes are primarily designed to aid service providers rather than the end users. For example, many service providers deploy automated systems to manage digital identities; however, these systems do not help end users, who must manage their digital identities manually.

In many isolated identity management systems, service providers authenticate users using an application layer technique (e.g. username and password), whereas user agents (e.g. web brows-

Figure 4. Isolated identity management model

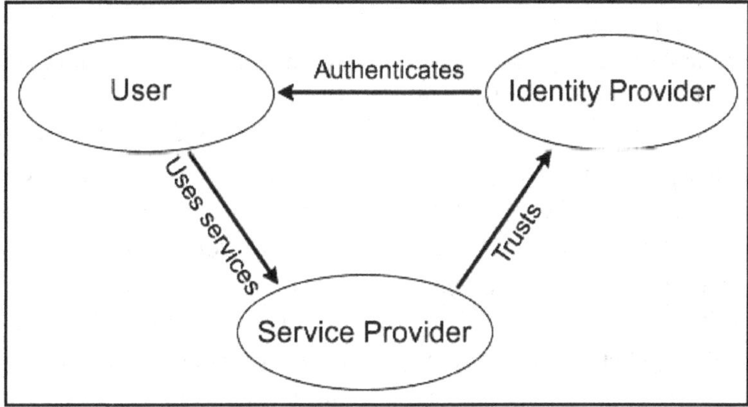

ers) authenticate service providers using a lower layer technique (such as SSL/TLS). Managing multiple digital identities and protecting the associated credentials in such an environment can become very difficult for users.

Information Card-Based Identity Management

An *Information Card-based* identity management (ICIM) scheme (also known as a claim-based identity management scheme (Bertocci, Serack, & Baker, 2008, Microsoft Corporation, 2005a)) is one which has the following properties:

- for each IdP with which the user has a relationship, there is a defined set of claims, i.e. pieces of PII for which the IdP is prepared to generate an assertion;
- when using the system, the user is presented with a choice of IdPs using a 'card-based' user interface;
- at least one proof-of-rightful-possession method is supported (see Section 3.1);
- users are capable of asserting their own claims; and
- IdP discovery is performed on the user machine.

ICIM schemes have been designed to make identity management easier for Internet users; such schemes enable users to employ their IdP-asserted PII to identify themselves to SPs, instead of using service provider specific identifiers (e.g. usernames) and access credentials (e.g. passwords).

In order to authenticate a user, the SP can request a 'security token' containing assertions of the values of certain pieces of user PII (i.e. claims). This security token must be signed by an IdP trusted by the SP. The user agent obtains a security token from an IdP, after being authenticated, and forwards it to the SP.

As stated above, ICIM schemes make use of virtual *Information Cards* (also referred to as InfoCards, or i-Cards), where IdPs issue such cards to users (typically in the form of XML files). Information Cards are stored on user machines, and hold (relatively) non-sensitive meta-information related to the user, including the types of claim that can be asserted (if required by the target SP), and information about the IdP that issued it (the next chapter provides more details on the contents of Information Cards used by specific examples of ICIM systems). During use, a user chooses one of the Information Cards stored on her/his machine to identify themselves to the SP that they wish to access. An IdP is able to assert the values of any claims listed in an Information Card it has issued. This is somewhat similar to the identification process we experience in real life, where we use physical ID cards (issued by a trusted authority) that have information about us stored in it and/or printed on it (e.g. a personal photo) in order to identify ourselves. Figure 5 shows the inter-entity relationships in the ICIM model.

In an ICIM system, an enabling component known as the *Identity Selector* (Microsoft Corporation, 2008) needs to be present on the user machine. This component performs several important tasks including: providing a user-friendly interface for Information Card management and security token viewing, negotiating the security requirements of the SPs and IdPs, supporting identity provider discovery, controlling and managing user authentication to the IdP, and generating self-issued security tokens. Self-issued tokens contain assertions made by the users about themselves, and are generated by the Self-issued Identity Provider (SIP), part of the Identity Selector.

Identity provider discovery in ICIM systems is performed by the user in conjunction with the user agent and the Identity Selector. The Identity Selector prompts the user to choose one of the Information Cards that support the claims which the target SP wishes to have asserted. By choosing an Information Card the user implicitly selects the IdP that will be asked for a security token,

Figure 5. Information Card-based identity management model

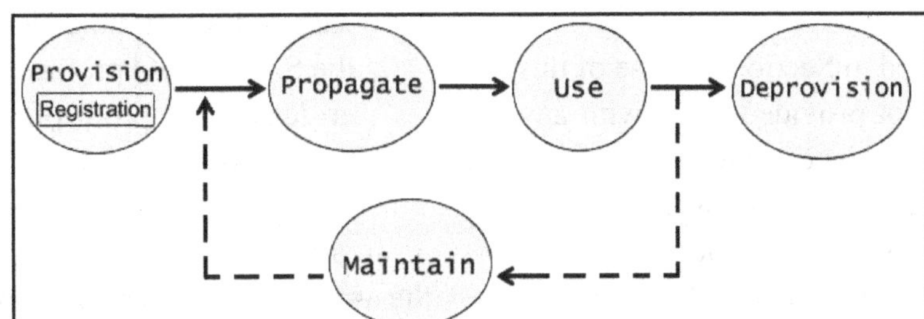

since Information Cards are specific to IdPs. We describe in greater detail how IdP discovery is performed in specific examples of ICIM systems in the next chapter.

In an ICIM system, the user is authenticated by the IdP through the Identity Selector. A user is required to present her security credentials to the Identity Selector (e.g. a username/password) so they can be passed to the IdP before it issues the requested security token. This authentication step must be performed every time before a security token can be issued, even if the user chooses to use the same InfoCard/IdP to access multiple SPs[8]. This means that an ICIM system cannot offer an SSO service, following the definition of the term given in Section 3.2.

Each Information Card typically has a global unique ID, and this ID can be used by the IdP to generate a new 'secret' long-term SP-specific ID (usually referred to as the *Private Personal Identifier* (PPID)) (Nanda, 2007). In the case of a self-issued Information Card, the SIP will generate the PPID. This PPID must be registered with the SP, and is known only by the IdP (or the SIP) and the SP; even the user cannot obtain a full PPID from the Identity Selector. PPIDs act as pseudonyms, and are used for identification purposes, e.g. by requesting the Identity Selector to obtain a security token from the IdP (or the SIP) that contains a specific PPID. Both types of ID, i.e. the global Information Card ID and the PPID, are treated as user claims.

A common feature of ICIM systems is that their identity management framework can be used for both authentication and authorisation. This is possible because the ICIM model allows SPs to request signed assertions of unique identifiers as well as other user attributes (they are all considered as claims).

ICIM systems typically offer three 'proof-of-rightful-possession' methods (Microsoft Corporation, 2008):

1. *Symmetric*. In this method, the Identity Selector must reveal to the IdP the identity of the SP to which the user is trying to log-in. The IdP generates a secret key, encrypts it with the SP's public key, and inserts it into the security token. This secret key is also sent directly to the Identity Selector (over an SSL/TLS channel) in a separate message. The Identity Selector can now use this secret key to prove rightful possession of the security token to the SP (e.g. by decrypting or MACing specific data using the secret key), since only the legitimate holder of the security token possesses the secret key.
2. *Asymmetric*. In this method, the Identity Selector generates an ephemeral RSA key pair, and sends the public key to the IdP. The IdP inserts this public key into the security token. The Identity Selector can then use the corresponding private key to prove rightful possession of the security token to the SP

(e.g. by signing specific data using the private key).

3. *Bearer*. As noted in Section 3.1, use of this method does not provide the SP with any cryptographic evidence that the user who forwarded a security token has the right to possess it. This means that the SP must assume that any user who provides a security token is the rightful owner. This method increases this risk of an imposter using a stolen security token to gain access to an SP.

The *Security Token Service* (STS) is a component of an ICIM system responsible for security policy and token management at the IdP and, optionally, at the SP (M. B. Jones, 2006).

The most widely discussed example of an ICIM system is Microsoft CardSpace[9]. Other ICIM systems include OpenInfoCard[10], Higgins[11], and DigitalMe[12]. DigitalMe is supported by the Bandit Project[13]. We will focus on Microsoft CardSpace because of its ubiquity as part of Windows Vista and Windows 7; however, many of the observations made in the remainder of this thesis regarding Microsoft CardSpace also apply to other ICIM systems since they have strong similarities to one another.

Finally we observe that, since they cannot provide SSO (as discussed above), ICIM systems do not adopt the SAML SSO profiles (Hughes et al., 2005). For further details see the next chapter.

Federated Identity Management

A *Federated* identity management (FIM) scheme is one which has the following properties:

- identity federation process is supported, in which the user SP-issued identity is linked with the user IdP-issued identity;
- the use of public global identifiers is not supported (as discussed below);
- SSO is supported;
- the scheme is built on an open, standardised, communication framework (e.g. the SAML SSO profiles); and
- at least one proof-of-rightful-possession method is supported.

In a Federated identity management system, the user might have one or more 'local' identities issued by SPs, in addition to a single identity issued by the IdP within a specific domain called a *circle of trust* (CoT). A typical CoT consists of a single IdP and multiple SPs. The IdPs of a CoT must be trusted by all the SPs within it. An SP can be a member of more that one CoT. A user can federate her/his IdP-issued identity with the local identities issued by SPs within the same CoT (ISO/IEC Second CD 24760, 2010, Windley, 2005).

Federating two identifies (where they exist) means linking them together so that if a user has been successfully authenticated as the holder of one (e.g. the IdP-issued identity), then he/she will be automatically deemed as the holder of the others, without the need for another authentication process in the same working session. This linking process is called *identity federation*. The process of identity federation has to be initiated by an SP; typically, when a user logs-in to an SP, the SP will check if that user has an IdP-issued identity. If so, then the SP can offer the user the opportunity to federate his/her local identity with his/her IdP-issued identity. Federating identities requires the user to separately authenticate to the SP and the IdP. If the user has federated several IdPs with an SP, then it is up to the SP to choose an IdP from amongst them, except in the enabled-client SSO profile (described in the next chapter) in which the user can be provided with a list of IdPs to choose from.

In order to support the above federation process, there must be a reliable means for an SP to discover whether or not the user has an IdP-issued identity. This can be achieved by using the 'common domain cookie' technique (Hughes et al., 2005). This technique involves establishing a CoT-specific common web domain to which every member of that CoT has access, in order for any member to be able to read cookies written by any other member. This would typically involve each member of the CoT owning its own web page under that domain.

For example, suppose that a CoT, *isgCoT* say, includes an IdP, *X* say, and two SPs, SP_1 and SP_2. The members of this CoT establish a common domain (isgCoT.com) say, and each member is assigned a sub-domain (e.g. IdPX.isgCoT.com, SP1.isgCoT.com, and SP2.isgCoT.com). The IdP *X* can then write a cookie from the domain IdPX.isgCoT.com that says, for example, '*I am IdP X, and I have issued an identity to this user*', and store this cookie on the machine of every user it has successfully authenticated (note that the identifier of the IdP-issued identity will never be revealed). Such a cookie is known as a *common domain cookie* (CDC). Subsequently, when a user that has already been authenticated by IdP *X* logs-in to SP_1 or SP_2, the service provider can read the CDC stored on the user's machine by redirecting the user agent to the service provider sub-domain. If the SP finds an entry from IdP *X* in the CDC, then they can assume that this user has an IdP-issued identity.

Once federation has taken place for a user's identities, an SP will know which IdP(s) it can ask to supply a token. The SP redirects the user agent (e.g. a web browser) to the relevant IdP. If the user has not already been authenticated during this working session, the IdP authenticates her/him, and redirects the user agent back to the SP with a signed assertion of the fact that this user has been successfully authenticated by the IdP using a specific method at a given time. Finally, the SP checks the information included within the assertion and verifies the IdP's signature; if the SP accepts the assertion, the user will be logged-in to the SP without the need for another authentication procedure. Figure 6 shows the inter-entity relationships in the Federated identity management model.

Typically, an IdP will only authenticate the user once during a single working session. Hence, almost all Federated identity management systems provide support for SSO functionality. Moreover, we observe that most of the Federated identity management systems are built on SAML SSO profiles (Cantor, Hirsch, Kemp, Philpott, & Maler, 2005, Hughes et al., 2005, Maler, Mishra, & Philpott, 2003).

Unique user identifiers make up a P3P[14] data category that must be protected in order to preserve user privacy (Wenning, 2006). Hence, these identifiers (either local or IdP-issued) must not be shared between CoT members. However, without sharing unique identifiers, it would be difficult to federate two identities belonging to the same user, since the SP and the IdP need to make sure that they are referring to a particular user in the system when they communicate. Typically, a federated identity management system solves this dilemma by using pseudonyms instead of the user's pre-issued identifiers, thereby providing unlinkability. The IdP and the SP must agree on specific pseudonyms (also known as *opaque handles*) as references to a particular user during the federation process; this agreement is an important part of what is known as a *federation agreement* procedure. The SAML Persistent ID (PID) field can be used to hold such a pseudonym in an SAML message. The PID is used for essentially the same purpose as the PPID described in Section 3.4.2.

As shown in Figure 7, the IdP and the SP may agree to use the same pseudonym to refer to a particular user, or they may use distinct pseudonyms. Regardless of how pseudonyms are used, it is clearly important that each party knows which pseudonym the other party will use to refer to a given user. For example, suppose that a user named *Alice* has three identities, an IdP-issued identity, *Alice@IdP*, and two local identities, *Alice.1@SP1* and *Alice.2@SP2*, issued by, SP_1 and SP_2, respectively. The IdP could use one pseudonym (*xxx*, say) to refer to *Alice* when it communicates with SP_1, and a different pseudonym (*yyy*, say) when

Figure 6. Federated identity management model

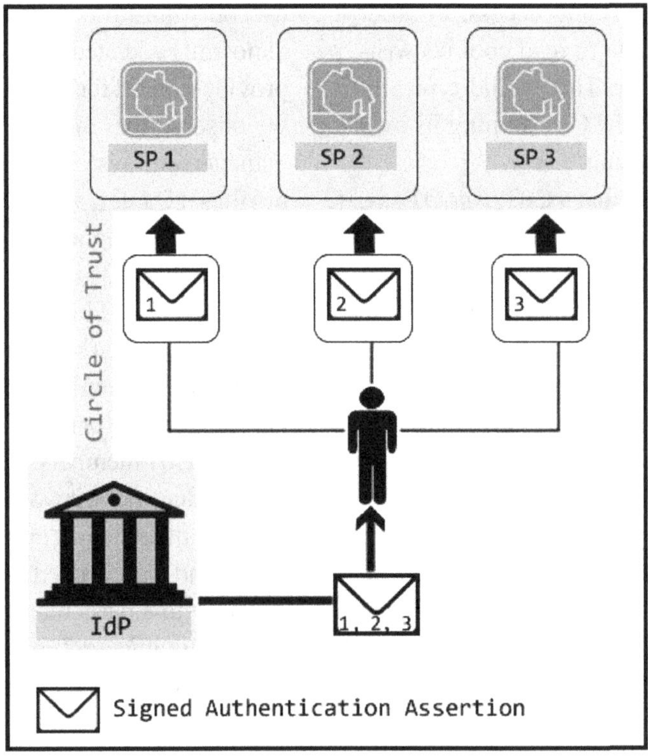

it communicates with SP_2. However, although the IdP is using the pseudonym *yyy* to refer to *Alice* when it communicates with SP_2, SP_2 may use a different pseudonym *y*123, say) to refer to the same user when it communicates with the IdP.

However, in some Federated identity management systems, the IdP and the SP do not agree on long-term pseudonyms for a particular user. Instead of using pseudonyms, the IdP and the SP use temporary IDs agreed during the authentication process. Such temporary IDs are typically only used for one working session (the use of temporary IDs is discussed in more detail in the next chapter in the context of specific examples of FIM systems). Of course the discovery method described above will not work in this case, because no federation process has taken place prior to the user log-in attempt. Therefore, another 'intermediary' discovery method is used, known as '*Where Are You From*' (WAYF). In this approach, the user is given a list of IdPs, and must select the IdP that issued the identity to be federated with the user's local identity. Although the user selects the IdP, the discovery is performed by the SP server (i.e. the SP redirects the user to the IdP, after it discovers the target IdP). More details on the WAYF method can be found in (Widdowson & Cantor, 2008).

Since most Federated identity management systems rely on the SAML SSO profiles, the IdP and SP can communicate directly by redirecting the user agent from one party to the other, assuming they use the SAML Web Browser profiles (Hughes et al., 2005). In this case, no enabling component needs to be installed on the user machine. However, if they use the SAML Enhanced Client profile, then an enabling component is required. These profiles are described in greater detail in the next chapter.

Figure 7. Pseudonyms in federated identity management

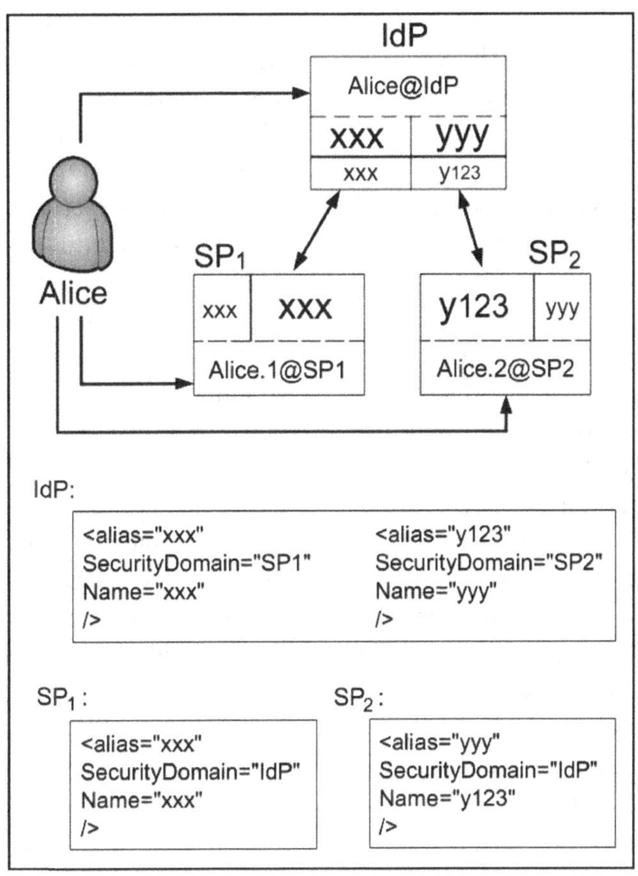

Federated identity management systems typically offer three 'proof-of-rightful-possession' methods (Monzillo, Kaler, Nadalin, & Hallem-Baker, 2006, Scavo, 2009):

1. *Holder-of-Key* (HoK). This method enables the user agent to prove its rightful possession of a specific assertion using a cryptographic key (either symmetric or asymmetric). If a symmetric key is used, then this key must be included in the signed assertion generated by the IdP, after being shared with the user. If an asymmetric private key is used, then the corresponding public key must be included in the signed assertion. How the IdP shares the symmetric secret key or the asymmetric public key with the user agent is usually left to the system implementers. Moreover, if a symmetric key is used, and unlike the ICIM 'symmetric' method, the IdP is not required to encrypt the symmetric (secret) key using the SP's public key. Of course this does not necessarily mean that the key is sent in the clear; it is typically sent over a secure channel (e.g. as provided by SSL/TLS or IPSec).
2. *Sender-Vouches*. This method is only used if the entity that presents the assertion to the SP is not the subject of the assertion, but nevertheless has the permission of the subject to present it to the SP on its behalf. Such an entity is called an *attesting entity*, and must have an existing trust relationship with the SP. The *subject* of an assertion is

the party whose attributes are asserted by the IdP-issued assertion. The subject could be an end user or another SP. The attesting entity must sign the assertion (even though it is already signed by the IdP) before forwarding it to the SP.

3. *Bearer*. This method is identical to the ICIM 'bearer' method described in Section 3.4.2 above.

These methods are known as the SAML proof-of-rightful-possession (or subject confirmation) methods, since they were first specified in the SAML specifications. Federated identity management systems typically rely on SAML assertions to hold the proof-of-rightful-possession data.

The Liberty Alliance Project[15] scheme is an example of a federated identity management system. Many of the observations we make in this here regarding the Liberty Alliance Project system also apply to other Federated identity management systems, since they have strong similarities to one another. Other examples of Federated identity management systems include the SAML 2.0 Federation Framework (Cantor, Kemp, Philpott, & Maler, 2005), WS-Federation (Nadalin & Kaler, 2006), and Shibboleth[16].

Although the OpenID[17] model is quite similar to the Federated identity management model, OpenID is not a Federated identity management system under the definition used in this chapter. This is because of the lack of explicit trust relationships in the OpenID model, the lack of 'federation' support, and the fact that OpenID does not support any proof-of-rightful-possession method. Further details of OpenID in the next chapter.

Finally, we observe that the concept of *User-centric identity management* (Ahn et al., 2008, Bramhall, Hansen, Rannenberg, & Roessler, 2007, ISO/IEC Second CD 24760, 2010, Jøsang & Pope, 2005, Jøsang, Zomai, & Suriadi, 2007) has been proposed as a means of easing the user task of managing digital identities by providing them with more control over their identities. A user-centric identity management system is one that is developed primarily from the perspective of end-users, enabling a user to maintain control over how user PII is created and used, thereby enhancing user privacy. Many identity management systems have been referred to as user-centric, including ICIM systems such as Microsoft CardSpace and PRIME (Camenisch et al., 2005), and Federated identity management systems such as UFed (Suriadi, Foo, & Jøsang, 2009).

Table 1. Information card-based versus federated identity management

Comparison Point	ICIM	FIM
Discovery of IdP	Performed on the user machine	Typically performed on the SP server
Pseudonyms	Used	Used
Identity federation	Not supported	Supported
Software enabling component on the user machine	Required	Typically not required
Self-issued assertions	Supported	Not supported
Single Sign-On	Not supported	Typically supported
Built on SAML SSO profiles	No	Yes
The IdP must be informed of all the accessed SPs	No	Yes
Proof-of-rightful-possession methods	Symmetric, Asymmetric, and Bearer	Holder-of-Key (Symmetric and Asymmetric), Sender-Vouches, and Bearer

CONCLUSION

In this chapter we have provided an overview of the notion of identity. Definitions of identity have been provided, along with a brief description of the identity lifecycle. We have also provided definitions of identity management and related terms such as authoritative source and identity authority.

A web-based conceptual model of identity management has been presented, as well as introductions to SSO systems and the concept of LoA. Finally, descriptions of three practical models of identity management systems have been provided, namely Isolated, Information Card-based, and Federated identity management. The Isolated model is related to the Isolated class discussed in Section 3.1, whereas the ICIM and FIM models can be either Centralised or Distributed.

Although the FIM and ICIM models share a number of the properties, as discussed in 3.4.2 and 3.4.3, each model has its own distinct properties. The FIM model does not support two of the ICIM model properties, namely the possession of a card-based interface, and support for users to assert their own claims[18]. On the other hand, the ICIM model does not support two of the FIM model properties, namely federation and SSO support.

Table 1 provides a comparison between Information Card-based and Federated identity management schemes.

REFERENCES

Ahn, G.-J., Ko, M., & Shehab, M. (2008). Portable user-centric identity management. In *Proceedings of the IFIP TC-11 23rd International Information Security Conference, IFIP 20th World Computer Congress*, IFIP SEC 2008, Milano, Italy (pp. 573-587). Springer-Verlag.

Bertocci, V., Serack, G., & Baker, C. (2008). *Understanding Windows CardSpace*. Addison-Wesley.

Bolten, J. B. (Director). (2003, December). *E-authentication guidance for federal agencies*. M-04-04. Office of Management and Budget (OMB), Executive Office of the President, The White House, Washington DC, USA.

Booth, D., Haas, H., McCabe, F., Newcomer, E., Champion, M., Ferris, C., et al. (2004, February). *Web services architecture*. The World Wide Web Consortium (W3C).

Bramhall, P., Hansen, M., Rannenberg, K., & Roessler, T. (2007, July/August). User-centric identity management: New trends in standardization and regulation. *IEEE Security & Privacy, 5*(4), 84–87. doi:10.1109/MSP.2007.99

Burr, W. E., Dodson, D. F., & Polk, W. T. (2006, April). *Electronic authentication guideline - Special publication 800-63 - Version 1.0.2*. Recommendations of the National Institute of Standards and Technology (NIST), USA.

Camenisch, J., Shelat, A., Sommer, D., Fischer-Hubner, S., Hansen, M., Krasemann, H., et al. (2005, November). Privacy and identity management for everyone. In *Proceedings of the 2005 Workshop on Digital Identity Management* (pp. 20-27). Fairfax, VA: ACM.

Cantor, S., Hirsch, F., Kemp, J., Philpott, R., & Maler, E. (Eds.). (2005, March). *Bindings for the OASIS security assertion markup language (SAML) V2.0. OASIS Standard Specification*. OASIS Open.

Chadwick, D. W. (2008). Federated identity management. In Aldini, A., Barthe, G., & Gorrieri, R. (Eds.), *Foundations of Security Analysis and Design V, FOSAD 2007/2008/2009 Tutorial Lectures* (*Vol. 5705*, pp. 96–120). Springer. doi:10.1007/978-3-642-03829-7_3

Claubeta, S., Kesdogan, D., & Kolsch, T. (2005). Privacy enhancing identity management: Protection against re-identification and profiling. In *Proceedings of the 2005 Workshop on Digital Identity Management*, Fairfax, VA, USA (pp. 84-93). ACM.

Gollmann, D. (2004). *Computer security*. John Wiley & Sons.

Graux, H., & Majava, J. (2007, December). *eID interoperability for PEGS - Proposal for a multi-level authentication mechanism and a mapping of existing authentication mechanisms*. The Interoperable Delivery of European eGovernment Services to public Administrations, Businesses and Citizens (IDABC). ENISA. (2008, November). *Mapping IDABC Authentication Assurance Levels to SAML v2.0 - Gap analysis and recommendations*.

Hughes, J., Cantor, S., Hodges, J., Hirsch, F., Mishra, P., Philpott, R., et al. (2005, March). *Profiles for the OASIS security assertion markup language (SAML) V2.0*. OASIS Standard Specification, OASIS Open.

ISO/IEC. (2010). *Second CD 24760 — Information technology — Security techniques — A framework for identity management*.

ITU-T. (2009). *X.1250 (X.idmreq), baseline capabilities for enhanced global identity management trust and interoperability.* Draft new Recommendation, 2009.

Jones, M., MacIntyre, R., Morrow, T., Nenadić, A., Pickles, S., & Zhang, N. (2006, November). *E-infrastructure security: Levels of assurance*. The Joint Information Systems Committee (JISC).

Jones, M. B. (2006, March). *A guide to supporting InfoCard v1.0 within web applications and browsers*. Microsoft Corporation.

Jøsang, A., & Pope, S. (2005). User centric identity management. In *Proceedings of Australian Computer Emergency Response Team Conference* (AUSCERT 2005).

Jøsang, A., Zomai, M. A., & Suriadi, S. (2007). Usability and privacy in identity management architectures. In *Proceedings of the Fifth Australasian Information Security Workshop Privacy Enhancing Technologies* (AISW 2007), Victoria, Australia (pp. 143-152). Australian Computer Society.

Maler, E., Mishra, P., & Philpott (editors), R. (2003, September). *Bindings and profiles for the OASIS security assertion markup language (SAML) V1.1*. OASIS Standard Specification, OASIS Open.

Microsoft Corporation. (2005a, May). *Microsoft's vision for an identity metasystem*.

Microsoft Corporation. (2008, July). *A guide to using the identity selector interoperability profile V1.5 within Web applications and browsers*.

Monzillo, R., Kaler, C., Nadalin, A., & Hallem-Baker, P. (Eds.). (2006, February). *Web services security: SAML Token profile 1.1*. OASIS Standard Specification. OASIS Open.

Nadalin, A., & Kaler, C. (Eds.). (2006, December). *Web services federation language: WS-Federation, version 1.1*.(BEA Systems, BMC Software, CA, IBM, Layer 7 Technologies, Microsoft, Novell, and VeriSign. Nanda, A. (2007, April). *Identity selector interoperability profile v1.0*. Microsoft Corporation.

Noor, A. (2008). Identity protection factor (IPF). In *The 7th Symposium on Identity and Trust on the Internet* (IDTrust 2008) (vol. 283, pp. 8-18). ACM.

Organisation for Economic Co-operation and Development (OECD). (1980). *OECD guidelines on the protection of privacy and transborder flows of personal data*.

Organisation for Economic Co-operation and Development (OECD). (2008). *At a crossroads: "Personhood" and digital identity in the information society.*

Scavo, T. (Ed.). (2009, November). SAML V2.0 holder-of-key assertion profile - Version 1.0 - committee draft 3. OASIS Open.

Suriadi, S., Foo, E., & Jøsang, A. (2009). A user-centric federated single sign-on system. *Journal of Network and Computer Applications, 32*, 388–401. doi:10.1016/j.jnca.2008.02.016

Taylor, J. A., Lips, M., & Organ, J. (2009). *Identification practices in government: Citizen surveillance and the quest for public service improvement. Identity in the Information Society*. Springer-Verlag.

Tiffany, E., Madsen, P., & Cantor, S. (Eds.). (2009, May). *Level of assurance authentication context profile for SAML 2.0 - Working Draft 03*. OASIS Open.

Wenning, R. (editors), Schunter, M. (2006, November). *The platform for privacy preferences*, version 1.1. W3C Working Group Note.

Widdowson, R., & Cantor, S. (Eds.). (2008, March). *Identity provider discovery service protocol and profile - Committee specification 01. OASIS Standard Specification*. OASIS Open.

Windley, P. (2005). *Digital identity*. O'Reilly Media.

Y.2720. (2008). *NGN identity management framework - Draft recommendation.*

ENDNOTES

1 http://www.w3.org/WWW
2 http://www.microsoft.com
3 http://www.nist.gov
4 http://www.whitehouse.gov/omb
5 http://ec.europa.eu/idabc
6 http://www.jisc.ac.uk
7 http://www.enisa.europa.eu
8 This has been verified by experiment for the CardSpace ICIM.
9 http://www.microsoft.com/net/cardspace.aspx
10 http://code.google.com/p/openinfocard
11 http://www.eclipse.org/higgins
12 More implementations are listed at: http://www.osis.idcommons.net
13 http://bandit-project.org
14 http://www.w3.org/P3P
15 http://www.projectliberty.org
16 http://shibboleth.internet2.edu
17 http://openid.net
18 Many FIM systems support the LEC profile, in which IdP discovery is performed on the user machine.

Chapter 18
Selecting and Implementing Identity and Access Management Technologies: The IAM Services Assessment Model

Peter Haag
Utrecht University, The Netherlands

Marco Spruit
Utrecht University, The Netherlands

ABSTRACT

This chapter investigates how organizations can be supported in selecting and implementing Identity and Access Management (IAM) services. Due to the ever growing number of applications that are being used in organizations, stricter regulations and changing relationships between organizations, a new approach towards login- and password administration, security, and compliance is needed. IAM services claim to provide this new approach. Unfortunately, IAM selection projects have not been very successful in the recent past. Therefore, this chapter presents the IAM Services Assessment Model which provides a useful and usable tool to support organizations in the selection and implementation of IAM services.

INTRODUCTION

During the recent decades, organizations have changed tremendously. One of the most important changes has been the mass-computerization, which has forced organizations to change the way they operate. This mass-computerization has been one of the most important enablers of the ongoing increase in both the size and the complexity of organizations. It is self-evident that those developments have had a wide range of consequences. Most have been positive, but during recent years

DOI: 10.4018/978-1-61350-498-7.ch018

some negative consequences of those developments have surfaced as well.

Some of those negative consequences are related to the way organizations manage identities and the access to their buildings and their IT-infrastructure. To deal with those negative consequences, the way in which the identification and authentication for access to an application is organized needs to be changed. During recent years, several major IT-suppliers like Oracle, IBM, Sun Microsystems, Novell and CA have introduced IAM systems in order to support organizations in doing so.

An article on the website of Wall Street Technology (Wall Street Technology, 2008) reports that a new research from Forrester estimates the market for IAM solutions to grow more than 20 percent over the next years. The total market is expected to grow from 2.6 billion dollars in 2006 to more than 12.3 billion dollar in 2014.

Despite the fact that these figures show that a growing amount of organizations is planning to implement IAM technologies, efforts to select and implement the right solutions have proven to be little successful (Becker & Drew, 2005). Therefore, the question arises if there is any way in which organizations can be supported in making the right decision with regard to the type of IAM solution they should implement. This chapter is aimed at developing a method to support organizations and their consultancy partners in effectively and efficiently selecting the right tools to cope with the challenges they have identified in the field of Identity and Access Management.

BACKGROUND

IAM has a relatively brief history. The directory management tools that emerged in the 1990's can be seen as the start of the development of IAM systems (Rizvi, 2006), although that term was not introduced until much later. Single Sign-on and Identity Administration followed, growing along with the number of applications used in organizations.

The current IAM market has its roots in a wide range of domains, as many of the different product areas within the IAM market have started out as separate markets that flowed together over time (Cser, 2008). However IAM is nowadays often considered to be a single market, the fragmented history of the field explains why the IAM market still contains a variety of vendors, from pure players to companies that offer comprehensive IAM solutions. A quote from the research vice president at Gartner describes the situation within the current IAM market perfectly: "No company has bought tools from one vendor, or implemented them all at once, They tend to solve their problems one at a time so most organizations are somewhere along the automations track, but very few have done it all." (Everett, 2007).

MAIN FOCUS OF THE CHAPTER

As mentioned before, the rising interest in IAM solutions, in combination with the limited success of IAM selection and implementation projects, raises the question how organizations can be supported in making the right decision with regard to the type of IAM solution they should implement. This chapter will elaborate on the creation of the IAM Services Assessment Model that was developed as an answer to that question. To start creating the IAM Services Assessment Model, eight carefully selected IAM services will be elaborated upon. The selection of the services is mainly based on the adoption of the services. The services that were selected are widely adopted in organizations and have proved to be potentially beneficial in practice. Another selection criteria was the universality of the services. The services that were selected are all vendor-independent and can represent several specific services that are aimed at the same challenge and provide comparable functionalities. The selection was validated during the expert interviews.

IAM CHALLENGES

As mentioned before, the ever increasing amount of applications that are being used in most organizations has some negative consequences. Those consequences are a challenge for organizations. This section will present the challenges in the field of IAM that were identified in literature.

During the analyses of the literature study results, and again during the introduction interviews, it became clear that the challenges in the field of IAM can be distinguished into several categories. In order to be able to present the challenges in a structured and conveniently arranged way, the challenge categories will be presented and elaborated upon first. The challenges will subsequently be discussed using the structure of this categorization.

The following types of challenges will be used: financial, security, regulatory compliance and ease of use. As mentioned before, the classification is based on both the literature found during the literature study and the introduction interviews. For instance, Becker & Drew (Becker & Drew, 2005) use exactly the same categorization. Furthermore, the categories are mentioned either as problem categories or as drivers for the implementation of IAM systems by others.

In the remainder of this section, the challenges will be discussed using the categorization described above. The challenges and the categorization of the challenges will be used together with the IAM services that will be elaborated upon later as a basis for the IAM Services Assessment Model.

Financial Challenges

Low user productivity: User productivity is negatively influenced by the wide array of login credentials that have to be managed by the user (Rizvi, 2006). Not only is valuable time lost if users have to log into every application separately, but productive time is also lost if an employee cannot enter an application or data that is needed for the execution of a task due to a lost or forgotten login name or password.

Redundant tasks: Because of the increasing number of applications, often in combination with an increasing number of users, it becomes very expensive to manage the login credentials for all applications, due to staff expenses, among others.

Many password calls: Every user in an organization has to remember all login credentials that are needed to access applications and data required for the execution of his or her job. As the number of applications increases, this is becoming impractical or even impossible. Especially for applications that are not used very often or require frequent password resets and strict password requirements, it is likely for the users to forget their login credentials from time to time. The helpdesk often has to manually reset the password every time a user forgets it. All those password calls combined account for a substantial part of the occupation of the helpdesk, and therefore for substantial costs (Rizvi, 2006).

Slow provisioning: Besides this, manual identity and access management processes cause an extensive lead time before new employees can be productive within the applications they need access to. This results in considerable loss due to a lower initial productivity of the new employee.

Security Challenges

Impractical security policies: A problem that surfaces more and more as the number of applications keeps growing, is that all login credentials need to be remembered by the users, and need to be securely stored by the system administrators. If users are forced to use more login credentials than they can reasonably remember, they are inclined to write the credentials down or record them in a text or spreadsheet document on their computers. This is even more likely to occur if password resets are time- and effort consuming procedures. Although understandable, such behavior is obviously a serious infringement on the security of the organization and both its digital and material possessions.

Inconsistent security policies: If the security policies are not enforced, for instance by a role model that can be used to determine access rights, it is almost impossible to be sure to comply with the security policies in the entire organization (Becker & Drew, 2005).

Inconsistent identity data: If there are many applications in use within the organization that all use their own data repository to keep track of user identities, it is very likely that the identity data will not be consistent throughout the organization (Rizvi, 2006).

Slow de-provisioning: Furthermore, as a result of the growing number of applications and users, it becomes harder to make sure that employees who leave the organization are immediately denied access to confidential information and applications. Due to application centric administration and authentication, there are multiple (and often many) identities of the same employee in use in different applications within the organization. It is very difficult and labor-intensive to make sure every one of those identities is deleted or changed to make sure the employee cannot access data or applications he or she does not need anymore. However, this is vital to guarantee the confidentiality, integrity and availability (CIA) of sensitive information/data that is stored in applications or databases.

Regulatory Compliance Challenges

Need for auditing: In the recent past, there have been a series of corporate and accounting scandals that have caused multiple organizations to lose a lot of money, or even go bankrupt. As a reaction to these scandals, a number of laws and regulations have been introduced (such as the Sarbanes-Oxley Act (SOx), HIPAA, Basel II, etc.). Failing to satisfy the demands of these regulations may result in criminal or civil penalties, not only for the organization, but also for managers who are now held personally responsible for any fraud or other misconducts that have taken place under their area of responsibility. Apart from these legal consequences, not complying to these regulations can also have consequences for the organization that are comparable to those experienced by the organizations that gave rise to the introduction of these laws and regulations. Enron, for instance, went bankrupt in 2001 after an extensive accounting fraud. To prevent any of these consequences, organizations have to be able to show audit and control data to demonstrate their regulatory compliance (Becker & Drew, 2005).

Privacy control issues: The emphasis of regulatory compliance differs based on the parts of the world in which the organization is active. Where law requires segregation of duties in the USA, the focus in Europe and particularly the Netherlands is directed more towards privacy control (Nieuwenhuizen, 2008). As a result of the laws on privacy control in the Netherlands, any organization that allows unauthorized employees (like a receptionist) access to customer data is breaking the law. This means that organizations are forced to make often significant changes to their IT-systems, processes and procedures to avoid liability to prosecution.

Need for segregation of duties: Many of the regulations like SOx, HIPAA and Basel II require segregation of duties. This means that controlling and supervising tasks are not allowed to be performed by the same individuals who perform the tasks that are controlled or supervised (Rizvi, 2006). In other words, employees are not allowed to control or supervise their own activities. However, as mentioned in the elaboration of the 'privacy control issues', the extent to which the need for segregation of duties is required by law is dependent on the parts of the world in which the organization is active. Segregation of duties is mainly an issue in organizations that are active within the USA (Nieuwenhuizen, 2008), but this doesn't mean that segregation of duties cannot provide advantages for organizations that are not operating in the USA.

Ease of Use Challenges

Increasing authentication complexity: when using application centric user authentication, the authentication to all applications that are needed for everyday operations becomes more complex. A user has to remember his or her login credentials for every application, and regularly also for (certain parts of) the building, operating systems, databases, etc. This obviously has a negative effect on the ease of use and the user experience of those systems.

Demand for personalized content: in many of today's organizations, knowledge is the main asset. It is therefore vital for the organization to be able to share the available knowledge among the employees. Many organizations have intranet sites or comparable initiatives to support knowledge sharing. As the amount of information in such a knowledge sharing environment increases, it becomes more difficult to find the specific piece of information that is required at that moment. Especially in large organizations with a wide variety of different expertise areas, making use of the knowledge gained by a colleague becomes difficult en time-consuming as a result. It would therefore be very convenient if the knowledge that is provided can be adapted to the roles of the users. Based on that role, information on the intranet site or any other knowledge sharing solution can be shown or hidden. The user is now only shown the information that is of interest for his role in the organization, instead of being overwhelmed with information that is not of interest for him.

Demand for self-service: as there are more applications in use that rely on application centric administration and authentication, the number of login credentials that need to be remembered grows accordingly. Therefore it becomes increasingly hard to remember all those credentials. Especially considering the fact that many applications require frequent password changes to ensure a high level of security. This results in employees forgetting some of the many credentials they need to memorize, and thus a password reset is needed before the employee has access to the application again. In those situations, employees would prefer to be able to arrange for a new password themselves, instead of being forced into a time- and effort consuming procedure to have their password changed by an admin. Other possibilities for self-service are enabling managers to make resource allocation decisions and allowing vendors to administer their own users (Becker & Drew, 2005). Providing users with this kind of self-service not only improves the ease of use and user experience, but also helps to make support for those activities more efficient. The same holds for the time and effort needed to get (and keep) access to the necessary applications. Not only is it inconvenient for the employee that he or she cannot access the application at that moment, but with a growing number of both applications and users it also gets very hard (and expensive) to have an efficient and fast procedure for passwords resets. Therefore, the employee is likely to write the password down. Again this is very likely to have a negative effect on their attitude towards the IT infrastructure and services.

Slow provisioning: Another effect of the increasing number of application in use within organizations is the frustration employees experience due to long start-up times and time and effort consuming procedures for password resets. The start-up time is the amount of time that is needed to provide a new employee with access to everything he or she needs, like access to the building, a pc or laptop, access to applications, etc. If an employee experiences that he or she cannot be as productive as possible right from the start, this will result in a negative effect on the attitude towards the IT infrastructure and services.

Final Notes on the Challenges in IAM

Most of the problems in the categories security, regulatory compliance and ease of use are likely to ultimately have financial consequences as well. However, the problems in the category financial have direct financial consequences, whereas the problems in the other categories primarily cause problems in their respective categories. Those primary problems may in turn cause financial consequences as well.

An example of a potential financial problem that is closely related to the problem described in the "compliance" and "security" sections is the loss of competitive advantage due to lacking compliance or security. If the increasing number of applications and users result in inadequate security, valuable and classified information may become available for competitors and other interested parties, resulting in potentially substantial losses for the organization. If compliance is compromised by the increasing number of applications and users, it may lead to a lack of control which in its turn can result in criminal or civil penalties and considerable financial losses.

IAM SERVICES

Following the elaboration on the challenges in the field of IAM in the section above, eight carefully selected IAM services will be elaborated upon to create the second dimension of the IAM Services Assessment Model. The selection of the services is mainly based on the adoption of the services. The services that were selected are widely adopted in organizations and have proved to be potentially beneficial in practice. Another selection criteria was the universality of the services. The services that were selected are all vendor-independent and can represent several specific services that are aimed at the same challenge and provide comparable functionalities. The selection was validated during the expert interviews.

The services that are elaborated upon in this section will be used together with the challenges as a basis for the IAM Services Assessment Model. As the IAM services will be linked to the IAM challenges in the model, this section sums up the 'Related IAM challenges' for each of the IAM services. Where applicable, it will be indicated for each of the related challenges from which literature reference this connection has been derived.

Provisioning

User provisioning systems "provide the administrative tools that link a user's business relationship to the electronic access privileges and physical resources (such as a telephone, credit card, or computer) required to perform a commercial function" (Becker & Drew, 2005). In other words, user provisioning makes sure that users have access to everything that is needed to do their jobs. This results in negative consequences on both the financial and ease of use aspects if the provisioning is not carried out fast enough. Therefore, user provisioning systems provide the tools for fast and efficient provisioning, even in complex environments. These tools are the most commonly used IAM tools, accounting for about 50% of the IAM expenditures in 2006. This number is even expected to further grow to 64% in 2014. (Wall Street Technology, 2008)

According to Becker & Drew (Becker & Drew, 2005) there are several functions provisioning systems perform:

- Detect changes in the user life cycle (hiring, role change, separation) by monitoring the key data elements in various systems.
- Define user access needs for electronic and physical assets based on those key data elements
- Create identities and credentials that provide access to electronic and physical assets before they are needed by the user.
- Apply the security policy organization-wide.

Table 1. Targeted IAM challenges by provisioning

IAM Challenge	Type	Key references
Low user productivity	Financial	Becker & Drew (2005)
Redundant tasks	Financial	
Slow provisioning	Financial	Becker & Drew (2005), Delio (2004)
Inconsistent security policies	Security	
Inconsistent identity Data	Security	
Need for segregation of duties	Compliance	Becker & Drew (2005), Delio (2004)
Increasing authentication complexity	Ease of use	

- Create an audit database to keep track of who has what access to applications and other resources, and who authorized it, when, and why.

There are several ways in which a user provisioning system can create and manage identities and credentials (Table 1). Most frequently, a network directory, like LDAP directory, Microsoft Active Directory or Novell eDirectory will be used. However, organizations often already have several of those systems implemented to manage the identification and authentication for various operating systems, applications and databases. Those different systems will very likely contain not only duplicate, but also proprietary data. There are two types of directory integration tools available to solve that problem: virtual directories and metadirectories (Delio, 2004). They will be elaborated upon below in the section Directory technologies.

Tools that provide provisioning services are also capable of de-provisioning (removing privileges). However, because provisioning and de-provisioning are related to different problem categories, they are discussed in separate sections in this document. De-provisioning will be discussed in the next section.

De-Provisioning

For de-provisioning, the same tools and services are used as for provisioning (Table 2). However, for de-provisioning purposes the definition that was given in the previous section can be adapted to "providing the administrative tools that remove a user's electronic access privileges and physical resources (such as a telephone, credit card, or computer) when they are not needed (anymore) to perform a commercial function.

As already mentioned previously, fast and efficient de-provisioning is very important for organizations to ensure the security of vital information. The same tools that enable fast and efficient provisioning can also make sure that an employee who leaves the organization or chang-

Table 2. Targeted IAM challenges by de-provisioning

IAM Challenge	Type	Key references
Redundant tasks	Financial	
Slow de-provisioning	Security	Becker & Drew (2005), Delio (2004)
Need for auditing	Compliance	Delio (2004), Rizvi (2006)
Privacy control issues	Compliance	Delio (2004)

Table 3. Targeted IAM challenges by credential management

IAM Challenge	Type	Key references
Redundant tasks	Financial	
Many password calls	Financial	
Inconsistent identity data	Security	
Increasing authentication complexity	Ease of use	

Table 4. Targeted IAM challenges by auditing

IAM Challenge	Type	Key references
Inconsistent security policies	Security	
Need for auditing	Security	Allan (2008)
Need for segregation of duties	Security	
Increasing authentication complexity	Ease of use	

es roles within the organization does not have access to any data or applications that are not needed anymore from the moment of the separation or role change.

Credential Management

Credentials management tools manage the life cycle of one or more type(s) of credentials, such as smart cards, certificates, biometric data, and proximity cards (Allan, 2008). This functionality is expected to be included into provisioning and single sign-on tools in the near future, but for now these are mostly separate tools that can only be integrated loosely into provisioning and single sign-on tools (Table 3). They support provisioning and single sign-on by offering an easy and time saving way to manage credentials over a broad range of target applications and systems.

Auditing

Auditing is "the process of documenting, reviewing and approving workflow, identity information and access controls (roles, segregation of duties rules and entitlements) for business applications and associated infrastructure components" (Allan, 2008).

The goal of auditing is to control aspects like workflow, identity information and access controls and making sure that those aspects are in line with both internal and external rules and legislation (Table 4). Obviously, this is vital for governance, and specifically for regulatory compliance.

In order to be able to accomplish that control, knowledge is required about (i) what privileges the user should have, based on the policy, (ii) what privileges the user has in practice (and is this consistent with the policy), and (iii) what privileges the user actually used.

(E)SSO (Enterprise) Single Sign-On

There are several disadvantages of having many different sets of login credentials:

Decreasing user productivity: If users have to log in to every application they need separately, this consumes valuable time and effort that can be used otherwise if a single sign-on is used. Furthermore, when users forget their password and have to contact the helpdesk to replace it, more time is lost due to both the time needed to

Table 5. Targeted IAM challenges by (Enterprise) single sign-on

IAM Challenge	Type	Key references
Low user productivity	Financial	Delio (2004)
Many password calls	Financial	Rizvi (2006)
Inconsistent security policies	Security	Delio (2004)
Increasing authentication complexity	Ease of use	Delio (2004)
Demand for personalized content	Ease of use	

contact the helpdesk and productivity lost because the user has no access to an application when needed. (Chinitz, 2000)

User inconvenience: It is inconvenient for a user to have many different sets of login credentials to remember, as it takes substantial time and effort to identify and authenticate time and time again for each application that is entered (Delio, 2004).

Ineffective or obvious passwords: When users have to sustain many different sets of login credentials, they are inclined to choose credentials that are easy to guess and therefore inherently insecure (Delio, 2004).

User negligence: If users are assigned strong passwords (for example by the IT department) they are likely to write down their credentials or record them in a digital file, which are often not kept in a secure place (Chinitz, 2000).

Lots of passwords resets: In many organizations, every time a user has forgotten a login credential, the IT-department has to be contacted to provide a new credential. In large organizations with application centric administration, this is a substantial burden on the IT department, which results in high support costs (Delio, 2004; Rizvi, 2006).

Off course, all these disadvantages will ultimately result in a financial disadvantage for the organization as well. The problems can be overcome by enabling users to access (almost) every operating system, application or database they need with a single set of login credentials.

Systems that provide that functionality have been around for quite some time (Table 5). However, early systems like Kerberos needed applications to be adapted to the use of the systems. With the broad landscape of security infrastructures in place at many organizations, this is not a practical solution anymore. Therefore, today's SSO systems need to be able to connect to every authentication system in use in an organization. They act as a authentication gateway (Chinitz, 2000).

However, not every organization should strive for a complete SSO. As mentioned by Delio: "The appropriate goal for many organizations will be reduced – rather than single – sign-on" (Delio, 2004). The decision on which information sources will be integrated into the SSO has to be taken based on a cost-benefit analysis. For a legacy system to which only a few people need access for a couple of times a year, it will probably not be worth the time and money to integrate it into the SSO system.

Authorization Services

Authorization services are responsible for providing privileges—such as permissions and access rights—o a user, based on the information that is available to the service (Table 6). There are different methods to determine which privileges have to be granted to a user. The most commonly used categories of methods are Discretionary Access Control (DAC), Mandatory Access Control (MAC), and Role-based Access Control (RBAC).

Discretionary Access Control: Identifies an owner for every object and delegates the distribution of privileges to that owner. In most cases, the

Table 6. Targeted IAM challenges by authorization services

IAM Challenge	Type	Key references
Redundant tasks	Financial	
Impractical security policies	Security	Delio (2004)
Inconsistent security policies	Security	Delio (2004)
Need for auditing	Compliance	
Need for segregation of duties	Compliance	
Increasing authentication complexity	Ease of use	Delio (2004)

owner is the user that created the object. As the owner is closely related to the object, he or she is expected to be able make a founded decision on who are allowed to access the object.

Mandatory Access Control: Relies on a combination of pre-established policies and security attributes of a user instead of the object owner to determine the access rights that have to be granted to a user. MAC compares the requirements for access to an object that are stated in a policy to the security attributes of a user. The user gets access to the object if his or her security attributes match the requirements for access to that object. Rule-based Access Control and Context-based Access Control are examples of authorization services that are based on this method.

Role-Based Access Control: Is by far the most commonly used method for user authorization. This method is based on a limited set of roles that are identified within the organization. Each of those roles is linked to a set of privileges. If a role is assigned to a user, that user automatically receives all privileges linked to the role.

Federation

Federated identity systems bring together two or more separately managed identity systems, often from different organizations, to perform mutual authentication and authorization tasks and to share identity attributes (Table 7). It "enables two organizations to administer their own users and interact with business partners utilizing industry standards" (Rizvi, 2006).

One of the most important parts of federation is to create solid and fair agreements between the federation partners. Those partners can be two different organizations, but also two departments form the same organizations, like the Human Resources and the Finance divisions (Windley, 2006).

Those agreements are vital for the success of federation, because each partner needs to be able to trust the other partner(s). For example, when two partners agree to provide access to their property and computer systems to employees of the other party, they have to be sure that their partner is careful enough in the employment, identification and authentication processes to be

Table 7. Targeted IAM challenges by federation

IAM Challenge	Type	Key references
Low user productivity	Financial	
Redundant tasks	Financial	
Slow provisioning	Financial, Ease of use	

Table 8. Targeted IAM challenges by directory technologies

IAM Challenge	Type	Key references
Inconsistent identity data	Security	
Need for segregation of duties	Compliance	Sturdevant (2005)

able to trust the employees of that partner. On the other hand, federation partners have to be careful to avoid creating agreements that are too strict, because this may cause the federation activities to become so expensive that the initial advantage of the federation is negated (Windley, 2006).

An example of the use of federation between organizations is provided by Chen (2005). She describes the way in which General Motors (GM) successfully used federation to make it easier for their 190.000 workers in the United States to access personal information, like health care and retirement benefits, through GM's employee portal MySocrates.

GM outsources many of the HR benefits they offer their employees. The result is that before the implementation of the federated identity management system, employees had to log in to everyone of those services separately. Now, as a result of the federated identity management system, users only have to log onto the MySocrates portal, and have access to all their personal information from there.

Directory Technologies

Directory technologies are products that "store and organize information about user identities and other resources within a network or domain and manage users' access to resources" (Allan, 2008). To enable these technologies to do this, they are equipped with extensive search possibilities and are optimized for reads. Directory technologies were once thought to be the answer to all IAM problems, but this has not come true (Table 8). However, many organizations use directory technologies as the backbone of their IAM architecture.

According to Gartner (Allan, 2008) many organizations can achieve about 60% of their functional IAM requirements with directory tools. However, there are some functions that cannot be provided by directory tools and have to be supplied by dedicated tools. There are several types of directory technologies, of which some are more established than others. The remainder of this section will elaborate on the most popular directory technologies, namely virtual directories and metadirectories.

Virtual directories: Virtual Directories are defined as "software products that create a logical (virtual) view of an LDAP directory by combining data from multiple repositories, or by combining multiple repositories into a single view" (Kreizman et al., 2007). In other words, a virtual directory is an intermediary between the data repository and applications. The virtual directory presents itself towards the application as a customized directory that provides exactly that information that is required by the application. To the data repositories on the other hand, the virtual directory presents itself as an application that asks for exactly the part of the needed information that can be supplied by the data repository in question (Sturdevant, 2005). By doing so, a virtual directory eliminates the need to synchronize multiple directories in order to provide a single view (Rizvi, 2006).

A virtual directory can pre-eminently be used to implement new applications or functionalities without the need to create a whole new physical data repository. An additional advantage of the fact that a virtual directory does not manipulate the data in any way can be found in situations in which ownership of the data is a delicate subject: "Virtual directories are excellent choices when

Table 9. Targeted IAM challenges by advanced self-service

IAM Challenge	Type	Key references
Low user productivity	Financial	
Many password calls	Financial	
Demand for personalized content	Ease of use	
Demand for self-service	Ease of use	

dealing with workgroups that have ownership issues concerning their data – since a virtual directory doesn't alter data, it just points to its location" (Delio, 2004).

Furthermore, as virtual directories are able to record which data has been accessed by which user, a virtual directory can help organizations to comply to regulation and legislation like SOx and HIPAA (Sturdevant, 2005).

Metadirectories: In contrast to virtual directories, which create a view in which data from different repositories is combined without moving the data, metadirectories create copies of directory data to combine data from several repositories into one large data repository (Sturdevant, 2005). "A metadirectory system establishes a single authoritative directory as the source of all data" (Delio, 2004).

While it can create an advantageous situation by physically storing all data on a single location, this solution requires a relatively complex and thus often costly infrastructure to enable replication and synchronization to ensure that the data are always up to date. It is especially useful when accuracy is considered the most important factor: "Metadirectories are ideal for situations where data accuracy across the board is critical. Everyone who has access sees the same information, period" (Delio, 2004).

Advanced Self-Service

Advanced Self-service functionalities enable users to perform tasks that were traditionally carried out by system administrators (Table 9). The reason why they are called 'advanced' self-services in this work is that some forms of self-service have been available for a long time, like the possibility provided by any operating systems to its users to change their password. The self-service functionalities in this section take over a task that was previously performed by system administrator, such as:

(SSO) Password resets: Users can reset their own passwords for applications, databases or even the entire Single Sing-On (SSO) system. The password is for instance changed to an automatically generated password that is sent to the e-mail address that is known by the system to belong to the user. The user can use this temporary password to change the password for a new, personal, password.

Requests for software licenses: A user who needs additional software often has to fill out a request and send that request to a system administrator. The system administrator then has to contact a manager or department staff to validate the request. Depending on the result of that validation, the administrator has to inform the user of a denial or provide the user with the requested software. Self-service functionalities can turn this into an automated process in which the request can be filled out digitally, and is redirected towards the manager (or staff) who is responsible for the validation of the request. The system administrator only receives a message that the user has to be provided with the requested software if the request is validated (electronically). This reduces the workload for system administrators and fastens the process for the user.

Table 10. Validation interview experts

Nr.	Position	Specialties
1	Principal Consultant at Capgemini	IS Architecture and Identity Management
2	Managing Consultant at Capgemini	Compliance governance architecture, Recertification, Authorisation Management, RBAC, Segregation of Duties, Recertification tools
3	Managing Consultant at Capgemini	Security, Security Convergence, Identity Management, Access Management, Access Control, Authorization Management
4	Managing Consultant at Capgemini	Identity and Access Management, RBAC, Security, GvIB
5	Managing Consultant at Capgemini	Specialist in Identity & Access Management
6	Principal Consultant at Domus Technica Editor of "Informatiebeveiliging" at PvIB	Identity and Access Management, Security Architecture
7	Managing Director at Domus Technica BV	Security, Risk Management, Compliancy, Business Continuity
8	Solution Architect at HP Computer & Network Security Consultant	Computer & Network Security

Requests for privileges: A request for privileges results in many cases in a process that is comparable to the one described above with regard to requests for software licenses. Self-service functionalities can therefore provide comparable services to reduce the workload for system administrators and fasten the process for the user.

Reporting problems and errors: Problems or errors that users encounter with systems can now be reported online, where they formerly were reported by phone. This saves system administrators lots of time, as the problems can be handled more efficiently this way.

The IAM Services Assessment Model

As both dimensions of the IAM Services Assessment Model have now been introduced and elaborated upon—i.e. IAM challenges and IAM services—the time has come to present the model itself. The objective of the model is to support organizations in selecting the right IAM service(s) to deal with their specific challenges with regard to IAM. The models shows the IAM services vertically (in the rows) and the challenges horizontally (in the columns). Each category of challenges was given a distinctive color to make it easier to read and use the model.

The IAM Services Assessment Model is depicted in Figure 1 and can be used bipartitely: the model can be used both service-centric and challenge-centric. The service-centric use of the model provides the user with an overview of the challenges that will be dealt with by a certain IAM service. The challenge -centric use of the model focuses on the challenges the user wants to deal with, and shows the user which IAM services are suitable to do so.

Validation

This section will elaborate on the validation of the IAM Services Assessment Model. A total of eight experts have been interviewed. During the interviews, the IAM experts were asked to fill out the IAM Services Assessment Model. They had no knowledge in any way about how the model in Figure 1 (that was based on the literature study) looks like. The only information that was given to the IAM experts was an explanation on the definition of the challenges and IAM technologies in the context of this research. The experts that were interviewed are shown in Table 10.

The model in Figure 2 shows the accumulated results of the model validation. The numbers in the cells show how many of the eight IAM experts

Figure 1. The concept IAM services assessment model based on literature

Challenges / IAM services	Financial				Security				Compliance			Ease of Use			
	Low user productivity	Redundant tasks	Many password calls	Slow provisioning	Impractical security policies	Inconsistent security policies	Inconsistent identity data	Slow de-provisioning	Need for auditing	Privacy control issues	Need for segregation of duties	Increasing authentication complexity	Demand for personalized content	Demand for self-service	Slow provisioning
Provisioning	X	X		X		X	X					X			X
De-provisioning		X						X	X	X					
Credential management		X	X				X					X			
Auditing						X			X		X	X			
Single Sign-On	X		X			X						X	X		
Authorisation (access control)		X			X	X			X		X	X			
Federation	X	X		X											X
Directory technologies							X				X				
Advanced self-service	X		X										X	X	

marked each cell, to indicate a direct link between the technology and the challenge. The red borders indicate which links are present in the model based on the literature study. The model was adapted based on the results of the validation in the following way:

- 0, 1 or 2 markings: the experts do not think that there is a direct connection between the technology and the challenge. If a connection was placed based on literature, that connection was removed.
- 3, 4 or 5 markings: the experts do not agree on if there is a direct connection between the technology and the challenge. No changes were made to the findings from the literature study.
- 6, 7 or 8 markings: the experts think that there is a direct connection between the technology and the challenge. If no connection was placed based on literature, a connection was added.

This method resulted in the changes shown in Table 11.

The adaptations result in the final IAM Services Assessment Model, which is shown in Figure 3.

FUTURE RESEARCH DIRECTIONS

Looking at the research that was carried out, there are some areas in which additional research can be performed.

The first and foremost is the validation of the IAM Services Assessment Model during actual selection processes in organizations that are planning to implement one or more IAM service(s). Due to time constraints and the limited set of organizations that are starting large IT-projects in

Figure 2. The IAM services assessment model with validation results

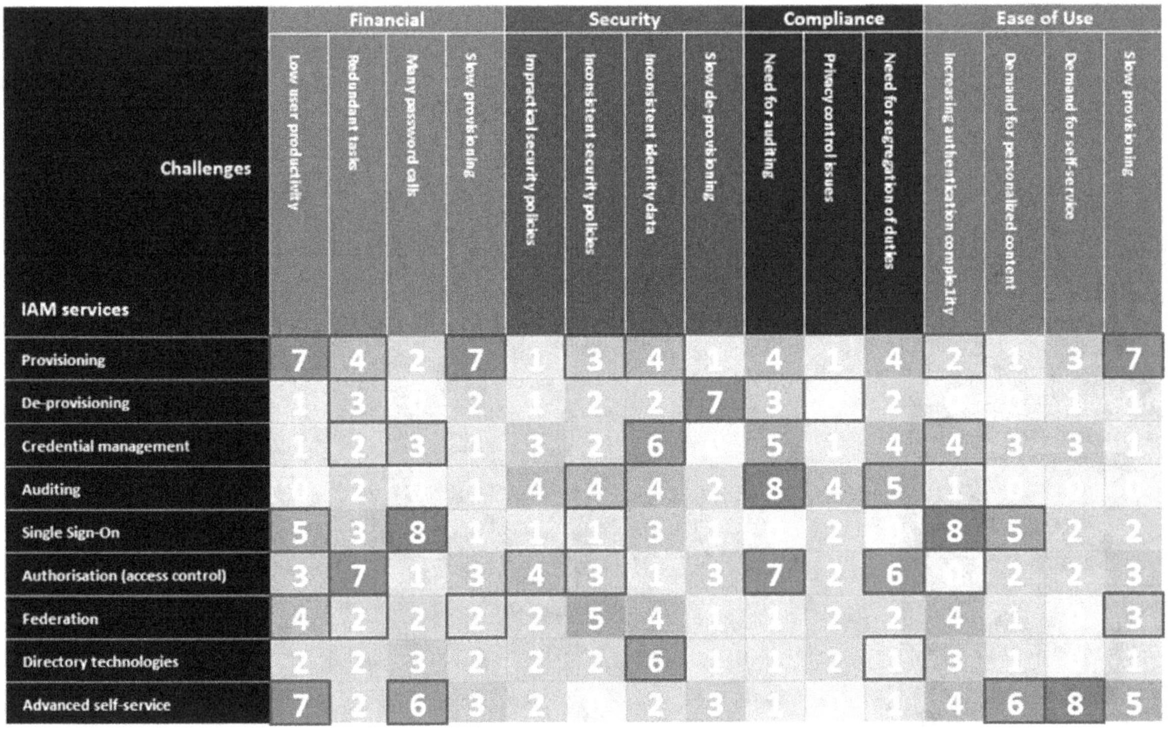

Challenges / IAM services	Financial: Low user productivity	Financial: Redundant tasks	Financial: Many password calls	Financial: Slow provisioning	Security: Impractical security policies	Security: Inconsistent security policies	Security: Inconsistent identity data	Security: Slow de-provisioning	Compliance: Need for auditing	Compliance: Privacy control issues	Compliance: Need for segregation of duties	Ease of Use: Increasing authentication complexity	Ease of Use: Demand for personalized content	Ease of Use: Demand for self-service	Ease of Use: Slow provisioning
Provisioning	7	4	2	7	1	3	4	1	4	1	4	2	1	3	7
De-provisioning	1	3	0	2	1	2	2	7	3		2	0	0	1	1
Credential management	1	2	3	1	3	2	6	0	5	1	4	4	3	3	1
Auditing	0	2	0	1	4	4	4	2	8	4	5	1	0	0	0
Single Sign-On	5	3	8	1	1	1	3	1	0	2	1	8	5	2	2
Authorisation (access control)	3	7	1	3	4	3	1	3	7	2	6	1	2	2	3
Federation	4	2	2	2	2	5	4	1	1	2	2	4	1	0	3
Directory technologies	2	2	3	2	2	2	6	1	1	2	1	3	1	0	1
Advanced self-service	7	2	6	3	2	0	2	3	1	0	1	4	6	8	5

these difficult economic times, it was unfortunately not possible to validate the model longitudinally in practice. Although the validation by IAM experts has produced a very usable and sound model, a validation based on multiple IAM service selections would make the model even more robust.

Something that was already mentioned in the validation section of this chapter, is that the IAM experts indicated that the challenges in the category Security are too similar to allow organizations to make a clear distinction between them. As a result of that remark, further research should be

Table 11. Removed IAM associations in the literature-based model shown in Figure 1 based on the expert validation results shown in Figure 2

Change #	IAM challenge type	IAM challenge	Removed IAM service link
1	Financial	Redundant tasks	Credential management
2	Financial	Redundant tasks	Federation
3	Financial	Slow provisioning	Federation
4	Security	Inconsistent security policies	Single Sign-On
5	Compliance	Privacy control issues	De-provisioning
6	Compliance	Need for segregation of duties	Directory technologies
7	Ease of use	Increasing authentication complexity	Provisioning
8	Ease of use	Increasing authentication complexity	Auditing
9	Ease of use	Increasing authentication complexity	Authorization

Figure 3. The validated IAM services assessment model

Challenges / IAM services	Financial				Security				Compliance			Ease of Use			
	Low user productivity	Redundant tasks	Many password calls	Slow provisioning	Impractical security policies	Inconsistent security policies	Inconsistent identity data	Slow de-provisioning	Need for auditing	Privacy control issues	Need for segregation of duties	Increasing authentication complexity	Demand for personalized content	Demand for self-service	Slow provisioning
Provisioning	X	X		X		X	X								X
De-provisioning		X						X	X						
Credential management			X				X					X			
Auditing						X			X		X				
Single Sign-On	X		X									X	X		
Authorisation (access control)		X			X	X			X		X				
Federation	X														X
Directory technologies							X								
Advanced self-service	X		X										X	X	

performed to assess the changes that can be made to the IAM Services Assessment Model to solve this problem.

A final suggestion with regard to further research based on this work concerns the adoption of the IAM Services Assessment Model with respect to the ongoing developments in the field of IAM services. The IAM services that were included in the model were selected based on their current level of adoption. However, some of the IAM services that were not included into the model at this time (because their current level of adoption is still rather low) may well develop into the leading IAM services of tomorrow. Therefore, especially in a few years from now, some additional research should be carried out to update the model in concordance with the IAM services that are leading in terms of adoption at that time.

CONCLUSION

The purpose of the research was to find an answer to the research question "How can organizations be supported in the process of selecting and implementing IAM technologies?". The answer to this research question was the development of the IAM Services Assessment Model that was presented in this chapter.

To come to this result, the research was started with a literature study. Based on that literature study, the initial IAM Services Assessment Model was developed as shown in Figure 1. Then, the model was validated with the help of eight IAM experts which were introduced in Table 10. Based on that validation, nine changes were made to the initial model as listed in Table 11. Figure 3, finally, shows the resulting validated version of the IAM Services Assessment Model.

The conclusion of this research—with regard to selecting the right IAM service to cope with the challenges the organization is faced with—is that the IAM Services Assessment Model provides a useful and successfully validated tool that can be used both service-centric and challenge-centric. The service-centric use of the model provides the user with an overview of the challenges that will be dealt with by a certain IAM service, while the challenge-centric use of the model focuses on the challenges the user wants to deal with, and shows the user which IAM services are suitable to do so. The IAM Services Assessment Model supports organizations in selecting the right IAM services efficiently and effectively, thereby providing a satisfactory answer to our research question.

REFERENCES

Allan, A. (2008). *Identity and access management technologies defined*. Stamford, CT: Gartner.

Becker, M., & Drew, M. (2005). Overcoming the challenges in deploying user provisioning/identity access management backbone. *BT Technology Journal*, *23*(4), 71–79. doi:10.1007/s10550-006-0009-x

Chinitz, J. (2000). Single sign-on: Is it really possible? *Information Systems Security*, *9*(3), 33–45. doi:10.1201/1086/43310.9.3.20000708/31359.5

Cser, A. (2008). *The Forrester Wave: Identity and access management, Q1 2008*. Cambridge, MA: Forrester.

Delio, M. (2004, September 6). Better security through identity. *Infoworld.com*, 35-42.

Everett, C. (2007). Piecing identity together. [Elsevier.]. *Infosecurity*, *4*(6), 22–25. doi:10.1016/S1754-4548(07)70145-6

Kreizman, G., Enck, J., Litan, A., Wagner, R., Orans, L., & Allan, A. (2007). *Hype cycle for identity and access management technologies*. Stamford, CT: Gartner.

Nieuwenhuizen, M. (2008). *Role based identity-en access management is makkelijker gezegd dan gedaan ['Role-based identity and access management is easier said than done']*. Retrieved July 28, 2008, from http://www.marqit.nl/securityschool-compliance-artikel2.aspx

Rizvi, H. (2006). I am who I say I am. *Quarterly Journal of the EDS Agility Alliance*, *1*(2), 46–57.

Sturdevant, C. (2005, June 6). Virtual directories ease quest for identity data. *eWEEK.com*, 43-46.

WallStreet Technology. (2008). *Identity and access management market to reach $12.3 billion in 2014*. Retrieved October 24, 2008, from http://www.wallstreetandtech.com/showArticle.jhtml?articleID=206904330

Windley, P. J. (2006, March 27). The hidden challenges of federated identity. *InfoWorld.com*, 27-33.

KEY TERMS AND DEFINITIONS

Authentication: the entity proofs that it is the rightful 'owner' of the identity by providing one or more credential(s).

Authorization: the entity is allowed a particular set of actions to be performed in the secured environment based on the combination of the identifier and the credential(s) provided by the entity.

Federation: linking two or more separate IT systems, enabling them to share authentication data and perform mutual identification, authentication and authorization services.

IAM system: a single set of hardware, software, databases, telecommunications, people, and procedures configured to collect, manipulate, store, and process data into information, supporting identifying individuals and controlling their access to resources, services and systems."

Identification: an entity claims an identity by providing an identifier.

Provisioning: linking a person (for example through his role) to the access rights (both physical and electronic) that are needed to do his/her job properly.

Single Sign-On (SSO): enabling users throughout the organization to log onto every system, application or database with a single set of credentials.

Compilation of References

1999/93/EC – Directive. (1999). *1999/93/EC of the European Parliament and of the Council of 13, December 1999 on a Community framework for electronic signature*.

Aberdeen Group. (2007). *Identity and access management critical to operations and security: Users find ROI, increased user productivity, tighter security*. March.

Adams, P. (2010). *Closing the gap between people's online and real life social network*. Paul Adams Presentations. Retrieved August 31, 2010, from http://www.slideshare.net/padday/the-real-life-social-network-v2

AdMob. (2010). *AdMob mobile metrics report*. Retrieved from http://metrics.admob.com/wp-content/uploads/2010/03/AdMob-Mobile-Metrics-Feb-10.pdf

Adobe Systems Incorporated. (2010). *Adobe Flashplayer*. Retrieved August 31, 2010, from http://www.adobe.com/products/flashplayer/

Aegis. (2009). *Article on identity management software, identity management solutions, identity access management*. Retrieved from http://www.aegisusa.com/

Aggarwal, G., Burzstein, E., Jackson, C., & Boneh, D. (2010). *An analysis of private browsing modes in modern browsers*. Proc. of Usenix Security.

Aguiar, R. L. (2010). *Deliverable DII-122*. Updated Daidalos II global architecture. Retrieved August 23rd, 2010, from http://www.ist-daidalos.org/

Ahn, G. J., Ko, M., & Shehab, M. (2008). Portable user-centric identity management. In Proceedings of the IFIP TC-11 23rd International Information Security Conference, IFIP 20th World Computer Congress, IFIP SEC 2008, Milano, Italy (pp. 573-587). Springer-Verlag.

Ahn, G., & Lam, J. (2005). Managing privacy preferences for federated identity management. In *Proceedings of the 2005 Workshop on Digital Identity Management,* DIM'05, ACM, Fairfax VA USA, (pp. 28-36).

Ahn, G.-J., & Sandhu, R. S. (1999). The RSL99 language for role-based separation of duty constraints. In *Proceedings of the 4th ACM Workshop on Role-Based Access Control*, (pp. 43–54).

Ahsant, M., Basney, J., & Mulmo, O. (2004, July). Grid delegation protocol (Technical Report No. YCS-2004-380). University of York, Department of Computer Science.

Akamai Technologies. (2006). *Retail web site performance*. Retrieved from http://www.akamai.com/4seconds

Allan, A. (2008). *Identity and access management technologies defined*. Stamford, CT: Gartner.

Allan, A., Perkins, E., Carpenter, P., and Wagner, R. (2008). *What is identity 2.0? Key issues for identity and access management*. Gartner Research Report, ID Number: G00157012.

Allison, D., El Yamany, H., & Capretz, M. (2009). Metamodel for privacy policies within SOA. *Proc. of the 5th IEEE International Workshop on Software Engineering for Secure Systems in conjunction with the 31st IEEE International Conference of Software Engineering*, Vancouver, Canada, May 19, (pp. 40-46).

Alrodhan, W. A., & Mitchell, C. J. (2009). Improving the security of CardSpace. *EURASIP Journal on Information Security*, *9*, 167216. doi:10.1186/1687-417X-2009-167216

Alrodhan, W. A., & Mitchell, C. J. (2007). Addressing privacy issues in CardSpace. In Proceedings of the Third International Symposium on Information Assurance and Security, IAS 2007, Manchester, UK (pp. 285–291). IEEE Computer Society.

Alrodhan, W. A., & Mitchell, C. J. (2008a). A client-side CardSpace-Liberty integration architecture. In Proceedings of the Seventh Symposium on Identity and Trust on the Internet, IDTrust 2008, NIST, Gaithersburg, USA (vol. 283, pp. 1-7). ACM International Conference Proceeding Series.

Alrodhan, W. A., & Mitchell, C. J. (2008b). A delegation framework for Liberty. In Proceedings of the Third Conference on Advances in Computer Security and Forensics, ACSF 2008, Liverpool, UK (pp. 67–73). Liverpool John Moores University.

Alrodhan, W. A., & Mitchell, C. J. (2010). Enhancing user authentication in claim-based identity management. In Proceedings of the 2010 International Symposium on Collaborative Technologies and Systems, CTS 2010, Chicago, Illinois, USA (pp. 75–83). IEEE.

Al-Sinani, H. S., Alrodhan, W. A., & Mitchell, C. J. (2010). CardSpace-Liberty integration for CardSpace users. In Proceedings of the 9th Symposium on Identity and Trust on the Internet, IDTrust 2010, Gaithersburg, Maryland, USA, April 13-15, 2010 (pp. 12-25). ACM.

Anderson, A., & Lockhart, H. (2005). *SAML2.0 profile of XACML v2.0.* OASIS Standard, 1 February 2005; Retrieved August 23rd, 2010, from http://docs.oasis-open.org/xacml/2.0

Anderson, J., Diaz, C., Bonneau, J., & Stajano, F. (2009). Privacy-enabling social networking over untrusted networks. In *Proc. of the 2nd ACM Workshop on Online Social Networks* (pp. 1-6). Barcelona, Spain: ACM Press. doi:10.1145/1592665.1592667

ANS. (2004). *Role based access control.* ANSI/INCITS 359.

Ardagna, C., Cremonini, M., Damiani, E., Capitani, S., Frati, F., & Samarati, P. (2006). *Privacy-enhanced identity management for e-services. Secure e-Government Web Services*. Idea Group Inc.

Arends, R., Austein, R., Larson, M., Massey, D., & Rose, S. (2005, March). DNS security introduction and requirements. RFC 4033, Internet Engineering Task Force.

Armando, A., & Compagna, L. (2008, January). SAT-based model-checking for security protocols analysis. *International Journal of Information Security*, *7*(1), 3–32. doi:10.1007/s10207-007-0041-y

Armando, A., Basin, D., Boichut, Y., Chevalier, Y., Compagna, L., Cuellar, J., et al. (2005). The AVISPA tool for the automated validation of internet security protocols and applications. In *Proceedings of the 17th International Conference on Computer Aided Verification (CAV'05)*. Springer-Verlag. Retrieved from www.avispa-project.org

Armando, A., Carbone, R., & Compagna, L. (2007, July). *LTL model checking for security protocols*. In 20th IEEE Computer Security Foundations Symposium (CSF20). Venice (Italy).

Armando, A., Carbone, R., Compagna, L., Cuéllar, J., & Tobarra, M. L. (2008, October). Formal analysis of SAML 2.0 Web browser single sign-on: Breaking the SAML-based single sign-on for Google Apps. In V. Shmatikov (Ed.), *Proceedings of the 6th ACM Workshop on Formal Methods in Security Engineering, FMSE 2008* (pp. 1–10). ACM.

Armando, A., Carbone, R., Compagna, L., Li, K., & Pellegrino, G. (2010, 6-10). Model-checking driven security testing of web-based applications. In *2010 Third International Conference on Software Testing, Verification, and Validation Workshops (ICSTW)* (pp. 361 -370).

Arnold, T. (2000). *Internet identity theft: A tragedy for victims*. White Paper, SIIA.

AT&T and The Economist Intelligence Unit. (2006). Avoiding safety culture shock. *AT&T Networking Views, 5*. Retrieved August 12, 2010, from http://www.business.att.com/content/emailmessage/assets/NV-Issue_5.pdf

Atwood, M., Conlan, R. M., Cook, B., Culver, L., Elliott-McCrea, K., & Halff, L. (2007, December). OAuth Core 1.0. OAuth Core Workgroup. Retrieved from http://oauth.net/core/1.0

Audun Jøsang, J. F. (2005). *Trust requirements in identity management*. Newcastle, Australia: Australasian Information Security Workshop 2005.

Aura, T., Nikander, P., & Leiwo, J. (2000). DOS-resistant authentication with clientpuzzles. *Lecture Notes in Computer Science. Proceeding of the Cambridge Security Protocols Workshop 2000* (pp. 170-177). Cambridge, UK. doi: 10.1.1.106.9259

Austel, P., Bhola, S., Chari, S., Koved, L., McIntosh, M., & Steiner, M. (2008). Secure delegation for Web 2.0 and mashups. A Position Statement for the 2008 Workshop on Web 2.0 Security and Privacy (W2SP). IBM Corporation.

Avatier. (2010). *Identity management, compliance management and password management software solutions at Avatier*. Retrieved from http://www.avatier.com/index.html

Axelrod, C. W. (2000). Systems and communications security during recovery and repair. In Doughty, K. (Ed.), *Business continuity planning: Protecting your organization's life*. Auerbach Best Practices Series. doi:10.1201/9780849390333.ch19

Azevedo, R. (2008). *SWIFT deliverable D.402 – Specification of identity-based service architecture with AAA function.* December 2008. Retrieved August 23rd, 2010, from http://www.ist-swift.org/

Babaguchi, N., & Yamada, S. (1999). *Jinkou chinou no kiso* [Basic of Artificial Intelligence]. Shokodo Co., Ltd.

Backstrom, L., Dwork, C., & Kleinberg, J. (2007). Wherefore art thou R3579X? Anonymized social networks, hidden patterns, and structural steganography. In *Proc. of the 16th International Conference on World Wide Web* (pp. 181-190). Banff, Canada: ACM Press. doi:10.1145/1242572.1242598

Bacon, J., Moody, K., & Yao, W. (2002). A model of OASIS role-based access control and its support for active security. *ACM Transactions on Information and System Security*, *5*(4), 492–540. doi:10.1145/581271.581276

Ballinger, K., Bissett, B., Box, D., Curbera, F., Ferguson, D., Graham, S., et al. (2006). *Web services metadata exchange* (WS-MetadataExchange). W3C.

Bandmann, O. L., Firozabadi, B. S., & Dam, M. (2002). Constrained delegation. In *IEEE Symposium on Security and Privacy*, (pp. 131–142).

Bankers' Ideanet. (2006, January 10). *Authentication techniques*. Retrieved April 2010, from http://www.sheshunoff.com/ideanet/index.php?itemid=204&catid=4

Barka, E. S., & Sandhu, R. (2000a). *Framework for role-based delegation models*. In 16th Annual Computer Security Applications Conference. Retrieved from http://www.acsac.org/2000/abstracts/34.html

Barka, E. S., & Sandhu, R. (2000b). *A role-based delegation model and some extensions*. In 23rd National Information Systems Security Conference. Retrieved from http://csrc.nist.gov/nissc/2000/proceedings/papers/021.pdf

Basin, D. (1999). Lazy infinite-state analysis of security protocols. In Baumgart, R. (Ed.), *Secure networking — CQRE (Secure) '99* (pp. 30–42). Springer-Verlag. doi:10.1007/3-540-46701-7_3

Bauer, D., Blough, D., & Cash, D. (2008). Minimum information disclosure with efficiently verifiable credentials. *Proceedings of the Fourth ACM Workshop on Digital Identity Management*, Association for Computing Machinery.

Beato, F., Kohlweiss, M., & Wouters, K. (2009). *Enforcing access control in social network sites*. Paper presented at the HotPET section of the 9th PET Symposium.

Becker, M., & Drew, M. (2005). Overcoming the challenges in deploying user provisioning/identity access management backbone. *BT Technology Journal*, *23*(4), 71–79. doi:10.1007/s10550-006-0009-x

Becker, M. Y., & Sewell, P. (2004). Cassandra: Flexible trust management, applied to electronic health records. In *Proceedings of the 17th IEEE Computer Security Foundations Workshop (CSFW04)*, (pp. 139–154).

Bell, D., & La Padula, L. (1973). Secure computer systems: Mathematical foundations. *MITRE Technical Report*, *2547*, 1.

Belsis, P., Gritzalis, S., & Katsikas, S. K. (2006). Optimized multi-domain secure interoperation using soft constraints. In *Artificial Intelligence Applications and Innovations*, vol. 204, (pp. 78–85). IFIP International Federation for Information Processing, Springer.

Benantar, M. (2006). *Access control systems: Security, identity management and trust models*. Berlin, Germany: Springer.

Benbasat, I., Goldstein, D. K., & Mead, M. (1987). The case research strategy in studies of Information Systems. *Management Information Systems Quarterly*, *11*(3), 369–386. doi:10.2307/248684

Bender, J., Fischlin, M., & Kügler, D. (2009). *Security analysis of the PACE key agreement protocol.* Paper presented at the Twelfth International Conference on Information Security (ISC 2009), Pisa, Italy.

Berners-Lee, T., Fielding, R., & Masinter, L. (2005, January). Uniform resource identifier (URI): Generic syntax. RFC 3986, Internet Engineering Task Force.

Bertino, E., Martino, L., Paci, F., & Squicciarini, A. (2009). *Security for Web services and service-oriented architectures*. Berlin, Germany: Springer.

Bertino, E., Khan, L., Sandhu, R., & Thuraisingham, B. (2006). Secure knowledge management: Confidentiality, trust and privacy. *IEEE Transactions on Systems, Man, and Cybernetics. Part A, Systems and Humans*, *36*(3), 429–438. doi:10.1109/TSMCA.2006.871796

Bertino, E. (2003). RBAC models – Concepts and trends. *Computers & Security*, *22*(6), 511–514. doi:10.1016/S0167-4048(03)00609-6

Bertino, E., & Martino, L. (2007). A service-oriented approach to security - Concepts and issues. *Proc. of the 8th International Symposium on Autonomous Decentralized Systems*, Sedona, AZ, USA, Mar. 21-23, (pp. 31-40).

Bertocci, V., Serack, G., & Baker, C. (2007). *Understanding Windows CardSpace: An introduction to the concepts and challenges of digital identities (independent technology guides)* (*Vol. 1*). Amsterdam, The Netherlands: Addison-Wesley Longman.

Beta Systems. (2010). *Beta Systems: SAM enterprise identity manager*. Retrieved from http://ww2.betasystems.com/en/

Beynon-Davies, P. (2006). Personal identity management in the information polity: The case of the UK national identity card. *Information Polity*, *11*, 3–19.

BeyondTrust. (2010). *Identity management, root access control, password management, privileged account management, UAC, Windows access control, admin rights control from BeyondTrust*. Retrieved from http://www.beyondtrust.com/

Beznosov, K., Flinn, D. J., Kawamoto, S., & Hartman, B. (2005). Introduction to Web services and their security. *Information Security Technical Report*, *10*, 2–14. doi:10.1016/j.istr.2005.02.001

Bhargav-Spantzel, A., Camenisch, J., Gross, A., & Sommer, D. (2007). User centricity: A taxonomy and open issues. *Journal of Computer Security*, *15*(5). IOS Press.

Bishop, M., & Klein, D. V. (1995). Improving system security via proactive password checking. *Computers & Security*, *14*(3), 233–249. doi:10.1016/0167-4048(95)00003-Q

BITS. (2003, April). *Fraud prevention strategies for internet banking*. Retrieved April 2010, from http://www.bits.org/downloads/Publications%20Page/mointernetwp.pdf

Bocan, V. (2004). Threshold puzzles. The evolution of DoS-resistant authentication. *Periodica Politehnica, Transaction on Automatic Control and Computer Science*, *49*(63). Timisoara, Romania.

Bocan, V., & Fagadar-Cosma, M. (2005, November). Adaptive threshold puzzles. *Proceedings of EUROCON 2005. The International Conference on "Computer as a Tool"* (pp. 644-647). Belgrade, Serbia. doi: 10.1109/EURCON.2005.1630012

Bocan, V., & Fagadar-Cosma, M. (2005, November). Towards DoS-resistant single sign-on systems. *Proceedings of EUROCON 2005. The International Conference on "Computer as a Tool"* (pp. 668-671). Belgrade, Serbia. doi: 10.1109/EURCON.2005.1630018

Bolten (director), J. B. (2003, December). E-authentication guidance for federal agencies — M-04-04. Office of Management and Budget (OMB), Executive Office of the President, The White House, Washington DC, USA.

Booth, D., Haas, H., McCabe, F., Newcomer, E., Champion, M., Ferris, C. (2004, February). Web services architecture. The World Wide Web Consortium (W3C).

Borcea, K., Donker, H., Franz, E., Liesebach, K., Pfitzmann, A., & Wahrig, H. (2005). Intra-application partitioning of personal data. In *Proc. of Workshop on Privacy-Enhanced Personalization.*

Borcea-Pfitzmann, K., Franz, E., & Pfitzmann, A. (2005). Usable presentation of secure pseudonyms. In *Proc. of the Workshop on Digital Identity Management, 2005* (pp. 70-76). Fairfax, VA: ACM Press. doi:10.1145/1102486.1102498

Boutin, P. (2009). How to block Facebook photos of yourself. *Gadgetwise Blog – NYTimes.com*. Retrieved August 31, 2010, from http://gadgetwise.blogs.nytimes.com/2009/05/05/how-to-block-facebook-photos-of-yourself/

Box, D., & Curbera, F. (Eds.). (2004, August). Web services addressing (ws-addressing). The World Wide Web Consortium (W3C).

Bramhall, P., Hansen, M., Rannenberg, K., & Roessler, T. (2007, July/August). User-centric identity management: New trends in standardization and regulation. *IEEE Security & Privacy*, *5*(4), 84–87. doi:10.1109/MSP.2007.99

Brands, S. (Ed.). (2009). *Rethinking public key infrastructures and digital certificates: Building in privacy*. MIT Press.

Brewer, D., & Nash, M. (1989). The Chinese Wall security policy. In *Proceedings of the 1989 IEEE Symposium on Security and Privacy*, (pp. 206–214).

Buecker, A., Ashley, P., Borrett, M., Lu, M., Muppidi, S., & Readshaw, N. (2007). Understanding SOA security design and implementation (2nd edition). Retrieved February 11, 2011, from http://www.redbooks.ibm.com/redbooks/pdfs/sg247310.pdf

Buell, A. D., & Sandhu, R. (2003). Noevmber). Identity management. *IEEE Internet Computing*, *7*(6), 26–28. doi:10.1109/MIC.2003.1250580

Bufu, J., & Daugherty, J. (Eds.). (2008, December). OpenID provider authentication policy extension 1.0.The OpenID Foundation. Retrieved from http://openid.net/specs/openid-provider-authentication-policy-extension-1_0.html

Buhler, J., & Wunder, G. (2010). Traffic-aware optimization of heterogeneous access management. *IEEE Transactions on Communications*, *58*(6), 1737–1747. doi:10.1109/TCOMM.2010.06.090182

Bunnell, J., Podd, J., Henderson, R., Napier, R., & Kennedy-Moffat, J. (1997). Cognitive, associative, and conventional passwords: Recall and guessing rates. *Computers & Security*, *16*(7), 645–657. doi:10.1016/S0167-4048(97)00008-4

Burr, W., Dodson, D., & Polk, T. (2006). *Electronic authentication guideline. National Institute of Standards and Technology (NIST), Special Publication 800-63, version 1.0.2*. Information Technology Laboratory.

Burton Group Inc. (n.d.). *Leading research and advisory services firm that focuses on providing practical, technically in-depth advice to front-line IT professionals*. Gartner Inc. Retrieved from http://www.burtongroup.com/

Byron, B. (2003, August 1). *The need for authentication and authorization*. Retrieved April 2010, from http://www.redbooks.ibm.com/abstracts/tips0266.html?Open

CA. (2010). *Identity manager*. Retrieved from http://www.ca.com/us/user-provisioning.aspx

CA/Browser forum. (2008, April). Guidelines for the issuance and management of extended validation certificates — version 1.1.

Cahill, C., & Hodges, J. (Eds.). (2006). *Liberty ID-WSF web services discovery service specification — Version 2.0*. Liberty Alliance Project.

Camenisch, J., & Saramati, P. (2009). *PrimeLife deliverable D2.1.1, first report on mechanisms*. Retrieved August 23rd, 2010, from http://www.primelife.eu

Camenisch, J., Shelat, A., Sommer, D., Fischer-Hübner, S., Hansen, M., & Krasemann, H. ... Tseng, J. (2005). Privacy and identity management for everyone. *Proceedings of the First ACM Workshop on Digital Identity Management*, Association for Computing Machinery.

Cameron, K. (2005). *Kim Cameron's identity weblog*. Retrieved 2010, from http://www.identityblog.com/stories/2004/12/09/thelaws.html

Cameron, K. (2005). *The laws of Identity*. Retrieved July 2010, from http://www.identityblog.com/stories/2005/05/13/TheLawsOfIdentity.pdf

Cameron, K., & Jones, M. B. (2006, February). Design rationale behind the identity metasystem architecture. Microsoft Corporation.

Canard, S., Malville, E., & Traoré, J. (2008). Identity federation and privacy: One step beyond. *Proceedings of the Fourth ACM Workshop on Digital Identity Management*, Association for Computing Machinery.

Cantor, S., Kemp, J., Maler, E., & Philpott, R. (2005). *Assertions and protocols for the OASIS security assertion markup language (SAML) V2.0. Organization for the Advancement of Structured Information Standards*. OASIS.

Cantor, S., Hirsch, F., Kemp, J., Philpott, R., & Maler, E. (Eds.). (2005, March). *Bindings for the OASIS security assertion markup language (SAML) V2.0. OASIS Standard Specification*. OASIS Open.

Cantor, S., & Kemp, J. (Eds.). (2004). *Liberty ID-FF protocols and schema specification — 1.2-errata-v3.0*. Liberty Alliance Project.

Cantor, S., Kemp, J., & Champagne, D. (Eds.). (2004). *Liberty ID-FF bindings and profiles specification — 1.2-errata-v2.0*. Liberty Alliance Project.

Cantor, S., Kemp, J., Philpott, R., & Maler, E. (Eds.). (2005, March). *Assertions and protocols for the OASIS security assertion markup language (SAML) V2.0. OASIS Standard Specification*. OASIS Open.

Cantor, S., Hirsch, F., Kemp, J., Philpott, R., & Maler, E. (Eds.). (2005, March). *Bindings for the OASIS security assertion markup language (SAML) V2.0. OASIS Standard Specification*. OASIS Open.

Cantor, S. (2008, January). Attribute release policies. Internet2. Retrieved from https://spaces.internet2.edu/display/SHIB/IdPARPConfig

Cantor, S. (Ed.). (2005a, October). SAML 2.0 single sign-on with constrained delegation. Internet2. Retrieved from http://shibboleth.internet2.edu/shibboleth-documents.html

Cantor, S. (Ed.). (2005b, September). Shibboleth architecture — Protocols and profiles. Internet2. Rerieved from http://shibboleth.internet2.edu/docs/internet2-mace-shibboleth-arch-protocols-200509.pdf

Cantor, S. (n.d.). User authentication and subject identifiers in Shibboleth. Retrieved from https://spaces.internet2.edu/display/SHIB/IdPUserAuthnConfig

Cantor, S., & Erdos, M. (2002). *Shibboleth-Architecture DRAFT v05*. Retrieved from http://shibboleth.internet2.edu/docs/draft-internet2-shibboleth-arch-v05.pdf

Cantor, S., Hodges, J., Kemp, J., & Thompson, P. (2003). Liberty ID-FF architecture overview (T. Wason, Ed.). Retrieved from http://projectliberty.org/liberty/content/download/318/2366/file/draft-liberty-idff-arch-overview-1.2-errata-v1.0.pdf

Cantor, S., Kemp, J., Philpott, R., & Maler, E. (2005). *Assertions and protocol for the OASIS security assertion markup language (SAML) V.2*. OASIS Standard, 15 March 2005. Retrieved August 23rd, 2010, from http://saml.xml.org/saml-specifications

Cao, Y., Yang, L., Fu, Z. B., & Yang, F. (2010). Identity management architecture: Paradigms and models. *Applied Mechanics and Materials, 40-41*, 647–651. doi:10.4028/www.scientific.net/AMM.40-41.647

Carver, B., Gomez, J., Pinnick, T., Soltani, A., Makker, S., & McCans, M. (2009). Know privacy, full report. *Know Privacy*. Retrieved August 31, 2010, from http://www.knowprivacy.org/report/KnowPrivacy_Final_Report.pdf

Casassa Mont, M., Bramhall, P., & Pato, J. (2003). *On adaptive identity management: The next generation of identity management technologies*. Retrieved from http://www.hpl.hp.com/techreports/2003/HPL-2003-149.pdf

Casassa, M., Bramhall, P., Gittler, M., Pato, J., & Rees, O. (2002). *Identity management: A key e-business enabler*. Presented at SSGR2002s, L'Aquila, Italy

Cavoukian, A., & Hamilton, T. (2002). *The privacy payoff: How successful businesses build customer trust*. Whitby, Canada: McGraw-Hill Ryerson Limited.

Central Union of Municipalities and Communities in Greece. (n.d.). *Index*. Retrieved from http://www.kedke.gr/index.asp

CEPIS. (2007, October 27). *Authentication approach for online banking*. Retrieved April 2010, from http://www.cepis.org/files/cepis/20090901104203_Authentication%20approaches%20for%20.pdf

Cha, S. (2008). Taxonomy of nominal type histogram distance measures. *Proceedings of the American Conference on Applied Mathematics*.

Chadwick, D. W., & Inman, G. (2009). Attribute aggregation in federated identity management. *IEEE Computer*, *42*(5), 33–40. doi:10.1109/MC.2009.143

Chadwick, D. W., Otenko, S., & Nguyen, T. A. (2009). Adding support to XACML for multi-domain user to user dynamic delegation of authority. *International Journal of Information Security*, *8*, 137–152. doi:10.1007/s10207-008-0073-y

Chadwick, D. W., Zhao, G., Otenko, S., Laborde, R., Su, L., & Nguyen, T. A. (2008). PERMIS: A modular authorization infrastructure. *Concurrency and Computation*, *20*(11), 1341–1357. doi:10.1002/cpe.1313

Chadwick, D. W. (2008). Federated identity management. In Aldini, A., Barthe, G., & Gorrieri, R. (Eds.), *Foundations of security analysis and design v, FOSAD 2007/2008/2009 Tutorial Lectures* (*Vol. 5705*, pp. 96–120). Springer. doi:10.1007/978-3-642-03829-7_3

Chadwick, D. W. (2005, April). Delegation issuing service for x.509. In Proceedings of the 4th Annual PKI R&D Workshop, USA (Vol. IR 7224, pp. 66-77). NIST Technical Publication.

Chanliau, M. (2010). *Oracle Identity Management 11G*. Retrieved from http://www.oracle.com/technetwork/middleware/id-mgmt/overview/idm-tech-wp-11g-r1-128261.pdf

Chappell, D. (2006). *Introducing Windows CardSpace*. MSDN Library. Retrieved from http://msdn.microsoft.com/enus/ library/aa480189.aspx

Chappell, D. (2006, April). *Introducing Windows CardSpace*. Retrieved from http://msdn.microsoft.com/en-us/library/Aa480189

Chappell, D. (2010). *Digital identity for. NET applications: A technology overview*. (C. &. Associates, Producer). Retrieved July 2010, from http://msdn2. microsoft.com/en-us/library/bb882216.aspx

Chau, P. Y. K., & Tam, K. Y. (1997). Factors affecting the adoption of open systems: An exploratory study. *Management Information Systems Quarterly*, *21*(1), 1–24. doi:10.2307/249740

Chaum, D. (1981). Untraceable electronic mail, return addresses, and digital pseudonyms. *Communications of the ACM*, *24*(2), 84–88. doi:10.1145/358549.358563

Chevalier, Y., Compagna, L., Cuellar, J., Hankes Drielsma, P., Mantovani, J., Mödersheim, S., et al. (2004). A high level protocol specification language for industrial security-sensitive protocols. In *Proc. SAPS'04*. Austrian Computer Society.

Chevalier, Y., Küsters, R., Rusinowitch, M., & Turuani, M. (2003). An NP decision procedure for protocol insecurity with XOR. In P. Kolaitis (Ed.), *Proceedings of LICS'2003*. IEEE.

Chew, M., Balfanz, D., & Laurie, B. (2008). (Under) mining privacy in social networks. In *Proc. of Web 2.0 Security and Privacy 2008*.

Chiasson, S., van Oorschot, P. C., & Biddle, R. (2008). Graphical password authentication using cued click points. *Lecture Notes in Computer Science*, *4734*, 359–374. doi:10.1007/978-3-540-74835-9_24

Chinitz, J. (2000). Single sign-on: Is it really possible? *Information Systems Security*, *9*(3), 33–45. doi:10.1201/1086/43310.9.3.20000708/31359.5

Christensen, E., Curbera, F., Meredith, G., & Weerawarana, S. (2001, March). Web services description language (WSDL) — Version 1.1. The World Wide Web Consortium (W3C).

Claub, S., & Kohntopp, M. (2001). Identity management and its support of multilateral security. *Computer Networks*, *37*(2), 205–219. doi:10.1016/S1389-1286(01)00217-1

Claubeta, S., Kesdogan, D., & Kölsch, T. (2005). Privacy enhancing identity management: protection against re-identification and profiling. In Proceedings of the the 2005 Workshop on Digital Identity Management, Fairfax, Va, USA (pp. 84-93). ACM.

Clippinger, J. H. (2009, December). Higgins towards a foundation layer for the social Web. Higgins — Working draft.

Coates, D., Adams, J., Dattilo, G., & Turner, M. (2000). *Identity theft and the Internet*. Colorado University.

Connolly, P. (2000, September 29). *Single sign-on dangles prospect of lower help desk costs*. Retrieved March 21, 2009, from http://www.infoworld.com/articles /es/xml/00/10/02/001002esnsso.html

Courion. (2010). *Courion identity and access management and compliance solutions*. Retrieved from http://www.courion.com/

Cover Pages, O. A. S. I. S. (2008, October). *Microsoft 'Geneva' framework supports SAML 2.0, WS-Federation, and WS-Trust*. Retrieved July 2010, from http://xml.coverpages.org/ni2008-10-29-a.html

Cover, R. (2003). *IBM releases updated enterprise privacy authorization language (EPAL) specification*. Retrieved February 11, 2011, from http://xml.coverpages.org/ni2003-07-09-a.html

Cragg, P. B., & King, M. (1993). Small firm computing: Motivators and inhibitors. *Management Information Systems Quarterly*, 47–60. doi:10.2307/249509

Cranor, L. F., Guduru, P., & Arjula, M. (2006). User interfaces for privacy agents. *ACM Trans. Comput.-Hum. Interact.*, *13*(2), 135-178. DOI=http://doi.acm.org/10.1145/1165734.1165735

Crosby, S. A., & Wallach, D. S. (2003, August). *Denial of service via algorithmic complexity attacks*. Paper presented at the 12th USENIX Security Symposium, Washington, DC.

Crowd. (2010). *Single sign-on (SSO) and identity management - Crowd*. Retrieved from http://www.atlassian.com/software/crowd/

Cser, A. (2008). *The Forrester Wave: Identity and access management, Q1 2008*. Cambridge, MA: Forrester.

Cser, A., & Penn, J. (2008). *Identity management market forecast: 2007 to 2014*. Forrester Research, February. Retrieved from http://www.forrester.com/rb/Research/identity_management_market_forecast_2007_to_2014/q/id/43842/t/2

Cuony, M. (2010). Install FireGPG. *FireGPG*. Retrieved August 31, 2010, from http://en.getfiregpg.org/s/install

Curbera, F., Parastatidis, S., & Schlimmer, J. (Eds.). (2006, August). Web services metadata exchange (WS-MetadataExchange) — Version 1.1. BEA Systems, Computer Associates, IBM, Microsoft, SAP AG, Sun Microsystems, and webmethods.

Cutillo, L. A., Molva, R., & Strufe, T. (2009). Safebook: A privacy-preserving online social network leveraging on real-life trust. *IEEE Communications Magazine*, *47*(12), 94–101. doi:10.1109/MCOM.2009.5350374

Cutler, R. (Ed.). (2008). *Liberty identity assurance framework — Version 1.1*. Liberty Alliance Project.

Cyberark. (2010). *Privileged identity management Suite from Cyber-Ark software*. Retrieved from http://www.cyber-ark.com/digital-vault-products/privileged-identity-management/index.asp

Dabrowski, M., & Pacyna, P. (2008). Modular reference framework architecture for identity management. In *Proceedings of the 11th IEEE International Conference on Communication Systems*, ICCS'08, Singapore, (pp. 743-749).

Danezis, G., Dingledine, R., & Mathewson, N. (2003). Mixminion: Design of a Type III anonymous remailer protocol. In *Proc. of Symposium on Security and Privacy, 2003* (pp. 2-15). Berkeley, CA: IEEE Computer Society.

D'Angelo, G., Vitali, F., & Zacchiroli, S. (2010). Content cloaking: Preserving privacy with Google Docs and other web applications. In *Proc. of the 25th Annual ACM Symposium on Applied Computing* (pp. 826-830). Sierre, Switzerland: ACM Press. doi:10.1145/1774088.1774259

Dantsin, E., Eiter, T., Gottlob, G., & Voronkov, A. (2001). Complexity and expressive power of logic programming. *ACM Computing Surveys*, *33*(3), 374–425. doi:10.1145/502807.502810

Davis, F. D. (1989). Perceived usefulness, perceived ease of use, and user acceptance of Information Technology. *Management Information Systems Quarterly*, *13*(3), 319–340. doi:10.2307/249008

Day, K. (2003). *Inside the security mind. Making the tough decisions*. Upper Saddle River, NJ: Prentice Hall.

Delio, M. (2004, September 6). Better security through identity. *Infoworld.com*, 35-42.

Diffie, W., & Hellman, M. E. (1976, November). New directions in cryptograph. *IEEE Transactions on Information Theory*, *IT-22*(6), 644–654. doi:10.1109/TIT.1976.1055638

DiMicco, J., Geyer, W., Millen, D., Dugan, C., & Brownholtz, B. (2009). People sensemaking and relationship building on an enterprise social network site. In *Proc. of the 42nd Hawaii International Conference on System Sciences* (pp. 1-10). Big Island, HI: IEEE Computer Society. doi:10.1109/HICSS.2009.343

Dingledine, R., Mathewson, N., & Syverson, P. (2004). Tor: The second-generation onion router. *Proceedings of the 13th USENIX Security Symposium*, USENIX Association.

Dolev, D., & Yao, A. (1983). On the security of public-key protocols. *IEEE Transactions on Information Theory*, *2*(29).

Duerst, M., & Suignard, M. (2005, January). Internationalized resource identifiers (iris). RFC 3987, Internet Engineering Task Force.

Durgin, N., Lincoln, P. D., Mitchell, J. C., & Scedrov, A. (1999). Undecidability of bounded security protocols. In *Proceedings of the FLOC'99 Workshop on Formal Methods and Security Protocols (FMSP'99).*

Dwork, C., & Naor, M. (1992). Pricing via processing or combating junk mail. [Berlin, Germany: Springer-Verlag.]. *Proceedings of CRYPTO*, *92*, 139–147.

Eap, T. M., Hatala, M., & Gasevic, D. (2007). Enabling user control with personal identity management. *Proceedings of the 2007 IEEE International Conference on Services Computing*, Institute of Electrical and Electronics Engineers.

Eastlake, D., & Reagle, J. (2002). *XML encryption syntax and processing.* Retrieved February 11, 2011, from http://www.w3.org/TR/xmlenc-core

e-Authentication Initiative. (2007). *E-authentication guidance for federal agencies.* US.

Eckersley, P. (2010). How unique is your web browser? *Panopticlick.* Retrieved August 31, 2010, from http://panopticlick.eff.org/browser-uniqueness.pdf

Egelman, S., Cranor, L. F., & Chowdhury, A. (2006). An analysis of P3P-enabled web sites among top-20 search results. In *Proceedings of the 8th international Conference on Electronic Commerce: The New E-Commerce: innovations For Conquering Current Barriers, Obstacles and Limitations To Conducting Successful Business on the Internet, ICEC '06, vol. 156,* Fredericton, New Brunswick, Canada, August 13 - 16, 2006, (pp.197-207). New York, NY: ACM. DOI=http://doi.acm.org/10.1145/1151454.1151492

Eichholz, J., Hühnlein, D., & Schwenk, J. (2009). *SAMLizing the European Citizen Card.* Paper presented at BIOSIG 2009 Special Interest Group on Biometrics and Electronic Signatures, September 2009, Darmstadt, Germany.

El Maliki, T., & Seigneur, J.-M. (2007). A survey of user-centric identity management technologies. *The International Conference on Emerging Security Information, Systems, and Technologies*, SecureWare 2007, 14-20 Oct. 2007 (pp. 12-17).

Elmufti, K., Weerasinghe, D., Rajarajan, M., & Rakocevic, V. (2008). Anonymous authentication for mobile Single Sign-On to protect user privacy. *International Journal of Mobile Communications, 6*(6), 760-769. ACM Press.

eMayor Project. (2004). *Electronic and secure municipal administration for European Citizens.* IST-2004-507217, Sixth Framework Programme.

Emig, C., Brandt, F., Abeck, S., Biermann, J., & Klarl, H. (2007). An access control metamodel for web service-oriented architecture. *Proc. of the 2nd IEEE International Conference on Software Engineering Advances*. Cap Esterel, France, Aug. 25-31, (pp. 57-64).

ENISA Report. (2008, November). Mapping IDABC authentication assurance levels to SAML v2.0 — Gap analysis and recommendations.

Erl, T. (2005). *Service-oriented architecture: Concepts, technology, and design.* Upper Saddle River, NJ: Pearson Education, Inc.

European Commission. (2006). *FIDIS Consortium: Structured overview on prototypes and concepts of identity management systems.* Retrieved from http://www.fidis.net/ fileadmin/fidis/deliverables/fidis-wp3-del3.1.overview_on_ IMS.final.pdf

European Commission. (2011). *Europe 2020: A strategy for smart, sustainable and inclusive growth*. Communication from the European Commission, Brussels. Retrieved from http://ec.europa.eu/eu2020/index_en.htm

European Parliament. (1997). Directive 97/66/EC of the European Parliament and of the Council of 15th December 1997 concerning the processing of personal data and the protection of privacy in the telecommunications sector. *Official Journal*, *24*, 1–8.

European Parliament. (2001). Directive 01/45/EC of the European Parliament and the Council of Ministers on the protection of individuals with regard to the processing of personal data by the Community institutions and bodies and on the free movement of such data. *Official Journal*, *8*, 1–22.

Everett, C. (2007). Piecing identity together. [Elsevier.]. *Infosecurity*, *4*(6), 22–25. doi:10.1016/S1754-4548(07)70145-6

FaceTime. (2008). *The collaborative internet: Usage trends, end user attitudes and IT impact*. Security, Management & Compliance for Unified Communications, Web 2.0 and Social Networks. Retrieved August 31, 2010, from http://www3.facetime.com/forms/survey08_request.aspx

Fagin, R. (1978). On an authorization mechanism. *ACM Transactions on Database Systems*, *3*(3), 310–319. doi:10.1145/320263.320288

Farahbod, R., Glasser, U., & Vajihollahi, M. (2007). An abstract machine architecture for web service based business process management. *International Journal of Business Process Integration and Management*, *1*, 279–291. doi:10.1504/IJBPIM.2006.012626

FengOffice. (2010). *Feng Office*. Retrieved August 31, 2010, from http://fengoffice.com/web/index.php

Ferraiolo, D. F., Kuhn, D. R., & Chandramouli, R. (2003). *Role-based access control*. Boston, MA: Artech House Publishers.

Ferraiolo, D. F., Sandhu, R., Gavrila, S., Kuhn, D. R., & Chandramouli, R. (2001). Proposed NIST standard for role-based access control. *ACM Transactions on Information and System Security*, *4*(3). doi:10.1145/501978.501980

Fischer-Hübner, S., Wästlund, E., & Raggett, D. (2009). *PrimeLife deliverable D4.3.1, UI prototypes, administration and presentation version 1*. Retrieved August 23rd, 2010, from http://www.primelife.eu

Fontana, J. (October 2003). *A national identity card for Canada? Report of the Standing Committee on Citizenship and Immigration*. Ottawa, Canada: House of Commons, Canada.

Forrester. (2007). *Identity management market forecast: 2007 to 2014*. Retrieved from http://www.forrester.com/rb/Research/identity_management_market_forecast_2007_to_2014/q/id/43842/t/2

Forward Consortium. (2009). *Managing emerging threats in ICT infrastructures*. Deliverable D3.1, FORWARD, 7th Framework Programme, Information & Communication Technologies Secure, dependable and trusted Infrastructures.

French Government. (2010). *Authentication, authorization and access control*. Retrieved April 2010, from http://eregie.premier-ministre.gouv.fr/manual/howto/auth.html

Furnell, S. M., Dowland, P. S., Illingworth, H. M., & Reynolds, P. L. (2000). Authentication and supervision: A survey of user attitudes. *Computers & Security*, *19*(6), 529–539. doi:10.1016/S0167-4048(00)06027-2

Gaedke, M., Meinecke, J., & Nussbaumer, M. (2005). *A modeling approach to federated identity and access management*. International World Wide Web Conference.

Gajek, S., Schwenk, J., Steiner, M., & Xuan, C. (2009). Risk of the CardSpace protocol. *Proceedings of the 12th International Conference on Information Security* (pp. 278–293), Springer.

Gamma, E., Helm, R., Johnson, R., & Vlissides, J. (2000). *Design patterns: Elements of reusable object-oriented software*. Reading, MA: Addison-Wesley Publishing Company.

Gauld, C., Beresford, A., & Rice, A. (2009). *Shadow and TorProxy*. Computer Laboratory: Digital Technology Group. Retrieved August 31, 2010, from http://www.cl.cam.ac.uk/research/dtg/android/tor/

Gollmann, D. (2004). *Computer security*. John Wiley & Sons.

Gomi, H., Hatakeyama, M., Hosono, S., & Fujita, S. (2005). A delegation framework for federated identity management. In Proceedings of the Workshop on Digital Identity Management (DIM '05) (pp. 94–103). New York, NY: ACM Press.

Goodner, M., Hondo, M., Nadalin, A., McIntosh, M., & Schmidt, D. (2007). *Understanding WS-Federation*, Version 1.0.

Goto. (2007). *Ebot Lite*. Retrieved from http://www.listbrowser.com/

Graux, H., & Majava, J. (2007, December). *eID interoperability for PEGS - Proposal for a multi-level authentication mechanism and a mapping of existing authentication mechanisms*. The Interoperable Delivery of European eGovernment Services to public Administrations, Businesses and Citizens (IDABC). ENISA. (2008, November). *Mapping IDABC Authentication Assurance Levels to SAML v2.0 - Gap analysis and recommendations*.

Griffiths, P. P., & Wade, B. W. (1976). An authorization mechanism for a relational database system. [TODS]. *ACM Transactions on Database Systems*, *1*(3), 242–255. doi:10.1145/320473.320482

Groß, T., Pfitzmann, B., & Sadeghi, A.-R. (2005). Browser model for security analysis of browser-based protocols. In di Vimercati, S. D. C., Syverson, P. F., & Gollmann, D. (Eds.), *ESORICS* (*Vol. 3679*, pp. 489–508). Springer. doi:10.1007/11555827_28

Groza, B., & Petrica, D. (2006, May). On chained cryptographic puzzles. *Proceedings of 3rd Romanian-Hungarian Joint Symposium on Applied Computational Intelligence, SACI'06* (pp. 182-191).Timisoara, Romania.

Guha, S., Tang, K., & Francis, P. (2008). NOYB: Privacy in online social networks. In *Proc. of the First Workshop on Online Social Networks* (pp. 49–54). Seattle, WA: ACM Press. doi:10.1145/1397735.1397747.

Gulyás, G., Schulcz, R., & Imre, S. (2009). Modeling role-based privacy in social networking services. In *Proc. of Third International Conference on Emerging Security Information, Systems and Technologies, 2009, SECURWARE '09* (pp. 173-178). Athens, Greece: IEEE. *Computers & Society*. doi:.doi:10.1109/SECURWARE.2009.34

Gulyás, G. Gy., Schulcz, R., & Imre, S. (2008). Comprehensive analysis of web privacy and anonymous web browsers: Are next generation services based on collaborative filtering? In *Proceedings of the Joint SPACE and TIME Workshops 2008* (pp. 17-32). Trondheim, Norway: CEUR-WS.

Gupta, M., & Sharman, R. (2008b). Dimensions of identity federation: A case study in financial services. [Dynamic Publishers.]. *Journal of Information Assurance and Security*, *3*(4), 244–256.

Gupta, M., Rao, H. R., & Upadhyaya, S. (2004). Electronic banking and information assurance issues: survey and synthesis. *Journal of Organizational and End User Computing*, *16*(3), 1–21. doi:10.4018/joeuc.2004070101

Gupta, M., & Sharman, R. (2008a). Security-efficient identity management using service provisioning (markup language). In Gupta, J. N. D., & Sharma, S. (Eds.), *Handbook of research on information security and assurance* (pp. 83–90). Hershey, PA: IGI Publishing. doi:10.4018/978-1-59904-855-0.ch040

Gupta, M., & Sharman, R. (2008c). Emerging frameworks in user-focused identity management. In Gupta, J. N. D., & Sharma, S. (Eds.), *Handbook of research on information security and assurance* (pp. 362–377). Hershey, PA: IGI Global Publishing. ISBN. doi:10.4018/978-1-59904-855-0

Gupta, M., Lee, J., & Rao, H. R. (2008). Implications of FFIEC guidance on authentication in electronic banking. In Gupta, J. N. D., & Sharma, S. (Eds.), *Handbook of research on information security and assurance*. Hershey, PA: IGI Publishing. doi:10.4018/978-1-59904-855-0.ch022

Gupta, M., & Sharman, R. (2010). Activity governance for managing risks in role design for SSO systems. *Journal of Information Assurance and Security, 5*(6). Dynamic Publishers.

Gürses, S., Rizk, R., & Günther, O. (2008). Privacy design in online social networks: Learning from privacy breaches and community feedback. In *Proc of International Conference on Information Systems*.

Hagstrom, A., Jajodia, S., Parisi-Presicce, F., & Wijesekera, D. (2001). Revocations: A classification. In *CSFW '01: Proceedings of the 14th IEEE Workshop on Computer Security Foundations*, (p. 44). IEEE Computer Society.

Hallam-Baker, P., & Maler, E. (2002). *Assertions and protocol for the OASIS security assertion markup language (SAML).* OASIS Standard, 5 November 2002. Retrieved August 23rd, 2010, from http://saml.xml.org/saml-specifications

Hammer-Lahav, E. (Ed.). (2009, June). OAuth Core 1.0 revisionA. OAuth Core Workgroup. Retrieved from http://oauth.net/core/1.0a

Hammer-Lahav, E., & Norris, W. (Eds.). (2009, November). Extensible resource descriptor (XRD) version 1.0 — Working draft 10. OASIS Open.

Hansen, M., Berlich, B., Camenish, J., Claus, S., Pfitzmann, A., & Waidner, M. (2004). Privacy-enhancing identity management. [Elsevier.]. *Information Security Technical Report, 9*(1), 35–44. doi:10.1016/S1363-4127(04)00014-7

Hansen, M., Berlich, P., Camenisch, J., Claub, S., Pfitzmann, A., & Waidner, M. (2004). Privacy-enhancing identity management. *Information Security Technical Report, 9*(1), 35–44. doi:10.1016/S1363-4127(04)00014-7

Hansen, S. M., Skriver, J., & Nielson, H. R. (2005). Using static analysis to validate the SAML single sign-on protocol. In *WITS '05: Proceedings of the 2005 Workshop on Issues in the Theory of sEcurity* (pp. 27–40). New York, NY: ACM Press.

Hardt, D., Bufu, J., & Hoyt, J. (2007, December). OpenID attribute exchange 1.0 — Final. The OpenID Foundation. Retrieved from http://openid.net/specs/openid-attribute-exchange-1_0.html

Harris, S. (2001, September). DoS defense. *Information Security Magazine*.

Hayashi, K. (2007). *Saishin netto koukoku no shikumi* [System of Latest Net Advertisement]. Nippon Jitsugyo Publishing.

Hishida. (2007). *xdoc2txt*. Retrieved from http://www31.ocn.ne.jp/~h_ishida/xdoc2txt.html

HitachWe ID Systems. (2010). *HitachWe ID systems: Identity and access management*. Retrieved from http://hitachi-id.com/

Hodges, J., & Aarts, R. (Eds.). (2005). *Liberty ID-WSF authentication service and single sign-on service specification — Version 1.1*. Liberty Alliance Project.

Hodges, J. (2009, July). Technical comparison: OpenID and SAML — Draft 07a. White paper. Retrieved from http://identitymeme.org/doc/draft-hodges-saml-openid-compare-05.html

Hogben, G. (2007). *Security issues and recommendations for online social networks*. ENISA Position Paper 1. Retrieved August 23rd, 2010, from http://www.enisa.europa.eu/act/res/other-areas/social-networks/security-issues-and-recommendations-for-online-social-networks

Howard, N., Rolland, C., & Qusaibaty, A. (2004). *Process complexity: Towards a theory of intent-oriented process design*. Paper presented at the 2nd International Conference of Information and Systems.

Hu, V., Ferraiolo, D., & Kuhn, D. (2006). *Assessment of access control systems*. Retrieved from http://csrc.nist.gov/publications/nistir/7316/NISTIR-7316.pdf

Huang, E. (2011). On improving privacy: Managing local storage in Flash player. *Adobe Flash Platform Blog*. Retrieved February 15, 2011, from http://blogs.adobe.com/flashplatform/2011/01/on-improving-privacy-managing-local-storage-in-flash-player.html

Hughes, J., Cantor, S., Hodges, J., Hirsch, F., Mishra, P., & Philpott, R. (2005, March). Profiles for the OASIS security assertion markup language (SAML) V2.0. OASIS Standard Specification, OASIS Open.

Hunt, P. (Ed.). (2006). *Client attribute requirements markup language (CARML) specification — Working draft 03*. Oracle.

Iacovou, C. L., Benbasat, I., & Dexter, A. S. (1995). Electronic data interchange and small organizations: Adoption and impact of technology. *Management Information Systems Quarterly*, 465–485. doi:10.2307/249629

IEEE. (2000). [Recommended practice for architectural description of software-intensive systems.]. *IEEE Standard, 1471*, 2000.

Imprivata. (n.d.). *Benefits of single sign on*. Retrieved March 22, 2009, from http://www.imprivata.com/contentmgr/showdet ails.php ?id=1170

InCommon Federation. (2008). *Identity assurance assessment framework.* Retrieved 2010, from http://www.incommonfederation.org/docs/assurance/ InC IAAF 1.0 Final.pdf

Intelcities Project. (2006). *Intelligent cities.* 6th Framework Programme, IST-2004-507860. Retrieved from http://intelcities.iti.gr/intelcities

Internet2. (2011). *Shibboleth Architecture.* Internet2 Middleware Iniative. Retrieved from http://shibboleth.internet2.edu

Investor Glossary. (2010). *Online banking.* Retrieved April 2010, from http://www.investorglossary.com/online-banking.htm

Irvine, C., & Levin, T. (2001). Quality of security service. *Proc. of the 2000 Workshop on New Security Paradigms.* Ballycotton, County Cork, Ireland, Sept. 18-21, (pp. 91-99).

ISO/IEC. (2010). *Second CD 24760 — Information technology — Security techniques — A framework for identity management.*

Itakura, Y., Kojima, T., & Miyaki, I. (2008). *A proposal of an architecture for effective utilization of personal information* (in Japanese). The 2008 Symposium on Cryptography and Information Security Miyazaki, Japan, Jan. 22-25, 2008, The Institute of Electronics, Information and Communication Engineers.

ITU-T X.1250. (2009, February). X.idmreq, Baseline capabilities for enhanced global identity management trust and interoperability — Draft new recommendation [Manuel de logiciel].

ITU-T. (2009). *X.1250 (X.idmreq), baseline capabilities for enhanced global identity management trust and interoperability.* Draft new Recommendation, 2009.

Jackson, M., & Ligertwood, J. (2006, December). Identity management: Is an identity card the solution for Australia? *Prometheus, 24*(4), 379–387. doi:10.1080/08109020601029953

Jacquemard, F., Rusinowitch, M., & Vigneron, L. (2000). Compiling and verifying security protocols. In M. Parigot & A. Voronkov (Eds.), *Proceedings of LPAR 2000* (pp. 131–160). Springer-Verlag.

Jain, A., Bolle, R., & Pankanti, S. (Eds.). (1998). *Biometrics: Personal identification in networked society.* Dordrecht, The Netherlands: Kluwer.

Jajodia, S., Samarati, P., & Subrahmanian, V. S. (1997). A logical language for expressing authorizations. In *SP '97: Proceedings of the 1997 IEEE Symposium on Security and Privacy*, (p. 31). Washington, DC: IEEE Computer Society.

Jensen, C., & Potts, C. (2004). Privacy policies as decision-making tools: an evaluation of online privacy notices. In *Proceedings of the SIGCHI Conference on Human Factors in Computing Systems CHI '04*, Vienna, Austria, April 24 - 29, 2004 (pp. 471-478). New York, NY: ACM. DOI=http://doi.acm.org/10.1145/985692.985752

Jentzsch, N. (2010, May). *Welfare analysis of secondary use of personal data.* Paper presented at the Ninth Workshop on the Economics of Information Security (WEIS 2010), Harvard University, USA.

Johansson, J., & Riley, S. (2005). *Protect your Windows network from perimeter to data.* Upper Saddle River, NJ: Addison-Wesley.

JonDos GmbH. (2010). JondoFox. *JondoNym.* Retrieved August 31, 2010, from http://anonymous-proxy-servers.net/en/jondofox/

Jones, M. B. (2006, March). A guide to supporting InfoCard v1.0 within web applications and browsers. Microsoft Corporation.

Jones, M. B., & McIntosh, M. (2009). *Identity metasystem interoperability version 1.0.* OASIS Standard, 1 July 2009. Retrieved August 23rd, 2010, from http://docs.oasis-open.org/imi/identity/v1.0/identity.html

Jones, M., & Cameron, K. (2005). *Design rationale behind the identity metasystem architecture.* Retrieved from http://www.identityblog.com/wp-content/resources/design_rationale.pdf

Jones, M., MacIntyre, R., Morrow, T., Nenadi?, A., Pickles, S., & Zhang, N. (2006, November). E-infrastructure security: Levels of assurance. The Joint Information Systems Committee (JISC).

Jørstada, I., van Thuan, D., Jønvikc, T., & van Thanh, D. (2007). Bridging CardSpace and Liberty Alliance with SIM authentication. In Proceedings of the 10th International Conference on Intelligence in Next Generation Networks, ICIN 2007, Bordeaux, France (pp. 8-13). ADERA.

Jøsang, A., Fabre, J., Hay, B., Dalziel, J., & Pope, S. (2005). Trust requirements in identity management. In Buyya, R., Coddington, P. D., Montague, P., Safavi-Naini, R., Sheppard, N. P., & Wendelborn, A. L. (Eds.), *ACSW Frontiers, 44* (pp. 99–108).

Jøsang, A., & Pope, S. (2005). User centric identity management. In Proceedings of Australian Computer Emergency Response Team Conference (AUSCERT 2005).

Jøsang, A., Al Zomai, M., & Suriadi, S. (2007). Usability and privacy in identity management architectures. In *The Proceedings of the Australasian Information Security Workshop* 2007, Ballarat, Australia.

Jøsang, A., Fabre, J., Hay, B., Dalziel, J., & Pope, S. (2005). *Trust requirements in identity management.* Newcastle, Australia: Australasian Information Security Workshop 2005.

Juels, A., & Brainard, J. (1999). Client puzzles: A Cryptographic countermeasure against connection depletion attacks. *Proceedings of the NDSS, 99*, 151–165.

Kaliontzoglou, A., Sklavos, P., Karantjias, A., & Polemi, N. (2005). A secure e-government platform architecture for small to medium sized public organizations. [Elsevier.]. *Electronic Commerce Research and Applications, 4*(2), 174–186. doi:10.1016/j.elerap.2004.09.002

Kantara Initiative. (2010). *Website.* Retrieved 2010, from http://kantarainitiative.org/

Karantjias, A., Papastergiou, S., & Polemi, N. (2009). Design principles of a secure federated e/m-government framework. *International Journal of Electronic Governance (IJEG)* [Inderscience Publishers.]. *Special Issue on Users and Uses of Electronic Governance, 2*(4), 402–423.

Karantjias, A., & Polemi, N. (2009). An innovative platform architecture for complex secure e/m government services. *International Journal of Electronic Security and Digital Forensics (IJESDF)* [Inderscience Publishers]. *Special Issue on Mobile Services Technological and Legal Issues, 2*(4), 338–354.

Karantjias, A., Stamati, T., & Martakos, D. (2010). Advanced e-government enterprise strategies & solutions. *International Journal of Electronic Governance (IJEG), Special Issue on Methodologies, Technologies and Tools Enabling e-Government, 3*(2), 170-188. Inderscience Publishers.

Karp, A. H. (2006). Authorization-based access control for the services oriented architecture. In: *Proceedings of the Fourth International Conference on Creating, Connecting and Collaborating through Computing* (C5'06), (pp. 160-167). IEEE Computer Society.

Kay, R. (2005, April 04). *Biometric authentication.* Retrieved April 2010, from http://www.computerworld.com/s/article/100772/Biometric_Authentication?taxonomyId=17&pageNumber=1

Kellomai, S. (Ed.). (2003). *Liberty ID-SIS employee profile service specification — Version 1.0.* Liberty Alliance Project.

Kellomäki, S. (2009). *TAS3 deliverable 2.1 – TAS3 architecture.* Retrieved August 23rd, 2010, from http://www.tas3.eu

Kemp, J., Cantor, S., Mishra, P., Philpott, R., & Maler, E. (Eds.). (2005, March). *Authentication context for the OASIS security assertion markup language (SAML) V2.0.* OASIS Open.

Kim, S. H., Choi, D. S., Kim, D. J., Kim, S. H., Noh, J. H., & Jung, K. S. (2009, October). OpenID authentication method using identity selector. United States Patent. (US 2009/0249078 A1).

Kim, Y., Lau, W. C., Chuah, M. C., & Chao, H. J. (2004). PacketScore: Statistics-based overload control against distributed denial-of-service attacks. *Proceedings of IEEE INFOCOM* (pp. 2594-2604). Hong Kong, SAR. doi: 10.1.1.137.6263

Koch, M., & Moslein, M. (2005). Identity management for e-commerce and collaborative applications. *International Journal of Electronic Commerce, 9*(3), 11–29.

Koch, M., & Worndl, W. (2001). *Community support and identity management.* Paper presented at the Seventh European Conference on Computer-Supported Cooperative Work, Bonn, Germany.

Komanduri, S., & Hutchings, D. (2008). Order and entropy in picture passwords. Proceedings of Graphics Interface 2008

Kormann, D. P., & Rubin, A. D. (2000). Risks of the passport single SignOn protocol. *Computer Networks, 33*(1-6), 51-58.

Kreizman, G., Enck, J., Litan, A., Wagner, R., Orans, L., & Allan, A. (2007). *Hype cycle for identity and access management technologies*. Stamford, CT: Gartner.

Krishnamurthy, B., & Wills, C. (2009). Privacy diffusion on the Web: A longitudinal perspective. In *Proc. of the 18th International Conference on World Wide Web* (pp. 541-550). Madrid, Spain: ACM Press. doi:10.1145/1526709.1526782

Kuhn, D. R. (1997). Mutual exclusion of roles as a means of implementing separation of duty in role-based access control systems. In *Proc. of the Second ACM Workshop on Role-based Access Control*.

Kylau, U., Thomas, I., Menzel, M., & Meinel, C. (2009). *Trust requirements in identity federation topologies*. International Conference on Advanced Information Networking and Applications (AINA-09). IEEE.

Lampson, B., Abadi, M., Burrows, M., & Wobber, E. (1992). Authentication in distributed systems: Theory and practice. *ACM Transactions on Computer Systems, 10*(4). Association for Computing Machinery.

Leenes, R., Schallabock, J., & Hansen, M. (2008). *PRIME White Paper – Third and final version*. Retrieved from https://www.prime-project.eu/prime_products/whitepaper/.

LGAF Project. (2009). *Local government access framework*. Sixth Framework Programme. Retrieved from http://lgaf.kedke.org/wiki

Liang, W., & Wang, W. (2005). *A quatitative study of authentication & QoS in wirless IP network*. Retrieved April 2010, from http://www.ece.ncsu.edu/netwis/papers/05LW-INFOCOM

Liberty Alliance Project. (2007a). *Liberty identity assurance framework*. Retrieved from http://www.projectliberty.org/liberty/content/download/4315/28869/file/liberty-identity-assurance-framework-v1.1.pdf

Liberty Alliance Project. (2007b). *An overview of the ID governance framework*. Retrieved from http://www.projectliberty.org/liberty/content/download/3500/23156/file/overview-id-governance-framework-v1.0.pdf

Liberty Alliance Project. (2010). *Liberty ID-FF protocols and schema specification 1.2*. Retrieved April 26, 2010, from http://www.projectliberty.org/liberty/content/view/full/179/(offset)/15/

Liberty Alliance Project. (2010). *Liberty specs tutorial*. Retrieved April 26, 2010, from http://www.projectliberty.org/liberty/specifications__1/

Liberty Alliance. (2003). *Liberty Alliance & WS-Federation: A comparative overview*. Retrieved from http://www.projectliberty.org/resources /whitepapers/.

Liberty Alliance. (n.d.). *Liberty ID-WSF Web services framework overview*, version 2.0. Retrieved from http://www.projectliberty.org

Liu, M., Guo, H., & Su, J. (2005). An attribute and role-based access control model for web services. *Proc. of the 4th International Conference on Machine Learning and Cybernetics*, Guangzhou, China, Aug. 18-21, (pp. 1302-1306).

Liu, S. (2004, February). *Authentication in ASP.NET web servers*. Retrieved April 2010, from http://progtutorials.tripod.com/Authen.htm

Lockhart, H., Andersen, S., Bohren, J., Sverdlov, Y., Hondo, M., Maruyama, H., et al. (2006, December). *Web services federation language* (WS-Federation), Version 1.1.

Lockheed Martin. (2010). *IronClads USB drive*. Lockheed Martin. Retrieved August 31, 2010, from http://lockheedmartinengineering.com/products/ironclad/index.html

Loh, Y., Yau, W., Wong, C., & Ho, W. (2006). Design and implementation of an XML-Firewall, *Proc. of the International Conference on Computational Intelligence and Security*, Guangzhou, China, Nov. 3-6, (pp. 1147-1150).

Lowe, G. (1996). Breaking and fixing the Needham-Schroeder public-key protocol using FDR. In T. Margaria & B. Steffen (Eds.), *Proceedings of TACAS'96* (pp. 147–166). Springer-Verlag.

Lowe, G. (1997). A hierarchy of authentication specifications. In *Proceedings of the 10th IEEE Computer Security Foundations Workshop (CSFW'97)* (pp. 31–43). IEEE Computer Society Press.

Lucas, M. M., & Borisov, N. (2008). FlyByNight: Mitigating the privacy risks of social networking. In *Proc. of the 7th ACM Workshop on Privacy in the Electronic Society* (pp. 1-8). Mountain View, CA: ACM Press. doi:10.1145/1456403.1456405.

Luo, W., Xie, Q., & Hengartner, U. (2009). FaceCloak: An architecture for user privacy on social networking sites. In *Proc. International Conference on Computational Science and Engineering, 2009* (pp. 26-33). Washington, DC: IEEE Computer Society. doi:10.1109/CSE.2009.387.

Ma, M. (2006, April). Mitigating denial of service attacks with password puzzles. *Proceedings of International Conference on Information Technology: Coding and Computing, Vol. 2* (pp. 621-626). Las Vegas, NV. doi: 10.1109/ITCC.2005.200

Madsen, P. (Ed.). (2008). Liberty IGF privacy constraints specification — Version 1.0-04. Liberty Alliance Project.

Madsen, P. (Ed.). (n.d.). Liberty ID-WSF people service — Federated social identity.

Madsen, P., & Maler, E. (2005). SAML V2.0 Executive Overview, Retrieved Feb. 11, 2011, from http://www.oasis-open.org/committees/download.php/13525/sstc-saml-exec-overview-2.0-cd-01-2col.pdf.

Magalhaes, R. M. (2001, November 19). *Understanding ISA's different types of authentication.* Retrieved April 2010, from http://www.isaserver.org/tutorials/Understanding_ISAs_different_Authentication_types.html

Maler, E., Mishra, P., & Philpott, R. (Eds.). (2003, September). Bindings and profiles for the OASIS security assertion markup language (SAML) V1.1. OASIS Standard Specification. OASIS Open.

Maler, E., Mishra, P., & Philpott, R. (2003). *Assertions and protocol for the OASIS security assertion markup language (SAML) V.1.1.* OASIS Standard, 2 September 2003. Retrieved August 23rd, 2010, from http://saml.xml.org/saml-specifications

Marlinspike, M. (2010). *GoogleSharing.* Retrieved August 31, 2010, from http://www.googlesharing.net

Mashima, D., & Ahamad, M. (2008) Towards a user-centric identity-usage monitoring system. *Proceedings of the Third International Conference on Internet Monitoring and Protection*, International Academic, Research, and Industry Association.

Mashima, D., & Ahamad, M. (2009b). Using identity credential usage logs to detect anomalous service accesses. *Proceedings of the Fifth ACM Workshop on Digital Identity Management,* Association for Computing Machinery.

Mashima, D., Ahamad, M., & Kannan, S. (2009a). User-centric handling of identity agent compromise. *Proceedings of the 14th European Symposium on Research in Computer Security* (pp. 19–36). Springer.

Massa, P., & Avesani, P. (2007). Trust-aware recommender systems. *Proc. of the 2007 ACM Conference on Recommender Systems*, Minneapolis, MN, USA, Oct. 19-20, (pp. 17-24).

Matthews, W., & Esterline, A. (2010). Personally identifiable information: Identifying unprotected PII using file-indexing search tools and quantitative analysis. In *Proceedings of the IEEE SoutheastCon 2010,* Concord, NC, (pp. 360-362).

Matyszczyk, C. (2009). Facebook entry gets office worker fired. *CNet News.* Retrieved August 31, 2010, from http://news.cnet.com/8301-17852_3-10172931-71.html

McKeon, M. (2010). *The evolution of privacy on Facebook.* Matt McKeon. Retrieved August 31, 2010, from http://mattmckeon.com/facebook-privacy/

Meadows, C. (1996). The NRL protocol analyzer: An overview. *The Journal of Logic Programming, 26*(2), 113–131. Retrieved from http://chacs.nrl.navy.mil/projects/crypto.html. doi:10.1016/0743-1066(95)00095-X

Meinecke, J., Nussbaumer, M., & Gaedke, M. (2005). Building blocks for identity federations. *Lecture Notes in Computer Science, 3579*, 203–208. doi:10.1007/11531371_29

Merkle, R. C. (1978). Secure communications over insecure channels. *Communications of the ACM, 21*(4). doi:10.1145/359460.359473

Microsoft Corporation. (2005a, May). Microsoft's vision for an identity metasystem.

Microsoft Corporation. (2005b, August). A technical reference for InfoCard v1.0 in Windows.

Microsoft Corporation. (2008, July). A guide to using the identity selector interoperability profile V1.5 within Web applications and browsers.

Microsoft Corporation and Ping Identity Corporation. (2005, August). A guide to integrating with InfoCard v1.0.

Microsoft Corporation. (2005a, May). *Microsoft's vision for an identity metasystem.*

Microsoft Corporation. (2008, July). *A guide to using the identity selector interoperability profile V1.5 within Web applications and browsers.*

Microsoft Research. (2009). *Online reputation in a connected world.* Online Reputation Research. Retrieved August 31, 2010, from http://www.microsoft.com/privacy/dpd/research.aspx

Millen, J. K., & Shmatikov, V. (2001). Constraint solving for bounded-process cryptographic protocol analysis. In *Proceedings of the ACM Conference on Computer and Communications Security CCS'01* (p. 166-175).

Miller, J. (Ed.). (2006, March). Yadis 1.0 (HTML). The Identity and Accountability Foundation for Web 2.0. Retrieved from http://yadis.org/wiki/Yadis_1.0_%28HTML%29.

Mindrum, C. (2008, January). It's in the cards. *Outlook*, 1.

Mishra, P. (Ed.). (2006). *AAPML: Attribute authority policy markup language — Working draft 08.* Oracle.

Mitra, N., & Lafon, Y. (Eds.). (2007, April). SOAP — Version 1.2. The World Wide Web Consortium (W3C).

Mödersheim, S., & Viganò, L. (2009). The open-source fixed-point model checker for symbolic analysis of security protocols. In *Fosad 2007-2008-2009* (vol. 5705, pp. 166–194). Springer-Verlag. Needham, R. M., & Schroeder, M. D. (1978). *Using encryption for authentication in large networks of computers* (Tech. Rep. No. CSL-78-4). Palo Alto, CA: Xerox Palo Alto Research Center.

Modinis-IDM Consortium. (2006). *D3.5 identity management initiative report 1 IIR1.* Deliverable of Modinis Project. Retrieved August 2nd, 2010, from https://www.cosic.esat.kuleuven.be/modinis-idm/twiki/pub/Main/ProjectDocs/modinis.D3.5_Identity_Management_Initiative_Report_1_IIR1.pdf

Mont, M. C., Bramhall, P., Gittler, M., Pato, J., & Rees, O. (2000). *Identity management: A key e-business enabler.* Retrieved from hpl.hp.com

Monzillo, R., Kaler, C., Nadalin, A., & Hallem-Baker, P. (Eds.). (2006, February). Web services security: SAML token profile 1.1. OASIS Standard Specification. OASIS Open.

Monzillo, R., Kaler, C., Nadalin, A., & Hallem-Baker, P. (Eds.). (2006, February). *Web services security: SAML Token profile 1.1.* OASIS Standard Specification. OASIS Open.

Morgan, B., Cantor, S., Hoehn, S. C. W., & Klingenstein, K. (2004). Federated security: The Shibboleth approach. *EDUCAUSE Quarterly*, *27*(4), 12–17.

Moses, T. (2005). eXtensible access control markup language (XACML) version 2.0. Retrieved February 11, 2011, from http://docs.oasis-open.org/xacml/2.0/access_control-xacml-2.0-core-spec-os.pdf

MS-Forefront. (2010). *Microsoft Forefront Identity Manager: Home page.* Retrieved from http://www.microsoft.com/forefront/identitymanager/en/us/default.aspx

MS-Live. (2010). *Home - Windows Live.* Retrieved April 14, 2010, from http://home.live.com/

Mule. (2008). *Technical Committee: Mule 2.0. release candidate 2.* Retrieved from http://mule.mulesource.org

Nadalin, A., Goodner, M., Gudgin, M., Barbir, A., & Granqvist, H. (2007). *WS-Trust 1.3. Organization for the Advancement of Structured Information Standards.* OASIS.

Nadalin, A., Goodner, M., Gudgin, M., Barbir, A., & Granqvist, H. (Eds.). (2007a, July). *WS-Security policy — Version 1.2.* OASIS Standard.

Nadalin, A., & Kaler, C. (Eds.). (2006, December). Web services federation language WS-Federation, version 1.1. BEA Systems, BMC Software, CA, IBM, Layer 7 Technologies, Microsoft, Novell, and VeriSign.

Nadalin, A., Kaler, C., Monzillo, R., & Hallam-Baker, P. (Eds.). (2006, February). Web services security: SOAP message security — Version 1.1. OASIS Standard Specification.

Nagao, M., & Iri, M. (1981). *Iwanami jouhou kagaku 23 - Kazu to siki no bun no syori* [Iwanami Lecture of Information Sciences 23 - Processing of sentence of number and expression]. Iwanami Shoten.

Namatame. (1999). *A. Maruchi eijento to hukuzatukei* [Multiagent and Complex System]. Morikita Publishing Co., Ltd.

Nanda, A. (2007, April). Identity selector interoperability profile v1.0. Microsoft Corporation.

Narayanan, A., & Shmatikov, V. (2009). De-anonymizing social networks. In *Proc. of the 30th IEEE Symposium on Security and Privacy, 2009* (pp. 173-187). Washington, DC: IEEE Computer Society. doi:10.1109/SP.2009.22

Nash, A., Duane, W., Joseph, C., & Brink, D. (2001). Pki: Implementing and managing e-security. Osborne/ McGraw-Hill.

National Institute of Standards and Technology. (2006). *Electronic authentication guideline*.

National Institute of Standards and Technology. (2003). *Electronic authentication: Guidance for selecting secure techniques*. Retrieved from http://www.itl.nist.gov/lab/ bulletns/bltnaug04.htm

Naumann, I., & Hogben, G. (2009). *Privacy features of European eID card specifications*. ENISA Position Paper. Retrieved August 23rd, 2010, from http://www.enisa.europa.eu/act/it/eid/eid-cards-en

Naumenko, A., & Luostarinen, K. (2006). Access control policies in (semantic) service-oriented architecture. *Proceedings of the Semantics 2006 Conference, Austrian Computing Society (OCG)*, (pp. 28–30).

Nieuwenhuizen, M. (2008). *Role based identity- en access management is makkelijker gezegd dan gedaan ['Role-based identity and access management is easier said than done']*. Retrieved July 28, 2008, from http://www.marqit.nl/securityschool-compliance-artikel2.aspx

NIST. (2001, May). Security requirements for cryptographic modules [Manuel de logiciel]. Gaithersburg, MD: NIST.

Noor, A. (2008). Identity protection factor (IPF). In The 7th Symposium on Identity and Trust on the Internet (IDTrust 2008) (vol. 283, pp. 8-18). ACM.

Novell. (2010). *Identity manager*. Retrieved from http://www.novell.com/products/identitymanager/

NSA. (2003, December). Guide to Sun Microsystems Java plug-in security, report number C43-022R-2003. Network Applications Team of the Systems and Network Attack Center (SNAC), National Security Agency (NSA), USA.

NSTC. (2008). *Standards and conformity assessment working group: NSTC Subcommittee on biometrics and identity management*. Retrieved from http://www.biometrics.gov/Standards/default.aspx

Nyanchama, M., & Osborn, S. (1999). The role graph model and conflict of interest. *ACM Transactions on Information and System Security*, *2*(1), 3–33. doi:10.1145/300830.300832

OASIS. (2005). *XACML technical committee: eXtensible access control markup language (XACML) version 2.0*. OASIS Standard Specification, February. Retrieved from http://docs.oasis-open.org/xacml/2.0/access_control-xacml-2.0-core-spec-os.pdf

OASIS. (2005a, April). *Security assertion markup language (SAML) v2.0*. Retrieved from http://www.oasis-open.org/committees/tc_home.php?wg_abbrev=security

OASIS. (2005b, July). *SSTC response to security analysis of the SAML single sign-on browser/artifact profile*. Retrieved from http://www.oasis-open.org/committees/tc_home.php?wg_abbrev=security

OASIS. (2007). *Web service secure exchange technical committee: OASIS WS-Trust 1.3*. OASIS Standard Specification. Retrieved from http://www.oasis-open.org

OASIS. (2007a). *Technical committee: Security assertion markup language v.2.0 – Technical overview*. OASIS Standard Specification. Retrieved from http://www.oasis-open.org

OASIS. (2008). *WSFED technical committee: Web services federation language version 1.2*. OASIS Standard Specification, Working Draft. Retrieved from http://www.oasis-open.org

OASIS. (2009, July). *Identity metasystem interoperability*, version 1.0. OASIS Standards.

OCC. (1999, October). *Internet banking*. Retrieved April 2010, from http://www.occ.treas.gov/handbook/intbank.pdf

Oda, K., Takahiro, N., Suda, S., & Yukawa, T. (2007). *Jisedai koukoku tekunorozi* [Next-generation Advertising Technology]. SOFTBANK Creative.

OECD. (1980). *OECD guidelines on the protection of privacy and transborder flows of personal data*. http://www.oecd.org/document/18/0,3343,en_2649_34255_1815186_1_1_1_1,00.html

OECD. (2008). *The Seoul Declaration of the future of the internet economy*. Retrieved from http://www.oecd.org/dataoecd/49/28/40839436.pdf

OECD. (2008, February). At a crossroads: "Personhood" and digital identity in the information society. Organisation for Economic Co-operation and Development.

Office of Security Management and Safeguards. (2003). *Further amendment to EO 12958, as amended, classified national security information*. Retrieved February 11, 2011, from http://nodis3.gsfc.nasa.gov/displayEO.cfm?id=EO_13292_

Office of the e-Envoy, UK. (2002). *Registration and authentication - e-Government strategy framework policy and guidelines*. Retrieved from http://www.cabinetoffice.gov.uk/csia/documents/pdf/ RegAndAuthentn0209v3.pdf

OMG. (2009). *Business process modeling notation (BPMN) version 1.2*. Object Management Group Specification. Retrieved from http://www.omg.org/spec/BPMN/1.2/

OpenView. (2006). *HP OpenView select identity software*. Retrieved from http://www.hp.com/hpinfo/newsroom/press_kits/2006/rsa/ds_hires_select_identity.pdf

Oracle-IDM. (2010). *Identity management*. Oracle Identity Management. Retrieved from http://www.oracle.com/us/products/middleware/identity-management/index.htm

Organisation for Economic Co-operation and Development. (1980). *OECD guidelines on the protection of privacy and transborder flows of personal data*. Retrieved February 11, 2011, from http://www.oecd.org/document/18/0,3343,en_2649_34255_1815186_1_1_1_1,00.html

Organisation for Economic Co-operation and Development (OECD). (2008). *At a crossroads: "Personhood" and digital identity in the information society*.

Paci, F., Bertino, E., Kerr, S., Squicciarini, A., & Woo, J. (2009). An overview of VeryIDX - A privacy-preserving digital identity management system for mobile devices. *Journal of Software*, *4*(7). doi:10.4304/jsw.4.7.696-706

Papastergiou, S., Karantjias, A., & Polemi, D. (2007). A federated privacy-enhancing identity management system (FPE-IMS). In *Proceedings of the 18th Annual IEEE International Symposium on Personal, Indoor and Mobile Radio Communications*, PIMRC 07, Athens Greece, IEEE Digital Library.

Paquin, C. (2010). *U-Prove technology integration into the identity metasystem V1.0*. Retrieved August 23rd, 2010, from http://connect.microsoft.com/site642/Downloads/DownloadDetails.aspx?DownloadID=26953

Park, J., Lee, Y., Lee, H., & Noh, B. (2003). A role-based delegation model using role hierarchy supporting restricted permission inheritance. In *Proceedings of the International Conference on Security and Management, SAM '03*, (pp. 294–302). CSREA Press.

Pashalidis, A., & Meyer, B. (2006). Linking anonymous transactions: The consistent view attack. In G. Danezis & P. Golle (Eds.), *Privacy Enhancing Technologies, 6th International Workshop, PET 2006, LNCS 4258,* Cambridge, UK, June 28–30, 2006, Revised Selected Papers (pp. 384-392). Berlin, Germany: Springer Verlag.

Pashalidis, A., & Mitchell, C. J. (2004). Limits to anonymity when using credentials. in: *Security Protocols, 12th International Workshop, LNCS 3957,* Cambridge, U.K., April 26-28. 2004, Revised Selected Papers (pp. 4-12). Berlin, Germany: Springer Verlag.

Passlogix. (2010). *Website*. Retrieved from http://www.passlogix.com/site/

Paulik, T., Földes, Á. M., & Gulyás, G. (2010). BlogCrypt: Private content publishing on the Web. In *Proc. of the Fourth International Conference on Emerging Security Information, Systems and Technologies, SECURWARE 2010*, Venice, Italy.

Pearsons, G. (2007). *Using international standards in your compliance program.* Retrieved 28 September, 2007, from http://www.securecomputing.net.au/feature/3759,using-international-standards-in-your-compliance-program.aspx

Penn, J. (2002). *IT trends 2002: Directories and directory- enabled applications*. GIGA Report.

Peyton, L., Doshi, Ch., & Seguin, P. (2007). An audit trail service to enhance privacy compliance in federated identity management. In *Proceedings of the 2007 Conference of the Center for Advanced Studies on Collaborative Research*, CASCON'07, ACM, Ontario Canada, (pp. 175-187).

Podio, F. L., & Dunn, J. S. (2001). *Biometric authentication technology.* Retrieved April 2010, from http://www.itl.nist.gov/div893/biometrics/Biometricsfromthemovies.pdf

Pond, R., Podd, J., Bunnell, J., & Henderson, R. (2000). Word association computer passwords: The effect of formulation techniques on recall and guessing rates. *Computers & Security, 19*(7), 645–656. doi:10.1016/S0167-4048(00)07023-1

Priebe, T., Dobmeier, W., Schlager, C., & Kamprath, N. (2007). Supporting attribute-based access control in authorization and authentication infrastructures with ontologies. *Journal of Software, 2*(1), 27–38. doi:10.4304/jsw.2.1.27-38

PRIME Project. (2005). *Privacy and identity management for Europe*. European RTD Integrated Project under the FP6/IST Programme. Retrieved from http://www.prime-project.eu.org/

Privacy International. (2011). *European privacy and human rights*. Privacy International. Retrieved February 15, 2011, from https://www.privacyinternational.org/ephr

Privacy Rating Jimukyoku & Westin. A. F. (Eds.). (2006). *White paper on the privacy in Japan 2007* (in Japanese). Yano Research Institute Ltd.

Privacy, V. P. N. (2010). *VPN privacy*. VPN Privacy Service. Retrieved August 31, 2010, from http://vpnprivacy.com

Quest. (2010). *Identity and access management software - Quest Software*. Retrieved from http://www.quest.com/identity-management/

Rahaman, M., & Schaad, A. (2007). SOAP-based secure conversation and collaboration. *Proc. of the International Conference on Web Services*, Salt Lake City, UT, USA, Jul. 9-13, (pp. 471-480).

Recordon, D., & Reed, D. (2006). OpenID 2.0: A platform for user-centric identity management. *Proceedings of the Second ACM Workshop on Digital Identity Management* (pp. 11–16). Association for Computing Machinery.

Recordon, D., Bufu, J., & Hoyt, J. (Eds.). (2007, December). OpenID authentication 2.0. The OpenID Foundation. Retrieved from http://openid.net/specs/openid-authentication-2_0.html.

Reed, D., & McAlpin, D. (Eds.). (2005, November). Extensible resource identifier (XRI) syntax V2.0. OASIS Open.

Renaud, K. (2009). On user involvement in production of images used in visual authentication. *Journal of Visual Languages and Computing, 20*(1), 1–15. doi:10.1016/j.jvlc.2008.04.001

Rieger, S., & Neumair, B. (2007). Towards usable and reasonable identity management in heterogeneous IT infrastructures. In *Proceedings of the 10th IFIP/IEEE International Symposium on Integrated Network Management* (IM '07), Munich, (pp. 560-574).

Rinocube. (2010). *MojoPac.* Retrieved August 31, 2010, from http://www.mojopac.com

Rivest, R. R., Shamir, A., & Wagner, D. A. (1996). Time-lock puzzles and timed-release cryptography. Retrieved April 26, 2010, from http://lcs.mit.edu/~rivest/Rivest-ShamirWagnertimelock.pdf

Rizvi, H. (2006). I am who I say I am. *Quarterly Journal of the EDS Agility Alliance*, *1*(2), 46–57.

Rolland, C. (1998). *A comprehensive view of process engineering*. Paper presented at the 10 International Conference CAISE'98, B. Lecture Notes in Computer Science.

Rotenberg, M., & Ngo, M. (May 2008). *Real ID implementation review: Few benefits, staggering costs*. Electornic Privacy Informatin Center.

Ruan, C., & Varadharajan, V. (2002). Resolving conflicts in authorization delegations. In *7th Australian Conference on Information Security and Privacy*, volume 2384 of *Lecture Notes in Computer Science*, (pp. 271–285). Springer.

Rusinowitch, M., & Turuani, M. (2001). Protocol insecurity with finite number of sessions is NP-complete. In *Proceedings of the 14th IEEE Computer Security Foundations Workshop.* IEEE Computer Society Press.

S.761. (2006). *The electronic signature in global and national commerce act*. US - S.761.

Sabadello, M., Trevithick, P., & Reed, D. (2009, April). Universal data identifiers. Parity Communications Inc.

Samy Kamkar. (2010). Evercookie -- Never forget. *Evercookie - virtually irrevocable persistent cookies*. Retrieved February 15, 2011, from http://samy.pl/evercookie/

Sánchez, M., Reverte, Ó. C., López, G., & Gómez-Skarmeta, A. F. (2008). Managing the lifecycle of XACML delegation policies in federated environments. In Proceedings of the IFIP TC-11 23rd International Information Security Conference, IFIP 20th World Computer Congress, IFIP SEC 2008, Milano, Italy (pp. 717-721). Springer-Verlag.

Sandhu, R., Coyne, E., Feinstein, H., & Youman, C. (1996). Role-based access control models. *IEEE Computer*, *29*(2), 38–47. doi:10.1109/2.485845

Scavo, T. (Ed.). (2009, November). SAML V2.0 holder-of-key assertion profile — Version 1.0 — Committee draft 3. OASIS Open.

Schneier, B. (2000, March). Distributed denial of service attacks. *Crypto-gram Newsletter*.

Schroeder, S. (2009). Are you sure those photos have really been deleted? *Mashable – The Social Media Guide.* Retrieved August 31, 2010, from http://mashable.com/2009/05/21/photos-deleted-facebook/

SearchSecurity. (2007, June 4). *Authentication*. Retrieved April 2010, from http://searchsecurity.techtarget.com/sDefinition/0,sid14_gci211621,00.html

Searls, D. (2007). *ProjectVRM*. Retrieved from http://cyber.law.harvard.edu/projectvrm/Main_Page.Bowman

Seifert, J. (2007). *Data mining and homeland security: An overview*. Retrieved February 11, 2011, from http://www.fas.org/sgp/crs/intel/RL31798.pdf

Seitz, L., Rissanen, E., Sandholm, T., Firozabadi, B. S., & Mulmo, O. (2005). Policy administration control and delegation using XACML and delegent. In Proceedings of the 6th IEEE/ACM International Conference on Grid Computing, Grid 2005, Seattle, Washington, USA (pp. 49-54). IEEE.

SETI @home Program. (2010). *Website*. Retrieved April 26, 2010, from http://setiathome.ssl.berkely.edu

Shen, H., & Hong, F. (2006). An attribute-based access control model for Web services. *Proc. of the 7th IEEE International Conference on Parallel and Distributed Computing, Applications and Technologies*, Taipei, Taiwan, Dec. 4-7, (pp. 74-79).

Siaterlis, C., & Maglaris, B. (2004). Towards multisensor data fusion for DoS detection. *Proceedings of the 2004 ACM Symposium on Applied Computing* (pp. 439-446). ACM Press. doi: 10.1.1.9.8572

Simon, R., & Zurko, M. E. (1997). Separation of duty in role-based environments. In *Proc. of the 10th Computer Security Foundations Workshop (CSFW '97).*

Singhal, A. (2009). Relevance meets the real-time web. *Official Google Blog.* Retrieved August 31, 2010, from http://googleblog.blogspot.com/2009/12/relevance-meets-real-time-web.html

Smedinghoff, T. J. (2010). *Building an online identity legal framework: The proposed national strategy. Privacy & Security Law Report*. The Bureau of National Affairs, Inc.

Snyder, J. (2008). *Refactoring networks: Five principles of integrated network security.* Paper presented at the SecurityPoint 2008, Sydney.

Soltani, A., Canty, S., Mayo, Q., Thomas, L., & Hoofnagle, C. J. (2009). *Flash cookies and privacy.* Social Science Research Network. Retrieved August 31, 2010, from http://papers.ssrn.com/sol3/papers.cfm?abstract_id=1446862

Sommer, D., Cassasa Mont, M., & Pearson, S. (2008). *PRIME deliverable D.14.2d – PRIME Architecture V3.* July 2008, Retrieved August 23rd, 2010, from https://www.prime-project.eu

Spatscheck, O., & Peterson, L. (1999). Defending against denial of service attacks in Scout. *Proceedings of the 1999 USENIX/ACM Symposium on OSDI* (pp. 59-72). doi: 10.1.1.37.157

Squicciarini, A., Trombetta, A., Bertino, E., & Braghin, S. (2008). Identity-based long running negotiations. In *Proceedings of the 4th ACM Workshop on Digital Identity Management*, Virginia USA, (pp. 97-106).

Stamm, S. (2010). Plugging the CSS history leak. *The Mozilla Blog*. Retrieved August 31, 2010, from http://blog.mozilla.com/security/2010/03/31/plugging-the-css-history-leak/

Stanton, J. M., Stam, K. R., Mastrangelo, P., & Jolton, J. (2005). Analysis of end user security behaviors. *Computers & Security*, *24*(2), 124–133. doi:10.1016/j.cose.2004.07.001

Sturdevant, C. (2005, June 6). Virtual directories ease quest for identity data. *eWEEK.com*, 43-46.

Sun-IDM. (2010). *Identity management.* Sun Microsystems. Retrieved from http://developers.sun.com/identity/index.jsp

Suriadi, S., Foo, E., & Jøsang, A. (2009). A user-centric federated single sign-on system. *Journal of Network and Computer Applications*, *32*, 388–401. doi:10.1016/j.jnca.2008.02.016

SWEB Project. (2008). *D4.1: SWEB platform development report. Project Deliverable.* Brussels: European Commission.

SWEB Project. (2006). *Secure, interoperable, cross border m-services contributing towards a trustful European cooperation with the non-EU member Western Balkan countries.* Sixth Framework Programme, IST-2006-2.6.5. Retrieved from www.sweb-project.org

Szabó, M. D., & Székely, I. (2005). Privacy and data protection at the workplace in Hungary. In Nouwt, S., & de Vries, B. R. (Eds.), *Reasonable expectations of privacy? Eleven country reports on camera surveillance and workplace privacy* (pp. 249–284). The Hague, The Netherlands: T. M. C. Asser Press, IT & Law Series. doi:10.1007/978-90-6704-589-6_10

Tamassia, R., Yao, D., & Winsborough, W. H. (2004). Role-based cascaded delegation. In *Proceedings of the 9th ACM Symposium on Access Control Models and Technologies*, (pp. 146–155). ACM.

Tang, Z., & Meclennan, J. (2005). *Data mining with SQL server 2005.* Hoboken, NJ: Wiley Publishing, Inc.

Taylor, J. A., Lips, M., & Organ, J. (2009). *Identification practices in government: Citizen surveillance and the quest for public service improvement. Identity in the Information Society.* Springer-Verlag.

The AVANTSSAR Team. (n.d.). *The AVANTSSAR project.* Retrieved from http://www.avantssar.eu/

The Bandit Project. (n.d.). *Digital me identity selector.* Retrieved 2010, from http://code.bandit-project.org/trac/wiki/DigitalMe

The Distributed.net Organization. (2010). *Website.* Retrieved April 26, 2010, from http://www.distributed.net

The Guardian Project. (2010). Open-source mobile security. *The Guardian Project.* Retrieved February 15, 2011, from https://guardianproject.info

The Open Group. (2002). *Identity management business scenario.* Retrieved from http://www.opengroup.org/bookstore/catalog/k023.htm

The OpenId Foundation. (2007). *OpenID authentication 2.0 - Final specification.* Retrieved 2010, from http://openid.net/specs

The Ponemon Institute. (2007). *Survey on identity compliance.* March.

Thigpen, S. (2005, July 17). *Banking authentication methods*. Retrieved April 2010, from http://www.infosecwriters.com/text_resources/pdf/Authentication_Methods_For_Banking.pdf

Thomas, I., & Meinel, C. (2009). *Enhancing claim-based identity management by adding a credibility level to the notion of claims*. International Conference on Services Computing. Bangalore, India: IEEE.

Thomas, I., & Meinel, C. (2010). *An identity provider to manage reliable digital identities for SOA and the web*. 9th Symposium on Identity and Trust on the Internet. Gaithersburg, MD: ACM.

Tiffany, E., Madsen, P., & Cantor, S. (Eds.). (2009, May). *Level of assurance authentication context profile for SAML 2.0 — Working Draft 03*. OASIS Open.

Tivoli. (2010). *IBM - Identity management software - TivolWe Identity Manager software*. Retrieved from http://www-01.ibm.com/software/tivoli/products/identity-mgr/

Toolware. (2010). *Identity management solutions by Advanced Toolware*. Retrieved from http://www.adv-toolware.com/

Tourzan, J., & Koga, Y. (Eds.), *(n.d.). Liberty ID-WSF web services framework overview — Version: 1.1*. Liberty Alliance Project.

Tracy, K. (2008). Identity management systems. [IEEE.]. *Potentials*, *27*(6), 34–37. doi:10.1109/MPOT.2008.929295

Trevithick, P. (2009, September). Relationship cards. Higgins Report 19 — Draft 0.46.

TrueCrypt Foundation. (2010). *TrueCrypt downloads*. TrueCrypt – Free Open-Source On-The-Fly Disk Encryption Software. Retrieved August 31, 2010, from http://www.truecrypt.org/downloads

Turuani, M. (2006). The CL-Atse protocol analyser. In *Term Rewriting and Applications (Proceedings of RTA '06)* (pp. 277-286).

US-CERT. (2008, Sep 2). *Vulnerability note VU#612636 - Google SAML single sign on vulnerability*. Retrieved from http://www.kb.cert.org/vuls/id/612636

Vittorio Bertocci, G. S. (2007). *Understanding Windows CardSpace: An introduction to the concepts and challenges of digital identities (independent technology guides)* (*Vol. 1*). Amsterdam, The Netherlands: Addison-Wesley Longman.

Wachob, G., Reed, D., Chasen, L., Tan, W., & Churchill, S. (Eds.). (2008, February). Extensible resource identifier (XRI) resolution version 2.0 — Committee draft 03. OASIS Open.

Wainer, J., Kumar, A., & Barthelmess, P. (2003). WRBAC - A workflow security model incorporating controlled overriding of constraints. *International Journal of Cooperative Information Systems*, *12*(4), 455–486. doi:10.1142/S0218843003000814

Wainer, J., Kumar, A., & Barthelmess, P. (2007). DW-RBAC: A formal security model of delegation and revocation in workflow systems. *Information Systems*, *32*, 365–384. doi:10.1016/j.is.2005.11.008

Wainer, J., & Kumar, A. (2005). A fine-grained, controllable, user-to-user delegation method in RBAC. In *SACMAT '05: Proceedings of the Tenth ACM Symposium on Access Control Models and Technologies*, (pp. 59–66). New York, NY: ACM Press.

WallStreet Technology. (2008). *Identity and access management market to reach $12.3 billion in 2014*. Retrieved October 24, 2008, from http://www.wallstreetandtech.com/showArticle.jhtml?articleID=206904330

Wang, J., Vecchio, D. D., & Humphrey, M. (2005). Extending the security assertion markup language to support delegation for web services and grid services. In Ieee International Conference on Web Services (ICWS 2005) (vol. 1, pp. 67-74). IEEE Computer Society.

Wang, Y., & Kobsa, A. (2009). Privacy in online social networking at workplace. In *Proc. of International Conference on Computational Science and Engineering, 2009, CSE '09* (pp. 975-978). Washington, DC: IEEE Computer Society. doi:10.1109/CSE.2009.438

Wason, T. (Ed.), *(n.d.). Liberty ID-FF architecture overview — Version: 1.2*. Liberty Alliance Project.

Waters, B., Juels, A., Halderman, J. A., & Felten, E. W. (2004). New client puzzle outsourcing techniques for DoS resistance. *Proceedings of 11th ACM Conference on Computer and Communications Security*. doi: 10.1.1.58.737

Weigold, T. K. (2006, March/April). *Secure internet banking and authentication*. Retrieved April 2010, from http://www.zurich.ibm.com/pdf/csc/SecureInternetBankingAuthentication.pdf

Wenning, R. (editors), Schunter, M. (2006, November). *The platform for privacy preferences*, version 1.1. W3C Working Group Note.

Wenning, R., & Cranor, L. (2007). *Platform for privacy preferences(P3P)*. Retrieved from http://www.w3c.org/P3P/

Wenning, R., et al. (Eds.). (2006, November). The platform for privacy preferences — version 1.1. W3C Working Group Note.

What They Know. (2010). What They Know. *WSJ Blogs*. Retrieved February 15, 2011, from http://blogs.wsj.com/wtk/

Whisper Systems. (2010). *RedPhone, TextSecure*. Whisper Systems. Retrieved August 31, 2010, from http://whispersys.com

White, P. (2009). *Managing enterprise complexity. The use of identity management architecture to control enterprise resources*. Saarbrucken, Germany: VDM Verlag.

White, P. (2008). *Identity management architecture in the Australian public sector.* Paper presented at the 5th International Conference on Information Technology and Applications ICITA 2008, Cairns, QLD.

White, P., Altas, I., Howarth, J., & Weckert, J. (2007). *An internal enterprise framework for identity based management*. Paper presented at the Australian Partnership for Advanced Computing Conference APAC07, Perth.

Whitehouse. (2009). *US President's cyberspace policy review*. Retrieved from http://www.whitehouse.gov/assets/documents/Cyberspace_Policy_Review_final.pdf

Widdowson, R., & Cantor, S. (Eds.). (2008, March). *Identity provider discovery service protocol and profile — Committee specification 01. OASIS Standard Specification*. OASIS Open.

Wiedenbeck, S., Waters, J., Birget, J., Brodskiy, A., & Memon, N. (2005). PassPoints: Design and longitudinal evaluation of a graphical password system. *International Journal of Human-Computer Studies*, *63*(1-2), 102–127. doi:10.1016/j.ijhcs.2005.04.010

Wielemaker, J., Schreiber, G., & Wielinga, B. (2003). Prolog-based infrastructure for RDF: Scalability and performance. In *The Semantic Web - Proceedings ISWC '03, LNCS 2870* (pp. 644–658). Springer.

Williamson, G. D. (2006). Enhanced authentication in online banking. *Journal of Economic Crime Management*, *4*(2).

Windley, P. (2005). *Digital identity*. Sebastopol, CA: O'Reilly Media Inc.

Windley, P. J. (2006, March 27). The hidden challenges of federated identity. *InfoWorld.com*, 27-33.

WinterGreen Research, Inc. (2009). *Worldwide Cloud Computing market opportunities and segment forecasts 2009 to 2015*. Retrieved from http://www.researchandmarkets.com/reportinfo.asp?report_id=1071781

Wohlgemuth, S., & Müller, G. (2006). Privacy with delegation of rights by identity management. In Proceedings of the Emerging Trends in Information and Communication Security, International Conference (ETRICS 2006) (vol. 3995, pp. 175-190). Springer-Verlag.

Wolter, C., Kohler, A., & Schaad, A. (2007). Classification model for access control constraints. In *WIA – Proceedings of the first International Workshop on Information Assurance*, (pp. 410-417).

Wondracek, G., Holz, T., Kirda, E., & Kruegel, C. (2010). A practical attack to de-anonymize social network users. In *Proc. of IEEE Symposium on Security and Privacy, 2010* (pp. 223-238). Washington, DC: IEEE Computer Society.

Wood, M. (2010). Google Buzz: Privacy nightmare. *CNet News*. Retrieved August 31, 2010, from http://news.cnet.com/8301-31322_3-10451428-256.html

Woodhouse, S., & White, P. (2007). *Identity based management: Extending the ISMS for federation.* Paper presented at the ISACA Oceania Computer Audit Control and Security Conference 2007, Auckland NZ.

X.509. (2000). Information Technology — Open systems interconnection — The directory: Public-key and attribute certificate frameworks [Manuel de logiciel].

X.509. (2005). Information Technology — Open systems interconnection — The directory: Public-key and attribute certificate frameworks [Manuel de logiciel].

X.680. (2002). Information Technology — Abstract syntax notation one (ASN.1): Specification of basic notation [Manuel de logiciel].

XAC. (2005). *eXtensible access control markup language (XACML)*. OASIS, version 2.0. Retrieved from http://docs.oasis-open.org/xacml/2.0/access_control-xacml-2.0-core-spec-os.pdf

Y.2720. (2008). *NGN identity management framework - Draft recommendation.*

Yang, Y.-J. (1997). *The security of electronic banking.* Retrieved April 2010, from http://csrc.nist.gov/nissc/1997/proceedings/041.pdf

Yao, W. (2003). Fidelis: A policy-driven trust management framework. In *Trust Management, First International Conference, iTrust, Lecture Notes in Computer Science 2692* (pp. 301–317). Springer.

Yasuharu, D., Atsushi, Y., Hideki, O., Hanae, K., & Toshinobu, O. (2007). *UniDic-chasen*. Retrieved from http://www.tokuteicorpus.jp/dist/

Zhang, L., Ahn, G.-J., & Chu, B.-T. (2003a). A rule-based framework for role-based delegation and revocation. *ACM Transactions on Information and System Security*, *6*(3), 404–441. doi:10.1145/937527.937530

Zhang, X., Oh, S., & Sandhu, R. (2003b). PBDM: A flexible delegation model in RBAC. In *SACMAT '03: Proceedings of the Eighth ACM Symposium on Access Control Models and Technologies*, (pp. 149–157). ACM Press.

Zhu, H. (2007). Strengthen access control with enterprise identity-management architecture. Retrieved 7 November, 2007, from http://msdn2.microsoft.com/en-us/library/bb447668.aspx

About the Contributors

Raj Sharman is an Associate Professor in the Management Science and Systems Department of the State University of New York at Buffalo. He received his B. Tech and M. Tech degree from IIT Bombay, India and his M.S degree in Industrial Engineering and PhD in Computer Science from Louisiana State University. His research streams include Information Assurance, Disaster Preparedness and Response Management, Patient Safety and Health Care Systems, Business Value of Information Technology investments, and Imaging Systems. He has published in National and International journals and is the recipient of several grants from university and external agencies, including the National Science Foundation. He serves as the Associate Editor for the Communications of the Association of Information Systems (CAIS), *Journal of Information Systems Security (JISSEC)* and as a Coordinating guest editor for Information Systems Frontiers (ISF).

Sanjukta Das Smith is an Assistant Professor of Management Science and Systems at the State University of New York at Buffalo, New York, USA. She has published in the *Information Systems Research, INFORMS Journal on Computing, Journal of Management Information Systems, ACM Transactions in Management Information Systems*, and the *Journal of Organizational Computing and Electronic Commerce*. She is a graduate of the University of Connecticut, Clarkson University, and Calcutta University.

Manish Gupta is an Information Security Professional in a Northeast US based bank. He received his PhD, in Management Science and Systems, and an MBA, in Information Systems and Finance, from State University of New York at Buffalo, NY, USA in 2011 and 2003, respectively. He received his Bachelor's degree in Mechanical Engineering from Institute of Engineering and Technology, Lucknow, India in 1998. He has more than twelve years of experience in information systems, security policies and technologies. He has also taught at School of Management at State University of New York at Buffalo, NY. He has published 4 books in the area of information security, ethics, and assurance. He has authored or co-authored more than 50 research articles in leading journals, conference proceedings, and books including *DSS, ACM Transactions, IEEE*, and *JOEUC*. He has also received two best paper awards. He serves in editorial boards of more than a dozen international journals and has served in program committees of several international conferences. He holds several professional designations including CISSP, CISA, CISM, CRISC, ISSPCS, CIW Security Analyst, and PMP. He is a member of Sigma Xi, Beta Gamma Sigma, ISACA, and ISC^2. He received prestigious 2008 ISC^2 information security scholarship (awarded to only 7 researchers around the world) and also received PhD Student Achievement Award from SUNY Buffalo.

* * *

Mustaque Ahamad currently serves as the Director of Georgia Tech Information Security Center (GTISC). He is a Professor in the School of Computer Science at the Georgia Institute of Technology, Atlanta, GA, USA. His research interests span distributed systems and middleware, computer security, and dependable systems. He has published over one hundred research papers in these areas and has advised over twenty doctoral students. He has also served on program committees of numerous conferences and has received awards for his research papers. As Director of GTISC, Dr. Ahamad has helped develop several major research thrusts in areas that include security of emerging converged communication networks and applications, identity and access management, and security of healthcare information technology systems. In his current role, Dr. Ahamad works extensively with local and national industry leaders to develop effective relationships to address the challenges associated with securing networked information systems. Dr. Ahamad received his Ph.D. in Computer Science from the State University of New York at Stony Brook in 1985. He received his undergraduate degree in electrical and electronics engineering from the Birla Institute of Technology and Science, Pilani, India.

David S. Allison is currently pursuing his PhD in Software Engineering at the University of Western Ontario, where he has previously completed his Master of Engineering Science and Bachelor of Engineering Science degrees, both specializing in Software Engineering. Mr. Allison was awarded an NSERC CGS D scholarship to help fund his PhD research. His Master's thesis focused on privacy for service-oriented architecture and Web services and was funded in part by an OGS scholarship. During his undergraduate studies, he partook in a sixteen month internship at IBM, where he worked as a database performance analyst.

Waleed A. Alrodhan has received a B.Sc. degree in Computer Sciences from King Saud University in 2002. He has received his M.Sc. degree (*with distinction*) in 2005, and his Ph.D. degree in 2011, both in *Information Security* from Royal Holloway, University of London. Two of Waleed's research papers (*Addressing privacy issues in CardSpace* and *Improving the Security of CardSpace*) have been chosen to be taught as an integral part of the (CS 590) M.Sc. course on Cloud Systems for Blind and Hearing Impaired, held by Purdue University, USA, 2010. Moreover, many of Waleed's research papers have been used and cited in a number of identity management related reports (e.g. reports by the Future of Identity in the Information Society (FIDIS) consortium) and books (e.g. The Future of Identity in the Information Society by Kai Rannenberg). Waleed is a reviewer for a number of well-known journals like, for example, *The Computer Journal*, Oxford Journals, Oxford University. He also reviewed many papers for a number of well-known international conferences (e.g. *NordSec* and *EuroPKI*). Currently, Waleed is an Assistant Professor at the College of Computer and Information Sciences in Imam Muhammed Ibn Saud University.

Alessandro Armando is Associate Professor at the Dipartimento of Informatica, Sistemistica e Telematica (DIST) of the University of Genova and Head of the Security & Trust Unit at the Center for Information Technologies of Bruno Kessler Foundation (FBK) in Trento. He got his PhD in 1994 at the University of Genova. His appointments include a research position at the University of Edinburgh and one at INRIA-Lorraine. He is co-founder and leader of the Artificial Intelligence Laboratory (AI-Lab) at DIST. He has contributed to the development and combination of automated reasoning techniques and their application to automatic program analysis and synthesis as well as to the automatic analysis of security protocols. He has coordinated a number of national and international research projects, including the AVISPA, V@PSI, and the SIAM projects, and has been principal investigator for several other research projects, including the AVISS, AVANTSSAR, and SPaCIoS projects.

C. Warren Axelrod, Ph.D. is a Senior Consultant with Delta Risk, a consultancy specializing in cyber security, risk management, and business resiliency, and Research Director for Financial Services for the U.S. Cyber Consequences Unit. Previously, he was the Business Information Security Officer and Chief Privacy Officer for US Trust, the Private Wealth Management division of Bank of America. He was a founding member of the Financial Services Information Sharing and Analysis Center (FS/ISAC) and represented financial services cyber security interests in the National Information Center in Washington, DC during the Y2K date rollover weekend. He testified before Congress in 2001 on the subject of cyber security. He recently led the Software Assurance Initiative for the Financial Services Technology Consortium (FSTC). Dr. Axelrod won the 2009 Michael Cangemi Best Book/Best Article Award for his article "Accounting for Value and Uncertainty in Security Metrics," published in the *ISACA Journal*, Volume 6, 2008. He was honored with the prestigious Information Security Executive (ISE) Luminary Leadership Award in 2007. He received a Computerworld Premier 100 IT Leaders Award in 2003. Dr. Axelrod has written three books, two of which are on computer management, and numerous articles on information technology and information security topics. His third book is *Outsourcing Information Security* (Artech House, 2004), and he was coordinating editor of *Enterprise Information Security and Privacy* (Artech House, 2009). He participated in the updating of the report *Security Guidance for Critical Areas of Focus in Cloud Computing*, and contributed major sections to the whitepaper *Domain 10: Guidance for Application Security*, both for the Cloud Security Alliance. He recently published two articles in *CrossTalk* magazine; one is "Investing in Software Resiliency," which appeared in the September/October 2009 issue, and the other is "The Need for Functional Security Testing," which is in the March/April 2011 issue. He holds a Ph.D. in Managerial Economics from Cornell University, as well as an honors M.A. in Economics and Statistics and a first-class honors B.Sc. in Electrical Engineering, both from the University of Glasgow. He is certified as a Certified Information Systems Security Professional (CISSP) and Certified Information Security Manager (CISM).

David Bauer holds a PhD, MS, and BS in Computer Engineering from Georgia Institute of Technology, with focuses on identity management, computer security, and computer architecture. He has contributed to several open-source projects in data analysis and statistical testing of random number generators. Previously, he has worked for the Department of Energy on distributed and large-scale data analysis. Currently, he works as a Reliability Analyst for the Department of Defense in Maryland.

Douglas M. Blough received the B.S. degree in Electrical Engineering and the M.S. and Ph.D. degrees in Computer Science from The Johns Hopkins University, Baltimore, MD, in 1984, 1986, and 1988, respectively. Since Fall 1999, he has been Professor of Electrical and Computer Engineering at the Georgia Institute of Technology, where he also holds a joint appointment in the School of Computer Science. From 1988 to 1999, he was on the faculty of Electrical and Computer Engineering at the University of California, Irvine. His research interests include distributed systems, dependability and security, and wireless multihop networks. He serves as Principal Investigator of the MedVault project.

Valer Bocan is a Senior System Analyst with the Wireless department of Alcatel-Lucent Romania. He received his B.Sc. in Computer Engineering from the Politehnica University of Timisoara in 1999 and a Ph.D. from the same university in 2009. He leads a team of talented software engineers whose main responsibility is designing tools for architecting, visualizing and measuring the quality of service of mobile networks. His research interests include network security and availability, compilers, parallel computing and functional programming languages. In his spare time Valer loves toying with the GPS tracker he installed on his car, hacking through the communication protocol and building his own car tracking service.

Miriam A. M. Capretz is currently an Associate Professor and Associate Dean (Acting), Research and Graduate at the Faculty of Engineering at the University of Western Ontario, Canada. Before joining the University of Western Ontario, she was an Assistant Professor in the Software Engineering Laboratory at the University of Aizu, Japan. Dr Capretz received her BSc and MESc degrees from UNICAMP, Brazil and her PhD from the University of Durham, UK. She has been involved with organization of several workshops and symposia as well as has been serving on program committee in several international conferences. She was a Program Co-Chair of the IEEE Workshop Web2Touch – living experience through web (W2T) in 2008 and 2009 and was the Program Chair of the IEEE Symposium on Human and Socio-Cultural Service Oriented Computing 2009. She has been working in the software engineering area for more than 25 years. Her current research interests include service oriented architecture, ontology and semantic integration, business process management, software security, and grid computing.

Roberto Carbone is a Researcher at the Security & Trust Unit of the Center for Information Technologies of Bruno Kessler Foundation (FBK) in Trento. He received his Master Degree in Computer Engineering from the University of Genova in 2005 and his Ph.D. in Electronic and Computer Engineering and Telecommunications from the same University, in 2009. His PhD Thesis, titled "LTL Model-Checking for Security Protocols", has been awarded the CLUSIT prize 2010 (by the Italian Association for Information Security.) His research mainly focuses on the formal analysis of security protocols and services. He is involved in some projects on automatic security protocol analysis, including the AVANTSSAR and the SIAM projects, and in the maintenance of the AVISPA tool. He has contributed to the development of some extensions of the SATMC model checker for security protocols and he is currently the main developer of SATMC.

Luca Compagna received his Master Degree in Informatic Engineering from the University of Genova in 2000 and his Ph.D. in Electronics and Computer Science Engineering from the University of Genova and the University of Edinburgh (joint programme) in 2005. Luca's research is mainly focused on security engineering, automated reasoning and their application to the modelling and analysis of industrial relevant case studies. He has been the main contributor to the development of the SAT-based Model-Checker for bounded model-checking of security protocols. He has contributed to various projects on information security, namely AVISS, AVISPA,V@PSI, Serenity, and AVANTSSAR, and he has published various scientific publications. Since March 2006, he is a member of SAP Research Center Sophia Antipolis where he is contributing to the Security and Trust (S&T) research program. Luca is currently responsible for the Security Engineering cluster of the S&T research program and managing the AVANTSSAR Project.

Rajanish Dass is a faculty member in the Computer & Information Systems Group at the Indian Institute of Management, Ahmedabad. His primary research and teaching interests are in the areas of strategic management of IT & analytics throughout its complete lifecycle (planning & prioritization, justification, benefits management, adoption and communication, project management and execution, value creation, impact analysis, innovation, along with sourcing and governance) ensuring alignment and co-evolution of the analytics road map, IS/IT portfolio planning of organizations, e-governance, business & competitive intelligence, and data mining. He has worked in a number of organizations on these issues as a part of his consulting and research projects. He has authored a number of research papers in national and international journals and conferences. At IIM Ahmedabad, he also coordinates a number of programs for working executives on strategic issues of Managing IT & Business Intelligence.

Igor Ribeiro de Assis graduated in Computer Engineering from University of Campinas - UNICAMP in 2009. He is currently a Master student in Computer Science at UNICAMP.

Hany F. El Yamany is an Assistant Professor in the Department of Computer Science Faculty of Computers and Informatics at Suez Canal University, Ismailia, Egypt. He received his PhD in Software Engineering at the University of Western Ontario, Canada. He has completed his Master's Degree in Computer Science from Ain Shams University, in Cairo, Egypt. Previously, he obtained his BSc in Computational Science from Suez Canal University, in Ismailia, Egypt. Dr. Hany El Yamany has more than 5 years of industry experience, working in the field of database applications. His research interests include software engineering, service-oriented architecture, Web Services, intelligent information security, and intelligent systems.

Mihai Fagadar-Cosma is a Project Team Leader in the Customer Care Centre of Excellence department at Alcatel-Lucent Romania. He has received his B. Sc. in Computer Engineering from the Politehnica University of Timisoara in 2004 and M. Sc. in Computer Engineering from the same university in 2005. From 2004 to 2007 he was in the Network Planning Tools team at Alcatel-Lucent, where he worked as Software Engineer and later as Technical Project Manager in the field of radio network planning algorithms. From 2007 Mihai has been working as project leader in the field of project management applications for the same company. His research interests include image processing and pattern recognition algorithms as well as GIS data mining and feature extraction.

Gábor György Gulyás received his M.Sc. degree in Computer Engineering in 2007. Between 2007 and 2010 he worked as a Ph.D. student at the University of Technology and Economics (BME), Department of Telecommunications, where currently he works as a Lecturer, and he is also a Researcher at the Mobile Communications and Computing Laboratory (MC2L). He is a member of IEEE. As being part of the editorial board and one of the founders of the International PET Portal and Blog (the portal of Privacy Enhancing Technologies) he regularly participates in social activities for promoting personal data protection and raising awareness on related issues. The focus of his research interests is on applying privacy-enhancing identity management on social networks, but he is also interested in other privacy and security issues of social networks, web privacy, data protection issues, and in using steganography for enhancing privacy.

Peter Haag is a Master's student in Business IT Alignment at the Department of Information and Computing Sciences at Utrecht University, The Netherlands. He has performed his thesis research on the subject of identity and access management and has developed the IAM Services Assessment Model to provide a useful and usable tool to support organizations in the selection and successful implementation of IAM services.

Sándor Imre was born in Budapest in 1969. He received the M.Sc. degree in Electrical Engineering from the Budapest University of Technology (BUTE) in 1993. Next he started his Ph. D. studies at BUTE and obtained Dr.Univ. degree in 1996, Ph.D. degree in 1999 and DSc degree in 2007. Currently he is carrying his activities as Professor and Head of Dept. of Telecommunications. He is member of Telecommunication Systems Committee of the Hungarian Academy of Sciences. He participates on the Editorial Board of two journals: *Infocommunications Journal* and *Hungarian Telecommunications*. He was invited to join the Mobile Innovation Centre as R&D Director in 2005. His research interest includes mobile and wireless systems. Especially, he has contributions on different wireless access technologies, mobility protocols, security and privacy, and reconfigurable systems.

Yukio Itakura was previously a President in NTT Data Technology Corporation. Prior to the NTT Data Technology, he had significant experience as a Vice President of NTT DATA Corporation. Yukio recieved his Dr. Eng. in Science and Engineering from Chuo University and is a Professor of Institute of Information Security, Japan. Yukio's interests include biometrics, information security and management, identification, and personal information protection. His educational background is as follows: Master in Science and Engineering, and most recently, a Dr. Eng in Science and Engineering (Chuo University) in 2002. His professional affiliations include: Auditor Information Processing Society of Japan, Director Japan Society of Security Management.

A. Karantjias has obtained the Degree of Electrical and Computer Engineering from University of Patras (Greece) in 2000 and a PhD in Computer Science from National Technical University of Athens (Greece) in 2005. He is currently Lecturer at the Department of Informatics of University of Piraeus (Greece). His current research interests include identification, design and evaluation of synchronous security, and interoperability issues on enterprise architectures and advanced wireless information systems.

Ryan Kendrick obtained his Bachelor of Science in Business Administration and Master of Science in Management Information Systems from the State University of New York at Buffalo where his prime area of study revolved around information security.

Takao Kojima was previously a Computer Engineer for six and a half years in the FUJITSU Limited group company. He had significant experience in Windows Server and related network and security products. Takao is a doctoral course student of Graduate School of Information Security, Institute of Information Security, Japan. Takao's interests include security and privacy for electronic services, and software engineering for security, privacy. His education includes: Bachelor in Social and Information Sciences and most recently a Master in Management Development (Nihon Fukushi University) in 2001. His professional affiliations have been: Student Member ACM, Student Member Information Processing Society of Japan, Student Member Japan Society of Security Management.

Pradeep Kumar is a Business Consultant in TEMENOS (Banking Software Company) in Chennai, India. He received his Master's degree from SRM University and SUNY Buffalo.

Daisuke Mashima is a Ph.D. candidate in Computer Science at Georgia Institute of Technology, USA since 2006 and is affiliated with Georgia Tech Information Security Center (GTISC). Before joining Georgia Tech, he worked as a Research Engineer at NTT Advanced Technology, Japan for 4 years, where he was engaged in a number of R&D projects related to security and contents sharing. He earned his B.E. and M.S. degree in Administration Engineering from Keio University, Japan. He is currently working on research in information security area, especially in online identity management, privacy in cyberspace, and security in E-healthcare systems.

Christoph Meinel is the CEO and President of the Hasso Plattner Institute for IT-Systems Engineering (HPI) and full Professor for Computer Science at the University of Potsdam since 2004. He studied Mathematics and Computer Sciences at the Humboldt-University, and received his PhD degree there in 1981. His habilitation thesis (1988) was about complexity theory. He worked in Humboldt University in Berlin, Max-Planck-Institut für Computer Science, and Paderborn University. In 1992 he was appointed a full Professor for Computer Science at the University of Trier. He is also a Professor both at the School of Computer Science of the Technical University of Beijing (China) and at the Luxembourg Institute of Advanced Studies in Information Technology. He is the author or co-author of 10 textbooks, various conference proceedings, and more than 350 peer-reviewed scientific papers. His research interests focus on in Internet Technology and Systems, particularly in the fields Trust and Security Engineering, Web-University and Innovation Research (Design Thinking). He is member of various scientific boards, chief editor of the scientific electronic journal "Electronic Colloquium on Computational Complexity" (http://eccc.hpi-web.de), of the "IT-Gipfelblog" (www.it-gipfelblog.de) and the tele-TASK archive (http://www.tele-task.de).

Chris J. Mitchell was appointed as Professor of Computer Science at Royal Holloway, University of London, in March 1990. Since joining Royal Holloway (http://www.rhul.ac.uk/), he has played a leading role in the development of the Information Security Group (http://www.isg.rhul.ac.uk/), and helped launch the MSc in Information Security in 1992, probably the first degree of its type. He has published well over 200 papers. He is co-editor-in- chief of *Designs, Codes and Cryptography* and is on the editorial boards of the *International Journal of Information Security, IEEE Communications Letters,* and *The Computer Journal*. He continues to act as a consultant on a variety of topics in information security.

Fabio Negrello graduated in Computer Engineering from University of Campinas - UNICAMP in 2003, Master's in Computer Science at UNICAMP in 2007. Professional experience includes 8 years working in areas of Access Control and Information Security for CPqD (Telecom Development and Research Center). Currently works as System Integration Specialist for IBM.

Sujoy Pal is currently working as a Researcher in Indian Institute of Management, Ahmedabad on various research projects related to Information Systems strategy and its applicability to different organizational scenarios. His latest work includes developing IT strategy and road map for various private and public organizations in India. He is involved in a cross-country project sponsored by UK India Education and Research Initiative (UKIERI) towards determining the drivers and inhibitors for adoption of mobile enabled financial services in India along with designing a framework for estimating demand for mobile banking and mobile payments. After obtaining a Masters in Computer Application, he has worked as a faculty in AES Institute of Computer Studies, Ahmedabad.

Andreas Pashalidis obtained his B.Sc. in Computer Science from the TEI of Athens (http://www.teiath.gr/?lang=en) in 1999, his M.Sc. in Computer and Information Networks from the University of Essex (http://www.essex.ac.uk/) in 2001, and his Ph.D. in Information Security from the Royal Holloway, University of London (http://www.rhul.ac.uk), in 2006. From 2005 to 2009 he worked as a research scientist on security, identity management, and privacy topics for the purposes of standardisation, business unit consulting, as well in the context of different EU-funded research projects - from 2005 to 2007 for Siemens (Munich) and, from 2007 to 2009, for NEC Laboratories Europe(Heidelberg). In 2009, he joined the Computer Security and Industrial Cryptography research group (COSIC) of KU Leuven in Belgium as a postdoctoral researcher.

Giancarlo Pellegrino is a PhD student at Institut Eurécom working as a Research Associate at SAP Labs France in Sophia-Antipolis. Since 2010 he is contributing to the AVANTSSAR Project and the SPaCIoS Project. Before joining SAP, he received a MSc in Computer Science at Universita' degli Studi di Catania (Italy) in 2009. His research topics include security testing, formal analysis of distributed web services, and networking.

N. Polemi has obtained the Degree in Applied Mathematics from Portland State University (USA) in 1984, PhD in Applied Mathematics (Coding Theory) from University of New York (Graduate Centre) in 1991. She held teaching positions in Queens College and Baruch College of City University of New York and was Assistant Professor in State University of New York at Farmingdale in the department of Mathematics. She is now Professor in the University of Piraeus, at the Department of Informatics. Her current research interests are in the fields of security.

H. R. Rao graduated from Krannert Graduate School of Management at Purdue University. His interests are in the areas of management information systems, decision support systems, e-business, emergency response management systems, and information assurance. He has chaired sessions at international conferences and presented numerous papers. He also has co-edited four books, of which one is on Information Assurance in Financial Services. He has authored or co-authored more than 175 technical papers, of which more than 100 are published in archival journals. His work has received best paper and best paper runner up awards at AMCIS and ICIS. Dr. Rao has received funding for his research from the National Science Foundation, the Department of Defense, and the Canadian Embassy, and he has received the University's prestigious Teaching Fellowship. He has also received the Fulbright fellowship in 2004. He is a co-editor of a special issue of *The Annals of Operations Research, the Communications of ACM,* Associate Editor *of Decision Support Systems, Information Systems Research* and *IEEE Transactions in Systems, Man and Cybernetics*, and co-Editor-in-Chief of *Information Systems Frontiers*. Dr. Rao also has a courtesy appointment with Computer Science and Engineering as Adjunct Professor. Professor Rao's PhD students have placed at Sogang U, UNCG, ASU, USF, FAU, MSU, OKState, FSU, PSU, and others. Professor Rao teaches Information Assurance, Networks, and E-commerce. Prof Rao is also the recipient of the 2007 State University of New York Chancellor's award for excellence in scholarship and creative activities. In 2010, Professor Rao was appointed a SUNY Distinguished Service Professor. He is the only School of Management Professor to be honored as a SUNY Distinguished Service Professor, which represents a promotion in rank above Full Professor. At ICIS, December 2010 in St. Louis USA, Professor Rao and his colleagues won the Best Paper Award in information Systems Research, for the year 2009. The article was entitled, "Two Stepping Stones for Successful E-commerce Relationships" (by Dan Kim, Don Ferrin, H. R. Rao). His recent book on Information Assurance Security and Privacy Services (edited by H. R. Rao and S. Upadhyaya) was published by Emerald Group Publishing (ISBN 978-1-84855-194-7).

Róbert Schulcz graduated in 2000 with MSc degree in Electrical Engineering from the Budapest University of Technology and Economics (BME) at the Department of Telecommunications. In 2009 he received the Master of Business Administration (MBA) degree from the same University. Between 2000 and 2003, he participated in the PhD course at the Department of Telecommunications and currently a Ph.D. candidate at BME. He is the Managing Director of the Mobile Innovation Centre (MIK), where he was the testbed Director previously, and he was responsible for the setup and operation of the testbed of MIK. He works as a Researcher at the Mobile Communications and Computing Laboratory (MC2L) since 2003. His research interests include mobility, mobile computing, IMS, security of next generation wireless, and heterogeneous networks. He is the member of IEEE and HTE (Scientific Association for Infocommunications Hungary). He is an author of several referred papers in international scientific journals and conferences.

Marco Spruit is an Assistant Professor at the Department of Information and Computing Sciences at Utrecht University, The Netherlands. He received his PhD from the University of Amsterdam, The Netherlands. His research revolves around knowledge discovery processes to help achieve organizational goals through data mining techniques, business intelligence methods, linguistic engineering techniques, and Social Web technologies. Additionally, he investigates information security models and cloud computing frameworks as infrastructural safeguards and enablers for knowledge discovery processes. His strategic research objective is to realize an interdisciplinary knowledge discovery platform. Please visit http://m.spru.it for more information.

Ivonne Thomas is a PhD student at Hasso Plattner Institute, University of Potsdam in Germany. She received her Master's degree in Software Systems Engineering in 2006. Ivonne Thomas has been working in the area of identity and trust management since more than four years including work placements at SAP Research in Brisbane, Australia as well as in the Security and Trust Group of SAP Research in Sophia Antipolis, France. Since three years she is working full-time on her PhD as a member of the HPI Research School on "Service-oriented Systems Engineering." As her PhD research, she is working on models and technologies towards a trustworthy and reliable management of digital identities in decentralized environments as SOA and the Internet.

Jacques Wainer is an Associate Professor at the Computing Institute – University of Campinas, since 1993. His research interests include artificial intelligence, information security, and social impacts of computing. He received his PhD from Pennsylvania State University in 1991.

Peter White is the Technical Services Architect (Operations) for the NSW Land & Property Management Authority and is an Adjunct Lecturer at Charles Sturt University. He holds a DInfoTech degree in Identity Management Architecture. Peter's research interests are in the areas of identity management architecture, multi-enterprise federation, and citizen authentication.

Index

A

B

C

D

E

F

G

H

I

K

L

M

N

O

P

Q

R

S

T

U

V

W

X